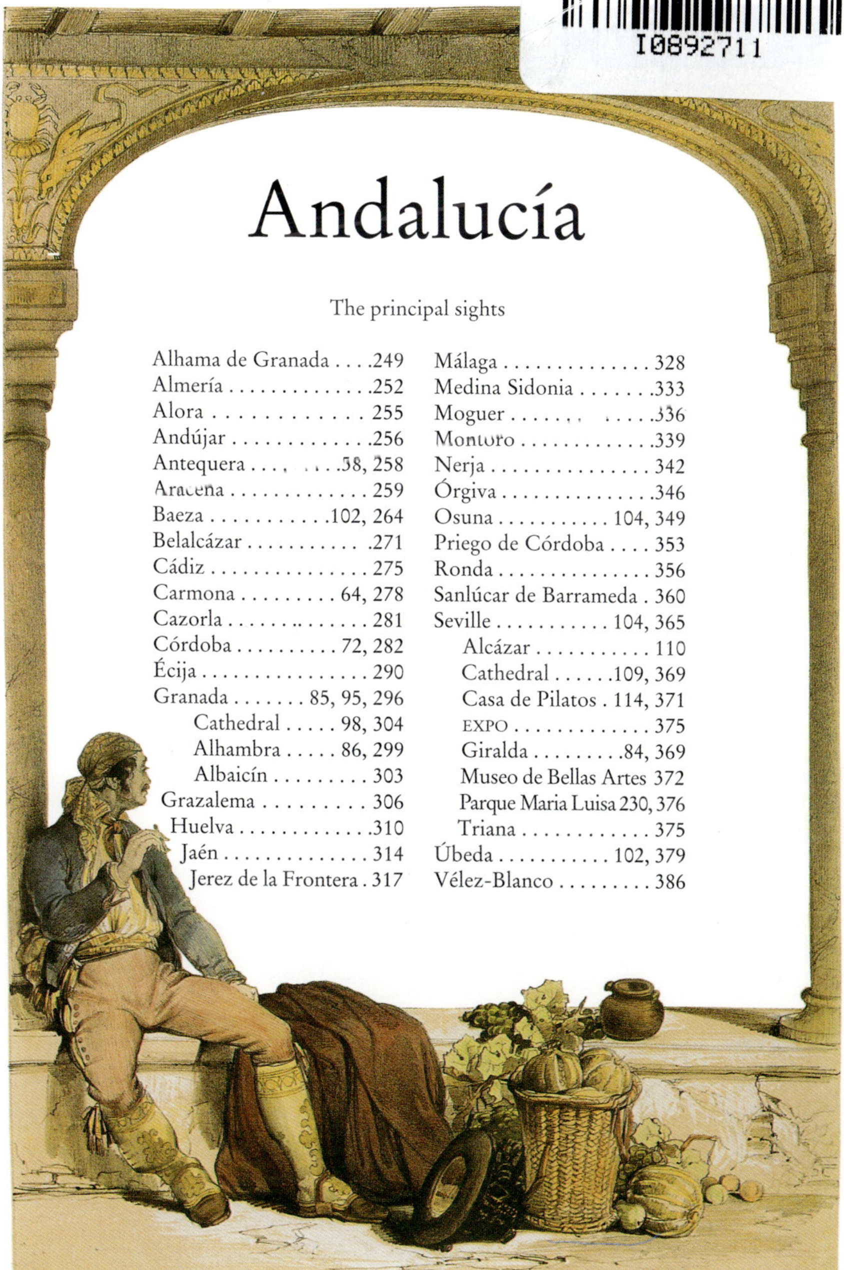

Andalucía

The principal sights

A
B
C
D
1
2
3
4
5
6
EXTREMADURA
PORTUGAL
Belalcázar
Sta Clara
Fuente Obejuna
Pozob
Peñarroya Pueblonuevo
Bélmez
Cumbres Mayores
Valdelarco
Galaroza
Jabugo
Aroche
Cortegana
Almonaster la Real
Fuenteheridos
Aracena
Alájar
Castaño del Robledo
Linares de la Sierra
Zufre
Sta Olalla del Cala
Alanís
Cazalla de la Sierra
Constantina
Las Ermitas
San Jerónimo
Medina Azahara
Almodóvar del Río
Castillo de Mulva
Palma del Río
Zalamea la Real
Nerva
Minas de Ríotinto
Lora del Río
La Carlot
La Luisiana
Écija
Santiponce
Olivares
Sanlúcar la Mayor
SEVILLE
Carmona
Marinaleda
Niebla
HUELVA
Lepe
Ayamonte
Moguer
Bolullos del Condado
Umbrete
Almonte
Palos de la Frontera
Monasterio de la Rábida
Castilleja de la Cuesta
Mairena del Alcor
Alcalá de Guadaira
Marchenilla
Marchena
Osuna
Estepa
Isla Canela
Isla Cristina
La Antilla
El Rompido
Punta Umbría
El Rocío
Villafranco del Guadalquivir
RÍO GUADALQUIVIR
Utrera
Morón de la Frontera
El Palmar de Troya
Matalascañas
Lebrija
Trebujena
Olvera
Ronda la Vieja
Setenil
Teba
Carratraca
La Algaida
Bonanza
Sanlúcar de Barrameda
Chipiona
Zahara
Grazalema
Acueducto
Ronda
Arcos de la Frontera
Cueva de la Pileta
Tolox
Jerez de la Frontera
Rota
Monasterio de la Cartuja
Ubrique
Buenalauría
Alhaurín el Grand
El Puerto de Sta María
Valdelagrana
Gaucín
CÁDIZ
Puerto Real
Medina-Sidonia
San Fernando
Sancti Petri
Chiclana de la Frontera
Jimena de la Frontera
Estepona
San Pedro
Marbell
OCÉANO ATLÁNTICO
Cueva del Tajo de las Figuras
Vejer de la Frontera
El Cuervo
Castellar de la Frontera
Conil de la Frontera
El Palmar
Zahora
San Roque
Los Caños de Meca
La Línea
GIBRALTAR
Barbate de Franco
Algeciras
Zahara de los Atunes
Tarifa
MEDIT
Ceuta
Ruina Romana de Bolonia
N
Tánger
MARRUECOS

F
G
H
J
1
2
3
4
5
6
CASTILLA - LA MANCHA
MURCIA
Desfiladero de Despeñaperros
La Carolina
Las Navas de Tolosa
Sanctuario Virgen de la Cabeza
Baños de la Encina
Segura de la Sierra
Hornos
Iznatoraf
Bailén
Andújar
Linares
Sabiote
Fuente Segura
Baeza
Úbeda
La Iruela
Arjonilla
Arjona
Bujalance
Porcuna
RIO GUADALQUIVIR
Cazorla
Quesada
Puebla de Don Fabrique
Huéscar
JAÉN
Galera
Orce
Vélez Blanco
Vélez Rubio
Cueva de los Letreros
Martos
Baena
Zújar
Zuheros
Ermita de NS de la Sierra
Alcalá la Real
Baza
Lucena
Priego de Córdoba
Purullena
Huércal Overa
Rute
Montefrío
Guadix
Cuevas del Almanzora
Valderrubio
Víznar
La Peza
Graena
Cóbdar
Vera
Palomares
Loja
Fuentevaqueros
GRANADA
Garrucha
Santa Fe
Gabia la Grande
Lacalahorra
Gérgal
Sorbas
Mojácar
Archidona
Monachil
Pico Veleta
Laujar de Andarax
Huétor Vega
Malá
Fondales
Tabernas
Capileira
Mecina
Trevélez
Alhama de Granada
Bérchules
Sta Fe de Mondújar
Mini Hollywood
Carboneras
Yegen
Bubión
Níjar
Necrópolis de los Millares
Cádiar
Castaras
Pampaneira
Pitres
Busquístar
Berja
Órgiva
Lanjarón
Rincón de la Victoria
Dalías
San Pedro
Cómpeta
Comares
Frigiliana
ALMERÍA
Motril
Vélez Málaga
Nerja
Adra
Roquetas de Mar
Cabo de Gata
MÁLAGA
Almuñécar
Salobreña
ÁNEO
KEY TO MAIN MAP
Roads
Motorway
Trunk Road
Major Road
Minor Road
Boundaries
Regional
Provincial
Altitude
2000m
1400
1200
1000
850
700
550
400
200
100
Sea level
Scale
50 Kilometres
FRANCE
SPAIN
Madrid
PORTUGAL
Lisbon
Córdoba
Huelva
Jaén
Seville
Granada
Cádiz
Málaga
Almería
MOROCCO
ALGERIA

Guadix

Coto Doñana

Bar in Seville

PROHIBIDO
TERMINANTEMENTE
EL CANTE
EL RINCONCILLO
CASA FUNDADA
AÑO 1670
ANÍS DEL MONO

michael jacobs

THE ANDALUCÍA GUIDE

Interlink Books

An imprint of Interlink Publishing Group, Inc.
Northampton, Massachusetts

Contents

Opposite: the Cathedral, Jaén

Holy Week procession, Granada

Preface and Acknowledgements

I was sixteen when I first came to Andalucía, and travelling alone for the first time. Andalucía seemed to me the most exotic place I had ever known, and I remember writing home ecstatically about jasmine-scented patios, Holy Week celebrations, and the mountain scenery near Ronda. I remember too an afternoon which began in a bodega near Córdoba. The wine went to my head, a gypsy appeared playing a guitar, and an old man told me of his friendship with the poet García Lorca. This first experience of the pleasant effects of drink ended up near some enchanted castle, which I now like to identify with Almodóvar del Río.

Andalucía has similarly bewitched thousands of travellers, many of whom have later gone on to record their impressions in a suitably flowery vein. I realize now the great extent to which such romantic visions of Andalucía have obscured the region's real identity. Though one of the tourist capitals of Europe, Andalucía remains remarkably little known, in terms not only of its countless unspoilt villages and forgotten monuments, but also of vital aspects of its culture.

Much of the enjoyment I have had in writing this book has been due to the exceptional amount of help and friendship which I have received in Spain. In Madrid, I must thank Maite Brik, Manolo Fernández, Pepe Llanos, Ian and Carole Gibson, and Carmen and Tito de la Guardia; Annie Bennett's hospitality made it difficult for me to leave the city, while Alicia Ríos – *consultadora gastronomica* – gave me an invaluable insight into Spanish food, and provided me with contacts in Andalucía that proved to be invaluable. Once I reached Andalucía, my debts soon became too numerous to list fully, and came to include people whom I encountered in town halls, tourist offices, churches, bars, restaurants, shops and museums in every corner of the region. The Junta de Andalucía, the former British Council in Seville, Equipo 28, and the Seville office of Longman Penguin España, were of great assistance to me, in particular Jerónimo Hernández, José Ramón Moreno, Fernando Olmedo, Rod Pryde, Cristina Soler, María Larreta and Javier Verdugo. On the pilgrimage to El Rocío in the spring of 1989, I was adopted by the Hermandad of Umbrete, and was excellently looked after by many people, including Lola Flores, Irene Kappel, Bignia Kuoni, Efraim Pintos, Andrés Modolell, Ana María Regén, Rosario Schlatter Navarro, Juana Alonso Vizcaíno, Mariano Zorrilla Vera, and Isabel Zorrilla Vera. Des Brennan, Louise

Opposite: one of the images of the Virgin on Easter procession in Granada

Byfield, Richard Cowan, Geoff Macdonald, Celine Morris, Louise Nicholson, Paul, Janis, Michael and Zoe Stirton, Michael Tamm, Sandro Trevisanello, Jim Urquhart, and Ruth Voggensperger, all came to see me in Sanlúcar de Barrameda during the summer of 1988, and helped in various ways. In the course of my stays and travels in Andalucía, I benefited also from the kindness and company of María Luisa Alías, Juan Carlos Alonso, David Baird, Berthus de Boer, Javier Barral, Diego Carrasco, Jerónimo Castañeda, Carlo and Anne Chinca, Richard Days, Ángel Díaz, John Dillon, Alfonso Duarte, Anchi, Jesús, and Lupe Flores, Ainara and Mamen Garrido Alías, José Garrido, Alberto González Morales, Francisco González Gómez, Cuqui González de Caldos, Javier Landa, Paco, Pisco and Sergio Lira, Marisa Lorena, Rosa Martínez, Begoña Medina, Eli Mendez Alcarazo, Berta Moreno, Carlos Ortega, Fernando Ortíz, Paco Pachón, Aurelio and Federico Patanchón, Encarnación Peinado Martínez, Manuel and Berta Perales, Nicolás Ramírez Moreno, Mabel Regidor, Juan Robles, Miguel Rodriguez Baeza, César Rodríguez Campos, Matthias Roskoschek, Francisco Salazar Romero ('Curro'), Jean and Hamo Sassoon, Pepe Schwartz Mosco, Magdalena Torres Hidalgo, and José Luis Valdivia. Above all, I am indebted to Esperanza Flores, whose generosity was quite exceptional, and through whom I came to know Andalucía incomparably better than I would otherwise have done.

I owe a distant debt to D. E. Brown, and Dr. Ernst Sanger, both of whom taught me Spanish, and helped greatly to foster my early enthusiasm for the country. I must also thank David and Mariagrazia Jacobs, Mic Cheetham of Anthony Sheil Associates, and the staff both of the Spanish Institute in London and of Viking/ Penguin, especially Eleo Gordon and Annie Lee. Jackie Rae, once again, made an immeasurable contribution through her helpful criticisms and unfailing support.

Michael Jacobs, Spring 1990

Preface to the second edition

This book first appeared at a time when Spain, and Andalucía in particular, was undergoing a period of radical change, encouraged by a Spanish government with strong Sevillian connections. In preparation for the Seville EXPO of 1992, Andalucía was made more accessible than ever before: the creation of a high-speed railway link and a new network of main roads put the region within two hours of Madrid and almost halved the time spent travelling between its principal towns.

Tourist interest in the Andalucían interior has grown accordingly, and many new guide-books have appeared to a region previously better served by romantic impressions than by anything of a more practical nature. However, for all this Andalucía can still be said to offer the traveller an extraordinary number of outstanding, little known sites and a stubbornly exotic, individualistic culture.

The reissuing of my 1990 guide-book has allowed me not only to take into account all the many recent changes, but also to add much new material acquired in the course of repeated long stays in a region which I almost regard now as a second home. While undertaking the revisions I was conscious of how much I had been affected in the late 1980's by the general bias of the time towards Seville and Western Andalucía at the expense of the region's eastern half. An excellent opportunity to redress the balance was provided by the charismatic founder of the Granada-based organization El Legado Andalusí, Jerónimo Paez, who commissioned me to write a book that involved extensive travels around the province of Granada, as well as a long period working in a large old house and garden situated directly under the Alhambra. I am greatly indebted both to him and to all the staff of El Legado Andalusí. I would like also to repeat my thanks to all those who helped me in the previous edition, and to acknowledge the kindness and help of the many new friends I have made in Andalucía in the intervening years, in particular Hourria and Mustafa Akalay, Lamine Benalou, Chelo Beltrán, Javier Blanco, Eduardo Castro, Nana Contreras Olmo, Juan Antonio Díaz, Tita Esperanza González, Francisco Fernández, Ian McCandless, Juan de Dios Morales Fregenal, Aurelio Ríos Rojas, Fernando Rodríguez Moreno, Isabel Sánchez Trigo ('la bandolera') and Pepe Zamora.

My thanks also to Bob Goodwin, William and Sonia Chislett, and of course, to my publisher Alexander Fyjis-Walker for reviving a commercially unfashionable type of guide-book that I would like to think of as being in the spirit of Andalucía – discursive, opinionated and idiosyncratic.

Michael Jacobs
London, Spring 1998

Preface to the fourth edition

Among the many new friendships I have made in the two years since this book was last reissued I owe a particular debt to the villagers of Frailes, above all to Antonio Cano, Manuel Caño, Merecedes and Isabel García, Custodio López, Carmen, Paqui and Mercedes Machuca, Miguel Montes, Ernesto del Moral, Fermín Mudarra, Paco Quirosa, Rafael Frías, and to that wisest and most generous of writers' patrons, Manuel Ruíz López ('El Sereno').Chris Stewart, Juan Infante, Jose Maria Suarez, Maria Paz del Moral, Santiago Campos, Juan Antonio Cabrera, Vicente Serrano, Jose Luis Revueltas, Julio Cerda, Julian Zulueta, Emilia Garrido, Rafael Aguilera, Gry Iverslien, Georgina Richmond, Carmen Suarez, Cristina Fuentes, Jonathan Cox, Manuel Molina.

Michael Jacobs
Frailes, Autumn 2005

Preface to the fifth edition

I have always preferred to write new books than to revise old ones. Yet my life-long love of Andalucía has compelled me to keep as up-to-date as possible a book that has been almost continually in print since its first publication in 1991 (when it was brought out, in a very different format, by Viking/Penguin). During the eight years since the last edition, Andalucía has changed more radically than ever, as have general attitudes towards guide-book literature. Though I have added new places, tried to keep abreast of recent developments, and removed a number of now sadly defunct bars and restaurants, I make no claims to be all-conclusive, nor to rival the sort of practical information best culled today from the internet. What I hope instead is that the book remains what it always has been: an idiosyncratic, informed and unfashionably personal account of what I still believe to be one of Europe's richest and most complex regions. My thanks again to my growing number of Andalucían friends, to the inhabitants of my adopted village of Frailes, to Jackie Rae, and to Carmen Suarez, whose librarian's eye has proved this time to be particularly invaluable.

Michael Jacobs
Frailes, Spring 2013

In memory of

Esperanza Flores

(1943-1999)

to whom this book

owes so much

The Generalife seen from the Casa del Chapiz, by J. F. Lewis

The Land and its People

Andalucía seems at times less of a real place than an invention of poets and storytellers. Situated at what was once the end of the known world, it faces both the Mediterranean and the Atlantic, and is protected on three sides by a mountain wall formed to the north by the Sierra Morena, and to the east and south by the Cordillera Bética. The Moors referred to the region as the *Yeşira Andalús*, 'The Island of Andalucía', and indeed its boundaries of sea and wild mountains effectively cut off the place from the rest of Spain. As with many a mythical land, the often daunting natural frontiers of Andalucía shield an interior famed for its abundant natural resources, luxuriant sensuality, and formidable history. For on the other side of these mineral-encrusted mountains, at the very heart of Andalucía, stretches the fabulously fertile basin of the Guadalquivir, the former homeland of what is traditionally Europe's oldest if also most elusive civilization, that of Tartessus.

Tartessus itself remains to this day hidden like some inland Atlantis, and the land of its people, the Tartessians, only begins to acquire a firmer historical identity following the arrival in Spain of the Phoenicians, the Carthaginians, the Greeks, and, most significantly, the Romans. The Romans ruled over the south of Spain for nearly four hundred years, and called the region Baetica after their name for its largest river, the Guadalquivir. Under the domination of the Moors, which began in the 8th century AD, Betis became part of al-Andalus, a name which was once fancifully thought to derive from the Vandal hordes who moved into 'Vandalucía' in the wake of the Romans. Southern Spain was divided by the Moors into the kingdoms of Seville, Córdoba, Jaén and Granada; Granada was the last of the Moors' Spanish possessions, falling to the Christians in 1492. After that date the term Andalucía to describe these former kingdoms came to be current, though this was not to begin with an official expression, nor did it have any administrative meaning. In the late 18th century Spain adopted a provincial structure, and in 1834 the provinces of Andalucía were established more or less in their present-day form, each one of these named after their most important town: Almería, Cádiz, Córdoba, Granada, Huelva, Jaén, Málaga, and Seville. After the death of Franco in 1975, opposition in

Spain to centralist government led to the Spanish regions acquiring a much greater degree of autonomy than hitherto, and in 1981, some time after the other regions, Andalucía acquired its own parliament, the Parlamento, based in Seville, and local regional government, the Junta de Andalucía. In contrast to Catalonia and the Basque Country, few people in Andalucía have ever seriously considered a complete break from the rest of Spain. The irony of this is that Andalucía is not only the Spanish region with the strongest geographical identity of its own, but also – in the eyes of many people – the one with the most idiosyncratic culture.

'Spain is different', ran a famous tourist slogan of the 1960's. But if Spain is different, Andalucía is even more so, for throughout history travellers who have crossed its borders have experienced a feeling of moving away from Europe and entering another continent. 'Once across the Sierra Morena', observed Théophile Gautier on a visit to Spain in 1840, 'the landscape changes completely. . . you feel truly in some other place; you are aware of having left Paris once and for all.' For him, as for most travellers to Andalucía, the change was seen in terms of an abrupt transition between Europe and Africa. It is often said that Africa begins with the Pyrenees, but it would be more accurate to claim that Africa begins with the Sierra Morena. Eight centuries of Moorish presence in Andalucía have clearly left their mark on such diverse aspects of the region as the architecture, the place names, the food, and even the physical types. In addition to all this are the remarkable geographical points in common between the two places: the Cordillera Bética belongs to the same geographical formation as the Atlas Mountains in Morocco; furthermore much of the flora and fauna of Andalucía is essentially African in type, for instance its palm trees, cacti, and the extraordinary pine tree called *pínsapo*, a relative of the Riffia Cedar from Ketawa in Morrocco, only found in Europe in Andalucía's Serranía de Ronda. Yet to define the exotic character of Andalucía purely in African terms is to oversimplify. Andalucía is neither Europe nor Africa but a potent mixture of the two. It is the proverbial meeting-ground of East and West, with, moreover, a strong suggestion of yet another continent. When the Guadalquivir river reaches the sea, having formed with its estuary the only significant gap in Andalucía's near-continuous mountain wall, it looks not to Africa or the rest of Europe, but across the Atlantic to America. From the Guadalquivir Columbus set off on his first journey to the New World, thus establishing the river for a while as the main point of departure and arrival for those plying between the two continents. Andalucía was now no longer at the end of the world, but at its centre. Reciprocal influences between Andalucía and Latin America were understandably enormous, and it is not surprising that the Colombian novelist García Marquez could note on a recent visit to Andalucía how much the character of the region reminded him of his native country.

Travellers to Andalucía have often described their arrival here in euphoric terms. The place was seen as a promised land, made all the more so by the inhospitable

The pass at Despeñaperros

countryside that came beforehand. The main overland route to Andalucía crosses the plains of La Mancha, possibly the dreariest landscape in Spain, and an area once known for its poor, infertile look. 'La Mancha', wrote a Moroccan ambassador in 1690, 'is above all a supremely dry country in relation to Andalucía; it is almost entirely lacking in water, its earth is scorched, and its villages are to be found in a primitive state, the very opposite of what you find in Andalucía.' For Gautier and countless other travellers who have journeyed south across La Mancha, the first sight of the Sierra Morena has always been an exciting one. 'Behind that line of purple mountains', exclaimed Gautier, 'was hidden the paradise of my dreams.' Approached from this side, Gautier's paradise had its gates, the Pass of Despeñaperros, the only breach in the Sierra Morena's three-hundred-mile wall. This is the traditional entrance to Andalucía, so much so that all the idiosyncratic and diverse phenomena of the region are sometimes covered by the oblique term *Despeñaperros por abajo*, 'below Despeñaperros'.

The route through Despeñaperros is as dramatic as the one across La Mancha is dull, and takes you through a gorge hemmed in by pine-covered slopes erupting into frenetically projecting outcrops of bare rock. The gorge opens out into the Guadalquivir valley, affording a monumental panorama over a rolling landscape studded with olive trees. Surveying the view, which extends beyond the valley to the distant peaks of the Cordillera Bética, Gautier was reminded of the visionary landscapes of the English painter John Martin. This same view, according to Gautier's predecessor Chateaubriand, so overwhelmed the French troops under Marshal Soult that they saluted it with their arms. Descending into the valley, your eyes will be dazzled in the spring months by a sparkling, jewel-like encrustation of poppies and other flowers. And as in representations of Paradise there are clusters of palm trees and – for most of the year – an uninterrupted blue sky so vivid in hue that even those living in other parts of Spain feel moved to comment on it.

'Andalucía intoxicates like alcohol and opium,' wrote the Seville poet Luis Cernuda. 'If I was ever asked what Andalucía means to me,' he said elsewhere, 'if I was asked what single word sums up the thousand sensations, suggestions and possibilities that unite the radiant surface of Andalucía, I would say: happiness.' 'I wandered around ancient Betis,' recalled Chateaubriand, 'where the poets had located happiness.' The Roman geographer Strabo likened the Guadalquivir Valley to the Elysian Fields, and emphasized, as writers always have done, the exceptional way in which Andalucía has been favoured by nature. Olives, vines and wheat brought great prosperity to the region in ancient times, as did the abundance of its fish, tuna from the coast near Cádiz and caviar from the sturgeons that once swam up the Guadalquivir being exported all over the Roman Empire. Not least abundant was Andalucía's mineral wealth, which was exploited long before the Romans, and once gave the region a reputation comparable to that of El Dorado: the first known mention of Tartessus is a line in the Old Testament refering to the mineral-laden ships of 'Tarshish'. The image of natural abundance which hangs over Andalucía like a cornucopia was furthered by the Moors, who introduced new elements such as cotton and silkworms, and who instigated remarkably sophisticated systems of irrigation that are still partially functioning. To them too Andalucía was a paradise, and their loss of the region and eventual expulsion from it has often been described in terms of the expulsion of Adam and Eve in the Bible. Long after the departure of the Moors, Andalucía maintained a reputation as the Spanish region most endowed with natural resources, and traveller after traveller has used the word 'paradise' to evoke the place's charms. 'When we entered Andalucía,' recollected an aristocratic Polish traveller, Jakob Sobieski, in 1611, 'our senses, tired after the monotonous desert we had crossed, were amply restored by the beauty, joy and abundance of products of this country. . . I thought I was in a Paradise.' 'Andalucía,' wrote the French visitor Etienne de Silhouette in 1750, 'is the best part of all Spain, the most fertile, the richest, in short the one in which all of nature's gifts have been best distributed.' 'The land overflows with oil and wine,' commented Richard Ford in his celebrated guidebook to Spain of 1845. All these views were summed up in 1848 by a Spanish writer, Cuendias, who suggested that the Pass of Despeñaperros was the frontier which separates 'the land of men from the land of gods'. And yet the more fulsome the praise becomes for Andalucía over the centuries, the more ironic the praise so often seems. The irony was in many cases fully intended.

The pass of Despeñaperros has been seen not just as the gates of Heaven, but as those of Hell. Andalucía has managed, paradoxically, to combine an image of great wealth and fecundity with one of extreme poverty: in modern times Andalucía, together with the neighbouring region of Extremadura, has been regarded as the poorest part of Spain. The marked discrepancy that has developed since the 17th century between Andalucía's economic potential and its economic reality, has prompted sad reflections from travellers. The French agriculturalist of the late 18th century, the Baron de Bourgoing, after having evoked Roman Baetica as a 'magic land in which happiness and abundance flourished', wrote that 'modern Baetica could be the same, and yet, despite its beautiful sky and estimable and varied crops, it only inspires nostalgia.'

The beauty and the tragedy of Andalucía was the subject of a well-known article of 1905 by the Spanish essayist and novelist Azorín. This article, entitled *La Andalucía Trágica*, begins with a description of a train journey between Madrid and Seville. After crossing La Mancha at night, the traveller wakes up in the morning in the Guadalquivir valley. Looking out of the window he is immediately enchanted and soothed by what he sees, for, in contrast to the harshness of central Spain, the landscape in front of him is of an 'inexpressable sweetness'; when he reaches Seville, the voluptuous and carefree character of the city almost overwhelms him. All this

Moorish irrigation channels in use today

Working in the aloe fields

serves as a prelude to a description of 'tragic Andalucía', an Andalucía which he finds in the small town of Lebrija, thirty miles to the south of Seville. Here he is struck by the emptiness of the place, by the deserted streets, and how only a handful of sad people fill the town's social club. Unemployment, normally high, has reached a drastic level, thanks to phylloxera in the neighbouring vines of Jerez. Few can afford to go out, or even have the energy to do so. People are literally dying of hunger. A local doctor provides the traveller with frightening statistics of death from malnutrition and tuberculosis. 'I don't know what the solution to our problem is,' says the doctor, all that I do know is that we cannot go on living like this. We are not living, we are dying.' The conditions of Andalucía's rural poor as described by Azorín in 1905 were scarcely to change for much of this century, and were to lead from the 1920's onwards to an exodus away from the country to the cities, and away from Andalucía itself. By the 1970's, when the exodus began to be curbed, Andalucía had come to be known as the emigration capital of Spain, and had suffered a severe demographic crisis: the region's rural population, which at the beginning of the century had exceeded the urban population, was now reduced to almost half of the latter. In the 1980's Andalucía's economy finally began to improve significantly, with once-poor areas such as Almería changing beyond recognition and even beginning to attract back former emigrés. However, since 1992, the region has been suffering again from severe recession, which has drawn renewed attention to such other problems as Seville's unemployment level, still the highest of any European city.

'The sky and earth are good,' goes an old Andalucían proverb, 'that which lies in between is bad.' Incompetence, corruption, greed, and the persistence of a ridiculous feudalism have joined forces to minimalize the untold natural advantages of Andalucía, and to ensure that what prosperity there has been has benefited only the very few. 'It has indeed,' wrote Richard Ford, 'required the utmost ingenuity and bad government of man to neutralize the prodigality of advantages which Paradise has lavished on this highly favoured land, and which, while under the domination of the Romans and Moors, represented an Eden, a garden of plenty and delight. . .' It is generally agreed that it was the expulsion of the Moors which contributed more than any other factor to the economic decline of Andalucía. The new Christian settlers, brought into Andalucía after 1492, represented only a fraction of the Moors who departed, and were hardly sufficient in number, or even willing enough, to look after the lands that the latter had so lovingly cultivated. As early as 1525 the Venetian ambassador Andrea Navagero lamented the ruinous state of countless gardens and plots of land that the Moors had been forced to abandon at Granada. The Moors, Navagero noted, had a remarkable ability to grow trees and plants, and to transform even the most meagre pieces of land into gentle, perfumed gardens with constant flowing water; the Spaniards meanwhile were 'not very industrious, and neither cultivate nor sow the land with any good will, but prefer instead to go to war or to the Indies to make their fortune.'

Of all the Moors' many gifts, it was their genius at irrigation which was to be most beneficial to them in Andalucía. The sun which lends the region such a smiling aspect for so much of the year is also a relentless, unremitting force that has dried out the land and created throughout Andalucía's history severe periods of drought. Zouch Turton, an English traveller of the 1870's, ridiculed the notion of Andalucía as the garden of Spain by saying that the only plants that flourished here of their own accord were the aloe and Barbary fig, and that almost everything else had to be brought in, planted and watered. The problem of water has been a constant one in Andalucía up to the present day, and was referred to in 1965 in a speech delivered by Franco at Huércal Overa, a desolate town in the middle of Almería, Andalucía's most arid and desert-like province. 'These lands,' the dictator shouted, 'are crying out for water, water, water.' Yet under the Moors, even Almería flourished. This fact was seized upon by the Catalan writer and socialist Juan Goytisolo, who in the

1950's brought out two controversial studies of poverty in Almería, *La Chanca* and *Campos de Níjar*. Reflecting on the lunar-like landscape of Almería, he wondered to what extent this was the cause of the region's poverty and to what extent the result of the expulsion of the Moors and the neglect of their irrigation systems.

Lack of water has by no means been the only problem affecting settlers in Andalucía. The Andalucían climate is one of extremes, long periods without rain being followed by intensive downpours that have often brought severe flooding, particularly in the Guadalquivir basin: it is known that the weather in Andalucía went through an especially changeable period in the early years of the 17th century, and that this undoubtedly consolidated the decline of the region's economy. Then there is the notorious wind called the *levante*, which seems to blow almost constantly around the coast of Cádiz, and has a popular reputation for causing insanity. Against such factors, not even the skills of the Moors could be of much avail. Nor could their impressive achievements hide the extraordinary fact that – according to a recent survey – 47% of Andalucía, this so-called 'Garden of Spain', is totally unsuitable for agriculture. But the main problem which has troubled Andalucía has nothing to do with weather or geography, but rather with the much thornier and still unresolved issue of the ownership of the land.

The enormous potential rewards of Andalucía's land have come only too rarely into the hands of those who have worked or lived on it. Andalucía's most profitable enterprises have been more often than not run by foreigners, the sherry industry being a well-known example of this. British merchants have been based in Jerez and the neighbouring sherry towns of El Puerto de Santa María and Sanlúcar de Barrameda since the middle ages, and the names Gordon Byass, Harvey, Osborne, Terry and so on testify to this day to the British domination of the trade. The British too, together with the Belgians and the French, have played the major role in the region's mining industry. While the Belgians and the French, respectively, controlled the lead mines in Almería province and the now exhausted coal mines in Peñarroya (Córdoba), the British were for a long while the beneficiaries of Andalucía's oldest and most famous mining concern, the copper mines of Río Tinto. A British syndicate bought the mines from the Spanish government in 1871 for a sum far less than their intrinsic value, and within a few years had achieved a leading position in the world market for copper and sulphur. The mines, which Franco often referred to as an 'economic Gibraltar', recently reverted to Spanish ownership, but by then the Rio Tinto Zinc Company had been able to expand its activities well beyond Europe, and was gaining notoriety for its involvement in Bolivia, South Africa and Wales. The Río Tinto mines are by no means the worst example of foreign exploitation of Andalucía's wealth. A far more disturbing and insidious phenomenon than this has been foreign involvement in the property boom of the Costa del Sol. The building companies that have transformed the once desperately poor coast between Gibraltar and Almuñecar into what is generally described as a concrete jungle are mainly foreign-owned, as are the burgeoning estate agencies. What is more many of the nearby inland villages are also becoming overrun by foreigners, many of whom, often without work permits, have taken up property speculation and other entrepreneurial activities.

The uneven distribution of Andalucía's wealth has been evident above all in agriculture, which is the traditional base of the region's economy. Agricultural oppression has always been symbolized here by the land structure of the latifundium or large estate. This structure has characterized other Spanish regions, most notably Castile and Extremadura, but whereas in these other places it declined in the early years of this century, in Andalucía it has prevailed to this day. The large estates of 200 hectares (494 acres) still represent only 1.4% of the region's farms in number, and yet continue to occupy over half the farmland. The latifundium remains as integral to the image of Andalucía as flamenco or bull-fighting. The word is Latin in origin, though the first latifundia might possibly date back to the Tartessian period. In any case it was not until the Roman occupation of Spain that the latifundium was to acquire what was later to be one of its most common features, namely an absentee landlord. When living in Rome, the Andalucían-born philosopher Seneca did not make his money purely from Stoicism; he seems also to have received an ample revenue from his property outside Córdoba. Another such landlord was one Marius, who gave his name to the Sierra Morena (a derivative of the Sierra Mariana) through owning there a vast estate later confiscated by the Emperor Tiberius.

The Roman fiscal system and the vandal hordes of the subsequent period destroyed the Roman latifundia, but they were reconstituted during the middle ages, the estates being given out as gifts to the feudal lords who had assisted the Spanish monarchs in their fight against the Moors. The majority of today's big estates, however, date from the 19th century, and were formed by the sale of the corporate landed property held by the Church and the municipalities. These sales were intended as a gesture of reform, as a way of widening the range of ownership and helping the landless. In the end of course they only had the effect of strengthening the position of the wealthy few, as these were the only people who could afford the newly available land. The landed élite and their allies formed a powerful oligarchy, which was able to block all the various attempts at land reform that were proposed from the mid 18th century onwards, and to accept only those reforms that were to be beneficial to them.

At the centre of the latifundium is the *cortijo*, a group of farm buildings surrounded by a relatively small, well cultivated area; the rest of the estate is traditionally divided up between wheat, grazing land and fallow. The surviving cortijos, all dating from after the 17th century, comprise a brilliantly white complex of buildings neatly arranged around a courtyard and dominated by a bell tower and large gate; a fringe of luxuriant tropical vegetation or even the nearby placing of a palm tree, lend to these places an added exotic quality. Grander and much less common versions of the cortijos are the *haciendas*, the equivalent of Roman or Palladian villas, and places that combine a farm and a country home; magnificent examples of these are to be found in the province of Seville, for instance the Hacienda Torquemada outside Bolullos de la Mitación.

Generally speaking, the more important the landlords, the less time they spend on their estates. Visits of leading aristocrats to their latifundia have been major events in local history. The Hispanist Gerald Brenan recalled in his book *The Spanish Labyrinth* (1943) how a visit made by the Duke of Alba in the 1920's to his estate near Córdoba took on almost the character of an African safari, the Duke equipping himself with tents and a convoy of lorries. When the landlords have directly worked their estates they have usually done so by putting an overseer in charge of the cortijo. Sometimes, however, they preferred to rent out their land, one of the advantages in the past of doing so being that they did not have to pay taxes on the property or spend money maintaining or improving it. The overseers of the cortijos and those who have rented these places, the *labradores*, have traditionally been portrayed as unattractive figures, hard on their employees, and often betrayers of their own class. They frequently took on the role of *caciques*, political bosses who manipulated and even falsified local electoral results.

Lower down the social scale from the labradores come the men (the *peletrines*) to whom the former would sometimes rent out the poorest or more distant parts of the estates. At the very bottom of the scale are the *braceros* or day-laboures, Andalucía's vast landless proletariat who to this day constitute one of the region's great social problems. The braceros are employed on a seasonal basis, which means that for much of the year they are redundant. They have never had their homes on the estates, but have lived in villages or towns often many miles away: this fact largely accounts for the emptiness of so much of the Andalucían countryside. When working on the estates, their employers have generally put them up, but in conditions that have often been pitiable. Blas Ibañez, in his novel *La Bodega* (1894), a study of a famous workers' strike in Jerez in 1892, describes how up to one hundred labourers and their families would be made to sleep on the floor of a long room called the *gañaría*; they would be fed purely on the cold garlic soup known as *gazpacho*, except at harvest time, when they would be given beans.

Andalucía's large and hungry landless proletariat, faced with huge estates and absentee landlords, caciques and ruthless employers, frequently rebelled. The Andalucían countryside has known periods of social unrest since at least the 15th century, but from the late 19th century right up to the Civil War of 1936-9 it was almost constantly troubled. Anarchism was particularly strong here, and, according to some historians, became closely associated with messianism, its message being often spread by itinerant lay preachers such as one Salvotea, a saintly figure heroized by the braceros. The great symbol of Andalucía's struggling rural population is the village of Fuente Obejuna, today a sad and slightly sinister place in the desolate northern half of Córdoba province. On 23 April 1476, the villagers rose up against their tyranical lord, Fernán Gómez, Comendador of the Order of Calatrava. An early account of the incident relates how they stormed his palace, threw him out of the window, finished him off with lances and swords, and then dragged his body to the main square, where it was hacked to pieces by men and women alike; later the village refused to single out any individual culprits, but assumed collective responsibility for what happened, thus giving rise to a popular saying, *Fuenteovejuna lo hizo* ('Fuenteovejuna did it'). This rebellion, which was one of several in the history of the village, is largely remembered today through its being turned into a drama of honour and revenge by the 17th-century playwright Lope de Vega. *Fuenteovejuna* (1612-14), perhaps Lope de Vega's best known work, was performed in the village in 1933 under the direction of the poet García Lorca. The production was staged in contemporary costume in front of the late 15th-century parish church which was built on the site of the Comendador's palace. Shortly before it was due to start, one of the actresses noticed a man wildly pacing up and down in the courtyard of the town hall. She was later told that the man was 'a dangerous anarchist', and was being kept under surveillance until the end of the play, just in case its contents incited his political feelings. With the help of Lorca she obtained his release. In gratitude for this the public surged on to the stage at the end of the production, thus apparently confirming the authorities' fears of the emotive qualities of the play: for a while Lorca was even afraid that the crowd would lynch the local caciques.

In 1979 a leading left-wing Andalucían journalist, Antonio Ramos Espejo, paid a visit to the village of Fuente Obejuna, and found that the basis of local discontent had remained fundamentally unchanged over the centuries. The seventy-year old mayor, questioned by Ramos Espejo on the subject of land ownership, replied: 'There are those who have a lot, and those who have nothing. There's nothing in between. It's either the landowner or the day labourer.' Of the 56,311 hectares of land falling within the territory of the village, 22,300 were owned by only 21 owners. The plight of the day-labourer was highlighted by the startlingly high level of emigration: the population of the village fell from 19,378 in 1940 to just over 7,000 in 1979.

'Andalucíans,' cried the writer Blas Infante, 'rise up; seek land and liberty.' The demand for land has been a constant one throughout Andalucía's history, though many agrarian reformers from the time of Charles III's enlightened agricultural minister, Aranda, have argued that the deep-rooted popular desire for a *reparto* or share-out of the land, does not represent a very practical solution to the problem of land ownership. Large areas of the latifundia consist of poor pasture which would never prosper as peasant farms; other areas are suitable only for monoculture and would require only two bad years of drought to force the peasant owner to sell them. The idea of a reparto was completely dropped by the Socialist government of

Felipe González. In 1984 this Government introduced an agrarian reform law – the first of its kind since 1932 – which did not call into question the actual ownership of the land, but stipulated instead that the farming rights of badly used land should be temporarily taken over and handed over, under contract, to co-operatives. As for the day-labourers, their position improved considerably with the introduction of state support for the months in which they are not working. None of these reforms, however, satisfy the demands of the workers' union known as the SOC (Sociedad de Obreros Campesinos), a radical organization in the tradition of Andalucían anarchism, but with an admixture of pacifist and ecological ideals. One of the main centres of this movement is the village of Marinaleda, in the easternmost part of the province of Seville.

Marinaleda is a small village in the middle of flat, wheat-growing country. It has a modern, undistinguished and fairly prosperous appearance, and bears the characteristically tasteless marks of recent civic improvements, such as an over-neat row of flower beds along the main street. There is nothing to hold the visitor's attention save for the name of the village square – Plaza de Libertad – and the banner flying over it, which bears the symbol of a dove and the words TIERRA DE LIBERTAD. On the square stands the Casa de Cultura, a worker's club, inside which you will find a portrait of a bearded, intensely serious young man standing in a field and addressing a group of admiring peasants. I thought the picture to be a representation of Jesus Christ in a modern setting, but it turned out to be of the man I had come to the village to meet, the village schoolteacher and mayor, Juan Manuel Sánchez Gordillo.

Thanks largely to Sánchez Gordillo, Marinaleda has a reputation as one of the most politically radical villages in the south of Spain, if not in Europe: its percentage of communists voters is virtually the highest in the western part of the continent. Sánchez Gordillo first caught the public eye in 1980, when he organized in Marinaleda 'a hunger strike against hunger.' Later he took up a policy of occupying nearby large estates, one of which, about sixteen kilometres from the village, belonged to one of Andalucía's largest landowners, the Duke of Infantado. I was able to track him down there in the spring of 1990. Attached to a post at the entrance of the estate were the words, ESTA TIERRA ES NUESTRA MARINALEDA, 'This land is our Marinaleda'. On the long drive up to the cortijo I passed a group of villagers, carrying hoes and rakes, the women dressed in black. They could have been straight out of a communist poster of the 1930's, and this impression was reinforced by the political badges they all were wearing. The scene outside the cortijo itself was more like a film set, the car I was in adding an incongruous note to what appeared to be a recreation of a pre-war agrarian strike. Dark, unshaven men and their families lay around in a large circle as if waiting for instructions. In the middle of all this prowled the leonine and instantly recognizable figure of Sánchez Gordillo wearing a Tolstoyan suit and a red sash. He addressed me in a slow, solemn voice, with no trace of a smile. I could not help feeling, con-

Labourer c. 1920

fronted by such a manner and appearance, that I was in the presence of one of the messianic figures who toured the Andalucían countryside in the 19th century. He talked of the inadequacy of the present agrarian reforms, of the great extent of the Duke of Infantado's properties, and of how the land in Andalucía continued to be in the hands of the very few. As he spoke, he gestured to a bucolic backdrop of shimmering wheat fields stretching towards the pale profile of distant mountains.

It is easy to romanticize Sánchez Gordillo, just as it is easy to romanticize the poverty, landlessness and exploitation that he has devoted his energies to eradicate. Tragedy and suffering are as integral to the traditional, stereotypical image of Andalucía as are joy and plenty. Travel writers have always loved to emphasize this dichotomy, which for many is symbolized in the clash between the blindingly white walls of Andalucía and the jet black grilles of their windows, or in the division of a bull-ring into *sol* and *sombra*, sun and shade. *Sol y Sombra* is the title of the chapter on Andalucía in Jan Morris' enormously successful *Spain* (first published in 1964), a chapter in which it is even hinted that this poverty, 'borne without grievance', has an attractive dignity: 'For one must admit that the earthiness of Spain, which is the cousin of backwardness, is often very beautiful to experience.' The poverty of Andalucía has to a certain extent become part of its tourist appeal, and it could even be argued that the interest shown by Goytisolo in what he terms the 'third-world' conditions of Almería was a fundamentally romantic one, for the primitive qualities that impressed him here were those that later made this sophisticated city-dweller fall in love with Morocco. Poverty in a southern, backward and preferably rural setting has often seemed exotic to many. However, these same people would be unlikely to find glamour in Andalucía's recently built areas of urban deprivation, such as Seville's dangerous and grafitti-scrawled suburb of Tres Mil Viviendas. The poverty in such places has nothing specifically Andalucían about it, and is little different from that found in the unexotic inner cities of Britain and America. This is a poverty which does not conform to the tidy and esentially poetic notion of sol y sombra.

The emphasis on the 'sun' and 'shade' of Andalucía is a reflection of how Spain itself has generally been characterized, as a land of extremes, of austerity and sensuality, passion and honour, grandeur and decay, fantasy and common sense. Hyperbole, the great sin of travel writing, has at times been ludicrously present in the literature on Spain. 'It has so long and annually been considered permissible,' wrote Richard Ford in 1845, 'when writing about Romantic Spain, to take leave of common sense, to ascend on stilts, and converse in the Cambysean vein, that those who descend to common-place matter-of-fact, are considered not only to be inaesthetic, unpoetical and unimaginative but deficient in truth and power of observation.' And what is true of Spain in general is doubly so of Andalucía, for this region has long been thought of as the distillation of all things Spanish. Almost everything that we consider as 'typically Spanish' is Andalucían in origin, from bull-fighting to flamenco. Andalucía is a compendium of every cliché that has ever been written about Spain, clichés that were wittily summarized in Mario Praz's wonderfully perverse and scabrous *Unromantic Spain* (1929): 'Old Spanish towns languorous beneath the warm sun and the scent of orange blossoms, castellated mansions and Moorish arabesques, a proud people hugging fierce passions beneath their cloaks, guitars and castanets, donkeys and courteous peasants, long white roads and snowy ribbed sierras, quaint old market squares, narrow streets with balconies atop and animated paseos, gardens everywhere, swimming in the sun.'

The Andalucíans are rightly angered by the cliché-ridden image of their region which is still promoted abroad. Yet this image has been as much the creation of their own writers as of foreign ones. For instance, the tediously sentimental plays written early this century by the Quintero brothers portrayed Andalucía as a land of endless gaiety and frivolity, while the works of the contemporary and widely successful gypsy playwright and director, Salvator Távora, represent the region misleadingly as a place which has known only suffering and oppression. The Andalucían writer who has done most to influence general attitudes towards Andalucía both in Spain and abroad has undoubtedly been Federico García Lorca. Lorca, in a talk which he gave about his most popular collection of poems, *El Romancero Gitano* or *Gypsy Ballads*, stressed how this book was 'anti-folklore, anti-local colour, and anti-flamenco,' and that it contained 'not one short jacket, suit of lights, wide-brimmed hat or Andalucían tambourine'. However, though Lorca's

Andalucía is radically different from that of his lightweight contemporaries, the Quinteros, it drew on and strenghtened all the clichés conveyed by the passionate chords and anguished wails of flamenco music. This is the Andalucía of the tragic, solitary gypsy, the Andalucía of *cante jondo* or 'deep song', a cry of pain from the mysterious, distant past, a cry heard in the wind which rustles through the olive trees, stirring up the passions that lie imprisoned behind barred windows, and permeating the very soul of the Andalucían people.

The clichés about Andalucía cannot always be ridiculed like this, and indeed are generally difficult to avoid and express much that is true. None the less they provide only the most limited view of the region. Flamenco, bull-fighting and gypsies are vital components of Andalucían culture, but not the only components; similarly Andalucía has its smiling and tragic faces, but it also has a wide range of moods in between. For a place which Ford was already describing in 1845 as 'the most popular destination for travellers to Spain,' and which has since become one of the main tourist centres of Europe, it is surprising how little known Andalucía remains. The fact that Ford's own *Handbook* contains what is still, nearly 150 years later, the best guide and general introduction to Andalucía is itself testimony to this. Our ignorance of Andalucía is reflected not just in our preconceptions of the place but in our knowledge of its towns, villages and landscapes. Most of Andalucía is as yet remarkably unspoilt, and away from the coast and main towns, you will find countless villages that have maintained folk and crafts traditions over the centuries, and where the tourist is still a welcome novelty. Travelling here should make you wary of generalizing too much about the character of the place. Andalucía constitutes a geographical and cultural identity of enormous individuality, and yet its apparent unity is belied by the startling variety of parts that make up the whole.

The size and emptiness of Andalucía will soon impress themselves on the traveller. The largest region in Spain, as large as a small country such as Hungary, Portugal or Switzerland, Andalucía is also one of the least densely populated areas in Europe, having 70 people per square kilometre, as opposed to 360 in England. Much of the terrain is wild and mountainous, and travel within the region has not always been easy. The main lines of communication have always been along the Guadalquivir valley. Those arriving in Andalucía by sea generally landed at Cádiz, and, up to the mid 19th century, would often continue their journey by sailing up the Guadalquivir to Seville. The main route connecting Seville with the rest of Spain was nicknamed by Lope de Vega 'the silver route', for it was along here that there once was transported to Madrid all the bounty from the Indies. Passing through Córdoba, the route follows the Guadalquivir almost up to its source in Jaén province, before turning abruptly north towards the Pass of Despeñaperros. Before beginning to silt up in the course of the 16th and 17th centuries the river was navigable up to Córdoba, thanks to the Romans, who once dug channels to prevent the

El Tempranillo

water level from dropping. As for the road from Seville to Despeñaperros, this was excellently modernized during the reign of Charles III, and was supplemented after 1870 by a railway. The coming of the railway to Andalucía in the late 19th century greatly improved links with places off the main Guadalquivir axis such as Huelva, Algeciras, Ronda, Málaga, Granada and Almería. However, anyone travelling to those parts had still to expect long and often arduous journeys. Málaga, which thanks to its airport is today the most popular point of arrival in Andalucía, was known until as late as the 1960's for its poor road communications with the rest of its province. Almería meanwhile is perhaps the most isolated major town in Spain. The railway link with Madrid was built principally to serve the mining industry, and well into this century travellers from Almería to the Spanish capital preferred to sail east to Cartagena or Murcia, and then make their way from there. The once notoriously bad inland route west from Almería was not improved until the 1970's, and it is only since 1992 that the drive from Almería to Seville has been reduced to a manageable five or six hours.

Travellers have loved to emphasize the adventurous nature of an Andalucían journey. The first thrills usually came while crossing Despeñaperros, and were inspired as much by jubilant feelings on arriving in Andalucía as by the reputation of the pass as a dangerous place. Travellers of the Romantic period evoked at such length the savage, primitive aspect of Despeñaperros that they almost all overlooked the fact that the road they were on, built in 1779 by the French architect Le Maur, was, with its tunnels, hair-pin bends and parapets, one of the great marvels of modern engineering: the Baron de Bourgoing described it in 1808 as 'one of the finest high roads in Europe'. The landscape took on for these travellers an exaggerated, wild appearance because they came here with heads filled with tales of wolves, and, above all, bandits. Andalucía was one of the notorious bandit areas of Europe, and banditry ended up by being one of the region's great attractions. Banditry here goes back at least to the time when gangs of Moors took to the roads to escape from their Christian persecutors, and reached its heyday during the 18th and early 20th centuries with the important trade in smuggled tobacco and other goods from Gibraltar. The empty, remote character of so much of Andalucía was a major contributory factor in the spread of banditry, which was concentrated largely in the mountainous and little populated areas of the region, above all in and around the Sierra Morena, the Alpujarras and the Serranía de Ronda.

The blatant social injustice expressed by Andalucía's land structure has also been suggested as a major cause of banditry. By the 19th century the Andalucían bandit had certainly gained popular fame as a latter-day Robin Hood, a friend and helper of the poor and a sworn enemy of the landlord and the cacique. He was seen as an essentially noble figure who had been driven into crime through justifiable outburts of passion. One such person was José Ulloa Tragabuches, a Ronda bullfighter in the school of the celebrated Pedro Romero (see page 167), who had been forced to abandon a promising career for a life of banditry after killing his adulterous wife in a passionate rage. The most legendary of Andalucía's bandits was José María Hinojosa Cabacho, known as El Tempranillo. Born in 1805 in Jauja (Córdoba), a fishing village on the banks of the river Genil, he was only thirteen when he killed a man during the pilgrimage festivities to the nearby hermitage of the Fuensanta. Why he did so is not clear, though in the various popular books and films that have dealt with his career, the motives have always been presented as honourable ones: that he was avenging either the murder of his father, or an attempt to take away his fiancée, or even the dishonouring of his mother. At all events, José María ran off and joined a notorious gang called the *Niños de Écija* (the 'Children of Écija'), and later established his own headquarters in the cave of Los Órganos, which is visible from the Despeñaperros road. He made travellers pay protection money to ensure a safe journey, but also earned respect for his courteous treatment of his victims and his consideration of the poor. In 1828 he declared that 'the King rules in Spain, but I rule in the sierra', and four years later the king acknowledged his noble reputation by granting him a royal pardon. An English traveller called George Dennis described him as five foot tall and with bow legs, but to Mérimée, the author of *Carmen*, he was a handsome, dashing figure, which is how he is portrayed on page 24 by the English artist John Lewis. He died in 1833, and his tomb can be seen in the village cemetery of Alameda (Córdoba) just to the south of Jauja; his gun is in the possession of a local family.

Not all bandits were so kind or civilized as José María was reputed to have been. White crosses marking the sites of roadside murders were numerous in the mountainous districts of Andalucía, and indicated that the dangers in travelling here were not purely figments of the Romantic imagination. However, as Ford noted, Romantic travellers vastly exaggerated the dangers so as to give added drama to an account of their adventures. It should be said that of the hundreds of travellers who wrote up their Spanish journeys, only one, a certain Alexander Slidell, actually exprienced a bandit attack, and this did not happen in Andalucía but in La Mancha. Travellers took a perverse delight in the feeling of danger, Disraeli even claiming that his fear of being assaulted on a journey in the Serranía de Ronda had raised his spirits enormously. To be deprived of danger came sometimes as a great disappointment, as Hans Christian Andersen found out when travelling across the Sierra Morena under the protection of armed soldiers: 'I felt myself so thoroughly safe that I was suddenly seized with a desire to witness a slight encounter with banditti. The whole country seems as if formed for it. . .' Andersen went on to relate an apocryphal story about Alexandre Dumas in which the Frenchman, before coming to Spain, had sent a cheque of 1000 francs to a bandit chief, asking him to arrange an attack on his party, on the condition, however, that no physical danger was to be run.

In the 1870's banditry began gradually to die out in Andalucía, thanks to the successful measures taken by the then Governor of Córdoba, Julián de Zugasti y Saenza, later the author of the first serious study of Andalucían banditry. The man generally thought to be the last Andalucían bandit was Juan Mingolla Gallardo, nicknamed *Pasos Largos* or 'Long Steps'. Born near Ronda in 1874, he was finally incarcerated in a penitentiary in El Puerto de Santa María in 1932. Here, suffering from tuberculosis, he almost ended his days, but he managed to escape, and died in a more worthy manner, shot while firing against the Guardia Civil in 1934. 'Is it true,' asked Gerald Brenan on a train journey across the Sierra Morena in 1949, 'that there are bandits in the Sierra?' 'You bet there are,' replied his Spanish travelling companion, 'all those rocks and peaks you see are full of them.' In fact the man was not really referring to bandits at all but to the 'Reds' who after the Civil War hid from the authorities in the same caves that had been used by the bandits. The legend of banditry lived on a long time in Andalucía, and as late as 1986, gullible travellers could still apparently be fooled by it. On a lonely road in Huelva, two policemen with a sense of humour stopped an English car, and interrogated its driver, the poet Ted Walker. They warned him of brigands along the road, but Walker paid no attention to this, until, shortly afterwards, a group of sinister men in check shirts and broad-belted corduroys blocked his way. Walker thought that his time had come, but it turned out that these men were merely employees of the Río Tinto Mining Company, and they were stopping him because of dynamiting ahead.

The rebuilding of the main road between Madrid and Seville, then the most used highway in Spain, was not the only step taken during the enlightened reign of Charles III to ensure the greater safety of travellers in Andalucía. Proposals were also put forward to populate the empty, lawless lands that lay immediately to the south of the Sierra Morena. Charles III's minister, Pablo de Olavide, administrator of Andalucía, suggested that colonies of foreigners should be established here, foreigners being preferred to Spaniards so as not to depopulate other parts of Spain. Eventually around 6,000 settlers came here, all of them Catholics, the great majority from Belgium and German-speaking countries, but also some from France, Switzerland and Italy, and even a handful from Greece. In charge of recruitment was a Bavarian officer called Johann Kaspar von Thürriegel, who, after serving in the Prussian army, had come to Spain to set up a sword factory. Among those whom he managed to enlist for the colonies was a group of convicts on the point of being shipped to the notorious French penal colony of Guyana. The French government had been glad to get rid of them.

La Carolina, the first village of any size that you come to after Despeñaperros, was the most important of the twelve colonies that were set up by Charles III and Olavide (among the others were La Carlota and La Luisiana, see page 291). As with the other colonies, and in complete contrast to most Andalucían villages, it was laid out on a grid pattern, with wide avenues and neatly arranged houses. As late as 1818, the American traveller George Ticknor could describe La Carolina as having a prosperous, comfortable appearance, so different from that of the squalid villages that he had just been through in La Mancha. The fortunes of La Carolina, however, had not been as smiling as they had appeared to Ticknor. The Baron de Bourgoing, who had visited the place ten years earlier, considered that a great decline had set in following the disgrace of Olavide in 1775. Olavide, as befitted an Enlightenment reformer, had settled in La Carolina, and had begun to witness at close hand his dreams for the place coming true. Unfortunately he had great political enemies, and these had arranged to make him fall foul of the Inquisition. The latter, after throwing him into prison and confiscating his property at La Carolina, accused him of possessing prohibited books, and of showing no regard to the faith. Condemned as a heretic, he was forced to spend eight years in a monastery reading books on piety. On the excuse of taking the waters in Catalonia, he escaped to France, and after the Revolution retired to the Loire. By then at least half of the foreign settlers in the Sierra Morena colonies had either died or gone home. The heat was unbearable to many of the northerners, though according to the English traveller Swinburne, the fatalities were mainly caused by 'eating unwholesome herbs, and drinking too much wine and brandy'. Those who remained married Spaniards, and gradually lost touch with their origins. By Bourgoing's day, a good twelve years had passed since the village had had any German-speaking priest. George Borrow, during his travels around Spain in the 1830's, came across a family of German descent, and was surprised by how they had forgotten the language and all the traditions of their ancestors. That La Carolina had had foreign settlers at all, and that it had been an experimental community of relatively recent foundation, was apparently unknown to one English traveller, William Pitt Byrne, who passed through the place in the 1860's. 'What a quaint old town it was,' he enthused. Pitt Byrne was one of the many travellers who had suffered the intoxicating effects of the Despeñaperros crossing, and had come to see everything through an oriental haze. 'The street architecture,' he wrote of La Carolina, 'was, to a certain extent, Moorish, and the mud walls, denuded *ventas*, jealously caged ground floor windows, mysterious arched entrances, and colonnaded *solanos*, contributed to its oriental character.'

The province which you reach at Despeñaperros is that of Jaén, a province only a three hours journey by car from Madrid and yet which is perhaps one of the least known parts of Andalucía. From La Carolina, as from the many villages in Jaén province with magnificent vantage points, you are confronted by an endless rolling landscape of red and white earth studded with regular lines of olive trees. There are over 150,000 of them in the province, making the place the largest olive-growing district in Spain. No landscape, you might think, could be more Andalucían, and you feel that it is only natural that in the middle of all these olives, in the town of Jaén, was baptized one of the Andalucíans best known abroad, the guitarist Andrés Segovia. But Jaén province has actually as much of the character of Castille as it does of Andalucía, and this ambiguous position between the regions seems even reflected in the Moorish name for Jaén, *Geen*, 'the caravan route'. The impressive yet monotonous regularity of the countryside has a note of Castilian sobriety, as do many of the province's towns and villages. The architecture is often heavy and sombre, quite unlike that of other parts of Andalucía. The twin towns of Úbeda and Baeza, two of the finest architectural showpieces of southern Spain, are filled with red stone renaissance palaces and churches that are completely Castilian in type. Appropriately, the poet, monk and leading exponent of the Castilian mystical tradition, Juan de la Cruz (St. John of the Cross), died at Úbeda, while at Baeza, the Seville-born poet Antonio Machado completed in 1917 one of the greatest books of poems ever dedicated to Castille, the *Campos de Castilla.*

While it is difficult to travel in European regions such as Provence or Tuscany without thinking of the painters who have worked there, in Andalucía it is the memories of poets that are everywhere present. In Baeza, the dark little schoolroom where Machado taught has been preserved as a charming, dusty and little visited memorial to him, and, on the edge of the town, the path where the poet loved to walk has been renamed the Paseo Antonio Machado. Here you will find a statue to

Machado, the poet's features turned east towards a landscape which often features in his work, a grandiose landscape rising up into a massive mountain wall formed by the parallel sierras of Cazorla and Segura.

This mountainous expanse, Spain's largest National Park, is the main natural attraction of Jaén province, and one of the great wildernesses of Europe, with ibex, deer and lynx. The attractive small town of Cazorla, directly facing Baeza on the lower eastern slopes of the Cazorla range, is now a popular summer resort, and within the National Park are such tourist attractions as nature trails and a wildlife preserve. Up to the 1950's there were scarcely any visitors at all to this area, and a French geographer, Dr. Bide, describing in the Alpine Club Annual of 1902 a climb up to the nearby peak of Mount Sagra, just to the west of the Segura range, relates the great difficulties that he had in crossing this forested and practically roadless part of Spain. Even today it is easy to shake off all other tourists, as you will probably find out if you decide to enter the Park by the rough track which leads up to the mountains from the road south from Cazorla to Quesada (see page 356). Soon you leave behind the ubiquitous olive fields of Jaén – the terrifying extent of which becomes more apparent than ever in the panoramic views to be had from this steeply winding road – and then enter a dense forest of pines. The trees spread up to the top of the Cazorla range and down into the long narrow valley which separates the range from that of Segura. Descending into this forested, unpopulated valley, you will find yourself near the source of the rushing mountain stream which runs the whole length of it. The world you are in seems more Appalachian than Andalucían, but the stream which is born in these mountains is that which once gave Andalucía its name. This is the river the Romans called Betis, and the Moors renamed Guad-al-Quivir, 'the Great River'. Born in the northeastern corner of Andalucía, and dying by Andalucía's Atlantic coast, it is a river entirely contained by the region, and the most important river in Spain. The ships that once plied it, laden with the region's abundant products and later with riches from the Indies, turned it into a symbol of Andalucía's wealth and greatness, and as such it has always been praised by poets. In the rock face above its source are inscribed famous lines by the Golden Age poet Luis de Góngora:

> *¡Oh gran río, gran rey de Andalucía,*
> *de arenas nobles, ya que no doradas!*
> O great river, great king of Andalucía,
> with your noble if not golden sands

Góngora came from Córdoba, and these lines are taken from a poem dedicated to his home town and its surroundings. Córdoba province adjoins Jaén, and sees the Guadalquivir valley opening up, the arable lands or *campaña* becoming yet more fertile. Jaén's olive belt extends into this province, and covers much of its southern

Source of the Guadalquivir

half, but there are more signs of other cultivation, for instance great expanses of wheat, brilliant yellow patches of sunflowers, orchards of oranges, cotton fields, and, around Montilla, extensive vineyards. Góngora's poem continues:

> *¡Oh fértil llano, oh sierras levantadas,*
> *que privilegia el cielo y dora el día!*
> O fertile plain, o soaring hills
> favoured by the sky and gilded by the day!

To Góngora this countryside was Arcadia, and in later life he retired to an isolated property outside Córdoba to find inspiration for his pastoral masterpiece, *The Solitudes.* Another writer to view the Córdoba landscape in terms of a pastoral idyll was the 19th-century novelist Juan Valera, who was born and brought up in the town of Cabra, in the south of the province. In his study of the women of Córdoba, *La Córdobesa*, Valera wrote: 'The fertile lands of Cabra are a paradise. There, if only mythology was in fashion, we could say that Pomona placed her throne, and, continuing in the same vein, and without the slightest exaggeration, we could add that Pallas has her own throne in the Hermitages [above Córdoba, see page 289], Ceres hers in the fields that stretch between Baena and Valenzuela, and Bacchus his in Los Moriles, the wine of which is far superior to that of all Jerez.' The villages of Cabra, Baena and Doña Mencía, where Valera set most of his novels of provincial life, mark the transition between the Guadalquivir valley and the foothills of Andalucía's southern ranges. They herald what might be called the most classical landscape of Andalucía. From here down into the provinces of Málaga and Granada extends a landscape of wheat- and olive-covered slopes alternating with bare, arid hills and sharp outcrops of rock, the whole intercut with winding ravines lined on their lower slopes with lush vegetation. This is a noble countryside structured like a landscape painting by a 17th-century artist such as Poussin, a world in which a pipe-playing goatherd would not seem out of place.

Córdoba province cannot and has not always been seen in the idyllic light evoked by Góngora and Valera. Even along the Guadalquivir Valley, almost up to Seville, there were dangerous desert-like stretches: two of Olavide's colonies, La Carlota and Luisiana (Seville), were established next to two such notorious areas, the *desiertos* of La Parilla and Moncloa. The sad, lonely quality which many find in Jaén province can also be found in that of Córdoba. Córdoba itself, with its cheerful white houses and flower-filled balconies, has come for many to express Andalucían gaiety, but the traditional view of the place is that of a melancholy, abandoned town. *Córdoba, lejana y sola* ('Córdoba, distant and lonely') is the opening of a famous poem by García Lorca. Directly above the town, hugging the northern banks of the Guadalquivir from Jaén province almost up to the town of Seville, looms the range of the Sierra Morena. The slopes above Córdoba, in which are situated the hermitages mentioned by Valera, are as verdant as those above Florence, but if you go beyond them you will reach one of the saddest districts in all Andalucía. Much of this northern half of Córdoba province is mountainous scrubland with a scattering of decayed and ugly towns such as Pozoblanco and Peñarroya Pueblonuevo, the latter a once-prosperous mining town now left to ruin following the exhaustion of its coal mines by a French company. Just to the west of Peñarroya is the Fuente Obejuna of Lope de Vega fame, while to the north, in the northernmost tip of Andalucía, is the village of Belalcázar, a place of enormous architectural interest but virtually unvisited, its historical monuments collapsing and its population rapidly dwindling (see page 271). In terms of architecture and atmosphere, there is even less of Andalucía in northern Córdoba than there is in Jaén. 'Although Pozoblano belongs to the province of Córdoba,' wrote Gerald Brenan, 'it cannot be said to lie in Andalucía. That low step up from the Guadalquivir valley to the *meseta* lands one in an altogether different geographical and ethnic region. Take architecture. The houses with their deep windows and granite lintels look cold and severe. . .'

From Fuente Obejuna a little used road through wild countryside, the C421, heads along the Sierra Morena in a southwesterly direction, into the province of Seville. Almost at the border between Córdoba and Seville provinces, the mountain scenery changes from bare and shrub-covered slopes to hillsides thick with oaks. The landscape is now mellow and welcoming, and the area is in fact a popular weekend and summer retreat for the people of Seville. The transformation which the Sierra Morena undergoes as it enters Seville province is symptomatic of the whole character of this province, which is the very opposite of austere. Seville itself lies just to the south of the sierra, at the fertile heart of the Guadalquivir basin. The heat intensifies as does the humidity, and at the height of summer not even the night brings any slackening of these conditions. Despite this, Seville and its surroundings have always been thought to encapsulate all the fertility and sensuality of Andalucía. In an essay on Don Juan (1921), Ortega y Gasset reflected that this libertine could not possibly have come from any other part of Spain, and that the environment induced in its inhabitants and visitors a perpetual, half-drunken state. Today, the old town of Seville has been enveloped by a large industrial and residential belt, but up to the end of the 19th century, it stood surrounded by its medieval walls in the middle of countryside that must have seemed like a great orchard. Dundas Murray, a British traveller of the 1840's, wrote that Seville was the 'Queen of Andalucía', and that 'her presence is aroused (in the visitor) by his entering a cloud of fragrance exhaled by her girdle of orange-groves; so heavy and luscious are the odours of this zone, that the senses feel oppressed.' Given the countless romantic descriptions of Seville such as these, it needed someone as down-to-earth as Richard Ford to point out that the odours that sometimes dominated the town were less sweet than those of oranges. In the early 19th century, in the interests of improving the navigability of the Guadalquivir, the river was diverted by a channel to the west of the town, and the much-admired stretch which divides old Seville from the former separate township of Triana, was blocked up at one end, and thus turned into a long stagnant backwater. Right up to 1992, when this stretch of water was allowed to run freely again, romantic feelings inspired by Seville were tempered somewhat by the rank, all-pervasive smells coming from the river.

Just above Seville the Guadalquivir heads away from the Sierra Morena and turns sharply south towards the sea, into which, to use a word of George Borrow, it 'disembogues' at Sanlúcar de Barrameda. Dundas Murray, though enraptured by Seville and its province, could not raise much enthusiasm for the Guadalquivir, particularly in its last stages, when it runs through unrelievedly flat, marshy terrain. He wrote of the stretch below Seville that 'its tide is dull, its water cloudy, its current lingering, and its banks canal-like and low. . . it divests itself by degrees of every feature of beauty till it becomes little else than a mighty drain, meandering leisurely through a vast flat.' Occasional pleasure boats ply today the stretch between Seville and Sanlúcar, and though the journey is tedious at times and very long (up to eight hours if the tide is low) you experience a certain haunting feeling as you gradually leave all villages and houses behind, eventually to pass, on the right banks of the river, a mysterious barrier of pines. The sense of mystery is compounded by the knowledge that behind these pines lies another of Andalucía's famed wildernesses, the Coto Doñana.

'Directly in front,' wrote Dundas Murray, 'was a tract of land that, from its singular contrast to the surrounding scenery, instantly arrested our eyes. "That," said our guide, "is the Coto of San Lucar [Coto Doñana]; it is a *despoblado* (empty area), and extends backwards from the river for seven or eight leagues; a lonely place it is, and as full of deer, wild boars and mountain cats, as the sea is full of fish; *vaya*! in all Spain there is no better place for game than the Coto of San Lucar!".' His interest thus aroused, Dundas Murray felt compelled to visit the place. 'My acquaintance with Andalucía,' he explained, 'having been as yet confined to its ancient cities and still more ancient roads, I was anxious to see something of its wilds; and this desolate expanse of sand and forest – a fragment, apparently, of some African desert, cast by a convulsion of nature on the shores of Spain – was just one of those solitudes with which the province was said to abound, and which I had long desired to explore.'

The Coto Doñana is a roadless expanse of over 27,000 hectacres, bordered to the south by the Guadalquivir, and to the west by the Atlantic. It comprises three main types of terrain. There are the pine forests, which are popularly thought to have provided the wood for the Spanish Armada and which were at one time far more extensive than they are now, having been brutally decimated in the early years of this century. Then there are the sand dunes, so wild and grand that they were even able to provide some of the settings for the film of *Lawrence of Arabia*. Finally come the great expanses of marshland and lakes, reduced in the summer months to a sinister desert of cracked mud. As with the Camargue – the geographically comparable wilderness formed by the estuary of the Rhône in the South of France – the Coto Doñana is a Mecca for naturalists. As in Dundas Murray's day you will find here wild cats, otters, lynx, wild cattle, the occasional wolf, and an abundance of wild boar and red and fallow deer, the Coto being the only place in Spain where red deer live permanently in a lowland area. Flamingo flocks land here in the spring, and you can also see such birds as egrets, kites, bee-eaters, hoopoes, vultures, and, if you are lucky, Spain's rarest bird, the imperial eagle. Among the only signs of human habitation in the Coto are a group of primitive stick and mud dwellings in the forest overlooking the Guadalquivir: these belong to charcoal burners and to some of the boatmen who ferry people over the river from Sanlúcar. Nearby is a charming neo-gothic summer villa built in the late 19th century for the Marquis of Villafranca. But the main residence in the Coto is the isolated former hunting hunting lodge of the Dukes of Medina Sidonia.

For over five hundred years the Coto was a hunting reserve to these Dukes, whose family home was at Sanlúcar. Their estate, which was originally known as that of 'Doña Ana' in homage to a wife of one of the Dukes, was first mentioned in a document of 1495 in which the 3rd Duke requested that the people of Sanlúcar obtain 'as many deer and stags as possible' for the restocking of the forest. From the 17th up to the 19th centuries, all the kings of Spain came to hunt here, the most important visit being that of Philip IV in 1624, in whose honour the original hunting lodge, the Casa del Bosque was enlarged into the present Palace. One of the many distinguished guests to have stayed in the Palace is thought to have been Goya, who might have painted here his portraits of the *Maja vestida* and the *Maja desnuda*. In the 1880's there hunted at the Coto an Englishman called Abel Chapman, who was later the author of *Wild Spain* (1894) and *Unexplored Spain* (1910). These two books were esentially manuals for the huntsman, but they were also among the first serious studies of the life of Spain's wildernesses. Chapman was the first to emphasize the importance of the Coto as a stopping-place for birds migrating between North Africa and the coast of Western Europe; he also published in *The Ibis* of 1884 an article which must certainly have heightened the mystique of this strange area. This article met with incredulity in England, dealing as it did with the sighting in the Coto of wild camels, and aquatic ones at that, who rushed at high speed across the swamps, creating clouds of spray. These camels were not the product of an over-imaginative mind but instead the offspring of a group of eighty camels brought over in 1820 from the Canary Islands to Cádiz by the Marquis of Villafranca. The Marquis' intention was to use these beasts as pack animals and for ploughing, but such was the fear they inspired and such their uselessness for the plough that in the end they were let loose in the Coto, where they successfully bred. Sixty remained in Chapman's day, but by 1950 there were only five, the majority of the camels having been caught and sold off as venison. Though a few more were brought in during the filming of *Lawrence of Arabia*, there are none surviving today.

In 1901 the Coto Doñana was sold by the Medina Sidonias to the sherry baron William Garvey, who supposedly recouped his investment in two years from the selling off of the Coto's pines. Successive purchases reduced the Coto to its present size, and caused growing concern about the future of this wildlife paradise. In 1958 another Englishman, Guy Mountfort, published *Portrait of a Wilderness*, a book which did much to draw world attention to the plight of the Coto. One result was the setting-up of the World Wildlife Fund in 1961, which four years later succeeded in persuading the Spanish authorities to turn the Coto into a National Park, thus stopping a projected highway across it and a large holiday camp along its coastline. Today it is possible to swim and even to drive your own car along its long and dirty Atlantic beach, but to visit the interior you are obliged either to take one of the slow and frankly boring Landrover tours organized by the Park authorities, or to ask beforehand for special permission, usually granted only to serious naturalists (see page 362). Many a time, lying on the Coto's beach, I was tempted to make illicit forays into the interior, and, one late afternooon, actually did so only to be turned back five minutes later, not by Park guards or by soldiers (for the Palace is now sometimes used as a retreat for Spain's prime ministers), but by a vicious cloud of mosquitoes.

The Guadalquivir, as it skirts the Coto Doñana, passes by three of Andalucía's provinces: that of Seville gives way to those of Huelva and Cádiz, which are divided from each other by the river. Huelva is Andalucía's westernmost province, and extends to the Portuguese border. It falls into two distinct geographical areas. Much of its southern coastal half is flat, sandy country covered with pines, and very reminiscent of the large, forested coastal stretch of the Landes in southwestern France; near the Portuguese border you come to rich strawberry country, a cultivation of recent date which has turned the town of Lepe – hitherto best known for the proverbial slowness of its inhabitants, the butt of many an Andalucían joke – into one of the wealthiest communities in Spain. The northern half of the province takes in the western end of the Sierra Morena, and is almost continuously mountainous and wooded. At the centre of this district is the beautiful Sierra de Aracena, the slopes of which abound in pines, oaks, chestnuts, apples, pears and recently planted eucalyptus trees; pigs thrive on the chestnuts, and the village of Jabugo produces many of the best hams in Spain. The mountains throughout northern Huelva are gently rounded and without dramatic features such as tall rocky outcrops or deep gorges. Their beauty comes from their wild extensiveness and rich mantle of trees. Arias Montano, a 16th-century poet and theologian who had worked in the Escorial, ended his days in the hermitage of Nuestra Señora de los Ángeles, enjoying one of the finest views to be had of this landscape, a view made up of an apparently infinite succession of undulating, dark green silhouettes. A Jesuit missionary visiting the area in Montano's day was struck by its wild primitive aspect and the poverty of its inhabitants, whose Spanish was almost impossible to understand. The villages here, with houses crowned by quaintly irregular wooden galleries, are silent secretive places hidden among the trees. However, their tourist potential has become increasingly exploited since the late 1980's, thanks partly to greatly improved road links with Seville, many of whose inhabitants have holiday homes here. More ominously, a handful of English people have bought houses in the area, believing this to be one of the most attractive, least spoilt areas of southern Spain. The English pioneering few have generally been the vanguard of a large-scale invasion, and it is quite possible that within a decade or so the quiet villages of northern Huelva will be filled with English voices.

The English have already left their mark on this district, quite literally so. The one major interruption in the forested landscape occurs just below the Sierra de Aracena, and takes the form of a gigantic cavity wrinkled by deep, terraced fissures. The steep slopes, turning at sunset from dusty pink to vermillion, are striped with bright green rivulets carrying iron that on contact with the air changes colour so that the rivulets form at the bottom of this infernal landscape what appears to be a meandering stream of blood. The river is the Río Tinto or 'Red River', and gives its name to what are perhaps the oldest worked mines in the world. Popular tradition has it that these were the fabled mines of King Solomon, and there is still a section of them known as the Cerro Salomón, a name from which is also derived the names of the nearby villages, Zalamea la Vieja (now known as Nerva), and Zalamea la Real. The Phoenicians and the Romans exploited the mines extensively, but they were afterwards abandoned, and only rediscovered in 1556 as a result of a search for mines instigated by Philip II with a view to replenishing the coffers of the Spanish crown. The search party, led by one Francisco Mendoza, was taken by a local guide to a large cave, in which they found impressive evidence of ancient workings. But for some reason the mines were not reopened until 1724, and even then were not worked as successfully as they could have been. Full exploitation was not to happen until after their sale to the British in 1873.

With the arrival of the British at Río Tinto there begins a curious chapter in the history of Huelva province. The company which bought the mines, though employing local labour, had an engineering and managerial staff which became increasingly British in its make-up, having in 1902 a ratio of sixty-four British members to only six Spanish ones. At the same time a growing rift developed between the two communities. Almost from the start the British at Río Tinto lived largely apart from the Spaniards, constructing on top of a woooded hill a group of tall Victorian villas based on suburban English prototypes, the only difference being that Spanish stone was used instead of English brick; after 1891 this community, known as Bella Vista, was served by a neo-gothic Presbyterian church, with a simple white interior completely at variance with local architectural tastes. The British community at Río Tinto was referred to by the Spaniards as the 'Colonia Inglesa', and the life they led there was certainly comparable to that of the British in India. Spaniards tended to be called disparagingly 'the natives', and were rigorously excluded from Bella Vista, which was protected by guarded gates. The British were actively discouraged from marrying Spanish women, and those that did so were no longer allowed to live within the colony. The one positive British contribution to Spanish life was the introduction of football, but otherwise the traditions that the British brought to Río Tinto must have seemed to the Spaniards at best bizarre, for instance the activities commemorating Queen Victoria's birthday, such as the egg-and-spoon race. Today it is possible to smile at stories of the British rule in Huelva province, but similar stories could easily be told of the British and other foreign communities that from the 1950's onwards have begun to take over the Andalucían coast and the villages behind it.

Contrary to what is often thought, Spain's southern coast is as yet not entirely dominated by foreigners or by high-rise development, and it is still possible to find quiet, little-spoilt and beautiful beaches. The Atlantic coast of Andalucía, the so-called Costa de Luz or 'Coast of Light', has certainly not suffered to the same degree as the adjoining Costa del Sol. The Huelva section of this coast remains

Río Tinto in the 19th century

popular largely with Spaniards, and is known for its extensive sandy beaches lined with pines: though tourist development is rapidly expanding, there are still beaches where you can be on your own and out of sight of any buildings, for instance the Playa de Canela, and the narrow sandbank or *barra* of El Rompido, best reached by boat (see page 264). The coast of Cádiz province begins at Sanlúcar de Barrameda, an enchanting old town with a quite special atmosphere, though with beaches polluted by being at the mouth of the Guadalquivir. The small area which extends east from here to Jerez and south to El Puerto de Santa María is sherry country, and is flat and densely agricultural. The coastline is uninspiring, with few trees and no cliffs, but with noisy resorts such as Chipiona and Rota, the latter booming with American voices from its controversial NATO base. South from Rota is Cádiz itself, one of the most animated and beautiful towns of Andalucía, but in the middle of a stretch of coast which combines, inexplicably, intense tourism with heavy industrialization. It is only in the southern half of Cádiz province that the scenery of the Costa de Luz begins again to excite. South of the pretty white coastal village of Conil de la Frontera, flat agricultural country is succeeded by the foothills of the Serranía de Ronda, which fall, uncultivated, down to the sea. The coast between Trafalgar and Tarifa, where the Costa del Sol begins, is one of the most attractive in southern Spain, with pine-covered slopes, steep cliffs, wide empty bays, and sweeping sand dunes (see page 270). Germans and nudists have taken to this coast in increasing numbers, but tourism here is relatively unobtrusive, and there are villages such as Barbate and Zahara de los Atunes where the fishing industry clearly predominates. That this area continues to be so unspoilt is due both to the fact that the Spanish army occupies much of the land between Barbate and Tarifa and to the *levante* wind, which is especially notorious here. This wind might create ideal conditions for wind-surfers – and at Tarifa, where the wind is strongest, there is indeed an important wind-surfing school – but it often makes it impossible to lie comfortably on the beach.

The rest of the Andalucían coast, from Tarifa eastwards is backed by high mountains, the wilderness of which forms a striking contrast to most of the coastal resorts below. The Serranía de Ronda covers much of both Cádiz and Málaga provinces, and was one of the areas of Andalucía most admired by Romantic travellers. These limestone mountains are savagely shaped, bare peaks and rocky crags jut out from wild woods and slopes lush with Mediterranean vegetation, villages perch like eagle-nests, and perilous ravines pock-marked with caves open up at every turn. This is classic bandit country, and it is also a landscape which has always greatly appealed to the English, whose tastes have been governed for so long by 19th-century notions of the picturesque. Richard Ford enthused over the dramatically situated town of Ronda, and since then the English have flocked there, even owning for a while its luxurious late 19th-century hotel, still called the Hotel Reina Victoria. More recently the English have begun to buy up houses in the pretty villages that abound in the area. One such place is the spectacular, isolated village of Gaucín, which appears superficially to have changed little since the time when it was a famous bandit's lair. I was walking admiringly through its streets when I noticed a sign in English advertising a Trivial Pursuits Society. Soon afterwards the Sevillian friend I was with entered a bar and failed to make herself understoood, for it turned out that the barman was English. Later a local boy asked if we were both English ('all strangers who come here are,' he said), and then pointed to a street which had only one Spanish family still living on it. At nearby Jimena de la Frontera, someone has quite rightly scrawled in large letters on one of the walls, *Pronto los Jimenatos serán los extranjeros* – 'soon the people of Jimena will be the foreigners'.

The Anglicization of the Serranía de Ronda is at least discreet, which is definitely not the case with the Costa del Sol, the name for the coast in between Tarifa and the frontier of Almería province. The English presence on the coast dates back to 1704, when Sir George Rooke and Sir Clowdisley Shovell hoisted the British flag on the massive Rock of Gibraltar; the Rock has been a British possession ever since. A visit to this place is a curious and potentially depressing experience, for you are suddenly confronted with British food and other products that you might well have come to Spain to forget about, and also with some of the worst and dingiest examples of British architecture and design of *circa* 1960. 'One moment,' wrote Gautier in 1841, 'you were in Andalucía, and the next you are in England. From the Moorish towns of the Kingdom of Granada and Murcia, you land all of a sudden in Ramsgate.' Gautier had finally been jolted out of the oriental reverie which had accompanied him since Despeñaperros, and knew that the time had come for him to go home. He went on caustically to observe: 'wherever an Englishman goes to, he lives exactly as he would in London; he needs his tea, his rump steaks, his rhubarb pies, his port and sherry if he is well, and camomile if he is ill.' The truth of this observation is borne out by the crowds of English residents in Andalucía who regularly descend on Gibraltar to do their shopping.

Tourism along the Costa del Sol was at first limited to the town of Málaga, which, with its temperate winter climate, became a popular wintering resort for the English from the early 19th century, and had the first English cemetery in Spain (founded in 1830). Outside Málaga the only luxurious hotel on the coast was for many years the Reina Cristina in Algeciras, which was built after the completion of the railway line to the town in 1873. The rest of the coast remained poor and neglected well into this century. 'The Costa del Sol they call this now,' reflected an old man from Míjas, 'the hunger coast is what it used to be.' After the Second World War English residents from Gibraltar took to using the unspoilt beaches between the Rock and Málaga, and in the 1950's parts of the coast became frequented by beatniks; finally, by the early 1960's, Franco's Minister for Tourism, Manuel Fraga, had given the go-ahead for the coast's full-scale exploitation. Today the stretch between Estepona and Málaga is a virtually uninterrupted series of high-rise buildings joined together by one of Europe's busiest and most dangerous roads. The English were at one time clearly in the majority, but other nationalities are now effectively imposing their own cultures, in particular the Germans and the Scandinavians.

East along the coast from Málaga, high-rise development is slightly less obtrusive, and east from Nerja and into Granada province, the resorts become more dispersed and the coastal road winds its way above impressive rocky bays. In recent years foreigners have moved in frightening numbers into the pretty villages such as Cómpeta and Frigiliana that cling to the steep slopes of the Sierra de Tejeda above Nerja; but beyond this range and throughout much of the interior of Granada province you are again in unspoilt countryside where foreigners are few and far apart. The interior of Málaga province changes considerably from west to east, as the Serranía de Ronda is succeeded by the bleaker slate range of the Sierra Nevada. The picturesque gives way to the surreal, as in the extraordinary twisted rock formations – comparable in shape to those in Arizona's Bryce Canyon – that comprise the National Park of El Torcal above Málaga. The increasingly arid look of much of the interior as you move east towards Almería contrasts with the areas of sub-tropical cultivation along the coast, such as the *vegas* or fertile plains of Málaga and Motril, which luxuriate in oranges, lemons, sweet muscatel grapes, sugar-cane, custard apples and prickly pears.

Granada province is the Andalucían province with the sharpest contrasts, and brings together the full range of Andalucía's scenery from fertile plains to high mountains and eroded wasteland. Granada itself is 67 kilometres to the north of the coast, at the eastern end of a long narrow vega which the Moors irrigated and planted with extensive wheat and tobacco fields. The view to the southeast is taken up by the highest peaks of the Sierra Nevada range, Mulhacén and the Pico Veleta, which are snow-capped for most of the year. García Lorca was born in the vega, spent much of his life there, and was probably executed on a lonely mountain spot

El Torcal

overlooking it. In common with most Romantic travellers to Granada he viewed the landscape with nostalgia, sensing that with the departure of the Moors it had acquired an underlying melancholy. He evoked too in his poetry the enclosed, isolated character of this province, a character which highlights the openness of that of Seville. One of his poems, entitled the *Ballad of the Three Rivers*, contrasts the navigable Guadalquivir with the Darro and Genil, two of the rivers that descend from the Sierra Nevada into the vega:

Para los barcos de vela
Sevilla tiene un camino;
por el agua de Granada
sólo reman los suspiros.
For the sailing boat
Seville has a passage;
Through the waters of Granada
There row only sighs.

The part of the province with perhaps the saddest and most isolated feel to it is the Alpujarra, which lies on the other side of the Sierra Nevada from the vega. The easiest approach is to take the main road south from Granada and then head east into the Alpujarra from near the spa resort of Lanjarón. But a far more adventurous and spectacular route is to go over the top of the Sierra Nevada range, a route which is only practicable during the summer months. The peaks of Mulhacén and La

Veleta, which are shown rising above Granada's Alhambra in countless picture postcards, have been endlessly admired, but, until recently, only too rarely climbed. When Gautier expressed a wish to go up Mulhacén, his friends from Granada warned him of the dangers, and tried hard, but to no avail, to dissuade him. Today there is an asphalted, well-graded modern road which takes you almost to the summit of La Veleta, passing on the way a major new ski resort. The old route, which joins the new one about three quarters of the way up the mountain, is a steep, rocky road just about manageable for those travelling in a strong car: it is still known by its original name, the Camino de los Neveros (the Road of the Snowfields), and was once used almost exclusively by the men who made their living gathering snow to be used for storage and ice-creams. Whatever route you chose, you will be struck by the greyish brown Icelandic barreness of the mountain's upper slopes, and the contrast between these and the ever more distant deep green of the vega below. From the top of La Veleta you look south over a landscape like a dark, crumpled cloth. This is the Alpujarra, an undulating stretch of land in between the Sierra Nevada and the arid coastal ranges of La Contraviesa and Gádor. On clear days, from La Veleta, you can see the Mediterranean and even Africa.

The road descending from La Veleta is unasphalted all the way, narrow, unprotected and definitely not for drivers lacking confidence or a head for heights. The views from the treeless, uncomforting landscape which you have to go through are sublime in the true sense of the word, combining beauty with a tinge of terror. Before the descent proper begins you have to drive underneath the neighbouring peak of Mulhacén, which at 3,482 metres is nearly 100 metres higher than La Veleta, and is the highest mountain in Spain; it is named after a Moorish king whose remains are popularly thought to be buried at its summit. As you descend you look directly down to distant Trevélez, famous for its hams and for being one of Europe's highest villages; but the first place you come to, after entering a belt of pine trees, is Capileira, at the top of the green, steeply descending riverbank of the Poqueira. This village, and the two immediately below it, Bubion and Pampaneira, have been recently much prettified, and draw most of today's visitors to the Alpujarra. Lower down, the Alpujarra has a dustier look, and the villages have a shabbiness and lack of architectural sophistication reflecting the great poverty which this area has often known.

The Alpujarra is the part of Andalucía where Moorish influence has persisted longest. The place rose to importance under the Moors in the 10th century, when its slopes were terraced and planted with mulberry trees to supply the silk looms of nearby Almería. The Moorish settlers who flocked here during this period were mainly Berbers, who had been used to mountain living in their North African homeland; later, when the Muslim population of Andalucía crowded into the Kingdom of Granada, it was above all the Berbers who favoured moving into the Alpujarra rather than into the towns. Even today the Alpujarra villages, in their layout and architecture, can be closely compared with Berber settlements in North Africa. The quaint cube-like houses, with whitewashed stone walls, and painted wooden beams, are compactly arranged one above the other, their flat grey stone roofs sometimes acting as terraces for the houses above. The tapestry industry which the Berbers introduced has also been maintained to this day, even though the original geometrical Islamic patterns have been supplemented by lion, eagle and crown motifs from Christian times.

After the loss of Granada in 1492, the last Moorish king, Boabdil, was briefly exiled to the Alpujarra, and many other Moorish refugees came here too. Forcible conversion of the Moors, and other measures later taken against them, led in the 16th century to two major revolts in the Alpujarra. The quelling of the second of these, in 1568, resulted in the Moors being finally expelled from the area, their place being taken by settlers from the mountainous districts of northern Spain. The silk farming was kept up until the early years of this century, but the Alpujarra became a forgotten district of Spain, and from the 17th up to the late 19th century was scarcely visited. The first person to reawaken an interest in the area was the writer Pedro Alarcón, who came from the town of Guadix in eastern Granada, and is best known outside Spain as the author of *The Three-Cornered Hat* (1874). In 1882 he published an account of a journey to the Alpujarra, a place, in his words 'known until recently only to its sons'. 'So much was this the case,' he wrote in the book's prologue, 'that there was hardly a map that represented it with any accuracy, and neither the foreigners who came from London or St. Petersburg in search of Moorish associations, nor the Spanish poets who sang of these associations as of a priceless heritage, had ever penetrated into that labyrinth of cliff faces and chasms, in which each rock, each cave, each tree testified to an episode in the Saracen domination.' For nearly 50 years after Alarcón's book appeared, the Alpujarra remained accessible only on foot or mule, but this did not put off a young Englishman, Gerald Brenan, from coming here in 1920 in search of a quiet place to live. He bought a house in the village of Yegen, and kept this until 1934, receiving visits from Bloomsbury intellectuals such as Lytton Strachey and Virginia Woolf. His book, *South from Granada* (1957), a record of these years and an excellent account of local history and folklore, finally secured the Alpujarra's international reputation. On his house at Yegen, a plaque commemorates 'the British Hispanist who universalized the name of Yegen and the customs and traditions of the Alpujarra'.

At Yegen, which borders on Almería province, there comes into view a strange, worn landscape. Eroded mountains, flat, arid wastes, and outright desert characterize almost the entire southeastern corner of Andalucía. The northern boundary of this area is formed by Jaén's Sierra de Segura, which on its southern slopes becomes increasingly parched, and then descends into a daunting, forsaken plateau. This belongs to Granada province, which in its northern half juts out to create a great wedge of land in between Jaén and Almería provinces. Off the N342, the main road

Yegen landscape, by Dora Carrington

which heads from Granada to the coast of Murcia, this is territory which has been virtually unvisited by the tourist. It is powerfully impressive country featuring ochre to pink expanses into which winding river courses have bitten like acid; oranges and palms cling to the narrow banks of dried-out streams, sheltering from the erosion which has eaten its way through the surrounding landscape. The gaping holes which have resulted have been converted into cave dwellings, most famously at Guadix, which has a district which brings to mind the fantastically shaped troglodytic village of Göreme in eastern Anatolia.

Cave dwellings are a notable feature of eastern Andalucía, and Granada province claims to have the highest number of inhabited caves in Europe. These caves were probably lived in during the Moorish period, but the first documented evidence of their habitation does not date until the 16th century. Thereafter travellers to Andalucía have rarely failed to comment on these dwellings, and have usually done so with a mixture of romantic fascination and revulsion, believing, quite wrongly, that the caves only housed the dirtiest and most poverty-stricken gypsies. Penelope Chetwode, describing a 1961 visit to Guadix, put matters right on this point:

'I would like above all to make it clear that the word "cave" is not synonomous with "slum" as some people in England seem to think. There are poor people and better-off people and some quite well-to-do people living in troglodyte colonies just as in any of our council estates; and most of the families living in them are of Spanish and not gypsy blood.' There is nonetheless no getting away from the fact that these caves, however affluent they might sometimes appear, suffer from humidity and lack of ventilation, and that these conditions have bred illnesses such as typhoid and tuberculosis. Since the 1950's the caves have slowly been abandoned.

The desolate scenery of northeastern Granada is continued into Almería province, and, on the southern side of the mournful Sierra de los Filabres, turns into Europe's most remarkable desert. Between Tabernas and Sorbas even the reassuring oasis-like vegetation of the river courses die out. No part of Andalucía looks more African than Almería, though its desert has been exploited by film-makers less for this than for its similarities with America's Wild West: at Tabernas you can visit 'Mini-Hollywood', an American town constructed originally for Sergio Leone's *A Fistful of Dollars*, and later used for various other 'spaghetti westerns'. The writer Juan Goytisolo fell in love with the Almería desert on his first visit here in the early 1950's. Stopping for a drink in a bar at Sorbas, he could not contain his enthusiasm any longer. 'It's the most beautiful landscape in the world,' he blurted out. But the barman reacted in a way which Goytisolo had not expected. He stopped what he was doing, stared reproachfully at the writer, and replied in a voice which Goytisolo was never to forget: 'For us, sir, it is an accursed country.'

Almería can be a very depressing province, and this might well be your first impression of the place if you drive to here along the coastal road from Málaga. Adra, the first town you come to across the Almería border, is dirty, modern and menacing. Its inhabitants, so unlike the Andalucíans in general, appear to have as little enthusiasm for their town as do its visitors: 'You've landed in a shit-hole of a place,' one surly Adra youth told me. The impression of poverty which Adra and other nearby towns give, however, is a misleading one, for the whole ugly stretch of land between here and the coastal town of Almería has become in recent years one of the wealthiest in Spain. This economic miracle has been brought about by what is known as the 'plastic culture', whereby much of the landscape has been covered by large sheets of plastic, which both encourage much-needed moisture and allow crops to ripen in the middle of winter. This might only be a short term solution to Almería's problems, as it is feared that eventually the 'plastic culture' will drain the province completely of its scant water resources. In the meantime the newly acquired wealth has been accompanied by numerous psychological problems, and the suicide rate has risen dramatically. To keep up the heightened productivity requires nearly constant work, and there is neither sufficient time nor the amenities to allow people to enjoy the money they have earned. The one major release has been gambling, the stakes for which have become increasingly preposterous, even to

Manuel Fraga in the atom-infested sea

the extent – apparently – of gambling away wives.

Interesting though the town of Almería itself is, it comes as a relief to leave all towns behind and continue east along what now becomes the wildest if also bleakest coast of Andalucía. A mere half hour's drive from Almería is the extraordinary mountainous peninsula known as the Cabo de Gata, where bare, bleached rock falls directly into the sea. The road ceases to be asphalted shortly after passing the cape's tip, and between the tiny, little-spoilt resorts of Las Negras and Agua Amarga, disintegrates into a rock-strewn track suitable really only for walkers. The Cabo de Gata has until recently been favoured largely by German hippies, and it is only to the north of here, around the town of Mojácar, that you meet the sort of coastal development that typifies most of the Costa del Sol.

Beyond Mojácar, almost before leaving Andalucía, you will pass a sign pointing to Palomares, a name which to many might have a familiar and sinister ring to it. Much of Almería province is how you would imagine the world to have looked like in prehistoric times, as well as how it might appear in the wake of a nuclear disaster. Appropriately enough, at Millares, near Almería town, is the largest Bronze Age site in Europe, while at Palomares there occured, in January 1966, an accident which might well have made the writing of this book unnecessary. An American bomber from the Rota base, fuelling in mid-air, collided with the tanker plane. Four bombs, each carrying sixteen times the explosive power of the Hiroshima bomb, fell near Palomares. Two landed intact, one into a river bed and another into the sea, but the other two directly hit the ground and their detonators went off. Safety devices fortunately prevented the actual plutonium and uranium from exploding, but the damaged bombs leaked considerable quantities of radioactivity. The two intact bombs were recovered, the one which ended up in the sea bed only after a lengthy search and the help of a fisherman, Francisco Simó, who later received the local nickname, 'Paco of the bomb'. Before this happened, Manuel Fraga, in his capacity as Minister of Tourism and Information, was rushed to the scene and photographed in his bathing costume, bravely putting on a smile in the cold and potentially explosive waters. The future of Andalucía's budding tourist industry was to not be jeopardized.

Richard Ford considered that no other part of Spain offered so much to the traveller as Andalucía, and the hurried tour of the region on which the reader has been taken over the previous pages has passed through landscapes of almost every conceivable type. Natural variety is reflected in the range of Andalucía's excellent if undeservedly little known food, and is also matched by the wealth of the region's monuments, for, as Baron Taylor said in 1840, 'is not Spain the land of the arts; and is not Andalucía of all Spain that portion which has produced the noblest monuments of artistic excellence and inspiration?' But the fascination which Andalucía has exerted over generations of travellers has often been inspired less by the region's landscapes, products and monuments than by its people. Andalucía is possibly unique among European regions in having an appeal based to a very great extent on a romantic view of its inhabitants. There is something unquestionably exotic and non-European about the looks of many Andalucíans, and there is also a deep-rooted paganism in the Andalucían character rarely to be found to the same degree elsewhere in Europe. What other European region, for instance, has such a strong and passionate tradition in dancing and singing as Andalucía, or such fanatical and exuberant religious celebrations? However, writers have loved to dwell on these folkloric and obviously picturesque aspects of Andalucían life without giving much serious thought to the mentality behind these activities. The interest taken in the Andalucíans has also been a very partial one, an enormous bias having been shown towards marginal figures in Andalucían society, such as bandits, bull-fighters, musicians and gypsies. Moreover, from the time of Gerald Brenan, writers on Andalucía, deeply nostalgic about vanishing rural traditions, have been interested more in the life of Andalucía's villages than in that of its towns. Finally, the foreign view of the Andalucíans has been influenced by the fact that the region gave birth to the world's two most famous sexual stereotypes, Carmen and Don Juan.

The study of Andalucían women, wrote a sociologist, David Gilmore, in 1987, 'is probably the most pressing unfinished task in Andalucían ethnography today'. If ethnographers have yet to write much about the women of the region, travel writers, novelists and poets have amply made up for the omission. Long before and long after Mérimée wrote his novella *Carmen* (1845), writers have praised the Andalucían woman as being the most beautiful in all Spain, if not Europe. Byron, who visited Spain in 1809, did much to promote this reputation:

> Oh never talk to me
> Of northern climes, and British ladies,
> It has not been your lot to see,
> Like me, the lovely girl of Cádiz...

Many British travellers, arriving at Cádiz from Britain, left their boats with hopes raised by Byron's poem, and were naturally often a trifle disappointed. George Dennis, who landed at Cádiz in 1839, found that Byron had greatly exaggerated the beauty of the local women, and that the 'darkness of the Spanish complexion contrasted unfavourably with the fair skins of the Devonshire and Cornish damsels.' By the end of his Andalucían stay, however, Dennis had overcome his initial disappointment, and was writing that 'the Andaluza takes precedence over all the women of Spain in point of beauty, grace and vivacity.' For Dennis' compatriot, A. C. Andros, the sight in 1860 of a group of young women gliding over the gas-lit *paseo*

An Andalucían beauty from a 19th-century postcard

of Seville had a quite overwhelming effect: 'My susceptible nature,' he wrote, 'is excited to such an alarming extent by the incomparable charms that I should tremble for the vows of celibacy made in dear phlegmatic old England, were my lot ever cast in the sunny climes of Andalucía.'

The physical attributes that made up the beauty of the Andalucían woman were frequently debated, but it was generally agreed that these were elegance of movement, and dark, expressive eyes; a reader of the London Library copy of Dennis' *Travels* entered the debate by illegally pencilling in the margin of the book 'and teeth', and Mérimée encouraged an ill-founded belief that Andalucían women were renowned for their small feet. All these various attributes were at any rate accompanied by a reputation for unbridled sensuality, a reputation which apparently goes back to classical times, when the lascivious dancing girls of Cádiz aroused much interest among the Romans. For Dennis, Andalucían women were more obsessed by 'love' than any other women he knew, and 'not pure exalted love but a much baser passion': 'I never was in the company of an Andaluza for ten minutes but the conversation was sure to turn upon *love*, to which she was generally the first to

Romero de Torres painting The Gipsy Muse

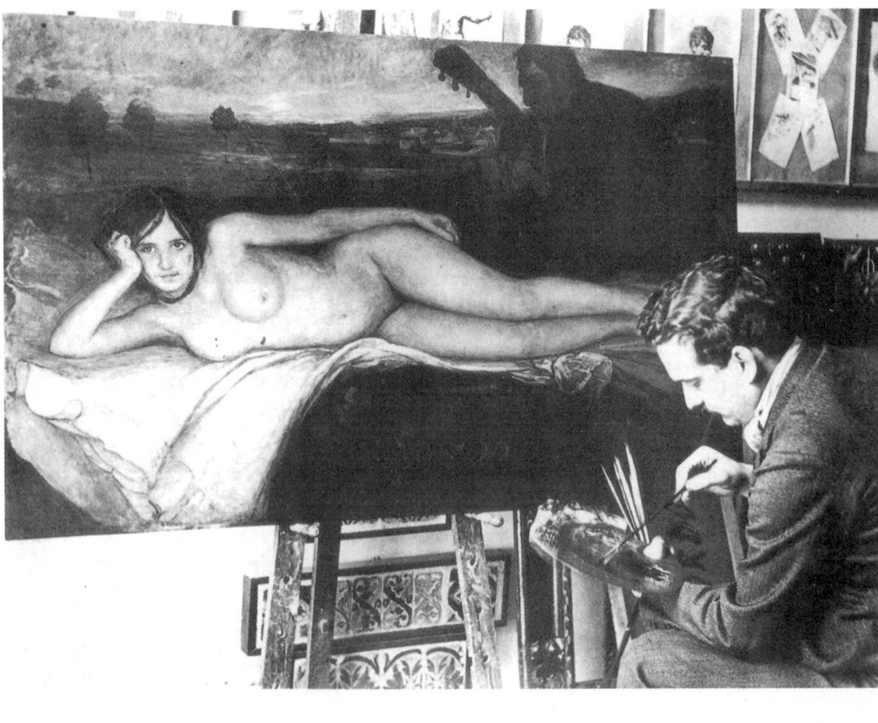

advert, either directly or otherwise.' 'The Andaluza,' Dennis concluded,' has not the charms of a refined and cultivated intellect; she is little more than a beautiful animal.' The Andalucían woman, stripped of personality, intellect, and even clothes, is the constant subject of the turgid and crudely symbolical canvases of the turn-of-the-century artist Julio Romero de Torres, to whom a whole dark and gloomy museum is devoted in his native Córdoba. These works, in which the female nude is generally portrayed with great candour and set alongside fully clothed guitar players, bullfighters or other such male Andalucían stereotypes, might strike the viewer as being little more than high kitsch, but they are immensely popular in Spain, and have inspired many a writer, even such an intelligent one as the Sicilian Leonardo Sciascia (see page 287). For the Andalucían poet and Falange supporter José María Pemán, the women of Romero de Torres were expressive of the 'deepest soul of this land of Andalucía'.

When I stayed in Córdoba during the Franco period, the Romero de Torres museum was a popular place for the young men of the town to take newly arrived foreign girls, in whom the men then placed their main hopes of sexual adventure. For much of Spanish history, even up to the death of Franco, the sort of Andalucían beauty who featured in Romero de Torres' imagination tended not just to be unobtainable outside marriage but protected from the physical advances of men by a code of behaviour almost unsurpassed in its rigidity anywhere in Europe. The aspect of Andalucían courtship which used to intrigue and amuse foreigners the most was the convention of men standing in the street and addressing or singing to their beloved through the iron grilles of the window. Ford wrote that while the aristocracy was gradually abandoning this convention ('either the ladies' hearts are less cold or the nights more so'), the 'lower order continue the old caterwauling plan'; indeed the convention was to be practiced well into this century. Of course there were those who maintained that the limitations of such courtship only intensified the erotic passion, and Ford himself noted that 'this metallic diet makes the lover as bold as fire-eating does elsewhere. . .' One of the more erotic scenes in Buñuel's film *That Obscure Object of Desire* was when the Carmen-like eponymous heroine (played alternately by two actresses to intensify the elusiveness) teases the man who unsuccesfully desires her by writhing naked behind the iron grille to which he desperately clutches. Gerald Brenan, who must have been the last if not the only English writer to court a Spanish woman through the bars of her house, showed how the outcome of such courtship was rather less glamorous than might have been imagined: when he eventually persuaded the exotic woman of his advances to meet him outside her house (in the company,of course, of a chaperone), he discovered that she was a lumpily formed midget who had been speaking to him standing on a chair. Ángel Ganivet, a Granada writer of the late 19th century, strongly disapproved of the conventions that forced the Andalucían woman to spend so much of her time at home, and found that the cities of Northern Europe, cold and grey though they were, were more cheerful than the ones in Andalucía because the streets, shops and restaurants were filled with women. A society, like that of Finland, where a woman working in a sauna could show not the slightest concern while washing a naked Ganivet, was for Ganivet a more natural one than that of Andalucía (the healthy effects of Finnish society, however, were not sufficient to prevent the writer from eventually throwing himself into the Dvina). Ganivet had also to admit that 'where there are no bolts to break, balconies to scale, third parties to bribe, nor vigilants to outwit, there could never be a Don Juan Tenorio.'

The legendary figure of Carmen, dark, passionate, mysterious and cruel, meets her match in the tireless and cynical seducer, Don Juan. The original Don Juan was the hero of a play by the 17th-century dramatist Tirso de Molina, *The Joker of Seville*, which is sometimes thought to be based on the life of an aristocratic contemporary of the dramatist, Don Miguel de Mañara. The story of the man and his seductions was later taken up, among others, by Molière, Mozart, Dumas and the 19th-century Spanish writer Zorilla, and is still so popular in Spain that every year a production of the Zorilla play is put on in almost every Spanish town on All Souls' Day. The Zorilla version is the one chosen because the tone is cheerful, and the ending happy, with Don Juan deciding to reform his ways. However, it is not always so easy to make fun of the Andalucían type whom the Don Juan legend reflects. Andalucían men, like the women of the region, enjoy a reputation for their good looks, but they are also thought to epitomize Spanish machoism at its worst. With the advent of modern psychology, the extreme machoism to be found in Don Juan has sometimes been considered as a sign of latent homosexuality. In any case, there is a male type, particularly common in Seville, who far prefers the company of other men to that of the women whom he regularly seduces, and who exudes an ambiguous sexuality. Good-looking and nattily dressed, he is the descendant of the 19th-century *majo* or dandy, a figure who caught the imagination of the Romantic traveller.

While remaining gullible to all the romantic stereotypes of Andalucían society, from the bandit to the majo, travellers have maintained at heart an ambivalent attitude towards the Andalucíans. Every cliché pertaining to Mediterranean peoples has been brought to bear on the description of the Andalucían character, and the end result has not always been very appealing. For though southerners are traditionally passionate, voluptuous and reckless, they are also hysterical, lazy, ostentatious, boastful and pleasure-loving. The Andalucíans have often been treated as ridiculous figures, just as have the Provençals or the Calabrians. 'The Andalucíans,' according to George Borrow, 'are in general held in the lowest estimation by the rest of the Spaniards,' a view with which Borrow was apparently in agreement: 'In a word, the Andalucíans, in all estimable traits of character, are as far below the other Spaniards as the country which they inhabit is superior in beauty and fertility to the other provinces of Spain.' Both Ford and Gerald Brenan held a completely contrary view

De Torres in Córdoban dress

to this, and stressed in their writings the great wit and sophistication of the Andalucíans. For Ford, they 'were, and always have been, the most elegant, refined and sensual inhabitants of the peninsula'; Brenan, contrasting the 'hard and dour' peasants to be found in other parts of Spain, with their 'lighter, more mobile' Andalucían equivalent, wrote that 'at heart all Andalucíans are town dwellers, quick, emotional, talkative and artistic.' Numerous travellers, Ford among them, have compared the Andalucíans to the Irish, and the comparison is an apt one, for the Irish, like the Andalucíans, have been the butt of many a joke while at the same time having a reputation for their sophisticated culture and rich poetic tradition. Both the Andalucíans and the Irish were for Ford 'impressionable as children, heedless of results, calculatory of contingencies, passive victims to violent impulse, gay, clever, good-humoured and light-hearted, and the most subservient dupes of plausible nonsense.'

An Irishman of this century, Walter Starkie, recognized that the 'stage-Andalucían' is as much a figure of Andalucía as the 'stage-Irishman' is of Ireland, for the Andalucíans have in general a love of playing up to what foreigners expect of them. Much of their life, it has been suggested, is a charade enacted for the benefit of tourists, and ruthlessly exploitative of every Andalucían cliché. The philosopher Ortega y Gasset, in an essay of 1921 entitled *The Theory of Andalucía*, attempted a radical assessment of the regional character. 'What is admirable, mysterious and profound about Andalucía,' he wrote, 'lies behind that multi-coloured farce which its inhabitants put on for the benefit of its tourists.' With great originality and eccentricity he proceeded to point out the similarities that exist between the Chinese and the Andalucíans, similarities that go beyond the fact that Mandarins and bull-fighters both had pigtails. The Andalucíans, like the Chinese, have had a history of passive resistance to the many foreign powers who have invaded their land. For Ortega y Gasset this was not a sign of cowardice, but of the inherent sophistication of the two races, both of which have always preferred peace to war, and have attached little importance to the role of the soldier in society. 'Foreigners,' continued Ortega y Gasset, 'are overcome by the sensuality of the Andalucían climate and become convinced that the Andalucíans must be a passionate, hot-blooded race, when in fact it is they themselves who are experiencing such violent emotions.' The Andalucíans have reacted to their climate in a completely opposite way to the foreigners, expending their emotions in the most economical way possible, developing a Chinese-like stoicism, and a sybaritic, serene contentment with their environment: 'instead of forcing himself to live, [the Andalucían] lives so as not to force himself, he makes the avoidance of effort the guiding principle of his existence.' In the end Ortega y Gasset's radical 'theory' of Andalucía turns out to be little more than an ingenious reassertion of the most harmful of all Andalucían clichés, namely that the Andalucíans are all lazy.

'Please don't write that the Andalucíans spend all their time drinking and enjoying themselves,' insisted a young Sevillian friend of mine at various stages during the research for this book. I am wary about making generalizations about the character of a particular race, but after only a few weeks in Seville, I realized that the life I was leading and the people I was with apparently confirmed all the preconceptions about Andalucía that I was hoping to get away from. The woman I was staying with, Esperanza Flores, was a maker of flamenco costumes, and the daughter of an exporter of oranges. Many of her friends sang and danced at every opportunity, and enjoyed endless socializing in bars. Few were conventionally religious, though several of them were passionate devotees of particular votive images of the Virgin, and never missed any of Seville's important religious festivities. Above all they tended to be anarchic in their behaviour, and to refuse to allow long-term problems interfere with the enjoyment of the present. Esperanza had no bank account, and believed in spending money as soon as she earned it. An after-lunch drink would turn into an evening and night of *cachondeo*, a word, much used in Andalucía, denoting 'riotous fun'. Conversations took the form of endless jokes and funny stories, and vicious mockery of others. I rarely got to bed before dawn.

Esperanza and her friends represented of course only one aspect of Seville society, and an aspect which many of the city's younger inhabitants find increasingly anachronistic. Moreover, Seville is not Andalucía, no matter how much the Sevillians like to think that they represent all that is best and most characteristic about the region. The Andalucíans themselves constantly remind you how the character of their people changes, not just between one province and another, but between towns and villages, and even between districts of a town. You might be told that the people of Cádiz and Seville provinces are the wittiest in Andalucía, while those from Málaga and Córdoba are, respectively, the most open and boorish. Idiotic behaviour might be excused on the grounds that the person comes from Huelva. The inhabitants of Granada are frequently characterized as reactionary and bourgeois, and few people are happy to admit that they come from Jerez, which is renowned for its snobbery and arrogance. The villagers of Mairena del Alcor are unable to speak clearly, and the men of the Aljarafe are nearly all homosexuals. The upper and lower towns of Sanlúcar de Barrameda produce completely different types of person. And so on. You might easily dismiss all this as nonsense, but there are often good historical reasons to explain these apparently arbitrary assessments.

The difficulties of reaching any straightforward conclusions about the Andalucíans are fully revealed as you begin to discuss the racial origins of these people. Who indeed are the Andalucíans? The romantic view is that they are essentially Moors, with a strong admixture of Jewish blood. To these races have been attributed a wide range of characteristics, from guiltless sexuality to fantastical imagination, fatalism, underlying melancholy, and large sexual organs; unmistakably Moorish are the facial features of many of today's Andalucíans. Yet, according to official versions of history, the Moors were all expelled from Andalucía and the region was largely repopulated by Castilians, Galicians, Asturians and others from north of Despeñaperros. The complex ethnic make-up of the Andalucíans was exacerbated by the later influx of settlers from outside Spain. The surviving Germans from the Sierra Morena colonies might soon have lost their languages and traditions, but they left a legacy of blond hair and blue eyes, as have many of the English and Irish who have moved to Spain in growing numbers since the Peninsular War. Intermarriage between foreigners and Andalucíans has often created a strange racial hybrid. I once met the Marqués Carlos Pickman, a descendant of an English family which had founded a famous ceramics factory in Seville in the early 19th century. Tall and fair, he had the look of an English aristocrat, and spoke Spanish with an English accent, but English with a Spanish one: he had never lived in Engand.

Andalucían nationalists like to think that the Christian forces of the so-called Reconquest tore out the cultural roots of their people, and prefer to ignore the racial transformation that Andalucía underwent after the time of the conquering Christians. This attitude is romantic and unhistorical, but in attempting to explain what it is about Andalucía that makes the place so different from the rest of Spain, it is clearly vital to look into those traces of earlier culture that survived the Christian invasion. In trying to unravel the mystery of Andalucía, you cannot simply stop at the Moors, but are forced to go further and further back in time, past the

Vandals, the Romans, the Greeks, the Phoenicians, and further still, back to the legendary civilization of the Tartessians.

From Tartessus to Granada

The cultural roots of Andalucía lie buried in a past distorted by myth and nostalgia. Andalucíans and foreigners alike have fancifully imagined that in the formative years of the region's history there was an age of universal prosperity and enlightenment. The Romans identified this golden age with the Tartessians, just as later generations looked back longingly to the time of the Romans. After the 16th century writers and travellers began to glorify the period of Moorish domination, and by the 19th century the fascination with Moorish Andalucía had grown to such proportions that the Kingdom of Granada, where this civilization enjoyed its final flowering, had acquired a character almost as mythical as that of Tartessus.

The Moorish monuments of Andalucía have for a long time been the main attraction for the sightseer to the region, to such an extent that the monuments of earlier and later periods are on the whole remarkably little known. Few people, for instance, are aware that Andalucía is one of the richest archaeological areas of Europe. The search for Andalucía's ancient and prehistoric past will take you to wild and exceptionally beautiful places, sometimes to territory which seems almost virgin. Most of the archaeological sites are poorly signposted, if signposted at all, many have been improperly excavated, and many more probably remain to be discovered; as yet there is no comprehensive catalogue of the sites, nor even any serious guide to direct you to them. The neglected condition of most of the sites will appal many a British traveller, and indeed the great difference in personality between the British and the Andalucíans is clearly brought out in their respective attitudes towards their past. In Britain the Department of the Environment surrounds even the most minor site with green wooden fences and neatly mown grass, establishes admission times and entrance fees, and erects clearly laid-out information panels. In Andalucía I have seen prehistoric dolmens used for storing farm equipment. A more caring approach towards monuments is developing, but in the meantime the future of many of these places is in jeopardy. The consolation is that the romantically inclined can find here an extraordinary continuity between past and present, and experience a sense of awe and wonder which is too often absent from Britain's well-tended sites.

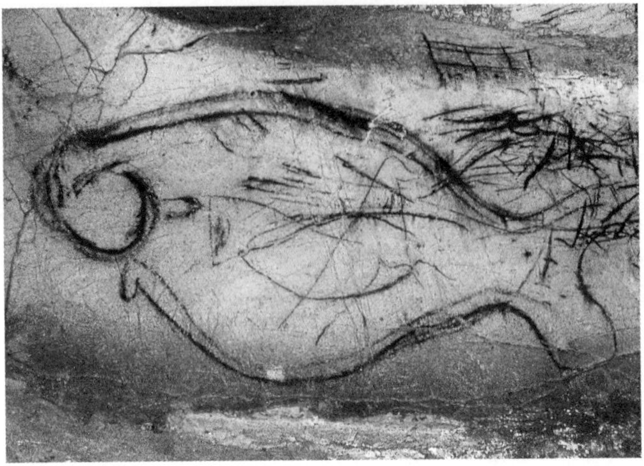

Flounder at La Pileta

I know of no other prehistoric cave paintings, still accessible to the public, that are so exciting to visit as those of the cave of La Pileta, high up in the Serranía de Ronda (see page 359). Even without its paintings, this is a special place: though tourists are coming here in growing numbers, it has yet to be commercialized in the same way as have some of Andalucía's many other famous caves, such as the Cave of Marvels at Aracena or the Cave of Nerja, both of which have been transformed by coloured lighting into what appears to be gaudy film sets. At La Pileta you can easily imagine what the place must have been like when used by prehistoric man, or when it was first entered in modern times. The cave was 'discovered' in 1905 by a farmer called José Cullón Lobato, and still remains in his family's possession, two of his nephews, José and Eloy, being the official guides. You reach it by climbing up a steep path carved into the rock face, and at the entrance are presented with an old-fashioned gas lamp. There is no other lighting inside, and the tour lasts for over an hour. You are led first into a massive chamber, at the top of which, fluttering around a narrow opening to the sky, you can make out the dark forms of hundreds of bats. Lobato had first been alerted to the cave by the sight of bats disappearing into the mountains, and had gone inside not out of curiosity but with a view to collect bat's droppings for his fields. Deep in the cave he came across prehistoric paintings, and, in later years, as various other chambers were discovered, it became clear that La Pileta contained one of the more extensive series of rock paintings in Europe. You soon lose all sense of direction as you are led up and down, squeezing your way between rocks, slipping on steep watery slopes, and finding at almost every turn wonderfully preserved examples of the art of early man.

The dating of La Pileta paintings is controversial, though it is generally thought that the beautifully naturalistic portrayals of goats, horses and other animals are of the Late Palaeolithic period, while the near-abstract drawings in black that cover in profusion the largest of the painted chambers date from Neolithic times. The cave was probably a sanctuary, as caves of such depth would have been impracticable for habitation; at any rate, by the 3rd millennium BC (the end of the Neolithic period), humans had begun living in cane huts, and used caves mainly for religious or burial purposes. In 1870 mineral prospectors uncovered in a cave in the northern foothills of the Serranía de Ronda one of the eeriest and most telling examples of Neolithic burial practice (see page 274). Immediately inside this cave, the Cueva de los Murciélagos, were three cadavers, one of which had a gold diadem. There were three more beyond, one wearing an esparto grass hat with traces of blood; further still was a group of twelve bodies, arranged in a semi-circle around a woman adorned with a collar of rings from which hung sea-shells. Fifty other bodies lay beyond, some in an apparently semi-mummified condition. Unfortunately the mining company which owned the cave later destroyed much of what was found, thus preventing further investigation. From the available evidence it was concluded that the cave was the burial chamber of a powerful chief who had insisted that his servants and close associates keep him company in death.

The paintings of La Pileta are almost certainly the oldest in Andalucía, and are the only ones known to have been executed deep down in a cave. The other so-called 'cave paintings' in the region are probably of the late Neolithic Period (*c.* 2000 BC) and are to be found in what should really be described as rock-shelters. The Abbé Breuil, the distinguished French scholar who studied the cave art of the Dordogne, was responsible in the early years of this century for publicizing two of the more important of these shelters, the Cueva de los Letreros near Vélez Blanco (see page 386), and the Cueva de Tajo de las Figuras near Benalup de Sidonia (see page 334). The former, situated in an appropriately primeval-looking landscape of arid mountains, is now protected from the graffiti-writer by an iron grille. However, I was strongly recommended in Vélez Blanco to bring with me a flask of water to throw at the paintings so as to bring out their colours; the present, near-illegible state of the paintings is sad evidence of the frequency of this practice. The Cueva de Tajo de las Figuras is the less accessible of the two caves, and requires a certain skill at rock-climbing to reach (a rope is provided to help those less sure of foot). Yet even here, the water-throwers have been at work, and the paintings are difficult to recognize as the ones described and drawn by the Abbé Breuil. Among the best preserved of the Andalucían shelter paintings are those of Laja Alta (the Cueva de Pacos) near Jimena de La Frontera, which are especially interesting because they include some of Europe's oldest known representations of boats (see page 319). The excellence of their condition, and the freshness of their colours, are due both to their very recent 'discovery' and to the fact that considerable determination and the services of a local guide are needed to get to them. An eight-kilometre climb up a non-asphalted mountain road, is followed by a forty minute trek through forest and undergrowth,

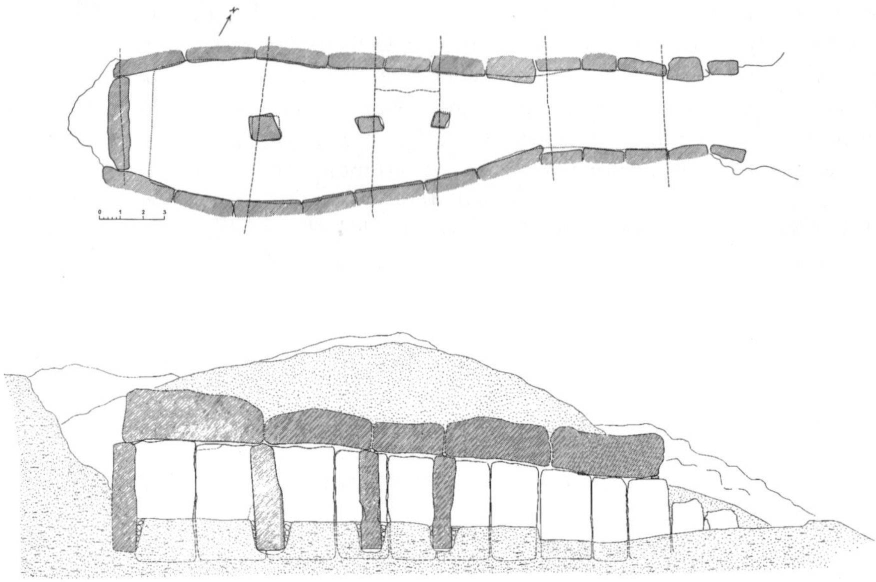

Antequera: plan and section

and eventually to a clamber, with virulent horse-flies in pursuit, and legs bleeding, up a sheer rock face. I was certainly surprised, having done this walk, to find attached to the shelter a beautifully written notice in Spanish and English, telling the visitor that the paintings are 'said to be over 2,000 years old, please do not throw water over them or in any way deface them.' The notice is, and could only have been, the work of an Englishman. It is a solitary and valiant gesture, and you can only hope that it does not have the opposite effect to the one intended: drawing attention to the paintings' importance might be a deterrent in England, but in Spain this appears mainly to incite the potential defacer.

The wealth of Andalucía's prehistoric legacy is evident not just in its cave culture. On the outskirts of Antequera stand three dolmens, the oldest of which, that of Menga, is the largest single dolmen in Western Europe. It was first recorded in 1645, and until the last century was thought to be a meeting place for druids. Dating back probably to the 5th millennium BC, it consists of a long white chamber formed of gigantic upright monoliths supporting equally massive slabs. Even more impressive, and in fact Andalucía's most extensive prehistoric site, is Los Millares, memorably located in the middle of a sinister, eroded landscape in Almería

Antequera

province. This site has been carbon-dated to around 2,340 BC, and is Europe's largest Bronze Age settlement. Built on top of a wide rock escarpment formed by the confluence of two dried-up rivers, it is surrounded today by a vast metal fence, and cannot be seen from the road. The site is not officially open to the public, nor in any way promoted, and the passing motorist might well think that a military rather than archaeological site lies beyond the fence. This encouraging evidence that steps are being taken to protect Andalucía's archaeological past is somewhat weakened when you discover that the key to this – one of the world's outstanding prehistoric sites – hangs above the bar in the nearby village of Santa Fe de Mondújar, and can be had just for the asking. With the key thus acquired you are allowed to wander at will around the site, in the knowledge that in the time you are there no-one else will be able to disturb the haunting peace of the place. The main site lies about a mile from the entrance gate, and features a series of tombs in front of a walled citadel, inside which are the ruins of Bronze Age habitations. Finds from the site – many of which are displayed in the small but excellent archaeological museum at Almería – reveal a civilization living not just off hunting as in the Stone Age, but off the breeding of sheep, goats and pigs, vegetable and cereal culture, the manufacture of cheese and lard, and the making of jewellery and basketwork. Some of the finds also indicate commercial relations with other Mediterranean peoples, for instance a pair of ivory sandals believed to be Egyptian.

Who were the people of Los Millares, and who were their ancestors? The Roman scholar Agrippa wrote that the inhabitants of Baetica were of African descent, and the earliest skulls to have been found in Andalucía are identical to ones of the same period discovered in Morocco. At the beginning of the Bronze Age, it seems that Andalucía was infiltrated by people of Cretan and Myceneaen origin, and it has even been suggested that the Spanish bull-fight owes its origins to the Cretan cult of the bull. They were joined towards the end of the 2nd millennium BC by Phoenician traders, who arrived in Andalucía by sea, and by Celtic tribes, who travelled to Spain over the Pyrenees. Greek traders had begun settling along the Mediterranean coast by 600 BC, and were soon followed by the Carthaginians. Finally, the Romans took possession of the whole of Spain by the 3rd century BC.

The term 'Iberian' is used to describe the multi-racial culture which had evolved in Spain by the time of the Romans. The study of Iberian culture began in the late 18th century, but it was not until very recent times that any extensive archaeological research on the subject was carried out. The first people to excavate at Los Millares, and at many other Copper and Bronze Age sites in Almería province, were the brothers Henri and Louis Siret, two Belgian mining engineers who settled in the province in the 1880's, building a house for themselves in a desolate place called Herrerías. They financed all their excavations on their modest salaries as engineers, and later claimed to have worked on more sites than all the Spanish archaeologists of their day put together. Louis Siret was still living at Herrerías in 1933, when Gerald Brenan visited him ('Fifty years at Herrerías!' Brenan exclaimed. 'This took some imagining!'). Brenan described him as a man 'of slightly crazy enthusiasm', and also found him embittered by the way his colleagues had not accepted many of his and his brother's findings. He told Brenan: *'Ce n'est pas une science, l'archéologie, c'est un combat à mort.'* Another eccentric archaeologist of this period, similarly obsessed by Andalucía's Iberian past, was an Englishman called George Bonsor, who worked among other places at the extraordinary necropolis at Carmona, and did for western Andalucía what the Sirets had done for the eastern half; he lived in the castle at Mairena del Alcor, which now has a small museum filled with his eclectic collections, and a number of Impressionist-style landscapes painted by him. But perhaps the craziest of these pioneering archaeologists was the German Adolf Schulten, who devoted most of his working life to the uncovering of the most mysterious aspect of Andalucía's Iberian past, the civilization of Tartessus.

Schulten was convinced that Tartessus was a glorious city-state, the capital of which lay buried under what is now the Coto Doñana. Thirty years of searching for it, however, failed to discover any proof of its existence, and in the end Schulten came to identify Tartessus with the equally elusive ancient city of Atlantis. Other archaeologists have tried with equal lack of success to locate Tartessus in Cádiz, Jerez, Sanlúcar de Barrameda, Huelva and Seville. The search for Tartessus has been one of the most pressing issues in Spanish archaeology this century, but despite numerous excavations, its existence is still only testified by literary rather than archaeological evidence. Furthermore these sources, derived from Phoenician traditions, are hopelessly contradictory, and suggest variously that Tartessus was the name of a kingdom, a city, a village, a mountain and even a river (the Guadalquivir). The one point on which all the sources are agreed is that the place was exceedingly rich in copper, silver and gold.

The Tartessian civilization is generally thought today to have flourished in the Guadalquivir basin, from the latter half of the 2nd millennium BC to around 500 BC, experiencing its greatest periods in the 8th and 9th centuries. The Tartessians were known to have been ruled by a monarchical dynasty, the origins of which belong now to the realm of mythology. The legends tell in fact of two Tartessian dynasties, one of which was headed by Geryon, a peaceful, flock-tending king whose only fault was to have had three bodies and three heads, for which he was killed by Hercules. Geryon's son, Nora, colonized Sardinia, and at this point mythology reflects historical fact, for there were strong commercial relations between the Guadalquivir and Sardinia from around 2000 BC. The other Tartessian dynasty begins with King Gargoris, the discoverer of honey, and a man whose incestuous relationship with one of his daughters produced a son, Habis. The moment he was born, Habis was abandoned to the wilds, where he was nurtured by the very animals who were expected to kill him. After a miraculous childhood, Habis was finally acknowledged by the king as his rightful successor. Habis proved to be a civilizing monarch, who taught his people how to plough with oxen, and who divided his subjects into seven social classes, the nobility being exempt from work. The legends of Geryon and Gargoris have been seen to throw much light on the real Tartessians. It says much of the ethnic make-up of these people that the two legends bring together Western and Eastern traditions, the tri-formed Geryon being a type frequently found in Celtic mythology, and the Gargoris story having parallels in legends of the Middle East. Furthermore the picture of Tartessian society which is suggested by the two legends – one which is peace-loving, monarchical, endogamous, well organized and highly sophisticated – is borne out by what is known about Tartessus from the time of of its first real monarch, King Arganthonios, who ruled around 1100 BC.

Though Tartessus itself has never been discovered, excavations at places such as Carmona, Niebla and Setefilla have uncovered numerous remains associated with Tartessian civilization. Just outside Andalucía, at Zalamea de la Serena in the Extremaduran province of Badajoz, there was recently found the ruins of a sanctuary dedicated to a goddess of the underworld, a cult which some believe to have been the dominant one of the Tartessians and the precursor of today's cult of the

The Lebrija Candlesticks: 70 cm high and made of gold

Virgin, which is very strong in the south of Spain. But the most spectacular discovery connected with the Tartessians occured in 1958 during the extension of a pigeon-shooting club at El Carambolo, just to the west of Seville. A walled town was revealed, as well as a dazzling horde of gold jewellery (now displayed in a darkened room of its own in Seville's Museo Arqueológico) which is a testimony to the proverbial wealth of the Tartessians. So rich is the soil of Andalucía in archaeological remains that discoveries continue frequently to be made, for instance the magnificent sculptures from the Iberian sanctuary at Porcuna in Jaén province (see page 314). The hope that one day Tartessus itself might surface is not an altogether forlorn one.

The Tartessians appear to have enjoyed relatively amicable trading relations with the Phoenicians and the Greeks, both of whom had been attracted to Andalucía by its famed mineral wealth. The Phoenicians and the Greeks founded many coastal colonies in Andalucía, the first and most important of which was the Phoenician town of Gadir, later known as Cádiz: though virtually nothing survives of the original Phoenician and Greek settlements, the important influence of these people on Andalucía is shown by the way in which the traditional unglazed pottery of such places as Lebrija and Utrera continues to follow prototypes established by them. In contrast to the Phoenicians and Greeks, the Carthaginians adopted a ruthless and hostile attitude towards the Tartessians; in fact it was probably they who succeeded in destroying the Tartessian civilization, either as a result of a major military victory or by gaining a monopoly on the trade in minerals. The growing power of the Carthaginians erupted in the 3rd century BC into a great struggle with the Romans to gain control over the western Mediterranean. Following the First Punic War (264-241 BC), the Carthaginians lost to the Romans Sicily, Sardinia and Corsica, and concentrated their forces on southeastern Spain. The Second Punic War (218-206 BC) led to their final defeat, and to the conquest of Spain by the Romans, who by 195 BC had made it clear that they intended to stay. Among those who had sided with the Romans against the Carthaginians were the descendents of the Tartessians, the Turdetanians. The Romans considered the Turdetanians the most civilized of the Iberian peoples, and in the 1st century AD Strabo was to write that the 'Turdetanians are ranked as the wisest of the Iberians; they make use of an alphabet, and possess records of their ancient history, poems and laws, written in verse, that are 6,000 years old.'

The Romans divided Spain at first into two separate provinces, Hispania Citerior, which embraced the whole eastern and northern parts of the peninsula, and Hispania Ulterior, which had Córdoba as its capital. The latter province was soon afterwards divided into Lusitania and Baetica, and at a much later date Hispania Citerior was broken up into the provinces of Gaellaecia, Carthaginensis, and Tarraconensis. The Romans, characteristically, were able to consolidate their hold over the country through a brilliant administrative system and the construction of an efficient network of roads. Their success in Spain was due also to their tolerance of, and integration with, the Iberian peoples, who were said to have been allowed to live in the same style as their conquerors.

Baetica played a vital role in the trading and commercial history of Roman Spain, and at Monte Testaccio in Rome there is even a great mound built of fragments of olive oil amphorae from this province. The importance of Baetica, however, was not simply a material one, for the place gave birth to Rome's first emperors from the provinces, Trajan and Hadrian, as well as to such outstanding figures in Roman intellectual history as Lucan and Seneca. The legacy of this Roman past is apparent in sites and monuments throughout Andalucía, many of which are scarcely better known than the ones from prehistoric times, and certainly no better treated: the main survivals from Roman Seville are three enormous columns sunk into a waterlogged, rubbish-strewn hole off the Calle Marmoles. Though Andalucía has no existing Roman monuments quite as distinguished or celebrated, say, as the theatre at Mérida or the aqueduct at Segovia, there are several monuments deserving special mention, for intance the magnificently preserved bridges at Córdoba and Andújar, and the massively-built theatre at Ronda la Vieja, which gains additional power from its isolated, hilltop position and the splendid panorama over the Serranía de Ronda.

Recently, work has begun on uncovering the rest of Ronda la Vieja, which like many Roman cities in the peninsula was built next to an earlier settlement. Lack of funds will ensure that the excavations are protracted over many years, but in the meantime there are extensive remains to be seen of other Roman townships in Andalucía. The least known of these is that of the Castillo de Mulva, which occupies a verdant hillside and features the ruins of houses, defensive walls, a mausoleum, a forum, and, dominating the site, a large sanctuary. Among the most beautifully situated ruins in Spain are those of the former town of Bolonia, which overlook a wild bay hemmed in by a great sweep of dunes and hills; the ruins come right down to a beach which until a few years ago was hardly frequented and even now shows only the most modest signs of tourist development. Bolonia in its present ruined state is probably a more romantic place than it once was, and certainly a less pungent one: it used to be a small port and industrial town, and the buildings nearest the shore, below the forum and basilica, contained vats in which tunny and mackerel were marinaded for several weeks in the preparation of a popular fish sauce known as *garum*, the Roman equivalent of Gentleman's Relish. Another of Andalucía's ruined townships is Carmona near Seville. The walls that enclose present-day Carmona, though restored in Moorish times, still have much of their Roman masonry; but the main Roman remains lie on the ugly outskirts of the town and consist of an overgrown theatre turned towards a block of flats, and, directly behind the theatre, one of Spain's most interesting necropolises. This has large rock-hewn family tombs built below ground and reached by steps; some have traces of ancient painted decoration, another has a statue of an elephant, one even has a bench and table intended for a funerary meal. The site is one of the best maintained in all Andalucía, and has the additional advantage of an excellent small museum of Roman finds.

Only a few kilometres from Seville, at the small and dusty village of Santiponce, are the most famous Roman ruins in Andalucía, those of Itálica. Founded by Scipio in 205 BC next to a Turdetanian settlement, Itálica was the first Roman town in Spain. Originally, it was simply a hospital and small military base, but it soon developed into an important port, and, in the first century AD gave birth first to Trajan and then to Hadrian; Hadrian took particular pride in his native town, and embellished it with many of the buildings that are to be seen today. Falling into ruin in the middle ages, it became during the renaissance a place of pilgrimage for Sevillian humanists, who regarded it as a Spanish Rome. However, vandalism had already begun to take its toll, and by the 14th century many of the columns from Itálica had been used in the building of the nearby monastery church of San Gerónimo. In 1595 and again in 1602 terrible floods forced the villagers of Santiponce to move closer to the site, and to use bricks from it for their new houses. A local 17th-century poet and archaeologist, Rodrigo Caro, was moved to write:

> *Estos, Fabio, ¡ay dolor! que ves ahora*
> *Campos de soledad, mustio collado,*
> *fueron ya tiempo Itálica famosa...*
> These empty fields before you,
> Fabio, this parched mound of earth,
> Were once, alas, the famed Itálica.

Elephant tomb at Carmona

Excavations began in earnest in the late 18th century, but if anything vandalism increased. The French marshal Soult took away many of the pieces that he found lying around, as did Wellington, and numerous Sevillanos anxious to decorate their houses. An American visitor of 1818, George Ticknor, was saddened by what he saw. 'Everything is neglected. The amphitheatre even is falling in every year; the mosaics, as I absolutely saw, are a part of a sheepfold, and, of course, more and more broken up every day, and the only person, I believe, who takes an interest in these curious remains, is a poor advocate of Seville, who comes out here on the feast days, and digs among them with his own hands. . .' The amphitheatre today, restored and surrounded by trees and parkland, is the focus in the summer months of a dance and opera festival. Many of the mosaics from the surrounding site have been moved to Seville's Museo Arquéologico, though many others can still be seen off the recently excavated grid of wide streets that cover the exposed hill above the amphitheatre. In Santiponce itself, you will find the now restored and rubbish-free theatre, which supports a picturesque accretion of houses, rather like those that were once attached to Rome's forum.

By the early 5th century AD, Rome's control of its Spanish provinces had weakened, and soon the Visigothic kings were the undisputed masters of the land, wresting power both from the Romans and other Barbarian tribes; by the late 6th century, the Visigoths had united Spain under a centralized authority, with Toledo as capital. However, Spain remained heavily under Roman influence; Romans lived alongside the Visigoths, and still held important civic and ecclesiastical positions.

The ruins at Itálica, c.1881

This situation was particularly true of Andalucía, whither the Emperor Justinian had even sent Byzantine troops in 572 (they were not expelled until 621). Few traces of Visigothic culture are to be found in Andalucía, and indeed the only important cultural contribution of this period was made by the scholar St. Isidore, who established an important school of learning in Seville in the 6th century.

The Visigoths themselves were not a united force, and throughout their stay in Spain were divided by internal conflicts, not least of which was that of religion. At first the Visigoths were separated from the Romans not only by language but also by religion, the Visigothic rulers adhering to a Christian heresy known as Arianism or Unitarianism (which denied the divinity of Christ). After 507 orthodox, Trinitarian Christianity became the official Visigothic religion, but a strong Arian undercurrent persisted, and came to be thought of as upholding the true spirit of the Visigoths. At the same time there was the growing problem of the Jews, who had probably arrived in Andalucía by the end of the first century AD, and who by Visigothic times made up a major portion of the merchant and artisan classes. In the course of the 7th century, they were subjected to increasingly harsh measures, such as confiscation of property, forced baptism, and persecution. In addition to these religious tensions there were grave economic problems, the nobility and the clergy enjoying all the privileges and wealth, and the peasantry being reduced to a state of serfdom; finally came feuds within the nobility itself, and the controversial problem of succession to the throne. So confused was the state of affairs in Spain by the early 8th century that the time was ripe for Arab intervention, an intervention probably encouraged by certain Visigothic factions, and certainly welcomed by the Jews. The legend goes that it was a Visigothic merchant called Julian who had encouraged the Arabs to come to Spain as a revenge upon the then ruler, Roderick, for having dishonoured Julian's daughter Florinda. Those more likely to have borne such a strong grudge against Roderick were the partisans of Achila, a Visigothic king whom he had deposed. But the closeness of Spain to Africa, and the legendary wealth of Andalucía, were reasons enough for the Arabs to want to come here.

In recent years it has become fashionable among historians to play down the notion of an Arab 'conquest' of Spain, and to emphasize instead how small were the forces that initially came here from Africa, how easily they took over the country, and how rapidly their religion and customs were assimilated by the indigenous population. These historians argue that all this was possible because of the strong African element already present in the ethnic make-up of the Spaniards, in particular the Andalucíans, and the fact that the Arian Unitarian movement has a parallel in an Islamic Unitarian movement. In other words the Arab take-over of Spain was a welcome and logical step, the idea of a ruthless and bloodthirsty military conquest by an alien force being merely an absurd exaggeration put forward by Arab and Christian fanatics from the 11th century onwards. There is nonetheless no getting away from the fact that the Arab presence in Spain was in keeping with an Islamic expansionist policy which had made vast progress since the death of Muhammad in the early 7th century.

Muhammad's immediate successors, known as Caliphs, managed soon after their master's death to impose Islam over an area that covered not only Arabia proper, but also Syria, Palestine, Iraq, Iran and Egypt. The twin religious and political capitals of this state were originally Mecca and Medina, but later the centre of political power shifted out of Arabia. The powerful Umayyad dynasty established the caliphate in the Syrian city of Damascus, and encouraged Islam to spread east to Central Asia and west to the Atlantic. The winning over of the whole of North Africa to Islam was not without its difficulties, but by 701 it had finally been achieved, and the Berber tribes pacified. The path was now clear to move into Spain. In July 710 an officer called Tarif went with a small force on a reconnaissance trip to Spain, and soon took possession of the peninsula's southern tip, where his memory is preserved in the name of a town with an impressive Arab citadel, Tarifa. Encouraged by the success of Tarif's mission, a full-scale expedition led by Tariq Ibn Ziyad was sent out to Spain in the following year. Tariq's forces made their headquarters at Gibraltar (the name of which is derived from the Arabic *Jabal Tariq,* or 'Rock of Tariq'), and went from there to win most of the peninsula, stopping short of the northern mountains, which were always to remain in Christian hands: it has been said that the Muslim invaders were never truly happy in places where olive trees did not grow.

The early years of Muslim domination of Spain were especially troubled and confusing ones, and matters were not helped by the lack of interest in Damascus, which was a good four months' journey away. Al-Andalus was the name given to the whole of Muslim Spain, and the part of it which we now know as Andalucía lacked the administrative unity which it had had during the Roman period, being divided into about fifteen provinces or *coras.* The governing of al-Andalus was left to an Emir, a position which at first changed hands with bewildering rapidity. During the brief period when Muslim forces spread over the peninsula, power in the land had been shared between Tariq and Musa Ibn Nusayr, a former governor of North Africa who had sent Tariq to Spain in the first place and had later joined him there, apparently jealous of the man's success, and wishing to have some credit in the victory. Musa's son, Abd al-Aziz Ibn Musa was appointed Emir by his father in 714, and immediately made Seville the capital of al-Andalus. His rule was able and very tolerant, but he was assassinated after only two years. The capital was moved to Córdoba, where it was to remain until the 11th century, despite initially being a scene of constant intrigues and in-fighting.

The Muslim occupants of Spain are commonly referred to as 'Moors', a term coined in the Middle Ages to describe the Muslims who stayed on in reclaimed Christian territory; *moro* was and still remains in Spain a term of abuse. The word, derived probably from the North African country of Mauritania, is at any rate a blanket term covering the many different races that make up the Muslim religion. The so-called Moors who came over to Spain in the 8th century consisted not simply of Arabs, but also of Syrians, Egyptians, and, above all, Berbers, who made up the bulk of Tariq's expeditionary forces of 711; the Arabs represented in fact the minority of the Muslim races in Spain, even if at first they were politically the strongest. Racial tensions between the Spanish Muslims were inevitable, and far more damaging to begin with than any threat from the Christians. They were complicated by opposing factions within the individual races, the situation thus created in 8th-century Córdoba being not unlike that of present-day Beirut. The greatest friction was between the Arabs and the Berbers, who felt quite rightly that the Arabs discriminated against them. A Berber revolt broke out in North Africa in 740, and soon threatened Córdoba. An army was sent from Damascus headed by Balj Ibn Bishr, who eventually defeated the Berbers at Córdoba, but then took the opportunity to make himself Emir. The partisans of the deposed Emir were mainly Yemenis or southern Arabs, and they entered a bloody conflict with the soldiers of Balj, who were mainly Qaysites or northern Arabs. Al-Andalus might have come to an end as quickly as it had been created had it not been for the arrival in Córdoba, a few years later, of a refugee from the Umayyad dynasty in Damascus.

In 750, after a period of grave political, social and economic crisis, the last Umayyad caliph in Damascus, Marwan II, was taken prisoner and executed, thus bringing to an end nearly 150 years of Umayyad rule. The usurping family, the Abbasids, were anxious to destroy any potential future threat from the Umayyads, and arranged that all its members should be treacherously killed at a banquet. As in a fairy tale, however, one of their number escaped, Prince Abd al-Rahman, who, with his faithful servant Badr, then wandered incognito through Palestine, Egypt and North Africa. Drumming up support from the Yemenis, he moved to Spain, and built up an army large enough to defeat the Qaysite ruler of Córdoba. In 756, aged 26, the prince became Emir of al-Andalus, and the founder of a new Umayyad dynasty, which was to rule until 1031. Under their rule Córdoba became one of the great cities of the world, rivalled in the Muslim countries only by Damascus, with which it was frequently compared. Its greatest period was to come after 929 when Abd al-Rahman III styled himself 'Commander of the Faithful', the legitimate Caliph, and in so doing transformed al-Andalus from an emirate into a caliphate.

By and large the period of Umayyad rule in al-Andalus can be characterized as one of prosperity, religious tolerance, relative stability, and intense cultural and scientific activity. The great natural resources of Andalucía were brilliantly exploited, and though the structure of land ownership had changed little since the Visigoths, the peasantry were no longer treated like serfs and now paid only 20% to 50% of their crops to their landlords as opposed to 50% to 80% previously. The Muslims of this period tolerated all those who were 'people of the Book', and, while extracting poll and land taxes in return for their protection, allowed Christians and Jews freely to practise their religions. The former were known as *mozarabs*, and, like the Jews, were fully conversant with the Arab language and traditions, and could rise to important positions in Muslim society; there were even those Christians of al-Andalus who joined the Muslims in fighting against their Christian brothers in the north of Spain. Marriage between Muslim men and Christian women was encouraged, the off-spring of such unions being called *muwalladun* (the Christians of the north referred to these people as renegades). The great majority of the Christians in al-Andalus, however, became *muslimah,* or Muslim converts, who were the most important social group in the country in terms both of numbers and their pre-eminence in the country's religious, political and intellectual life. Another group which should be mentioned were the *saqaliba*, who were originally slaves from Northern Spain, France, Germany and Eastern European countries. Indoctrinated into Arab ways, they came to be trusted by the Umayyad rulers more than the Arabs and Berbers, and were indeed preferred to them as palace employees by Abd al-Rahman III. From their lowly social position, they rose to posts of great importance, and acquired large estates.

Though the Umayyads managed to stay in power for so long, and to avert all religious conflict, they were only just able to contain the many internal quarrels provoked by the ever greater social diversity of Muslim Spain. The greatest challenge to Umayyad authority was offered by a muwallad from Ronda called Ibn Hafsun. His life was a picturesque one, and began, like that of many 19th-century bandits, by his killing a man and leading the life of a highway robber in the mountains. Escaping from justice, he went over to North Africa, where he became apprenticed to a tailor. He returned to al-Andalus, and by 880 had gathered together a rebel army with its headquarters at Bobastro, an isolated mountain-top fortress in the northernmost part of the Serranía de Ronda. Exploiting the dissent felt against the Arab rulers of al-Andalus, he attracted an ever-growing number of followers, particularly among his fellow muwalladun. Various successful campaigns were mounted against him, at the end of one of which his enemies had one of his commanders, Ayshun, crucified with a pig at his right and a dog at his left. Despite all this Ibn Hafsun was able to maintain a strong hold over southern al-Andalus, and this did not even weaken after 899, when he converted to Christianity and thereby lost many of his Arab supporters. He died in 917, and his son continued fighting for his cause for a further ten years. His castle at Bobastro was never taken. Today the scant ruins of the place are difficult to locate, but the site is a beautiful and peaceful one, near the end of a small road which climbs its way up through wild and verdant mountain scenery. Immediately below the castle ruins, and a ten minute walk from the road, stands an enchanting Mozarabic church (see page 256). Built into the rock, this ruined church, with it overgrown horse-shoe arch, and superb views, is one of the most romantic sites in all Andalucía. This was Ibn Hafsun's final resting place.

The negative aspects of Umayyad rule are outweighed by the positive ones, which for many are reflected above all in the cultural and scientific achievements of the period. These achievements must be seen in the context of the whole Muslim world, which in the fields of arts and sciences was far more advanced at this time than Christian Europe: Arab physicians, for instance, were dissecting before the 10th century, whereas European ones only did so after the renaissance. The specific part which al-Andalus itself played has only rarely been looked at in any serious, critical way, the many who have written on Muslim Spain having generally eulogized the place unreservedly, often with little or no knowledge of Muslim culture or Arabic. At first al-Andalus was in fact a backward place in relation to other Muslim countries, which was perhaps inevitable given its distant provincial status at this time, and initial minority of Arabic speakers. The first great figures in the country's cultural and intellectual life were imports fom the East, such as the musician Ziryab, who came from Bagdhad in the early 9th century to work at the court of Abd al-Rahman II (822-852): he was famous not only for his minstrel singing and lute accompaniment, but as a pioneer in the arts of hairdressing, perfumes, fashion and cooking (it was he who introduced to Europe an orderly sequence in which dishes should be presented, ending with the dessert).

Not until the second half of the 9th century, when the population of al-Andalus had become thoroughly immersed in Arab ways, did a flourishing of native talent begin to be apparent. In the 10th century Córdoba emerged as a major centre of patronage and learning, with al-Hakam II (961-976) building up in the city one of the great libraries of the world; at the same time the wealthy of Europe descended upon the city to be treated by doctors such as Rhazes, who distinguished measles from smallpox, and popularized animal gut for stitching. Few scholars or writers of great originality, however, were produced during this period. Philosophy and jurisprudence (the latter being the fulcrum of Muslim intellectual life) continued to be dominated in al-Andalus by the views of the Arabian jurist Malik Ibn Anan, who had been an outspoken opponent of all philosophical and religious speculation; his rigid beliefs – the so-called Malikite orthodoxy – had been adopted in al-Andalus under Hisham I (788-796), and were probably responsible for the relative poverty of philosophic literature in Muslim Spain. Poetry, the main literary form in al-Andalus was likewise based largely on eastern models, and recent claims to find in it specifically Spanish features such as an underlying melancholy have not been convincing.

Whereas Córdoba was known for its learning, Malága became celebrated for singing, and Seville for the making of music instruments. Singing, dancing and lute

Poetry at court in the 13th century

music were among the great passions of al-Andalus, even though Muhammad had disapproved of these activities. There is a famous account of an Arab traveller, Ahmad al-Yamani, staying in Málaga around 1016, and being unable to sleep because of the constant sounds of lutes, harps, drums and song. One such night, however, he heard instrumental music of such beauty and mystery that all his anxiety and irritation vanished and he was filled with a great happiness. Then a woman began to sing with ' a voice more brilliant than the flowers after the rain and more pleasant than is the freshness of the embrace to the ardent lover'. Finally he was unable to contain his curiosity any longer, and got up to see where the music was coming from. He soon found himself in a large courtyard, in the middle of which sat about twenty men, holding fruits and drinks. In front of them were slave girls with lutes, tambourines, flutes and other instruments, but they were silent at the time, absorbed, like everybody else, in the music of one of their number, who was accompanying herself with a lute as she sang.

The form which dancing took is not known, but to judge from the many poems describing dancers of the time, it was highly sensual. One poem even describes how a slave girl dances to the chords of a lute until finally she slips out of her dress to appear 'like a bud unfolding from a cluster of blossoms'. Sensuality and sybaritism featured prominently in the Romantic image of Muslim Spain, but it would be difficult to form a different impression of this society. Despite the famous libraries of al-Andalus, leisure time here seems not to have been spent in reading and studying, as Muslim religious leaders would have liked, but instead in playing chess, listening to music and poetry, drinking, watching dancing, and indulging in love-making. One of the few themes to which poetry could be devoted was – strangely enough for a Muslim society – wine and its pleasurable effects. But the most popular of these themes was love, which was portrayed in all its guises, but above all in the physical one. Love was an activity expressed by poets in ever more novel and absurd ways. 'Such was my kissing,' wrote one poet, 'such my sucking of his mouth that he was almost made toothless.'

A strong sensuality characterizes much of the architecture of Muslim Spain. There evolved here a style radically opposed to that of the classical tradition, and one which was fundamentally unintellectual in its approach. Intead of an architecture based on strict rules of proportions and the rational ordering of space, the Muslim architects favoured curiously intangible structures, in which there was much mysterious play of light and shadow, and intricate decorative effects on an unprecedently large scale. All these qualities can be seen in the Great Mosque or Mezquita at Córdoba, which was the major architectural work carried out in Spain under the Umayyads, and arguably the most original achievement in Spanish culture of this period.

Originally a modest structure built under Abd al-Rahman I around 780, it was continually enlarged and embellished under succcessive Umayyad rulers until

The Mezquita, Córdoba

eventually it was virtually unrivalled in size and splendour in the Muslim world, and indeed was described by early Arab travellers as the greatest mosque ever built. The exterior is relatively severe and ungainly, and gives little idea of the richness within. The European traveller, accustomed to Christian churches with their prominent west portals, might well be perplexed by the Mezquita's apparent lack of an obvious main entrance, and will certainly have no idea of where to turn the moment on entering the building. In a Christian church your eyes would immediately be led down the central nave to the High Altar, but here you are confronted by what has been described unfailingly since the Middle Ages as a 'forest' of marble columns, of which there were originally 1,293. Somewhere in here is the *mihrab*, or prayer niche indicating the direction of Mecca, but this too is off centre and difficult to find. Even the great Christian structure built within the Mosque in the 16th century, after the building had been turned into a cathedral, is almost lost in the forest. Charles V, who had authorized the construction of this later addition, subsequently believed that he had 'destroyed what was unique in the world'. Damaged rather than destroyed, however, would have been a better word, for the place today remains so magical that it is impossible to imagine what it must have been like with all its columns, mosaics, gold decorations and multitude of candles, lamps and copper chandeliers, one of which held reputedly 1,000 lights. Traveller upon traveller has gaped with astonisment inside the Mezquita, and yet the building must have been deeply disconcerting to classical sensibilities. The German art historian, Meier-Graafe, visiting Córdoba in the 1880's was one of the few people honest enough to express his reservations about the building. Confronted with the forest of columns, this rationally minded, and slightly puritanical scholar was unable, as it were, to see the wood for the trees. 'I can't make head or tail of the Mosque,' he wrote, 'the impression is there of course, but I don't know what to do with it and I am not sufficiently enthusiastic to think about it. . . The mosque lacks altogether the living power of *matière*, the multiple quality of intelligible proportions.' What Meier-Graafe considered an intellectual failing, however, was in fact an indication of a radically different religious mentality from that of Christianity. This is a mentality that does not believe in any priestly hierarchy, and sees no need to have any rigid structural format in a place of worship. The centre of a mosque is anywhere in the building you want to pray.

The earliest mosques in the Muslim world were simple square enclosures, with almost bare interiors, but as Islam moved from desert surroundings to urban centres, the structures became more and more sophisticated, with domes, minarets and a profusion of decoration. Islam frowns on the representation of the human form, and the religious message of a building was conveyed by inscriptions. These inscriptions became an ever more prominent element in the decoration of a building, and the complex forms of Arab calligraphy seem in turn to have inspired the Muslim craftsmen to create increasingly intricate and extensive decorative framing motifs to surround them; the skill of Muslim craftsmen, in all materials, was proverbial. The first outstanding examples of Muslim religious architecture are the Dome of the Rock in Jerusalem and the Umayyad Great Mosque in Damascus, which date respectively from the 7th and 8th centuries. Córdoba's Mezquita, like many mosques throughout the Muslim world, has many echoes of these two buildings, but its most noticeable feature is completely without precedent in a mosque, and is a masterly example of the adoption of western elements to an eastern setting. This is the super-imposition of one row of arches on top of another, so as to double the height of the building. The actual arches, horse-shoe in shape as in most Muslim buildings, are probably of Visigothic origin, but the doubling of them is clearly inspired by Roman acqueducts such as that of Mérida.

The other outstanding innovations of the Córdoba Mezquita are in the part added by al-Hakam II in the 960's. The breathtakingly elaborate ornamentation which had come to characterize Muslim art and architecture of this period is here applied to structures of revolutionary complexity. The decorative possibilities of arcading, as revealed in the main body of the mosque, are exploited to a far greater degree in the *maqsura*, or royal gallery of the Caliph: in this the arches are interlaced and have small semi-circular segments cut out of them so as to form what are known as poly-

Córdoba

lobed arches. In front of the mihrab – a dazzlingly ornate structure in coloured marbles – is a vestibule lined with mosaics and covered with an ethereal dome, supported on vaulting shaped like a star and with openings through which light floods in. In transforming sturdy simple forms such as arches and domes into delicate and fascinatingly complex ones, the architects employed by al-Hakam II greatly encouraged the Muslim trend towards an architecture in which the distinction between structure and decoration becomes ever more blurred.

The many other mosques constructed in Spain during the Umayyad period were either destroyed or ruthlessly converted into churches. As for the once highly praised secular buildings of this period, these have fared little better, and there remain today only a handful of castles – most notably the much restored and enlarged Alcazaba of Almería and the scant ruins of the extraordinary palace of Medina Azahara, which ranked with the Mezquita at Córdoba as one of the great wonders of the world. Medina Azahara was begun in 939 and intended as the summer palace of Abd al-Rahman III, who was perhaps the Umayyad ruler to have devoted the most money to architectural work. He is said to have spent over a third of the state revenue on public construction, and the building boom which he instigated at Córdoba was to turn the place by the end of the century into a vast metropolis containing – according to the 17th-century Arab historian al-Maqqari – 1,600 mosques, 900 public baths, 60,300 mansions for the wealthy, 213,077 ordinary homes, and 80,455 shops. These figures are obviously greatly exaggerated (and if true would mean that Córdoba had a population of over a million), but at least they give some idea of how much has been lost.

Sentimental travellers can indulge in dreams of former glory by visiting what is left of Medina Azahara. Lying eight kilometres to the east of Córdoba, it occupies a quiet, isolated site on the lower slopes of the Sierra Morena, and has extensive views over the Guadalquivir Valley. To describe this place simply as a 'summer palace' is misleading, for it was actually a great architectural complex comprising several palaces, a mosque, gardens, a zoo, an aviary, and manufactories for weapons; its name in fact means 'city of Azahara' (Azahara being probably a favourite mistress of Abd al-Rahman III). Supposedly, 10,000 workers and 1,500 beasts of burden were employed in its construction, during which period 6,000 carved stones were used daily. Marble was imported from Almería and Carthage, and engraved basins from Constantinople and Syria; the roof tiles were covered in gold and silver.

In 1009 a rebellion broke out in Córdoba, and rioters pillaged and destroyed Medina Azahara, and rendered it uninhabitable. The ruins were gradually buried, and the remaining parts plundered for their stone. 'But for the testimony of historians,' wrote Dundas Murray on a visit to the site in 1849, 'it would be hard to believe that Medina Azahara ever rose from the ground to cover a wide space with sumptuous edifices.' Gerald Brenan came here over a hundred years later and found that the ruins were 'scarcely worth seeing, since all the stones were being carried off to

Medina Azahara

build a monastery on the hill'. I first came here in 1968 and was confronted, in what had been the main hall of the palace, with a monumental jigsaw of masonry and plasterwork. Since then the jigsaw has been miraculously put together, and the profusely decorated reconstructed hall gives an excellent idea of what the building must originally have been like. Moreover, excavations elsewhere in the site continue to reveal more and more of the original complex. Its astonishing extent has become clearer than it has been for centuries.

The fate of Medina Azahara mirrored that of Córdoba after the fall of the Umayyad dynasty. The Umayyads had maintained a strong rule right up to 1009, thanks mainly to a dynasty of chamberlains headed by the brilliant al-Mansur, who had risen to power after the death of al-Hakam II in 976 and had virtually governed the country single-handed until his own death in 1002. Al-Mansur's family, the Amirids fell from favour in 1009 following the reckless, dissolute and over-ambitious behaviour of al-Mansur's second son, Abd al-Rahman. With their fall, the Umayyad dynasty itself collapsed. The revolts that had led to the sacking of Medina Azahara in 1009 turned into a bloody civil war, which soon reduced al-Andalus to chaos. In 1023, the Umayyads were briefly and half-heartedly reinstated, but they were ousted for good eight years later. Córdoba's days of greatness were finally over. The celebrated library of al-Hakam II had been pillaged and burnt, and the population of the city had begun to decline. In the late 12th century an Arab traveller, Muhmmad al-Idrisi, was to marvel at the splendour of Córdoba and its monuments, and to describe the place as 'the most famous town in all of Spain'. He

Jewish girl in Moorish architecture, by J. F. Lewis

had to add, however: 'At the time of writing the town of Córdoba has been torn apart by discord; its situation has been altered by harsh fortune, and its population is no longer large.' Visitors of later centuries, while generally unqualified in their enthusiasm for the Mezquita, had little good to say about the town itself. 'Córdoba,' wrote Dundas Murray in 1849, 'is a very dull place; the life has utterly departed from it, and to roam through its streets is like wandering among the tombs. If any one desires to know what a silent and desolate city is, let him come here.' Murray's contemporary Richard Ford was no more complimentary about the town. 'Córdoba is soon seen. This Athens under the Moors is now a poor Boetian place, the residence of local authorities. . . and a library of no particular consequence: a day will amply suffice for everything.'

With the ousting of the Umayyads in 1031, al-Andalus came to be broken up into twelve small kingdoms or *taifas*, the boundaries of which were based to a large extent on the provinces or coras that had been established in the early 8th century. The kingdom of Córdoba was soon outstripped in power and prestige by that of Seville, which under the rule of the Abbasid kings rose to become the most important and populated town of the peninsula. Intense rivalry between the various courts of al-Andalus had a disastrous effect on the political life of the country, and the quarrels were eventually to facilitate the first stages of the so-called Christian

Reconquest at the end of the 11th century. However, what with each court vying to outdo the other in splendour, this rivalry might also be held partially responsible for what has been described as the greatest period in the cultural history of al-Andalus.

The 11th century was above all a period of exceptional writers, in particular poets, the works of whom may well have been a major influence on the troubadours of France. The most versatile of these new writers was the Córdoba-born Ibn Hazm (994-1064), a man sometimes regarded as the first intellectual giant of Muslim Spain. He wrote on numerous topics, in verse and in prose, though perhaps his most popular work was *The Ring of the Dove*, a youthful treatise on love in which he praised the spiritual aspects of love, attacked sexual excesses and recommended continence. Love remained the major preoccupation of the Muslim poets, though whether they followed Ibn Hazm's advice on this matter seems doubtful, to judge by what is known of some of their lives and by the passionate, physical descriptions of love that they put in their works. One of the most distinguished of these poets was Ibn Zaydun (1003 -1070) from Córdoba, who in his twenties fell in love with the daughter of the Caliph al-Mustakfi, Princess Walladah. The princess wrote skilful poetry herself, and enjoyed a lifestyle which gives an interesting insight into the relative freedom then enjoyed by women in Arab society: she completely disregarded the veil, regularly frequented the higher circles of Córdoba society, and openly went out at night to meet her lover, Ibn Zaydun. The two corresponded in poems, until eventually the Princess began responding to the attentions of a wealthy, influential man called Ibn Abdus. The rejected poet wrote a particularly vituperative piece characterizing his rival as a stupid, vulgar and loathsome creature no better than a fly or mosquito, but this did little to further his own suit, and in fact landed him briefly in jail. Finally freed, he took refuge in Medina Azahara, where he expressed his anguish at losing the Princess's love in a poem in which each of its fifty verses rhymes in *nun*. This is considered one of the finest love poems in the Arab language.

Among the plethora of poets who worked at Seville in the 11th cenury, the two best known are Ibn Ammar (1031-86), and the poet-king of Seville, al-Mutamid (reigned 1069-91). The former, a man of humble origin, began his career as a wandering poet composing works in praise of anyone who would pay him. He ended up working at Seville in the court of al-Mutamid's father, al-Mutatid, for whom he wrote a poem celebrating a recent victory over the Berbers. At the court he became intimate friends with his fellow poet, al-Mutamid, but incurred the father's displeasure and was exiled. When al-Mutamid himself succeded to the throne of Seville in 1068, Ibn Ammar was reinstated at the court, but the friendship betwen the two soon began to fall apart, until finally they became political enemies, and wrote vicious poems against each other. Ibn Ammar was forced to escape to the north of Spain, but al-Mutamid had him brought back to Seville, and there, insensible to a poem begging for forgiveness, killed his former friend with repeated blows from an axe. Al-Mutamid was himelf to have an unhappy end, exiled to Morocco, and composing bitter poems bemoaning his fate as 'a stranger, a captive in the Maghreb'. In better days he had been the ruler of a powerful kingdom, and had celebrated the joys of wine and women. His great love had been one Itimad, separation from whom in the course of his duties as a king had once inspired the lines:

> I am pining because of being separated from you,
> Inebriated with the wine of my longing for you,
> Crazed with the desire to be with you,
> To sip your lips and to embrace you.

The outpouring of poetic talent in 11th-century Spain reflected a new confidence among the country's poets and a diminishing of once firmly held feelings of inferiority towards the poets of the east. Nonetheless eastern models continued to be faithfully imitated, and the subject-matter and verse forms of classical Arabic poetry in Spain remained as rigid as before. What is more there were those who continued to feel that poetry and scholarship were still not taken seriously enough in Spain, one such person being Ibn Hazm, who once complained that he would have been far better appreciated had he been born outside the country. The one indisputably original and indigenous contribution made by Spain to Arabic poetry took the form of popular verse, of which there were two known genres, the *muwashshah* and the *zayal*. Written in colloquial rather than classical Arabic, simple and spontaneous, and owing nothing to eastern connections, these types of verse were frowned upon by most purists, and indeed scarcely considered to be poetry. Yet, after 1100, when classical Arabic poetry began to decline, the muwashshah and the zayal flourished more than ever, and have even lived on, some say, in the lyrics of flamenco.

In considering the poetry of al-Andalus, mention must finally be made of the many great Jewish poets who emerged in Spain after 1000. Whereas the Jewish scholars and philosophers of Spain wrote in Arabic, these poets composed almost exclusively in Hebrew, partly because many of their works were liturgical, and partly because the Hebrew language had a greater flexibility when applied to poetry than it had with philosophy. Though writing in Hebrew, the Jewish poets followed classical Arabic forms of verse, and adopted the same themes. Thus Samuel Ha-Nagid, the first important Jewish poet of Spain, wrote a poem in praise of wine:

> Red in appearance, sweet to taste
> Vintage of Spain, yet renowned in the East
> Feeble in the cup, but once in the brain,
> It rules over heads that cannot gain.
> The bereaved, whose blood is mixed with his tears,

The blood of the grape diminishes his fears.
Friends, passing the cup from hand to hand,
Seem to be gambling for a precious diamond.

Ha-Nagid had a remarkable life. Born in Córdoba in 993, he left the town in the course of the troubles following the rebellion of 1009. Settling in Málaga, his skill with Arabic calligraphy reputedly attracted the attention of the vizier Abu-al-Kassim Ibn al-Arif, who made him his private scretary. Later, at Granada, he became vizier himself, and a commander of the king of Granada's armies. No wonder he could once write a poem entitled *The Power of the Pen*, for apparently only one other Jew was ever to command a Muslim army, and that was his son, Joseph. Many of his poems deal with war and bereavement, and his long descriptions of battles in which he was involved are unique examples of Jewish martial poetry in Spain.

Two other memorable Jewish poets were Moses Ibn Ezra and Judah Ha-Levi, both of whom witnessed and suffered from the collapse of the taifa dynasties after 1089. Moses Ibn Ezra, who was born no later than 1055, established an early reputation as a poet among the intellectual circles of his native Granada, but was left destitute after the city's devastation by the Berbers in 1090. Reluctant to abandon the town, as many members of his family had done, he stayed on here for a while, but eventually a personal quarrel compelled him to leave it for good. His last years were spent in Christian Spain, longing for the physical and intellectual environment of his native town. Judah Ha-Levi, generally regarded as the finest of Spain's Jewish poets, if not the greatest of all post-Biblical Hebrew poets, also spent an important part of his life in Granada, where indeed he befriended Moses Ibn Ezra. After 1090, he appears to have moved first to Lucena, near Seville, and then to Seville itself, before finally going on to Toledo, which had recently been reclaimed by the Christian armies of Alfonso VI. Persecution of Jews in Christian Castille in 1109 sent him back again to al-Andalus, where he stayed in Córdoba. The position of Jews in Spain, in both the Christian and Muslim parts of the peninsula, was becoming increasingly difficult, and Ha-Levi saw the only hope for his people in an eventual return to the Holy Land. In the end he himself decided to leave Spain altogether, and to go to the Middle East. Friends tried to dissuade him, and he also had his own fears to contend with, as he later set down in a poem:

He trembles. His tears begin to fall.
He fears to leave Spain, to travel through the world,
To embark on board ship, to cross the desert,
By the lion's den and the leopard's mountain lair.
He rebukes his friends, and decides to go.
He leaves his home and lives in the wasteland.

The Court of Lions, Granada

Ha-Levi probably died in Egypt, though the story goes that he was killed by a Muslim horseman just as he had reached the gates of Jerusalem.

Religious intolerance, which had barely existed under the Umayyads, began gradually to take hold of Spain from the late 11th century onwards, under the influence first of all of the ever growing threat from the Christian north, and then of the fanatical Muslim beliefs held by the two succeeding Berber dynasties who were to rule over al-Andalus in the 12th and 13th centuries. The turning-point in the history of al-Andalus was the capture of Toledo by Alfonso VI in 1085. This marks the beginning of what came to be known as the 'Reconquest', but was actually a 'Conquest' of lands which after nearly four centuries of Muslim rule were far more Muslim than Christian in their ethnic and cultural make-up. The loss of Toledo was at any rate deeply disconcerting to the taifa rulers in the south of Spain, particularly as Alfonso VI had already declared war on Seville. In 1086 the poet-king al-Mutamid of Seville felt that he had no other option but to invite to Spain a Berber sect which had recently come to power in northwest Africa, the Almoravids.

The situation in northwest Africa in the first half of the 11th century was roughly comparable to that of al-Andalus at that time, the whole place being divided up into lands ruled by different Berber tribes. One of these desert tribes, the Sanhajahs, visited Mecca around 1039, and on their way back fell under the influence of a religious teacher called Ibn Yasin. This man later established a retreat or *ribat* for his followers, who became known in consequence as *al-murabitun*, from which the word 'Almoravids' is derived. The Almoravids rapidly gained a hold over northwest Africa and in 1062 founded the city of Marrakush (Marrakesh), which they made the capital of their state. After being called over to Spain in 1086, they immediately defeated the forces of Alfonso VI near Badajoz, but then returned to Africa. Summoned again to Spain two years later, their leader Yusuf Ibn Tashufin decided to make an all-out attempt to take possession himself of al-Andalus, and in so doing to secure the cause of Islam. Granada was captured by him in 1089, al-Mutamid was deposed and sent to his exile in Morocco the following year, and one by one all the taifa kingdoms fell to the Almoravids. The turbulent mood of this period is vividly evoked in the extraordinary autobiography written in exile in Morocco by the last of the Zirid Kings of Granada, Abd Allah Ibn Bulluyyin.

The success of the Almoravids was due largely to their winning over of the Muslim lower classes through their religious fervour and austerity, and their strongly anti-intellectual stance. However, their success was short-lived, for in the early 12th century, another equally fanatic Berber group, the Almohads, begun to win over Almoravid territory. The Almohads were Berbers from the Atlas Mountains, and their religious leader was one Ibn Tumart, who had been born a lamplighter's son in around 1084. Ibn Tumart styled himself the *mahdi*, or divinely chosen leader, and his followers were referred to as *muwahhidun* (hence 'Almohads') after their leader's advocacy of the concept of the unity or *tawhid* of

God. The man who brought the Almohads to political power was a potter's son called Abd al-Mumin, who in 1147 seized Marrakesh and thus brought about the collapse of the Almoravids. The Almohads then moved over to al-Andalus, but only gained possession over the whole country by about 1170, following years of political turmoil there. As with the Almoravids, their hold over such a heterogeneous society as that of Spain had only been possible through the fanaticism of their beliefs, but once this fanaticism began to wane, they were left deeply vulnerable. They were to survive in Spain no longer than had the Almoravids, being crushingly defeated by Alfonso VIII at Las Navas de Tolosa in 1212. The event, commemorated today by a large and hideous sculptural group on the site, was romantically described by Théophile Gautier as presaging the end of Spain's happiness and prosperity. The natives of al-Andalus, however, cannot have been too saddened by the defeat of the Almohads, whose intervention in their country's affairs had been welcomed by them with far less enthusiasm than had that of the Almoravids. In fact the Spanish Muslims probably felt that they had less in common with the Almohads than they had with the Christians of northern Spain. As more and more of their country came into the hands of the Christians, many of these Muslims were happy to stay on in Christian territory, and able to carry on with their lives much as before. The Christian conquest of Spain made rapid progress after 1212, and met with little serious resistance. When Seville was taken in 1248, only the western half of Andalucía remained under Muslim control.

The Almoravids and the Almohads have often been portrayed as uncouth, and barely literate people, with little interest in the arts and sciences. This is a great exaggeration. Under their rule standards of scholarship remained as high as ever in al-Andalus, and the country produced two of the outstanding intellectual figures in the history of Islam, the jurist, physician and Aristotelian scholar Averroes, and the Jewish philosopher and theologian Maimonides. Nonetheless, the patronage of literature declined significantly, and few major architectural works were produced. Our knowledge of both Almoravid and Almohad architecture is in fact largely based on what they built in Africa. From these buildings it could be said that the Almoravids maintained the trend in Islamic architecture towards ever more extensive surface decoration, in complete contrast to the Almohads, who reacted against such decorative excesses and favoured a style of great austerity. However, the latter's architectural masterpiece in Spain, the Giralda tower in Seville (built between 1172 and 1195) is notable as an elegant structure with exquisite ornamentation, and is thought by some to illustrate the civilizing influence of al-Andalus on these people. A virtuoso intricacy of detailing was always to be kept up by the Muslim craftsmen in Spain, throughout the turbulent history of al-Andalus, and long after the Christian conquest of the country. Those of the craftsmen who worked for the Christians were happy to incorporate Christian motifs into their designs, and also to apply these designs to structures of a radically opposed style. The work of these craftsmen is referred to as *mudéjar*, a term originally used in reference to Muslims who remained in Christian Spain without converting to Christianity (the word is derived from the Arabic *mudaijir*, which means 'to stay on', but also implies 'to be tamed'). Some of the great buildings of medieval Spain are essentially the work of the mudéjar craftsmen, such as the magnificent Alcázar in Seville, a Moorish building transformed in the late 13th century into a palace for the Christian king Pedro the Cruel.

By 1248, when most of al-Andalus had been reclaimed by the Christians, the monuments of Muslim Spain that were to have the greatest impact on the Western imagination had yet to be built. That al-Andalus managed to survive at all after 1248, let alone to do so for nearly two and a half centuries, and to create during this period some of Islam's most remarkable works, was an extraordinary achievement due in no small part to the ambitions and clever manoeuvering of a man who claimed noble Arab descent, Muhammad Ibn Nasr, founder of the Nasrid dynasty. He had come to power during the chaotic years following the collapse of the Almohads, and had created a small state in his native province of Jaén. Jaén fell to the Christian army of Ferdinand III in 1245, after which Ibn Nasr made Granada the capital of a kingdom which extended from just north of Granada itself down to the Mediterranean, and from Tarifa to Almería. The Kingdom of Granada had a precarious existence, being coveted both by the Christians, and by a tribe now powerful in Morocco, the Marinids. To lessen the Christian threat, Ibn Nasr signed a peace treaty with Ferdinand III in 1245, but this compelled him to swear allegiance to the Spanish kings, pay them an annual tribute, and even assist them in fighting should the occasion arise. The terms of the treaty put Ibn Nasr in the unenviable position of having to help Ferdinand in the siege of Seville of 1248, an act which did much to antagonize his fellow Muslims. Later Ibn Nasr had to call in the Marinids to fight off the Christians, and the help of these Moroccans was further sought by his son and successor, Muhammad II. The Christians could easily have been provoked by these actions into mounting an all-out attack on Granada, but the mountainous terrain of this kingdom, its proximity to Africa, and the usefulness of its tribute money, deterred them from doing so, at least for the time being. Alliance between Granada and the Marinids may nevertheless have incited the Christians to adopt increasingly severe measures against the Muslims in their own territories. These people began pouring into Granada in ever increasing numbers, and the population of the kingdom became almost exclusively Muslim.

Under the Nasrids the town of Granada came to draw from Arab travellers the lavish praise which they had once bestowed upon Córdoba. Their praise has been echoed by countless travellers up to the present day, for whereas Córdoba has lost much of what had made it famous, Granada has retained more of its Islamic past than any other Spanish town. Built on and around two hills underneath the Sierra Nevada, Granada has Muslim houses and monuments dispersed over a wide area.

Even in the middle of the bustling lower town, which was radically altered in the late 19th century, you will come across such an important Muslim building as the 14th-century Casa del Carbón, with its grand, horse-shoe arched entrance way, and excellently preserved three storey courtyard in brick. The building, the only one of its kind to survive intact in Spain, was originally both a warehouse and a place of lodging for merchants, who would set up their tents in its courtyard just as they would have done in one of the caravanserais of the east. Across the road from it is a lively market, which though a 19th-century Moorish pastiche, marks the site of the original market and has much of the character of an Oriental bazaar. But the part of town which gives perhaps the best idea of what everyday life was like in Muslim Granada is the hill of the Albaicín. This largely residential area has been much smartened up in recent years, but its maze of steps and alleys, and dense cluster of tiny white houses and hanging gardens remain otherwise much as they were in Muslim times, with even a sufficient amount of noise, smells and animation to give a life-like quality to this vision of the past. (A number of Sufi Muslims have even begun returning to the area in recent times, bringing with them several Arab tea rooms and shops selling oriental goods.) Hidden within the warren of the Albaicín are splendid Moorish palaces that are virtually unvisited by the tourist; and by knocking at the door of a modest private house on the Calle Darro, you will have a surprise similar to the one you might have had by rubbing Aladdin's lamp. For behind the door, which the house's owner is only too willing to open for you, lie a series of darkened, atmospheric chambers which were once Moorish public baths. Should you come here in the middle of the day, when narrow shafts of brilliant sunlight pierce through the star-shaped openings in the vaults, you might indeed feel that you have entered some Arabian fairy tale.

Predictably, and with wearying regularity, the world of fairy tales has been invoked to describe what are Granada's, if not Andalucía's, most celebrated monuments, the palaces and gardens of the Alhambra and Generalife. Seen from the Albaicín, they appear to float on the crest of a verdant hill, their picturesque silhouettes highlighted against a backdrop of snow-capped mountains. Towards evening, large groups of tourists climb up to the Albaicín to enjoy the sun setting behind this enchanted apparition. By day the two places are as crowded with visitors as descriptions of them are congested with superlatives. Their appeal is easy to understand – the luxuriance of their gardens, their coolness even at the height of summer, their magnificent setting, their abundance of pools, fountains and running water, and the way in which their architecture positively drips with ornamentation as in some Hollywood recreation of an oriental scene. They fulfill popular notions of what Paradise must be like, and have been described by writers as if they were the work of angels rather than of real architects, craftsmen and landscape gardeners. From what you can read about them, you might also conclude that they were places dedicated solely to pleasure, but this is really only true of the Generalife, which was intended as a summer retreat. The Alhambra was both a private residence for the Nasrid kings, and a vast complex of government buildings. Its finest parts date from the late 14th century, and are remakable for the lightness of their architecture, the complexity of their vaulting, and, above all, for their ornamentation, which though heavily restored, is more overwhelming in its intricacy than that of any other Moorish monument in Europe. Mario Praz, whose book *Unromantic Spain* contained a cruel and witty attack on Romantic attitudes to the Alhambra, found, perversely, that the end result of all this ornamentation was mind-numbing monotony. Praz might perhaps more profitably have pointed out that it was largely executed in the cheap materials of plaster and wood, and that this was evidence that the Nasrids had far less wealth at their disposal than did the Umayyads, who had used in Medina Azahara only the finest marbles and other rich materials. The Alhambra, furthermore, has none of the architectural innovations of Córdoba's Mezquita. Its greatness, like that of Nasrid culture in general, lies in its dazzling synthesis of centuries of Islamic achievement, rather than in any original contribution of its own.

The Moorish baths at Ronda

An Arab visitor to Granada in 1465 compared the town in size and in cultural splendour to Damascus, and wrote that 'it is a meeting place of illustrious people, poets, scientists, artists; there are here some of the finest men of our time, grandiose monuments, charming little corners. . . with its Alhambra it is one of the great cities of Islam.' 'Yet,' he added ominously, 'the Infidels are close at hand and have taken the greater part of this land of al-Andalus.' Three years previously the Christians had conquered the Rock of Gibraltar, which the famous 14th-century traveller Ibn Battuta had once described as the 'citadel of Islam'. The loss of Gibraltar accentuated the Spanish Muslims' sense of being cut off from Africa, a feeling which had grown with the decline of Marinid power in the second half of the 14th century. More isolated than ever before, they turned for help to Egypt and then to the Ottoman Empire, but in vain. The end of the Nasrids was spelt out in 1481, when their forces rashly seized the castle of Zahara from the Christians. This action made the Spanish monarchs Ferdinand and Isabella resolve to conquer the Kingdom of Granada. In 1482, the Christians, led by Rodrigo Ponce de León, made a brazen incursion right into the heart of Islamic territory, and took the Moors completely by surprise at Alhama de Granada, a town greatly favoured by the Nasrids on account of its hot springs. Ronda was captured in 1485, Málaga in 1487, Almería in 1489, and in 1492 the Christians were at the gates of Granada itself.

The last Nasrid ruler, Abur Abd Allah, known in Spanish as Boabdil, ignominiously surrended to the Christians in 1492. Abandoning Granada, he went first into the Alpujarras, then to the coastal town of Adra, and finally ended up in North Africa. Legend has it that at a place marked today by a large petrol station and a scattering of characterless modern houses, the escaping Boabdil turned around to catch his final glimpse of his beloved Granada, and heaved a great sigh (this place is now known as the Puerta del Suspiro or the 'Pass of the Sigh'). 'Weep like a woman,' his mother told him, 'you who have not defended your kingdom like a man.' For many, the collapse of the Nasrid dynasty brought to an end a golden age in Spanish history. Yet, according to official versions of this history, the Golden Age had only just begun.

The Golden Age

1492 was a momentous year in Spanish history, and its fifth centenary was the subject in Spain of major and controversial celebrations. The year which had begun with the surrender of Granada and the consequent unification of Spain under Ferdinand and Isabella, was to end with Columbus' pioneering voyage to America, and the claiming of the lands there for the Spanish crown. The new era which the two events heralded has traditionally been described as 'The Golden Age', and not without reason. A period of great economic prosperity in which gold flowed into Spain from America turned eventually into a magnificent flowering of the arts. Andalucía was to play the central role in this new Spain, and yet the Andalucíans, more than any other Spanish peoples, are prone to look back at 1492 with scepticism. The 19th-century chronicler of Spain and her empire, Prescott, referred to the reign of Ferdinand and Isabella as the most 'glorious epoch in the annals of Spain'. Yet the basis of this glory was a Reconquest that was not really a reconquest, and a Discovery that was not a discovery. Both these achievements should really be seen in terms of a brutal subjugation of other peoples, and it is singularly appropriate that the coat of arms of Ferdinand and Isabella should consist of arrows and a yoke. The Golden Age was an age of great paradox, and it has become a commonplace among historians to emphasize that the years of Spain's greatness contained the seeds of her decline. Even while Spain recently commemorated the glories of 1492, the Spanish state felt also the need to make an official apology for having expelled in that year the country's Jewish population – an act with disastrous consequences and with a particularly ironic resonance in view of the many protagonists of that era with Jewish blood, including Ferdinand himself and almost certainly Columbus.

The early years of Columbus' life are shrouded in mystery, and perhaps Columbus later intended them to be so. He is said to have been born in the Italian town of Genoa around 1445, though he was always to write in Spanish, and never to show the slightest pride in his supposed birthplace. His mother was almost certainly a Spanish Jewess, and it has recently been suggested that in Spain Jews were sometimes referred to as 'Genoese', both races being legendary for their avarice. In any case he married in the 1470's the daughter of a Spanish captain, from whom he

The tabernacle at La Rábida

would inherit numerous maps and nautical instruments, as well as documents relating to various journeys and discoveries that this captain had made. These documents apparently encouraged Columbus in his belief that it would be possible to reach the East by sailing to it across the Atlantic. There is also a story that Columbus had a meeting with a pilot who had actually done this journey by accident, his boat having been swept drastically off course while sailing between Spain and England; his story, related for the first time in a book of 1535, and afterwards frequently repeated, was later omitted in the biography of Columbus written by his son Hernando.

As is well known, Columbus spent many years trying without success to raise money for his Atlantic enterprise. By 1485, his wife had died, his hair had gone prematurely white, and he had just received another serious rebuttal, from the court of Portugal. Undeterred he went straight from Portugal to Andalucía, hoping to arrange a meeting with Ferdinand and Isabella, who were then residing at Córdoba. His first stop was at Huelva, where his sister-in-law was living. He stayed a few kilometres outside the town, at the monastery of La Rábida, and it was here that he established a friendship with Fray Antonio Marchena, with whom he had lengthy discussions on astronomy, cosmography and philosophy. From La Rábida he went to Seville, and made contact with the Duke of Medinaceli, who was able to secure for Columbus his first meeting with the Catholic Monarchs. This was not a success, and Columbus was compelled to continue his search for financial backing, approaching, among others, the Duke of Medina Sidonia, and Henry VIII of England. In 1491 Columbus was reported to be in a deeply depressed state, and in the autumn of that year he was back at La Rábida.

Few places seem more suited for the relief of melancholy than the charming monastery of La Rábida, which is now the place in Andalucía most evocative of Columbus' memory. Though situated on the ugly estuary of the Río Tinto, and with views towards the industrial town of Huelva, it is fortunately shielded from its surroundings by a forest of pines, and a colourful garden filled with palms and exotic flowers. The monastery was badly damaged after the earthquake in 1755 that also destroyed Lisbon, and has been subject to extensive restoration and rebuilding; but it still has a pleasantly homely and intimate character. This character is completely at variance with the murals of Columbus's life painted in one of the monastery's rooms early this century by a local artist, Daniel Vázquez Díaz (see page 311). These works, executed in a highly stylized manner, have epic pretensions, and even include a scene of a monk embracing Columbus which the artist intended as symbolizing the meeting of the medieval and modern worlds.

The voyage which Vázquez Díaz and countless others were so heroically to envisage was finally made possible on the intervention of La Rábida's abbot, Fray Juan Pérez. Pérez had once been a confessor to Isabella, and he wrote her a letter strongly supporting Columbus' project. By the time the letter arrived, early in January 1492, Granada had just been surrendered, and the queen was thus well disposed to finance a project which might conceivably further Spain's glory. Shortly afterwards Columbus was finally able to prepare for the journey, and recruited his crew largely fom the two villages closest to La Rábida, Palos de la Frontera and Moguer de la Frontera; he chose as the captain of one of the three ships that he intended to take with him a Palos man called Martín Alonso Pinzón, who had a considerable local reputation as a sailor. Columbus was finally able to leave at the beginning of August 1492, and enjoyed a farewell supper at La Rábida in the simply furnished refectory that still survives. He set sail early the next morning from Palos, a place which is described today as 'the cradle of the Americas'. Approached from La Rábida, you have to drive along a road known as the Calle de las Americas, which is lined with ceramic plaques listing the countries that now make up the new continents. The village itself is a characterless place, and two of its few buildings of interest are the house which belonged to the Pinzón family (currently being turned into a museum) and the modest late gothic church of St. George, where Columbus and his crews were blessed on the morning of their departure. They set off from the small bay directly underneath this church, and reached the New World just over two months later. On the return journey Columbus had a serious quarrel with Pinzón, who arrived back in Spain gravely ill and died at La Rábida in March 1493.

Columbus' pioneering voyage brought him not only great fame but also a considerable amount of money, for he had managed to secure before leaving Spain an excellent financial deal should his mission be successful. It says much of Columbus' character that he decided also to keep for himself the large reward which he had offered to the first sailor to sight land; the poor sailor in question afterwards went off to Morocco, where he was never heard of again. Columbus was later to see his mission of colonizing the New World as being divinely inspired, but he had been trained as a merchant, and he remained a merchant at heart. Religious fervour competed in him with a greed that was to lead ultimately to great personal unhappiness. He returned three more times to America, but proved to be inept at administering the lands that he had 'discovered'; he acquired many ambitious rivals, was deposed as governor, and ended up a disillusioned man in Spain, where he died in Valladolid in 1506. His remains were transferred to Seville's Charterhouse (the ruins of which were transformed into the centrepiece for this city's 1492 celebrations) and then many years later to Seville Cathedral, where they were given a splendid memorial in the transept, only to be disinterred yet again, and shipped off to the West Indian island of San Domingo.

Greed dominated the lives of many of the so-called *conquistadores* who followed in Columbus' footsteps to the New World. And several of these lives also ended miserably. Cortes, the conqueror of Mexico, died an embittered and forgotten man at a village near Seville called Castilleja de la Cuesta, a place remembered today mainly for its biscuits and for being the ancestral home of Rita Hayworth. Pizarro, the conqueror of Peru, was killed there in 1541, finished off not by the Indians but by his fellow Spaniards, who set upon him with the brutality that had typified his own exploits in the New World. The Spanish conquerors left in America a legacy of violence and lawlessness which has survived to this day. But they were able to settle the continent probably faster than any other European power of the time could have done: the English, for instance, discovered Nova Scotia in 1497, but were not to have any settlement in America until the 17th century. The Spaniards succeeded in colonizing and Europeanizing America so quickly because they had spent over four hundred years doing exactly this in their own country.

The unification of Spain under Ferdinand and Isabella was accomplished in a spirit of brutal fanaticism. Isabella had an obsession with racial purity, and tried to impose this on a country which had always been exceptionally diverse in its ethnic make-up: even Ferdinand himself had a Jewish mother. Andalucía, the most heterogeneous of all Spanish regions, was consequently the one most affected by Isabella's racial policies. In 1480 the notorious Spanish Inquisition was set up in Seville, and in the following year the first victims of this were burnt at an *auto-da-fe* in this city. Among those persecuted by the Inquisition were homosexuals, the act of sodomy having always been considered one of the gravest offences possible for a Christian: a German traveller visiting Andalucía in the 1490's, Hieronymus Münzer, found in Almería the corpses of six Italian sodomites who had been hung up first by their necks and then by their feet, and, before finally dying, had had their genitals cut off and attached underneath their chins. But the majority of those killed in the name of Christianity were those Jews who had been converted to it. Known as *conversos* they often came under the suspicion of the Inquisition on the grounds that their conversions had not been genuine. Converted or not, Jews were by now hated figures in Spanish society, and they were still associated with that most despised of professions, money-lending. The Inquisition stirred up popular resentment towards them as a way of strengthening support for Ferdinand and Isabella. As with the exploits of the conquistadors, greed too was a major motivation behind the activities of the Inquisition. Anyone falling foul of this body had their property taken away from them, even before guilt could be proved. In this way the Church and many of her inquisitors such as the dreaded Torquemada (himself, ironically, a secret converso) acquired great wealth. Much of this wealth was directed towards the Granada campaign, a campaign which was also financed by Jewish backers. Only converted Jews were allowed to remain in Spain after 1492, and those who failed to disguise their origins stayed on to an increasingly uncertain fate.

The Muslims who remained in eastern Andalucía after 1492 fared at first rather better than Spain's conversos, and indeed had surrendered to the Christians on quite favourable terms. They were allowed to keep their religion, costumes and traditions on the one condition that they stayed away from their fortified settlements such as the Alhambra. The Muslim population of the former Kingdom of Granada was now about a quarter of a million, a further quarter of a million having left Spain voluntarily or been killed in the hostilities. The Christian colonizing of this part of Andalucía was by no means an even one, the southern towns such as Málaga and Marbella becoming largely Christian, and the eastern half acquiring only small and isolated Christian communities. Only in the northern towns, including Granada itself, could converso Christians and Muslims be found in equal numbers. The Muslim population of Granada was concentrated on the Albaicín, and continued to bring wealth to the town with their trade in raw and patterned silk. The many western visitors to the town after 1492 were fascinated by the Muslims and their exotic costumes, in the same way as are tourists in Morocco today: of especial interest was what one traveller described as the 'fantastical' white robes of the women, which trailed down to the ground and almost completely covered the face. Though the two races were now strictly segregated, the Spanish Christians continued to adapt to Muslim ways as they had always done. Christians came to eat much the same food as the Muslims, learnt from them the silk trade, took up the strange Muslim habit of nibbling at pieces of porcelain, and even began wearing some of their clothing, to judge from a few wardrobe inventories of the time. Even the Moorish love of frequent washing, which the Christians condemned as a sign of promiscuity, caught on among some of the Andalucían Christians, and the ritual of the public bath was to remain an important feature of their social life well into the 17th century.

The first Bishop of Granada after 1492, Fray Hernando de Talavera, was a tolerant, enlightened man who believed that the Muslims would gradually assimilate to Christianity, and should not have the religion forced upon them. However, political enemies of his and numerous Christian fanatics were anxious to discredit him, particularly in view of growing fears of a Muslim invasion supported from Africa.

Muslim-style costume worn in Mochagar-Vejer at the turn of this century

The feared rebellion broke out in 1499, following the arrival in Granada of the fanatical Cardinal Cisneros, who ordered the baptism of 60,000 Muslims. The revolt broke out in the Alpujarras, but soon spread throughout eastern Andalucía, and was only put down in 1501. The Spaniards afterwards attempted to safeguard Andalucía by capturing the North African towns of Ceuta and Melilla, and have held on to these places to this day. Meanwhile in Andalucía itself, they threw out all the unconverted Muslims, and forced the others to wear western clothes and speak in Spanish. These last measures were difficult to impose, and seem to have been ignored by most of the Muslims. The Venetian ambassador Andrea Navagero, in a fascinating description of Granada in 1526, described how the converted Muslims (who were referred to as *moriscos*) continued not just to wear their own costumes and speak their own language but also to practise their traditional faith. They held the Christians in utter contempt, which did not surprise Navagero, who thought that they had been terribly treated. Navagero hoped that the Inquisition would stay away from Granada, and that no more severe measures would be imposed on the moriscos, for, in his view, such measures would seriously damage both the prosperity and the beauty of the town. His pleas for tolerance were not to be heeded, for in 1568 Philip II tried to stamp out Muslim culture far more forcibly than before. Another revolt was sparked off, this one breaking out in the Albaicín, and then retreating into the Alpujarras, where it was finally quelled in 1571. The cost of this rebellion was the final expulsion of all the moriscos from Granada and its former kingdom.

When Ferdinand and Isabella marched into the town of Granada in 1492, they had before them the task not simply of introducing Christianity and Western customs into a place which had been under Muslim rule for over seven centuries. They were also determined to create in what had been one of the great urban wonders of the Islamic world memorials worthy of the spirit of the Christian Reconquest. This spirit may not in itself have been so admirable, but no-one can deny that the works of art and architecture that it inspired were of outstanding quality. Visitors to Granada today see the place essentially as a Muslim city, and yet in the 16th century Granada developed also into one of the main centres of renaissance Europe.

In the creation of renaissance Granada, a remarkable amount of care was taken not to destroy the major monuments that had been left by the Muslims. Ferdinand and Isabella are known to have had a great love for the Alhambra, and were happy to adapt to the Moorish style of living and to use the place as a palace, just as their predecessors had done with the Alcázar in Seville. The place had in fact been left by the Nasrids in a slightly decayed state, and the Catholic Monarchs had Muslim craftsmen brought in to restore it to its former magnificence. The main new building which was put up in the Alhambra by Ferdinand and Isabella was a Franciscan monastery, built over a former Arab bath and palace belonging, it is thought, to a Nasrid prince; the monastery is now one of the most exclusive of the Government-run hotels known as paradors. The temptation to create within the Alhambra a massive cathedral that would rise up above the surrounding infidel structures to proclaim the greater glories of the Church was wisely avoided. Before a cathedral could be built elsewhere in the town, however, a temporary one was established in the Alhambra's mosque, the building in which the first mass of the Reconquest had been celebrated. This mosque, re-dedicated to the Virgin and pulled down in the late 16th century to make way for an austere church, was one of the few mosques in Granada taken over by the Christians in the early years of their rule here; most of the others, including the principal one, kept on functioning as before. The Christians also left largely undisturbed the main residential district of the Muslims – the hills of the Albaicín and Alcazaba. The only important building founded by the Catholic Monarchs on these hills was the modest convent of Santa Isabel, which stands on top of the Alcazaba and has a church adorned with a delightful portal in a playful late gothic style. The two monarchs' dreams of a great Christian city were reserved essentially for the lower town of Granada.

The reign of Ferdinand and Isabella saw the emergence of an architectural style known as the plateresque. Derived from the word for 'silversmith', *platero*, the term was coined to describe the highly intricate decoration to be found in many of the buildings of this period. The actual decorative forms of the plateresque – gothic in the earlier years of the style, and classical in the later ones – are European in origin, but the love of intricacy was a legacy of Spain's Muslim past. Spanish architecture of the late medieval and early renaissance periods is imbued with a Muslim presence. As the term plateresque suggests, the Spaniards inherited from the Muslims an essentially decorative approach to architecture. Spain's great gothic cathedrals are not notable for their harmony of proportion, as are those of France, but instead often gain their power from the profusely decorated surfaces, and chaotic cluster of rich furnishings: as with the Great Mosque at Córdoba, it is often difficult in a Spanish church to grasp the overall structure, and you are not even given a clear view down the nave, as this is blocked by a sumptuously carved choir. Spanish buildings may also show specifically Muslim borrowings, for instance the use of decorative bands of lettering on a large scale. Furthermore, as has already been noted (see page 85), mudéjar craftsmen were themselves responsible for wholly Muslim elements within these buildings: among the most popular Spanish ceilings up to the early 17th century were the *artesonado* ones, which were mudéjar ceilings in wooden inlay imitating traditional Muslim leatherwork. But Spanish architecture is one of great contrasts, and alongside the Muslim-inspired love of decorative richness is an inherently Spanish love of the austere. The most elaborate portals are sometimes set against bare slabs of granite; breathtakingly sumptuous decoration is

A plateresque door to Málaga Cathedral, of a style almost identical to the late gothic Royal Chapel at Granada

applied to structures of exceptional severity. In the course of the 16th century, the austere elements in Spanish architecture were to gain the upper hand, a development that can be seen in its early stages in Granada.

Ferdinand and Isabella envisaged the new cathedral of Granada as dominating the lower town, and to be built, like that of Seville, on the site of the town's main mosque. The mosque was transformed into a church in 1501, but the cathedral itself was not begun until over twenty years later. In the meantime there was erected next to the former mosque a chapel intended to house the tombs of Ferdinand and Isabella. The two monarchs had originally planned to be buried in the church of San Juan de los Reyes in Toledo, but a year before the queen's death in 1504 they decided that it would be more fitting to have their mausoleum in the town where they had known their greatest triumph. They chose as their architect for this chapel a man then engaged in work for Toledo Cathedral, Enrique Egas, who, like most of the leading architects and artists in Spain at this time, was of Flemish descent. This Flemish generation is associated with what is called the Isabelline or Gothic plateresque, a style of late gothic fantasy in which playful naturalistic detail abounds. San Juan de los Reyes, the work of the Flemish-born architect Juan Guas, is one of the masterpieces of this style, and its sumptuous and fantastical ornamentation make the Egas Chapel at Granada seem restrained in comparison. The Granada chapel was not finished until 1527, a good twenty years after the completion of the Toledo church, and though Egas himself was a pronounced gothicist there worked with him younger men of more classical leanings: the chapel's exuberant gothic north portal, which now stands inside the cathedral, contrasts with the more measured classical archway through which you enter the building from the street. Isabella's own taste was for the charming, minutely executed naturalism of Flemish art, and in the chapel's sacristy can be seen part of her celebrated collection of Flemish paintings. But tastes in Spain had changed considerably since her death in 1504, and her own tomb and that of her husband were the work of an Italian artist, Domenico Fancelli, who favoured a simpler and bolder monument than a Flemish artist would have liked. Egas also had the commission to build Granada's cathedral, but after starting on the foundations, he left Granada for good in around 1525, thus clearing the way for the classical, Italianate, artists and architects preferred by Ferdinand and Isabella's grandson Charles V.

The lower town of Granada had been a scene of intense building activity since the beginning of the 16th century. A massive Franciscan monastery (now a military headquarters) was erected on the site of the demolished Jewish quarter, and a great hospital (now the University) put up outside the town's walls. Numerous other palaces and churches were built, Moorish towers pulled down, abandoned palaces restored, streets widened, and a series of impressive squares created – the Plazas

The grille in the Royal Chapel in Granada, with the royal tombs beyond

Nueva, Bibarrambla, and del Príncipe. Despite the remaining Moorish monuments the lower town of Granada acquired in the 16th century a character very unlike that of most other Andalucían towns; its regular street plan, squares and predominance of grey stone buildings bring to mind an Italian renaissance town rather than any place in Andalucía. Among the more important buildings dating from the early 16th century was the church of San Domingo, which has a triple arched classical portico covered in frescos, and could easily be mistaken for some Italian creation. Contemporary with this is the enormous Monastery of San Jerónimo, a structure of gothic proportions but classical detailing, designed by two of the leading exponents of the classical style in Granada, the Italian Jacopo Florentino and the great genius of the Spanish renaissance, Diego de Siloe.

Andalucía was the part of Spain where the gothic style made the least impact. In the case of Granada, it was supplanted almost immediately by the classical style, which was far better suited to express the uncompromising spirit of the new Spain. Granada was never intended as the capital of Spain, but it was in the 16th century an important commercial and university town, and a courtly centre invested with a major symbolical role. The man who did most to emphasize this role was the Holy Roman Emperor Charles V. He entered Granada for the first time in 1526, just after

Pillars and vaulting in the Cathedral, Granada

marrying Isabel of Portugal in Seville. They were on their honeymoon, and took up residence in the Alhambra. Most people today could hardly dream of a better place for a honeymoon, but Charles V and his queen had been spoilt by the luxuries of modern life and found the place uncomfortable, and difficult to warm. Isabel was apparently so horrified by her bedroom that she immediately took off with her retinue to San Jerónimo in the lower town. Many of Charles' courtiers would have liked to have done the same, as they too complained bitterly about their assigned lodgings. When Charles finally decided that he wanted to turn Granada into a permanent residence of the court, he clearly felt that he had to do something about the Alhambra, particularly so as he considered the place totally unsuitable for receiving ambassadors. Both his mother, Juana la Loca (Joan the Mad), and his grandparents, Ferdinand and Isabella, had urged him not to destroy the Alhambra, and he himself had only recently been to Córdoba and been horrified by the effects of his allowing a cathedral to be built within the town's Mezquita. In the end Charles V barely touched the main Nasrid palaces, but built alongside these a mighty palace of his own. He entrusted the work to one Pedro Machuca, a man who had received his architectural training in Italy. Machuca made no attempt to create a building that would harmonize with its architectural surroundings, but designed instead an imposing and scarcely ornamented square block containing a colonnaded circular courtyard. This was a building unprecedented in Spain in its classical severity, and indeed revolutionary even in an Italian context. When seen alongside the romantically old-fashioned palaces of the Nasrids, it must have struck contemporaries as a powerful statement of the aspirations of Golden Age Spain.

An indication of what was to become of these aspirations is the fact that the building was abandoned before being completed, and, like the Alhambra, was left to decay. Charles V's ambitious plans for Granada were to be forgotten in the course of his subsequent military exploits throughout Europe. Before leaving Granada for ever in 1527, he expressed a wish to be buried in the town's cathedral, work on which had only just begun. Even this wish was to come to nothing, but at least it gave new impetus to the construction of this building, and an opportunity to reassess the existing plans for it. Egas' design was considered too old-fashioned, and in 1528 the projct was taken over by Diego de Siloe. Siloe was an architect and sculptor of Flemish descent whose father, Gil, had been responsible for some of the most exciting works of the Isabelline plateresque, including the overwhelmingly intricate tombs of Juan II and Isabel of Portugal in the Charterhouse of Miraflores outside Burgos. In Diego's own work can be seen a transition from the Isabelline to the classical plateresque, and then, in his cathedral at Granada, to a classicism as bold and daring as that of Pedro Machuca. In fact so uncompromising were his plans for the cathedral that even Charles V, when he got to hear of them in 1529, began to be worried: Siloe had to go to the Emperor to defend himself, and to reassure him of the suitability of having a great classical structure next to the gothic

Royal Chapel built by Egas. It comes indeed as a considerable shock to move from this homely chapel into the cathedral proper. You find yourself at first in a towering circular chancel inspired by the Holy Sepulchre in Jerusalem; as you walk towards the nave, the massive size of the place becomes quite overpowering. Throughout the interior runs a giant order of classical columns and pilasters that were originally intended to support barrel vaulting (the present gothic vaulting was an alteration made to Siloe's plan in the late 16th century). The whole place is saved from being heavy and oppressive by its spaciousness and by being painted all over a brilliant white. I was once lucky enough to attend High Mass here on Corpus Christi and was able to appreciate the building's theatricality to the full when, to the accompaniment of the cathedral's superb late baroque organ, dazzlingly coloured confetti fell from the incense loft like manna from the heavens. The theatricality of the place, greatly heightened during the baroque period, has often proved too much for the English traveller; John Harvey, was not alone in believing that the building was 'one of the world's architectural tragedies, one of the saddest of wasted opportunities'. Such prejudices seem to be echoed by the tourists who today happily crowd into the Royal Chapel, but do not even bother to enter the cathedral proper. This is a telling reflection of the neglect from which so many of Andalucía's Golden Age monuments have suffered.

Granada's cathedral was just one of a number constructed in Andalucía in the wake of 1492. At Córdoba, Almería, Guadix, Málaga and Jaén, lofty new cathedrals rose up in celebration of the triumph of Spain and the Catholic Church. For all their lingering gothic elements, all showed an obsessive interest in the new classical style; in common with Granada Cathedral, most of these buildings were not to receive their final coating of splendour until the baroque period. Córdoba Cathedral, so derided because of its unfortunate position within the town's Mezquita, is the most unified of these structures, and is a rich and fascinating blend of the mudéjar and the classical plateresque. Almería cathedral is heavy and fortress-like, a true bulwark of the Faith; Guadix is grey and austere; Málaga has much of the theatricality of Granada Cathedral though it is fussier in its detailing; and Jaén has the most commanding situation of them all, a true giant dwarfing the town below. Diego de Siloe had a hand in the cathedrals of Almería and Guadix, while those of Málaga and Jaén were designed by Siloe's successor as the leading classical architect active in Andalucía, Andrés de Vandelvira.

Vandelvira was a prolific architect, but the bulk of his work is to be found in the twin towns of Úbeda and Baeza, which are richer in renaissance palaces and churches than almost any other towns in Spain. A thriving textile industry brought enormous prosperity to Úbeda and Baeza in the 16th century, and their importance was increased by Úbeda being the home town of the man who virtually ruled Spain during the first half of the century, Charles V's secretary, Francisco de los Cobos y Molina. This man founded, and is buried in, what is the most striking of Úbeda's

Jaén

many fine churches, the chapel of San Salvador. Designed by Diego de Siloe but executed by Vandelvira, this is the great rarity in Spain, a renaissance church built within a very short period of time, untouched in later centuries, and containing most of its original furnishings: the excellence of the architecture is matched by the superlative quality of these fittings, among which is a powerful retable by Spain's leading renaissance sculptor, Alonso de Berruguete, a pupil of Michelangelo.

Baeza has not any single monument equal in quality to San Salvador, but in many ways it is the more attractive of the two towns, having fortunately been spared the ugly modern development which has grown up around Úbeda. To wander around the quiet, and excellently preserved streets of Baeza is to turn the pages of some manual of renaissance architecture. The delicate classicism of Vandelvira and his followers is everywhere apparent, but the building that claims the visitor's attention most is the extraordinary and fantastical Palacio de Jabalquinto: whether or not this was the work of Juan Guas, the architect of Toledo's San Juan de los Reyes, it is indisputably the most striking example of the Isabelline plateresque in the south of Spain. I was standing admiringly in front of this building when a group of schoolchildren came up to ask me what I was doing. They seemed amazed that any foreigner should take an interest in their town. Baeza's decline into obscurity after the 16th century has been quite remarkable, and I found it hard to believe that the school from which these children came – a harmonious classical building adjoining the Palacio del Jabalquinto – had been founded in 1535 as one of Spain's earliest universities.

Another of Andalucía's improbable former university towns is Osuna near Seville. Osuna too is a little-visited place and exceptionally rich in monuments. Hardly a single modern building spoils its perfect 16th- to 17th- century character, and, what is more, the old buildings give directly on to the countryside. Its two major renaissance monuments rise up on a gaunt hill above the town. One is the old University, which was founded in 1548, and is now also a school. The other is the splendid Collegiate Church, which has an exquisite classical plateresque portal adorning an otherwise rather severe west façade, and a light and spacious interior. The building was magnificently endowed with 16th- and 17th-century furnishings and paintings, but the highpoint of a visit here is the 16th-century pantheon of the Dukes of Osuna, which is like a church in miniature, with doll-like choir stalls, and jewel-like renaissance ornamentation.

The monuments of Osuna might be undeservedly little visited, but at least they have been excellently looked after. The same cannot be said of the castles of Lacalahorra and Vélez Blanco. Both places were designed and embellished in the early years of the 16th century by Italian architects and craftsmen, and were among the first buildings in Spain in an Italian renaissance style. The former, situated in a forlorn village fifteen kilometres south of Guadix, stands on top of what seems like a great mound of rubble; its exterior is particularly sturdy and forbidding, but inside is a sumptuous Italian renaissance courtyard crumbling away. Vélez Blanco is an even less likely place for the introduction of Italian renaissance ideals to Spain, being in the middle of the wild, uninviting landscape of Almería province, an area which in the early 16th century was still largely inhabited by people of Muslim descent. This castle has an elegant and well preserved exterior, and the tourist, not forewarned, might well approach the building with mounting excitement. Inside, however, there is nothing. The celebrated courtyard, with its rich marble decoration by Italian craftsmen, was sold off in 1903, and has since been reconstructed in the Metropolitan Museum of Art in New York.

The glory, the squalor, and the decline of Golden Age Andalucía are illustrated above all in the history of Seville. While Granada and its former kingdom suffered in the 16th century from racial strife and major demographic changes, the western half of Andalucía experienced a great surge in prosperity. This was the part of Spain that most benefited from the settlement of the New World, and its thriving centre, well into the 17th century, was Seville. Seville had already become Spain's largest city in the 12th century, and its importance had been recently emphasized by its becoming the headquarters of the Spanish Inquisition. But its fame was finally assured in 1503, when the Spanish court decreed the setting up here of a Casa de Contratacción, a royal agency responsible for the administration of trade and politics in the New World. From now on all ships sailing between Europe and the New World would have to pass through Seville. As a monk observed in 1587, 'was not Seville and all Andalucía the furthest point and the end of all land? and now it is the middle to which come the best and most esteemed of the Old World. . . to be carried to the New.' In the early years of the century the exodus to the New World, together with losses from plagues, resulted in a temporary fall in Seville's population. When Andrea Navagero came here in 1525 he found the place to be 'poorly populated and almost in the hands of women'. This situation was soon to change: between 1530 and 1580 the population doubled, to reach an estimated 85,000, which made the town the largest in Europe after Venice and Rome. Seville's boom-town atmosphere attracted people here from all over Spain and Europe. Merchants from Flanders, Germany, England and Scotland settled here, as did many of the moriscos expelled from Granada in 1570. The racial muddle of Seville was compounded by the influx of mainly black African slaves, who were to turn the place into the greatest centre of the slave trade in Europe after Lisbon. And in the wake of all these people grew up a notorious underworld of thieves, murderers, muggers, swindlers, card-sharps, prostitutes, pimps, entrepreneurs, black marketeers, and all kinds of seekers of fortunes and refugees from justice. A priest of the time described Seville as a *mare magnum*, a 'great sea', and criminals referred to the place in their slang as *Babylonia*. The celebrated Golden Age poet Luis de Góngora addressed Seville as 'great Babylon of Spain, map of all nations'; and the Seville poet Fernando de Herrera said 'you are not a city, but a world.' In the 16th century, Granada acted as the symbolical capital of Spain, and Madrid became the political one; but the economical and cultural capital was unquestionably Seville.

'A powerful gentleman is Mr. Money,' wrote the cruel satirist Francisco Quevedo, whose smirking, bespectacled face was portrayed by the Seville-born painter, Diego Velázquez. The obsession with money was one which united all the social classes in 16th- and 17th-century Seville. The traditional image of the aloof Spanish aristocrat refusing to demean himself by involvement in trade has to be forgotten when discussing the Seville of this period. The Seville aristocrat speculated in money no less avidly than the merchants; moreover, an increasing number of these merchants – many of whom, incidentally, were secret conversos – were able to buy their way into the aristocracy. 'Money,' continued Quevedo, 'is born in the Indies, dies in Spain, and is buried in Genoa.' Sixty to one hundred boats a year would bring back the bounty from America, bounty which greatly increased in value after 1560 when a new way was discovered of processing silver. One of the most profitable investments to be made in Seville was to buy a boat or even a whole fleet, but much money was also acquired through the stocking up of these ships for their long journeys, and through exports to the New World. The biscuit business flourished in 16th-century Seville as did more traditional enterprises such as the making of wine and olive oil, vast quantities of which were required for America. Gunpowder was needed for the protection of those working in America and for the safeguarding of the goods that came from there: the Seville suburb of Triana had one of the largest gun-powder factories in Europe, until 1579, when it blew up, causing great loss of life. Less explosive, but no less profitable Seville activities included the making of ceramics, and the manufacture of soap from olive oil (an industry which had been introduced by the Muslims). Nor should one forget the various trades dependent on the mineral wealth of the New World, such as the silversmiths, the jewellers, and those involved in minting the metals into coin.

Great fortunes were to be made in Seville, but a high proportion of the population was barely able to subsist. The enormous marginal element in Seville society provided many of the victims for the Inquisition, which further increased this element by depriving the livelihoods of those whom they arrested. The real underdogs were the moriscos, who were subject to constant racial harassment, and sometimes responded with violence themselves. They stayed close together, and many of them even lived in those ghettos that had once been allotted to the Muslims, who had been chased out of the city between 1502 and 1505. In common with slaves and conversos, the moriscos were strictly excluded from the guilds, and thus could only take on unskilled or semi-skilled jobs. One of the common sights in 16th-century Seville was that of morisco men selling fritters, while their wives sold roasted chestnuts, buttercakes and sweets. These people were often the lucky ones; many others resorted to more desperate measures.

Cervantes described Seville as the 'asylum of the poor, and the refuge of the outlaw'. The place abounded in beggars, among whom were so many false cripples that by 1597 a license was needed to beg. Numerous women took up prostitution, thereby risking the new and dreadful disease of syphilis, which had reputedly been brought over from the New World. Seville's criminal reputation was legendary, and the city has retained it to this day, though with increasingly less justification. In the 16th century the risk of assault was so great that everyone carried arms for protection. The part of the city where the silversmiths worked had its own walls and guards, but otherwise the policing of Seville was scant and ineffective. Criminals could easily evade the law by moving into another district of the city, taking sanctuary in the cathedral, or, as a final resort, going to America, which, as Cervantes said, was 'the refuge and shelter of all desperate folk in Spain, the sanctuary of bankrupts, the safe-conduct of murderers, the protection and cover of those gamblers known by the experts in the craft as sharpers, the general decoy for loose women, where many go to be deceived, and few get out of their difficulties.' The picaresque novel, the novel of the wandering rogue or *pícaro*, was born in 16th-century Spain, and Cervantes was one of the many Golden Age writers to take their inspiration from the low life of Seville. In one of his *Exemplary Stories*, he tells of two impoverished boys who come to Seville, and soon take to thieving, despite initial reservations. 'What's wrong with it?' asks the person who persuades them into thieving. 'Isn't it worse to be a heretic or a renegade, or to kill one's father and mother, or to be a solomite [sic]?' One of the boys finally ends up 'shocked by the slackness of the law in that famous city of Seville, where pernicious and perverted people could live almost openly'.

The English writer Laurie Lee, evoking the Seville he had known in the 1930's, spoke of the place as a 'city where, more than in any other, one may bite on the air and taste the multitudinous flavours of Spain – acid, sugary, intoxicating, sickening but flavours which, above all in a synthetic world, are real as nowhere else.' Thanks to a wealth of 16th- and 17th-century documents and literary accounts, it is possible vividly to experience what the city must have been like in the Golden Age, down to the place's very sounds and smells. Up to 1500, the place had changed little since Muslim times. It had kept the irregular street plan characteristic of a Muslim city, and its whitewashed houses had been left plain on the outside, in accordance with Muslim taste. In the course of the 16th century streets were widened, but the irregularity of the layout remained, as it does today. The houses meanwhile were given often lavish exterior decoration, while retaining what has always been their most enchanting feature – their patios. 'What a pleasure for both the sight and sound is a Seville patio!' enthused in 1587 the normally rather reticent priest, Padre Alonso de Morgado. These patios were filled, as they are today, with jasmine, rose-bushes, orange trees, and flower pots containing, in Morgado's words, 'a thousand different kinds of fragrant flowers and plants'. The patios were renowned for their cleanliness, and Cervantes described one as 'so spotlessly clean that it shone as if it had been rubbed with the finest vermilion'. Outside, in the streets, a rather different world awaited you, filthy and foul-smelling. Navagero was impressed by the way the streets were paved with bricks, but most people commented on the way these streets were piled high with rubbish. In 1597 an assistant to the Seville Court of Justice found that the 'conditions in the ciy are shameful', and that all the streets had 'become little more than dung heaps'. Added to the smells of rubbish was a rather more sinister odour. While the Moors and the Jews had had the sense to bury their dead outside the city, the Christians preferred to do so in shallow graves in the cloisters of the city's monasteries and convents. Through the streets of jasmine-scented Seville wafted in the summer months the odour of decomposing flesh and inner organs.

Seville was and remains a city of violent contrasts, the beautiful and the ugly, wealth and poverty existing in close proximity. *Quien no ha visto Sevilla no ha visto meravilla*, 'He who has not seen Seville has not seen marvels' is a saying which has been unfailingly repeated by travellers over the centuries. Yet this city, praised for its marvels, has been equally famous for its slums and wastes. Only a few minutes' walk from the cathedral was El Arenal, an area of inhabited swampland between the city walls and the Guadalquivir. This was one of the famed meeting-places for the city's underworld, and it was sometimes referred to as 'El Corral del Arenal' after the name of Seville's largest brothel, which was once to be found here. Another grim and dangerous part of Seville was an area of polluted, marshy land now known as the Alameda de Hercules. Situated in the northern half of the city, this was such

The Alameda of Hercules

an eyesore that in 1574 a nobleman gave money for it to be transformed into a tree-lined promenade or *alameda*. Two ancient columns were re-erected at one end of it, and on these were put statues of Hercules and Caesar. The promenade later reverted back to the dirty, depressing state of the former wasteland, and for much of its history was the centrepiece of a part of the city notorious for its prostitutes and drug addicts.

The poor and the rich were roughly divided in the 16th century between the northern and southern halves of Seville, and this division remains much the same today. The decline of northern Seville was probably accelerated in the 15th century, when the Muslim quarter, or *Morería*, was moved from a favourable situation near the cathedral to the outlying northern parish of San Marcos; this parish later became populated by moriscos, and, after them, gypsies. Moriscos and gypsies were also to be associated with the suburb of Triana, which lies on the eastern side of the Guadalquivir and is considered by some to be a separate town. It was until recently a notoriously depressed area, even though many of Seville's important industries had once been situated here. Described by Dundas Murray in 1849 as 'the abode of robbers and desperate characters', it had had a reputation since the 16th century as a place of heavy crime and lax morals. The irony was that Triana's most prominent building – until coastal floods eventually forced its demolition in the late 17th century – was the lugubrious castle of the Inquisition.

'What Seville lacks,' complained one Francisco de Siguenza in 1579, 'is a good central square.' The most important square in the 16th century was that of San Francisco, around which were situated the town's main prison, and the newly built Mint, High Court and Town Hall; but this was hardly a square to be compared with the monumental public spaces to be found in northern and central Spain, such as Madrid's Plaza Real. The traditional meeting-place in most Andalucían towns had always been the intersection of four streets. Seville had also its cathedral, which acted as an extraordinary magnet for all levels of Seville society and all kinds of activities. On the *gradas* or steps of the cathedral took place many of the Inquisition's autos-da-fe, and, for most of the 16th century, nearly all the city's business transactions. The cathedral's descration by commercial enterprise finally led in 1572 to Archbishop Cristóbal de Rojas making a complaint to Philip II; only then was work begun on the construction of the city's Exchange or *Lonja*. Well after the expulsion of the merchants and bankers, the cathedral and its surroundings continued to attract many of the city's criminal types. The roughest elements in Seville society were drawn to the Corral de los Olmos – a small square, no longer surviving, between the cathedral and the Archbishop's Palace – where there was a cheap and very popular eating place. The elite of the criminal world preferred to gather in the cathedral's charming Courtyard of the Oranges (Patio de los Naranjos), which owed much of its popularity to its being within the sanctuary area of the cathedral. Refugees from justice could stay here untouched throughout the day, and make their escape at night. So many criminals did this that in 1586 a law was introduced limiting sanctuary within the church to eight days, banning entrance to women, and forbidding gambling.

Today it is mainly tourists who converge here in vast numbers, the cathedral being Seville's major attraction, along with the neighbouring palace and gardens of the Alcázar. As with the Alcázar, the cathedral complex has parts dating back to Muslim times. After the taking of Seville from the Muslims in 1248, the Christians had used as their cathedral the town's mosque. The 15th-century mudéjar gateway through which you enter the Patio de Los Naranjos has two of the mosque's 12th-century bronze doors, both of which feature inscriptions fom the Koran. But the principal survival of the old mosque is the Giralda (see page 84), a former minaret turned by the Christians into a bell-tower. The elegance of this structure contrasts with the squat, heavy profile of the cathedral itself, a building which Laurie Lee evocatively described as 'hugging the ground like an encrusted turtle'. Begun in 1401, its main body was complete by 1504. A Polish traveller of 1484, Nicolas Popielovo, found to his surprise that the building was even larger than Cologne Cathedral; it has in fact the reputation of being the largest gothic cathedral in the world. The impression on entering the gloomy interior is of enormous space though not of soaring proportions. So dark and vast is the place that you are at first barely aware of the wealth of 16th- and 17th-century paintings and furnishings. The Golden Age not only provided the cathedral with its greatest works of art, but also

Bronze doorway of Patio de los Naranjos

with some outstanding architectural additions. Two of the architectural highpoints of the interior are the Great Sacristy, in a classical plateresque style, and the Chapter House, a pioneering elliptical structure designed by Diego de Siloe.

The Alcázar too was splendidly embellished during the 16th century, some of the work coinciding with the marriage here of Charles V in 1525. The greatest transformation was to the Moorish gardens, which acquired numerous features of the Italian renaissance, such as a delicate and perfectly proportioned arcaded pavilion (known as the Pavilion of Charles V), statues and grottoes dedicated to figures of classical mythology, and one of those many light-hearted inventions typical of 16th-century Italy – an hydraulic organ. The harmonious combination of Muslim gardening skills and Italian whimsy and inventiveness created in the Alcázar one of Europe's finest gardens. A successful intermingling of Moorish and renaissance elements can also be found in another remarkable Seville residence, the Casa de Pilatos. Begun around 1480, and completed in the early 16th century by Pedro Afán de Rivera, this has many of the enchanting characteristics of the Alcázar with the added charm that it is relatively little visited. Classical arcading, Roman statues, and plateresque ornamentation vie with mudéjar craftsmanship, and a Moorish luxuriance and sensuality. During the 16th century Seville also saw the construction of many other impressive buildings, ranging from the lavishly ornamented plateresque Town Hall to the austerely classical Exchange, designed by the architect of the Escorial, Juan de Herrera. But none of these buildings have the originality of the Casa de Pilatos, and few of them are so unmistakeably Sevillian in character. Appropriately, under Afán de Rivera's grandson, the 3rd Duke of Alcalá, the Casa de Pilatos was to turn into one of the main centres of the city's culture.

In the second half of the 16th century, long after Seville's economic importance had been established, cultural life began to flourish as it had not done since Muslim times. The beginnings of this renaissance can be seen in the literary gatherings that took place after 1559 in the house of Columbus' great grand-son, Álvaro Colón y Portugal, Count of Gelves. Seville had at this time only a modest, recently founded university college, and in the absence of a full-scale university, the meetings in Álvaro's house assumed a particular importance: they were an early example of what was to be a vital ingredient in Spain's cultural life, the *tertulia* or salon. Among the writers in this circle were the humanist scholar and teacher Mal-Lara, and Juan de la Cueva and Lope de Rueda, who are among Spain's greatest dramatists prior to Lope de Vega. The most revered poet of the group was Fernando de Herrera, known to his contemporaries as the 'divine'. A great admirer of Petrarch, this shy and retiring man found his Laura in Álvaro's wife, Leonor, to whom he constantly referred in his Petrarch-inspired love poetry. All his poetry is high-flown, rhetorical and rather alien to present-day tastes, but he was a highly influential figure. His commentary on the work of Spain's early 16th-century poet, Garcilaso de la Vega, was the most important poetic treatise of the Golden Age; and his own poems, with their striking abundance of words expressing colour, prefigured the works of the great Córdoba poet of the 17th century, Luis de Góngora. A totally different poet from Herrera, and a far livelier and more vivid personality, was Baltasar del Alcázar. He too belonged to the Álvaro circle, though he lacked the pretensions of its other members, did not consider his works worth publishing, and made a living as a soldier. Alone among the Seville writers of this time, he displayed in his works the great wit for which the people of Seville are renowned, and their love of good living. His humour and obsession with eating well come together in two of his best known works. One, *The Comic Meal*, has the poet trying to relate a romantic tale, but being constantly side-tracked by the delicious food which he is eating. In the second he describes the three great loves of his life:

Tres cosas me tienen preso
de amores el corazón:
la bella Inés, el jamón
y berengenas con queso.
There are three things
that hold my heart love's captive:
the fair Inés, raw ham,
and aubergines with cheese.

Alcázar was also greatly esteemed as a madrigalist, though his reputation as a musician was far eclipsed by that of another member of the Álvaro circle, Francisco Guerrero. Guerrero, and his Seville contemporary Cristóbal de Morales, were two

Casa de Pilatos

of Spain's leading polyphonists of the 16th century, and their work was noted for its simplicity and spontaneity of inspiration, particularly in opposition to the exagerated artifices of Flemish composition. The vitality of the Seville musical world of the 16th century – of which two other luminaries were the organist Francisco Peraza and Mudarra, who played the *vihuela*, a kind of lute – owed much to the presence in the city of the Biblioteca Colombina, which included the largest group of musical manuscripts in Spain outside the Escorial; the whole library had been amassed by Columbus' son, Hernando, and presented to the cathedral after his death.

The great age of Sevillian painting and sculpture was to come, but there were many important artists working here in the 16th century. The arts in Seville at the beginning of the century were dominated, as they were throughout Spain, by artists and craftmen of Northern descent. Lorenzo Mercadante, Miguel Perrin, and Pedro Millán, the sculptor responsible for the naturalistic carvings that decorate the cathedral's exterior, all came originally from France. However, Italian art was coming into fashion, and various Italian artists had started moving to Seville. One of these was Niculoso Pisano, who executed for the north portal of the convent church of Santa Paula a yellow and white terracotta lunette imitative of the works of the Florentine artists, the della Robbias. The Florentine sculptor Pietro Torrigiano was another and more important arrival to the city. His life had been a restless one ever since he had been expelled from Florence for breaking Michelangelo's nose: he had wandered around Italy and the Netherlands, and had introduced the renaissance style to England in the tomb of Henry VII in Westminster Abbey. In Seville he carved a kneeling figure of St. Jerome (now in the Museo de Bellas Artes) which in later centuries was to serve as a maquette for students at Seville's art academy; but his propensity for getting into trouble led to his being denounced as a heretic by the Inquisition and thrown into prison, where he died in 1528.

The greatest painter active in Seville in the early years of the century was Alejo Fernández, an artist of German origin who had married a woman from Córdoba and taken on her name. His art shows Italian influence in its use of perspective and architectural detailing, but it is essentially Flemish in its intimate naturalism: one of his most charming works is the *Virgin of the Navigators* (now in the Alcázar), in which the Virgin protects under her capacious cloak many of the more famous people involved in the colonization of America. A later artist, also torn between Italy and Flanders, was Pedro de Campaña. Born Pierre de Kempreneer in Brussels in 1504, he had been trained as a painter first in his native city and then in Italy, and had settled in Seville by 1537. In Italy he had fallen heavily under Raphael's influence, though his colouring, landscape backgrounds and naturalistic detailing were always to remain very Flemish in character. The major work in his career was the multi-panelled altarpiece of the *Deposition* in the Mariscal Chapel of Seville Cathedral: it is a work of great emotional power, yet it was apparently not a success, and the artist afterwards returned in disgust to Brussels.

A fully-fledged Italian style was achieved in the works of the Seville painter Luis de Vargas, who had also spent part of his youth in Italy. Back in Seville by 1551, he later began to frequent the house of Álvaro Colón, and became a true figure of the renaissance by developing an additional talent as a musician. His retable of the *Genealogy of Christ* in Seville cathedral, and his *Pietá* in the church of Santa María la Blanca, reveal an artist blindly emulating the example of Raphael. One of the Spaniards who most lived up to the Italian renaissance ideal of the artist was Francisco Pacheco. Born in Sanlúcar de Barrameda in 1564, Pacheco soon moved to Seville, and became a central figure in the city's cultural life. His uncle, a canon at Seville cathedral, had been a leading member of the Álvaro circle, and he instead became closely associated with the literary gatherings that superseded Álvaro's in the last years of the century – those held by the 3rd Duke of Alcalá in the Casa de Pilatos. Pacheco believed that the artist should be a person of great learning rather than a mere craftsman, and he himself was a poet, a scholar and the author of a biographical survey of the Seville artists and writers of his day. His own paintings are stiff and academic, and his attempts at mythology and allegory – as can be seen in the Casa de Pilatos – are frankly ludicrous. Yet he was an outstanding teacher of painting, and was to have among his pupils artists whose fame would extend well beyond the frontiers of Seville.

The finest achievements of Spain's Golden Age date mainly from a period of political and economic decline. Despite the great riches coming from America, the money which came into the hands of the State had largely been squandered in expensive military campaigns. The financial crisis which developed in Spain towards the end of the 16th century was to have a particularly strong effect on Seville, where it was aided by a major demographic upheaval. Plagues had swept through the city repeatedly during the 16th century, though none with greater virulence than that of 1599-1601, which decimated Seville's population. It had barely had time to recover when, in 1609, all of Spain's moriscos were finally expelled from the country. The majority of the moriscos were from Seville, and their growing numbers and the separateness of their existence had become of increasing concern to the city's authorities, who were worried that they might support an invasion from North Africa or even become allies of the English. A law had been introduced limiting the number of moriscos in a specific building, and there had even been talk of providing all of them with an identity badge. In the end expulsion seemed the only solution. Most of the moriscos went directly to North Africa, but a law prohibiting them to take children under seven to non-Christian lands forced many to go first to Marseilles or to other European ports: this was a dangerous undertaking, and there were those who decided simply to abandon their children in Seville. A significant proportion of the moriscos was clearly able to evade the expulsion order, for in 1623 a traveller to Seville commented on how many 'Moorish men and women' there were in the city; later in the century a Moroccan ambassador was to describe

2 GRANADA Plasterwork in the Alhambra
◁ 1 CÓRDOBA The Mezquita
3 GRANADA Tilework in the Alhambra

SEVILLE Tilework in the Casa de Pilatos

SEVILLE Tilework in the Plaza de España, Parque María Luisa

6. ÚBEDA Chapel of San Salvador: altar by Alonso Berruguete

7 & 8 ZURBARAN Sts. Antelmo and Antony, from the Charterhouse at Jerez (now Museo de Bellas Artes, Cádiz)

9 RONDA The Bullring ▷

10 OLVERA ▷ ▷

SOL

SOMBRA

CAFETERIA BAR POSTAL
PANADERIA
BAR
LA GITANA GUERRA

12 SEVILLE Courtyard of the Casa de Pilatos

◁ 11 SEVILLE Street scene

13 SEVILLE Pavilion in the Parque María Luisa

4 BAEZA Palacio de Jabalquinto

5 CÓRDOBA Courtyard of La Merced

16 SEVILLE Nineteenth-century windows

17 SEVILLE Mudéjar windows

18 ROCÍO Approaching the Raya Real

20 ROCÍO Persuading a cart onwards ▷

19 ROCÍO Rocieros

21 SEVILLE Cathedral: Columbus' tomb ▷

the population of the nearby town of Lebrija as being almost wholly Muslim in origin. The moriscos who ended up in Africa were to stick as closely together there as they had done in Spain, and they have done so to this day, retaining as well a sense of superiority to their neighbours.

In the course of the 17th century great areas of Seville thus became emptied of people, and where there had once been houses orchards were planted. By 1630 Seville had been overtaken by Madrid as Spain's largest city, and in 1649 the place suffered its worst plague ever. The process of decline was accelerated greatly by Seville's notoriously inefficient government (of which even Philip III complained), and, above all, by the silting up of the Guadalquivir, which forced the Casa de Contratacción to move from Seville to Cádiz in 1620. Cádiz prospered while Seville stagnated. Other Andalucían towns also fared rather better than Seville in the 17th century, including Granada and other places that in the previous century had been Seville's poor relations. But Seville remained the cultural capital of Spain, and it was during these years of decline that many of her greatest works of art and architecture were produced.

The baroque period had no less great an impact on the look and character of present-day Andalucía than the Muslim period. The region's wealth of baroque monuments and works of art, and the continuing baroque traditions in craftsmanship and religious art, make Andalucía one of the European centres of this style. Yet, ironically, most of the travellers who have lavishly praised Andalucía have had only a limited appreciation of baroque art and architecture, in particular the British, whose country is one of the least baroque in the continent. The one aspect of this period's culture to be universally admired is its painting, thanks largely to three artists, Velázquez, Zurbarán and Murillo.

The story of Spanish 17th-century painting begins in Seville, the churches and monastic institutions of which continued to offer artists numerous and lucrative commissions in the early years of the century. One of the leading painters of this period was Juan de Roelas, who had probably been trained in Italy, and been influenced by the Venetian painter Tintoretto: his masterpiece, the *Martyrdom of St. Andrew* in the Seville Museum, is dark, dramatic, and has that peculiarly Spanish combination of mysticism and acute realism. The renewed realism in Seville art of this time was a reaction against the Raphael-inspired idealism of the preceding period. Strange though this at first might seem, the new realism was advocated principally by Francisco Pacheco, whose studio was by far the most important in the city. Pacheco's dry and academic manner was belied by the advice that he gave his pupils 'to go to Nature for everything'. One of these pupils was Alonso Cano, the most versatile of Spain's great baroque artists. Though born in Granada of Castilian parentage, Cano's early years as an artist were spent entirely in Seville, where he was trained both as a painter and sculptor. In later life he was also to become known as an architect and draughtsman, and this versatility earned him the reputation as 'the Spanish Michelangelo', despite there being otherwise very little in common between the two artists. Cano's paintings and sculptures have a quiet, unsensational realism tinged with considerable sentimentality: among his most popular works were his countless Immaculate Conceptions, a subject much depicted by members of Pacheco's studio. The sweet nature of Cano's art was contradicted by a troubled life which gave rise to much malicious gossip. His second wife, whom he had married when she was only twelve, was brutally murdered in 1644, six years after he had moved from Seville to Madrid. The murderer, an unidentified Italian, fled without trace, and suspicion immediately fell on Cano, who was proved innocent only after undergoing torture. During his last years Cano mainly worked for Granada Cathedral, and managed also to be ordained priest there, despite opposition from the ecclesiastical authorities. He died in Granada in 1667, apparently in poverty, and uncommemorated.

In his youth in Seville Cano would have been able to witness at close hand the rapid rise to fame of his fellow pupil at Pacheco's studio, Diego Velázquez. Born in Seville in 1599, Velázquez became apprenticed to Pacheco when he was little more than ten, and was so precocious that he soon surpassed his master. Pacheco recognized the superior gifts of his pupil, but, far from being jealous, gave him every possible encouragement, and even the hand of his daughter in marriage. It says much for the changing economic situation in Seville that Velázquez, like Cano and many other ambitious artists of the time, tried to further his career by seeking work in Madrid. He paid a brief visit to Madrid in 1622, and painted there a portrait of his fellow Andalucían, the poet Luis de Góngora. In the following year he was recalled to the capital by Philip IV's powerful minister, the Count-Duke Olivares, who was himself from Seville. After painting a portrait of the king, Velázquez was appointed court painter, and remained based in Madrid for the rest of his life, enjoying a friendship with the king of remarkable closeness. Velázquez is not one of those geniuses whose lives can be embellished by tales of tortured private life and destructive jealousy on the part of others. The ease of his success was comparable to the ease with which he painted, and his was a life which until recently had seemed completely free of discord. In 1983 documents were discovered revealing that on a visit to Rome in the 1640's he had had an affair with a widow called Martha, who had given him an illegitimate son, Antonio. Such details might seem barely relevant, but they do help to give a more human dimension to this almost too perfect of artists.

When Pacheco urged his pupils to turn to nature for inspiration, he could hardly have imagined such extraordinary naturalism as that shown by Velázquez even in his early teens. Virtually no other artist before or after him has given so life-like a quality to the painted image. The history of art is filled with ridiculous stories of

The Water Carrier of Seville, by Velázquez

birds picking at painted cherries, servants mistaking portraits of their masters for the masters themselves, and so on; but in the case of Velázquez such confusion between art and reality seems almost plausible. In the works that he painted in Seville, he used this realism to portray scenes of everyday life, such as an old woman stirring eggs, and an old man selling water to a young boy: these scenes are treated with extreme seriousness, and not with that patronizing humour or sentimentality with which many of Velázquez' contemporaries might have handled such subject-matter. He also painted a handful of religious works during this period, and displayed in these too a similarly restrained realism: in a couple of them he might even have used his wife as the model for the Virgin. Velázquez appears to have preferred genre scenes to religious ones, and in two of his Seville works he reduced the religious element to a sketchily portrayed event glimpsed in the background of a contemporary domestic scene.

Unfortunately almost nothing of Velázquez' work can be seen in his native town. In the 19th century foreign visitors to Seville stripped the city of many of the paintings that they most admired. Most of Velázquez' genre scenes ended up in British collections, for these were exactly the sort of paintings that the British could appreciate, paintings mercifully devoid of all the morbid religious fervour generally thought characteristic of Spanish art. It is to the Prado in Madrid, however, that the traveller must go to study the full range of Velázquez' art. Here you will see how his style changes between his Seville and Madrid years, how his palette lightens and his brushwork loosens, and how in his last works he achieves the most life-like effects with what seems from close-up a random series of hasty brush-strokes: as a Spanish 18th-century critic put it, 'you cannot understand [the technique] if standing too close, but from a distance it is a miracle'. The naturalism of Velázquez' late art is endowed with an almost supernatural quality.

Velázquez' works would not have been widely known at the time, as hardly any of them were made for public places. Zurbarán, on the other hand, painted almost exclusively for churches and religious institutions. Extremaduran by birth, he came to Seville in his teens, and studied painting at the same time as Velázquez. The Seville Guild of Painters, like the other guilds in the city, was not welcoming to people fom other parts of Spain, especially not to those who came from such a provincial backwater as Extremadura. After completing his studies, Zurbarán had great difficulties in finding work in Seville, and had to go back for a time to his native town of Fuente de Cantor. Only in 1629, after marrying as his second wife a woman from an influential family, was he finally able to establish himself in Seville; he was to be based here throughout his most successful years. Zurbarán's naturalism is of a very different kind from Velázquez', and has an austerity which has been seen as a reflection of the character of his native region. Simplified and tightly executed forms and figures, set against plain, sombre backgrounds, are given a solemn monumentality. The sturdy simplicity of Zurbarán's art is very much to present-day tastes, but it is easy to see how this same quality could once have been interpreted as a sign of naïveté; his art was in fact to go out of fashion even in his lifetime, and it was not until the 19th century that its reputation was to be revived, and its originality recognized.

Many of Zurbarán's paintings remain in Andalucía, but only a fraction of these are in the settings for which they were originally intended. He painted his major works mainly for monasteries and convents, and most of these institutions either fell on hard times in later years or else were dissolved: in either case 19th-century collectors, responding to the growing fashion for his art, made every possible effort to acquire the paintings. Two of Zurbarán's most important Andalucían commissions were for the Charterhouses at Jerez de la Frontera and Seville. A visit to the former institution greatly helps an understanding of Zurbarán's art, even though all his paintings that were once there have long been dispersed. The Charterhouse lies in fertile, undulating countryside several kilometres to the east of Jerez. In the early baroque period its church was given a sumptuously ornate facade and embellished inside; but the greater part of the complex was finished in the late 15th to early 16th centuries, and is in a gothic style. It is the only Charterhouse still functioning in Andalucía, and can only be visited with special permission. In September 1998 the abbot finally allowed women to pass through its gates.

The Carthusian monks are few in number and occupy only a small area of the original vast complex. Unable now to work the large orchard which they own, they dedicate much of their spare time to maintaining the surviving parts of the Charterhouse in a state of spotless cleanliness. The odd monk in his coarse white garment and with shaved head walks silently by, disappearing into the darker recesses of a sharply lit cloister. The atmosphere is of perfect order and complete silence. Zurbarán was the ideal artist to produce work for such an environment, and his pictorial style was also excellently suited to portray the austere robes of the Carthusians. The placing of these robes against the artist's characteristic dark backgrounds creates a most powerful effect, as can be seen in Zurbarán's panels of saints now in the Museo de Bellas Artes at Cádiz. These and a group of other other small panels in Cádiz are all that remains in Andalucía of his Jerez altarpiece. In the Museo de Bellas Artes in Seville, however, you can see the three large works that Zurbarán executed for the Sacristy of Seville's own Charterhouse. The most impressive of these works depicts the moment when the Carthusian bishop St. Hugo observes a bowl of meat turning into ashes, thus offering him divine justification of the Carthusian practice of vegetarianism and abstinence. A group of Carthusians is shown in stiff, hieratic formation behind a long refectory table. For those lucky few who have been to the Charterhouse at Jerez, memories of the refectory there will come back as you look at this scene, which reveals to the full Zurbarán's genius as a painter of simple still-lives in which the humblest object is invested with tranquil dignity. The table is covered in a plain white cloth, and sparingly laid with the same

St John the Evangelist's Vision of Jerusalem, by Alonso Cano

blue and white ceramic bowls and mugs that are still in use in Jerez's Charterhouse today.

The plague of 1649-50 killed off many of Zurbarán's family, including apparently all his children from his second marriage. Finding life hard in Seville in the 1650's, Zurbarán finally moved to Madrid, where he died in 1664, not poverty-stricken, as is sometimes said, but certainly in no great state of wealth. His last paintings lack the power of his earlier ones, his technique having lost its former precision in an attempt to imitate the more flowing, vaporous style then in fashion. The master of this style was Bartolomé Murillo, who in the late 1640's had displaced Zurbarán as Seville's leading painter.

Murillo's career illustrates how possible it still was for an artist to prosper even in the depressed Seville of the late 17th century. He constantly received commissions in this, his native city, right up to his fatal fall from scaffolding in 1682, and in 1660 had even founded an institution which had given new dignity to the arts in Seville, an Academy of Painting. After Velázquez' death, in 1660, Murillo was indisputably Spain's most renowned painter and was soon to be considered, in the eyes of the rest of Europe, as one of the greatest artists of all time. This reputation was maintained well into the 19th century, and then fell as quickly as it had risen, his works being dismissed as facile and cloyingly sentimental. Today Murillo is coming more into fashion again, especially now that his own works are being distinguished from those of his numerous and slap-dash followers and copyists. The technical virtuosity of his art is undeniable, and even though he is often sweetly sentimental, there is also a darker, more forceful side to his personality. His international reputation was once based mainly on his radiant Immaculate Conceptions, and his genre scenes, which are mainly of pretty-faced beggar boys in picturesque rags. Most of the latter works found their way into British collections, but a large proportion of his religious paintings remain in Seville, and these include some of his most powerful works. The Museo de Bellas Artes is filled with his paintings, but many others are still in the buildings for which they were originally commissioned, most notably the Cathedral, the Archbishop's Palace, and the churches of Santa María la Blanca, and the Caridad. Murillo's *St. John of God Carrying an Ill Man*, and *St. Isabel of Hungary Feeding the Lepers* deserve special mention, for they show the artist to have been as capable of conveying drama and deep emotion as he was of portraying celestial visions. The two paintings are both in the Caridad, and really need to be seen in the context of this hospital church, a building distinguished not just for its paintings, but for being a magnificent sculptural and architectural complex.

The sculpture and architecture of the Andalucían baroque are no less worthy of attention than the region's paintings of this period, and yet have been ignored by most foreigners, even one as conscientious and open-minded as Richard Ford. The prejudices that are still held against the sculptures of the baroque are strongly connected with a puritanical belief in truth to materials, and a distaste for the religious

Nuestra Señora de La Macarena

sensationalism which came to the fore after the Reformation. From the late 16th century, the favourite medium in Spanish sculpture had been polychromed wood, and this medium was used to create ever more life-like effects. The first great Seville sculptor in this style was Martínez Montañés, a friend and contemporary of Pacheco, who was in fact responsible for polychroming many of the artist's works. Known in his time as the 'God of Wood', Montañés was famous for his ability to give human semblance to his sculptures, and some of his portrait heads, such as that of St. Francis of Borja (Francis Borgia) in the Museo de Bellas Artes in Seville, do indeed seem to be creatures of flesh and blood. The succeeding generation of Seville sculptors persevered in this realistic vein, while at the same time abandoning the restraint which Montañes had always reserved for the gestures and emotions of his figures. The outstanding sculptor of the middle and latter years of the century was Pedro Roldán, whose retable for the altarpiece of the Caridad features a frenetically agitated *Deposition*. It is in the work of Roldán's followers, however, that critics of the baroque see Spanish art descending into out-and-out vulgarity. Eye-sockets are filled with glass, beads imitate tears, and real clothing and even hair are used. It is certainly wrong to discuss these works simply in artistic terms, for they are much more than mere sculptures: they are images that continue to play a central role in Andalucían life of today. Adorned in different finery for different occasions, paraded through the streets during the region's celebrated Easter processions, they inspire a devotion in people who are not even religious, and are talked about as if

Nuestra Señora de la Esperanza de Triana

they had magical powers. The respective merits of these images are hotly debated, and allegiance to a particular one is often seen as defining someone's personality. The most famous of Andalucía's sculptures is Seville's Virgin of the Macarena, attributed to Roldán's daughter, Luisa. To most foreigners, this Virgin is the epitome of shallowness of emotion and crude artifice, but thousands of Sevillians praise her beauty and mystery, and are moved to tears by the sight of her face. I have even known those who would not dream of living with anyone who does not worship the Macarena above all other images of the Virgin.

The baroque architecture of Andalucía has at times an appeal as visceral as that of much of the region's sculpture, and can leave many feeling distinctly queasy. The baroque style was actually slow to evolve here, and the buildings put up in the first half of the 17th century, such as the Convent de la Merced in Seville (now the Museo de Bellas Artes) largely perpetuated the mannered classicism of the preceding century. The feature which makes them unmistakeably Sevillian, and which looks ahead to later developments, is their dazzling colour: the lines of the architecture are accentuated by bright pastels, and expanses of white plaster alternate with shining ceramics and pink to russet red brickwork. In the last quarter of the century, colour was to combine with ornamental inventiveness to create baroque effects of mesmerizing power. But in many ways the most striking Seville monument of the 17th century was a building in a transitional style dating from the middle years of the century. This, the Church and Hospital de la Caridad, has a history as fascinating as its architecture and decoration.

Miguel de Mañara, the founder of the Caridad, was a wealthy aristocrat popularly thought to have been the model for Tirso de Molina's Don Juan. He would actually have been far too young for this, but he was certainly an intriguing figure who in middle age decided to live frugally and give away most of his wealth to the construction of a building intended for the care of the poor and sick. Legend has it that he had led a dissolute philandering life until one day, seeing a funeral cortège pass by, he had asked who was inside the coffin, and was told that it was himself. Little is in fact known of Mañara's youth, though there is good reason to suppose that he was not very proud of it. The latter half of his life was devoted entirely to his hospital of the Caridad and to self-punishment, and when he lay dying in 1679 he insisted on being treated in the same room as the paupers. His tomb at the entrance to the Caridad church bears, as he had requested, the following inscription, worded with characteristic Sevillian exaggeration: 'Here lie the bones and ashes of the worst man who has ever lived.' Immediately inside the church are two paintings by Valdés Leal that testify to Mañara's obsession with death: one, *In Ictu Oculi*, has a gleeful skeleton standing over a pile of discarded books, and insignia of wealth and power; the other, *Finis Gloriae Mundi*, shows in savage close-up the decomposing, insect-ridden bodies of a cardinal and a soldier. Yet the building itself is by no means sombre. Its principle baroque feature, the superb retable supporting Roldán's *Deposition* is a joyous, gilded structure with swirling columns. The interior is light and colourful, and the white exterior is inset with large ceramic panels as intensely blue as the Andalucían sky. The architecture and decoration of the Caridad, and the life-story of Mañara himself are an interesting reflection of the Andalucían mentality, a mentality in which a love of suffering is frequently the obverse of a passion for life.

The paintings, sculptures and other furnishings of the Caridad are integral to the architecture, but they do not overlap with each other and are neatly contained by the regular lines of the building. Towards the end of the century the Andalucían architects went in more and more for shock tactics, and completely broke down the remaining barriers between architecture and the visual arts. Underneath all these buildings' lavish accretions is usually a simple and unoriginal structure, but the initial impact is nonetheless quite staggering. A foretaste of what was to come is provided by the Seville church of Santa María la Blanca (1751-3), a simple cruciform building made exciting by an extraordinary ceiling of frothing plaster foam. The greatest and most prolific Seville architect of the late 17th and early 18th centuries was Leonardo de Figueroa, whose many churches for the city, such as the Magdalena and San Luis, revel in ceramics, polychroming, and a plethora of busy, ornamental forms of plateresque derivation. In his frontispiece for the former monastery of San Telmo, these forms seem almost to be pitted against each other in a struggle to be seen, rather like the anarchically behaved traffic which congests the Seville streets. Izquierdo Hurtado, a contemporary of Figueroa's, went in for partic-

The Charity of St Thomas Villanueva, by Murillo

ularly dramatic ornamentation, and his masterpiece in Seville, the chapel of San José, has a retable resembling a gilded lava flow churning up a flotsam of limbs and architectural bric-à-brac.

Outside Seville the main centre of the Andalucían baroque was Granada, and it was in this city's Charterhouse that the style reached a point of ornamental exuberance beyond which it could scarcely go any further. Hurtado worked in the monastery church, producing in the chancel a blaze of gold and coloured marble of enormous theatricality; but it was an unknown architect who was responsible for the building's most startling feature, its Sacristy. Entering this from the nave is to be drawn suddenly into a blizzard, from which you emerge reeling and with eyes dazed by the brilliant whiteness. Not a single part of the walls is left undecorated, and many visitors such as Mario Praz have found parallels with the Alhambra, though the intended effect of all this decoration was not to soothe, as in the latter's case, but to exhilarate.

The exhilarating, emotionally charged architecture of 17th- and 18th-century Andalucía was successfully transposed to Latin America, where its ornamental

Palace of the Marquis of Gomera, Osuna

fantasies gave much inspiration to the native craftsmen. It was an architecture too which travelled far beyond the main cities and often ended up in what are now the humblest of places. Rural Andalucía is rich in lavish monuments of this period, particularly the small towns and villages of the Guadalquivir basin, where the wealthy owners of latifundia once had homes. Lucena boasts a Sagrario chapel in the parish church of San Mateo of an ornamental intricacy unsurpassed even in Seville and Granada. Écija has a splendid series of polychromed baroque towers described by Gautier as being in 'sublime bad taste'. Meanwhile on the magnificent palace-lined street of San Pablo in nearby Osuna, you can see the rivetingly bizarre palace of the Dukes of Gomera, which has an asymetrical, undulating skyline inspired by the fantastical engravings of German rococo artists. The enchanting small town of Priego de Córdoba, beautifully situated above a ravine, has perhaps two of the most surprising baroque monuments of them all, a great public fountain with mythological statues playing under more than a hundred jets of water, and an unexpectedly large Sagrario chapel overwhelming an otherwise modest parish church. Few structures can have such a claim to be compared to a wedding cake as this circular chapel of soaring proportions and plaster-coated balconies which recent restoration has revealed to be a glistening white. Gerald Brenan doubted whether the showy virtuosity as revealed in this chapel could be the source of 'great art', and Jan Morris, reflecting on both the monuments of Priego de Córdoba and the Charterhouse of Granada, wrote that for her taste 'they are too flippant, too frothy, and their practitioners stand in relation to the masters of Spanish austerity as a gifted interior designer might stand to the engineer of a pyramid.'

The transition in Andalucía between the baroque and neoclassical periods is shown in the evolution of Cádiz. The Cádiz of ancient fame was by the early 17th century a small, inconsequential place, the scant remains of which constitute today a decrepit prostitute quarter in the shadow of the city's cathedral. The importance of Cádiz grew considerably in the course of the century, but it was not until the following century, when the place enjoyed a 45-year monopoly of trade with America, that it became a scene of major urban and architectural development. None of the new buildings was of outstanding architectural merit, least of all the massive and clumsy cathedral, which was begun in a heavy baroque style in 1722 and completed in a neoclassical one in 1856. Cádiz nonetheless grew into a most elegant town, thanks largely to a programme of urban reform carried out after 1775, during the period of governorship by a Spanish general of Irish descent, Alexander O'Neill. The houses, churches and regular street plan of 18th- and early 19th-century Cádiz have survived to this day, grimy but virtually intact, and contained within the massive encircling walls put up by the French in 1810. Cádiz, today one of the finest and best preserved towns of this period in Spain, impressed and disappointed travellers of the Romantic period by its modernity. Many of these travellers caught at Cádiz their first glimpse of Andalucía, a region to which they had come expecting a journey back in time. Stepping off the boat, they found themselves instead in a city which had the first sewage system in Spain, as well as a sparkling new architecture, some of it imitative of that of revolutionary France. 'There was nothing of the sombre aspect I had been accustomed in fancy to associate with the streets of Spain,' wrote Dundas Murray on a visit to Cádiz in 1849, 'every edifice appeared modern and new, or, if ancient, was painted "up to the eyes".'

The contrast between Cádiz and Seville in the early 19th century was a striking one. For Dundas Murray, Seville was a city locked in a glorious past: 'Her fame in the present day rests upon the traditions of the past, and upon the undoubted signs of a wealth and magnificence which once rolled through her streets.' Murray's English contemporary George Dennis described the vast abandoned cannnon factory in Seville, and found this to be a poignant reflection of the city's economic decline. Yet in Murray's and Dennis' day, there was one industry still flourishing in the city – tobacco. The construction of the city's Tobacco Factory between 1728 and 1757 had brought new vitality to the city, and had resulted in a building which Dennis was to describe as 'one of the wonders of Seville'. This vast factory, which is today the city's main university building, contains an apparently endless series of courtyards, and is crowned by the monumental figure of Fame blowing her trumpet. It was the last great monument of Andalucía's Golden Age, and it was also a pioneering example of industrial architecture. However, the many tourists who visited the place from the early 19th century onwards, took a diminishing interest in the actual architecture or in the building's industrial implications. These were people who failed to take seriously Andalucía's role in the modern world, and were dreaming instead of a region of mystery and romance, colourful costumes and lascivious dancing, Moorish monuments and voluptuous maidens. The Tobacco Factory was not for them a factory but a harem, where thousands of sultry beauties lay imprisoned, scantily dressed owing to the great heat, and provocative in their behaviour. One of these legendary employees was a gypsy woman called Carmen.

Gypsies

The image of Andalucía had changed significantly by the middle of the 19th century. The region that had once been one of the economic centres of Europe was by now living mainly off its reputation as an exotic land. This new image had been greatly fostered by a group of people whose origins were mysterious and whose life style inspired a mixture of revulsion, fascination and sentimentality.

The word 'gypsies' which is used to describe these people covers in fact a large number of different ethnic groups spread today between India, Europe, North Africa and America. Traditionally all these groups lead a nomadic existence, speak variants of the same language, Romany, and make their living through ironmongery, horse-trading and thieving. Their origins have been endlessly discussed, often in a malicious way. Many have identified the gypsies as the accursed descendants of Cain, others have seen them as people condemned to perpetual wandering for having forged the nails of the Crucifixion. The most fantastical hypothesis concerns specifically the gypsies of Spain, Southern France and North Africa, who have been related to the Guanches, an ancient people from the Canary Islands sometimes considered to be the last survivors of Atlantis. The eccentric poet-rancher of the Camargue, the Marquis Baroncelli-Javon, pursued this line further after he had invited Sitting Bull and other native Americans to come and visit him in his Provençal home. So struck was he by the similarities between the Indians and the local gypsies, that he concluded that all were descended from red-skinned nomads dispersed after Atlantis' destruction.

The general belief today is that all gypsies were originally from India, and that, after reaching the Bosphorus, some went directly to Europe, and others travelled along the southern shores of the Mediterranean, eventually crossing the Straits of Gibraltar. The Spanish and Provençal gypsies probably chose the latter route, as they are referred to respectively as *gitanos* and *gitans*, which are derived from the Spanish and French words for 'Egyptian'. There is the complication, however, that the Andalucían gypsies are also often known as *flamencos*, or 'Flemings'. Were the gypsies described as such because their colourful costumes were similar to those brought back by Spanish soldiers from Flanders? Or was it because these people

The Prince of the Gypsies, Granada, end of the 19th century

came from Central Europe, the Spaniards of the time being unable to distinguish Flemings from Germans? Numerous interpretations of the word 'flamenco' have been offered, and there is the strong possibility that it has nothing to do with Flanders at all. For instance, it might derive from the Arabic word for a fugitive peasant (*felagmengu*), or even from the supposed flamingo-like appearance of gypsy men, with their brightly coloured trousers clinging to spindly legs (see also page 143).

Whatever their origins, gypsies had first come to Europe by 1425, and by the end of the century had formed considerable communities in Spain. A great many of the Spanish gypsies were drawn to the Nasrid Kingdom of Granada, and sentimentalists have argued that they went there out of an innate preference for the Moors over the Christians. However, Andalucían gypsies supported the Christians after 1481, and might even have forged the projectiles used by Ferdinand and Isabella in the siege of Granada in 1492. In all probability the gypsies were driven largely by opportunistic motives, and at heart cared as little for one nation as for the other.

The gypsies were spared the early stages of the Inquisition, probably because they were too poor to be worth bothering about, rather than as a gesture of goodwill for their having helped the Catholic Monarchs. Isabella certainly had no great love for them, and in 1499 issued a decree giving them sixty days to stop their wanderings and to find stable employment, or else to be exiled for life. Subsequent Spanish monarchs were to be no less harsh on them. Philip II did not conceive of them as a race but as a 'collection of vicious people drawn from the dregs of Spanish society'; Philip IV saw them as useless Spaniards, and called for their colonies to be broken up. Between 1499 and 1783 at least twelve laws were to be passed limiting their activities and life style. The gypsies did their best to ignore these.

After the departure of the moriscos in 1609 the gypsies became the main objects of Spanish racial abuse and hostility. Significantly, they moved into areas that had once been frequented by moriscos such as Triana in Seville and the Albaicín in Granada, and took over some of the casual unskilled trades that the moriscos had vacated. Yet they inspired much greater fear and hatred than the latter had done. They did not share the moriscos' concern with personal cleanliness, and lived unwashed in the filthiest surroundings. They were thought capable only of deceit and thieving. 'Gypsies,' wrote Cervantes, 'seem to have been born into the world for the sole purpose of being thieves: they were born of thieving parents, they are brought up with thieves, they study in order to be thieves, and they end up past masters in the art of thieving.' The most feared of Andalucía's infamous highway robbers were gypsies, who were supposed to have no mercy on their victims, and have none of the nobility of character associated with bandits such as José María. They were quite happy to kill for the smallest amounts of money, because they belonged to a race notorious for its complete lack of scruples and morals.

Much of what was thought about the gypsies was based on the disdain which these people often showed to those not of their race. The 19th-century author George Borrow, one of the first to write about the gypsies with both sympathy and learning, noted how among themselves they behaved according to the strictest of moral codes. This was particularly true as regards personal loyalty and sexual behaviour. One of the great myths about the gypsies was that they were extremely promiscuous. Yet they held virginity and fidelity to one's partner to be sacrosanct, and punished terribly those who violated their laws. Gypsy women might frequently appear to behave in a provocative manner towards outsiders, but Borrow insisted that none of them would ever dream of committing an indiscretion. Prosper Mérimée, not surprisingly for the author of *Carmen*, dismissed Borrow's views on gypsy chastity as rather naïve, though he himself had to concede that the women displayed extraordinary loyalty towards their husbands.

Some of the qualities attributed to the gypsies were wholly fanciful. Their tendency to work with furnaces and live in caves made many think that they were in league with the devil. Involvement with the black arts was apparently confirmed by their interests in palmistry and by the strange culinary concoctions brewed up in large pots by the women. One of the most unfounded and widespread beliefs about the gypsies was that they practised cannibalism. This belief was the cause of much persecution in 17th- and 18th-century Spain, and yet there was not a single shred of evidence to support it.

In 1783 Charles III, a true figure of the Enlightenment, tried to dispel many of the prejudices held against the gypsies, and to integrate them into Spanish society. He passed a law forbidding the gypsies their costume, wanderings, and language, while at the same time permiting them to chose virtually any profession that they wanted, and penalizing any non-gypsy for refusing either to employ them or to allow them entry into a public place; he also insisted that they were no longer to be referred to as *gitanos* - a word which they have always hated - but rather as 'New Castilians'. Charles III's law came at a time when the gypsy contribution to Spanish culture was beginning to be recognized. The following century saw great changes in Spanish attitudes towards gypsies and in the gypsy life-style itself. Spanish gypsies found a great champion in George Borrow, whose *The Zincali* (1841) did much to promote tolerance and understanding of them: in other parts of Europe, such as Moldavia, gypsies were still being thrown into slavery. In 1889 Spain became the first country in the world to have a special school for gypsy children. It was founded in a cave in Granada's Sacromonte by an eccentric priest called Padre Manjón, a man whom Walter Starkie was to remember in the 1920's as a saintly figure ambling down cactus-lined paths on a donkey. Padre Manjón's small school grew into a large institution, and the priest's belief that the gypsies could be turned into good Catholics helped to pave the way for the gypsy pilgrimage to Rome in 1956 to seek the protection of Paul IX.

Spain's gypsies are today more integrated into their country's society than those

Gipsy and his wife, by Gustave Doré

elsewhere in Europe. Unlike most other gypsies, their first language is not Romany, and they are no longer nomadic, the gypsy encampments that you occasionally see in Andalucía being generally made up of Portuguese gypsies. Nonetheless, the Spanish gypsies have continued to stick closely together, and have retained their idiosyncratic culture, contrary to fears that Charles III's 1783 law would deprive them of much of their individuality. Triana is no longer a gypsy suburb, and few gypsies remain in the Albaicín; but there are many other urban areas in Andalucía that are still largely inhabited by gypsies. Two such districts are that of Santiago in Guadix and La Chanca in Almería, both of which have many cave dwellings and are thus considered picturesque by passing tourists. Some of these caves are still lived in, but those in Granada's famous Sacromonte are now only used by the gypsies to put on tourist entertainments. Walter Starkie remembered Sacromonte when its caves were still in everyday use, glowing at night with the fires of countless furnaces, transforming the hillside into 'some island of Vulcan'. Serious flooding in

1963 compelled the Grenadine authorities to move the gypsies to make-shift 'temporary' homes in the suburb of La Chana. They are still there. La Chana, one of Granada's ugliest, poorest and most crime-ridden districts, is typical of many places in Andalucía where gypsies have been forced to live. Romantically inclined tourists might pine for the days of gypsy caravans and gypsy caves, but places such as La Chana serve as a useful reminder that gypsy life is anything but picturesque, and remains in many ways as hard today as it always was.

The fact that gypsies have managed to keep a strong cultural identity despite the constant attempts of others to suppress it is an indication of the strength of their laws, social ties and pride. Secret gypsy tribunals continue to be held, and gypsies still obey unwritten laws of loyalty to the clan. Marrying a non-gypsy is not encouraged, and those who do so have to make their partners adjust entirely to gypsy ways. Cultural conservatism is further ensured by gypsy parents allowing their children almost total participation in the adult world; the adult appearance and behaviour of these children can be quite disconcerting for the outsider. Underlying, and strengthening the gypsy mentality is a belief in the superiority of gypsies to other beings. The Spanish gypsy still refers to the non-gypsy as *payo*, which translates as 'peasant' or 'serf'; the exclamation *¡que gitano!* ('how gypsy-like!') is used meanwhile to express approval of non-gypsy people, acts or things. In the Romany dialect of Spain called Calí, the word 'to know' is *chanelear*, which means not simply 'to know' but 'to know by intuition'. To some people this is an indication that the gypsy mentality is indeed a more advanced one than that of the payo.

The gypsies' contemptuous attitude towards the non-gypsy is an understandable one in view of the prejudices that are still held against them throughout the world. This century they have in fact been subject to the worst persecutions in their history, when Hitler sent 400,000 of them to die in the concentration camps. The Spaniards pride themselves on being more tolerant towards the gypsies than any other nation, and fail to recognize how strong their racial prejudices still are. One of the most detailed recent books in Spanish on the subject of gypsies, *Los Gitanos Españoles* by Helena Sánchez, bears the extraordinary dedication, 'To my father, lover of flamenco, although not of gypsies'. A medical research student whom I met in Málaga uncovered three cases of leprosy in parts of the city which were very poor and happened to be largely populated by gypsies. The publication of his research had the effect of ostracizing all gypsy children in Málaga schools.

The hatred which has always been felt against gypsies has been balanced by a tradition of romantic infatuation with them. Cervantes' short story *The Little Gypsy Girl* describes a wealthy aristocrat falling in love with a beautiful gypsy, to whom he proves his love by leaving his family, and taking up a gypsy life of wandering and stealing. Cervantes, the nephew of a gypsy, expressed in this story the yearning for the simple gypsy life that has been experienced by many young men of privileged background. The yearning was to become particularly strong from the early 19th century onwards, when the gypsy was to acquire a heroic status. Travellers to Andalucía up to then had mentioned gypsies only rarely, and had usually done so in a derogatory way. The Marquis de Layle, visiting the region in 1784, wondered how anyone could put up with them, 'a people. . . who hold nothing sacred, and have neither religion, laws nor strength of character'. Bourgoing, thirteen years later, believed that they should have been 'purged from society a long time ago'. However, by 1830, Gautier was describing the gypsy women of Granada as if they were goddesses: 'Nearly all of them carry themselves so naturally, and with such innate dignity, and they have such ease of posture when sitting, that, despite their rags, filth and poverty, they seem imbued with an awareness of the antiquity and unsullied purity of their race. . .'

Gautier's romantic attitude towards gypsies was to be shared by a growing number of travellers and writers. The rapid industrial and capitalist expansion of the 19th century made the untrammelled, non-conforming lifesyle of the gypsies seem increasingly attractive. Many of those who wrote on it had nomadic tendencies themselves, like George Borrow. Borrow's fascination with gypsies had begun as a child, when he had been allowed a privileged glimpse of a gypsy encampment in Norfolk; his fascination grew in the course of his extensive travels around England, France, Germany, Russia and Spain. He developed a particular empathy for the Spanish gypsies, perhaps because he himself, as an eccentric, wandering Englishman selling Protestant bibles, must often have felt an outcast in this country. The combination of scholarship and romanticism with which he wrote on gypsies was to typify many later studies of these people. In 1888, the Gypsy Lore Society was founded in London with the intention of recording gypsy traditions. Its presidents have included several colourful figures, such as the painter Augustus John, and the writer Walter Starkie, both of whom espoused a gypsy lifestyle. Starkie had had his first encounter with gypsies in Italy at the end of the First World War, meeting a Transylvanian gypsy musician who became his blood brother. In fulfilment of a pledge that he would one day go and meet this man in Transylvania, Starkie set off on a long journey through Hungary and Romania, earning his living as an itinerant musician. By 1921 he was in the south of Spain, still with his fiddle, and still spending most of his time with gypsies: the outcome of this latter trip was *Don Gypsy* (1936).

In the 1920's and 1930's many romantic young travellers journeyed like to Starkie, with little money, and frequently on foot or donkey; and many of these, like Starkie, ended up in Andalucía: Gerald Brenan for instance, and Laurie Lee. These two decades saw also a great surge of writings on gypsies, among which were those by an American called Irving Brown, who was of gypsy blood himself. Augustus John, Starkie, Brenan and Irving Brown were all in Granada at the beginning of the 1920's . The place had by now become as famous for its gypsies as for its Moorish monuments, and John found that the gypsies here were 'wholly given up

Gipsy music, end of 19th century

to the entertainment of tourists'. The character of Granada's Sacromonte became ever more bogus in the following decades, as indeed did so many other apects of gypsy life that were exposed to the public. Yet the fascination with this life has lasted to this day, together with numerous romantic preconceptions about it. Jean-Paul Clébert, the author of one of the most scholarly recent books on gypsies, despises all the sentimental literature on the subject, yet he himself was undoubtedly attracted to it for sentimental reasons: he has gloried for many years in self-imposed isolation in the Provençal countryside, after first making his name with a book on down-and-outs and other social outcasts in Paris, *Paris Insolite*. If Clébert had written about low life in Seville rather than Paris, he would undoubtedly have had a few words to say about 'Lucy'. Lucy is an elderly American woman who for the past thirty years has lived in Seville, claiming to write a book on the gypsies. She is well known to those who frequent the Seville bars, and spends much of her day propped up at one of them. Dishevelled, and always mumbling to herself, she speaks hardly a word of Spanish, but is understood by everyone. Many of those who talk to her are gypsies, though whether they seek her company out of genuine affection or simply in a mocking spirit is sometimes difficult to tell. In any case this enigmatic figure exemplifies an extreme type of gypsy enthusiast.

No other region in the world has an attraction based to such an extent on its gypsies as Andalucía. Towards the middle of the 19th century Andalucían gypsies began to realize the tourist potential of their music and dancing, and by the end of the century had made flamenco famous throughout Europe and America. They created a vogue for their flashy flamenco costumes, and brought new panache to that traditionally Andalucían art of bull-fighting: this century the most elegant and exciting of Spain's bull-fighters have frequently been Andalucían gypsies, such as Joselito, Rafael el Gallo, and Curro Romero. Numerous writers, musicians and painters have taken their inspiration from Andalucían gypsy themes, and their works have in turn done much to promote gypsy fashions: Bizet's 1873 opera based on Mérimée's *Carmen* is a notable example of this, and established Andalucía once and for all as the land of the glamorous gypsy. The gypsies have no written tradition, and it has been left to non-gypsies to invent a gypsy literature. Already in the late 18th century, pseudo-gypsy ballads began to appear in Andalucía; but it was not until the time of García Lorca, that this literary tradition was to achieve real distinction. The most popular of Lorca's collections of poetry was his *Romancero Gitano* (1928) or *Gypsy Ballads*, which both drew on gypsy themes and emulated the moving simplicity of gypsy song. Lorca, who did more than any other writer this century to influence attitudes towards Andalucía, encouraged his readers to look at the region through gypsy eyes.

Flamenco and bull-fighting are the two most obvious aspects of gypsy culture in Andalucía. The fascination with the Andalucían gypsy has much more to it than just an interest in these two activities; it is inseparable from other essential elements of the region's appeal. To travellers nostalgic for Moorish Andalucía, the gypsies have often seemed to represent an unbroken link with this Moorish past. They have a suitably exotic appearance, and had of course until recently lived in districts such as the Albaicín and Triana that had previously been the haunts of moriscos; occasionally they themselves had even been referred to as Moors. Gautier fancifully believed the Granada gypsies to be at heart 'Arabs and Muslims', and numerous other visitors to this city, staring across to the Albaicín from the Alhambra, have had their oriental reveries confused with gypsy fantasies. 'In 1921,' wrote Starkie, 'on my first visit to Granada I started the day in the Alhambra in the company of Abenamar, Zaïda, and the heroes and heroines of the Moorish ballads; but I finished it in the caves of the dancing gypsies. Whenever I gazed out of the arched windows of the Alhambra, my mind travelled over to the Albaicín. . .'

The Andalucían gypsy, who has often been thought of as the most beautiful of all gypsies, has also fulfilled travellers' visions of exotic Andalucían beauty: Carmen was after all a gypsy. But more than living up to the ideal physical image of the Andalucían, the gypsy encapsulates those aspects of the Andalucían personality that have most intrigued foreigners. Gypsies are known for their ability to adapt to other cultures, but the amount that they have in common with the Andalucíans suggests that the influence has been mutual, and that there is a fundamental empathy between these two peoples.

It is difficult to get to know the gypsies, and foreigners especially have to be wary in their dealings with them. Gypsies generally assume, often rightly, that foreigners are interested in them purely out of an interest in flamenco culture. Many promise to accompany foreigners to 'real' flamenco events, convince them of their wholly friendly motives for doing so, and then extort from them as much money as possible. Even if you are an Andalucían, to be accepted by the gypsies to an extent that a genuine friendship develops is not always easy, and depends to a great degree on your being introduced to them through a payo they already trust. One such payo is Esperanza Flores, who, as a celebrated maker of flamenco costumes, and as someone who had once run one of the Seville bars most popular with gypsies, is a figure well known and much loved in the gypsy world. Through her I got to know more gypsies than I would otherwise have done, but I was also made more aware than before of the ties that link the gypsy with the Andalucían payo.

Driving once in a car with Esperanza, I innocently pointed to a large snake which was crossing the road. Without realizing it, I had touched on one of the great superstitious fears common to both gypsies and Andalucíans: the very mention of the word 'snake' is meant to bring on bad luck, and the only remedy is to shout out afterwards *lagarto* or 'lizard'. Esperanza and many in her payo circle in Seville shared a great number of the superstitious fears of the gypsies, and rarely had I encountered such superstition among urban-living people. Every day I discovered new sources of bad luck, ranging from the colour yellow to a chance encounter with a funeral procession. A terribly unlucky act is to refuse to buy one of the sprigs of rosemary that are constantly being hawked by passing gypsies: not only do you have to buy one, but you also have to keep it afterwards in your house, and only get rid of it by burning. Magic and superstition also play a vital role in both the Andalucían and gypsy attitudes towards religion, along with an obsessive dwelling on death and suffering, and a love of exuberant spectacle. Gypsy rites are perfectly in keeping with the Andalucían brand of Catholicism : the famous pilgrimage to the Rocío (see page 170ff) has much in common with the spectacular gypsy gatherings at Les-Saintes-Maries-de-la-Mer in Southern France, and for over three hundred years the church authorities in Granada have employed gypsy dancers and singers in their Easter processions.

The infamous machoism of the Andalucían is matched in its strength only by that of the gypsy. Once I found myself standing at a bar next to a well-known group of male gypsy singers. Esperanza was friendly with all of them, but told me that, as a woman, she could not introduce them to me at that moment, as this would entail her breaking into an exclusively male gathering, and thus being contemptuously received. In gypsy society women lead a life completely separate from that of the men, but what is remarkable is that they frequently support their husbands, and far

Tiles at La Caridad, Seville

prefer to do so than to see these men working. Such an attitude is in fact common in Andalucía generally, and had certainly worn off onto Esperanza, much of whose life has been spent selflessly looking after men with little money and large drink problems.

Visitors to Andalucía, and to Seville in particular, frequently comment on the amount of time that people appear to spend doing little other than drink, sleep, and enjoy themselves. Such indolence, constantly made fun of by outsiders to the region, reflects a philosophy of life common to both gypsies and Andalucíans: some call it by the more dignified name of 'fatalism'. To the gypsy, and to many Andalucíans the ideal in life is to be free, not to be tied down by work, social obligations, or thoughts about the future. To these people, of whom Esperanza is one, the careful way in which most westerners plan their lives, is utterly incomprehensible. In their philosphy, to be practical is to be boring and not to appreciate life to the full. As Irving Brown wrote: 'Gypsies are not content with spending their last cent: in order to be happy they must defy all sense of practicality.' It is a philosophy which leads to great extremes of pleasure and pain. Esperanza once had a birthday in the middle of which she quarrelled with her employer, decided that the job she had was curtailing her freedom too much, and gave it up then and here, thus losing the only secure source of income which she had had in years. Her subsequent reaction was to spend the rest of her birthday getting rid of all her remaining money by an afternoon and night of trailing the Seville bars with an ever-growing crowd of friends and acquaintances, whom she lavishly regaled with food and drinks. Excessive pleasure is the main way for many Andalucíans of coping with sadness, as it is for gypsies. A gypsy funeral is renowned as an orgy of gaiety.

Social restraints generally prevent Andalucíans from behaving with quite the same excessiveness as do the gypsies and Esperanza and her friends. An underlying love of riotous pleasure is nonetheless shown in the Andalucían obsession with *ferias*. All the social classes are united in these occasions in a whirlwind of drinking, dancing and singing. And to be able to enjoy yourself without the slightest inhibitions about such whole-hearted hedonism, it has been customary since the 19th century to dress up for these occasions in flamenco costumes.

Flamenco

The sounds of dancing, plucked strings and plaintive song have echoed through Andalucía's history. The famed sensuality of the dancing girls of Roman Cádiz was taken up in Moorish times by slave girls, whose bodies swayed to the rhythms of tambourines and lutes. The minstrel Ziryab pioneered in Umayyad Córdoba the use of the lute as an accompaniment to singing, and this instrument was further developed by the brilliant musician of 16th-century Seville, Alonso de Mudarra. By the 18th century a passion for the lute had given way to one for the guitar, and a sensual new dance form had emerged with the fandango. Guitar, song, and dance are the main components of flamenco, a type of popular music and dancing which has affected the way we look today both at Andalucía and at Spain itself. Flamenco lies at the mythical heart of a region which has constantly been shrouded in myth. It expresses much that is genuinely mysterious about Andalucía, and much that is bogus.

There are many commonly held preconceptions about flamenco, which is not surprising given the fanciful, vague, contradictory and purely speculative nature of most of what has been written on it. Probably the greatest of all these misconceptions is the belief that the flamenco artist is respecting an age-old tradition. It is one thing to show how deep-rooted is the Andalucían love of music and dance, it is quite another to say that flamenco has gradually evolved over the centuries. The composer Manuel de Falla did much to propagate this fallacy in a short essay which he wrote in 1922 on the origins of what is always considered the purest form of flamenco, *cante jondo* or 'deep song'. Falla saw as the three major influences on its development the adoption in Visigothic Spain of Byzantine chant, the Muslim invasion, and the settlement in Spain of numerous groups of gypsies. Walter Starkie added as a fourth influence the festival songs of the Jews, and also suggested – on the basis of a conversation with a Jewish bookseller in Tetuan – that the word *jondo* came from the Hebrew *jon tob*, which means 'good day' or 'festival'. With García Lorca the discussion of cante jondo evaporated completely into hot air, the style becoming a blend of influences in which the 'emotion of history, its lasting light without dates or facts, takes refuge'.

Flamenco, which Lorca once described as 'one of the most gigantic creations of

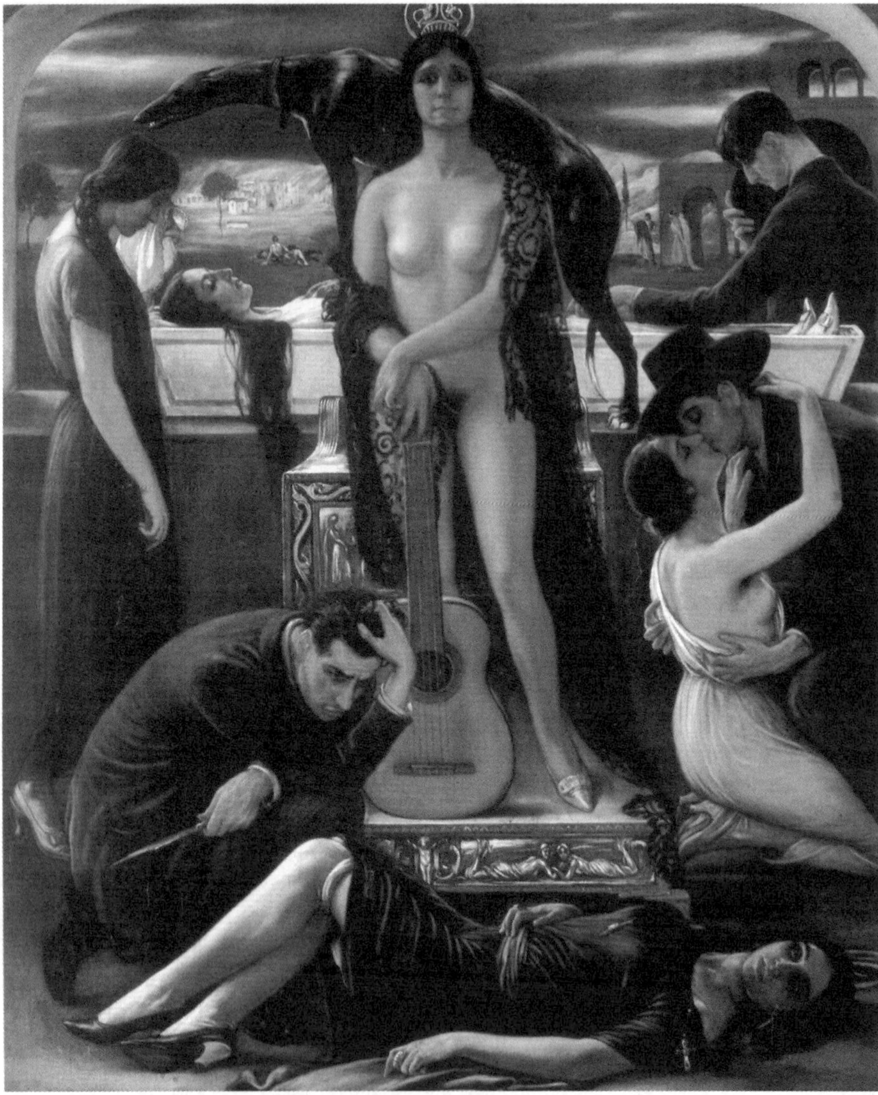

Cante Jondo, by Julio Romero de Torres

the Spanish people', and which many have characterized as the proverbial soul of Andalucía, probably dates no further back than the late 18th century. The word itself is not known to have been used before 1837, and is possibly derived from the 18th-century slang for a 'boaster'. Used initially to describe gypsies, the word was only in later years applied to a specific tradition of music and dancing. This tradition was essentially the creation of gypsies, and appears to have begun after 1783, when Charles III issued the edict compelling them to integrate themselves into Spanish society. The place of origin is thought by many to have been the Guadalquivir basin, more specifically a triangle area of land incorporating Seville, Jerez and Cádiz, the three Atlantic-facing towns that are often regarded as the Holy Trinity of flamenco. The triangle itself, referred to variously as the 'Tartessian' or 'Golden' Triangle, has as much mystery attached to it as that of Bermuda. Nonetheless scholars have been able to show that almost all the many songs and dances of flamenco are native to this area.

The tragic lyrics and tone of much flamenco is generally seen to reflect the sufferings of the gypsy people. Understandably the gypsies were anxious initially to keep their songs and dances to themselves, and probably did not understand how outsiders could take an interest in an art of such personal significance. They performed them at their weddings, funerals and baptisms, and at *juergas* or 'sprees', spontaneous gatherings of musicians and musical enthusiasts. Flamenco evolved in the homes of gypsies, above all in their patios. One of the first *payos* or non-gypsies to describe a gypsy festival at length was the Seville writer Estébanez Calderón, who in 1847 published an account of singing and dancing in Triana, the Seville centre of flamenco. Antonio Mairena, one of the finest gypsy singers of recent times, believed that Estébanez Calderón had been made fun of by the gypsies, because many of his observations on their traditions were frankly ridiculous. To this day, gypsies have exploited the gullibility of payos to relate all manner of nonsense about their music. A recent example of this was a BBC documentary which purported to show 'flamenco as it has never been seen before'. Each of the performers interviewed stressed how they were *gitano puro* or 'pure gypsy', as if this made incontrovertible everything that they said about flamenco. You had the impression that they were enjoying themselves leading the programme's director on, convincing her that she was witnessing flamenco in its authentic state.

It is certainly difficult to know what, and what not, to believe about flamenco. That music runs in the blood of all gypsies is clearly untrue, for only a tiny proportion of gypsies are musicians. But you cannot so easily dismiss the widely held view that only gypsies can successfully perform flamenco. I spoke about this with the guitarist Paco Peña, and as a non-gypsy himself, he was undestandably contemptuous about this point of view, referring me to a book called *Payos Too Know How To Sing*. He himself has an enormous reputation outside Spain, though not, interestingly enough, in Spain itself, where it is sometimes thought that he lacks the feeling

Gypsies dancing the Zorongo (a dance from Granada's Sacromonte), by Gustave Doré

that only a gypsy can have. This 'feeling' is obviously not exclusive to gypsies, as one of the most influential of all flamenco singers was the half-Italian, half-Andalucían payo of the last century, Silverio Franconetti; furthermore two of the most exciting flamenco artists of today are also payos, the guitarist Paco de Lucía and the dancer Cristina Hoyos. Yet the fact remains that most of the finest flamenco performers are and have been gypsies. The reason for this might not be as mysterious as it seems. Flamenco music, with its chromatic inflections and subdivisions, and its free and complex rhythms that do not conform to any regular measurement, is very difficult to transcribe with modern European musical notation. To be able to learn and perform such music, it is obviously a great advantage to have been exposed to it from an early age: a great many of the flamenco performers come from musical dynasties that stretch back for decades.

Flamenco depends much on spontaneity and improvisation, yet it also obeys strict rules and conventions that, like the lyrics of the songs, appear mainly to have

The Sevillana in Seville,
by Gustave Doré

been formulated in the last century. Flamenco singing, to the uninitiated, can seem monotonous and unvarying. The singers or *cantaores* are usually seated, and sing one at a time, the palms of their hands outstretched and shaking, their faces becoming ever redder, and the veins on their foreheads more prominent, until eventually apoplexy seems forthcoming; the same note is often endlessly repeated, and there are frequent shouts of *¡ay!*, which often appear to to express genuine pain. Those knowledgeable about flamenco, the *aficionados*, will usually be able to tell you what type of song the singer is performing, though I have known people who have listened enthusiastically to flamenco most of their lives and are still unable to distinguish between certain of these types. They fall into two main groups, only one of which, confusingly, is actually known as 'flamenco'. This group, the *cante flamenco* or *cante chico* ('small song') includes light-hearted, lyrical songs such as *bulerías*, *alegrías*, *fandangos gitanos* and *malagueñas*. Far more primitive, and anguished are the songs in the other group, the *cante jondo* or *cante grande* ('big song'). Two of these songs, the *siguirilla gitana*, and the *solea*, are unrelievedly sad (the word *solea* is derived from *soledad*, or solitude), and are considered by all aficionados as the greatest works in the flamenco repertory. Less common songs in the same group are the *martinetes* and *deblas*, which today are sung completely unaccompanied, and might originally have evolved in the gypsy forges, the beat being provided either by the workings of the bellows or the hammering of the metal. Another type of cante jondo is the *saeta*, which is an 'arrow of song' (to use Starkie's words) directed towards the images of a religious procession: the cantaor Antonio Mairena first made his name during the Seville Holy Week of 1933, after jumping out of a crowd watching one of the processions, and singing so well that the procession was halted and he was carried in triumph around the city's streets. Commonly confused with flamenco, though not belonging either to cante jondo or cante chico, are those traditional Andalucían or Latin American folk songs that have been greatly influenced by flamenco : the most famous of these, and the ones that you constantly hear today throughout both Andalucía and Spain generally are the *sevillanas*.

Flamenco songs are usually accompanied by the tapping of feet (*zapoteo*) or the clapping of hands (*tapoteo*). Audiences frequently join in the clapping themselves, often without realizing that the tapoteo is quite an art in itself, and that three people who are good at it can make as much noise as ten novices. For fast rhythms, the middle three fingers of the right hand are used to strike the extended palm of the left, the sound sometimes being supplemented by the clacking of tongues; for a deeper, more hollow sound, suitable to more solemn singing, the palms of both hands are cupped. Essential to any flamenco performance are shouts of encouragement, the one most travestied by foreigners being *¡olé!*; other popular exclamations are *¡anda!* ('bravo!') and *¡así se canta!* ('that's singing!').

The importance of the guitar in a flamenco performance has greatly increased over the years. To begin with the flamenco guitar was used as a simple accompanying instrument; but at the beginning of this century, under the influence of the great Ramón Montoya, it was made to adopt some of the techniques of the classical guitar, such as the tremolo and arpeggio. The playing of the flamenco guitar has become an exceedingly difficult task, requiring not only great skills at interpreting composition, but also at improvising to match the mood of the other performers. Flamenco guitarists have created further difficulties for themselves by having kept, out of pride, the traditional flamenco practice of resting the guitar on the right thigh: this awkward posture is particularly unsuited to the more classical style of guitar playing developed by Montoya. Another difference between the flamenco and classical guitarist is the use of the *capo*, a moveable bridge which allows the tuning of the guitar to be raised or lowered without having to retune each string.

Whereas the guitarist is often the least acclaimed player in a public performance of flamenco, the dancer generally receives most of the attention, especially from the foreigners in the audience. The costumes worn by the women dancers borrow traditional Andalucían streetwear of the 19th century, such as the *peinetas* or large combs, and *mantillas*, or fringed shawls; peculiar to gypsy dancers are the polka-dotted fabrics, and the trailing frilly dresses known as the *batas de cola*. Flamenco dancing involves movement of the hands and torso rather than of the feet, and in its purest form rarely requires castanets. The strong erotic element in the dance is undeniable, though is of a different kind from that which you find in the dancing of sevillanas: whereas sevillanas are danced with sinuous, voluptuous sensuality, flamenco at its best is performed with intermittent outbursts of frenetic, hysterical passion. With a bad dancer such passion can verge on the ludicrous.

All aficionados are agreed that the greatest performances of flamenco require an element called *duende*, a word which literally means 'fairy'. Lorca, quoting Goethe on Paganini, referred to duende as 'a mysterious power which everyone senses and no philosopher explains'; 'all that has black sounds has duende,' wrote a music critic after hearing Falla play his own *Nights in the Gardens of Spain*. Duende, Lorca emphasized, is very different from the muse, being violent, discordant, and only present when 'he sees that death is possible'. To perform flamenco with *duende* technical virtuosity alone is not sufficient. Lorca's contemporary, Manuel Torres, a celebrated cantaor known to sing from the chest rather than from the throat, told a singer: 'You have a voice, you know the styles, but you will never triumph, because you have no duende.' Even if a singer has this quality, it is unlikely that it will be brought out during a public performance of flamenco, as these performances require a professionalism and discipline that are anathema to it. The most memorable performances of flamenco are nearly always the gypsy juergas, spontaneous musical gatherings put on purely for the benefit of the musicians and a handful of aficionados.

Lorca undoubtedly glamourized the notion of duende, and gave it much more romantic mystery than it actually has. Drink and drugs are as likely to induce duende as deep spiritual passion, and Lorca himself suggested this in his description of a performance given by a singer called Pastora Pavón. At first she had sung beautifully, but had left the audience unmoved; only later, after drinking half a bottle of aguardiente did she begin to hold everyone's attention, singing 'with scorched throat, without voice, without breath or colour, but with duende'. The juergas are notorious for the amount of drink and drugs consumed, and have often involved prostitutes. They also tend to last for hours and even days on end, the stamina required to endure them having frequently to be maintained with cocaine. So many of the flamenco singers, including the great Silverio Franconetti, have died of heart attacks, and Lorca and others have loved to stress that these were caused by the emotional intensity required of these performances. A more likely reason would be found in the excesses of their lifestyle, which is similar to that of many rock stars, but with the difference that in their case it reflects the gypsy and Andalucían

Flamenco
c. 1880

philosophy of life brought to its ultimate conclusion. The juergas begin in a spirit of fooling around, but as the hours wear on, the search for pleasure is carried to such a degree that it can turn into self-destructiveness. And this is perhaps when the duende enters.

Duende may be incompatible with commercial flamenco, but flamenco would not have enjoyed any great popularity, and might not even have survived at all had it not been commercialized. Up to about 1860, flamenco had been restricted almost entrely to gypsy homes, and it was only after this date that it came to be widely known. The years 1860-1915 are often referred to as the 'Golden Age of flamenco', and correspond exactly to the period of the *cafés cantantes*. Cafés and bars began to allow private juergas to take place in their back rooms, and eventually arranged for flamenco artists to perform in public. One of the most famous of these cafés cantantes was the Café Silverio in Seville,which was founded by Silverio Franconetti in 1869 on his return from a long period in Latin America. Another well-known one was the Café de Chinitas in Málaga, a favourite haunt not only of musicians, but also of bull-fighters and poets; it is now a dress shop, but there is a plaque outside recording the days when Lorca loved to come here.

The new prospect of earning money from flamenco encouraged numerous gypsies to take up music. There was certainly a remarkable number of major flamenco performers in the second half of the 19th century. This was also the period which produced the first serious writer on flamenco, Antonio Machado y Álvarez, the father of the poets Antonio and Manuel Machado; he usually wrote under the pseudonym 'Demófilo', because he was a 'lover of the people'.

The considerable number of adherents that flamenco gained in the late 19th century was matched by a small but vociferous group of opponents. Among these were many of the writers and intellectuals belonging to the Generation of '98, including the philosopher Ortega y Gasset, who thought of flamenco as part of the 'southern copperware' which Andalucía employed to hide its real identity. Ortega y Gasset and many others who criticized flamenco had probably never witnessed any outstanding flamenco performance, for by 1900 commercialization had already had the inevitable effect of vulgarizing the genre. The success which flamenco artists began to enjoy abroad, combined with the international impact of Bizet's *Carmen*, led in Andalucía to countless gypsy shows intended primarily for tourists. A taste for 'Flamenco Operas' developed, gypsies and dancers came to be increasingly self-conscious in their looks and performances, castanets and other accessories were introduced, and cante jondo came to be abandoned in favour of the cante chico.

Manuel de Falla, with the assistance of Lorca and others, attempted in 1922 to halt flamenco's decline by instigating a cante jondo competition in Granada. In his rules for competitors, Falla warned 'most earnestly that preference will be given to those whose styles abide by the old practice of the classical cantaores and which avoid every kind of improper flourish, thus restoring the cante jondo to its admirable sobriety, which was one of its beauties, and is now regrettably lost.' The competition represented an important moment in Andalucía's cultural history, but it did little to stop the cante jondo's continuing decline. Walter Starkie made a pilgrimage in the early 1930's to the Triana home of a celebrated cantaor of the old generation, Fernando de Triana. He found the aged singer bitterly upset about recent developments in flamenco, ranging from the craze for castanets to the mixing up in dancing of the *cuadro Andaluz* with the *cuadro flamenco.* Then the singer got on to the subject of the cante jondo. 'There are,' he said, 'only a few of us left here in Triana who remember the great old days of cante jondo, when gypsy singing was as different to Andalucían singing as brandy is to Jerez. When Niña de los Peines and a few others have gone there will be nothing to remind us of the proud, metallic harshness of the gypsy voice.' Fortunately the singer did not get to hear of the experiences while visiting Granada of an English contemporary of Starkie called Marguerite Steen. Steen found herself entertained in a cave in Granada by a group of gypsy boys who had never even heard of a *solea*. What is worse they 'insulted' her ears with a rendition of *Slow Boat to China.*

La Argentinita

The cafés cantantes died out in the first quarter of the century, and were replaced by institutions devoted exclusively to putting on flamenco *tablaos*. These tablaos show flamenco at its most debased, but they have maintained flamenco's international popularity to this day and still remain one of Andalucía's major tourist attractions. The most popular centre of the tablao is Granada's Sacromonte, where a night club called La Zambra was opened in one of the caves in 1908. The place enjoyed an immediate success among the chic and wealthy, and more and more of the surrounding caves were subsequently transformed for the putting on of tablaos. Walter Starkie recalled how the Granada dancer Lola Medina 'enlisted the services of a well-known Madrid architect to create a sophisticated residence out of her cave and furnished it with illuminated alabaster baths and cocktail bars.' Starkie had known Lola as a plain-looking girl, but now she was 'a glamorous gypsy princess wearing the diamond bracelets and emeralds of the Duchess of La Rochefoucauld, her humble devotee, who humbly waited for her in her cave.' Today the Granada caves cater solely for tablaos, though these generally attract rather more modest tourists than before. Every hotel will try to sell you tickets for a tablao, which usually consists of the offer of a weak glass of sangría followed by an indifferent display of dancing in which the audience is eventually invited to join.

In the 1950's a renewal of serious interest in flamenco was marked by the birth of the flamenco festival. The first festival took place in Córdoba in 1956, and was soon followed by others in Chiclana, Morón, Lebrija, Utrera, Jerez, and Mairena del Alcor, the latter founded by the town's greatest singer, Antonio Mairena. The rapid spread of these festivals was accompanied by the emergence of a growing number of critics and historians describing themselves as 'flamencologists'; it was a period, wrote Mairena, in which the intelligentsia was concerned with Andalucían gypsy singing. Flamenco festivals are now held in the summer months throughout Andalucía, and usually take the form of a single, protracted concert, involving many musicians and dancers, among whom is always a local celebrity. Mairena himself described the festivals as offering 'the most spectacular but least genuine form of flamenco', and the phoniness of the occasions is emphasized by the way in which many of them are named after 'typical' Andalucían dishes, such as the *Gazpacho* of Morón, the *Potaje* ('stew') of Utrera, the *Caracol* ('snail') of Lebrija: these names serve only to highlight the myth that the gypsy has no food. Nonetheless the festivals are surprisingly free of tourists, are well attended by both gypsies and aficionados, and offer an opportunity to hear often excellent cante jondo: without them it is unlikely that the purest forms of flamenco would have survived. As with the juergas, the concerts are interminably long, beginning usually around midnight (about two hours after the official start), do not get really animated until around three in the morning, and last well into the dawn. The toilets are filled with men sniffing cocaine, but the festivals are also attended by families with small children who seem happy to endure the ordeal to the very end. It is important not to go to the festivals in the same spirit that you would go to a classical concert, for not even the greatest aficionados can comfortably sit for up to eight hours seriously engrossed in the music. The success of a festival depends much on the proximity of the bar to the stage. The first and best festival I went to, the Caracol of Lebrija, had an excellently situated bar where most of the musicians and aficionados spent the greater part of the night, interrupting their lively banter only by the occasional glance at the nearby performers. On occasions such as these, some of the character of the juergas survives into the festivals. I remember also a memorable scene at the Potaje of Utrera when the successful singer 'El Lebrijano', not scheduled to appear that night, spontaneously joined in the proceedings. A woman was singing on stage, and El Lebrijano stood up from the audience and sang back at her. In a drunken state, and continuing to sing, he advanced towards her, precariously balanced on a wall, from which he eventually fell and broke his arm. Even this incident did not stop his singing, which was quite magnificent and well appreciated by an equally drunk audience. Whether or not the duende took possession of him, it is incidents such as these that remind one that the best of flamenco is the unplanned.

Foreign visitors to Andalucía are constantly asking where the 'real flamenco' can be heard. Many journalists, including from the BBC, end up by asking this question to Paco Lira, the quiet but charismatic owner of Seville's large and attractive bar, the Carbonería. Paco, a payo greatly respected by gypsies and musicians, is one of those people who is aware of everything which is going on around him, and can even overhear conversations across a crowded, noisy room. He knows more than anyone where the best flamenco can be heard on a particular night, and holds informal flamenco sessions every Thursday night at his own bar – events whose atmosphere has been diluted of late by the place's growing element of poseurs and naïve young foreigners. Increasingly few bars in Andalucía allow juergas, the tradition having been killed off by the ubiquitous bar television and by the new licensing laws that permit only a few bars to remain open throughout the night. You are more likely to hear flamenco in a truly sympathetic environment in one of the private clubs known as *Peñas Flamencas*. It was at the Peña Flamenca at the village of Trebujena, near Sanlúcar de Barrameda, that I experienced the most exciting flamenco performance that I have yet attended. The occasion, unpromisingly, was a recital of 'Flamenco Piano' given by an elderly music teacher from Seville, Pepe Romero. I would not have gone had I not met Pepe a few days earlier in Seville, and been impressed by his sparkling and engagingly eccentric personality. He is largely unrecognized in Spain, though he has been referred to, much to his amusement, as the 'Chopin of flamenco', and has a small but passionate group of devotees who feel that he is one of Spain's greatest pianists. I arrived at the concert an hour after its scheduled time of ten o'clock and found Pepe incongruously in dinner jacket and bow tie in the middle of an almost empty room. At midnight, with still only a handful of people present, he decided to begin playing, and within fifteen minutes the room began to

Flamenco today

fill with villagers, and was soon packed out. Never had I expected a piano recital to be interspersed with constant shouts of *¡olé!*, *¡Anda Pepe!*, and other expressions of passionate enthusiasm; one old man was so carried away that he got up in the middle of the concert to thank Pepe for sharing with the audience his genius. Others were crying.

That the piano could lend itself so well to flamenco is an indication of the music's potential adaptability. Purists are critical of any changes to the canon, and yet change is perhaps needed if flamenco in its public form is to survive other than as an exotic entertainment or as an historical curiosity preserved by such institutions as the International Centre of Flamencology at Jerez de la Frontera. Some of the liveliest and most successful flamenco artists of today – the guitarist Paco de Lucía, the erstwhile heroin addict Camarón de la Isla, and the gypsy group Pata Negra – have all maintained a popularity through concessions to modern forms of music, Pata Negra even having gone as far as to combine flamenco with rock. The artists who have resisted such modern innovations as the use of an electronic bass guitar, and have kept their integrity and purity of style are once again facing difficulties in Spain. The audiences at the festivals are beginning sharply to decline, and many of the artists are forced to make a living abroad, where flamenco is largely understood in terms of 'Spanish colour'.

If the future of flamenco is at present in jeopardy, the singing and dancing of sevillanas are more popular than ever before, and a fashion for this music has caught on throughout Spain. In their commercial form, sevillanas combine folk with pop music, lyrics about sad love affairs with ones in praise of the processional virgin of the Rocío. I once went to a concert of sevillanas which lasted as long as a flamenco festival but was completely sold out, and was far livelier if also more ridiculous than most of these festivals. The climax, at four o'clock in the morning, was the arrival on stage of a famous, middle-aged group of musicians known as the Romeros de la Puebla. They emerged, out of a cloud of dry ice, dressed in the traditional leather gear of the horsemen of the Rocío; they began with a homage to Andalucía, and ended up with a song to the Virgin, during which many of the audience held up lighted candles. As an example of spectacular kitsch, this concert took some beating. But sevillanas should not really be seen in a concert performance, for they are essentially the songs and dances of everyday people rather than of professionals. Most people in Andalucía know how to sing and dance sevillanas, and foreigners are frequently surprised by the professionalism with which they are danced by the youngest children. Esperanza Flores, brought up during some of the worst years of the Franco period, told me that for the women of her generation these songs and dances were among the main means of expression and escape. Today you will always see people interrupting an afternoon's drinking or an evening paseo by bursting into sevillanas. Above all, however, it is in the *ferias* and in the pilgrimage to the Rocío that these songs and dances come into their own, performed by a myriad of women dressed in the gaily coloured flamenco costumes. Tourists at these occasions might be clicking their cameras and exclaiming at the quaintness of it all, but those involved are not performing for their benefit. They are perpetuating what must be one of Europe's liveliest, strongest and most genuine folkloric traditions.

Fiestas and Ferias

'Great doings in the Cathedral, churches and convents, great consumption of incense, torches, oil tapers. I wonder how the lower orders manage to keep themselves, as every day seems to be a holiday.' Richard Ford's first impressions on reaching Andalucía in 1830 typify those of most people visiting the region today. Every possible occasion, religious or otherwise, seems an excuse for a holiday or *fiesta*, and it is often hard to imagine how any work gets done. Spectacular religious celebrations, noisy local festivals, bull-fights, gaudily striped marquees, women in polka-dotted costumes, men with wide-brimmed hats, gaily bridled horses, and perpetual singing, dancing and drinking, all feature prominently in travel-writers' accounts of Andalucía. Festive Andalucía is deeply seductive, but is is generally trivialized by writers, portrayed simply in terms of 'Spanish colour' rather than as the expression of a complex culture.

Wherever you go in Andalucía, and at whatever time of the year, you are bound to encounter some festival. Furthermore the passion for festivals is increasing now that many of the restrictions imposed on them during the Franco period have been lifted. Events such as *romerías* (outings to a shrine) and parties known as *cruces de mayo* were heavily frowned upon by Franco for their blatant mingling of religion with the purely secular. Carnivals meanwhile, with their highly subversive element, were banned altogether, the one at Cádiz surviving only under a different name and at a different time of the year. The Cádiz Carnival is now back in its original form, and is held once again in the second week of February. It is the first major festival of the Andalucían year, and one of the most local in its significance. Through the streets of the town raucous, costumed groups parade themselves, enacting humorous tableaux. The visual puns are extremely funny and sophisticated, but virtually incomprehensible to anyone unfamiliar with the Andalucían brand of humour, or with local events and personalities.

The festival season begins in earnest in the spring, which most Andalucíans consider to be the finest time of year. Seville certainly is at its best during this period, bursting with flowers and redolent of jasmine and citrus-fruits rather than of the rank odours that pervade the town during the impossibly hot summer months.

From Palm Sunday to the Whitsun pilgrimage to the Rocío, the town is the scene of near constant festive activity. The Sevillians are traditionally the most pleasure-seeking of all Spaniards, and much of their year is spent in anticipation of the spring period, and remembering events that happened in previous festivals. Not surprisingly, Seville boasts the two Spanish festivals best known abroad, those of its Holy Week and *Feria*.

Holy Week or *Semana Santa* is celebrated very differently in Andalucía than it is in Castille, where the occasion is much more sombre and mystical. Religious fanaticism plays a surprisingly small part in an Andalucían Holy Week, and in Seville itself the religious element of the occasion is far from a conventional one. Most of those taking part in the processions, or crying while watching the religious images pass by, would never dream of attending a mass, and frequently have a hatred of the Church and its priests. Yet the emotions that they experience during this week are integral to their lives. The Sevillian obsession with Holy Week is evident in the many photographs of its processions and religious images that decorate the houses and bars of the town: there was even one bar, El Joven Costalero, which used to have a constant video show of the week (see page 374). Preparations for the week take up most of the year, the sounds of bands practising for it being heard every evening by the Torre de Oro.

When Palm Sunday finally arrives, the whole of Seville flocks to the streets, and most of the bars in the town centre are open day and night. Hotel rooms for Semana Santa are booked up for months in advance, yet to the ever growing number of tourists who come to the town during this week, the occasion must be a very baffling one. Foreign tourists tend to stay around the cathedral, not realizing that to get the most of Semana Santa you need to be constantly on the move and to be at particular places at particular moments. A good knowledge of Seville's streets is obviously an advantage, and it also helps if you buy your daily copy of the newspaper ABC, which publishes a detailed guide to the day's processions, and suggests the best places and times to watch them. Better still is to be guided by somebody from Seville, in whose company you will begin to become aware of the more subtle and myserious aspects of the Semana Santa, such as the way an image is carried, the way in which it is decorated, and the emotional importance attached to it.

The Semana Santa processions are organized by lay confraternities (*cofradías*), who also own the images that are paraded. There are on average eleven processions a day, each lasting between three and twelve hours, all passing through the cathedral, and beginning and ending in the church where the images are kept: the itinerary chosen by each confraternity rarely varies from year to year, and the slightest change made to it becomes a major talking-point. Up to Good Friday all the processions start from noon onwards, the mornings being the traditional time for the Sevillians to visit the images in their churches, where they will also receive a badge of the appropriate confraternity. Semana Santa begins in a particularly festive

Santísimo Cristo de la Pasión

fashion, and a good place to be on Palm Sunday is at one of the open-air bars of the María Luisa park, through which the confraternity of La Paz passes. Monday, in contrast, is the most sober day of the week, at least two of the processions being completely silent. The festive atmosphere of the Sunday does not fully reassert itself until late on Wednesday, which is when the Sevillians are officially freed from work, the following two days being a public holiday in Spain. Maundy Thursday and Good Friday are the highpoint of the Seville Semana Santa. On the Thursday, the men of the town put on dark suits, while the women wear combs in their hair and black mantilla shawls. Most of the town is up all night, for no sooner do the Thursday processions end than the Friday morning ones begin, among which are those of the three most celebrated confraternities, El Gran Poder, La Esperanza de Triana, and La Macarena. There are so many people on the streets during this night that it can take up to an hour to walk a distance that would normally be covered in five minutes. On Good Friday, the Macarena procession finally enters its chapel, watched by cheering thousands. From now on the excitement of the Semana Santa begins to wane, the afternoon processions of the Friday being less interesting than the morning ones, and the energy to watch them being considerably diminished. On the Saturday there are only four minor processions, and on the Easter Sunday the main event of the day is not a religious one but the first bull-fight of the season.

The Sevillians heavily dispute among themselves which are the best parts of the town in which to see a particular procession, but most are agreed that the processions are at their most beautiful at night (when the participants carry long candles), while passing along a narrow street, or while leaving or entering their churches. The most curious of these 'departures' (*salidas*) and 'entries' (*entradas*) are those of the confraternity of San Esteban, which take place along a narrow street crammed with people who have been waiting for up to two hours: the interest comes from seeing the processional images pass through the small ogee-arched portal of the church, a movement that requires exceptional skill. Other much appreciated moments of the Semana Santa include the Confraternity of El Museo passing alongside the Town Hall, the Esperanza de Triana crossing the Bridge of Triana, and the first rays of dawn illuminating the Virgin of the Macarena as she leaves the Calle Cuna and enters the Plaza Villasis. Outside the cathedral, on the Town Hall Square, along the Calle Sierpes, and around the Campana, there is special seating for those wishing to watch the processions, but rights to these seats are frequently held by the same families for years. Whether the Semana Santa should be seen sitting down is another matter, for the processions are interminably long, with constant stops. The most comfortable way of seeing them is undoubtedly from the balcony of a private house, the owner of which will probably treat you indoors to drinks and food during the more boring moments. But Semana Santa should really be experienced while standing in the treets, jostling with the crowds, and becoming physically as well as emotionally involved in the occasions. As you move slowly from one part of Seville

A Nazareno in Seville

to the other, the town is transformed into a vast stage set enlivened by thousands of actors, of whom you are one: you see the place with fresh eyes, modest streets and squares that you might once have ignored acquiring in the excitement of the occasion a magical aspect.

The processions vary little in their make-up. First come row upon row of draped men wearing the same peaked hats used by the Inquisition and later adapted by the Ku Klux Klan in America. In Seville these men are known as *Nazarenos*, elsewhere in Andalucía they are called *Penitentes* (Penitents), a name which in Seville is used in reference only to those Nazarenos who carry crosses; until the 1950's some of the Penitentes would also bear chains, and, up to the early 19th century, would even flagellate themselves. Anyone can be a Nazareno or Penitente, the only condition being that you pay the annual membership fees of the Confraternity, and sign yourself up for the processions several months in advance. There is no limit in age on the number of members taking part: boys no more than four years old are frequently to be seen, and some of the processions have over two thousand participants. Many people become Nazarenos or Penitentes as an act of penance, but a love of spectacle and dressing up is a more common reason for doing so.

The longer a Nazareno has belonged to a confraternity, the nearer he is allowed to the processional images. The wait for these images can seem endless, especially as a gap or *corte* often develops in the processions: a confraternity has to return to its church by a given time, though some of the confraternities prefer to pay a fine than to do this, that of the Gitanos or Gypsies being notorious in this respect. The longed-for arrival of the *pasos*, or processional floats bearing the religious images of the confraternity, is signalled by the appearance of men carrying long silver candlesticks known as *ciriales*: a stir of excitement runs through the crowd at this moment. Between the ciriales and the pasos are the church dignitaries, leading members of the confraternity, and enthusiastic members of the crowd, the latter walking backwards and sliding their feet along the ground, their eyes always fixed on the images. The pasos are nearly always two in number, the first always bearing a sculpture af Christ, and the second an image of the Virgin. Behind the pasos is usually a band,

Roman Centurions in Seville, c. 1900

and between them another double row of Nazarenos. In Málaga – after Seville the Andalucían town most famous for its Semana Santa celebrations – the men supporting the pasos (the *costaleros*) walk on either side of the floats, but in Seville they are hidden underneath them. The costaleros were once all professional, but in recent years these professionals have been replaced by members of the confraternities, who willingly undertake this most physically demanding of jobs. They suffer from infernally hot and claustrophobic conditions, their backs will ache for weeks afteward, and their necks – on which most of the weight of the *paso* is placed – swell up and are rubbed raw. But all this is as nothing to the feeling that they experience of working together to carry as well as they can the image they adore.

The respective merits of the processional images are much debated, and a tactless comment made outside the church of their origin could well lead you into a fight. Two of the most beautiful and famous Christs are those of the Salvador and the Gran Poder, the works respectively of Martínez Montañés and Pedro Roldán: both are life-size representations of Christ carrying the Cross, and it is a matter of personal taste and family tradition whether you consider the one to be more 'noble' and 'moving' than the other. The other outstanding and much revered Christ is that of the Cachorro, the masterpiece of the obscure late 17th-century artist Francisco Ruiz Gijón: tradition has it that for this portrayal of the crucified Christ the artist was inspired by the body of gypsy killed in a knife fight in Triana. Other Christs feature in enormous and slightly ridiculous tableaux, for instance that of the *Lanzada*, in which the soldier driving the lance through Christ's body sits atop a horse that could have come straight out of a fun-fair. An especially popular tableau is of *Christ before Pilate*, a processional float paraded by the Confraternity of the Macarena. Costumes comparable to those of the Roman soldiers in this tableau are worn by the men walking in front and behind it: these absurd 'centurions', who seem to be participating in an amateur drama, provoke much mirth among the crowd, and provide the necessary note of bathos prior to the arrival of the Virgin of the Macarena.

The processional Virgins are all of identical composition, and are borne on elaborate baroque floats crowned by a canopy. Foreigners generally are unable to recognize the difference between the expressions of these Virgins, and cannot understand the fanatical devotion of Sevillians to a particular Virgin. The main rivalry is between the Virgin of the Esperanza de Triana and that of the Macarena (see pages 122-3). The latter undoubtedly incites the most ecstatic reaction among the crowd, being always greeted with shouts of *Macarena¡ Guapa! ¡Guapa! ¡Guapa!'* ('Macarena, beautiful, beautiful, beautiful!'*)*. Intense emotion for all the processional images is expressed most movingly in the singing of *saetas*. Sometimes a professional singer is hired to sing these most difficult of songs from a balcony near the entrance to the confraternity's church. Normally, however, members of the crowd burst spontaneously into song when the images pass by; sometimes the saetas

A saeta, c. 1880

are sung by people as an act of penance, in which case the singing is particularly bad and at the same time particularly moving. The finest saeta I have ever heard was sung by a woman in her late 90's, who was both deaf and blind, and had to be told by the nurse who was with her when the paso had stopped so that she could begin.

The emotion generated by the processional images depends on factors that most foreigners fail to perceive entirely. Of particular importance is the way the image and its paso are adorned, the type of flowers that are placed on the float, the particular mantle which the Virgin is wearing, and so on: it is common to hear the Sevillians make such comments as 'the Virgin of the Macarena is more beautiful this year than she has been for ages.' But above all it is the way an image is carried which can affect the enthusiasm of the crowd. Much depends on the competence of the man known as the *capataz*, who stands directly in front of the paso, shouts out instructions to the costaleros, and strikes a hammer telling them either to stop or to start. The skill needed by the costaleros to negotiate the portal of San Esteban (the pasos have to be moved by the costaleros on their knees) is evident to all. The other, more normal manifestations of the costalero's art are not so obvious. A paso lifted in a single swift movement, or carried smoothly, is much appreciated, as is the occasional spontaneous flourish, such as a rhythmical swaying to the band's music. A particular way of carrying a paso sometimes characterizes a particular confraternity, the Christ of El Gran Poder, for instance, always being carried at the same fast pace every year. Occasionally there is a complete departure from tradition: the full-circle turn performed by the Virgin of Montesión in the Holy Week of 1989 was admiringly commented on by the Sevillians for weeks afterwards. There are ultimately no fixed rules determining whether or not a paso is carried well or not, for, to appropriate Lorca's definition of duende, this is something which everyone feels but no-one can explain. Foreigners tend to think of the Seville Semana Santa as a picturesque display of superstition and fanaticism by a culturally backward people. They are largely unaware of the refinement of the occasion, of the great degree to which it depends on *arte*, a word much used by the Andalucíans, and meaning more than just 'art' or 'skill', but also 'grace', 'wit', 'intelligence' and 'subtlety', the attributes in other words of a highly sophisticated culture.

Depending on whether or not Easter falls late or early in a particular year, the Sevillians have between one and two weeks to recover from the Semana Santa and prepare themselves for their *Feria*, which can be described as the ultimate secular manifestation of the baroque spirit of Andalucía. The ferias of Spain have their origins in the market fairs held from the middle ages onwards with a view to selling and promoting local products. Today ferias exist almost exclusively for the pursuit of pleasure, and are comparable in their activities to village *fiestas*, or to those urban district festivals known as *veladas*, for instance the *Velá de Sant Ana* of Triana. The transformation of Seville's horse and cattle fairgrounds into a place of entertainment took place after 1847, following the example of the nearby town of Mairena del

Alcor; Mairena del Alcor, in view of its pioneering position in the history of the Andalucían feria, always holds its festival several days before that of Seville. The Seville Feria grew rapidly in size and popularity, and today occupies a vast precinct in the modern district of Los Remedios. Part of this space is taken up by fairground attractions, but the greater part of it is given over to *casetas*, or marquees. These casetas, lined along streets named after famous Sevillian bull-fighters, were once all owned by individual families, though today they are largely paid for by companies, societies, or by groups of families clubbing together; the number of casetas put up is strictly limited, and in the run-up to 1992, the rights to a caseta were being acquired by certain companies for exorbitant sums.

The women of Seville, traditionally frustrated at not being able to dress up as Nazarenos in the Semana Santa, get their own back on the men by wearing flamenco or 'Gypsy' costumes for the Feria. These brightly coloured costumes featuring floral or polka-dotted material, are worn for a maximum of two weeks in the year – for the week of the Feria, for the Cruzes de Mayo, and for the pilgimage to El Rocío. More women now wear flamenco costume than ever before, and the style of these costumes is improving slightly after a long period of decadence. When Esperanza Flores started making flamenco costumes in the early 1960's, she was virtually alone in being interested in their style and design; at that time Seville high society spurned flamenco costumes as being vulgar, and Esperanza herself was once refused admission to a caseta for wearing one. Esperanza brought back good taste into the wearing of flamenco, and the costumes she makes herself are among the most sought-after in the town. As a true artist, however, she refuses to commercialize her talents, and makes costumes usually only for friends, who allow her complete freedom to chose the materials and style.

Talk about flamenco costumes, combined with an intensive slimming programme, take up much of the week prior to the Feria. An equal amount of time is spent putting up the casetas and discussing how they will be decorated, prizes being later awarded to those casetas considered by a jury to be the most beautiful. The casetas – made normally out of blue or red striped canvas – are adorned inside with a baroque abundance of streamers, paper flowers and gilded mirrors. The final touches to them are made on the Sunday, by which time people are already streaming into the Feria precinct, even though the Feria does not officially open until the Tuesday. On the Monday night a sit-down banquet is organized for the associates of the casetas, and at midnight the Feria is declared open by the turning on of a sea of coloured lights. From this moment onwards the colour, movement, and animation of the place become quite overwhelming.

The Seville Feria is essentially one continual party lasting from the Monday night through to the dawn of the following Monday. The whole of Seville is on holiday, and the town shuts down almost completely; on the instigation of the anarchic one-time director of the festival, José Luis Ortiz Nuevo, the Monday after the Feria is

Esperanza Flores at the Feria of Seville

now also a public holiday, and is referred to by everyone as 'Hang-Over Monday' (*Lunes de la Resaca*). A typical Feria day begins around mid-day, continues until eleven or twelve at night, after which you might try and catch a couple of hours sleep before returning to the Feria at around two in the morning, where many remain for at least another six hours, enjoying before going home to sleep a breakfast of chocolate and *churros* or doughnut fritters. By day the Feria ground is packed with parading horses and riders, Andalucía being perhaps the part of Europe where equine culture is strongest. Women in flamenco costumes sit side-saddle behind men with leather breeches, grey waistcoats and wide-brimmed hats; other people ride around in horse and carriage. Despite the bustle of the streets, the life of the Feria is centred mainly inside the casetas, which are used by their owners as places for inviting their friends and family; if you know many people in Seville, you can spend your day going from one caseta to another. Inside the casetas you will be

The Feria

treated to numerous tapas of ham, cheese, and shell-fish, but rarely will you be offered anything lavish to eat, as that might dissipate the great stamina necessary to survive the Feria. The main drink is sherry or manzanilla (see page 184), and every year journalists try and calculate how much of these fortified wines is drunk in the Feria, the usual estimate being that this equals the quantity consumed by the whole of Spain in one year. The effects of the drink are compensated by the constant dancing of sevillanas. In the best casetas, music for this dancing never comes out of loudspeakers. Instead a circle is formed around the dancers, with somone beating the rhythm on a drum, another person singing, and the others clapping their hands. In a handful of the more snobbish casetas belonging to Seville's high society, there continues the bizarre and condescending tradition of gypsies performing flamenco to men and women dressed in evening attire.

In the old days the Seville Feria was crowded with turbaned Indian princes, Arab sheikhs, bejewelled European aristocracy, and American film stars such as Orson Welles. Today it is still customary for foreign dignitaries and celebrities to visit the Feria. Nonetheless the Feria is essentially a festival for the inhabitants of Seville, and the welcome given to outsiders is a guarded one. Families from Madrid have managed in recent years to acquire casetas, and these people are commonly thought by the Sevillians to be spoiling the character of the Feria, as are the countless people from other parts of Spain who pour into the Feria at the week-end. The Feria is one of the great tourist attractions of Andalucía, and yet the tourists who come here will encounter one of the most private of public festivals, where full enjoyment is only possible if you can secure entry into the closely guarded private casetas. The owners of the casetas are more welcoming to foreigners than they are to other Spaniards, but it is rare for the foreign tourist without friends in Seville to be invited inside the casetas for more than a single glass of wine.

Acceptance into the superficially open, but at heart very closed society of Seville is difficult for a foreigner. One person who managed this in the 1950's was a tall and kilted Scotsman known as 'Pepe el Escocés', who came to Seville every year for the Feria, and was invited into almost every caseta, where he delighted everyone with his vigorous if arhythmical dancing of sevillanas. He became such a feature of the Feria that journalists used to report his arrival in Seville as a sign that the Feria had at last begun. Acceptance like this demands the following of certain unwritten codes of behaviour. High spirits and wit are greatly admired, but excessive drunkeness and gauche behaviour are deeply frowned upon. Most people are slightly tipsy, but considering the amount of alcohol which is consumed in the Feria, it is surprising how rarely drunken brawls break out. Even drinking and enjoying yourself requires arte in Seville, and the Feria must be one of the most inherently refined of public festivities. Within the casetas, social and family barriers are broken down in the common pursuit of pleasure. Money is never talked about, but spent thoughtlessly, the private bills in the casetas amounting to hundreds of pounds a day. Wit flows as abundantly as the wine, and all the cares of life are temporarily put aside. No wonder that the Sevillians, with their ability to reject all material proccupations, sometimes consider themselves to be the upholders of the spiritual values of Europe.

The notion of the Feria as a highly sophisticated occasion seems to many people incompatible with the fact that it coincides with the principal bull-fights of the Seville year. Bull-fighting, considered by most foreigners and a growing number of Spaniards to be the most barbaric of all sports, has for many years been a major component of all Spanish festivals, but it was originally an essentially Andalucían speciality. The rules of the game were drawn up in the mid 18th-century in Ronda, a town which produced during that period one of the most legendary of all Spanish fighters or *matadors*, Pedro Romero, whose last fight was given at the age of eighty-six. The bull-rings at Ronda and Seville are the oldest and most beautiful in Spain, the latter, known as the Maestranza, being a supremely elegant late baroque creation in white and vivid ochre. During the Feria, fights or *corridas* are held in the Maestranza daily, and these are generally the most exciting fights of the year, as the bullring is always packed to capacity with a particularly enthusiastic audience: the mood of the crowd is vital to the enjoyment of a corrida. The one drawback of the Feria corridas is that good seats have to be booked a long time in advance, and the price of the tickets – very high for all bull-fights – becomes ridiculously exorbitant.

The very attending of a bull-fight demands a certain amount of ritual. Ideally you should arrive at the Maestranza in a horse and carriage, and enjoy a glass or two of aguardiente in one of the animated bars beside the building before the fight. Do not

Pedro Romero

get too carried away, however, as bull-fights are renowned as one of the few Andalucían activities that always begin exactly on time. To the sounds of a band and to general applause, the participants of the fight walk into the ring, preceded by two costumed men on horseback responsible for maintaining order in the Maestranza. The three matadors fight in order of seniority, and have to kill two bulls each. Directing the fight is the President, who sits behind a balcony facing the arch through which the bull enters the ring; the weight of each bull is recorded in a notice above this arch. The first moments of the fight give the matador a chance to assess the calibre of the bull, and to show off his own skill with the cape. After a few minutes without any blood being shed, the President signals for the *picadors* to be brought in. These men, mounted on horse-back, carry long lances with which they gore the bull. Since the 1920's the horse have always been padded, thus sparing the spectator the once common sight of horses having their entrails quickly sewn up so that they can face the bull again. The skill of the picador is to stick the lance into the bull in such a way as to reduce slightly its energy without in any way destroying its fighting spirit. Then follow the *banderilleros*, men who run at the bull and have to place as elegantly as possible two coloured banners into its neck. Finally the matador is left alone in the ring with the bull, a moment of impressive silence. If the matador performs well with his cape, the band starts to play in preparation for the kill. The matador's reward for a good display of fighting is to be given the bull's ear, both ears if his performance is thought to have been truly outstanding. In the latter case – a rare event in Seville, where the public is an especially demanding one – the matador is carried in triumph through the main gate of the ring. The bull's corpse

Matador's costume, 19th century

meanwhile is dragged off to be cut up by eagerly awaiting butchers, who sell off parts of it to the town's bars and restaurants.

Many of the finer points of bull-fighting can be learnt by observing the reactions of the crowd, who will shout out for a weak bull to be replaced, wave their handkerchiefs to demand that the matador be awarded an ear, and will constantly make such comments as 'the President knows his bulls', or 'good' (*¡bien!*), 'well done!' (*¡bien hecho!*), and *¡olé!* Furthermore there are countless books in English on bull-fighting, generally written in an emotional, macho vein by those who claim to have a unique insight into the sport: two of the most famous are by Ernest Hemingway and the drama critic Kenneth Tynan, both of whom, incidentally, had relatively little experience of the Seville Maestranza. What you rarely read is that the great majority of the fights are very poor in quality, and that bull-fighting today has lost much of its former greatness. One of the reasons for the decline might be that the desire to escape from poverty was once the main spur to the matador, and that extreme poverty of this kind is no longer so widespread in Spain.

A Seville matador currently near the top of Spanish bull-fighting is Espártaco, who is exceptionally brave and skilful, and can always be relied upon to give a good fight. However, he lacks *arte*, a quality which for many Sevillians can only be found today in Curro Romero, a native of the neighbouring town of Camas. Curro Romero, in his late 60's but still fighting, is a living legend who already has a street named after him in the precinct of the Feria. As cowardly as Espártaco is brave, he has been known to go to prison for his refusal to kill a particularly dangerous bull (failure to kill a bull constitutes a breach in the bull-fighter's contract). It is said that you never see Curro fight badly, for he either fights well, or not at all. Most of the time he does the latter, but occasionally he has moments of unsurpassed brilliance, an event which makes newspaper headlines: following a fight of his in the Seville Feria of 1989, the front page of ABC bore the enormous headline CURRO FOUGHT! I was present at one such fight of his, and for little more than two magical minutes the crowd rose and gaped in astonishment, some people even starting to cry. No account can hope to explain exactly what he did in those two minutes, but the arte was immediately sensed, just as it is in the finest of flamenco, or in the truly successful carrying of a Semana Santa float. It is in rare moments such as these that bull-fighting transcends the level of mere butchery or sport to become one of the more moving and mysterious of human activities.

No sooner is the Seville Feria over than the *Cruz de Mayo* parties begin. These are put on in private or communal patios, and in some of the town's smaller squares, for instance the Plaza de Santa Cruz in the Barrio de Santa Cruz. The essential component is a cross decorated with flowers, in front of which people in flamenco costumes, sing, dance and drink. The parties are sometimes said to commemorate the discovery of the True Cross by St. Helena, but parallels can be drawn with maypole celebrations and ancient fertility rites. The blending of the religious and the secular is certainly striking, though not as much as it is in the Whitsun pilgrimage to El Rocío, which brings together elements of the Semana Santa and the Feria to create what is not only the culminating festival of the Andalucían year, but also one of the most fervently supported festivals in Europe today.

The story of the pilgrimage goes back to the 15th century when a man from the Huelva village of Villamanrique discovered while hunting a miraculous image of the Virgin hidden in a tree. A small hermitage was built, known at first as Nuestra Señora de las Rocinas. Around 1600 the villagers of nearby Almonte claimed the Virgin as theirs, and changed the name of the hermitage to the Virgen del Rocío ('The Virgin of the Dew'; she is also often referred to as *La Blanca Paloma* or 'The White Dove'). From around that time a regular pilgrimage to the shrine began, which soon attracted a growing number of people. Pilgrimages of this sort are known as *romerías*, of which there are a great many in Andalucía. All the other romerías are completed within a single day, but the shrine of El Rocío is so isolated that it takes a day simply to reach it on foot from the neighbouring village of Villamanrique. From at least the early 19th century pilgrims were setting off for El Rocío from various places throughout the provinces of Huelva, Cádiz and Seville, arriving at the Hermitage by the Saturday after a journey taking up to four days. The journey or *camino* to El Rocío became as important a part of the romería as the celebrations at the Hermitage itself. The popularity of the Rocío pilgrimage has increased yet further in recent years. Up to as late as the 1950's there was just a scattering of houses around the Hermitage, the pilgrims all camping in their waggons. A significant proportion of the pilgrims then were wealthy young men with a love of horses and practical jokes, who would attempt to seduce the woman pilgrims behind the plentiful trees that you pass through on the camino. The pilgrims to the Rocío today form a representative cross-section of society, and come from many-parts of Spain, including the Canary Islands. The hamlet of El Rocío has swollen to an extensive village, where houses are rented out for astronomical sums of money, and where an estimated half a million people congregate for the Whitsun celebrations. To many people, known as *rocieros*, the pilgrimage is the most important event of their year, and they are happy to devote to it all their annual savings.

The pilgrimage to El Rocío from the various villages and towns of Spain is organized by local *Hermandades*, or 'Brotherhoods', at the head of which is a *mayordomo*. An annual meeting of mayordomos (of which there were seventy in 1989) establishes the exact itinerary and timetable which each Hermandad has to follow. The 'brothers' of the Hermandad carry their belongings in decorated waggons, pulled today mainly by tractors; some of the older Hermandades, such as that of Triana, still have the traditional ox-drawn waggons shaped like those that once crossed America's Wild West. At the head of the long line of waggons is always the *simpecado*, a banner of the Virgin transported under an elaborately decorated canopy pulled by oxen. In front of the simpecado go pilgrims on foot, horseback, or in horse-drawn carriages. The women are all dressed in flamenco costumes, while most of the men have cloth caps, black sashes, braces and grey and black striped trousers known as *pantalones Rocieros*. All the foot pilgrims carry large sticks, the ones of the women decorated with flowers and sprigs of rosemary. Rosemary (worn by the men in their caps) is as essential an attribute of the Rocío pilgrims as the scallop shell is to those going to Santiago de Compostela, and indeed a pilgrim on this route is referred to as a *romero* or 'rosemary'.

The three major and most traditional routes to El Rocío run from Sanlúcar de Barrameda, Huelva and Triana; most of the Hermandades eventually join one of these routes. The camino from Sanlúcar is the most beautiful, crossing as it does the Guadalquivir and the protected section of the Coto Doñana National Park; the Huelva route is the dullest, while the Triana one goes through the most varied scenery of the three. Whatever route is chosen, the last day and a half before reaching El Rocío is spent in a wild and virtually uninhabited area formed by the estuary of the Guadalquivir and called the Marismas. Covered in marshes, sand and pine-trees, the area was turned by Alfonso X into a royal hunting ground in the 13th century. Triangular in shape, the Marismas have a great deal of mystery attached to them, and many like to locate the legendary Tartessus here. At the centre of the triangle, surrounded by marshes, lies El Rocío, and it is quite possible that long before the place became a shrine to the Virgin an important maternity and fertility cult was celebrated here. Most people who come to El Rocío are convinced of the magical properties of the place, and claim to experience a great renewal of energy whenever they visit it.

Procession of El Rocío

I embarked on my first pilgrimage with considerable scepticism, believing that the event would be little more than a colourful folkloric pageant set in attractive countryside. But I was immediately entranced and have returned regularly since then. Though remaining unconvinced about the cosmic energy supposedly emanating from El Rocío, I have always found it an event that takes you completely outside the realm of everyday experience. On this first occasion I went with a group of friends from Seville, who hired three waggons, and attached themselves to one of the oldest of the Hermandades, that of Umbrete. Umbrete is one of the prettiest villages in Seville's Aljarafe, and the one perhaps most obessed with the Rocío. To prepare themselves to be Rocieros, the children of the village have their own annual pilgrimage to an old pine tree near the village, a journey undertaken in miniature waggons and with a simpecado pulled by dogs.

Nearly a third of the village's three thousand inhabitants took part in the pilgrimage which I was on. After an early morning mass in the village church, we set off, serenaded by the village band and warmly applauded by the remaining villagers. A man playing a pipe and drum accompanied the simpecado throughout its journey, and rockets were let off in front of it at all the key moments, such as entering a village or passing a chapel. Angelus would always be said in front of the simpecado at 12 o'clock each morning, and there were frequent stops for singing and dancing; at the end of each main halt the mayordomo would shout out, *¡Viva la Virgen del Rocío! ¡Viva la Blanca Paloma! ¡Viva la Hermandad de Umbrete!* A strong emotional attachment developed between the pilgrims and the simpecado and among the pilgrims themselves. Conversations were easily struck up, and those of us on foot were constantly being offered food and drink by the people travelling in the carriages.

Only an hour into our first day we left the asphalted road, and for the next three days followed tracks through the dust and sand. The sensation of leaving the twentieth century developed, on reaching the Marismas, into one of alighting on another planet. The procession of flamenco costumes and gaily coloured waggons through ever changing countryside provided an endless succession of beautiful images whose dream-like quality was only occasionally disturbed by the intrusion of an ugly and often absurd reality – the strewing of vast quantities of rubbish, the mounting chaos, the queues and floods of tears accompanying such renowned moments of the journey as the crossing of the River Quema, where, in a parody of the River Jordan baptism, capfuls of murky water were thrown over the heads of new pilgrims. At the end of each day, our eighty or so waggons would group together around the simpecado, near to where various other Hermandades had encamped. Rockets exploded all night, and around the countless camp fires sevillanas were endlessly sung and danced, the rhythms provided not only by clapping and drums, but also by the shaking of special reeds.

Late on a Friday afternoon, nearly three days after leaving Umbrete, we reached El Rocío, the entrance to which is marked by the Ajolí, a mosquito-infested but much-sung rivulet regularly replenished by tears from both arriving pilgrims and the emotional crowds who come to greet them here. In the village the Hermandades all have their own houses, in the patios of which the waggons set up camp in the fashion of some Arabian caravanserai. I meanwhile stayed in the house of friends who who were not really rocieros at all, but Sevillians who enjoy the Rocío for its spirit of conviviality and for the energy which they say the place gives them. The life they lead here is comparable to that of the Seville Feria, a continuous round of drinking, eating, dancing, singing and visiting friends. The main difference is that a spirit of total anarchy rules in El Rocío, and you lose altogether any sense of time and social responsibility. The village itself is unlike anywhere in Andalucía if not in Europe, resembling a Wild West town gone mad, with thousands of horses parading up and down dusty streets lined with arcades. From Friday afternoon to Tuesday morning the pandemonium increases with the constant arrival and departure of the Hermandades – events greeted by fireworks, and people rushing to the doors of their houses to sing to the passing pilgrims.

The religious functions taking place in El Rocío – organized by the Hermandad of Almonte – lack both the moving simplicity of those of the camino and the sophistication of the Seville Semana Santa; what they do have are moments of quite primeval intensity. The present Hermitage is a white modern building in a curious neo-baroque style; as for the image of the Virgin kept inside, this is a stiff, hieratic object with no trace of the subtle expressiveness to be found in some of the baroque Virgins of Seville. Throughout the Saturday the Hermandades take it in turn to file past the open doors of the Hermitage to pay their respects to the Virgin. Loudspeakers constantly shout out instructions to those taking part in the processions, a ridiculous touch that would be unthinkable in any religious occasion in Seville. The Sevillians and most of the Rocieros have a low opinion of the people of Almonte (the Almonteños) whom they consider stupid, brutal and arrogant. The Almonteños are noted for their predominance of blonds, and there is a theory that they are the descendants of a band of Vikings who got lost in the Marismas.

The boorish behaviour of the Almonteños is noticeable to everyone on the night of Whitsun. Only they have the right to carry the Virgin, and they defend this right in a vicious manner. At an unspecified time in the early hours of the Monday morning the Virgin is carried outside of the Hermitage and around the main square. The scene inside the Hermitage before this happens is quite terrifying with a surging, hysterical mass of bodies sweating under tropical conditions. After a given signal the Almonteños (recognizable by their khaki shirts) jump over the railings that protect the Virgin and fight among themselves for the honour of carrying her. For a long time, both inside and outside the Hermitage, the Virgin is rushed backwards and forwards in the anarchic fashion characteristic of El Rocío. The hysteria and crush of the crowd are unceasing, and once when I was there, the Almonteños smashed the cameras of two television crews whom they thought had not paid enough for the privilege of filming the event. Miraculously it seems no-one has ever been killed during this night. With the first light of dawn, the Virgin is finally carried in a slightly more orderly fashion, and taken in turn to each of the houses of the Hermandades. The magic of El Rocío reasserts itself, and as the Virgin becomes ever brighter in the rays of the rising sun, people are everywhere crying with joy, believing that she has looked directly at them, and will grant them their every wish.

The Hermandad of Umbrete began their return later that Monday, the chaos and violent emotions of the weekend giving way to the pleasures of human company and of being united in a common endeavour. The journey back was very different from the outward one, more leisurely and intimate. Our last night and much of the last day were spent in the grounds of an 18th-century estate, where in the courtyard of the finca, midday mass was said to the accompaniment of sevillanas; after this a large cake was shared out to commemorate the appointment of next year's mayordomo. We arrived in Umbrete shortly after sunset on the Wednesday, welcomed by fireworks and cheering villagers. I had slept for little more than ten hours in the entire week but the sense of well-being counteracted the exhaustion. Good

Manolo Perales dancing at El Rocío

friendships had been formed by this stage, and departure was a genuinely sad occcasion. The shock later that night of being back in Seville and of returning to the twentieth century was a considerable one. But Andalucía from the spring onwards leaves you with little time for serious reflection. The cruzes de mayo were continuing, and there was much talk of the following week's Corpus Christi celebrations, and of a special procession in which the Macarena was brought to the Cathedral. From this time onwards there would also be weekly fiestas in every village surrounding Seville, and throughout Andalucía. Meanwhile, in a bar in Umbrete, a noticeboard conscientiously records the days left to next year's Rocío. 'How we suffer to enjoy ourselves,' said Esperanza Flores.

Food and Drink

It is inconceivable that people as hedonistic as the Andalucíans should not take an interest in what they eat. Yet the Andalucíans, more than all other Spaniards, have been constantly criticized by foreigners for the poverty of their food. The idea that Spanish food in general is poor is another of the myths about Spain propagated by the Romantic travellers of the last century. Even someone as impartial and perceptive as Richard Ford could instruct the traveller to Spain not to 'lumber himself with much batterie de cuisine; it is not much needed in the imperfect gastronomy of the Peninsula, where men eat like the beasts which perish.'

'Spanish cuisine,' concluded Benjamin Disraeli after a few weeks' stay in Andalucía, 'is not to my taste, for garlic and bad oil predominate.' Oil and garlic were what 19th-century travellers loathed most about Spanish food, and Andalucía is perhaps the Spanish region which makes the most use of these ingredients. To these travellers the ultimate culinary abomination was Andalucía's most famous dish, *gazpacho*, a cold soup featuring garlic and olive oil mixed with large quantities of water. Dundas Murray's description of his Andalucían servant making this dish has the tone of someone recording a barbaric practice: 'Of this savoury mess, he offered me a share; but half-a-dozen spoonfuls sufficed to satisfy my curiosity. . .' Gautier went even further in his criticism of this dish: 'In our country, no dog with the slightest breeding would deign to put his muzzle in such a mixture. It is the favourite food of the Andalucíans, and even the prettiest of the women here have no hesitations in swallowing every evening large spoonfuls of this infernal brew.'

In the course of the present century the long-held prejudices against oil and garlic have slowly been dropped, and the healthy properties of a cuisine heavily dependent on them have come to be widely recognized. The once much despised food of traditionally poor Mediterranean regions such as Provence is today very much in fashion, and even Spanish food is becoming increasingly popular. Nonetheless the food of Andalucía remains remarkably little known, and it is still widely looked down upon, even in Spain itself. Elsewhere in Spain Andalucía is disparagingly referred to as 'the land of the fried fish', and before moving to the region from Madrid, I was endlessly warned about how bad and unimaginative the food here

Collecting eggs and making tortillas in the Marismas of the Guadalquivir

was. The food I ate in Andalucía turned out to be one of the great revelations of this constantly surprising region.

The widespread ignorance of Andalucían food is explained to a large extent by the lack here of any long-standing tradition of eating in restaurants. Until comparatively recently the restaurants of the region catered mainly for tourists, and offered few truly local dishes. Today there are a number of outstanding Andalucían restaurants, but even so you are much more likely to encounter good food not only in people's homes, but also in bars, modest roadside inns (*ventas*) and other seemingly unpromising establishments that few tourists would think of entering. A certain spirit of adventurousness is needed to be able fully to appreciate Andalucían food. Certainly you have to adapt to what must be the most idiosyncratic of European eating habits. The Andalucíans eat later than all other Spaniards, and it is not uncommon to have lunch as late as five in the afternoon or to dine at midnight. If you do insist on eating in a restaurant at times to which you have been used elsewhere in Europe, you will probably end up in the blandest of establishments. But you must also remember that Andalucíans frequently forsake conventional meals altogether in favour of the *tapa* or bar-snack.

Andalucía is the traditional home of the tapa. In some of the region's bars, particularly in the provinces of Jaén and Granada, you will automatically be given a tapa whenever you order an alcoholic drink. In all other bars, you will almost certainly be asked if you want one, and if you answer yes, the waiter will probably recite at great speed a long list which would baffle most Spaniards. The tradition of the tapa is usually said to have developed as a result of poverty and great heat, two factors that can make impracticable the eating of a large meal. The tapa, however, also reflects a very refined attitude towards eating and drinking. It prolongs the amount of time you can drink without getting drunk, turning lunchtime or an evening into a protracted eating experience which does not leave you bloated; and it never impedes the flow of conversation. Above all it offers you an opportunity to taste an enormous variety of dishes, a variety that is the hallmark of Andalucían food. Even when sitting down to a meal, at home or in a restaurant, the Andalucíans tend to cover the table with a large selection of small dishes, all of which are shared out (the only thing which is not shared in a restaurant is the bill, which is usually magnanimously taken up by one person). With their belief in eating well but in tiny quantities at a time, the Andalucíans can perhaps claim to be more advanced in their eating habits than most other peoples. While others have traditionally regarded them as a culinary backward people, they understandably feel that most foreigners do not have the same understanding of food as they do. They are perhaps the most gastronomically conscious of all Spaniards, and it is not coincidental that Seville should have more gastronomic societies than Madrid, and that Andalucía should have produced such a food-obsessed poet as Baltasar del Alcázar (see page 111), and two of Spain's pioneering food historians, Doctor Thebussem (see page 334), and

Dioniso Pérez (known as 'Post-Thebussem'), author of the excellent *Guía del Buen Comer Español.*

That Andalucía should have such an excellent and varied cuisine should not really astonish if you pause to think of the region's traditional fame for natural abundance, its having both an Atlantic and Mediterranean coastline, the presence of the immensely fertile Guadalquivir Valley, the introduction of so many new crops and fruits by the Greeks, Romans and Moors, and the fact that Andalucía was the first European region to benefit from American imports such as the tomato and pepper. In the history of Andalucían cuisine, a particularly important role was played by the Moors. Andalucía under the Umayyads was as advanced gastronomically in relation to the rest of Europe as it was in all other cultural and scientific fields: it is worth remembering that the great Ziryab – an innovator in pastries and the man who introduced into Europe a fashion for eating according to a rational sequence of dishes – flourished in 10th-century Córdoba (see page 70-1). The Moors encouraged the Andalucíans to flavour their dishes with spices such as saffron, pounded ingredients together to create fine pastes (the basis of many Andalucían dishes of today such as gazpacho) and created a tradition of pastries and sweets. Numerous Andalucían specialities are wholly Moorish in origin, incluing *ajo blanco* (see below) and all the region's many almond and honey-based pastries and biscuits such as *alfajors* and *polvorones.* At present there is also great interest in Andalucía in the revival of Moorish food, and two of the region's most renowned restaurants both specialize in this, the Molino de Lecrín near Granada (run by the Gastronomic Society of Granada) and the Caballo Rojo in Córdoba. Among the famed dishes prepared by the latter are lamb in a honey-flavoured sauce (*cordero a la miel*), and ray with raisins (*rape Mozárabe*), two excellent examples of the Moorish love of combining sweet and savoury flavours.

The great size of Andalucía, the variety of its terrain, and the traditional isolation of many of its towns and villages, have led to a range of cuisine perhaps unrivalled in any other European region. It would be impossible to list and describe all the region's specialities, and the best way to find out about these is to make a point of visiting village bars, where there will always be someone to advise you on the characteristic tapas of the locality. In the following few pages I have given only the broadest outline of Andalucían specialities.

Gazpacho alone exists in countless variations. In its most common form it consists of a blend of tomatoes, peppers, garlic and stale bread to which olive oil and wine vinegar from Jerez have been added, the whole watered down to the required consistency. Most people make the dish today in an electric blender, but it is really at its best when the ingredients have been slowly pounded by hand in a special terracotta bowl known as a *dornillo*; either way, the dish should be eaten as soon as possible after it is made, and cooled with cubes of ice. Diced cucumber is today often served with it, as are diced peppers, tomatoes, onions, eggs, and fried croutons (a particular aberration). The dish is ideal for an Andalucían summer, and though now considered mainly as a starter, it was traditionally drunk after a meal, to refresh the palate. *Salmorejo*, a Córdoban speciality, is a dense version of gazpacho, prepared without water; *gazpacho verde* comes from Huelva Province and uses both parsley and other green herbs rather than tomatoes. *Ajo blanco*, a white gazpacho from Málaga, is especially good and one of the most Moorish of Spanish dishes: made with blanched almonds it is always served either with peeled muscatel grapes, or, less commonly, chunks of honey-dew melon.

Seafood and fish provide Andalucía with some of its greatest dishes, and are apparently consumed here in greater quantities than in any other part of Europe. The best seafood is from the Atlantic coast of Cádiz and Huelva. Sanlúcar de Barrameda is renowned throughout Spain for its prawns (*langostinos*), while Huelva is known for its shrimps (*gambas*), clams (*coquilas*), razor-shells (*navajas*), and, above all, crayfish (*cigalas*), the finest of which are the females, recognizable by their lack of a large appendage, under the head, and the presence of a delicious coral-coloured roe inside. Seafood in this western part of Andalucía is usually cooked boiled in water flavoured with oil and bay-leaves; from Málaga eastwards, there is more of a tendency to fry the seafood on a hot metal plate. *Arroz marinera* is a saffron-flavoured sea-food rice dish of soup-like consistency, made with the excellent rice from the Guadalquivir estuary (considered by many to be superior to that of Valencia).

Though the Andalucíans are sneered at for their love of frying most fish in batter, considerable skill and excellent, spanking-fresh fish are needed for successful frying. The prerequisite texture is for the fish to be crisp on the outside and succulent inside. It is ironic that the English tradition for frying fish in oil – a tradition which generally leads to the saddest, soggiest results – was probably introduced into the country by English merchants who had lived in Jerez. The English fish and chips shops of today have certainly nothing in common with Andalucía's *freidurías*, where exquisite fried fish is sold throughout the day. The fish most commonly fried in Huelva and Cádiz are *lenguados* (soles), *pijotes*, *acedías* (small soles), and *salmonetes* (red mullet); Málaga meanwhile is celebrated for its fried *boquerones victorianas* (a kind of anchovy), and *chanquetes* (whitebait), the latter described by the painter Zuloaga as 'crisp sea-spray'. *Adobo* is any white fish fried after being marinaded in wine. A selection of all these is often served in large platters in restaurants and bars.

Despite Andalucía's reputation as the 'land of the fried fish', fish is prepared here in a great variety of ways, ranging from being grilled over charcoal (this is how the *Malagueños* like to cook their delicious small sardines) to being stuffed with minced meat, tomato, parsley and bread crumbs, as in *chipirones rellenos* (stuffed squid). Three outstanding elaborate dishes are *raya al pimiento* (skate in a pimento sauce), *chocos con habas* (cuttle-fish with broad beans) and *urta a la roteña* (bream with peppers and tomatoes); the first two are specialities of Huelva, the last of Cádiz. The roe (*huevas*) of chocos and other Andalucían fish are frequently served in salads, and make a popular tapa. Mention should finally be made of the region's tunny fish (*atún*), which has been caught since at least Roman times along the coast of Barbate de la Frontera and Zahara de los Atunes. The main catches of the year (the *almadrabas*) take place in late May and early June, and are extraordinary spectacles with some of the excitement and brutality of a bull-fight, the huge fish struggling on board deck as men lance at them with long knives. Throughout the year the bars of Barbate offer an enormous variety of tunny-fish tapas, including *mojama* (dried tunny-fish) and *atún encobellado* (tunny cooked in a wine and onion-based sauce). The most sophisticated of all Andalucían tunny-fish dishes is *mechado de atún*, a speciality of the Huelva town of Isla Cristina and featuring tunny-fish minced with bacon, garlic and parsley, covered in flour and lard, and cooked in the oven with a sauce of onions, garlic, wine and herbs; it is served either hot or cold.

Few sheep or cattle are raised in Andalucía, and thus there is little tradition here for eating most meats; the idea of a large bleeding steak is at any rate anathema to the majority of Andalucíans. Pig-raising, however, is common to many parts of Andalucía, and the Andalucíans have a particular love of cured hams, as is evident from Baltasar del Alcázar's famous poem quoted on page 111. Del Alcázar specified in this work that the ham he liked most came from the Sierra de Aracena in Huelva. The Sierra village of Jabugo produces among the best hams in Spain, rivalled in fame only by those of Trevélez high up in the Alpujarras of Granada: the latter perhaps are better known abroad, but the former are the most popular in Andalucía. Granada province, however, is undoubtedly superior in its charcuterie products (*embutidos*), in particular its *chorizo* (spiced sausage), *salsichón* (salami) and *morcilla* (blood sausage). A great many of the bars and ventas of this area make their own charcuterie, including the Venta Bienvenido on the southern outskirts of Granada town, where I have enjoyed some of the cheapest and best meals I have ever had in Andalucía (see page 305). Lovers of morcilla should also make a pilgrimage to the Málaga village of Cártama, where some of the best of Spain's blood sausage is made. In bars throughout Andalucía, but particularly in those in the Seville area, large vats of *manteca* or lard are placed on the counters at breakfast time for those wishing to spread it on their *tostada* or toast; unique to the region is the *manteca colora*, which is flavoured with pimento. Another Andalucían speciality not for the faint-hearted or the calory-conscious is bull's tail (*rabo de toro*), though this is not exactly what you most care to eat after a bull-fight, nor on a hot day, as it is a very rich dish served always in a thick and heavy wine sauce (much appreciated in Córdoba). Poultry is not popular in Andalucía, but game is often served in rural bars during the hunting season; all kinds of birds are cooked in the Guadalquivir estuary village of Villafranca del Guadalquivir, while good partridge pâté from the Sierra Morena is tinned in the Jaén town of La Carolina, as game is in Villafranca.

Most Andalucían dishes are accompanied by a salad of lettuce and tomatoes, but

Hams curing in a farmhouse, Laujar de Andarax

rarely by any other greens. Vegetables are served mainly as dishes on their own, and take frequently the form of stews made with fresh vegetables and pulses. Spinach cooked with chick peas (known simply as *espinacas*) is a great favourite of western Andalucía, while in the early summer months you should try the baby asparagus from around Trigueros in Huelva (*espárragos trigueros*) which are stewed with onions, coriander and lemon juice. Broad beans cooked with little pieces of cured ham (*favas al jamón*) is common to the Granada area. *Huevos a la flamenca*, a dish now found throughout Spain, was originally from Seville, and consists at its best of eggs cooked in a terracotta dish together with pieces of cured ham and a selection of the abundant vegetables of the Guadalquivir valley, including artichokes, asparagus and peas.

The most national of Spanish dishes is the *cocido*, a stew featuring a selection of meats, pulses and fresh vegetables, the whole served as two, three or even four separate courses. The exact ingredients and way of serving cocido differ from region to region, and there are numerous variations within Andalucía alone. The main difference between the Andalucían brands of cocido and those of other parts of Spain is that the dish here always includes cauliflower and is served in no more than two courses: first come the vegetables with the cooking broth, and then the meats (usually chicken, mutton, chorizo and morcilla) which the Andalucíans tend to cut finely on their plates to form what is known as *pringá*. Cocido was the only Andalucían dish enjoyed by Disraeli, but he claimed that the vegetable medley included slices of melon, a variant found today only in Valencia. A humbler form of cocido is the *puchero*, which leaves out chorizo and morcilla and uses meat bones. The broth from a puchero, together with a sprig of mint, is dished out in great quantities in festivals, being renowned as a great pick-me-up and a cure for hang-overs.

Cheeses are always eaten as tapas rather than at the end of a meal in Andalucía. The region's cheeses – all made of goat or sheep's milk – are hardly encountered outside their village of origin, the one nationally known brand being the sheep's cheese of Pedroches, near the Córdoba town of Pozoblanco. Most Andalucíans end a meal with coffee rather than with fruit or dessert: however, a great after-meal treat in the summer months is the *chirimoya* or custard apple, grown around Motril in Granada. Pastries and sweets are traditionally eaten around Christmas and Easter only, and many of the finest specialities of this kind are unobtainable at other times of the year: if you find yourself in Seville during Holy Week you should try *torrijos*, which are slices of bread that have been steeped in white wine and honey, coated in egg yolk and then fried. Estepa near Seville is famous for its crumbly almond-based biscuits called *polvorones*; Cádiz and its neighbouring towns make a rich variant of crème caramel known as *tocinos de cielo*; the large, thin cinnamon coated *tortas* of Castilleja de la Cuesta are exported throughout Spain; and Medina Sidonia is traditionally known for its *alfajores* (pastries made of lard, honey and almonds) dating back to Moorish times. The best places to buy these all these specialities are in convents, Spanish nuns having been engaged in the making of sweet things since at least the time when St. Teresa distributed the sugar and egg-yolk *yemas* to the poor of Ávila (the outstanding yemas of Andalucía are those of the convent of San Leandro in Seville).

Lager beer, served extremely cold and often taken away from you as soon as it begins to get warm, is Andalucía's most popular drink; the main brand is Cruzcampo, which is far preferable to the Castilian Mahon or San Miguel, and is regarded by many Andalucíans as one of Europe's best beers. Andalucía's table wines are nearly all white, and hardly any of these are marketed, for instance the excellent *costa* from near Granada, and the *mosto* of Umbrete, both of which are young wines that should not be drunk more than five or six month after the grapes have been harvested. The Sanlúcar firm of Antonio Barbadillo has recently had an enormous success promoting Castillo de San Diego, a light white wine of no great character but which goes very well with all fish and sea-food.

The fame of Andalucía as a wine centre is based entirely on its fortified wines, the ones from the Jerez area being traditionally Spain's most popular wines abroad, and the ones that gave rise to the word 'sherry'. *Fino* is the dry, classic sherry, the most popular brand being Tío Pepe; *amontillado* is mellower and darker in colour, while *oloroso*, the most matured of these sherries, is the deepest in texture, and can be slightly sweet. *Manzanilla* is a wine from the sherry area which can only be made in

Bar in Granada

Sanlúcar de Barrameda, the cool sea-breezes of this town being essential to its fermenting process. This wine has a slight tang of the sea, and a reputation of tasting at its best not just in Sanlúcar itself, but in the part of the town nearest the sea; many also claim that it is less likely to leave you with a hang-over than the wines of Jerez. The other Andalucían area known for its fortified wines is Montilla in Córdoba, but these are slightly coarser in quality. Most foreigners tend to think of all these wines essentially as aperitif wines, and indeed there can be few drinks that so perfectly complement tapas : many Andalucíans can conceive of little better than to sip a glass of manzanilla while enjoying one of Sanlúcar's celebrated prawns. However, sherry, manzanilla, and Montilla are also regularly drunk here as an accompaniment to a full meal, a tradition which has yet to catch on elsewhere.

Most of Spain's renowned brandies come also from the Jerez area, among the most refined being Carlos I, Cardenal Mendoza and Gran Duque de Alba. Sweet dessert wines made in the Jerez and Montilla areas include Pedro Ximénez and Solera; but the dessert wines best known abroad are those of Málaga, which enjoyed a great vogue in England in the Victorian and Edwardian periods, and of which the finest are those of the Bodegas Scholtz. A drink manufactured in various parts of

Andalucía is *aguardiente* or anis, which can be both sweet or dry. Zalamea (Huelva), Rute (Córdoba) and Cazalla de la Sierra (Seville) are among the main places where it is made, the latter producing also an attractive cherry-flavoured drink known as *aguardiente de cereza*. Significantly all three places are in traditional mining areas, a glass of aguardiente being a necessary boost before a day's work in the mines. An early morning aguardiente will also be appreciated by those who have undergone the rigours of a characteristically Andalucían night of drinks, tapas and banter.

Romantic Andalucía

In the years 1811-12, at the height of the Peninsular War, a group of radical patriots took refuge in Cádiz and set up the Spanish Parliament or Cortes. They held their meetings in the baroque oratory of San Felipe Neri, an oval-shaped building encircled with balconies as in a theatre. When the French laid siege to the town in 1812, these patriots drew up a constitution which was to have a major impact on European politics. This document, demolishing the basis of the old monarchy, and upholding the sovereignty of the people, used the word 'liberal' for the first time in a political context, and became a model for future revolutionaries all over Europe. From the time of the Peninsular War, the attention of Europe was turned increasingly towards Spain, and in particular Andalucía, which was considered by some to be the liberal centre of the country. 'In no other part of Spain,' wrote George Dennis in 1839, 'is the liberal party stronger than in Andalucía. Whether this arrives from the great commercial intercourse with foreigners, from the vicinity of Gibraltar, or from the naturally independent spirit of the inhabitants, the fact is certain.' Foreigners tended to romanticize and oversimplify the Spanish political situation, often reducing it to a straightforward conflict between the forces of 'liberalism' and reaction. In any case those tourists who came here in growing numbers in the 19th century had usually only a superficial interest in the politics of Spain, preferring instead to dwell on the country's exotic past and traditions. The tourists who passed through Cádiz seem certainly to have given little thought to the great event which had taken place in 1812 in the Oratory of San Felipe Neri. Even the young Benjamin Disraeli had anything but politics on his mind when he visited the town in 1870. He had not even reached Seville, and yet already the sounds of opera were ringing in his ears. 'Figaro is in every street,' he enthused, 'Rosina on every balcony.'

The Romantic rapture which came to affect all travellers to Spain in the course of the 19th century developed against a background of near constant political turmoil. Since 1700 Spain had been ruled by the Bourbons, and in 1762 the Spanish and French branches of the family had signed a Family Compact whereby their two countries entered a closer alliance with each other. The ruling Spanish king was then

Charles III, under whose reign Spain at last appeared to to be enjoying again an image as a progressive nation in touch with the latest European ideas. Charles III's edict of tolerance towards the gypsies, his expulsion from Spain of the Jesuits, and his programme of land reform – which had included the establishment of the Sierra Morena colonies -were all acts fully in accordance with Enlightenment ideals. Reform ceased to be fashionable, however, after his death in 1788. His successor, Charles IV, a weak and unintelligent man, was given in a famous group portrait by Goya an appearance which has been described as that of a contented grocer. Power in Spain came largely into the hands of the king's minister Godoy, who enjoyed both the favour and the bed of the queen, María Luisa. Godoy, who failed to prevent the execution of the French king Louis XVI, compromised with the French revolutionaries, and eventually became actively involved in Napoleonic schemes. Off Cape Trafalgar, today one of the wildest and most beautiful spots on the Andalucían coast, the Spanish and French fleets came together in 1805 to attack the British, and retired shattered to Cádiz. Two years late an irate mob stormed Godoy's house at Aranjuez near Madrid. The overthrow of Godoy was followed shortly afterwards by the abdication of Charles IV, the flight of the Spanish royal family to Paris, and the arrival in Madrid of French troops under Murat, whose atrocities were later recorded in Goya's horrific *2nd of May*. One of the first deeds committed by the French on their coming to power in Spain was to suppress the country's monasteries and convents.

The events of 1808 provided a great dilemma to Spanish liberals. On the one hand they welcomed French revolutionary ideas, and on the other resented a foreign power in their land. The Seville-born writer and theologian Blanco White escaped from Madrid to Seville in 1808, and was overjoyed to hear of the French defeat at Bailén by General Castaños. However, he reported that the news was received with mixed feelings by a liberal friend of his: 'To my friend and companion, whose anti-Catholic prejudices are the main source of his mental suffering, the religious character which the revolution has assumed, is like a dense mist concealing or disfiguring even objects which otherwise would glorify his mind.' When finally the French, under Marshal Soult, succeeded in entering Seville, the local intellectuals collaborated fully with the invaders, the reformist priest and poet Lista even becoming a Freemason and journalist in the Marshal's pay.

Humiliatingly, the Spanish nationalists had to rely heavily on their country's traditional enemy, the English, to oust the French. The Peninsular War dragged on until 1814, one of the main French defeats taking place at Borrosa in Andalucía. In 1814, with English help, the Bourbon monarchy was restored in the person of Charles IV's son Ferdinand. Ferdinand VII, universally described by his contemporaries as an odious figure, agreed to abide by the 1812 Constitution, but soon repudiated it. He attempted to stifle all liberal opposition, introduced rigid censorship, and brought back both the Jesuits and the dreaded Inquisition. A revolt in

1820 led to a short period of liberal rule, which came to an end in 1823 after French troops put Ferdinand back in power. He continued to be as repressive as ever, one of his notorious deeds being to order the in 1831 of a young Granada woman called Mariana Pineda, whose crime had simply been to sew a liberal flag, and to refuse to denounce the people for whom she had made it. Transformed by a popular legend into a woman of remarkable beauty and virtue, Mariana Pineda was commemorated a few years afterwards by a statue outside her house, and she later was made the eponymous heroine of an early play by García Lorca. In the play Mariana's decision to go to the scaffold rather than to betray her ideals causes particular dismay to her lover, whom she rebukes with the following words: 'Do you love your little Mariana more than you do Liberty? Well I shall be the very Liberty which you should adore.' Other liberals of the time made comparable gestures of defiance against Ferdinand, but did so in more bungled and inglorious fashion. One of these people was the exile Torrijos, who in 1831 landed with a small force near Málaga, only to be immediately arrested. He had been accompanied by an Irish adventurer, Robert Boyd, whose execution, together with that of Torrijos, provided the British cemetery at Málaga with its first corpse. The British, still not fully recovered from their

Málaga

rage at the unchivalrous treatment of Mariana Pineda, were made virtually apoplectic by news of what had happened to Boyd. Richard Ford, however, took a different view from his compatriots: 'Certainly,' he wrote, 'if anybody of the party deserved shooting, it is a meddling *Foreigner*.'

To everyone's relief Ferdinand died in 1833, but not before ensuring that on his death the country would be plunged into chaos. Three years earlier he had married María Cristina, by whom he had had his only children, both of whom were girls. Altering a law which would have granted succession to his brother Don Carlos, he had appointed as his heir his eldest daughter Isabel. On his death María Cristina was forced to enlist the support of the liberals, and was also lent a hand by the British, again much to the disapproval of Ford. A treaty in María Cristina's favour was signed in 1839, but the confusion of Spanish political life only worsened, and continued to do so for the rest of the century. Isabel II, who had been declared of age in 1843, was forced to abdicate in 1868 following a rebellion raised in Andalucía by a group of liberals under General Prim. In 1873-4 Spain experimented with a republic, but growing anarchism in Andalucía and Catalonia brought this to an end just over a year later, by which time the Second Carlist War had broken out in the north.

It was in these latter years of the century that the great economic decline of Andalucía was consolidated, thus turning what had once been Spain's wealthiest region into one of the poorest. The loss of Spain's Latin American possessions, which had begun after 1812, had affected Andalucía more than any other Spanish region, but it had still remained relatively prosperous up to as late as 1868: what with the expansion of the region's mining industry, the development of its ports, and the continued success of traditional industries such as textiles, tobacco, olive oil and wine, Andalucía could even claim to have been one of the most industrialized parts of Spain. Growing political confusion, however, the ever greater involvement of foreign companies in the region's industries, and the emergence of the region after 1850 as one of the main monarchist centres of Spain, were all contributory factors in Andalucía's economic collapse in the late 19th century. In the 1880's a phylloxera epidemic spread from the vineyards of France, first to those of Málaga and then those of Jerez de la Frontera, sparking off in the latter town one of the most virulent of the many strikes that had repeatedly paralysed Andalucía's industries from the early 1870's onwards. Blasco Ibáñez gave an embellished account of the strike in his novel *La Bodega*, but his journalist contemporary Leopoldo Alas had actually been present at the strike, and had described the way in which the protesters, in their fury, had lashed out at anyone who wore glasses and was well dressed. This was certainly a different rural world from the bucolic one of the early years of the century as evoked nostalgically by Alarcón in his novella *The Three-Cornered Hat* (1874).

Misery and backwardness were among the features that made the country picturesque for the Romantic traveller. Previously they had deterred many from coming here. Until the late 18th century Spain had not in fact been a country particularly popular with tourists: most of those who had visited and written about the place had been merchants, diplomats or politicians. In the mid-18th century Voltaire was writing that 'Spain is a country which we know no better than the wildest parts of Africa and which does not merit being better known.' Charles III's enlightened policies helped change European attitudes towards Spain, and encouraged in the last years of the century a sudden rise in tourism, as is made evident by the appearance of numerous detailed travel books about the country, such as those by Jacob Twiss, Peyron, Swinburne, Townsend and the Baron de Bourgoing. Many of these travellers commented with admiration on such aspects of modern Spain as the excellent new road between Madrid and Seville, and the Sierra Morena colonies. A new, cheerful and optimistic image of Spain began to emerge, and Andalucía was the part of the country which most lived up to this image. The Spain of morbid gloom and inflexible moral codes gave way to a country much more in keeping with the free-thinking spirit of the Enlightenment, a country of great gaiety and sensuality, where everyone endlessly courted, and indulged in such exuberant and provocative dances as the bolero and the fandango. The popularity of this new Spain was mirrored and furthered by the success of Beaumarchais' two plays, *The Barber of Seville*, and *The Marriage of Figaro*. Beaumarchais had not even been to Spain, let alone Seville, and neither had Rossini or Mozart, who set these plays to music.

The Peninsular War, though hardly strengthening the lively carefree image of Spain, made more people aware of the country than ever before. Accounts of Spain written by foreign soldiers who had been involved in the war proliferated, heightening people's curiosity about the place, as well as fuelling many British readers with a desire to visit the sites where their compatriots had excelled: Dundas Murray was not alone among British travellers in touring battle sites such as that of Borrosa armed with a copy of Napier's *History of the Peninsular War*. In the years following the war, knowledge of and enthusiasm for Spain were further increased by the large numbers of Spanish political exiles, most of whom took refuge in England: an especially large community of Spanish exiles grew up in the London district of Somers Town. Among the Spanish liberals resident in Britain was Blanco White, who had left Spain in 1810, subsequently dropping his Spanish name of José María Blanco y Crespo. A man of Irish parentage, he had been brought up as a Catholic in Seville, but had become disillusioned with the church's teachings around 1800: after converting to Anglicanism in England, he ended up as a Unitarian. His *Letters from Spain* of 1822 are full of vivid details of Andalucían life in the early years of the century, and were much read by the English. With a critical eye, a loathing of Spanish fanaticism and superstition, and a belief in the essential superiority of British over Spanish culture, he described at length such popular aspects of Andalucían life as bull-fighting and the Seville Holy Week. Of a particular event from the latter he wrote: 'I have carefully glided over such parts of this absurd performance as would shock many an English reader even in narrative. Yet such is the strange mixture of superstition and profaneness in the people.' Blanco White succeeded in informing and fascinating the English, and also confirmed many of their prejudices about the Spaniards.

For all the interest that the Peninsular War generated, it was not until the end of the 1820's that tourists started visiting Spain in significant numbers. They had allowed a sufficient amount of time to pass for the country to recover somewhat from its ruined state, but not so much time as to prevent them from benefiting from its impoverishment: one of the new incentives of a journey to Spain was the realization that there were countless works of art to be had for the smallest sums of money. Between 1829 and 1850, there was published a great range of travellers' accounts of Spain, including four of the most successful ever written, Washington Irving's *Tales of the Alhambra*, George Borrow's *A Bible in Spain*, Richard Ford's *A Handbook for Spain* and Théophile Gautier's *Voyage en Espagne*. The majority of the travellers were either British or French, not surprisingly given their countries' vested interests in Spain. A genuine adventurous spirit was still required of this generation of travellers to Spain, even though they generally much exaggerated their bravery with constant tales of bad roads and banditry. The appearance of Ford's *Handbook*, the greater safety of travellers ensured by the Guardia Civil, founded in 1848, and the spread of the Spanish railway network after the 1850's, made journeys through Spain increasingly easy for foreigners, so much so that in 1887 Disraeli's nephew, recollecting his uncle's trip in the 1830's, could write that 'in these days of easy travel the whole of this foreign tour reads almost like a romance.' In the second half of the century, there was no falling off in the number of travel books on Spain, though there was in their quality. The observations of Spanish life seem second-hand, and the attempts to stir the reader's interest with evocations of adventure and romance have an increasingly hollow ring. Spain had changed considerably since the 1830's and 40's, but attitudes towards the country remained those that had been formulated in that earlier period. Some of these attitudes are still held today.

Andalucía continued to represent for Romantic travellers all that was most typical of Spain. But these travellers saw the region in a markedly different way from their predecessors. It was still a region of all-embracing sensuality, but this sensuality had lost some of its innocence; a mood of cheerful flirtatiousness had developed into one of dangerous passion. The region's Moorish past, which had interested 18th-century travellers in an essentially archaeological way, now became a reflection of this sensuality, a consuming obsession, an ideal of civilization, and, not least, an excuse for British travellers to air their anti-Catholic prejudices. Whereas earlier travel writers gave equal emphasis to the modern and traditional aspects of Andalucía, Romantic writers were far less impartial, and reserved their enthusiasm for those aspects of the region that for them made the place exotic and remote from

In the monastery, *by J. F. Lewis*

the rest of Europe. Richard Ford was thinking above all of Andalucía when he described going to Spain as 'flying from the dull uniformity, the polished uniformity of Europe, to the racy freshness of that original, unchanged and unchangeable country'.

A striking feature of Romantic attitudes towards Spain is that travellers often criticized the place for the same reasons that they found it so exciting. They loved Spain for being 'unchanged and unchangeable' to the extent that they greatly exaggerated its backwardness; and yet they complained much of the time about poor inns, bureaucratic inefficiency, the laziness of the inhabitants, the lack of modern comforts and so on. They were stimulated by the sensual atmosphere of Andalucía, but frequently censured the women for the looseness of their morals. They were fascinated by the spectacular religious processions and other manifestations of religious fanaticism in the region, the painter David Roberts going apparently out of his way to put monks and priests into his Andalucían views. Yet they generally loathed the clergy and found excuses to criticize priests wherever possible: William Jacob even wrote that the pretty women of Andalucía were rarely to be seen in the streets because they were always being entertained in priests' houses. No visit to Spain, above all to Andalucía, could be made without going to a bull-fight. But few bull-fights could be seen without some reference either to the barbarity of the sport or the sadism of the spectators.

British travellers – the most adventurous and visible of the foreign visitors to Spain – often prided themselves on their adaptability to Spanish manners. Richard Ford took to wearing traditional Spanish costumes, and thought that this was sufficient to hide his nationality and thus make him less of a prey to bandits. Clearly he loved the charade of trying to appear Spanish, as did many of the British travellers who later imitated his example. When Gautier went to a tailor's in Granada in 1845, he was told that the only people to buy such costumes were the English. The Spaniards' belief in the eccentricity of the English was constantly being confirmed. Dundas Murray had only to propose going on foot from Cádiz to Sanlúcar for a Spaniard to mutter 'mad Englishmen'; but, as Murray observed, 'in this quarter of the world Englishmen have the reputation of doing all sorts of odd things.' Ford wrote shortly after settling with his family in Seville that 'the natives are interested and surprised at all our proceedings, and verily believe we have arrived from the moon.' Considering that the English had been the traditional enemies of the Spaniards since the time of Philip II, the fact that the Spaniards regarded them at worst with bewildered amusement, and rarely in any hostile way, is remarkable. On the other hand the English were almost without exception patronising towards the Spaniards, and convinced of their own superiority. These feelings usually rose to the surface the moment the British traveller entered Gibraltar. 'On again setting foot on British ground,' wrote George Dennis in 1839, 'to that thrill of delight which can

. . .and also procured a swell sombrero, *literally the* nobbiest *of hats, after an innocent pantomimic flirtation with a captivating little shopwoman...*
A. C. Andros, A Scamper in Spain, *1860*

only be experienced on passing immediately from a strange land to one's native soil, I felt added pride, when with the neglected fortifications and squalid troops at the Spanish barrier fresh in my memory, I looked round on the clean, well-accoutred soldiery ... Freedom in England, has brought knowledge, enterprise, wealth, power, in its train. Despotism, religious and political, has rendered Spain ignorant, superstitious, slothful, poor and impotent.' A. C. Andros put all this more succinctly in the concluding line of his own book of Spanish travels: 'Thank God! I am an Englishman!'

Few of the British 19th-century travellers had actually much close contact with the Spaniards, and most of them were greatly dependent on the help and companionship of compatriots of theirs already resident in Spain. In Granada British visitors were often looked after in the first half of the century by General O'Lawlor, the Lieutenant-Governor of the province, and the man appointed by the Duke of Wellington to supervise the running of the vast estate nearby which the Duke had been awarded after the Peninsular War. Elsewhere in Andalucía the British could expect considerable hospitality from their consuls at Cádiz, Seville and Málaga. Brackenbury held the post at Cádiz during the 1830's and 40's; Julian Williams ('Don Julian') was consul at Seville during this time, and was later succeeded by his son Manuel; for most of the century the consulate at Málaga was run by members of the Mark family, beginning with William Mark. Brackenbury, Julian Williams and William Mark had all taken on the poorly paid job of consuls after having fallen in love with Andalucía in the course of working there as merchants. They were knowledgeable about the area and had amassed important collections of works of art, antiques, and curios. The arrival of British travellers offered a welcome opportunity to share their knowledge and enthusiasm and to show their collections to people who, they believed, knew how to appreciate them.

Cádiz, Gibraltar, Málaga, Seville and Granada were the main centres around which the Romantic traveller's tour of Andalucía was usually based. Córdoba was visited quickly, being generally considered, in the words of Borrow, 'a mean, dark, gloomy place'; nor did it have any important foreign residents to take care of the visitor. Otherwise the traveller's attitude towards the Andalucían interior was very similar to that of today's tourist. Then, as now, travellers tended to visit few of the out-of-way towns and villages, and generally hurried between one main centre and the other. The one part of the countryside which many people made a special detour to go and see was the Serranía de Ronda, which was as popular then with the British as it is today. It was an area which managed to be conveniently near to Gibraltar while its savage aspect, notorious roads, and fame as a bandit centre satisfied to the full the traveller's love of adventure. Describing a journey there in 1810, William Jacob wrote: 'It has not been unattended with fatigues, privations, and even dangers; but the scenes through which I have passed, the character of the people I have seen, and especially the bold features of the most picturesque country in

Europe, will afford recollections which I shall dwell upon with pleasure through the remainder of my life.' Ronda itself, with its spectacular cliff-top situation, and deep gorge cleaving the town in two, was the archetypal Romantic site. Owing to its isolated and wild situation Ronda was not thought at first to be a suitable place for the woman traveller, but in the second half of the century a belief in the beneficial qualities of its mountain air led to the town gaining some of the character of a genteel health resort.

Though the Andalucían coast was not to be extensively developed until this century, the town of Málaga enjoyed an ever growing popularity from the 1830's onwards, and by 1850 had become a thriving winter resort for the British. Its consul, William Mark, who described the town as a 'Second Paradise', did much to encourage the British to come here. He was also able to allay British travellers' fears of dying on Spanish soil by founding at Málaga, in 1830, Spain's first British cemetery. Up to then Protestant visitors to this country had been treated at death like infidels, and in Málaga had been buried on the beach in a standing position. The locals had vague ideas about Protestantism, and were surprised by the cross which was put up at the entrance of the British cemetery: they did not know that 'these Jews' worshipped the same symbol as they did. The cemetery became an obsession of Mark's, and he spent much of his life prettifying it. He had to wait a long time for its first corpse, and, as Ford cruelly suggested, he might even have been secretly pleased by the execution in Málaga in 1831 of Torrijos' Protestant companion Don Boyd: 'In heart,' Ford wrote in a letter, 'I believe he was as glad as a young surgeon to get a subject for his new churchyard. He has certainly a hankering after my wife's body, not her live body, but, hearing of her ill health, tried all in his power to get me to Málaga to have a pretty female specimen in his sepulchral museum.' When, shortly afterwards a child of Ford's died and was buried in an orange grove at Seville, Ford doubted whether Mark would ever forgive him. However, it was not to be long before the cemetery began filling with the corpses of the British invalids who had come to Málaga to try and recover their health. As Málaga developed into a wintering resort (Augustus Hare wondered why so many invalids came here, as the place was thick with dust), the town acquired an elegant promenade with numerous trees planted by Mark. The cemetery meanwhile was further embellished by Mark's son and became quite a tourist attraction. Hans Christian Andersen, one of its many admirers, wrote that he could 'well understand how a splenetic Englishman might take his own life in order to be buried in this place'. Its former sea views have today been blocked by extensive modern development, but the cemetery is still a place of evocative charm, and much visited by an old-fashioned type of English tourist.

Granada and Seville were the foremost Andalucían destinations of the Romantic traveller, the former being praised above all for its monuments, the latter for its paintings and colourful life. Travellers to Granada would take a look at the Royal

Inside the Tower, Alhambra, by J. F. Lewis

Chapel in the lower town, and the more adventurous of them would go to the gypsy quarters of the Sacromonte and the Albaicín. But their time would be largely taken up in the Alhambra, which Ford called 'that magical word which in the minds of Englishmen is the sum and substance of Granada'. Both the Alhambra, and the adjoining gardens of the Generalife (an essential part of any Alhambra tour) had been left to decay ever since the late 16th century, and remained in a piteous state for much of the 19th century. Into the vast precinct of the Alhambra had moved a considerable population of gypsies, and other impoverished people, while the palace itself had served as a military hospital and as a prison both for debtors and galley slaves. After 1798 the palace had suffered further damage by being turned into an official residence of the Governor of Granada, who used much of the woodwork for fires, and allowed farm animals to run around the halls. During the Peninsular War, the French invaders kept soldiers, prisoners, stolen goods, and dynamite here, and, as a parting gesture, blew up eight of the Alhambra's Moorish towers. In 1810 William Jacob had predicted that 'without repair, to which the finances of Spain are inadequate, it will in a few years be a pile of ruins; its voluptuous apartments, its stately columns, and its lofty walls, will be mingled together, and no memorial be left in Spain of a people who once governed the peninsula.' Its ruined state, though causing alarm, undoubtedly contributed to its appeal for the Romantic travellers who started flocking here from the late 1820's onwards. Ford, in his magnificent descriptions of the Alhambra, relished the effects of bathos achieved through evoking one moment the sublime beauty of the place and then going on to observe such details of its decline as the sight of a group of galley slaves converting part of the building into a storehouse for salt fish. He was there in 1831 and 1833, and at that time the Governor of Granada employed a peasant woman called Francisca de Molina to look after the palace with the help of her two nieces. 'Tía Antonia', as she was called, made among the first tentative attempts to 'restore' the palace by clearing away the accumulated debris of centuries and by setting on their legs the famous lions of the Lions' Courtyard. Other, more important restoration campaigns were subsequently carried out, but Spain's constant political troubles in the 19th century led to equally numerous interruptions. Only after 1870, when the Alhambra was declared a National Monument, was the future of the place finally safeguarded.

The Alhambra has always been regarded as one of the great wonders of the world, but in the 17th and 18th centuries many travellers were content simply to repeat the praise of others, and did not see the place for themselves. The Valencian writer Antonio Ponz, the author of the most detailed topographical account of Spain published in the 18th century, went to every part of Spain except Granada, as did the similarly meticulous French travel writer, the Baron de Bourgoing. The French were in fact notoriously lax about visiting Granada, and several of the 18th-century accounts of the Alhambra are copied from other works. Characteristically it was the British who pioneered tourism to Granada in the 18th century. One of the few

French writers to go there himself, Peyron, found in one of the Alhambra's rooms grafitti by the English writer Henry Swinburne. Swinburne and his companion Thomas Gascoigne had inscribed their names, a short poem and the date 'January, 1775'. Another Frenchman, Nicolas Masiari, staying in Granada as a prisoner in 1792, wrote that 'the town and province of Granada are more famous than they are known. The English come to see the place, to say that they have seen it, then rush away after having grabbed some of the stones from the palace of the Moorish kings, without even being stopped by the Spaniards, who merely register surprise that anyone should have come such a long way to look at stones.'

At this early date, the Moorish remains of the Alhambra were not the exclusive concern of travellers, the renaissance Palace of Charles V apparently being an equal source of wonder. William Jacob was lavish in his praise of this palace, and in his *Travels to the South of Spain* of 1811 there appears an engraving in which the building dominates the Alhambra as it never does in views by later artists. With the fashion for orientalism which was soon to develop, Charles V's renaissance addition was to be largely ignored. One of the great instigators of the new fashion was Chateaubriand, who came to the Alhambra in 1807, recording his visit with a signature in the gallery above the Court of Lions. 'It is,' he wrote of the Alhambra,'one of those building from the Thousand and One Nights, that one sees less in reality than in dream.' By 1826, when he published his Moorish romance set in 16th-century Spain and called *The Last of the Abencerages*, memories of the Alhambra had indeed ceased to bear much resemblance to a real place. The enormous success of

Tourists in the Alhambra, by Gustave Doré

Washington Irving

this book was soon rivalled by that of Victor Hugo's epic poem *Les Orientales* (1829), which turned orientalism from a fashion into a mania, and featured a beautiful evocation of the Alhambra, a place that Hugo had never seen. Two years earlier a little known English draughtsman, T. H. S. Estcourt, had published the first major series of engravings of the Alhambra, thus enabling the European public to have a much clearer idea of what the place actually looked like. Over the next few years many other engraved views of Granada were to appear, the most influential of which being those of David Roberts: as in his other Andalucían works, Roberts greatly exaggerated the proportions of both the buildings and the surrounding mountains, and in so doing enhanced the fairy-tale aspect of the place. But the man who did most to influence foreign attitudes towards the Alhambra, and to fire travellers with an enthusiasm for seeing it, was a young American diplomat who arrived in Granada the same year that Hugo's *Les Orientales* was published.

Washington Irving, born in New York in 1783 of an English father, first came to Spain in 1826 to work for the American Legation in Madrid. He had already earned a certain reputation as a writer, but in Madrid he dedicated himself to his first major work of scholarship, a biography of Columbus. His energy was prodigious, and when writing his biography he was known to rise sometimes as early as two o'clock in the morning, a time when most people in Madrid today have usually not gone to bed. With a view both to completing this work, and to researching another on the conquest of Granada, he set off to Seville in March 1828. His travelling companion was a German called Stoffenegen, who 'having never before been so far to the south' was 'in continual transport with the luxurious indications of a southern climate'.

Irving remained based in Seville for over a year, spending much of his time in the archives, and also going on a long excursion to the sites near Huelva associated with Columbus such as the Monastery of La Rábida. In Seville he spent much time with the Scottish painter David Wilkie, whom he had first met in Madrid, and who was one of the most important of the Romantic artists to tour Spain. Irving was later to dedicate his famous book on the Alhambra to Wilkie, and in his preface to this was to recall how the two of them, in Seville together, 'were more than once struck with scenes and incidents in the street, which reminded us of passages in the Arabian Nights'.

In April 1829, Irving moved on to Granada, in the company of a Russian prince, Prince Dolorouki, Secretary to the Russian Legation. Over a month later Irving was writing to a friend to say how he and the prince were '*royally* quartered', the governor of Granada having offered them the use of his rooms in the Alhambra. 'Here, then,' Irving continued, 'I am nestled in one of the most remarkable, romantic and delicious spots in the world. I breakfast in the Saloon of the Ambassadors, among the flowers and fountains in the Court of Lions, and when I am not occupied with my pen I lounge with my book about these oriental apartments, or stroll about the courts, and gardens, and arcades, by day or night, with no one to interrupt me. It absolutely appears to me like a dream, or as if I am spell-bound in some fairy palace.' He and his Russian friend had virtually the palace to themselves, among the only other occupants being the Governor's house-keeper Tía Antonia, and her two nieces. Tía Antonia, whom Irving described as a 'woman of strong and intelligent, though uncultivated mind', looked after the two guests with enormous devotion. When Prince Dolorouki eventually left, Tía Antonia was most critical of Irving's decision to change apartments and to move into a remoter and more isolated part of the palace: she feared that he would be too vulnerable there to the many criminals and people of bad character who lived within the Alhambra precinct. Irving, however, was too enchanted by his new surroundings to worry much about personal safety. These rooms, adjoining the gallery where Chateaubriand had signed his name, now form a small Irving museum, which can only be visited by special permission (see page 300). After jostling with the crowds of tourists that daily throng the Alhambra, a visit to this museum affords a pleasant respite. It consists of a suite of four small rooms, which differ from all other parts of the palace not only by their silence, but also by their sombre, murky and neglected character: suddenly you have an inkling of what the Alhambra must have been like in Irving's day. In these sparsely furnished rooms, dating back to the 16th century but thoroughly 19th century in character, you will find the only furniture still left in the palace, including Irving's bed and writing-desk. The sitting-room juts out above the verdant northern slopes of the Alhambra hill, and from its window the writer's eyes must often have wandered over the rising line of fortifications up to the hanging gardens of the Generalife. While staying here, Irving completed his *Conquest of Granada* and began work on the book by which he is best known in Spain today, *The Alhambra: A Series of Tales*. In this book, today on sale in various languages throughout Andalucía, Irving combined romantic tales of the Alhambra's history with descriptions of the place and of the memorable personalities whom he got to know there such as Tía Antonia. Fact and fantasy were intermingled in the book, as they have generally been in the minds of the thousands of tourists who have come to the Alhambra in Irving's footsteps.

Summoned to work at the American legation in London, Irving left the Alhambra on July 29th, 'after having passed between two or three months in a kind of oriental dream'. Two years after his departure, Richard Ford arrived with his family and English servants in Granada, and was also offered the possibility of staying in the Alhambra. The place was described to him as being in such a poor state that at first he was reluctant to take this up. '. . .as my children and English servants,' Ford wrote in a letter to his friend Addington, 'have no taste for the Moorish picturesque, but a great notion of the more humble gratifications proceeding from a comfortable home and well-appointed kitchen, I am rather inclined to put up with the unromantic reality of some good ready-furnished house.' In the end, however, practical considerations were outweighed by romantic feelings, though not before Ford had arranged for carpenters and decorators thoroughly to overhaul the rooms where he and his entourage were to be put up. This was the part of the palace where Tía Antonia and her nieces lived, and they treated Ford no less well than they had Irving. Ford was a more restless traveller however, and while staying at the Alhambra toured Granada and its surroundings rather more extensively than Irving appears to have done: he even made the arduous ascent up to the peak of Pico Veleta, accompanied by his wife, who thus became the first woman to do the climb. But, like Irving, he found the surroundings of the Alhambra to be so congenial that he took relatively little part in the life of the town below. Later travellers would nearly all try and stay on the Alhambra hill, and though the actual palace was soon to be no longer available to them as a residence, various hotels were to be built on the hill, including the Hotel Washington Irving, described in 1870 as 'the most comfortable hotel in Spain'. Visitors to Granada in the 19th century stayed in their ivory towers, ignoring as best they could the real world at their feet.

Of the French Romantic travellers to write about Granada, the most influential after Chateaubriand was unquestionably Théophile Gautier. Born in 1811 in Gascony near the Spanish border, Gautier was always to pride himself on having a southern temperament and even Spanish looks. In Paris in 1829, he studied to be a painter, but changed his vocation to writing after reading Hugo's *Orientales* and meeting the great man himself. Soon afterwards he started going around Paris dressed in Egyptian costume. By the end of 1839 he was beginning to tire of Paris, and toyed with the idea of visiting Turkey. A wealthy friend of his, Eugène Piot, suggested that they should go instead to Spain. Piot's motives for wanting to go

Théophile Gautier

there were not wholly romantic ones, for he pointed out to Gautier that as Spain had been impoverished by the Carlist War, antiques and works of art would be cheap to buy. They set off for Spain in May 1840, arriving in Madrid in June; by July 1st they were in Granada, and remained there until August 12th. They stayed in the lower town, and, unusually, did not have any regrets in doing so. Gautier was one of the first and last writers to describe Granada as a town of great gaiety and animation. Most people have usually commented on how dull the place is socially, but Gautier was in elated spirits, and was seeing everything through rose-tinted spectacles. He had found Madrid grim and provincial, but had started to become excited the moment he had crossed the Sierra Morena and entered Andalucía. Granada was his first taste of an Andalucían town, and it was the place in Spain which was to make the greatest impression on him: he dreamt one day of building a reproduction of the Court of Lions in his Paris garden.

After Granada, Gautier was able quickly to finish off the rest of Andalucía: three days were adequate for Málaga, two for Córdoba, and a week each for Seville and Cádiz; he was back in France by the beginning of October, his return having been delayed by an enforced stay in Valencia. On the basis of what had been little more than a four and a half-month stay in Spain, Gautier wrote his best-selling *Voyage en Espagne* (1841). It is a book with many fresh and humorous observations, and is admirable for its open-minded attitude towards such reviled aspects of Spanish culture as food and baroque architecture. Yet at other times Gautier merely repeated by now hackneyed Romantic responses to Spain, and he too often uses as his visual point of reference the orientalist canvases of fashionable contemporary painters such as Delacroix and Decamps. Mario Praz, in his *Unromantic Spain*, put much of the blame on Gautier for 'faking a mannered Spain' which was later to be 'consecrated in the lyric prose style of Thos. Cook & Son Ltd'.

Descriptions of the Alhambra after Gautier became ever more delirious and tedious. The French painter, Henri Regnault, visiting the place in 1869, was so overwhelmed that he was totally unable to do any sketching for several days. He concluded that the civilization of the Spanish Moors was infinitely superior to that of the West, and heavily criticized Charles V for having built within the Alhambra 'a horrible, enormous block'. Among the most purple passages inspired by the Alhambra were those by the once highly revered Italian author, Edmondo de Amicis, author of the sentimental novel *Cuore*. De Amicis, putting forward the oft-repeated idea that the architecture of the Alhambra is an expression not of power but of love and voluptuousness, wrote: 'There is thus a strong link, a harmony between the beauty of this Alhambra and the souls of those who have been love at sixteen, when desires are dreams and visions.'

In view of Granada's development from the late 19th century onwards into a pretentious and ugly modern town, the oriental ecstasies that the Alhambra continued to provoke came to seem increasingly anachronistic. The magical name 'Alhambra' had by now been appropriated by theatres, cinemas and night-clubs throughout Europe, and the architecture of the place had been parodied in countless hotels and vulgar wealthy villas; even a sewage works in London's Wapping was given an Alhambra-inspired interior. It was left to Praz brilliantly to deflate the whole tradition of Romantic attitudes towards the Alhambra:

> Reader, I did not take up my abode between the magic walls of the Alhambra for four days and and as many nights, with the tacit consent of the authorities, neither did I dwell there for several months attended by houris and escorted by valets descended from the Moorish kings. . . None of the bits of luck which fell to the lot of Washington Irving and Théophile Gautier was repeated for me. My mind was not haunted by any of the many delicious follies, pleasant whim-whams, and gentle absurdities that the tearful Edmondo de Amicis claims to have thought and uttered between the Court of the Myrtles and the Court of the Lions. While visiting the Alhambra I did not tremble like an aspen leaf; while leaving it I did not tremble like an aspen leaf; while leaving it I did not bid farewell to all the illusions of youth and to that love which will never live again.

Seville's appeal for the Romantic traveller was altogether different from that of Granada. In the first half of the century, the town could boast Moorish monuments such as the Giralda and the Alcázar that were in a far better state of preservation than the Alhambra; moreover, the cathedral here was far more admired than

Granada's, and indeed was considered one of the finest in Spain. But the sightseer was drawn to Seville less for its architecture than for its 17th-century paintings. Murillo was still regarded as one of the greatest artists of all time, Velázquez was enjoying ever-greater popularity, Alonso Cano was far more widely appreciated than he is today, and Zurbarán had suddenly come into fashion after over a century and a half of neglect. Under these circumstances, Seville came to be thought of as one of the great art centres of Europe, as William Jacob wrote in 1811: 'Few places in Europe, with the exception of London or Paris, contain so many good pictures as are to be found in this city.'

Not content merely to look at these pictures, travellers made every effort to acquire them, and could do so at first with remarkable ease and minimum expenditure. Marshal Soult, occupying Seville at the time when its religious foundations were particularly vulnerable, began the collecting trend by ruthlessly requisitioning paintings; by the 1830's the Seville art market was as thriving as Venice's had been in the previous century. Two of the main collectors were the consul Julian Williams, and a British businessman resident in Seville, Hall Standish. The former, who owned a renowned group of Murillos, was described by Irving as a 'man of great taste' and by Disraeli as 'the greatest connoisseur of paintings in Spain': it was under his influence and that of the Cádiz consul Brackenbury, that Ford himself became a considerable collector, acquiring among other works a magnificent Zurbarán of *The Martyrdom of St. Serapion* (now in Dumbarton Oaks). Hall Standish, referred to by Ford as 'Maecenas Standish', was much more than a collector, being additionally a celebrated dandy, and the author of a biography of Voltaire: 'He is,' wrote Disraeli, 'a most singular character – a spoiled child of fortune, who thinks himself, and who is perhaps now, a sort of philosopher.' His collection, comprising both a wide range of Spanish old masters and numerous contemporary Seville works, was later to be offered by him to the British Government in return for his receiving a baronetcy. The offer was turned down, and the collection ended up in 1841 in the famous Spanish Gallery founded by Louis-Philippe in Paris.

Louis-Philippe, a passionate enthusiast of Spanish art, had sent to Spain in 1835 a colourful personality called Baron Taylor to amass works of art for him. Baron Taylor, a Belgian-born soldier who had travelled extensively around Europe, spent two years in Spain, based much of the time in Seville. His mission was an enormous success, and when the Spanish Gallery was opened to the public in the Louvre in 1838 it caused a sensation, inspiring a fashion for all things Spanish. By this time, however, the people of Seville had begun to show concern at their rapidly disappearing heritage. Following the further suppression of monasteries and convents in 1836, Dean Manuel López Cepero tried to save as many works of art for the city as he could, and he made these the nucleus of Seville's Museo de Bellas Artes, which was established in the former monastery of La Merced. Without the intervention of López Cepero, Seville's reputation as an artistic centre would have been greatly diminished, and the town would not have had an art gallery rivalled in Spain only by the Prado.

Fortunately Seville was not just treated as a repository of potentially lucrative objects. Travellers loved coming here for its people, social life, and festivities, generally regarded as the most lively and exotic in the whole of Spain. Colourfully dressed women and majos paraded the streets, the sounds of singing and dancing were constantly being heard, and any excuse seemed sufficient for organizing an exuberant religious procession. The town's theatrical life was and still is notoriously bad, but in compensation the streets provided a constant human spectacle, and the whole place seemed to many like a living opera: 19th-century travellers were finding on every corner Figaro, Don Giovanni, and Carmen. One of the greatest promoters of Seville's charms was Richard Ford, who was also one of the few people to write perceptively about its people, with their caustic humour, refusal to be hurried, and wild outbursts of child-like enthusiasm. Describing Granada, Ford wrote that 'to those who arrive from Seville, the inhabitants do not look either so well dressed, gay or intelligent. There are fewer majos, and the women are inferior walkers and talkers.' Ford had a passion for the Alhambra, but Seville was his favourite Spanish town, and it was here that he had decided to base himself when he first came to Spain in 1830.

The son of a minor politician and an amateur painter, Ford was born in London in 1796. He studied for the law, but never practised, and in 1824 married Harriet Capel, the pretty daughter of George, 5th Earl of Essex. Harriet was always in delicate health, and Ford thought that a stay in a southern climate would do her good. Most people in his position would have chosen to have gone to the French Riviera or Italy, but Ford, eccentrically, settled on Andalucía, a region which was still considered too wild to be wholly suitable for aristocrats travelling with their families, and especially not for ailing women. Ford's interest in visiting Spain might have developed through his friendship both with the Duke of Wellington, and with the then British Envoy Extraordinary at Madrid, Henry Unwin Addington, whom Ford had known since schooldays; he had also been much enthused by a talk on Granada given by Irving in London in 1829.

Ford and his family and servants, including a nanny called Oggy, arrived in Seville in October 1830, and rented a house belonging to Hall Standish; they were to spend three consecutive winters in Seville, moving in their second year into a large 16th-century palace, the Palacio Monsalves. Ford had a letter of introduction from the Duke of Wellington to a leading Seville family, and with his evidently engaging manner was popular with most Spaniards. At the Palacio Monsalves, he put on balls that were well attended by the local nobility, in particular one which was held in honour of the daughter of 'Míster Mark' of Málaga. The Seville painter José Bécquer did a portrait of Ford wearing the majo costume of which he was so proud; another local artist, José Gutierrez depicted him and his wife as

Richard Ford dressed as a majo

17th-century Spanish grandees. More than most other British travellers of his generation, Ford tried to immerse himself in Spanish life, and is still remembered in Seville as one of the few foreigners to be accepted by the outwardly open though at heart closed society of this town. Nonetheless Ford's social life still revolved largely around the town's foreign community, a community which always looked forward to the arrival of visitors from abroad. Among those who came to see Ford in Seville were the collector Sir William Eden, and the artist J. F. Lewis, for whom Ford was to arrange an introduction to the bandit king José María (see page 25). To his regret, Ford was away from Seville when the French painter Delacroix passed by on his way to Morocco; Delacroix profited from his absence by openly flirting with Harriet. Ford at the time was on a lengthy and arduous sketching trip to Extremadura, one of several such excursions that he made from Seville. Like many of his compatriots, Ford had a passion for sketching, an activity he described as being as incomprehensible to the Spaniards as reading. Outside Seville and Granada sketching was met not simply with bewilderment but with deep suspicion, and was liable to have its perpetrator landed in gaol on charges of spying. Ford was much braver, more inquisitive and persistent than most other sketchers, and as a result came to know the Spanish towns and countryside more intimately than nearly all his compatriots. But it was not until many years after leaving Spain that he was to put this knowledge to any great use.

Shortly before the outbreak of the First Carlist War, Ford, worried by the worsening political situation in Spain, decided to return with his family to England. Furthermore Harriet and he had been having a difficult time together during the previous months, exacerbated no doubt by the growing isolation which she had experienced in the course of her husband's long absences fom Seville. When they reached England in October 1823, they separated, he moving to Exeter, she staying in London, where she died four years later. Ford bought a house in the country, Heavitree House, and refurbished it enthusiastically, indulging in the occasional Spanish touch: he decorated one of its towers with 'Arabesque lienzo' and confessed to Addington that the end result was 'prettier than the Puerta del Vino of the Alhambra'. Though he was never to return to Spain, Ford kept himself well informed about everything that happened there, and read all that he could on the country. In 1839 the publisher John Murray approached him for advice as to who should write the volume on Spain in the popular guide book series known as *Murray's Handbooks*. Under the influence of wine and a good dinner, Ford proposed himself, and soon found that he had taken on far more than he had bargained for. For the next five years he remained largely tied to his desk, dressed in a Spanish jacket of black sheepskin, and surrounded by growing piles of manuscripts and books. A very sociable person with a love of the good life, Ford did not have the makings of a scholarly recluse, and in the end was thoroughly bored by the whole project. After withdrawing the first edition at great expense to incorporate changes suggested by Addington, the *Handbook* finally appeared in 1845. Despite being a two-volumed work densely printed in double columns, it was an immediate success, and the long introductory section was soon afterwards reprinted separately as *Gatherings from Spain*, a work intended mainly for the arm-chair traveller; the *Handbook* itself was reissued numerous times in the 19th century, though the only popular edition now available is in Spanish.

By making the section on Andalucía the first and largest part of the *Handbook*, Ford greatly strengthened the misleading view that Andalucía is the quintessential Spanish region; he also shared and reinforced several other British prejudices about Spain, such as hatred for baroque sculpture and architecture. These cavils apart, the *Handbook* remains without doubt the best general introduction to Spain ever written, and one of the liveliest and most informative guide-books to have appeared on any country. Partly because of its healthy mixture of enthusiasm and down-to-earth observation, it conveys the feel of the country far more acutely than do the sentimental, high-flown ramblings of most travel writers on Spain; that it was written in England and so long after its author had left the country makes the achievement even more remarkable. His prodigious scholarship is worn lightly, and the book is endlessly entertaining, showing no evidence of the tedium that such an encyclopaedic task always entails. Ford kept himself and his readers amused by peppering his text with witticisms that make you want to laugh out loud. His turn of phrase was masterly. 'So great a literary achievement,' a contemporary summed up, 'had never before been performed under so unpretending an appellation.' Had the book been published today, it would probably scarcely be reviewed, a distinction having now been made between travel and guide-books: the former are considered as literature, the latter are not.

Several other members of the British community in Seville tried their hand at writing about Spain and their Spanish experiences. Hall Standish brought out a dreary book on Seville in 1840, and Captain S. E. Cook ('not *the* Captain Cook', as Ford stressed in a letter to Addington) wrote two general works on the country. Ford had known Cook well in Seville, and found that the man's first book on Spain was not as bad as he had feared: its main failings for Ford were its artistic judgements, Cook being someone who did not know 'a Murillo from a mainmast'. A writer on Spain for whom Ford had unqualified admiration was George Borrow. John Murray had published Borrow's *Zincali: The Gypsies of Spain* in 1841, and it was quite clear from this idiosyncratic work that the adventures in Spain of the man who wrote it would make an equally fascinating read. Ford encouraged Murray to go ahead and publish them, and later wrote a letter to Addington referring to the 'extraordinary fellow George Borrow, who went out to Spain to convert the *gypsies*. He is about to publish his failure, and a curious book it will be.'

Six foot three inches tall with a shock of prematurely white hair, a semitic nose, a direct and aggressive way of looking at people, Borrow must have cut an eccentric

George Borrow

figure in Spain; certainly he was the great individualist among the British travellers to the country, and the great outsider. The son of a recruiting officer, Borrow was born in 1803, and schooled in Norwich. In addition to his interest in gypsies, he developed an obsession with languages and the Vikings. With such a background he could hardly fail to turn to a life of roving, which began in 1824 when he abandoned his training as a solicitor, and walked to London. Between then and 1833, the story of his life, as gleaned from his later autobiographical writings, is difficult to follow and even more difficult to believe. Prone to wild exaggeration, and to complete invention, Borrow nonetheless turns out demonstrably to be telling the truth when his tales seem least plausible. He may have gone around the world before 1833, almost certainly experienced life as a wandering tinker, and travelled widely around Europe. In 1833, he found the perfect job to suit his travelling instincts when he joined the London Bible Society, the aims of which were to sell the Bible to as many countries as possible and in as many languages. The job took him around Russia between 1833 and 1835, and then to Spain shortly after his return from Russia to England. The First Carlist War was at its height and most British travellers of the time had the sense to be leaving Spain rather than going to it. Borrow was always at variance with the rest of society.

Borrow's first trip lasted until September 1836, but he was back two months later, this time visiting Andalucía for the first time. He went from England directly to Cádiz, where he took a room in the Hotel de Paris. Characteristically, he went out of his way to avoid the hotel's middle-class cosmopolitan clients. Unlike most other British travellers in Spain, he had no desire to meet his compatriots, and had a life-long loathing for the niceties of British middle-class behaviour. In Cádiz he spent much of his time in coffee-houses and 'seeking out those parts of the town where the lower classes principally reside.' He went afterwards to Seville, and was not unnaturally drawn to Triana which he said 'is inhabited by the dregs of the populace, and abounds with Gitanos or Gypsies'. While at Seville he was delighted by a chance encounter with Baron Taylor, a man whom he was always running into in various parts of the world, and whom he clearly regarded as a kindred spirit. 'Whenever he descries me,' Borrow wrote of Taylor, 'whether in the street or the desert, the brilliant hall or amongst Bedouin haimas, at Novgorod or Stambul, he flings up his arms and exclaims, "O ciel! I have again the felicity of seeing my cherished and most respectable B__!"'

Borrow's second trip to Spain ended dramatically in Madrid with his being thrown into prison as a result of his evangelizing activities. His imprisonment seems to have upset people in England more than it upset him, and he benefited from his stay in gaol by studying the dialect of thieves. Released in September 1838, he returned to England, but then set off again almost immediately to Spain, despite the by now wary attitude towards him of his employers at the Bible Society. On this third and final visit to Spain, he was based mainly in Seville, which he described as 'this terrestrial paradise'. Unknown to the Bible Society and hardly in accordance with their conventional Christian morality, Borrow was joined in Seville by an English widow, Mrs. Mary Clarke, with whom he lived out of wedlock for the rest of his time in Spain. This secret liaison is indicative of how nominal Borrow's work for the Bible Society in fact was, and he probably regarded it largely as an excuse for adventure and travel. Back in England in April 1840, Borrow broke off his association with the Society, married Mary Clarke, and devoted the rest of his life to writing. *The Bible in Spain* (1842), written in a solitary hamlet in a remote part of England, was immensely popular with the English reading public. In comparison with so many other travellers' accounts of Spain, Borrow's is startlingly original and unconventional; his emphasis is on his encounters with strange people, but even when he looks at places, he does so in an unusual way, as for instance when he evokes the ruins of Itálica by concentrating on a vulture standing grotesquely over the pitiful corpse of a horse. He feels no necessity to praise at length the Moorish and other monuments to which his fellow travellers devoted so much of their tiringly romantic descriptive prose: the Alhambra is thankfully absent from the book. The most that he shares with other British travellers is his condescending attitude towards the Spaniards, above all to the Andalucíans (see page 50). The Sevillians, however, bear no resentment towards him, and remember him to this day as a loveable eccentric who sold his Bibles in the town's flea-market. By a curious turn of fate, he is probably better known in Seville than he is today in England, and still referred to by the endearing nickname of 'Don Jorgito'.

With so many foreigners describing Spain and the Spaniards, it is easy to forget that the Spaniards themselves turned their attention to the same exotic aspects of their country that intrigued their visitors. Seville in the 19th century played an important role in the history of *costumbrismo*, a movement in art and literature dedicated to the portrayal of manners and customs peculiar to the Spanish regions. The

Don Juan

professed aims of its literary members were to record Spanish life in as impartial and objective way as possible, avoiding the romantic embellishment common to foreign descriptions; in practice the writers tended to reinforce foreign stereotypes of the Spaniards. One of the leading writers in this genre in Seville was in fact of foreign extraction even though she always regarded herself as a Sevillian. Cecilia Boehl von Faber, who wrote under the name 'Fernan Caballero', was born in Switzerland of a German father and a mother who was half Spanish and half Irish. Her father, a Catholic convert, was a well known Hispanist and the German consul at Cádiz. Cecilia, after being schooled at a French pension in Hamburg, settled in Seville, and lived there most of her life, marrying three times to members of prominent Seville families. Her literary reputation is based on *La Gaviota* (1844), which is set mainly in Seville and deals with the failed marriage of a German doctor to a fisherman's daughter. She later falls in love with a bull-fighter, leaves her huband to take up a career of singing, and then, her voice ruined, returns to her home village to marry a barber. The book is filled with local colour, dwelling precisely on those aspects of Andalucía such as bull-fighting and beautiful singers that are essential to the region's picturesque appeal. Another example of Andalucían costumbrismo is Serafín Estébanez Calderón's *Escenas Andaluzas* (1847), a series of mannered though charming vignettes of Andalucían life. The author was born in Málaga but the finest of his essays are devoted to Seville, such as his account of dancing in Triana (see page 143). Colourful, light-hearted and filled with people prone to wild

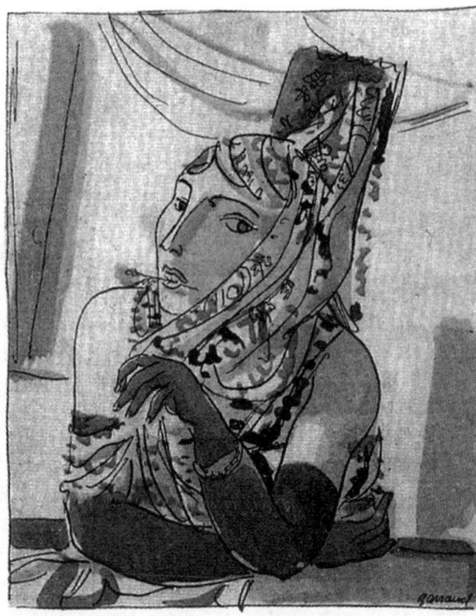

exaggeration, the Seville of Estébanez Calderón is little different from that evoked in countless accounts by Romantic travellers.

Seville was above all a centre of costumbrista painters. In contrast to their counterparts in Madrid, who took their lead from Goya and looked at Spanish life in a dark and savage fashion, the Seville costumbristas were sentimental, anecdotal, and heavily reliant on the local tourist industry. Their subjects were those that appealed to tourists – the Giralda, the Feria, dancers, majos, gypsies, cigarette girls, and so on. The head of the school was José Bécquer, who was so successful with tourists such as Ford that he sometimes had to employ a cousin, Joaquín, to help him out with his commissions. His two sons were Valeriano and Gustavo Adolfo, the former another well-known costumbrista painter, the latter Seville's leading 19th-century poet, and the author of *Rime*, the most popular Spanish collection of poems before García Lorca's *Romancero Gitano*. Gustavo Adolfo had begun his career as a painter, and his decision to change to poetry shocked his god-mother, who reputedly said: 'The English will always buy Andalucían scenes, but who will buy verses?' In the 1850's a Scottish painter and pupil of Wilkie, John Phillip, came to Seville and emulated the local costumbrista school. His animated and brightly coloured canvases of Seville life earned him the nickname 'Philip of Spain', but were criticized by Ruskin for missing 'the wayward, half-melancholy mystery of Spanish beauty.' The Romantic traveller needed a hint of tragedy to turn the brightly coloured surface of Andalucían life into a setting of great art.

It was left to a foreigner, Prosper Mérimée, to appropriate the subjects of Andalucían costumbrismo and create out of them a story that would seize the European imagination in a way which no Spanish work was ever to do. Mérimée first visited Spain in 1830, and came to know Estébanez Calderón as well as to hear from an Andalucían family the story which many years later was to form the basis of *Carmen*. The first of his works inspired by Andalucía was *The Souls of Purgatory* (1834), a fictional account of a man with whom all travellers to Seville in the early 19th century were obsessed, Don Miguel Mañara. The music of Mozart's *Don Giovanni* fresh in their minds, these travellers came to Seville determined to find sites associated with Don Juan, and convinced themselves that Miguel Mañara and Juan Tenorio were, in the words of Hans Christian Andersen, 'unquestionably one and the same person'. The Hospital of La Caridad, founded by the man who came to be known even in Mérimée's story as 'Don Juan Mañara', was one of the high-points of the Romantic traveller's tour of Seville. Many of its visitors loved to speculate about what had happened to Mañara in his youth to justify his reputation as 'the worst man who had ever lived'. Mérimée, in his *Ames du Purgatoire* came up with an unconvincing story, as did Alexandre Dumas and various other Romantic authors who gave fictional treatment to Mañara.

Having exploited one of Andalucía's existing myths, Mérimée went on to create a new one in *Carmen* (1845). Before writing this he had returned to Andalucía to carry out archaeological research to determine the site of the battle of Munda, in which Julius Caesar had defeated the followers of Pompey: his findings were to be published in the *Revue Archéologique* of June 1844. The narrator of Carmen is an archaeologist engaged in the same research as Mérimée had just done. On a field trip to the Serranía de Ronda he befriends an unkempt but well educated man who is later revealed as a notorious bandit. The second part of the story finds the narrator in Córdoba, where he strikes up a conversation with Carmen, a beautiful gypsy whom he accompanies to her home. To his surprise the bandit bursts into the room and starts quarrelling with Carmen. The narrator makes his escape. In the next and principal section of the book, he is once again in Córdoba several weeks later, and discovers that the bandit has murdered Carmen and is shortly to be executed. Visiting him in prison, the narrator learns the man's tragic story, how he had been a respectable army officer whose obsession with Carmen had led him into banditry, and of how he had killed her in a jealous rage over her flirtation with a bull-fighter. The story's concluding section is a general account of Spanish gypsies. Though based on a supposedly true story, and written up as if it were a historical document, *Carmen* manages to bring together every conceivable element which made Andalucía popular to the Romantic tourist, from banditry to gypsies, beautiful women to majos, dancers to bull-fighters, from the Serranía de Ronda to the Tobacco Factory at Seville.

The Tobacco Factory, where the unfortunate hero of Mérimée's story first sets

The Tobacco Factory, Seville

eyes on Carmen, was an essential component of Romantic Andalucía, and as obligatory to any visit to Seville as the cathedral. Travellers' fanciful conceptions of the place, when compared with the reality of the life which was led there, are an interesting reflection on the Romantic distortion of Andalucía. Early visitors to the factory had merely expressed wonder at the monumental dimensions of the building, at the efficiency with which it was run, and at the great number of people and mules employed there. By Mérimée's day the interest of foreigners was concentrated on four connected rooms at the very centre of the immense complex, for here were gathered a reputed three thousand female cigar makers, chattering away, their colourful street clothes hanging around the walls. One of Andalucía's great attractions was its beautiful women, and these four rooms, with their steamy, hot-house atmosphere, seemed to offer travellers unlimited possibilities for studying these women in a suitably sensual environment. Richard Ford greatly enhanced these women's reputation for animosity and provocative behaviour when he wrote that they were known to be 'more impertinent than chaste', and would sometimes smuggle out 'the weed in a manner her most Catholic majesty never dreamt of'; when

A. C. Andros visited the place in 1860 he was turned away on the grounds that 'owing to the intense heat, the *eight thousand* females employed in making cigars are working in all but *puris naturalibus*'. The strong-minded, cheeky, beautiful and overwhelmingly sensual Carmen represented all that Romantic travellers had come to expect of the women of the the Tobacco Factory. Naturally, the hopes being so greatly raised, numerous travellers came away bitterly disappointed, and went afterwards to opposite extremes to describe the women. 'I have never beheld such an assemblage of uglinesses,' wrote George Dennis. William Baxter in 1875 considered that the complexion of Spanish women was never their strong point and that 'in the Tobacco Factory it is absolutely repulsive. . . in this pest-house [the women] look as if they had breathed the deadly malaria of the Pontine marshes and were becoming prematurely mummified. Sallow, shrunken, shrivelled specimens of humanity, life seems to have but little hold upon the older of the operatives.' Baxter was one of the few 19th-century travellers to show concern at the working conditions within the factory. According to him, the cigar-makers worked twelve hours a day, with only an hour's break for lunch, which was provided in the building to lessen chances of smuggling; furthermore the poorly ventilated, nicotine-filled atmosphere was thought by him to be very detrimental to the health, nicotine 'being among the deadliest of poisons'. The reward for all this hardship were the most meagre of wages, and only three years before the publication of *Carmen* the cigar-makers had gone out on strike to demand better pay. Yet for as long as the Factory functioned, tourists would continue coming here in search of exotic beauty. As late as 1929, the sexual reformer Havelock Ellis, in an essay on Spanish women in his *The Soul of Spain*, described the place as 'one of the most delightful spots in this delightful city, and one of the most picturesque'.

The impact of Mérimée's *Carmen* on European attitudes towards Andalucía was as nothing in comparison with that of Bizet's 1875 musical adaptation of the story. By this date the primitive, bandit-infested region that Mérimée had portrayed bore even less resemblance to reality than it had before; but when the opera was premièred critics savagely attacked it for its realism. Bizet did not live to see the work's prodigious success, and died shortly after the première, expiring on the very night when the principal singer, enacting the moment when Carmen foretells her own death, collapsed on stage. Four years later the opera was ecstactically received in Vienna, and in 1887 created a sensation when first put on in Madrid. In his later years Nietzsche forsook his idol Wagner in favour of Bizet's Carmen. 'With Carmen,' he reflected, 'we take leave of the damp north, of all the mists of the Wagnerian ideal. This music possesses the limpid, dry atmosphere of southern climes.' Mario Praz was later to think that Nietzsche was already showing signs of his future dementia when he said this, but the great man's opinion was shared by countless of his younger contemporaries, who turned towards the south, and Andalucía in particular, with renewed passion.

Cigarreras, c. 1901

Music and dancing brought to Andalucía in the latter years of the century a popularity greater and more widespread than it had ever had. Bizet did much to encourage the fashion for Andalucían music, even though the so-called Andalucían elements in his own music had little to do with the region and were derived more from the folk music introduced into Europe by Cuban refugees. Unlike Bizet, the Russian composer Glinka had actually been to Spain, where he had befriended a gypsy guitarist during a stay in Granada in 1847. Andalucían gypsy music had a major influence on Glinka, whose works were in turn to affect the development of a national style in Russian music. In the wake of Glinka, and with Andalucía principally in mind, numerous European composers wrote Spanish works, including Rimsky-Korsakov, Rubinstein, Saint-Saëns, Chabrier, and Lalo. Their knowledge of Spain itself was often minimal, Rimsky-Korsakov basing his *Capricho Español* on a three-day stay in Cádiz, and Ravel, composer of *L'Heure Espagnole*, experiencing

Worker in today's cigarette factory

a mere twenty-four Spanish hours. A popular source of inspiration was the Alhambra, and the *Alhambrista* music of foreign composers even began to influence Spanish classical composers such as Pedrell, the master of Falla. Confusion between what was genuinely Andalucían and was thought to be Andalucían developed too in dancing, as dance-rooms called Alhambra proliferated in Europe and America, and Andalucían dancers adopted foreign fashions, while foreign dancers pretended to be Andalucían.

Ortega y Gasset wrote in 1927 that a craze for Andalucía and Andalucían culture had dominated the history of 19th-century Spain. The craze survived into this century, though with the difference that the Romantic image which accompanied it was the creation less of foreigners than of the Andalucíans themselves.

Poetry and War

Laurie Lee remembered Spain in the 1930's as a place where almost everyone was writing poetry. Spain is still such a place. In England, few people will admit to writing poetry, let alone show it to you, but in Spain, as in other southern countries, poetry is shamelessly written by an exceptionally wide range of people. The passion for poetry is especially strong in Andalucía, where poems are penned on the slightest pretext, and people are constantly being presented to you as poets, even though they will rarely have had works published, or show any intentions of doing so. In the 1920's and 1930's Andalucían poets were in the forefront of what is sometimes referred to as Spain's Second Golden Age. Shelley's line about the poet being the unacknowledged legislator of the world has rarely rung so true as in those years, when poetry became enmeshed in politics, culminating in the Spanish Civil War, with the onrush of poets to the front, and the political assassination of one of the greatest of all their number, Federico García Lorca.

Spain's transformation early this century into what Gerald Brenan described as a 'poetic Klondike' must be set against the ever more fraught political history of the time. The twentieth century began only two years after Spain had lost Puerto Rico, Cuba and the Philippines in the space of a few months: its economy had reached one of its lowest points, and the social unrest which had troubled the country for much of the previous century was worsening. *The Lost Grove* (1948), the autobiography of the poet Rafael Alberti, opens with the words: '1902 – year of great agitation and activity among the peasant masses of Andalucía, a year of preparation for the revolutionary uprisings to come. December 16 – date of my birth, on an unexpectedly stormy night.' Alberti's native region of Andalucía, a traditional stronghold of anarchism, now emerged also as a major centre of communism, and was soon to produce, in the Málaga-born José Díaz, Spain's first communist deputy. At the same time the regionalist movement known as *Andalucismo* gained momentum with intellectuals such as Blas Infante calling out not only for 'land and liberty' but also for a greater Andalucían autonomy. Seville's Ateneo (the city's cultural institute), where Blas Infante held court, became a focus of this movement, the aims of which were further discussed in a series of important conferences held in the early years of the century at Ronda and Córdoba. Andalucismo was nonetheless to have more of a cultural than a political significance, one of the main barriers to autonomy being the continuing division between the eastern and western halves of the region.

Social unrest took on an especially savage character in Spain in the years between 1918 and 1923, with Andalucía and Barcelona being once more at the centre of the troubles. Spain's neutrality during the First World War, however, had led to a brief improvement in the nation's economy, and to a revival of commerce, mining and agriculture. In Andalucía renewed capitalist investment had also been inspired by the prospect of the great Ibero-American Exhibition planned for 1929. The idea for such an exhibition had first been mooted in 1910, and preparations for it had already got under way by 1914. The exhibition received a further boost following the collapse in 1923 of Spain's parliamentary monarchy, and the coming to power of the right-wing dictatorship of Miguel Primo de Rivera. The dictator came from Jerez de la Frontera, and was thus keen to promote an exhibition which was thought would bring back to Andalucía something of its Golden Age glory. Spain generally prospered in the early years of Primo de Rivera's rule, which at first was widely supported. Its popularity waned as soon as the prosperity on which it was based began to be threatened: 1929, the year when the Ibero-American Exhibition opened, was described by Primo de Rivera's son, José Antonio, as 'the year of the dictator's agony'. Students and intellectuals had been largely unfavourable towards Primo de Rivera from the start, García Lorca, for instance, implicitly criticizing his rule in a history play about freedom and political oppression, *Mariana Pineda* (1927). By the late 1920's, those intellectuals who had been allies of the dictator such as Ortega y Gasset and the poet Manuel Machado, changed their allegiance to the opposition. At a time when intellectuals had a greater influence than ever before on Spanish political life, the complete loss of their support was of particular consequence. The army and the king, Alfonso XIII, soon followed suit, and in January 1930, Primo de Rivera was finally forced to resign.

Spain's leading intellectuals of this time either belonged to, or were heavily influenced by the 'Generation of 98', a group of writers who believed that the key to the revival of Spain lay in the spiritual and ideological regeneration of the individual. The major poet associated with the group, indeed one of the most popular of all Spanish poets, was Antonio Machado. He came from a most talented Sevillian family, his father being the pioneering folklorist and student of flamenco known as 'Demófilo' (see page 149), and his brother Manuel being another outstanding poet. The father – married to the daughter of a sweet-seller from Triana – was a middle-class intellectual who had actively supported the revolution of 1868. Shortly after the restoration of the monarchy in 1874, he had lost his job in Seville and had moved to Madrid, where in 1881 he had founded Spain's first Folklore Society. His family joined him there in 1883, when Manuel was nine years old, and Antonio

Antonio Machado

Manuel Machado

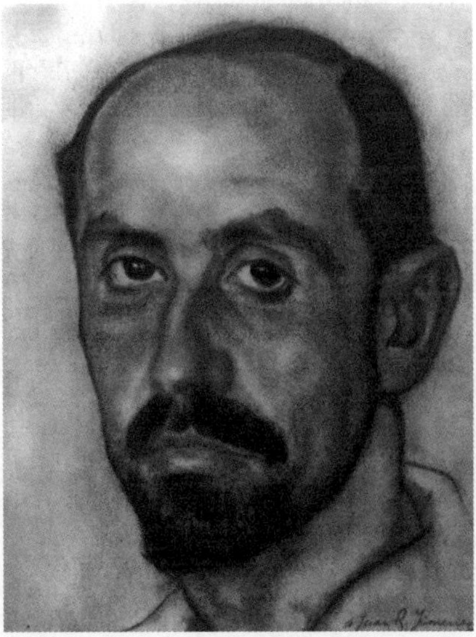

Juan Ramón Jiménez

Federico García Lorca

eight, but he died of a stroke and overwork in 1893, aged forty-six, after having sailed alone to Puerto Rico to take up a post as a minor civil servant. Antonio and Manuel were both educated at Madrid's Institución Libre de Enseñanza, a revolutionary university which had recently been set up in protest against existing educational methods. As with so many Spanish writers and artists of their generation, both Antonio and Manuel continued their training in Paris, where they became involved in the bohemian life of the city.

Antonio led the very antithesis of a bohemian life after 1907, when he returned to Spain and took up as a post as French teacher in Soria in northern Castille. In Soria he fell in love with and married the sixteen-year-old daughter of his landlady, but his young wife died in 1912. Feeling unable to remain in the town any longer, he went on to teach at Baeza, a town filled today with his memories (see page 265f). The views towards the Sierra de la Segura enchanted him, but his mind was always drifting back to Castille and to his dead wife. The melancholy of these thoughts inspired the second part of his *Campos de Castilla*, a collection of poems evoking the loneliness and grandeur of the Castilian landscape, and reflecting on the decline of modern Spain. When he left Baeza in 1919, he went back to Castille, settling in Segovia. Remembered by Alberti as a man whose appearance of a timid schoolteacher gone to seed was belied by a great dignity, Machado became a prophet-like figure to Spain's poets in the 1920's.

Whereas Antonio Machado felt an exile in his native Andalucía, his brother Manuel exalted this region, and in particular Seville, which he described as 'bull-loving, witty and animated'. In 1896 and 1897 he stayed with his mother's family in Triana, and during this period became obsessed by bull-fighting, frequented the famous café cantante of Silverio Franconetti, and enthusiastically attended the town's Holy Week processions and feria; the poet Juan Ramón Jiménez claimed even to have seen Manuel – the son of an avowed atheist – dressed up as a penitent in the procession of the Brotherhood of Silence. Not long after his final return from Paris in 1909, he went to Seville to marry a cousin of his, to whom he had been unfaithfully engaged for thirteen years. Though they subsequently moved to Madrid, his poetry constantly harked back to Andalucían themes. His works, for instance his *Cantares*, were often inspired by the lyrics of flamenco songs, and can be seen as prefiguring many of the themes of García Lorca's poetry.

Juan Ramón Jiménez, known usually as 'Juan Ramón', ranks with Antonio Machado as one of the father figures of 20th-century Spanish verse. The village of Moguer de la Frontera where he was born and spent much of his life was once exclusively a place of pilgrimage for those in search of Columbus associations, but has since become an obligatory destination for anyone seriously interested in Juan Ramón's works. It is an especially attractive village, rising gently above fertile plains a short distance away from the Río Tinto estuary, and living off a combination of

Moguer

agriculture and fishing. Juan Ramón, the son of a wealthy wine-merchant, was born in 1881 in the 'Casa Grande', at Calle de la Ribera 2. From this imposing, and now rather decayed, late 19th-century mansion, the young Juan Ramón endlessly observed his surroundings, his attention fixed above all on a house opposite, which he studied 'on clear evenings, during rainy afternoon siestas, at each slight change of each day and each hour'. Later the family moved to Calle Nueva 10 (now Calle Ramón Jiménez 5) directly in front of a house where Columbus is reputed to have spent his last night before moving in February 1492 to the monastery of La Rábida (see page 91). One of the poet's girl-friends was, curiously enough, Blanca Hernández Pinzón, a direct descendent of the captain who accompanied Columbus on his 1492 voyage.

Schooled at a strict Jesuit college in El Puerto de Santa María, Juan Ramón later attended Seville University, at this stage harbouring ambitions to become a painter rather than a poet. By 1899, when he went to Madrid, he had begun to concentrate on poetry, and was shortly to become unofficial poet-in-residence at the Institución Libre de Enseñanza, where he met and befriended Antonio Machado. A supreme aesthete, with the sickly, languid temperament which traditionally characterizes such a person, Juan Ramón was to dedicate himself single-mindedly to poetry for the rest of his life. In 1905, after having spent much of the previous four years in sanatoria in Madrid and Bordeaux, he returned to Moguer and remained there until 1912. During this period he developed a particular passion for the countryside surrounding the village, and frequently buried himself in the family's country home of

Fuentepiña, a twenty-five minute walk from the centre. It was at this time that he wrote his best loved work, *Platero and I*, a series of prose poems dedicated to his mule, Platero. In this mixture of delicate observation and childhood memory, a detailed if rather sentimental portrait of Moguer emerges; quotations from the book are now recorded in ceramic plaques liberally placed in appropriate sites throughout the villlage. From 1912 until the outbreak of the Civil War, Juan Ramón was largely based in Madrid, where he became closely associated with the Residencia de los Estudiantes, a progressive institution comparable to the Institución de Libre Enseñanza. He regularly returned to Moguer during the summer months, and, like Manuel Machado, constantly evoked Andalucía in his poetry. After 1916 his poetry underwent a process of what he described as *depuración* ('purification'), whereby it was reduced to its self-conscious essence, to a state in which musical rhythms became more important than content.

While Juan Ramón's poetry aspired increasingly towards music, the music of Manuel de Falla blazes with images that have inspired poetry. Falla, another father figure to Spanish intellectuals of the 1920's, was born in Cádiz in 1876, spending his boyhood in a house in the Calle Ancha, and later in the Fonda de Cádiz in the Plaza de la Constitución. His family moved to Madrid in 1896, and he studied music there

Falla

under Felipe Pedrell, the composer who did most to influence the development of a Spanish national style in music. From Madrid Falla went to Paris, where he formed a life-long friendship with Debussy. The French composer was one of many in Paris who had been deeply impressed by a performance given by gypsy singers at the Paris International Exhibition of 1900. Memories of their singing were later to inspire passages of his *Ibéria,* which Lorca described as 'a truly genial work in which Andalucían perfumes and essences dreamily float'; to Alberti, this tone poem was a 'reflection by the most transparent composer in France on the exotic aroma of an imagined Andalucía'. Debussy was never to visit Spain, and it was his friendship with Falla that helped him in his two musical evocations of Granada, *Soirée en Grenade* and *La Puerta del Vino,* the latter based on a postcard of the Alhambra sent to him by Falla. Lorca found in the latter composition 'all the emotional themes of the Granada night, the blue remoteness of the vega, the Sierra greeting the tremulous Mediterranean, the enormous barbs of the clouds sunk into the distance, the admirable rubato of the city, the hallucinatory poetry of its underground waters'.

Gypsy and Andalucían themes permeated Falla's own work from the time of his *Vida Breve* and *Amor Brujo*, both of which were premièred on his return from Paris to Madrid in 1914. *The Three-Cornered Hat* (1919), a ballet version of Alarcón's tale of the Alpujarras, was intended for Diaghilev, who also toyed with the idea of turning Falla's piano and orchestral piece, *Nights in the Gardens of Spain* (1916), into a ballet: Diaghilev imagined it in terms of a fiesta set at night in the gardens of the Generalife, the women wearing mantillas, the men in evening dress. Granada was perhaps the main influence on Falla's life and music, though it was not until after the death of his parents in Madrid in 1919 that he eventually settled there. In 1921 he acquired a tiny villa or *carmen* high up on the southern slopes of the Alhambra hill, and he was to live here, together with his sister María del Carmen, up to 1939. This modest house and garden has been kept almost in the state in which he left it, and despite recent restoration it remains one of the most charming of Andalucía's small museums. In its white doll's house rooms there are some costume designs by Picasso for *The Three-Cornered Hat*, a drawing by Zuloaga dedicated to Falla, various photographs cut out by the composer from books, and a small design by him for a ceramic plaque to mark the site of the Granada pension where Théophile Gautier had stayed. You will also find the composer's upright piano, and his monk's cell of a bedroom, adorned with a plain white cross above the tiny bed. Falla's was an ascetic and deeply religious household, and in his sister's bedroom are numerous sacred objects. To its garden, with its extensive views over Granada, there came in the 1920's and early 30's, Lorca, Segovia and many other of the poets, musicians and intellectuals from Spain and abroad who gave to the town during this period a cultural life such as it had scarcely known since Moorish times.

The Moorish and gypsy Granada which inspired Falla and his circle contrasted with the ever more intrusive modern town of Granada, a place with a distinctly northern and unexotic character, sober and notoriously philistine. This latter reputation had already been acquired in the 19th century. Richard Ford referred to its people as stagnating in 'bookless ignorance' and remarked on how little they appeared to appreciate the Alhambra. From the 19th century onwards, these inhabitants have made little positive contribution to the appearance of the town and have distinguished themselves largely by destroying much of what they have inherited. A particularly insensitive act was the construction in the 1880's and 1890's of the Gran Vía. This main street, lined with heavy and monstrously out-of-scale shops and apartments, had radically altered the character of Granada, cutting as it did a great swathe through the town's Moorish and renaissance centre. Ángel Ganivet, an associate of the Generation of '98, wrote a book heavily critical of the urban changes to his native town, finding them symptomatic of Spain's spiritual decay. Juan Ramón Jiménez, visiting Granada in 1924, could not help contrasting the 'tempered mysticism and delicate sensuality' emanating from the town's Moorish monuments, with the deeply unaesthetic nature of its present-day people. But the greatest critic of modern Granada was the man who, together with Falla, did most to animate the town during the 1920's, García Lorca.

'Granada is horrible,' Lorca wrote in 1924 in a letter to a friend. 'This is not Andalucía. Andalucía is something else. It's in the people. And here they're Galician. I, who am an Andalucían and an Andalucían through and through, sigh for Málaga, for Córdoba, for Sanlúcar la Mayor, for Algeciras, for authentic and high-toned Cádiz, for Alcalá de los Gazules, for that which is *intimately* Andalucía. The real Granada has vanished, and now appears dead beneath greenish and delirious gas lights. The other Andalucía is alive, for example Málaga.' Lorca, who in the early 1920's whimsically contemplated setting up in Granada a cultural centre commemorating the town's Moorish heritage, was entirely convinced that the decline of the place had set in from 1492. He was to put forward this view in a most outspoken fashion in an interview which he gave to the newspaper *El Sol* shortly before his death in August 1936. In this he spoke about 1492 as a 'disastrous event. An admirable civilization, and a poetry, architecture and delicacy unique in the world – all were lost, to give way to an impoverished, cowed town, a wasteland populated by the worst bourgeoisie in Spain today.' A statement such as this served only to strengthen the resentment harboured by many in the town towards him. This resentment has survived in certain quarters to this day.

Granada and its surroundings are rich in places closely associated with Lorca's life, though until comparatively recently the visitor to these places might well have aroused local suspicion. In the immediate aftermath of the Spanish Civil War, Lorca was a virtually unmentionable name in Spain, and it was not until the mid 1960's that he was officially re-instated here. Even so, the opening in 1986, fifty years after the poet's death, of the memorial park to him at Víznar, and of the museum in the house where he was born at Fuentevaqueros, would have been unthinkable during the Franco era.

Fuentevaqueros, a prosperous village sixteen kilometres northwest of Granada, is a flat and architecturally unremarkable place set among fields of tobacco, sugar-cane and wheat, and backed to the north by grey, rocky mountains. It lies in the middle of 'El Soto de Roma', a vast estate awarded to the Duke of Wellington, though never visited by the Duke himself. The estate had lain idle for much of the 19th century, but towards the end of the century its economic potential had finally been realized by its English administrators, and the area had begun to be populated and to prosper. Lorca's father was a wealthy farmer, and his mother the local schoolteacher, a woman much loved in the village and still fondly remembered here. Federico García Lorca was born on 11 June 1898 in what is now Calle Poeta García Lorca 4. The museum which now occupies this simple white building is beautifully and lovingly laid out, but the building itself has been heavily altered and modernized, and bears little resemblance to what it must have been like in Lorca's day. A small selection of family items has been gathered together in the house, including the cot used by the baby Lorca. Of similar sentimental interest is the *geranio Vicent*, a pale-coloured geranium, grown from the seeds of a plant which Lorca's mother, Vicenta, always kept in her classroom.

In 1907 Lorca's family moved to a village with the unfortunate name of Asquerosa, or 'Repulsive', four kilometres north of Fuentevaqueros: in the 1920's the poet was to mount a campaign to have this name changed to the present one of Valderrubio. The Lorca home here, at Calle Iglesia 20, is as full of character as the birthplace is lacking in it, having always remained in the family's possession and featuring many of its original furnishings, as well as a pleasantly decayed character (it is now leased to the local Socialist Party, the members of which will be glad to show you round, if you can find them). Two years after buying this place, Lorca's parents decided to install themselves in the very centre of Granada (in a house, now gone, on the Acera del Darro), and to keep their Asquerosa home merely as a summer retreat. In 1914, after a schooling in Almería, Lorca became registered as a law student at Granada University. As well as a budding interest in poetry, Lorca had by now developed his life-long passion for the piano and the guitar: a recording played in the Fuentevaqueros museum of Lorca accompanying on the piano the singer La Argentinita gives some idea of his great facility as a musician. His cultural and intellectual interests were hardly satisfied by Granada University itself, let alone by his law course. But he did find stimulus in the *tertulias* or cultural gatherings that took place in the Café Alameda, a large café attached to the 18th-century palace now used by Granada's Town Council: the café itself has been replaced by the tackily decorated Cafés Coimbra and Chikito, the latter occupying the reading-room where the meetings were held. The Café Alameda group, known as the 'Rinconcillo', included among its members the art historian and author of the best

Fuente de la Teja

guide to Granada, Gallego Burín, and a colourful personality sometimes thought of as Granada's Oscar Wilde, Francisco Soriano Lapresa. The most significant contact Lorca made at the Café Alameda was with Manuel de Falla, whom he met in 1919.

Lorca joined Madrid's Residencia de Estudiantes in that same year, but he always returned to Granada during the summer months, and was thus able to pursue his frienship with Falla. A mutual interest in puppets led in 1921 to their collaboration on a puppet show, first performed in the Lorca home at Asquerosa. A more significant venture was their organizing, with the painter Zuloaga, of the famous cante jondo festival in 1922, held in the courtyard of Charles V's palace and intended to halt the declining standards in flamenco singing (see page 149). This memorable and much publicized event attracted a wide range of listeners and performers, including the distinguished English Hispanist J. B. Trend, the American Romany gypsy Irving Brown, the guitarist Andrés Segovia, and two of the celebrated gypsy singers from the Café Silverio, Manuel Torres and Antonio Chacón. To accompany the festival, Lorca delivered his famous lecture on the cante jondo, a text combining historical and musical exposition with great flights of fantasy.

The deep popular roots that Lorca romantically claimed for the cante jondo were exactly those that he considered as nourishing his own verse. He felt an empathy both for the gypsies and for the countryfolk among whom he had grown up. Undeniably he was a man whose charm communicated itself to all levels of society, and his work itself was loved by the people who had inspired it. A revelation for me was a visit to the Fuente de la Teja, a spring by a wooded river bank, situated a kilometre across fields from Asquerosa. In this quiet and enchanting spot sat a group of men drinking the spring water and talking. On a fridge were painted the words: 'Fuente de la Teja, where Federico García Lorca used to come and write.' In his summers spent in the early 1920's at Asquerosa, Lorca would sit for hours by this spring, his attempts at writing habitually interrupted in the late afternoon by the arrival of farm-workers, who gathered here when their day's work was done to talk to the poet, discuss with him their problems, and to hear him recite. These occasions were vividly related to me by one of the men whom I myself met at the spring, a man in his mid nineties, partially blind and deaf, but with a perfect recollection of the young Lorca. The tradition of coming to the spring at the end of the day is still regularly maintained by the local men, and even though the great poet himself is no longer with them, the spirit of poetry has apparently lingered on among them. Before I left, the old man's son-in-law had opened the fridge and pulled out a cloth bag in which he kept poems written by himself in this very spot. There was a respectful silence as he then started to recite an ode to Spain's Socialist prime minister, Felipe González, a poem shortly followed by one inspired by Lorca, and telling of a young woman who forsook her husband so that she could come and meet the poet by his spring.

Though deriving inspiration for much of his verse from the countryside, Lorca had to look elsewhere for intellectual stimulus, and this he found in the 1920's above all in Madrid's Residencia de los Estudiantes. The Residencia, or 'Resi', as it was often known, was during this period the cultural centre of Spain, and certainly there was nowhere in Andalucía to compete with it, least of all Granada University. At the 'Resi' Lorca met Juan Ramón Jiménez, whose work he revered, and also made friends with his fellow students Salvador Dalí, Luis Buñuel and Rafael Alberti. The latter had had, like Juan Ramón, early ambitions to be a painter, but had been side-tracked by poetry, and for a while enjoyed a greater recognition as a poet than Lorca. This happened after 1924, with the publication of his enormously popular *Marinero en Tierra*, a series of poems inspired by the environment of his native Cádiz. In 1927, Alberti, Lorca, and a number of their talented young poet contemporaries decided to celebrate the third centenary of the then disgracefully neglected Luis de Góngora, a poet whose pure aestheticism, constant use of metaphor, and delight in descriptions of colour and sounds, was very much to their own hearts. This generation of Spanish poets, united in their admiration for Góngora, are generally known as the 'Generation of '27', though they are sometimes referred to as 'the Generation of the Dictatorship' and even as 'the

Grandchildren of '98'. A significant number of them were from Andalucía, for apart from Lorca and Alberti, the group included Emilio Prados and Manuel Altolaguirre from Málaga, and Vicente Aleixandre and Luis Cernuda from Seville.

The Góngora celebrations, which consisted of lectures and poetry recitals, were held not in Góngora's native Córdoba but in Seville, a town which Juan Ramón had described as the 'ideal capital of poetry'. Juan Ramón did not mean by this that Seville was a place filled with distinguished poets, but was thinking instead of the intense blue of its skies, the luxuriance of its vegetation, and the liveliness of its inhabitants. As a cultural and intellectual centre, Seville in the early years of this century was in fact scarcely more advanced than Granada. The mainstreams in European culture and thought had largely passed the town by, no-one, for instance, paying any attention to the visit here in 1909 of the Dadaist painter Picabia or to that of the German poet Rainer Maria Rilke in 1912-13. Picabia's canvas inspired by the town's Holy Week processions, *Procession in Seville*, was far more original than any treatment of this subject by a native artist. Seville continued to be dominated by an increasingly anachronistic costumbrismo, which can be seen as much in the repellently sentimental domestic dramas of the Quintero brothers as in the music of Joaquín Turina, the latter evoking such hackneyed aspects of Andalucía as the Seville Feria and the procession to El Rocío.

The most exciting developments in Seville in these years were undoubtedly in the fields of architecture and town-planning, the whole town being in a state of great activity in preparation for the Ibero-American Exhibition of 1929. The buildings that were being put up were by no means examples of the avant-garde, but instead structures that reflected the growing regional pride of the Andalucíans, and drew heavily on traditional Andalucían and, in particular, Moorish elements. One of the leading architects of the town was Espiau, who designed the Edificio Ciudad de Londres in the Calle de la Cerrajaría, a splendid neo-Moorish pastiche with dazzling ceramics set against a white background (see page 372). In 1916 Espiau won the competition to build the Hotel Alfonso XIII, which was intended as the main hotel for the 1929 Exhibition, and the most luxurious hotel in Europe: Espiau's grandiose structure, rivalling in scale even the nearby Tobacco Factory, brilliantly combines Moorish with Andalucían renaissance architecture, thus bringing together the two greatest periods in the city's history. A similar combination of styles characterizes the work of Anibal González, the architect responsible for the main Exhibition buildings, most notably the monumental, curved mass of tiles, red brick, and towers which dominates the landscaped Plaza de América. As a setting for these buildings, the María Luisa Park was created, one of Europe's finest parks and comparable only to parks in Latin America in its jungle-like anarchy and vegetation. On the other side of the park to the Hotel Alfonso XIII the wealthy residential area of El Porvenir developed, the name of which means 'the future', but the architecture of which looks back to Seville's past, the houses being in a traditional Seville style, white, adorned with black grilles, and centred around small jasmine-filled patios.

The visit to Seville in 1927 of Lorca, Alberti and this circle was certainly a major moment in their lives, and the optimistic mood of the town as it prepared for 1929 might well have had an added effect on them. Through Alberti Lorca met one of the more extraordinary personalities in Seville at that time, Fernando Villalón, Count of Miraflores, a Góngora-inspired poet who terrified Lorca with the speed with which he drove his car. A more important encounter was with Ignacio Sánchez Mejías, a bull-fighter who wrote plays and poetry, and had a great interest in modern artists such as Picasso. While Sánchez Mejías yearned for the literary life, Alberti had a secret ambition to become a bull-fighter, though after a short practice bout in the ring with Sánchez Mejías he decided not to pursue this career. Alberti and Lorca became good friends with Sánchez Mejías, and one of their most memorable evenings in Seville was spent in the latter's house, where they were treated to the voice of the illiterate Triana singer Manuel Torres (the 'Niño de Jerez'), who was to die in poverty only a few years later. News of the company which Alberti and Lorca were keeping in Seville reached the ears of Juan Ramón Jiménez, who was quite horrified, believing that through this association with Sánchez Mejías they had lost their way as poets: 'I have heard,' he wrote to a friend, 'that Alberti is involved with gypsies, banderilleros, and other low-living types.' Later in the year Lorca published his *Romancero Gitano* ('Gypsy Ballads'), the subject-matter of which bothered many of its more snobbish readers such as Juan Ramón and Salvador Dalí. However, it was this work which was to turn Lorca into the most popular of all Spanish poets.

Many of the Generation of '27 had their works published in Seville's *Mediodía*, which was described by Alberti as 'a somewhat offbeat poetry magazine started by a group of young people in Seville'. In March 1928 Lorca brought out in Granada a similar magazine called *Gallo*, and soon reported that it had created a great stir in the town, that the edition had sold out within two days, that a big fight had broken out in the University between the 'Gallistas' and 'Anti-Gallistas', and that everyone in the town was talking about it, in cafés, clubs and houses. This being Granada, however, the excitement soon died down, and, in the words of Lorca, 'in the two months between issues, Granada had regained her usual serenity and indifference'; there was not to be a third issue. It was high time for Lorca to broaden his horizons, and to get away not just from Andalucía, but from Spain. In 1929, the year of the Ibero-American Exhibition, Lorca left for America. The exhibition itself turned out to be less of an event than the preparations leading up to it. Anibal González, its main architect, died two weeks after its opening, and Miguel Primo de Rivera, one of its most enthusiastic promoters, was experiencing the disastrous last months of his dictatorship. When the Exhibition eventually closed, it left a saddened and bankrupt Seville. Sir Peter Chalmers-Mitchell, a former Secretary of the London Zoological Society, and looking forward to what he hoped would be a quiet retirment in Málaga, passed through Seville shortly afterwards, and went out to see 'the deserted and faded splendour of the unsuccessful Great Exhibition'. 'Few things,' he reflected, 'are more tragic than tattered splendour, whether it be of bright dresses or of painted pavillions.'

1929 was also the year that Gerald Brenan completed his last long stay at the Alpujarra village of Yegen, a place where he had been living periodically since January 1920 (see page 42). He had first come here with scarcely any knowledge of Spanish, and had intended his stay then to be merely a stage on a journey around the world. His yearning for travel had begun in his early teens, when he had run away from his conventional middle-class home, and had set out to walk to Jerusalem in the company of an older and eccentric compatriot, Hope-Johnstone. At Yegen he tried to make up for his lack of a university education by devoting himself to reading and studying, concentrating in particular on classical literature, and on the language and culture of Spain. Though friendly with the villagers, and very observant of their activities, he kept his distance from them, and relied heavily on the company of visiting English friends. Even when travelling elsewhere in Andalucía, the future Hispanist had little close contact with the Spaniards, and played virtually no part in the exciting cultural life of this period. In his description of Granada in the 1920's, he mentions having met Lorca, but says that his encounters with him were too slight to be worth recording; instead he gives long accounts of the town's English community, the members of which lived in elitist isolation on the Alhambra hill. Hope-Johnstone came to live with him at Yegen, and he received several visits from members of the Bloomsbury group, inluding Dora Carrington, who stayed here in 1920 when married to an old friend of Brenan, Ralph Partridge. Brenan's passionate but essentially platonic affair with Carrington began then, and was to absorb much of his energy in the following years.

Brenan resolved to become a writer, and dreamt of being a poet or even a novelist, but devoted much of his early literary output to long letters to the feckless Carrington. Finally, back in England in the mid 1920's, he embarked on a life of St. Teresa of Ávila, and spent many hours in the British Museum Library. The book progressed slowly, and, early in 1929, he returned to Yegen, hoping that the place would provide the peaceful atmosphere in which to write, yet soon becoming distracted by sexual frustration. For a man with an apparently enormous libido, an Alpujarran village in the 1920's might not on the surface seem the most promising place to be. Yet soon Brenan had embarked on an affair with a fifteen-year old local girl called Juana, which turned out to be as physical as his affair with Carrington had been cerebral. Making love several times a day wreaked havoc on his biography of St. Teresa, and Brenan later confessed that he was left in a state of mental lethargy. To recover he went off on a visit to the Seville Exhibition, but soon became involved there in other amorous adventures. Eventually, at the end of the year, he packed up and went off to England, leaving Juana pregnant with his child.

Gerald Brenan by Dora Carrington

Back in England, he married an American authoress, Gamel Woolsey, and attended the funeral of Carrington, who had killed herself a few days after the death of her second husband, Lytton Strachey. Brenan was not to return to Spain until 1934, missing four critical and complex years in the country's political history.

With the resignation in January 1930 of Primo de Rivera, the most unpopular man in Spain was now Alfonso XIII, whose name had just been given to a newly completed luxury hotel in Seville. Later that year King Alfonso decided that it would be unwise to winter, as he normally did, in Málaga's Hotel Príncipe Asturias, (the name of which was soon to change to the uncontroversial Miramar) and he abdicated in April 1931. Spain's Second Republic was declared. In the village of Míjas above Fuengirola, 'there was great joy,' according to the local barber Manuel Cortes, shortly to be elected deputy mayor of his village. The people of Míjas were also to support the further swing to the left which occurred in December of that year, when Manuel Azaña came to power. Cortes, whose remarkable life was later the subject of Ronald Fraser's *In Hiding*, was typical of many left-wing Republicans. An atheist, who welcomed the Republic's land and other reforms, and the introduction of civic marriage, he was nonetheless far from radical in his views, and was strongly opposed to communism. He and his kind were hardly the dangerous 'Reds' whom many believed to be now ruling in Spain.

Alberti related how in general Spain's intellectuals, authors and artists celebrated the advent of the Republic. For Lorca, who had recently come back from America, the first two and a half years of the Republic must have been particularly auspicious.

In 1931 celebrations were put on at Fuentevaqueros to coincide with the naming of a street after him. After the election of Azaña, he was appointed the director of the Government-sponsored theatre company, La Barraca, the aims of which were to employ university students to bring drama to the provinces, an enterprise typifying the initial spirit of the Republic, progressive and optimistic. The only surviving film shots of Lorca – shown to visitors to the Fuentevaqueros Museum – are of the poet with smiling face travelling with his company to their next engagement. Such was La Barraca's success that it was invited in 1933 to tour Argentina, where it remained until the end of the year. A bleaker and more troubled Spain awaited Lorca on his return.

On 17 June 1934, Ignacio Sánchez Mejías was fatally gored at the bullring of Manzanares near Madrid, an event commemorated by Lorca in an ode with the insistently ominous refrain, 'It was exactly five in the afternoon': *Eran las cinco en punto de la tarde.* The poem, one of Lorca's greatest, is full of foreboding:

> *¡Oh blanco muro de España!*
> *¡Oh negro toro de pena!*
> O white wall of Spain!
> O black bull of grief!

The political situation in Spain was rapidly deteriorating, Azaña's government having been ousted in November 1933, and a rightwing backlash having set in following the appointment of Lerroux as prime-minister. Land-owners, caciques and their allies were taking their revenge on those who had opposed them; the extreme right-wing party, the Falange, recently founded by Primo de Rivera's son, José Antonio, was growing at an alarming rate. The various left-wing opponents of Lerroux finally came together in January 1936 to form the Popular Front, which managed to defeat the Right in the elections held one month later. Manuel Cortes was made major of Míjas, an unenviable position at a time when his country was clearly heading for civil war.

The breakdown of Spain in the years immmediately preceding the Civil War is described in Ralph Bates' novel *The Olive Grove*, which is set mainly in the imaginary Andalucían village of Olivares. Bates, an English communist as fully opposed to anarchism as he was to the Church, gives a detailed picture of Andalucían society, from the down-trodden day-labourer to the aloof landlord lost in his mystical day-dreams; at the centre of the novel are two friends, one a guitar-playing anarchist, the other an anarchist who becomes opposed to violence. The novel has many of the Romantic clichés of Andalucía, and a rather heavy-handed symbolism; but it has the advantage of being written by someone who had both extensive personal experience of working in an Andalucían olive grove, and an informed knowledge of the Spanish political scene. Most of the British who came to Spain during this period recognized the mounting political tensions in the country, but failed to take these seriously enough, and continued merely to rhapsodize the beauty and picturesqueness of the land that they were in.

The mood of Spain during the Easter of 1936, and the attitudes towards the country of the British traveller, are memorably evoked in Louis MacNeice's poem, *But they Remember Spain*. Recalling a journey made with the art historian and future Russian spy Anthony Blunt, MacNeice describes attending a boring bull-fight in Seville, catching a cold on a rainy day in Córdoba, and failing to find the right light in which to take a photograph; he meets an obnoxious Cambridge don who shows off his Spanish by ordering anis at a café.

> But only an inch behind
> The map of olive and ilex, this painted hoarding,
> Careless of visitors the people's mind
> Was tunnelling like a mole to day and danger.
> And the day before we left
> We saw the mob in flower at Algeciras,
> Outside a toothless door, a church bereft
> Of its image and its aura.

Chalmers-Mitchell, now happily settled in his retirement home at Málaga, and enjoying life among the large British community there, remembered the spring of 1936 as 'a particularly beautiful spring', so much so that 'many who were in Málaga for the first time were considering buying or building villas for permanent residence.' 'There was,' he continued, 'much bridge at the club; golf on a rather inefficient but beautiful course recently opened, motoring into the neighbourhood, walks and mutual visits for luncheons or dinners or tea.' Living nearby, in the exclusive residential district of Churriana, were Gerald Brenan and his wife Gamel Woolsey. On the afternoon of 18 July, both Chalmers-Mitchell and Woolsey were sitting in their respective luxuriant gardens, the former reading a book, the latter resting after a lunch of fried sardines. 'It was the most beautiful day of the summer,' she wrote in her memoir *Death's Other Kingdom* (1939). But suddenly shots rang out, and soon reports were coming in of buildings been set alight. The temperature was 97° Fahrenheit, 'not a good day for burning houses,' Woolsey reflected. Meanwhile in a garden on Granada's Alhambra hill, Lady Nicholson, recently arrived from a damp and depressing London, was being troubled by similar uncalled-for disturbances. She had come to stay with her daughter and Spanish son-in-law, and had up to now been thoroughly enjoying herself. 'The nightingales were singing in the Alhambra woods, the fountains were playing in the gardens of the Generalife, and after a wet winter the countryside was extraordinarily green, and dotted with clumps of wild pink oleander, which had an intoxicating fragrance. The

The view from Lorca's window at La Huerta de San Vicente

sun shone on the vega, and on the snow-capped peaks of the Sierra Nevada. Who wanted to think of politics in such surroundings as these ? Assuredly not I. . .' The young Laurie Lee, nearing the end of the Spanish idyll which he would record in *As I Walked Out One Midsummer Morning*, found himself on the Granada coast, at Salobreña, on that fateful day of July 18. 'There were no announcements, no newspapers, just a whimpering in the street and the sound of a woman weeping.'

On July 17 a military uprising led by General Franco had broken out in Morocco and had soon spread to the mainland. By the end of the following day, the entire western half of Andalucía, as well as the town of Granada, had fallen to the rebels. Andalucía had been taken by surprise, but the suddeness of its capture had been very much in keeping with the region's response to invaders throughout its history. Furthermore, the uprising had been almost universally supported by the great landowners of Jerez, Cádiz and Seville, whose wealthy estates were providing food for Franco's troops. Romanticism and Andalucían machoism fuelled the enthusiasm for Franco among the younger landlords, some of whom were to form cavalry batallions with horses and riders harnessed as if they were going to the ferias at

Seville or Jerez; one such young man, known as *Cañoncito pum* ('little cannonfire') toured Seville's Aljarafe on 19 July frightening villagers into submission with the cannon he was carrying.

Seville itself, the first Spanish city to welcome Franco, was taken with insolent ease by General Queipo de Llano, who simply walked into the city's military headquarters, and arrested those officers who were too timid to join the revolt. Within hours he was delivering from here the first of his celebrated radio broadcasts, which were avidly listened to by everyone, though less for their inspirational than amusement value. Gamel Woolsey was not alone in believing that the General gave these while under the influence of the local wine, for he had 'the cheerful wandering manner of the habitual drinker'. On one occasion, according to both Woolsey and Brenan, he referred to the 'villainous *fascistas*', and was quietly corrected by someone at his side, 'No, no, General, *marxistas.*' 'What difference does it make?' he apparently replied, 'both are villainous.' Arthur Koestler, then active as a journalist, had the privilege of seeing the General at the microphone, in a decrepit, make-shift studio, ranting like the buffooonish demagogue in Bertholt Brecht's *The Resistible Rise of Arturo Ui.* As examples of the contents of his broadcasts, Koestler quoted the following: 'The Marxist are ravening beasts, but we are gentlemen. Señor Companys deserves to be stuck like a pig'; 'I have given orders for three members of the families of each of the sailors of the loyalist cruisers that bombarded La Línea to be shot. . . To conclude my talk I should like to tell my daughter in Paris that we are all in excellent health and that we should like to hear from her.'

García Lorca had returned from Madrid to Granada on 14 July, and gone to stay at his parents' new estate, La Huerta de San Vicente, just beyond the town's western outskirts (see page 306). This house, the most beautiful of the surviving Lorca homes, was to remain in the family's possession up to 1986, and is still looked after by a man who has worked for the family for over forty years. Though now lying within sight of the ugly modern apartment blocks that line Granada's wide street known as the Ronda, it had remained surrounded by orchards and fields until as late as 1992, when a characterless commemorative park was created. In Lorca's time, the Alhambra was clearly visible from the house, and the peace and beauty of the place must have been quite idyllic. Only four days after Lorca's arrival here that July, the town entered one of the darkest phases in its history.

By 20 July, the insurgents had captured Granada, encountering resistance only in the maze of streets in the Albaicín, which finally capitulated on 22 July. Surrounded at first on all sides by enemy territory, the Granada insurgents felt understandably insecure in their position, and responded by executing as many as possible of the town's potential trouble-makers. Every day, early in the morning, lorries would climb up the Alhambra hill carrying prisoners to be shot in the magnificently situated cemetery. William Davenhill, British Consul at Granada, closed his ears to this morbid convoy, which also passed right next to the Hotel Washington Irving, where many of the journalists and foreign visitors to the town were gathered. Lady Nicholson, by no means a sympathizer of the 'Reds', came to dread these morning shootings, though they were to provide her with the title of her odious memoir, *Death in the Morning*. To calm her nerves she drank endless cups of tea, much to the amusement of her Spanish son-in-law. 'The English are an extraordinary people,' he used to say. 'Always in a crisis they drink tea!'

Lorca stayed on at the Huerta de San Vicente until at least 9 August, then decided that it would be safer for him to move into the centre of the town. He chose not to stay with Falla, with whom he had recently fallen out after having dedicated to him his *Ode to the Holy Sacrament*, a poem which had offended the composer's religious sensibilities. Instead he went to a house at Calle Argulo 1 which belonged to the family of Luis Rosales, a writer friend whose brother was a prominent Falangist. Lorca believed that this connection with the Falange would protect him, but he was arrested on the 16th of August, and executed either late on the 18th or early on the 19th. The Nationalists attempted to minimize the outcry which news of his death might provoke by making the fake claim on the 19th of August that the 'Marxists' had murdered the Quintero brothers, a piece of news which might well have pleased playgoers of all political persuasions. Reports that Lorca had been assassinated were not confirmed by the Nationalists, though after weeks of speculation, they were eventually accepted as true by a horrified Europe. The first Spaniard to react to the news with a poem was Antonio Machado:

> He was seen to fade in air. . .
> Cut, friends,
> in stone and dreams, in Alhambra,
> a tomb for the poet,
> over a fountain where the water weeps
> and eternally cries:
> the crime took place in Granada. . . his
> Granada.
> *que fue en Granada el crimen*
> *sabed – pobre Granada! – en su Granada!...*

The reasons why Lorca was killed have been much discussed, and no easy answer can be given to the question. Unlike Alberti, a member of the Communist Party, Lorca was never actively involved in politics, though neither was he apolitical, as was later claimed during the Franco period: he was an enthusiastic supporter of the Popular Front. A poem of his portraying the Guardia Civil as a symbol of death and evil, together with his homosexuality, might not have endeared him to certain Spanish circles; but it was probably his left-wing views combined with his outspoken comments on Granada's philistine bourgeoisie that were held most against him.

His assassination was at any rate an acute embarrassment to Franco and his supporters, who later hampered all attempts to investigate the death. One of the finest sections in Gerald Brenan's *The Face of Spain* is an account of the author's search for the place where Lorca died. Local conversations led Brenan to conclude that Lorca was driven up into the mountains near Víznar and shot in an execution ground commanding an extensive view over the vega. Appropriately this site, known as the Fuente Grande, was near a spring which had been greatly admired by the Islamic poets of Granada, and around which various Islamic villas had been built. Brenan had been driven to Víznar by taxi, but the taxi-driver had become suspicious of him, and the author was soon intercepted by the local police. The taxi-driver who took me to Víznar in September 1988 talked openly about Lorca's death, and had even read the stimulating book on the subject by Ian Gibson, a work which had been banned during the Franco period. This man helped me to climb over the gates of the ugly commemorative park which had been opened in 1986 near a large luxury residential block (see page 306). The circumstances of my visit to Víznar could hardly have been more different to Brenan's, yet the subject of the poet's death is still not without its controversy. A handful of extreme right-wing families continue to play a dominant role in Granada life, and I was even told about one Lorca expert who is given police protection every time he appears in Granada for a lecture or book-signing.

Mass executions such as those that took place at Granada were also perpetuated by the Nationalists at Seville and Córdoba: the commander in charge of the latter town, Major Bruno Ibañez, was in fact so brutal in his recriminations against the Republicans that he was finally removed from the town, the Nationalists fearing that he would end up by doing away with most of the population. Republican resistance in eastern Andalucía was centred mainly on the villages, which were the scene of constant reprisals by both left and right. Terrible atrocities, still vividly remembered in the villages today, were committed by both sides, though, after the Civil War, blame for these was put almost wholly on the 'Reds'. The 'Reds' too were accused of the most appalling brutalities in Málaga, where they had managed to defeat the July uprising and to keep the town until February 1937.

Chalmers-Mitchell, who prided himself on being a neutral observer, wrote that the 'Reds' had behaved almost impeccably in Málaga, and that on his daily visits into the centre of the town, he had witnessed no instances of cruelty on their part. Brenan, who later confessed to a dislike of Chalmers-Mitchell, believed that the man had developed a pathological left-wing ideology as a result of an oppressive religious background in Scotland. Yet Chalmers-Mitchell, like Brenan and Woolsey, had sheltered a Nationalist family in his Málaga home, and had helped many other Nationalists to escape from the town. Whatever his political views, he was certainly a most intriguing figure, a parody of proverbial British imperturbability, refusing to be flustered at the height of a crisis, and dressed always in immaculate summer clothes with a fresh flower in his button hole. When the Nationalists were on the point of seizing Málaga, and most of the British community had been evacuated from the town, Chalmers-Mitchell decided to stay on here so as to be able to observe subsequent developments. Arthur Koestler, who had come to Málaga in January, bravely resolved to stay with him.

No-one believed that the Republicans would be able to hold on to the town, least of all Koestler, who had driven up to the nearby Sierra de Torcal to examine the town's defensive measures. Here he had found one Captain Pizarro (a reputed descendant of the conqueror of Peru) seated next to a telephone which was intended to relay any news of an enemy advance: the captain had anticipated the likely event of the telephone not working by rigging up a wire and a bell to the military post below, but the wire was constantly being pecked at by birds. The Nationalists captured the town on 9 February, and both Chalmers-Mitchell and Koestler were arrested, thanks largely to the ungrateful behaviour of a Nationalist whom Chalmers-Mitchell had previously saved from the 'Reds'. Chalmers-Mitchell was released immediately, and he returned to England, but Koestler spent many months in prison, and narrowly escaped execution. His experiences later served as the basis of his novel *Darkness at Noon*.

The Civil War dragged on until April 1939, the Republicans holding on to Almería and the eastern corner of Andalucía almost until the end of the war. The mayor of Míjas, Manuel Cortes, and Rafael Alberti were both fighting for the Republicans at Valencia when their side finally surrendered. Cortes returned to his home village, intending to surrender himself to the authorities, but then decided to to go into hiding. Alberti was able to escape from Spain, and emigrated to Argentina, the first stage of an exile which was to last until 1977. Most of Spain's prominent intellectuals, artists, musicians and writers were likewise forced to leave their country. Antonio Machado fled with his mother and other refugees to Collioure across the French border, but died there almost immediately. His brother, Manuel, from whom he had become estranged at the beginning of the war owing to their differing political views, had gone to Collioure to see him, but had arrived too late. Juan Ramón Jiménez escaped across the Atlantic, and found temporary homes in Puerto Rico, Argentina, Cuba, Florida and, finally, Washington, where he was to die in 1958, eighteen months after receiving the Nobel Prize; as he had wished, a museum to him was later set up in his family home at Moguer, bearing both his name and that of his wife Zenobia, who had lived for only a few days after the news of the Nobel Prize. Manuel de Falla, too ill to leave Granada in 1936, left for Argentina at the end of the war, and spent his last seven years in a beautiful hilly area of the country known as 'New Andalucía', the capital of which was another Córdoba. Alberti went once to visit him there, and the two men recollected past times. On the subject of Lorca, Falla remained silent, until after they had exchanged their farewells, when he hesitatingly said: 'I'm sorry, dear Alberti. . . I know such horrible things about that. . . but my conscience prevents me from speaking.'

Andalucía, as with the rest of Spain, was left after the Civil War an impoverished place, both physically and spiritually. Few Andalucían writers are worth singling out in the post-war period, the literary output of Nationalists such as José María Pemán – the author of a book on Andalucía – being singularly mediocre. Gerald Brenan paid a visit to the region in 1949, and recorded the sad impressions of his journey in *The Face of Spain*. These impressions, however, did not prevent him and Gamel Woolsey from returning to live in Churriana in 1953. Brenan stayed in the area for much of his remaining life, dying in 1986 at nearby Alhaurín el Grande, after having been rescued by the Spanish Government from the oblivion of an old people's home in England.

In the years that Brenan had spent in England he had finally found himself as a writer, his first important book being *The Spanish Labyrinth* (1943), an attempt by someone of slightly naïve political views to explain as simply as possible the complexities of the Spanish Civil War. Later, in *The Literature of the Spanish People* (1951), he had bravely taken on the whole literary history of Spain, a history of which the English-speaking world was, and still is, shamefully ignorant: once again the tone is that of an inquisitive enthusiast, who prefers his own spontaneous observations to years of painstaking scholarship. Not until 1957, four years after having moved to Churriana, did he finally publish *South from Granada*, the book by which he was to be best remembered. This account of Yegen and of his experiences in the village is admirably unsentimental, though it had the effect of inspiring a romantic yearning for Andalucían village life among many of its readers. The Andalucían people are among the most urban-minded in Europe, but, thanks partly to Brenan, the British came to believe that the 'real Andalucía' is to be found in the region's traditional rural communities.

South from Granada appeared at a time when the coast near Brenan's home was beginning to be radically transformed by tourism. Torremolinos, described by one 19th-century traveller as 'a delightful small fishing village', was by now being taken over by pot-smoking beatniks, most of whom, according to Brenan, were New York Jews. Brenan, with his love of bohemian life, rather welcomed these new arrivals, especially the uninhibited young women, some of whom came to stay with him. However, when Torremolinos, Fuengirola and other coastal villages near Málaga began to be increasingly commercialized in the 1960's, even such a tolerant and adaptable foreigner as Brenan became deeply depressed. Manuel Cortes, having spent thirty-three years in hiding in his native village of Míjas, emerged in 1968, and saw this coastal development for the first time. The shock of seeing what had happened to the former fishing village of Fuengirola, immediately below Míjas, must have been a considerable one. To Cortes, who had known Míjas in its days of great poverty, there was at least the consolation that a new era of prosperity had begun. One wonders, though, what he would have thought of Míjas today, which is virtually a suburb of Fuengirola, and overrun by coachloads of tourists. Some of the older inhabitants can be seen leading these tourists around the chic white streets of this 'typical Andalucían village' on gaily bridled donkeys known as *Burro-Taxis*.

Laurie Lee, in an interview at the end of his life, regretted not only the transformation of the Spanish coast into a 'concrete cliff' but also other aspects of modern Spain. 'Spaniards,' he said, 'have been poisoned by soap, by *Dallas* and *Dynasty*, as have all the once culturally-clean peoples of Europe and the Middle East. They have lost their identity. They don't known where they are any more.' Many foreigners would love Spain to be the 'unchanged and unchangeable' country that Ford had described in the 1840's. But Spain, since the death of Franco, has changed more rapidly than almost any other Europen country. Andalucía itself, reduced to a backwater during the Franco period, received vast funds in the 1980's from a government headed by a Sevillian, Felipe González. The Seville World Exhibition of 1992 set in motion major social and architectural projects, and prompted a radical improvement in the region's communications network. Hopes were even raised that Seville would regain some of the international importance that it had had in the 16th century.

Andalucía today, like the rest of Spain, continues to suffer from what the Spaniards refer to as 'the hangover of '92', a condition brought on by the collapse of the many small businesses created in anticipation of an economic boom, and by tales of corruption surrounding the recently defeated government of Felipe González, a government whose increasing unpopularity had been compounded by the way it had favoured Seville at the expense of other parts of Spain. To make matters worse the region was affected after 1992 by one of the most serious droughts this century, a consequence of which was the postponement in 1995 of an event with which Granada had hoped to attract some of the world attention that had previously been directed towards Seville – the World Skiing Championships.

For all the changes that Andalucía has experienced over the past three decades, romantic attitudes towards the region remain as prevalent as ever. The image of a dynamic, progressive Andalucía that the Seville EXPO had tried so hard to promote has proved less persuasive than the more familiar image of a festive, seductive region living in the shadow of its Moorish past. Indeed the disappointments of the present have now led the Andalucíans themselves to dwell in this past with a degree of obsessiveness recalling the orientalist delusions of the Romantic traveller. As if in expiation of their guilt in celebrating the defeat of the Moors in 1492, the Andalusians have begun to forge links with Morocco and have encouraged a massive programme of research into the Islamic heritage. Islamic names are being given, inappropriately, to a growing number of bars and discothèques; Sufism and Islamic tea-rooms have taken hold in Granada; and an organization called *El Legado Andalusi* has created within Andalucía a series of Islamic cultural 'routes' for tourists to follow. One of these has even been named after Washington Irving.

EXPO in Seville

The many clichés and prejudices that have grown up around Andalucía will be difficult to dispel. For the moment one can only hope that first-time visitors to the region, embarking perhaps on one of the so-called 'Routes of al-Andalus', will come here with an open mind and find a place which is not only romantic and exotic, but also sophisticated, complex, and with one of the richest cultural histories of any part of Europe.

A Gazetteer of Andalucía

Andalucía is a vast and perplexing region, much of it unknown even to its inhabitants. In the gazetteer below I have been able only to hint at the enormous variety of the region's attractions, and have made no attempt to write a comprehensive guide. My selection of lesser places is a personal one, and the information given under all the entries unshamedly idiosyncratic. Methodical tourism is alien to the Andalucían mentality, and the immense heat which affects the region for much of the year greatly reduces the amount of conventional sight-seeing that can be done. The leisurely pace and anarchic character of Andalucía soon take hold of the traveller, and I hope that the following pages will convince the reader that the region is best seen in this way, slowly, meanderingly, and with lengthy stops at bars to try out local food and drinks.

The gazetteer is arranged alphabetically, though frequently I have included under a single location a variety of villages, monuments and scenic attractions that can be conveniently visited from it. The references at the beginning of each entry are to the map printed inside the front cover, but the reader is strongly advised to use the gazetteer in conjunction with Michelin Map No. 446 (*Andalucía, Costa del Sol*), which is clear, detailed, and well indexed.

I have avoided describing hotels, unless they are of historical or architectural interest, or have considerable character. Bars on the other hand have frequently been included, owing to their central role in the life of the Andalucían village – my emphasis has been on those with eccentric and old-fashioned interiors, strong cultural associations, and renowned tapas or bar snacks. Details of food and craft specialities are given, with occasional indications as to where these can be bought. Every village, every town, and every district of a town has its own festivals, and I have mentioned in the entries only those that are particularly unusual or famous. A fuller list of festivals, together with further information and opening times, hotels, restaurants, tourist offices, holiday activities and so one, are featured in the yellow pages towards the back of the book.

Entries in **bold** are the principal reference to any place. Towns mentioned in SMALL CAPITALS have a full reference of their own in the gazetteer.

Boabdil (detail of modern statue in Granada)

ADRA [4G]: The last king of the Moors, the unfortunate Boabdil, stayed in Adra immediately before leaving Spain for good. If he sighed when fleeing from Granada, he would have sighed even more had Adra in the 15th century been anything like the place which it is today. Backed by black, depressing mountains, Adra can only be recommended for those with a love of seedy ports. Should you wish to visit the Moorish castle where Boabdil was put up, you will just be able to make out a few remaining fragments lying off the Calle Castillo, surrounded by dereliction and grey modern blocks. The lead-mining town of **Berja**, 17 km inland, is similarly grim despite references in certain guide-books to its 'magnificent' palaces.

To the east of Adra stretches the **Campo de Dalías**, flat land which in recent years has been made exceptionally fertile owing to the introduction of 'plastic culture' (see page 44). The N340 to Almería is today virtually one long, featureless town.

ALCALÁ DE GUADAIRA [3C], one of the liveliest towns on the outskirts of Seville, is popularly known as Alcalá de los Panaderos ('Alcalá of the Bakers') because it was from here that much of the bread for Seville was baked. It is dominated by its massive Moorish fortress or *al-Kala*, the largest surviviving one built by the Almohads in Spain. The castle is incorporated into a slightly seedy public park, and you are free to wander around it, and to climb its many disintegrating square towers. The views down to the River Alcaira are delightful, but the ones towards Seville are obscured by industrial pollution.

Four kilometres to the south of the town off the C342 to Morón de la Frontera is another impressive ruin of a castle, the **Castillo de Marchenilla**, which has parts dating back to Roman time, and machicolated round towers of the 14th century; the place is now used as a warehouse.

ALCALÁ LA REAL [3F]: Near the southern border of Jaén province, Alcalá looks over a rolling landscape of olive trees and wheatfields that is terminated to the south by the distant range of the Sierra Nevada. The early history of the town is centred entirely on the parched, ship-like escarpment of La Mota, which was inhabited in prehistoric times and turned by the Moors into a heavily fortified citadel (*al-Kala* – hence the name 'Alcalá'). The town's Moorish heyday was the 12th century, when it formed an independent fiefdom within Almoravid Spain; subsequently it came under repeated attack from the Christians, who were interested in its strategic position at the northern approach to Granada's vega. Its capture by Alfonso XI in 1341, when it was given the title of *Real* or 'Royal', brought the Christians to within 52 km of the Nasrid capital. After 1492, with the disappearance of the Moorish threat, the townspeople gradually moved down from the citadel to develop the present large and busy lower town, where one of the greatest of Andalucía's Golden Age sculptors, Juan Martínez Montañés, was born in 1568 (see page 122).

Though several 16th- to 18th-century churches and palaces can be found in the new town (and a delightful main square with a late Renaissance town hall), the visitor to Alcalá will be drawn immediately towards the exciting walled profile of the citadel, which can be reached by following an attractive and steeply ascending street of white houses, the Calle Real. Leaving behind the last of the houses you will climb up steps to the Puerta de las Lanzas, immediately below which is a gate leading to the ruins of the church of Santo Domingo de Silos: the first Christian structure to be erected within the Moorish town, this dates back to 1341 and is thought to have replaced a mosque. The Puerta de las Lanzas, which brings the visitor into the upper citadel, was built in the 16th century, when the Moorish walls were extensively remodelled.

Further up is the large and impressive Puerta de la Imagen (so-called because of a statue of the Virgin which was placed here after the Christian conquest), which is a largely unaltered Moorish gate recalling the Puerta de la Justicia in the Alhambra. Attached to the gate is a plaque commemorating the lively Islamic scholar Ibn Said al-Andalusi, who was born in Alcalá in 1243 but moved as a young man to Seville, and thereafter led an itinerant life in North Africa and the Middle East, probably dying in Damascus in 1274; in Cairo he wrote an enormous work on Andalucía, which includes the first anthology of Hispano-Moorish poetry (translated in English by A. J. Arberry as *Moorish Poetry*, Cambridge 1953); the anthology is arranged according to place, the section on Alcalá being largely taken up by poems by his family and himself.

Beyond the gate you continue ascending between walls up to the highest level of the citadel, a large area strewn with rocks and ruins dominated by the imposing structures of a Moorish keep and the former convent church of Santa María la Mayor de la Mota. The citadel's rapid deterioration since the 17th century has been halted in recent years by a brash and ongoing restoration campaign that has led to much rebuilding and a proliferation of audio-visual displays. A massive video screen blocks today the east end of Santa María, a 14th-century foundation transformed in the sixteenth into a spacious and impressive late gothic building with Renaissance detailing. Fragments of the original church, together with Palaeolithic and later tombs, and remains of Roman and Moorish structures, can be seen in the now exposed foundations, which have been covered by a glass floor. The keep, with its inner Umayyad gate, contains today horrible costumed figures, but is worth visiting for the steep climb up to its battlements, from where superb views can be had of the Sierra Nevada. The numerous archaeological finds once displayed inside the building have been transferred to the excellent museum now housed in the former Bishop's Palace in the lower town.

With the conquest of Alcalá by the Christians in 1341, the burden of protecting Granada from the north fell heavily on nearby **Moclín**, which Ferdinand V was to describe as 'the key to the vega'. Moclín, a small and pleasant village 25 km from Alcalá, is reached by driving south for 21 km on the main Granada road, and then turning left at Puerto Lope. The citadel, with its well preserved rings of walls rising above the village on a steep rocky outcrop, fell to the Christians immediately after the conquest of LOJA in 1486, which also led to the capture of the nearby castles of MONTEFRÍO and Colomera (of which only the scantiest ruins survive). A modest restaurant with an enchanting terrace stands near the citadel's entrance, from which it is a short walk on a level path to the Church of the Paño, a heavily restored and remodelled structure founded by the Catholic Kings over a mosque. The bus-loads of visitors that occasionally descend on this out-of-the-way and otherwise little visited site are primarily interested in this church, which houses the miraculous image of the *Christ of the Paño*, an unappealing 16th-century canvas said to have cured a sacristan of his cataracts (an illness known at the time as *la enfermedad del Paño*): the festive pilgrimage honouring this image at the beginning of October is one of the most popular in eastern Andalucía.

Few visitors continue beyond the church to scramble over rocks up to the top of the citadel, a walk which is rewarded on clear days by one of the most exhilarating panoramas to be seen of Granada's vega backed by the luminous, snowy expanse of the Sierra Nevada.

ALCAUDETE [5D]: Strategically situated on what was once the frontier between Moorish and Christian Spain, Alcaudete changed hands repeatedly from 1085 to 1340, when it was definitively conquered by the Christian King Alfonso XI. Overlooking a broad valley of wheat fields, with distant views towards the Sierra de Cordova, and with a backcloth of rocky mountains, the town today is known largely for its baby broad beans, and for being Andalucía's second largest producer of the delicate biscuits knows as polvorones and mantecados (see ESTEPA). The old, upper town, has a pleasantly old-fashioned main square, with a bar that seems straight out of the 1920's. Further up are a 16th-century prison (newly converted into a stylish hotel and restaurant), a superbly ornate late Renaissance and early baroque parish church, and one of Andalucía's finest castles. The latter, privately owned until recently, stands starkly atop a bare outcrop of rock. Dramatically restored by the Town Hall, it features today the inevitable audio-visual displays, though these at least are entertaining and informative. The castle, dating back to the 11th century, was guarded from 1340 onwards by the military religious order of the Knights of Calatrava.

Next to the park in the modern town is the excellent and very friendly Restaurante Almocaden, which serves light and imaginative interpretations of traditional local food. Those in search of an unchanged, family-run establishment dating back to the 1950's and still serving cheap and excellent local specialities should head off to the wonderful Casa Morejon in nearby Doña Mencía – the establishment, with its colourful long and narrow patio, is one of the few remaining ones of its kind in Andalucía.

ALGECIRAS [5D]: After driving along the Costa del Sol from Málaga, Algeciras comes as a pleasant relief: though it is an indisputably ugly town, at least it has a life of its own independent of tourism. Founded in Roman times, and occupied by the Moors from 713 to 1344, it has kept virtually nothing of its past, and is cramped with dirty 19th- and 20th-century blocks. Much of its life is centred around the port, Algeciras being the main point of departure for those going to Ceuta, Tangiers and other Moroccan towns. The place also boasts the first hotel on the Andalucían coast, the luxurious Hotel Reina Cristina, which is set in a large park on the western edge of the town. Sir Alexander Harrison, a British philanthropist, decided to build the hotel in 1890 after his firm, Henderson Associates, completed the construction of the Bobadilla to Algeciras railway. The architect of the hotel was British, and the building (gutted by fire in 1928 and extensively remodelled) has much in common with the Hotel Reina Victoria in Ronda. Two plaques on the reception desk record the signatures of some of the many famous and diverse guests who have stayed in the hotel, including Alfonso XII, Sir Arthur Conan Doyle, W. B. Yeats, Orson Welles, Ava Gardner, Cole Porter and Rock Hudson.

ALHAMA DE GRANADA [4F]: 'Alas for my Alhama!' groaned Richard Ford, lying in his flea-ridden inn here, and thinking of the famous refrain of a popular medieval ballad which Byron, Southey, Mérimée and other Romantics translated. The words of the ballad referred to the surprise attack made on the town in 1482 by Rodrigo Ponce de Léon (see page 88) – an attack which heralded the last stage in the Christian conquest of Spain. The governor of this reputedly impregnable town had been away at the time at a wedding in Málaga, and the Christians merely had to kill a solitary guard lying on the battlements to gain entry into the citadel. They met with far greater resistance while making their way from here into the actual town; and by the time that the Nasrid king Abd al-Hasan arrived with his troops from Granada to help the beleaguered townspeople, he was met by the sight of hundreds of Moorish corpses thrown over the walls to be eaten by carrion and dogs; he

View of the gorge of Alhama

immediately ordered the dogs to be shot ('not even the city's dogs could remain alive,' observed one contemporary), but failed to recapture the town, and was eventually called away by reports of a large Christian army advancing towards LOJA. The events of the siege were vividly chonicled by a Christian eyewitness, Fernando del Pulgar, secretary to the Catholic Monarchs.

The sadness caused by the loss of Alhama is easy to understand, for the place is one of the most beautiful of Andalucía's small towns, and situated in a landscape of classical nobility, featuring meadows, ravines, olive trees, streams and picturesquely shaped outcrops of rock. Approaching the town on the C340 from Granada, turn right 2 km before the village, and you will soon reach a tiny gorge formed by the fast-flowing Río Alhama. At the entrance to the gorge the river is spanned by a Roman bridge, just as it would be in a classical landscape painting of the 17th or 18th centuries. The small road follows the gorge as it descends into an oasis of trees shading a popular spa resort, the waters of which, apparently beneficial for those suffering from rheumatism and stress, have been famous since Roman times. Fernando del Pulgar, searching for a reason why 'it had pleased God to show his wrath so suddenly and cruelly against [the Moors]' found the answer in these thermal springs. 'We discovered,' he wrote, 'that very close [to Alhama] there are baths in a beautiful building where there is a natural hot spring. Thither men used to resort, both from the town itself and from the surrounding region in order to bathe. These baths were the cause of a certain softness in their bodies, from which there proceeded idleness and other deceits and evil dealings that they inflicted on one another in order to sustain the ease to which they were accustomed.'

The original spa buildings have been replaced by the modern Hotel Balneario, but if you go inside this hotel and ask to be shown the Moorish Baths (*Termas Árabes*), you will be taken downstairs through the modern baths until eventually a door is opened from behind which emanates a great heat (the word *al-Hamma* means 'hot springs' in Arabic). Suddenly, you will be confronted by what appears to be a half-submerged mosque, with two enormous and dramatically spotlit horseshoe arches standing in the water and supporting a sturdy octagonal vault. This is not, in fact, an actual bath, but merely the cistern built over the thermal source, from which water was channelled into baths (now gone) on either side, one of which was for women, and the other for men. The use of stone rather than brick suggests this structure dates back to the time of the Caliphs; there are also stones with Roman inscriptions indicating the Roman origin of the spa itself. Should you wish to take a thermal bath, you might find it more enjoyable not to do so in the hotel but to go outside and lie in the pool where the hot waters join the river (just below the modern bridge at the entrance to the hotel's grounds). In the autumn and winter months, when the hotel is closed, many people from the town and even from as far away as Granada come here late at night, after the discothèques have closed, to steam off their alcoholic intake by lying naked in the river. Pulgar would not have approved.

The town of Alhama is perched on top of a rock ledge, and on its southern side looks precipitously down to a wide and deep gorge, lined at the bottom with mills, following the verdant banks of the Alhama as it winds its way down from its source high up in the Sierra de Almijara. The best views are from the terrace behind the 17th- to 18th-century church of the Carmen, a simple austere structure formed of massive blocks of stone; the much damaged but recently restored interior has draperies dramatically hung behind the high altar.

The small, tree-lined main square is framed at one end by its Moorish castle, now a decayed private residence which in the 19th century was given toy-like battlements. A narrow street flanking the castle leads into the tiny, late medieval heart of Alhama, dominated by its parish church given by Ferdinand and Isabella; the tall, uncluttered interior is one of the finest late gothic structures in the province of Granada, and there is the added pleasure of the sacristy, which has vestments with borders supposedly embroidered by Isabella herself. The elegant renaissance bell-tower at the eastern end of the church was designed by the famous Diego de Siloe (see page 101) and faces an enchanting small square with a well preserved 16th-century warehouse or *pósito*.

Behind the square you will reach the sorry, rubbish-filled shell of the Church of Las Angustias, a fine early baroque structure which fell into disrepair in the 1930's. From here you can begin the steep and exciting descent into the gorge, passing a ruined Moorish dungeon built into the rock; some of the chains of Christian prisoners that were placed on the outer walls of the church of San Juan de los Reyes in Toledo were reputedly taken from here. This echoing, urine-smelling cavern seems popular now with heroin addicts. Returning to the parish church, and following its southern side back to the town's main square you will skirt the so-called Casa de la Inquisición, notable for its amusing Isabelline plateresque façade.

Some 19 km along the C335 to Vélez-Málaga you pass through **Ventas de Zafarraya**, where there is a deep cleft in the Sierra de Tejeda which has served as a pass since ancient times. On the other side you enter the province of Málaga, and there are beautiful views over a verdant, fertile landscape down to the distant Mediterranean.

ALMERÍA [4H], the most African of Spanish towns, feels cut off from the rest of Spain, and indeed until comparatively recently was best reached by sea. Its heyday was during its period of Moorish domination. In the mid 10th century, the Caliph of Córdoba, Abd al-Rahman III, had a great fortress and arsenal built here, and transformed the place into the most important maritime town in al-Andalus. After the fall of the Caliphate in 1031, Almería became the capital of a Moorish principality rivalled only by that of Seville. Poetry and philosophy flourished here, and the town's economy prospered as never before through the expansion of its silk and ceramics industries. 'When Almería was Almería,' runs a famous old saying, 'Granada was but its farm.' The town was captured by Alfonso VII in 1147, and though regained by the Moors only three months later, it did not fare so well under its new Moorish rulers. In the two centuries following the surrender to Ferdinand and Isabella in 1481, the town's decline was compounded by a series of devastating earthquakes, one of which, in 1658, reduced its population to 500. The redevelopment of the local mining industry, and the construction of a railway line and a new port, led to a revival of the town's fortunes in the late 19th century, but only in very recent times has the place managed to shake off much of its overwhelming atmosphere of decay. Brenan frequented its brothels in the 1920s, though the town's slightly decadent notoriety peaked from the 1950s onwards, when the place became a major centre of the film industry. The fishing district of El Campillo was transformed with ugly blocks to accommodate film crews and their hangers-on, with passing celebrities being put up in the Gran Hotel. Ringo Starr stayed there in 1968, though the main member of the Beatles associated with Almeriá was John Lennon, who came to the town in 1966 to film *How I Won the War*, and to whom there is now a statue outside the Hotel Torreluz. Lennon started writing his hit song *Strawberry Fields* while staying in a seaside house at the end of the C/García Cañas; later he moved to a grand villa on the town's outskirts, now converted into a cinema museum known as the Casa del Cine. Almería's links with popular music were strengthened in the 1980s by the Irish rock group The Pogues, whose song *Fiesta in Almería* evoked the tackiness of a drunken spree here.

The 20th-century heart of Almería, with its beaches, luxury hotels, and regular grid of streets, is the eastern half of the town, which is separated from the western half by an enormous wide avenue known as the Ramblas. The main monument of interest in this part of town is the Archaeological Museum on the Calle de Javier Sanz. In its hospital-like rooms are displayed a remarkable series of prehistoric and ancient finds, most of which were donated by the eccentric Belgian engineer and archaeologist Louis Siret (see page 60); of special interest are the objects from the Bronze Age site of Los Millares (see TABERNAS). The western, older half of town is bordered to the west by barren slopes falling directly down to the sea, and to the north by the tall rocky outcrop supporting the vast Moorish fortress or *Alcazaba*. Along the sea-front runs an elegant palm-lined promenade, sheltering the town slightly from its port. The main thoroughfare through western Almería is the lively Paseo de Almería, which runs diagonally off the Ramblas, and, with its restaurants, open-air bars, and elegant turn-of-the-century buildings gone slightly to seed, bears a strong resemblance to the famous Cannebière in Marseille. At No. 56 is one of Almería's finest 19th-century buildings, the neo-baroque Círculo Mercantil, a club which on the outside could easily be mistaken for an opera house; its bar has a splendid ceramic decoration.

The area of the old town in between the sea-front and the Paseo de Almería, now dramatically prettified and heavily pedestrianized, was filled until only a few years back with dark, dirty and decaying 19th-century buildings, and was positively sinister at night. One of the few old establishments that has avoided recent refurbishment is the famous Casa Puga on the Calle Real (at the junction with the C/Jovellanos), a small and popular bar which has been in the ownership of the same family since 1870; in addition to its excellent tapas, and the attractive, barrel-filled interior, the place, despite its modest appearance, has the most extensive wine list you are ever likely to encounter in Spain, and even includes in this the exorbitantly priced and difficult-to-obtain Vega Sicilia – a Ribera del Duero wine that Prince Charles ineffectually tried to secure for his wedding. At the very centre of the old town is the squat and sturdy 16th-

The Cathedral, Almería

The Moorish walls of Almería

century cathedral, begun in 1524 on the site of a mosque destroyed in the earthquake of 1522. The crenellations on its exterior, and the overall fortress-like appearance of the building are due to Almería's being constantly under attack in the 16th century by pirates and rebellious moriscos. The military character of the outer walls is belied by the renaissance elegance and rich sculptural decoration of its west and north portals. The original plans for the building were drawn up by Diego de Siloe (see page 101), but executed by Juan de Orea, a pupil of Pedro Machuca (see page 101). The interior is an appealing blend of gothic and classical elements, and there is a rather austere renaissance cloister, shaded by palms. To the north of the cathedral is the 17th-century Plaza de la Constitución, an arcaded square in a grand Castilian style, but with dingy, ochre-coloured houses and sliding metal gates closing off some of its arches. On the Calle de San Juan to the east of the cathedral is the austere church of San Juan, where you can still see the mihrab (prayer niche) and some of the ornamentation from the mosque that stood on this site.

The Alcazaba, to which you climb from a rocky path leading off the Calle Almanzor, is one of the major surviving structures from the time of the Córdoba Caliphs, and the most important Moorish fortress in Spain after the Alhambra. A pair of camels is sometimes to be found sitting next to the path, waiting for tourists to be photographed with them. The fortress is divided into three levels, the lower of which contains a luxuriant and neatly arranged park, a refreshing contrast to the grime and starkness of the town below. From its northern battlements the town's surviving Moorish walls fall down into a dusty, African-looking valley and then rise up over the hill of San Cristóbal. The second level was once crowded with Moorish places, baths, prisons and other buildings, but is now a parched, unshaded and empty space; an Arab tent has been set up in the middle, where you can squat down and drink mint tea served by men in Arab costume. The third and highest level has a tower bearing the arms of Charles V. The sensation which you might have had throughout your stay in Almería that you are not in Spain but in Africa seems confirmed by looking down over the northern walls, and seeing immediately below you a group of Sahara gazelles running across a stretch of desert: the animals in fact form part of the Sahara Wildlife Rescue Centre, a research centre dedicated to the study of animals that are in danger of disappearing in their original habitat (this place can only be visited on previous application). From this part of the Alcazaba you can also see, to the west, the poor district of Almería known as La Chanca. The novelist Juan Goytisolo first became aware of this district following a climb up to the Alcazaba, and was later moved to write a powerful book publicizing the desperate plight of its inhabitants (see pages 15-16). To tourists and artists, however, La Chanca was once wonderfully picturesque, with a maze of white and colourfully painted walls clustered under an arid cliff. The poverty has been ameliorated in recent years, but to the loss of the district's once striking appearance: the former hovels have now been replaced by uniform grey housing.'

A restful and unusual place to stay near Almeria is the spa hotel at **Baños de Alhamilla**, which is situated high in the barren Sierra de Alhamilla, 20 km to the north of the town (follow the N340 for 10 km, then turn right into the industrial suburb of Pechina, from where the spa is clearly marked). The hotel, surrounded by palms and with extensive views towards the sea, is an austere late 18th-century structure centred around a double, arcaded patio; it has recently been modernized and embellished with neo-Moorish details. In the basement are sunken marble baths built by the Romans, taken over by the Moors, and still used today by the hotel's predominantly German clientèle. The 13th-century Islamic author al-Qizini wrote that ill people always got over their ailments after bathing in the waters here.

ALMONTE [3B], a dull small town in the middle of flat, pine-forested country, has as its main architectural attraction a fanciful late baroque church by A. M. de Figueroa, who was also responsible for the colourful church of San Juan Bautista at **La Palma del Condado**, 16 km to the north along the H612. The fame of Almonte derives entirely from the town's possession of the celebrated Virgin of the Rocío. The village of El Rocío, where this Virgin is kept, lies 15 km to the south, and is a curious place with the look of a town from America's Wild West. Dazzling and anarchic at the time of its celebrated Whitsun festivities (see page 170ff), El Rocío has for the rest of the year a quality of haunting stillness. The large and ungainly neo-baroque sanctuary housing the Virgin is at its most impressive when seen from across the marshland in front of it. A beautiful six-hour walk can be made from El Rocío to the village of **Villamanrique**, about 20 km to the north. On the way you pass by a splendid late 18th-century hacienda, and go across the sands and pine forests of the former royal hunting district known as the Raya Real. The village of Villamanrique is a charming small place boasting a baroque palace set in a magnificent exotic garden; the present owner of the palace is heir to the imperial throne of Brazil.

ALORA [4E], a former Roman municipality, and a Moorish possession until 1484, is a lively small town with a ruined 14th-century castle standing in isolation on a parched hill at the eastern edge of the town. From Alora a short round trip can be made to the three most unusual places in Málaga province. Leave the town on the MA 441 towards Ardales, and you will reach, after a winding uphill journey of 16 km, the first of these, the tiny spa town of **Carratraca**. The waters here were known to the Greeks and Romans, but the spa then fell into disuse, to be revived after the 16th century. The heyday of Carratraca was the 19th and early 20th centuries. Ferdinand VII had a small palace constructed here in 1830, three gambling halls were opened, and numerous celebrities came to stay, including Lord Byron, Alexandre Dumas, Gustave Doré, Juan Valera, Romero de Torres and Rainer Maria Rilke. Badly damaged in the 1930's during the Civil War, the baths have been recently restored, but the appeal of the place lies in its distinctly faded atmosphere. Ferdinand VII's palace is now a delightfully old-fashioned and remarkably cheap hotel known as the Hostal del Príncipe. You can use the staircase of the hotel to reach the upper street of the village, on which are located the baths; an attendant will show you the tub used by the wife of Napoleon III, the Empress Eugénie (Eugenia de Montijo).

The mountainous and wooded landscape around Carratraca is known, ridiculously, as the 'Switzerland of Andalucía'. Its character is unmistakeably Mediterranean, and becomes no more Swiss after Ardales, when you turn right on to the MA446, passing alongside a series of interconnected artificial lakes. After 6 km take the road to the right marked El Chorro, and turn off it after 2 km to the road leading up to ruins of **Bobastro**, the former stronghold of the Moorish rebel leader, Ibn Hafsun (see page 79). Before reaching the top of the hill a sign on the right indicates the footpath to the *Iglesia Mozárabe Rupestre*, the evocative remains of the 9th-century church built by Ibn Hafsun into an outcrop of rock. The ruins of his citadel are further up the hill, but these are scant and difficult to recognize.

The slightly sinister hamlet of **El Chorro** (which can be reached by train from Málaga) is the starting point for a walk which should definitely be avoided by those without a head for heights. In 1921, during the construction of the local hydroelectric station, a catwalk was built following the narrow gorge of El Chorro. This catwalk, known as the Camino del Rey, clings perilously to the vertical cliff and was once one of the great wonders of Spain. Today its condition is dilapidated, and there are the added thrills of the odd gap and missing portion of balcony.

ANDÚJAR [2F], on the right bank of the Guadalquivir, is a prosperous market town and centre of light industries, with a long-standing ceramics tradition. Of the original Roman settlement of Iliturgi there survives a heavily restored bridge dating back probably to the time of the Emperor Trajan. Andújar developed considerably during the Muslim period, thanks to its proximity to Córdoba and to the strategically important pass of Despeñaperros. Captured by Ferdinand III in 1225, it became the first walled town in Andalucía in Christian possession. The walls survive now only in small fragments, and the Moorish castle – of which the celebrated epic poet Jorge Manrique was governor – has gone altogether. The appearance of present-day Andújar is mainly modern and unprepossessing, though there still remain a handful of interesting old monuments centred around the ungainly Plaza de España. On one side of the square stands the 16th-century church of San Miguel, which has a fine classical plateresque west portal: the porch which shelters this has two splendid polychromed wooden angels supporting the roof. The Calle Feria leads from the Plaza de España into the most attractive corner of Andújar, the long and narrow Plaza de Santa María, which contains at one end a rather Italianate medieval bell-tower: this structure, renewed in the 19th century, probably replaced a minaret. The church of Santa María, which takes up one of the long sides of the square, is Gothic in origin, but was heavily remodelled in the 17th century. In the chapel to the left of the high altar is a characteristically stiff *Immaculate Conception* by Velázquez' teacher, Pacheco. The church's greatest treasure is in the second chapel in the left aisle. This, a *Christ on the Mount of Olives* by El Greco, would alone make a visit to Andújar worthwhile, and is indeed one of the few outstanding paintings still to be seen in a provincial Andalucían church: the work originally formed part of the church's high altar, the other panels of which were all sold off in the 19th century. Returning to the Plaza de España, turn right by the Town Hall and you will come to the Calle Maestra, where No.16 has an amusing late renaissance façade featuring boldly if crudely executed carvings, two of which are of Roman soldiers sporting feathered helmets; the façade, preceded by an overgrown forecourt, is in a sad condition and is all that remains of the building known as the Casa-Palacio de los Niños de Gomez.

The ceramic products of present-day Andújar are all of modern design, the last remaining potter to produce the traditional blue and white Andújar ware having recently died. This man, José Castillo, lived at No. 7 of the tiny street now named after him, off the Calle Monja. Among his products were the amusingly shaped *jarra de estudiante* ('student's jug'), so-called because apprentice potters used to make them to show their skill. Of far more elaborate design was the *jarra grotesca*, a jug in four elaborate pieces crowned by an angel with a hat thought by some to be imitative of that of Napoleon: this wonderful example of popular baroque seems originally to have been used in the making of home-made liquor, but has now a purely decorative function. Other more modest pieces made by José Castillo included horses with riders, another traditional Andújar speciality.

The most attractive nearby village to Andújar is **Arjona**, 14 km to the south on the 3219. The Roman settlement here was the scene of martyrdom of the obscure Christian brothers, Sts. Boroso and Maximilian. The two saints are commemorated by statues in the heavily restored late gothic church of Santa María, which stands on a charming, decayed square on top of the village; on the other side of this square is a 17th-century reliquary chapel containing the martyrs' bones and a gruesome collection of other relics. The views from the upper village over roof-tops and endless rolling expanses of olive-groves are splendid. Another possible excursion from Andújar is to the sanctuary of the **Virgen de la Cabeza**, situated in a wooded mountainous setting 31 km to the north of the town on the J501. Little remains of the original sanctuary, which was founded in the 13th century to house a miraculous statue of the Virgin; the present building is a bleak example of post-civil war Spanish fascism. The drive here is magnificent though, and on the first Sunday of every April a colourful pilgrimage is made to the sanctuary from Andújar.

ANTEQUERA [4E], backed by steep, barren peaks, and with extensive views over flat fertile country, was known even to the Romans as the 'Ancient City', or Antikaria. On the northern outskirts of the town, off the Granada road, are three dolmens that are among the most important prehistoric monuments in southern Spain (see page 58). The two nearest the town, the Cuevas de Viera and Mengal, are in an enclosed precinct with the same opening hours as the town's museum (10 am-1.30 pm, and 5-7 pm). The Mengal dolmen, which is reputedly about 4,500 years old, consists of a vast underground gallery supported by vertical monoliths and adorned with engravings of symbols and human figures; it was probably the burial place of an important nobleman, and is the third largest monument of its kind in Europe. The Viera dolmen, opened for you by the guardian of the site, is thought to be of slightly later date, and consists of a long and narrow tunnel leading to a small burial chamber, into which you have to stoop to enter. If you have a car, the guardian will accompany you to the dolmen of El Romeral, 3 km to the north. This is the most recent in date and the most sophisticated of the three tombs, having two chambers domed in brick: the smallest of these chambers was a votive chamber, where offerings to the dead would have been placed.

The medieval town of Antequera, captured by the Christians in 1410, was built on top of a hill, but from the 17th century onwards expanded down into the plain. In the late 16th century the town had emerged as a flourishing cultural centre, the grammar school attached to the former Collegiate Church of Santa María la Mayor becoming an important focus for poets and humanists. Numerous fine churches and aristocratic palaces were erected from then right up to the late baroque period, turning the place into what is today one of the architectural showpieces of Andalucía. The town continued to prosper throughout the 19th century, but thereafter went into a sharp decline, from which it has been rescued only in recent years.

Heading west into the centre of the town from the Cuevas de Viera and Mengal, you will pass the delightful small square of Santiago, containing the late baroque churches of Santiago and Santa Eufemia. Continuing west along the Carrera you will eventually reach the Plaza San Sebastian, with its late 16th-century parish church; just off the street leading to it is the town's excellent archaeological museum, attractively housed in the 18th-century palace of Najera and containing prehistoric and Roman finds, among which stands out a Roman bronze of a nude boy known as the 'Ephebus of Antequera' (1st century AD). The bustling Calle Infante Don Fernando leads north from the Plaza San Sebastian into the heart of 19th-century Antequera, opening up eventually into a square on which stands the town's attractive mid-19th-century bullring (an elegant bar and restaurant have been built in its basement). Half way along the street is the Town Hall, occupying a late baroque monastery.

The Cuesta Zapateros climbs steeply up into the quietest part of Antequera. The Arco de los Gigantes (the 'Giant's Arch') at the top of the hill was built to display a group of Roman sculptures and inscriptions, and is thus claimed to be Spain's oldest public museum; at any rate it typifies the humanist spirit of late 16th-century Antequera. Adjoining the arch are the ruins of the town's medieval castle (now turned into a formal garden, with good views of the lower town), while beyond it is the former Collegiate Church of Santa María, distinguished by a most elegant early renaissance west façade in the form of a Roman triumphal arch. To the east of the square is the district of El Carmen, dominated by the church of that name, which has a good 18th-century interior and one of the finest and most elaborate of Andalucía's late baroque altarpieces. Another masterpiece of the 18th century is to the west of the Collegiate square, on the enchanting Plaza del Portichuelo: here you will find the brick porticoed chapel of the Virgen del Socorro (known popularly as the 'Portichuelo'), a very idiosyncratic building in a style which could only be described as baroque-mudéjar.

Classical keystone on the Arco de los Gigantes, Antequera

The outstanding natural attraction in the area is the National Park of **El Torcal**, 15 km to the south of the town off the Málaga road. This is a large area of bizarrely-shaped calcareous rocks, which give the impression of being the work of some contemporary sculptor rather than the result of erosion. Leaving your car at the small hotel in the middle of it, you can follow one of two footpaths which encircle the park: the shorter of the two (marked with yellow arrows) takes 45 minutes to an hour, the other (marked in red) about 2 hours. There are magnificent and extensive views over wild countryside down to the distant coast of Málaga.

ARACENA [2B] is the main town of a beautiful district of low mountains covered in oaks, cork trees, fruit trees and recently planted eucalyptus. The Río Tinto mines (see MINAS DE RÍO TINTO), made the Sierra de Aracena very important in ancient times, and the collapse of the mining industry in the second century AD led to a serious fall in the district's population. The late Middle Ages were marked by frequent border disputes with Portugal, reflected today in the numerous and splendid surviving castles. In recent years this once neglected district has become an ever more popular holiday destination for the inhabitants of Seville, which can be reached from Aracena in little more than an hour.

Dominating the town of Aracena is a bare hill crowned by a 13th-century castle and the church of Nuestra Señora de los Dolores, perhaps the finest medieval church in Huelva province. Begun at the same time as the castle, it was brought to completion in the 15th century, and has a mudéjar tower with ornamentation inspired by that of the Giralda in Seville. The short track leading up to the church from the town passes through a charming 16th-century brick gate. The parish church of Nuestra Señora de la Asunción in the centre of Aracena was never completed and is now an exposed shell, revealing elegant renaissance workmanship. The 16th-century Town Hall next to it is one of the oldest in Huelva province, and has an impressive main entrance designed by the Seville architect Hernán Ruiz. An exquisitely ornamented turn-of-the-century Casino by Anibal González (the architect of Seville's Plaza de América) towers over the town's lively and elegant main square, off the southern side of which is the Confitería Rufino, which since 1875 has been producing some of the finest sweets and pastries in Andalucía.

The principal tourist attraction of Aracena lies on the eastern outskirts. This, the cave known as the Gruta de las Maravillas, is entered through a modern building surrounded by tourist kiosks, shops selling local ceramics (of rather poor quality) and by a group of hideous contemporary sculptures forming the grandly-named 'Museum of Contemporary Sculpture'. The cave extends right under the castle hill, and the compulsory guided tour of it lasts up to an hour. The place, with its underground lakes, and garishly illuminated stalactites and stalagmites resembles a film set, and indeed this place has been used for several films, including *Journey to the Centre of the Earth*.

There is a whole series of pretty villages near Aracena hidden in woods, dotted with small orchards, and characterized by their wooden-beam houses supporting picturesquely askew balconies decorated with a riot of flowers. Among these are **Linares de la Sierra**, **Fuenteheridos** and **Galaroza**; two of the best preserved are **Valdelarco** and **Castaño del Robledo**, both with cobbled streets, the latter with a very rustic wooden-beam bar ('La Bodeguita'). One of the famed sites of the area is the **Hermitage of Nuestra Señora de los Ángeles**, situated on a rock ledge in between Alájar and Fuenteheridos, and with magnificently extensive views towards Río Tinto. The hermitage, to which an annual pilgrimage is made on the 7th and 8th of September from Alájar, was lived in for many years by the 16th-century philosopher, naturalist and theologian Arias Montano, who had previously been librarian at the monastery of the Escorial near Madrid: Philip II had an enormous respect for this mystic, and came to see him here (an obelisk records this visit). The climb between here and Fuenteheridos is particularly attractive, and there is an excellent viewing-point at the top of the hill. Another memorable walk is from the village of **Cortelazor** to the 'Charco Malo' or 'Evil Pool' (3 km to the south-east) – a deep and freezing pool flanked by rocks, trees and a waterfall.

Some of the district's finest monuments are to be found in the neighbouring villages of **Cortegana** and **Almonaster la Real**. The former, a particularly friendly and animated place, has a well-preserved 15th/16th-century castle, as well as a dark and evocatively decayed Casino, in a style best described as Art Nouveau Baroque. A 10th-century former mosque, with an excellently restored interior, and spectacular views from its minaret, sits on top of the citadel of Almonaster la Real, whose cobbled streets and absence of modern buildings make this one of Andalucía's most beautiful villages; the Casa García, at the entrance to the village, is a small hotel with an outstanding restaurant.

Places of interest further away include AROCHE to the west, CUMBRES MAYORES to the north, Zufre (see SANTA OLALLA DEL CALA) to the east and Zalamea la Real (see MINAS DE RÍO TINTO) to the south. Pig-raising is one of the principal local activities, and you should not leave the area without paying a visit to the hill-top village of **Jabugo**, which produces some of the best hams in Spain: you can buy a whole ham, or just content yourself with a ham tapa in one of the local bars.

ARCHIDONA [4E], the name of which is derived from the Roman Estelduna, meaning 'oil mill', is built against the slopes of a mountain, and overlooks a landscape of olive trees extending towards the Guadalquivir Basin. The most remarkable feature of the pretty town centre is the octagonal square built between 1780 and 1786 by Francisco Astorga and Antonio González Sevillano. Constructed with stones from the nearby Sierra del Torcal (see ANTEQUERA), the square has remained much as it was in the 18th century, the main modern addition being the unappealing modern arrangement of benches and hedgerows at its centre.

Just outside the village in the Loja direction is a tiny road leading vertiginously up the rock face to the mountain-top ruins of Archidona's Moorish castle and palace. Next to these scant but magnificently situated ruins is the Sanctuary of the Virgen de la Gracia, a simple, heavily restored brick structure which was originally a mosque; inside is a ceramic baptismal font of múdejar design presented as a gift by Isabel la Católica.

Legend has it that a Moorish girl from the palace of Archidona fell in love with a Christian, and that the two of them, realizing the impossibility of their love, decided to commit suicide by throwing themselves off the prominent, isolated rock which stands half-way between Archidona and Antequera. This rock, known as the Peña de los Enamorados ('Lovers' Rock') is thought variously to have the shape of an embracing couple and a girl's head.

ARCOS DE LA FRONTERA [4C]: The spectacular position of Arcos is best appreciated when approached from the east along the C344 from Ronda. The town is seen from here to hang above a sheer cliff face, into the darker recesses of which dive the occasional kestrels. Fortunately, the extensive modern development which has grown up on the western side of the town is shielded from view.

The history of Arcos goes back to Celtic times, though all of the town's important monuments date from after its capture by the Christians in 1250; as with all the towns and villages in this area named de la Frontera ('of the frontier'), the place once marked the limits of Christian territory. Almost all the town's hotels and restaurants are in the animated lower half of the town, lining the long main street. This street becomes progressively steeper as it climbs the hill, and eventually turns into the Cuesta Belén, which goes through the old heart of Arcos. This part of the town, very silent at night, is crammed with tall white houses, and beautiful palaces, convents and churches with crumbling stone façades. Continuing uphill from the Cuesta Belén you will see on your left the charmingly decorated late gothic façade of the Convent of the Encarnación; on the right is the parish church of Santa María, to enter which you should retrace your steps a few yards and climb up the steps leading to the magnificent west façade, a masterpiece of the Isabelline plateresque style; the interior has splendid late gothic vaulting, impressive baroque choir stalls by Diego Roldán, and a rich treasury with a painting dubiously attributed to Zurbarán. Once outside again make your way round to the church's south side, which has an impressive 18th-century bell-tower (which can be climbed) facing a large open square. On one side of the square is the town's privately owned castle, while on the other side is the grand late 18th-century parador, which was once, ironically, a poor people's home; it hugs the cliff edge and has been closed down twice recently as a result of subsidence. On the side of the square directly opposite the bell-tower of Santa María is a balcony with a breathtaking view down the cliff. The church which you see to your left is that of San Pedro, which can be reached by following the street adjoining the parador. This church, perilously poised at the highest and narrowest part of the town, has a baroque façade and a late gothic interior with a striking 15th-century polychromed retable. The highpoint, in two senses, of a visit to San Pedro, is the climb up onto the roof, an experience not to be recommended to those with a fear of heights, for there is nothing to prevent you from falling; the view over the village and across to the Serranía de Ronda is quite exhilarating.

Directly below the town, and accessible from the C344, is a small artificial lake, where you can sail, swim or relax by the shaded shores.

AROCHE [2A]: On the edge of the sparsely forested and far less visited Sierra de Aracena (see ARACENA) this attractive, little-changed village near the Portuguese border has, at one end, a ruined castle containing a tiny and rustic bullring, and an even more primitive local museum. The famously eccentric collection of rosaries known as the Museo del Santo Rosario, once housed in the oppressively decorated home of its founder Paulino G. Diaz Alcaide, has now been transferred to a less atmospheric setting next to the Guardia Civil (near the main entrance to the village): among the profusion of rosaries to be seen here are one that belonged to General Franco and another presented, mysteriously, by President Nixon, a non-Catholic.

3 km north of the village, following a track that begins in front of the petrol station, and passing next to a grand 18th-century cortijo with the wonderful name of La Belleza ('Beauty'), you will come to the quaintly rustic 13th-century hermitage of **San Mamés**, which is the object every May of a popular romería. The surrounding mountains are the home of some of Europe's last black vultures.

AYAMONTE [3A]: On the estuary of the Guadiana and overlooking the Portuguese town of Villa Real de Santo Antonio, Ayamonte is a fishing port and sprawling border town. The modern, lower part is filled with bars and restaurants, where you will find numerous tourists on their way to and from the Portuguese coast of the Algarve. It all has a slightly run-down character, rather like the boats that once plied between here and Portugal; this boat service has now been superseded by a bridge, which has further devastated the town's economy. The old town, a considerable walk from the port, rises on a gentle slope up to the 16th-century church of San Francisco, from the tower of which there is a good view over the Guadiana; the ugly modern parador lies in an isolated setting a short distance away.

Between Ayamonte and Huelva is a landscape of estuaries, marshland, long sandy beaches, and extensive stretches of pine forest; the coastal towns and villages are famous for their sea-food, in particular for their shrimps, razor-shells, crayfish and clams. The nearest long beach to Ayamonte is that of **Isla Canela**, a modern resort at the southernmost end of a flat, marshy and treeless area lying between two estuaries. More interesting, if also slightly sinister, is the town of **Isla Cristina** to the east, which is both a fishing port and a resort containing a number of strange turn-of-the-century villas and other buildings; its bars and restaurants specialize in two unusual fish dishes, *raya con tomate* (skate in a piquant tomato sauce), and *mechado de atún*, a magnificent tunny fish concoction (see page 182). East from Isla Cristina the coastline is backed almost uninterruptedly by pine trees; the Playa de la Antilla, one of the finest sandy beaches in the province, leads on to the long sandbank of El Rompido, which lies between the sea and the estuary of the Río Piedras, and is an excellent place for swimming, camping, and for being on one's own. Situated 5 km inland from the resort of **La Antilla** is the modern and very prosperous town of **Lepe**, known for its strawberries and for being the subject of nearly all Andalucían jokes; in 1988 the civic authorities responded with good grace to this latter reputation by instituting an annual festival of humour, which takes place in the last week of May. On the eastern side of the Río Piedras estuary is the tiny and very attractive village of **El Rompido**, which has charming bars situated on the jetties; a fishing boat can be hired to take you over to the south bank opposite. An attractive but now extensively developed coastline of dunes, trees and secluded stretches of beach extends from El Rompido almost all the way to Punta Umbria (see HUELVA).

BAENA [3E], straddling a ridge in between gently rolling agricultural countryside to the north, and wild hills and rock escarpments to the south, has a long and important history. Situated in an area rich in prehistoric finds dating back to palaeolithic times, Baena was a major town in Moorish times, and in the 15th century had one of the largest populations in Andalucía. Baena was one of the Andalucían towns which suffered most from emigration; indeed so many of its citizens left that one group was able to found in northern Spain a town known as Nueva Baena, or 'New Baena'. Most of its finest monuments are in the upper town. You can begin your tour from the Plaza de la Constitución, on one side of which is an elegant arcaded warehouse or *pósito* dating from the 18th century; part of this is a cultural centre, and another part the Mesón Casa del Monte, a bar with excellent tapas. From the square the Calle Fray D. Henares leads up to the early 16th-century church of Santa María, the bell-tower of which incorporates what was probably the minaret of a mosque built by Abd al-Rahman II. You are now at the top of the town's ridge, and should turn sharply left, passing alongside the ruins of a castle erected by the Moors on Roman foundations. The furthest point which you can reach is the early 16th-century convent of the Madre de Dios, notable for a beautiful mudéjar portal and a renaissance choir. The Semana Santa processions of Baena are famed for their noise: between the Wednesday and Friday, the streets echo to upwards of 2,000 drums.

BAEZA [2G], crowning a hill dotted with olive trees, has views of ÚBEDA to the east and the Cazorla range to the south. An important city in Roman times, then a Visigothic bishopric, Baeza under the Moors became the thriving capital of an extensive city state. As with Úbeda, its greatest period was the 16th century, when its population increased enormously, and its economy, based on agriculture, cattle-raising and textiles, prospered as never before: it was in that period too that it acquired its university, which survived until 1824. Though Baeza has not quite the same quantity of architectural treasures as Úbeda, it is still one of Spain's outstanding renaissance towns, and has the advantage over its neighbour in its not having been affected this century by ugly urban development (see page 103).

The Calle San Pablo leads from the town's eastern outskirts (where the bus station is situated) to its centre. Walking along it in this direction, you will pass on the left-hand side three small renaissance palaces with impressive façades – the Casas

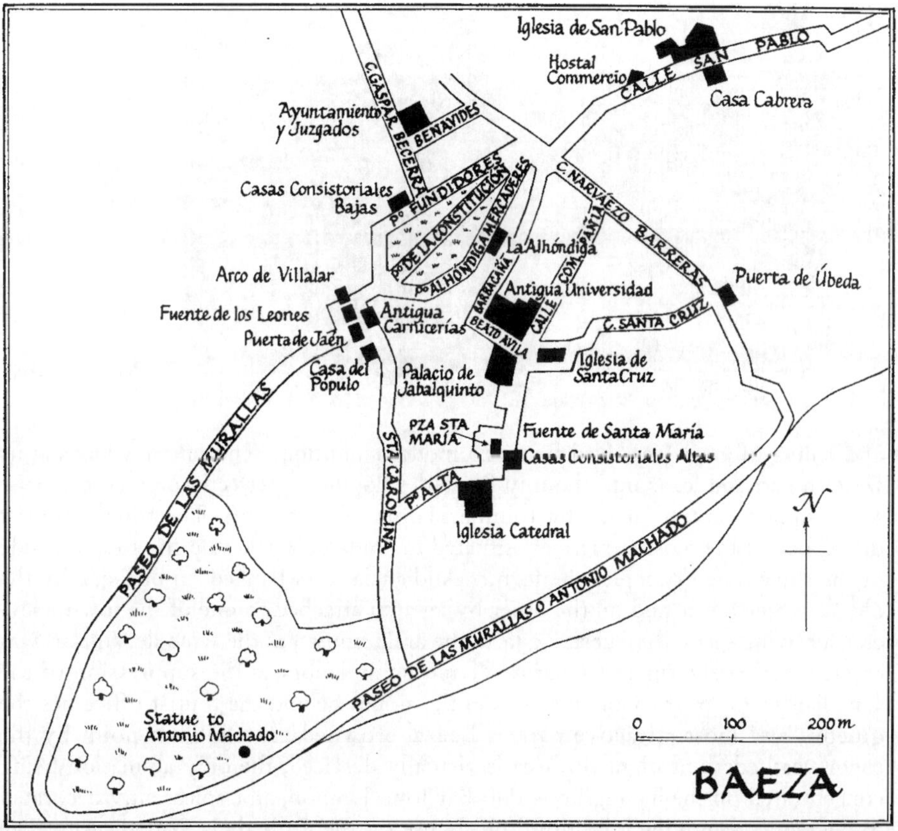

Cabrera and Acuña, and the Palacio Cerón. On the other side of the street is the 15th-century church of San Pablo, where Pablo de Olavide, promoter of the Sierra Morena colonies, lies in an unmarked tomb (see page 27). Further along the street, at No. 21, is the Hostal Comercio, a hotel which will appeal to the impecunious tourist with a nostalgia for the old days of Spanish travel. This extraordinarily cheap establishment, patronized by a largely ageing clientèle, and with a lugubrious tiled decoration, seems to have changed little since the early days of this century, when the poet Antonio Machado stayed here: if you do not mind the feeling of being in a morgue, you should eat in its splendidly oppressive dining room, where the food, incidentally, is far better value than that of any other establishment in this town. The Calle San Pablo takes you into the town's bar-lined main square, which, at night, is more animated than anywhere in Úbeda. The large and elegant arcaded building on its southern side was built in the 16th century as a place for the buying

Puerta de Jaén, Baeza

and selling of grain (the third floor is a modern addition). The square widens at its western end and leads into the tiny Plaza del Pópulo, a perfectly preserved renaissance square centred around a fountain adorned with lions. The town's tourist office, one of the most attractively situated in Andalucía, takes up the southern side of the square, and occupies the former Audiencia. It is flanked on one side by the old slaughter house and on the other by an arch attached to one of the town's several surviving gates, the Puerta de Jaén: the arch, known as the Arco de Villalar, was erected during the time of Charles V, and commemorates the suppression of the Castilian revolt of the Comuneros. On the slopes behind the tourist office lies the quietest and most attractive part of Baeza, crowned at its highest point by the town's cathedral; at night the area is virtually deserted, the only animation being concentrated on the incongruous Pub Bar John Lennon, an unpleasantly decorated discothèque occupying a beautiful old house on the Calle de la Portada Alta. The Cuesta de San Gil ascends from the tourist office towards the cathedral. An alternative and much longer way of reaching this building from the Plaza del Pópulo is to go through the Puerta de Jaén, and follow the path which skirts the top of the town's extensive fortifications. This path makes a loop through open countryside and takes you round the southern edge of the town, offering magnificent views of the Cazorla range. The southern stretch of the path has now been named after Antonio Machado, who worked as a teacher in Baeza between 1912 and 1919, and who loved to walk along these walls, and contemplate the views from here: 'Land of Baeza,' he wrote, 'I shall dream of you when I cannot see you' (see page 222). Leaving the 'Paseo Antonio Machado' after passing the recent memorial to the poet, you will soon reach the cathedral.

Built over a former mosque, the cathedral was begun in the 13th century and has an attractive 14th-century window on its west façade. The joyfully light and spacious interior retains its late gothic chancel, but was given a magnificent renaissance

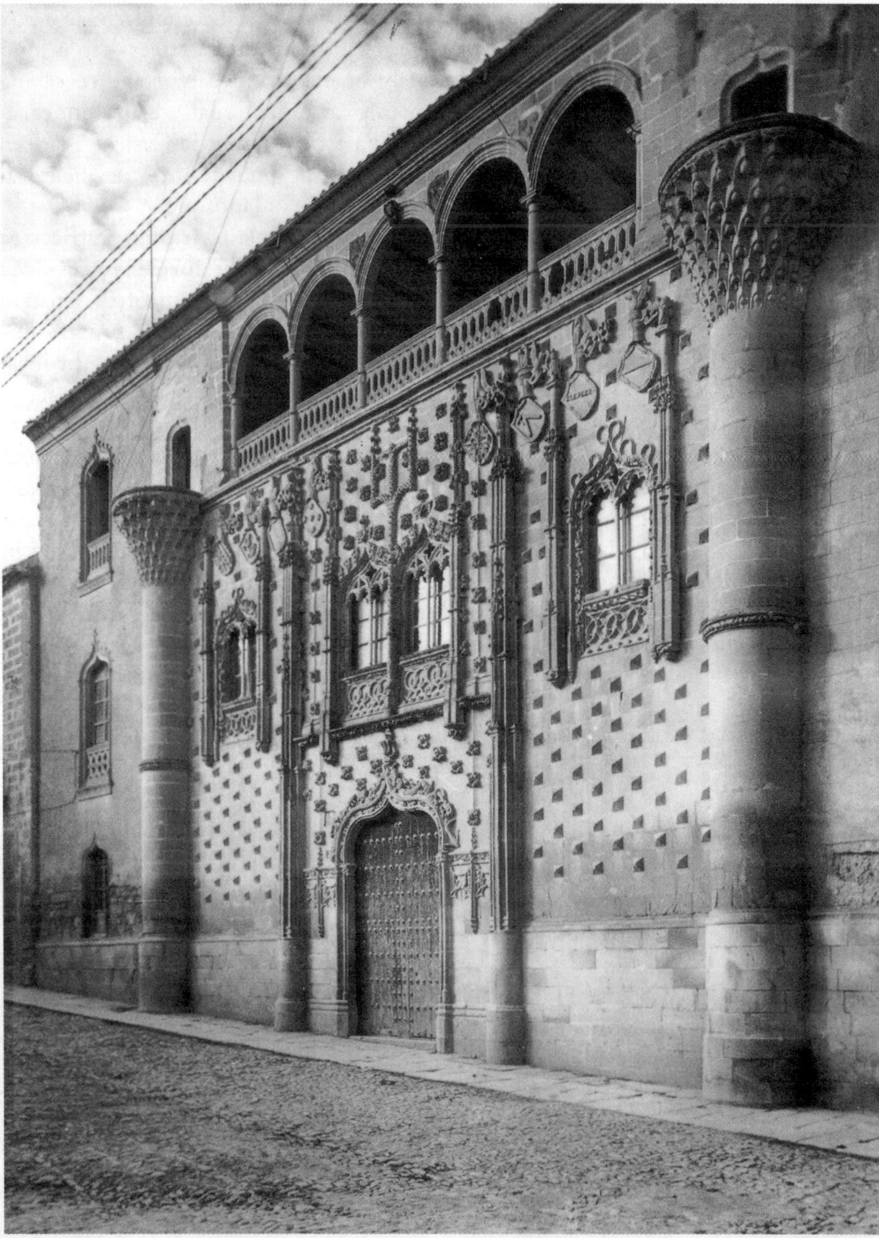

Palacio de Jabalquinto, Baeza

nave by Andrés de Vandelvira in the mid 16th century. A small coin, placed in a box innocently marked *Custodia* in the left aisle, has a remarkable effect – to a loud musical accompaniment a door is mysteriously opened to reveal a stand revolving against a red velvet background and supporting an exceptionally elaborate early 18th-century silverwork *custodia* by the Córdoba artist Nuñez de Castro. You can recover from the shock of this experience by walking outside into the medieval cloister, the vaulting of which is the main survival of the old mosque.

The north portal of the cathedral rises on steps above a charming traffic-free square, the Plaza Santa María; adjacent to this building is the former renaissance Town Hall, with Isabelline plateresque detailing. Standing in front of the austere 17th-century Jesuit Seminary on the north side of the square is a 16th-century fountain in the form of a classical triumphal arch: this crudely carved work, by the local man responsible for the town's water system, has an engagingly provincial character.

On the beautiful Cuesta de San Felipe, which leads down from the Plaza Santa María in the direction of the town's main square, is the 15th-century Palacio Jabalquinto, the most striking and unusually decorated building in Baeza (see page 103). In complete contrast to this fantastically ornamental masterpiece of the Isabelline plateresque is the romanesque simplicity of the church of Santa Cruz in front of it. Further down the hill, on the left-hand side, is the former University building, which was founded in 1542, and transformed in 1875 into the Instituto de Enseñanza Media, the school where Machado taught French for eight years. One of the rooms, with 16th-century tiered seating, was originally the main hall of the university. Next to this is Machado's classroom, kept almost exactly as it was in his day, with the addition of a small collection of documents and photographs relating to his stay in Baeza, and a heavy covering of dust. After initially putting up at the Hostal Comercio, Machado moved on to a private home, at Plaza Cardinal Benavides 21, just to the north of the main square. His house, marked by a plaque, looks across the Plaza to the richly decorated Town Hall, the most interesting building in the northern part of the town and one of the finest examples of the classical plateresque style in Andalucía.

Fountain and Seminary, Baeza

BAILÉN [2F], a town of largely modern appearance, is famous as the place where the Spanish General Castaños defeated French troops under the command of General Dupont in 1808, a crucial setback for Napoleon (see page 188). Castaños is buried in the gothic parish church of the Encarnación, which has a sculpture attributed to Alonso Cano.

Baños de la Encina

The outstanding attraction of the area is the village of **Baños de la Encina**, which stands on a hill 11 km to the north of Bailén, dominated by its excellently preserved Moorish castle. The charming small village has a fine 15th- to 16th-century parish church in salmon-pink stone; the toy-like square on which it is situated also has an attractive early 16th-century Town Hall bearing a prominent coat of arms. From here you can obtain the key to the castle, which is a few minutes' walk away. Completed in the mid 10th century by order of the Caliph al-Hakam II, it comprises 14 square towers and a large round keep facing the village. You enter it through a horse-shoe shaped gate, and can climb up to the battlements, from which there are magnificent views across a rolling landscape of olive trees towards the distant and majestic profile of the Sierra de Segura (see CAZORLA); at the eastern end of the castle you look down to a reservoir encased by barren slopes.

BARBATE DE FRANCO [5C]: In the middle of one of the most beautiful stretches of the Andalucían coast, Barbate is an ugly modern town which nonetheless has the attraction of being a place where fishing rather than tourism predominates. Tunny-fishing is the great speciality of the place, and in every bar you can savour a wide variety of tunny snacks. A beautiful small road (the 169) to the west of the town leads up a pine-coated hill before descending to the tiny resort of **Los Caños de Meca**. This resort has been built up over the last fifteen years, and until recently has attracted people mainly from Cádiz and Seville; although a growing number of Germans are now coming here, it is still an extremely quiet place for most of the year (the worst times being summer weekends and the whole month of August). It has a reputation for attracting unorthodox people, one of whom, known to everyone as 'La Francesa', runs the resort's oldest bar and restaurant, the Trafalgar. The resort's main hotel, the Miramar, is a few hundred metres to the west, and is a popular meeting place at breakfast time. The beautifully situated Bar Pirata lies just across the road from the Trafalgar, while to the east is the Bar Discoteca, a spacious and amusing modern building perched above a recently much expanded sandy beach. An attractive walk, climbing over rocks and nudists, can be made underneath the cliffs that stretch all the way to Barbate; the furthest point to which you can go is a place where jets of water from a spring shoot over the cliff face to form an excellent natural shower. An alternative trip in the opposite direction can be made either by car or on foot (half an hour's walk) to the celebrated **Cape Trafalgar**, where there took place on 21 October 1805 the decisive naval action of the Napoleonic Wars. Admiral Nelson, leading a British fleet of only twenty-seven ships of the line and four frigates, managed to defeat the much larger but more drawn-out French fleet led by Villeneuve. Britain was left in an unchallenged position of maritime supremacy while gaining one of its most romantic and inspirational heroes in Nelson, who died from his wounds shortly after being informed of his victory, around 4.30 am, following the cessation of sporadic gunfire that had lasted throughout the night. 'TRAFALGAR!' reflected Richard Ford, in one of his rare sentimental moments. 'Is not the name enough to animate every English sailor to do his duty to the end of creation?' Hearts can still be stirred by this enchanting site, which is also one of the best places along the Cádiz coast to watch the sunset. However, those not wishing to meet here their own Trafalgar should be wary about swimming too far from the cape, for the currents are notorious and regularly claim the lives of even the most experienced swimmers. Excellent sandy beaches extend all the way north from here to the old hill village and popular resort of **Conil de la Frontera**.

Nearly 10 km to the south of Barbate is **Zahara de los Atunes**, which has a large and crumbling fortress on its extensive beach. Much of this area of the coast is owned by the army, and to continue to the ruins of Roman Baelo Claudia at **Bolonia** (see page 64) you have to return to the main Cádiz to Algeciras road and turn off it after 15 km. To wander around the ruins you have to follow a guided tour, but they can be well seen from outside their wire perimeter. Bolonia itself has a scattering of bars, and a small, recently built hotel; the beach is magnificent, but suffers terribly from the levante wind.

BAZA [3H], in the middle of the wild, little populated expanse of northeastern Granada, stands in an oasis of cultivated fields surrounded by erosion and distant barren mountains. In 1971 a beautiful polychromed Iberian statue of a goddess was discovered on the outskirts of the town; this work, known as the Dama de Baza, is to be found alongside the equally famous Dama de Elche in the National Archaeological Museum of Madrid. Under the name of Basti, Baza was the capital of the Roman province of Bastetania; a Visigothic bishopric until at least the 4th century, the town was occupied by the Moors up to 1489. Baza has suffered periodically from earthquakes, and the present town has little of architectural interest. The main legacy of the Moors is the warren of small streets in the centre, and the tiny, much restored baths that lie in a basement in the former Jewish quarter behind the church of Santiago (the woman who looks after these lives at Calle Caniles 19). The town has a curious annual event mentioned by Cervantes and dating back to the late 15th century, when a bricklayer discovered a miraculous image of the Virgin in a local church. The nearby town of Guadix quarrelled with Baza over the rights to possess this Virgin, and the quarrel is commemorated on 9 September each year when a man from Guadix, dressed as the buffoon-like 'Cascamorras', arrives at Baza and is prevented from taking the Virgin by a crowd who taunt and pursue him; returning to Guadix empty-handed he receives a similar treatment there. The unfortunate man who plays the part of the 'Cascamorras' often does so as an act of penance, but he reputedly never gets badly hurt.

The landscape to the north of Baza is dominated by the bizarrely impressive Jabalcon, an enormous, isolated outcrop of rock as changing in its colouring as Australia's Ayers' Rock. Below it, 11 km from Baza, is the bleak village of **Zújar**, which has been known since Roman times for its thermal waters. The nearby spa hotel – once frequented, I was assured, by elegant German women – was pulled down in the 1970's to make way for the now much depleted reservoir 10 km to the north. At the point where the old road to Cortes de Baza reaches the reservoir there is still a natural thermal pool where families come to bathe throughout the year. To lie in its steaming waters on a winter's evening is a particularly magical experience.

BELALCÁZAR [1D]: Those who wish to know what travelling in Spain was once like should come to Belalcázar, a place redolent of a great past, yet in a romantic state of decay, and far from all tourist routes. It lies at the most northerly point of Andalucía, in an area in which the sobriety of its architecture and people is entirely Castilian in character. The old part of Belalcázar is built on high ground, facing another hill to the north on which stands the village's enormous and ramshackle castle. In the dip between the two hills is an old fountain where many of the villagers come to wash their clothes. A stony path overgrown with thistles leads through land strewn with olive trees to the castle, which is one of the most impressive not simply in Andalucía but in the whole of Spain. Known by 1466 as Belalcázar or 'the beautiful castle', it had been constructed some twenty years earlier within Moorish fortifications captured in 1240 by Ferdinand III; a plateresque palace was added in the 16th century. The fiefdom of the man who commissioned the 15th-century castle, Gutierre de Sotomayor, Master of the Order of Calatrava,

Belalcázar

was one of the most important in Spain, and came to stretch almost all the way from Córdoba to Badajoz and north to Toledo. In apparent deference to the former County of Belalcázar, there is today a curious bus service, which, following historical rather than commercial logic, connects the forgotten village of Belalcázar with Badajoz, passing on the way Gutierre de Sotomayor's properties in the so-called 'Extremaduran Siberia'.

The castle remained in the hands of Gutierre's descendents, the Counts of Belalcázar, right up to the Peninsular War, when it was heavily damaged by Napoleon's troops. The present eccentric owner has admirably resisted government offers to purchase the place and turn it into a luxury parador. But, following the injury from falling masonry of a recent visitor, he has blocked up the main entrance and thus made it impossible now for anyone to look inside. Of the rapidly disintegrating exterior the most distinguished feature is the impressively high keep which is crowned with bizarrely decorated machicolations that appear to be the whim of some extravagantly imaginative if heavy-handed pastry chef. On the south side of the castle are elegant renaissance medallions. The sad fragments of the earlier fortifications lie scattered and half-buried in the surrounding fields.

On the run-down main square of the village, the Plaza de la Constitución, is the massive church of Santiago, dating from the 15th century, but with an 18th-century granite façade and bell-tower; the interior was gutted during the Civil War. The ruins of the late 15th-century monastery and church of San Francisco stand in farmland on the eastern side of the village; the beautiful late gothic shell of the church is remarkably complete, but is now used as a pigsty. In a hamlet on the southern outskirts of the village, off the C420 to Hinojosa del Duque, can be found the convent of Santa Clara de la Columna, which was founded in 1476 by the first Countess of Belalcázar. Nuns still live here, but with no money to repair the sadly decayed late gothic church and cloister; the convent can be visited during the mornings and late afternoons.

BUJALANCE [2E]: The Moorish castle dating back to the time of Abd al-Rahman II lies in ruins, but the rest of this village is well preserved, and has an attractive medieval parish church with delightfully intricate late gothic vaulting in the chancel. Next to the church is a most elegant late 17th-century Town Hall, and in the middle of the long, narrow and tree-lined main square is a statue to the painter and writer on art Antonio Palomino: born in Bujalance in 1653, Palomino settled in Madrid, and is best known today for his biographies of Spanish artists, to which he dedicated the last years of his life.

Heading east of Bujalance, across an interminable expanse of olive trees, you will enter what had been a frontier zone between Republican and Nationalist Spain during the Civil War. The remains of Nationalist bunkers can be seen next to the bridge shortly before reaching **Lopera** (18 kms north-east of Bujalance) a delightful Córdoban style village with an interesting castle and a sole surviving Bodega producing an excellent fortified wine. Just to the east of the village, off the quiet road that once linked Córdoba with Madrid, is the spot where the British writers John Cornford and Ralph Fox were killed while travelling with Republican reinforcements in December 1936; the two men are commemorated in the village itself by a harsh modern memorial in a square named after 'the English poets' ('*los poetas Ingleses*').

Within sight of Lopera is the rival village of **Porcuna**, a lively and historically important town known in Iberian times as Obulco; Iberian finds and copies of the famous works now in the Museum of Jaén (see page 314) are distributed around the Town Hall and the local museum housed in the remains of the village's medieval castle. Other attractions include murals by the Córdoban artist Julio Romero de Torres (see page 49) in the modern parish church, and an amusing and much loved 20th century folly called the Casa de Piedra, a house built entirely in stone by an eccentric local quarryman. In addition, the village has an outstanding and always packed restaurant (it is still known after the adjoining Casino), and a friendly and ancient bar (the Epi) that is probably the smallest in Andalucía. In the last weekend of May the village's main street is covered in sand and parading horses in honour of the annual *romería* to the nearby sanctuary of La Aharilla.

CABO DE GATA [4J]: The lunar-like volcanic peninsula of the Cabo de Gata is one of the least spoilt and most haunting sections of Spain's southern coast. The Phoenicians referred to it as the 'promontory of cornelians and agates', a name which the Arabs translated as Cabpta-Gata. Driving to it from Almería, you will pass the small resort of Cabo de Gata, after which you follow a group of salt flats until you reach the tip of the promontory, marked by a lighthouse. From here there are wonderful views of the bleached mountainous coastline to the east. The coastal road begins to climb after the lighthouse, and then turns into a dust-track, just about manageable by car. After 10 km of uninhabited and treeless landscape you approach the popular resort of **San José**, which is backed by an African-looking landscape of palms and cacti and has an excellent sandy beach just to the south (at **El Morrón de los Genoveses**). The coast road north from here to the small and slightly sinister resort of **Las Negras** is asphalted, and passes next to **Los Escullos,** from where a track leads south to a sandy beach lying below dunes; further on is the coastal hamlet of **La Isleta del Moro**, which has a small, modest and outstandingly situated hotel, behind which local women still wash clothes in a municipal fountain. After Las Negras a rough track continues to hug the coast, and can be followed in a Land Rover to the top of the barren hill to to the north of the village. The point where you can go no further is indicated by the abandoned, rusty shell of a car inscribed in English with the words 'Welcome to the pleasure zone'. You now have to continue on foot, descending on a spectacular footpath to the ruined finca of San Pedro, which is frequented by hippies; the coastal path joins an asphalted road 10 km further on, at **Agua Amarga**. The whole coast of the Cabo de Gata is particularly popular with Germans, whose taste for nudism and primitive living accords well with the prehistoric surroundings.

CABRA [3E], a Roman colony and later a Visigothic bishopric, is today a small town with much old-fashioned charm and a beautiful situation. Standing above a group of palms and cypresses at the western end of the town is the 16th-century church of the Asunción, adjoining which are ramparts, with views directly down to a rolling landscape covered with olive trees; in the distance, rising above the village, are barren peaks, one of which is crowned by the hermitage of the Virgen de la Sierra. On the other side of the Asunción is the former palace of the Counts of Cabra (now a school), which has a heavily restored mudéjar tower containing a gloomy neo-Moorish saloon. Off the tiny green square below the Asunción runs the village's main street, the Avenida Solis Ruiz. The grand but somewhat decayed early 19th-century house at No. 13, its yellow paint flaking away from its pilastered façade, was the birthplace of the novelist Juan Valera (see page 30). Valera, a diplomat for much of his life, spent relatively little time in his native Cabra, but repeatedly used the place and its surroundings in his novels.

Pepita Jimenez, the first and one of the best known of Valera's novels, is set in Cabra, and deals with the love affair between the eponymous heroine and an older man, a characteristic theme of Valera's writings. In the book the **Hermitage of the Virgen de la Sierra** is evocatively described at sunset. To reach the Hermitage take the C336 in the direction of Priego de Córdoba; on the outskirts of the town you will pass a natural spring shaded by trees, a popular picnic spot; the village's spacious swimming pool is on the other side of the road. The winding, steeply ascending road to the Hermitage leads off to the left after 7 km. The Hermitage is supposed to be at the very centre of Andalucía, and there are extensive views on all sides, embracing both the Guadalquivir and the Sierra Nevada. Some 14 km to the north of Cabra is the village of **Doña Mencía**, where Valera lived for several years, and which he featured (under the name Villalegre) as the setting of his novel *Juanita la Larga*. His house is in the lower end of the village, at Calle Llana 6, off what is now the Calle Juan Valera; at the end of his street is a ruined castle.

CABRA DEL SANTO CRISTO: A remote, wonderfully preserved large village, high up in the dramatically shaped Sierra de Mágina, with a spectacular views towards Baeza and Úbeda. The Casa de Cultura displays the pioneering photos of Arturo Cerdá y Rico, who lived in the village at the beginning of the last century, and created some of the most memorable images ever of traditional Andalucían life. The Restaurante Herminia, housed in one of the village's two former cinemas, serves wonderful local food including an outstanding partridge pâté.

CÁDIZ [5B]: Encased in its sturdy late 18th-century defensive walls, the old town of Cádiz is surrounded on three sides by sea and joined to the mainland by a long and narrow strip of land. Cádiz claims to be the oldest town in the west, its origins being in the Phoenician settlement of Gaadir, which was founded, according to classical sources, in 1100 BC, only a few years after the end of the Trojan War. Used by the Carthaginians as a base for their military campaigns in Spain, Cádiz later prospered under the Romans, and acquired a reputation for its lascivious dancing girls. Captured by the Goths in the 5th century AD, Cádiz entered a long decline, and was a place of little significance under the Moors. Trade with the New World revived its fortunes in the 16th century, but then in 1596 over a third of the town was destroyed during an English naval raid led by the Earl of Essex. Only after 1717, with the transfer here from Seville of the Chamber of Commerce of the Americas (the Casa de Contratacción; see page 115), was Cádiz finally established again as one of the leading towns of Spain. In 1812 the Spanish Parliament or *Cortes* was temporarily set up here, proclaiming on 19 March the first Spanish Constitution (see page 187).

Cádiz today is one of the most beautiful of Andalucía's towns, and yet has been barely affected by tourism. Most of the old town consists of long, straight and narrow streets lined with tall 18th- and early 19th-century houses with projecting windows. Elegance is blended with evocative decay. The inhabitants of this lively town are the people with whom the Sevillians have traditionally the most in common. They are famed both for their wit and gastronomy. Their celebrated Carnival, held in February, is a riot of sophisticated humour (see page 155), while their bars, restaurants and freidurías offer a delectable and imaginative range of fish and seafood.

The town's massive cathedral stands in the southern half of the old town, occupying a site betweeen the Plaza Catedral and the western sea-front. Built over the 17th and 18th centuries, it has an interior notable more for its size than its subtlety, and a west façade curiously fusing baroque movement and sober neo-classical detailing; attached to the building is a small museum housing a collection of opulent ecclesiastical silverwork and some dingy 17th- and 18th-century religious paintings of dubious attribution. On the south side of the Plaza Catedral is a medieval arch marking the entrance to the Barrio del Pópulo. This tiny district – all that remains of medieval Cádiz – is crammed with picturesque if filthy small streets and buildings, among which is the Mesón del Pópulo, a dilapidated inn dating back to the early 17th century. On the highest part of this district is the former Cathedral of

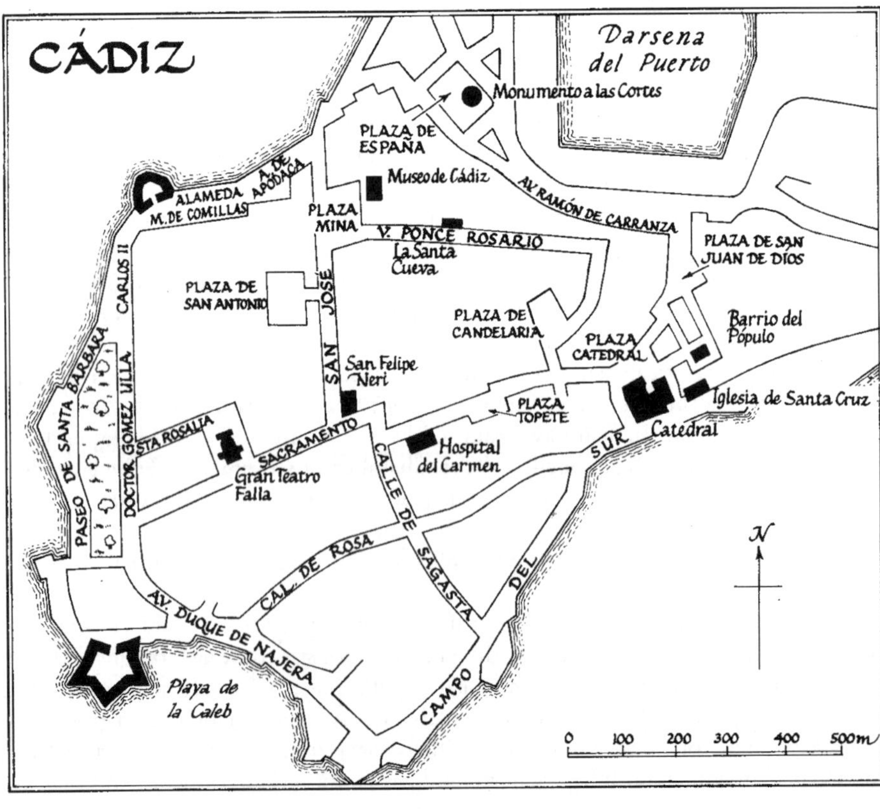

Cádiz, now the Iglesia de Santa Cruz: built after 1260 over a mosque, this is an attractive small building with an interior remodelled in the early 17th century in a sober renaissance style.

The Calle Campania leads north from the Plaza Catedral into the Plaza Topete, which contains a pretty flower market; the town's fish, meat and vegetable market lies just beyond, a 19th-century building surrounded by excellent bars. Heading north from here along the Calle Obispo Calvo y Valero you will pass on the left-hand side the late baroque hospice of the Carmen, which boasts a signed canvas by El Greco of the *Ecstasy of St. Francis*. Turn east shortly afterwards on to the Calle San José, and you will arrive at the oratory of San Felipe Neri, where the Cortes assembled in 1812; this celebrated historical site adjoins the town's excellent history museum, which is housed in a 19th-century mansion and contains documents connected with the Cortes and a model of the city in 1777.

A few minutes' walk north of San Felipe Neri along the Calle Sacramento will take you to the town's splendid turn-of-the-century theatre, a neo-Moorish building in brick now named after one of Cádiz's best known sons, Manuel de Falla. The elegant, ultra-modern parador (Hotel Atlántico) lies further north, on a site overlooking the sea; follow the sea wall west from here and you will soon reach a sign advertising the Faro restaurant, which is at the junction of the Calles Ecuador and Felix. This restaurant, the best in town, is one of the outstanding fish and sea-food restaurants of Andalucía; if you do not feel like a full meal, you can enjoy delicious tapas at its bar.

East from San Felipe Neri, the Calle San José crosses the Calle Ancha, where at No. 18 is the Casa Mora, an impressive early 19th-century mansion, open to the public on Tuesday mornings. The Calle San José comes to an end in the Plaza Mina, a delightful square with luxuriant gardens. The house at No. 3, on the western side of the square, is the birthplace of Falla (plaque; see page 224). The southern side of the square is taken up by the Museo de Cádiz, which has good collections of archaeology, ethnography and the fine arts displayed in a light, spacious and imaginatively modernized setting. The highpoints of the archaeological section are two large and powerfully carved Phoenician tombs, one discovered in 1896, the other in 1980; the finest of the paintings are those by Zurbarán, most notably a large *St. Francis receiving the Stigmata*, and a series of panels from the High Altar of the Jerez Charterhouse, featuring Carthusian saints (see page 119). Leaving the square by the street off its southwestern corner you will pass a large art-nouveau bar and café (El Castellón del Tinte) and eventually come to the late 18th-century church of La Santa Cueva, where there is a heavily decorated chapel featuring sober frescos by Goya. Due east of the Plaza Mina are the small and charming seaside gardens of the Alameda de Apodaca, while to the south-east is the large Plaza de España, dominated by a massive early 20th-century monument celebrating the Cortes of Cádiz.

South of the old town of Cádiz is a district of residential blocks lining the sandy

Cádiz

Playa de la Victoria, the continuation of which, the Playa de Cortaduna, follows the NIV all the way to **San Fernando**, a sprawling town of mainly modern appearance, but with a long-established naval base. **Puerto Real**, to the east of Cádiz, is a similarly unprepossessing town, founded as a port by Ferdinand and Isabella after 1492; it has a small archaeological museum, with interesting Phoenician finds, and a splendid and recently restored 18th-century theatre. The current mayor, Juan Barroso, was notorious for his stand against Spain's 1992 celebrations, and even commissioned an ambitious and never-to-be-executed monument from a Mexican artist recording the disastrous consequences of the so-called Discovery of America. **Chiclana de la Frontera**, to the south of the Bay of Cádiz, is an ugly small town, but with a celebrated flamenco festival in July. West of Chiclana, 9 km along a tiny road, is **Sancti Petri**, a hamlet situated on an as-yet-unspoilt stretch of coast (a large resort is being planned). At low tide you can walk out to the Island of Sancti Petri, on which stand the ruins of a Roman temple dedicated to Hercules.

CARMONA [3C]: 'Like the morning star at dawn, so shines Carmona in Andalucía,' Ferdinand III is supposed to have said after capturing the town in 1247.

These words are now incorporated in the coat of arms of Carmona, a place which is indeed one of the most beautiful and interesting small towns in the whole of Andalucía. Built on a bluff projecting from the fertile Guadalquivir basin, Carmona was inhabited as far back as Neolithic times. Numerous finds from the Tartessian period have been uncovered, and the place later developed as a major Roman town on the Via Augusta. Under the Moors Carmona was capital of a city state, and in the late 14th century it was a favourite residence of the Castilian king Pedro the Cruel.

In the modern outskirts of the town, off the Seville road, is an overgrown Roman theatre, and, directly in front is the entrance to the necropolis used by the Romans from the 2nd century BC to the 4th century AD (see page 64). Excavated in 1881 this remarkable and excellently looked-after site also has a small archaeological museum containing funerary offerings, bronze figures, busts and other finds from the area.

Walking towards the centre of Carmona from the Necropolis, and just before entering the old town the church of San Pedro, you will pass a 15th-century church remodelled in the 17th century, and given a bell-tower imitative of the Giralda in Seville; the interior is notable mainly for its sumptuously ornate mid-18th-century Sagrario chapel, the work of A. de Figueroa. The old town of Carmona is entirely encircled by the walls constructed by the Romans and strengthened by the Moors. You enter through the impressive double Seville Gate (Puerta de Sevilla), which is attached to a well-preserved castle and now houses a tourist office and a local museum. Beyond, lining the steep slope on which this part of the town is built, lies a whole series of quiet streets bordered by palaces, convents, churches and numerous other buildings, mostly painted in a brilliant white. The Calle Prim climbs up the slope to the cheerful and shaded main square, off which stands a former 17th-century monastery which serves today as the Town Hall; you should go inside to see the Roman mosaic of Medusa, discovered in 1929 and now placed in the main courtyard of the building. Almost adjoining the building is the arcaded market square or Plaza de Abastos where there is an eccentric bar, An Ca Carmela which serves the most imaginative *tapas.* Continuing uphill along the Calle Martín I, you soon reach the priory church of Santa María, built between 1424 and 1518 over a mosque, of which the charming Courtyard of the Oranges (on the north side of the building) survives. Just to the north of this courtyard, on the small Plaza de Lasso, is the 16th-century Palacio de los Lasso de la Vega, which has been tastefully transformed into the Casa de Carmona, one of the most stylish and homely of Spain's ultra-luxurious hotels. Comparably elegant, and housed in a neighbouring old palace is a late-night bar named after the nearby Puerta de Córdoba. This beautiful Roman gate, flanked by octagonal Moorish towers, was remodelled in the 17th century and turned into a triumphal arch. A short walk away, at the highest point of the town, stands the castle, which Pedro the Cruel transformed into a sumptuous residence, employing the same mudéjar craftsmen who worked for him in the Alcázar in Seville. Now part of it has been drastically converted into a luxury parador, the main attractions of which are the extensive views of the surrounding countryside: non-residents can use its neo-Moorish bar and walk out on to the spectacularly situated terraces.

CASTRIL: Thrust above a lush valley in between the eroded expanses north of Guadix (see page 309) and the pine-covered slopes of a nature reserve, Castril is a well preserved and spectacularly situated hill village dominated by a fine renaissance church and the ruins of a citadel. The delightful Café Bar Emilio in the main square serves excellent local dishes, such as the red pepper stew known as *maimones*. An exciting short walk can be done along the newly created 'nature path' at the bottom of the village's gorge; there is also a well displayed local museum in the Visitor's Centre at the entrance to the nature reserve. The village has a foundation named after the Nobel prize-winning Portuguese author José Saramago, who is married to a locally born journalist and presides over an annual arts festival that was inaugurated in July 2004.

CAZALLA DE LA SIERRA [2C] is in the middle of a gentle and extensively wooded mountain area popular with week-enders from Seville. Linked to Seville by train, it lies at the end of what becomes in its last stages one of the most attractive railway lines in southern Spain. From the isolated station, surrounded by oaks and olive trees, you will have to complete the remaining 4 km by taxi. The road passes next to the currently closed hotel complex of Las Villas, which is designed as a terraced and landscaped village that beautifully and sensitively exploits a panoramic, hill-side position. Visible from here and more unusual still is a small hotel built within the monastic buildings of a ruined 15th-century Charterhouse, the present and eccentric owner of which welcomes artists, writers and musicians to her establishment, and sends away the more boring-looking prospective clients to the rival Las Villas. The Charterhouse itself was founded in 1476 by the prior of the Sevillian Charterhouse of Las Cuevas, Don Fernando de Cerezuela, who described the surroundings as a 'piece of Paradise'. The enormous shell of its church, evocatively overgrown, was extensively altered in the 18th century.

The town, of Roman origin, is at the top of the hill. Though lacking a central focus, and damaged by insensitive recent development, it has cheerful, whitewashed streets, in one of which is a spacious old bodega where you can eat meats grilled on a wood fire and tapas of the excellent local game. The incomplete and massive church of Nuestra Señora de la Consolación is an architectural mess, though with interesting parts, notably a renaissance chancel with strange honey-combed vaulting. The Calle Virgen del Monte in front of the church's northern portal leads you into the animated market area of town. In the middle of this, off the Calle Carmelo Meclana, is the former monastery church of San Francisco, which has now been turned into the cellar and sales outlet of a well known brand of local aguardiente, Miura. Cazalla is famous for its cherry brandy, and at the Miura store you can taste one of the best examples of this while looking up at the crumbling baroque decoration on the church's ceiling. An excellent place to watch aguardiente being distilled according to traditional, safety-defying methods is the small and attractive 'Destileria Clavel' at 8 c/S. Benito.

About 6 km to the south of Cazalla is the **Hermitage of Nuestra Señora del Monte**, which was built after 1756 in commemoration of an appearance made by the Virgin to a local shepherd. On 7 August each year a pilgrimage is made to this enchanting shaded spot overlooking a valley densely covered with oaks and olive trees; a tiny rustic bar has been placed at the side of this building. The cheerful, palm-fringed town of **Constantina**, 25 km to the west of Cazalla, was an important colony in Roman times, but was much damaged during the Peninsular War; its main monument is its 16th-century parish church of La Encarnación, which has a beautiful if slightly deteriorated classical plateresque portal by Hernán Ruiz. **Alanis**, 16 km to the north of Cazalla, has a castle sitting on top of the conical hill which rises above the village: the building, reached by an overgrown footpath, was built by the Moors, greatly damaged during the French occupation of 1808, and has recently been crudely restored. East of Alanis begins a winding and beautiful stretch of road (the C21) crossing, wild, uninhabited countryside which becomes suddenly parched and bare soon after entering the province of Córdoba.

CAZORLA [2G], on the western slopes of the Sierra de Cazorla, is a popular mountain resort, and the main base for excursions into the National Park of Cazorla and Segura and the nearby village of La Iruela. The bustling centre has a largely modern aspect, and betrays little of Cazorla's formidable history, which goes back to an Iberian settlement of the first century BC and includes a period as one of Spain's earliest bishoprics, founded by St. Isacius. West of the Town Hall, Cazorla has a completely different character, and you descend into a district of picturesque white houses clinging to the sides of a ravine. The centre of this very quiet part of town is the beautiful Plaza de Santa María, which has a renaissance fountain and the imposing ruins of a 16th-century church designed by Vandelvira. Thrust up high on the steep rocky slopes above is the tower of the Moorish castle of La Yedra.

La Iruela

On the northern outskirts of the town, on the road to La Iruela, you will find the main information office of the National Park of Cazorla and Segura, which will provide details about hunting, fishing and other activities. The village of **La Iruela**, only 1 km from Cazorla is known for its basketwork (ask for the house of 'Esteban'). At its far end is another 16th-century ruined church (Santo Domingo de Silos), also perhaps designed by Vandelvira. The ruins of the castle next to this, perched almost implausibly on a near-vertical pinnacle of rock, seem to be the figment of a stage-designer's imagination; it is just about possible to climb up to it, though a certain skill at rock-climbing is an advantage. The road beyond the castle continues its relatively easy ascent into the National Park. Once over the pass you can turn right to the modern Parador of El Adelantado, or take the unasphalted road below this to the source of the Guadalquivir (see QUESADA). The most popular route through the park is to head left 4 km before the turning for the parador, and follow the J704 in the direction of Segura. Shortly before reaching the reservoir of El Tranco, there is the Torre del Vinagre, which has stuffed animals, photographs and other objects relating to the park; next to this is a garden bringing together the diverse flora and fauna of the region. At the southern end of the reservoir is an area unappealingly named the Cirugertic Park, which is a wild life park with a path leading to a viewing balcony where you might see in the far distance some rather bored-looking red deer.

CÓRDOBA [2E]: Built on the northern banks of the Guadalquivir, underneath the Sierra Morena, Córdoba rose to fame in Roman times when it became the capital of Baetica, the largest town in Spain and the birthplace of Lucan and Seneca. The Moors made it the capital of al-Andalus, and between 755 and 1031 it was ruled by the Umayyad dynasty. In the 10th century, under the caliphs Abd al-Rahman III and al-Hakam II, Córdoba enjoyed a reputation as one of the great cities of the world in terms of size, the splendour of its architecture, and the vitality of its cultural and intellectual life. The decline set in after the fall of the Umayyads, and was consolidated by the capture of the town by the Christians in 1236. For much of its subsequent history travellers have tended to describe Córdoba as a sad, bleak and empty town, living off memories of its past (see page 78). However, since the Civil War of 1936-9, 'the distant and lonely' town evoked by García Lorca has developed into a thriving commercial town and one of the major tourist centres of Spain.

At the heart of the present-day Córdoba is the bustling but ugly Plaza de las Tendillas, which has, attached to one of its tall and pretentious buildings, a much loved clock chiming flamenco music. The usual tourist instinct is to head off from here as soon as possible down to the Mezquita; but a pleasant detour before doing so is to walk north to the neighbouring small square of San Miguel, where you will find one of the liveliest of this city's many surviving old bars, El Pisto: virtually unchanged in its decoration since the early years of this century, it has a covered

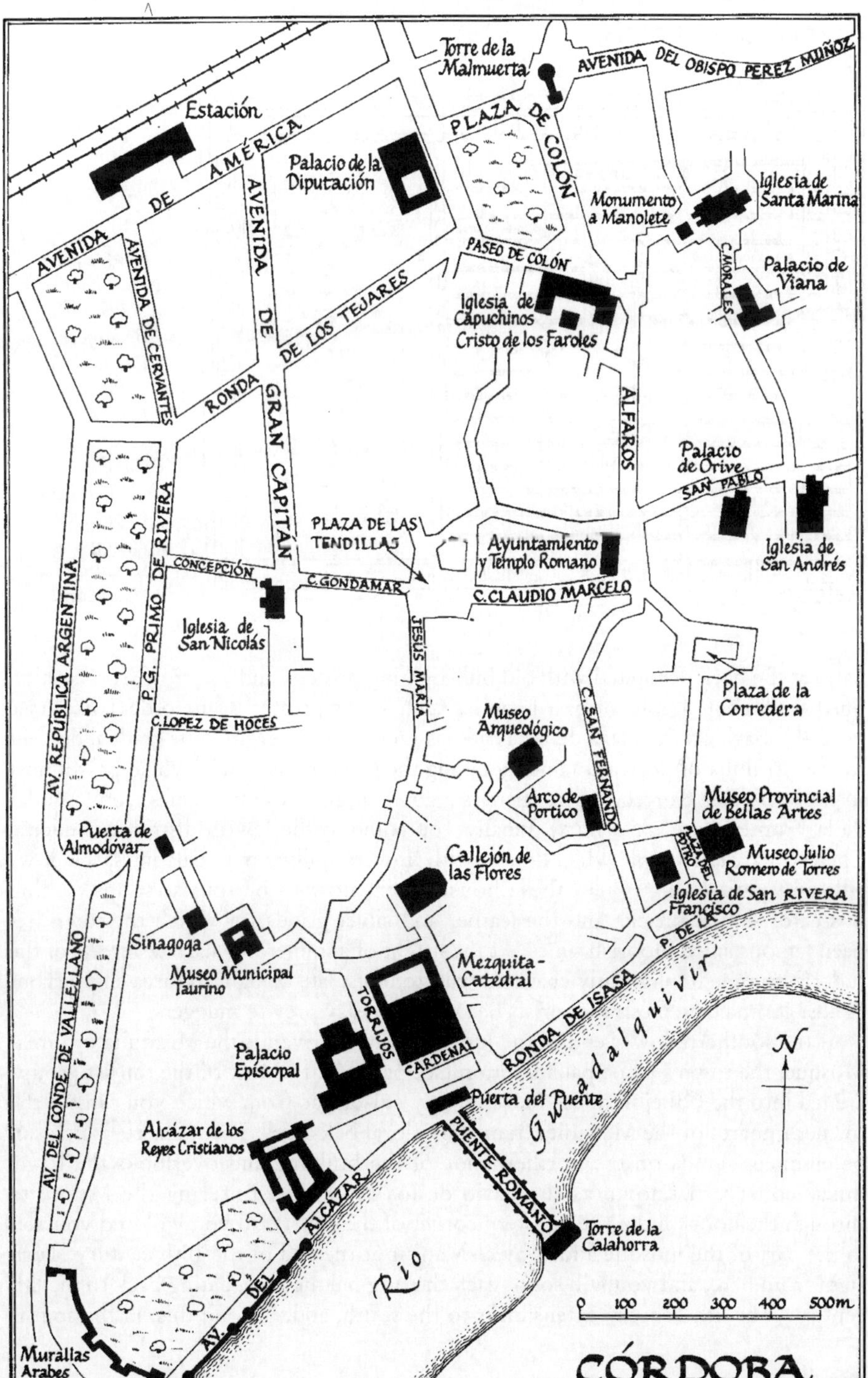

Torre de la Malmuerta
Avenida del Obispo Pérez Muñoz
Estación
Avenida de América
Plaza de Colón
Palacio de la Diputación
Monumento a Manolete
Iglesia de Santa Marina
Avenida de Cervantes
Avenida de Gran Capitán
Ronda de los Tejares
Paseo de Colón
Iglesia de Capuchinos
Cristo de los Faroles
C. Morales
Palacio de Viana
Alfaros
Palacio de Orive
San Pablo
Iglesia de San Andrés
Plaza de las Tendillas
Ayuntamiento y Templo Romano
Concepción
C. Gondamar
C. Claudio Marcelo
P. G. Primo de Rivera
Iglesia de San Nicolás
Av. República Argentina
Jesús María
C. San Fernando
Plaza de la Corredera
C. Lopez de Hoces
Museo Arqueológico
Arco de Portico
Museo Provincial de Bellas Artes
Plaza del Potro
Museo Julio Romero de Torres
Puerta de Almodóvar
Callejón de las Flores
Iglesia de San Francisco
P. de la Rivera
Sinagoga
Museo Municipal Taurino
Mezquita-Catedral
Torrijos
Ronda de Isasa
Guadalquivir
N
Av. del Conde de Vallellano
Palacio Episcopal
Cardenal
Puerta del Puente
Alcázar de los Reyes Cristianos
Puente Romano
Torre de la Calahorra
Av. del Alcázar
Rio
0 100 200 300 400 500m
Murallas Arabes
CÓRDOBA

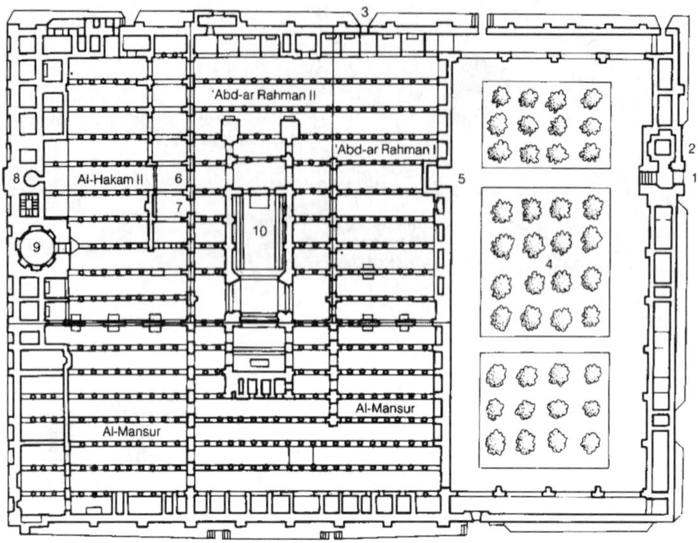

The Mezquita
1 Puerta del Perdón
2 Bell tower
3 Puerta de San Esteban
4 Patio de los Naranjos
6 Capilla Villaviciosa
7 Capilla Real
8 Mihrab
9 Sacristy
10 Cathedral

patio at the back decorated with old bull-fighting posters, and a narrow front section lined with photographs of past habitués such as the painter Romero de Torres (see page 49). Back on the Plaza de las Tendillas you can now begin your gradual descent to the Córdoba of postcard fame by taking the Calle Jesus María, which passes next to the small Bar Correo, where there is a good supply of white wines from Aguilar de la Frontera (see MONTILLA). Finally you come to the Jewish district or Judería. This is an area of simple white houses with flowers spilling over balconies, window-sills and patios. Almost all these houses seem now to be tourist shops, selling postcards, knick-knacks and the leather and silver goods for which the town has been famous since Moorish times. At the height of summer, the narrow streets of the Judería become unpleasantly crowded with tourists; late at night the area empties out almost completely, its stray tourists becoming an easy prey to muggers.

At the southern, lower end of the Judería, near the river, is the Mezquita or Great Mosque, the town's principal attraction (see pages 72ff). Most of the tourist groups are led into the Callejón de las Flores, a tiny cul-de-sac from which you can see the former minaret of the Mezquita framed by floral balconies. The minaret, which can be climbed, stands on the northern side of the building and overlooks the large, dusty courtyard known as the Patio de los Naranjos. Entering the Mezquita through the door on the southeastern corner of the courtyard you will find yourself in the part of the mosque added by al-Mansur at the end of the 10th century. Turn right from here, and you will soon reach the original mosque, dating back to the 8th century. The 9th-century extension is to the south, and, beyond this, in the south-

The Capilla Villaviciosa, by J. F. Lewis

eastern corner of the building, is the section built by al-Hakam II in the 10th century; this last section is the most elaborate in its architecture and decoration, and contains the third mihrab, the maq-surah, and a 13th-century mudéjar chapel, called the Capilla Villaviciosa. The 16th-century cathedral in the middle of the Mezquita is a remarkable structure mingling late gothic and renaissance elements, with 18th-century carved choir stalls that blend well with the intricate ornamentation of the rest of the cathedral.

Córdoba is famous for its gastronomy, and off the northwestern corner of the Mezquita a tiny alley leads to one of Andalucía's better known, the Caballo Rojo, which specializes in Hispano-Moorish dishes such as lamb with honey. The fame of this establishment has been superseded in recent years by two of its neighbours, the beautiful and labyrithine Churrasco and the rather more animated Casa Pepe, which has emerged of late as a place of great culinary invention. West from here are an extensive section of the medieval walls (behind the Calle Maimonides), a charming 14th-century synagogue, and the Museo Taurino, a rather characterless modern display of local crafts and bull-fighting souvenirs; a number of these souvenirs are of the Córdoban bull-fighter of the 1960's and early 1970's, El Cordobés, better known for his gimmickry and rock star presence than for his artistry. The city's main bull-fighting *peña,* or club, holds its meetings in the attractive Bodega Guzmán, further north on the same street as the synagogue. At the northern end of the Judería, on the Calle Barroso, is the church of San Juan, attached to which is an impressive 9th-century minaret.

Running down the western side of the Mezquita is the Calle Torrijos, on which stands the Episcopal Palace. This building, marking the site both of the palace of the Roman and Visigothic governors of Córdoba and of the original Moorish Alcázar, today houses the spacious Diocesan Museum, which is worth a visit largely for its well-restored baroque setting. The adjoining Casa de Expósitos, or Foundling Hospital, containing the town's tourist office and a restful bar, is used in July and September by Paco Peña's guitar school and during these two months echoes with the sounds of flamenco. The new Alcázar, begun by Alfonso X in the late 13th century, is entered from the Calle Almodóvar del Río, just to the south of the Episcopal Palace; its main interests are its Roman mosaics and beautiful gardens. The Calle Torrijos leads into a tiny square featuring a curious late baroque monument to St Raphael and a Roman gate restored in the Renaissance period. Córdoba's celebrated Roman bridge, below the gate, crosses an especially beautiful stretch of the river, overhung with greenery, and cradling the evocative ruins of Moorish mills. The views of the town from the tower on the opposite bank are quite magnificent. The tower itself, known as the Torre de la Calahorra, now has a museum evoking Córdoba's Moorish past with the aid of waxworks, changing lighting, music, and pretentious commentary.

The area to the east of the Mezquita has much of the charm of the Judería, but with fewer tourist shops. On the Plaza de Jerónimo Paez – reached from the Mezquita by following the Calle Encarnación – is a renaissance palace with an attractively ornate façade and a cool, patio-dominated interior housing the town's archaeological museum; among its most important pieces are finds from the caliph's summer palace at Medina Azahara. The narrow Plaza del Potro, further east, is one of Córdoba's most delightful small squares, and comes down almost to the river. The house at the top of the square belongs to the guitarist Paco Peña, and is the headquarters of his guitar school. On the square's western side is a building which was once the 'Potro Inn', an inn mentioned by Cervantes; built around a narrow courtyard with wooden balconies, this has now been restored to house a permanent display of old Cordovan leatherwork from medieval times up to the 18th century. Opposite is the former Charity Hospital, founded under the Catholic monarchs and now containing the town's Fine Arts Museum and a museum dedicated to the local painter Julio Romero de Torres (see page 49). A plaque outside the latter indicates the the building was the birthplace of Romero de Torres, and that he also lived and died here. The interior is dark and gloomy, rather like Torres's paintings, which are nearly all of naked Córdoba women. One of the artist's best-known works is *La Chiquita Piconera*, which features a sultry, provocatively clad girl stirring the ashes of a brazier; another work on show here is *Viva el Pelo*, which is rapturously described in *1912 + 1* (1986), a novella by the Sicilian writer Leonardo Sciascia. The Fine Arts Museum includes other works by Romero de Torres, and a large painting of the *Last Sacrament* by his father, Rafael. A staircase with a mudéjar ceiling and 16th-century murals leads up to the holdings of old masters, which range from a fine *Christ at the Column* by Alejo Fernández to slight works by Zurbarán and Goya.

Casa Jerónimo Paez

By now the time has probably come for some gastronomic refreshment. For a proper meal you could do no better than walk to the bottom of the square and turn left, you will soon find the Bodegas Campos, a dazzlingly white and seductive bar and restaurant complex that has been formed by the joining together of a convent, two bodegas and several private houses (including one with a courtyard dating back to the 16th century); the

Santa Marina

superlative and imaginative food, not to mention the excellent selection of local wines and the warm welcome given by the head waitress Manoli, make the place one of the highpoints of any visit to Córdoba. For a shorter stop, for just a drink and a *tapa*, you could head instead to the delightful Taberna de San Francisco, which is built around a glazed patio just off the Plaza del Potro's north-western corner (it can be entered from either the Calle de San Francisco or the parallel Calle Romero Barro). Dating back to 1872, this was for over a century the headquarters of the Sociedad de Plateros (Society of Silver Workers), which was founded in 1868 to assist silver-workers who had fallen on hard times. The large room off the patio is now used as a Flamenco Club, attended by the likes of Paco Peña; but the place is still in the possession of the Sociedad de Plateros, who indeed own some of the finest of Córdoba's old taverns, including, until recently, the nearby and exceptionally beautiful Bar Los Plateros (on the Plaza de Seneca), which has columns supporting a wooden beam ceiling.

The Calle Armas leads north from the Plaza del Potro to La Corredera, a large 17th century arcaded square inspired by Castilian models; used once for bull-fights, theatrical spectacles and other public entertainments, this has now been transformed into an elegant and fashionable space lined with cafes and bars. It is a short walk from here back to the Plaza de las Tendillas, passing the excellent Taberna Salinas (a late 19th-century bar with traditional Córdoban food) and then the main façade of the ugly modern Town Hall in front of which are the much-restored columns of a

Roman temple. Alternatively you could turn east from the Town Hall on to the Calle San Pablo and enter a fascinating but little visited part of Córdoba. Half-way down the Calle San Pablo, on the Plazuela de Orive, is the House of Villalones, a small, elegant renaissance structure crowned by a loggia. The pleasant Plaza San Andrés, further down the street, features a late medieval church and another modest renaissance house. Further east still, in distinctly seedy surroundings, is the very impressive gothic church of San Lorenzo, the west face of which has a beautifully ornamented rose window.

A five-minute walk north of the Plaza San Andrés will take you to one of the most enjoyable of Córdoba's architectural attractions. This, the Palacio de los Marqueses de Viana, is a 14th- to 18th-century building boasting no fewer than fourteen patios and gardens; the interior, which can be visited, is splendidly furnished and has a well-known collection of Cordovan leatherwork. In front of the nearby medieval church of Santa Marina is a monument to the bull-fighter Manolete, and a bar – once much frequented by matadors – decorated with bull-fighting souvenirs and specializing in deep-fried boquerones. West from here, along the Calle Conde de Priego, is the Plaza del Cristo de los Faroles, bordered by a 17th-century convent and adorned in its centre with a statue of Christ encased by black railings supporting lanterns; this square is particularly attractive at night.

The square backs on to the spacious Plaza de Colón, which has in its northeastern corner a 15th-century brick tower forming part of the town's original fortifications. Called the Torre de la Malmuerta ('Bad Death'), it was reputedly built as an act of contrition by a nobleman who had killed his adulterous wife and her servants. Much of the western side of the square is taken up by the former 18th-century convent of

La Merced

La Merced (now the seat of local government offices), the most important and colourful of Córdoba's baroque buildings. The town's train station is a short distance away to the west, on the Avenida de América. Running south from the Avenida are a wide, park-lined avenue marking the town's western fortifications, and the Avenida del Gran Capitán, lined with Córdoba's finest modern buildings. At the southern end of the latter street is the church of San Nicolás, with a tall bell-tower which was once a minaret; the Calle Gondomar leads east from here back to the Plaza de las Tendillas.

An enjoyable trip from Córdoba can be made to **Las Ermitas** (the Hermitages) and the ruins of the Moorish summer palace of **Medina Azahara** (see pages 76-77). The former – a group of hermits' cells – are situated high on the verdant hills above the town and command beautiful views of the Guadalquivir valley; the winding 10 km road which leads to them passes through the luxurious northern suburbs of Córdoba, in which are to be found the town's parador and one of Andalucía's most fanciful discothèques, Sheherazade. From the Hermitages you can meander slowly west along the ridge of hills in the direction of Medina Azahara; before descending to the latter you will pass the Bar Restaurante Cruce, an excellent lunch stop, where you can eat locally hunted wild boar. The ruins of Medina Azahara, attractively contained within gardens coloured by bougainvillea, are best seen either in the early morning or late afternoon. Above the ruins is the 16th-century monastery of San Jerónimo (now a private residence), which was built with some of the stones from the palace. In the far distance, to the west, can just be made out the castle of **Almodóvar del Río**, sitting on top of a tall barren mound directly above the Guadalquivir river. This impressive if heavily restored castle, 17 km from Córdoba on the C431, can be visited; it is now rented out to the controversial Catholic society Opus Dei.

CUMBRES MAYORES [2B] lies at the northwestern extremity of Andalucía, and already the densely wooded hills of the Sierra de Aracena (see ARACENA) have given way to the starker more barren landscape characteristic of Extremadura. The village, which has the sombre aspect typical too of that region, has an impressive castle, the keys for which can be had from the house at Plaza Portugal 3 directly in front of the building. The castle is entered through an enormously tall gate, beyond which you reach, to your surprise, an overgrown football pitch. The walk around the well-preserved battlements is rewarded by extensive views.

ÉCIJA [3D], sunk in a depression formed by the river Genil, has inspired one of the silliest lines in the *Green Guide to Spain*: 'Écija enjoys a moderate climate except in summer, when it is known as the Furnace of Andalucía.' An important Roman settlement known as Astigi (the scant ruins of which can be seen on the town's outskirts), Écija developed in early Christian times as one of the main bishoprics of Spain, visited reputedly by St. Paul. Under the Moors it began to decline, but in the

17th and 18th centuries it flourished owing to its being surrounded by prosperous latifundia, the owners of which had palaces built in the town. After being devastated by the earthquake that also destroyed Lisbon in 1755, many of its churches were rebuilt and Écija acquired the splendid series of late baroque church towers that have earned it the nickname of 'the city of towers.' Away from the ugly outskirts that have grown up alongside the main Seville to Córdoba road (the NIV/E25), Écija reveals itself to be the most architecturally impressive of all the small towns near Seville with an unrivalled number of aristocratic palaces, grand churches and stage-like streets and corners. The Avenida Miguel de Cervantes leads from the NIV/E25 to the long and picturesquely variegated Plaza de España, which is lined with arcaded 'miradors', from where the town's aristocrats once watched the world go by. The square's magnificence is marred only by the endless excavations which have unearthed numerous Roman statues and Islamic tombs. A jumble of Iberian, Roman and medieval finds can be seen in the charming small cloister of the adjoining church of Santa Maria which is notable also for its massive 18th century entrance arch. The finest survival from the early Christian period in Écija is a sarcophagus in the 18th-century church of Santa Cruz, on the Plazuela Virgen del Valle, to the north of the Plaza de España. The baroque monuments of Écija are the town's greatest attractions, though few travellers have hitherto been able to appreciate these: one of the few was Théophile Gautier, who was enraptured by what he described as 'the sublime bad taste' of the local architecture. Of the town's many baroque towers, the most spectacular is that of the church of San Juan Bautista, which stands to the east of the Plaza de España, on the Calle San Antonio: this fantastical tower is dripping with volutes and coloured with brilliant blue ceramic tiles shining against a background of red brick. The former convent church of La Limpia Concepción de Nuestra Señora (Las Descalzas), on the eastern edge of the old town, boasts the most elaborate of Écija's church interiors: the building was begun in 1511, but completely remodelled after the earthquake and given its magnificent polychromed stucco interior, which oozes rococco forms. There are various impressive palaces in the town,

Palace of the Marqueses de Peñaflor

the most charming and unusual being that of the Marqueses de Peñaflor on the Calle de Castellar (near the church of San Juan Bautista and now used for occasional exhibitions): dating from 1726, it has a curving main façade covered in 18th-century decorations, and featuring a frontispiece crowned with Solomonic columns; leading off its beautiful patio is an intriguing staircase with columns in red marble and an elaborate plasterwork ceiling. The outstanding palace in Écija is that of the Peñaflor's great rivals, the Marqueses de Benameji (on the Calle Castillo, behind the Church of Santa María), now a smart bar and restaurant and home to the town's excellent Archaeological Museum. It was built about the same time as the Peñaflor Palace, and has a particularly imposing frontispiece in grey and white stone, supporting a gigantic coat of arms. Among the numerous other palaces of interest are the privately owned Casa Palacio (Plaza Nuestra Señora de la Valle, open daily from 12 to 2) and (on the calle Emilio Castellar) the Casa Palacio Palacio de Valdehermoso with its enchanting renaissance façade and the newly opened Hotel Palacio de los Granados, perhaps the most stylish of Andalucia's palace hotels.

La Luisiana and **La Carlota**, two of the colonies founded in the late 18th century by Charles III and his minister Olavide (see LA CAROLINA) lie respectively 15 km to the west of Écija, and 21 km to the east, both along the main Seville to Córdoba road. As with the other colonies, these are both laid out on a regular grid plan. La Luisiana, the smaller and less interesting of the two, has a tiny and pretty square flanked by a modest Town Hall and a neoclassical church highlighted in pink. The Town Hall of La Carlota, standing besides the main road, is a more notable building than that of La Luisiana: faced with giant pilasters, it is a true structure of the Enlightenment in its mixture of grandeur and simplicity. On the other side of the road is an attractive 18th-century red brick coaching inn (Real Casa de las Postas), while further along the road is a statue to Charles III and Olavide, recording how these two men 'came to transform these sterile and deserted lands into productive villages'. Set back from the road is the harmonious Plaza de las Iglesias, dominated by a large parish church featuring a triple-arched portico, and two bell-towers.

EL CARPIO [2E]: Near the uninspiring hill village of El Carpio is one of Andalucía's most remarkable examples of turn-of-the-century industrial architecture. Take the main road (NIV/E25) east from El Carpio for 4 km, then turn onto the small CO412. After crossing the Guadalquivir on a dam flanked by neo-Moorish towers, you will find on the left-hand side of the road a gate marked Central Carpio. Go through this, and, taking care to bear always to the right (if you turn left you will end up in the private estate of the Dukes of Alba) you will reach an extraordinary electrical power station designed, like the dam, by an eccentric Madrilenian architect of Scottish ancestry, Casto Fernández Shaw. Crowned by mosque-like domes, this neo-Moorish fantasy has, on its river side, a balcony supported by magnificent elephants' heads. The adjoining estate of the Dukes of Alba was where Goya stayed in

1796, enjoying an affair with the Duchess, who inspired several erotic drawings of his, and who is sometimes said, implausibly, to have posed for the *Maja Desnuda*.

EL PUERTO DE SANTA MARÍA [5B] stands at the mouth of the River Guadelete overlooking the heavily industrialized Bay of Cádiz. Founded by the Greeks, it developed in the 15th century as a major port, and wine-exporting town; today it is a popular summer resort, much frequented by the inhabitants of nearby Jerez de la Frontera. The poet Rafael Alberti, who was born here in 1902, described the town rapturously in his sentimental autobiography, *La Arboleda Perdida* (see page 219). Extensive modern development has considerably spoilt the place in recent years, but there is a pleasant old quarter, which, with its regular grid of streets and late 18th- to early 19th-century houses, is highly reminiscent of that of Cádiz. The main church of the town is the 15th- to 17th-century Iglesia Mayor Prioral, which has an imposing classical plateresque south portal. Of great historical and architctural interest is the heavily restored Castle of San Marcos, a largely 13th-century structure built by Alfonso X (the Wise) on the site of a Moorish watch tower and mosque: the monarch referred to the construction of this building in one of his famous *Cantigas*. The foundations of the mosque, together with some Roman columns discovered here, were incorporated into the castle's small and delightful church. In the 19th century the castle was lived in by a strange variety of people and as such inspired two novels by the costumbrista writer Fernán Caballero (see page 212).

The town's enormous but elegant bullring was built in 1880, and is much loved by bullfighting enthusiasts: a ceramic plaque placed at one of its main entrances records the fighter Joselito as saying that 'he who has not seen bulls at El Puerto does not know what a bullfight is like.' The square's other attractions are its bodegas, most of which can be visited: the oldest and prettiest is the 17th-century Bodega Terry on the Calle General Mola. In the summer months an enjoyable journey from El Puerto to Cádiz can be done on a small old boat called the *vapor*; the service has been run since its inception in 1929 by the same Galician family.

The beach resort of El Puerto is the western suburb of Valdelagrana, the chic appearance of which is belied by the industrial landscape that surrounds it. A nearby resort is that of **Rota**, 15 km further east, which has, on its northern side, good clean beaches that are fortunately out of sight of Cádiz's industries. Rota itself is an old village with a pretty central square featuring an austere 14th/15th-century church and a much restored castle; its most offensive feature is the American military base on its outskirts, which has all the appearance of a gigantic prison camp.

ESTEPA [3E]: When the Romans entered Estepa in 208 BC they found that its inhabitants had killed themselves and burnt their own property, preferring this to surrendering to the enemy. To most Spaniards the name 'Estepa' does not recall this valiant action but instead the dry, fragile biscuits known as *polvorones* and *mantecados*, which are eaten generally at Christmas time and are manufactured in various small factories in the lower half of the village. The old town of Estepa, which lies higher up, is like a small and not so well-preserved version of nearby Osuna. The church of the Carmen, on the small but lively village central square, the Plaza del Carmen, has an extraordinary, elaborate baroque façade of 1768, comprising a rhythmical interplay of convex and concave forms in black and white stone. Walking from this square down to the village's cheerful main thoroughfare, the Calle Mesones and its continuation, the Calle Castillejos, you have good views of the rugged rocky crags of the Sierra de Machuca; at Calle Castillejos 18 is the fine 18th-century Palace of the Marqueses de Cerverales with an animated frontispiece made up of Solomonic columns. Above the village stand the ruins of a castle, dating back to Iberian times, rebuilt by the Romans, and given its sturdy keep in the late 13th century.

14 km north of Estepa is the communist village of **Marinaleda**, notorious for its charismatic mayor, Sánchez Gordillo (see page 20).

FRAILES [2F], though by no means a place of great architectural beauty, is an exceptionally friendly village in the foothills Sierra Sur de Jaén. Its best known resident today is the much-loved El Sereno, whose house at the top of the village contains the smallest olive mill in the world. Off the village's lower street are the Bars La Cueva (of interest for its cave setting) and El Choto, which has outstanding home cooking and charcuterie. An unexpected treat in the neighbouring village of **Ribera Alta** is the innovative and elegant Rey de Copas, one of the finest restaurants in eastern Andalucía. On the other side of Frailes you can drive into countryside famed for its saintly dynasty of faith healers, the most important of whom was the 'Santo Custodio', who died in 1960. The rock shelter where this unofficial saint prayed is to be found outside the hamlet of **La Hoya del Salobral** (10 km north-east of Frailes) and enjoys a magnificent panorama towards the snow capped Sierra de Nevada.

FUENTE OBEJUNA [1D], a sad and sinister town in a depressed area of Córdoba province, is famous for its insurrection of 1476 against its tyrannical governor (see page 19). The event was commemorated in a play by Lope de Vega, who is remembered here in the name of the main square and in a plaque opposite the parish church praising him for having 'celebrated the civic virtues of our citizens'. The governor's palace was pulled down shortly after the tyrant's death, and replaced by this church, whose delicate late gothic interior contains a beautiful 16th-century polychrome altar, and an altarpiece with Hispano-Flemish painted panels.

GAUCÍN [5D], with its eagle's-nest setting and former notoriety as a bandit's lair, had an obvious attraction to the Romantic traveller. The bandits have now been replaced by the British, who have bought up whole streets in this picturesque and superficially unchanged village. There is an excellent cheap and old-fashioned Fonda (the Nacional) and a British-run bar popular with the teenage children of the foreign residents. Jutting out on rocky ground above the ridge to which the village clings are the ruins of a castle, from which you can see as far as Gibraltar on clear days. Some 10 km to the north, off the C341 to Ronda, is the hamlet of **Benalauria**, the castle of which encloses the village church and cemetery. The old road to the south of Gaucín (MA539) descends perilously to the coast, passing on the left the attractive village of **Casares**.

GIBRALTAR [5D]: The Rock of Gibraltar, one of the famed landmarks of the Mediterranean, was thought of in ancient times as one of the pillars of Hercules, and as such marked the western end of the known world. Its present name was acquired after 711 AD when the Berber leader Tariq ibn Ziyad landed here and called the Rock Jebel Tariq, 'the Mountain of Tariq' (see page 68). Under Moorish domination up to 1309, and then again from 1333, Gibraltar was definitively captured by the Christians in 1462, an event which presaged the imminent collapse of the Nasrid dynasty. Early on during the War of Spanish Succession, in 1704, the Rock was taken by the English, who in 1782 brilliantly defended it against the combined

Spain from Gibraltar

forces of the French and Spanish. Thereafter the British transformed it into a British colony, which it remains to this day. Spanish antagonism towards the British presence here led in 1969 to the Rock being made inaccessible from the Spanish mainland; access was only re-established in 1985. In 1988 the Rock acquired further notoriety when British police shot down and killed three apparently unarmed Irishmen suspected of being terrorists. The British government subsequently went to absurd lengths to cover up the facts of the incident, despite international outcry.

Gibraltar is an unquestionably ugly place, and for those who have been relishing the sensuality of southern Spain, the shock of arriving here from the mainland can be considerable (see page 38). The architecture of the town is almost wholly English, and even the local ice-cream van plays Greensleeves to remind you of the mother country. Yet for all the Englishness of Gibraltar the place has a curious hybrid character. The bilingual inhabitants speak a mixture of English and Spanish, and the streets are packed with a fascinating variety of peoples, from blond British soldiers to Jewish traders and veiled Moroccan women.

The oldest and most interesting part of Gibraltar is North Town, the main street of which provides a constant human spectacle. Of this district's more obvious attractions, mention should be made of the neo-Moorish Anglican Cathedral of 1821 (on Cathedral Square) and the Gibraltar Museum, which retains an English drabness despite incorporating an old Moorish bath. From the southern end of North Town you can take a cable car up to the top of the Rock. Walking down from here, along St. Michael's Road, you will pass next to the gigantic St. Michael's Cave, where ballets and other shows are sometimes put on; the look of this garishly lit cave is very artificial. Further down the Rock you will come to the Apes' Den, a popular meeting-place both for tourists and Gibraltar's famous Barbary apes: the apes were probably first brought over from Africa by the Moors, and are the only tribe of monkeys living wild on the continent of Europe. The Queen's Road leads from near here to the steeply sloping northern half of the Rock, inside which an impressive series of defensive tunnels was dug out in 1782; these tunnels, which can be visited, are known as the Upper Galleries. From here you can walk back to North Town by way of the much restored Moorish Castle, the phoniness of which is emphasized by the waxwork Moorish figures which have been placed on its battlements.

GRANADA [3F/4G]: Built beneath the snowcapped peaks of the Sierra Nevada, at the easternmost edge of the fertile plain or *vega* formed by the River Genil, Granada is one of the most beautifully situated of all Spanish towns, and has been since the early 19th century one of the principal tourist destinations of Europe. This town of fabled reputation was actually an obscure place in ancient and early Christian times, and even under the Moors it only rose to fame after 1241 when Ibn Nasr, founder of the Nasrid dynasty, established here the capital of his empire (see

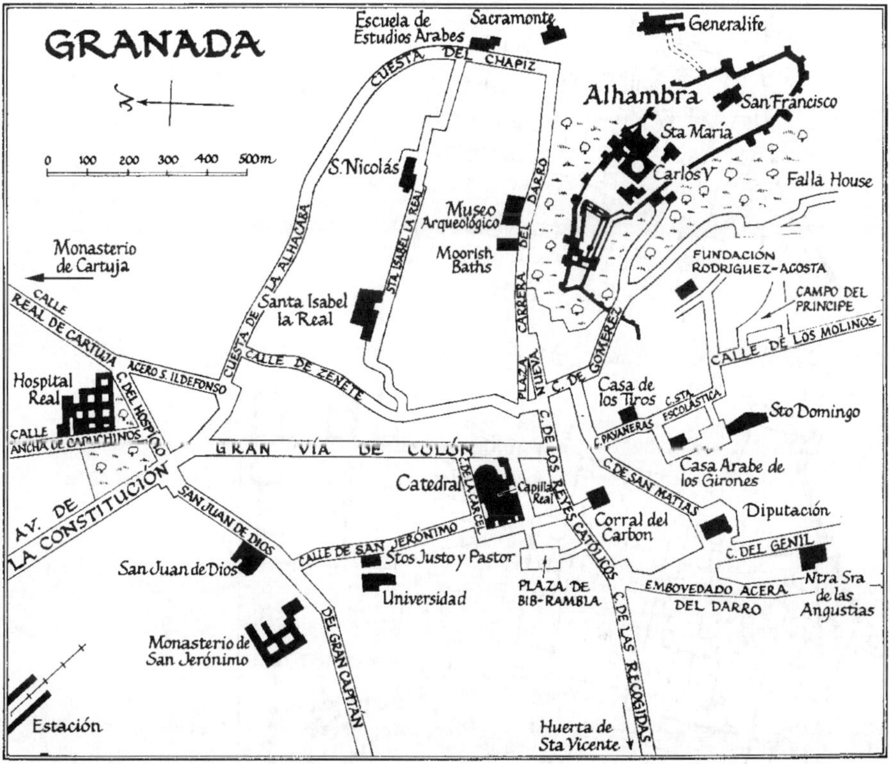

page 85). After its capture by Ferdinand and Isabella in 1492, the town was troubled by racial tensions, yet it continued to have a great cultural importance and was embellished by numerous splendid renaissance buildings (see page 95). Later the town became the main baroque centre of Andalucía after Seville, and among the distinguished figures of the period who worked here were the painter, sculptor and architect Alonso Cano (the 'Spanish Michelangelo'; see page 115), the sculptor Pedro de Mena, the painter Sánchez Cotán and the architect Hurtado Izquierdo (see page 124). Cultural decline set in during the late 18th century and coincided with the town's growth as a tourist centre. In the 1920's the poet García Lorca and the musician Manuel de Falla brought new distinction to the cultural life of Granada, but both were depressed by the modern aspects of the town and preferred to dream about its Moorish past. By their date much of medieval, renaissance and baroque Granada had been badly affected by insensitive modern development. To this day charming old corners of the town are being brutally pulled down.

García Lorca described the people of Granada as 'the worst bourgeoisie in the

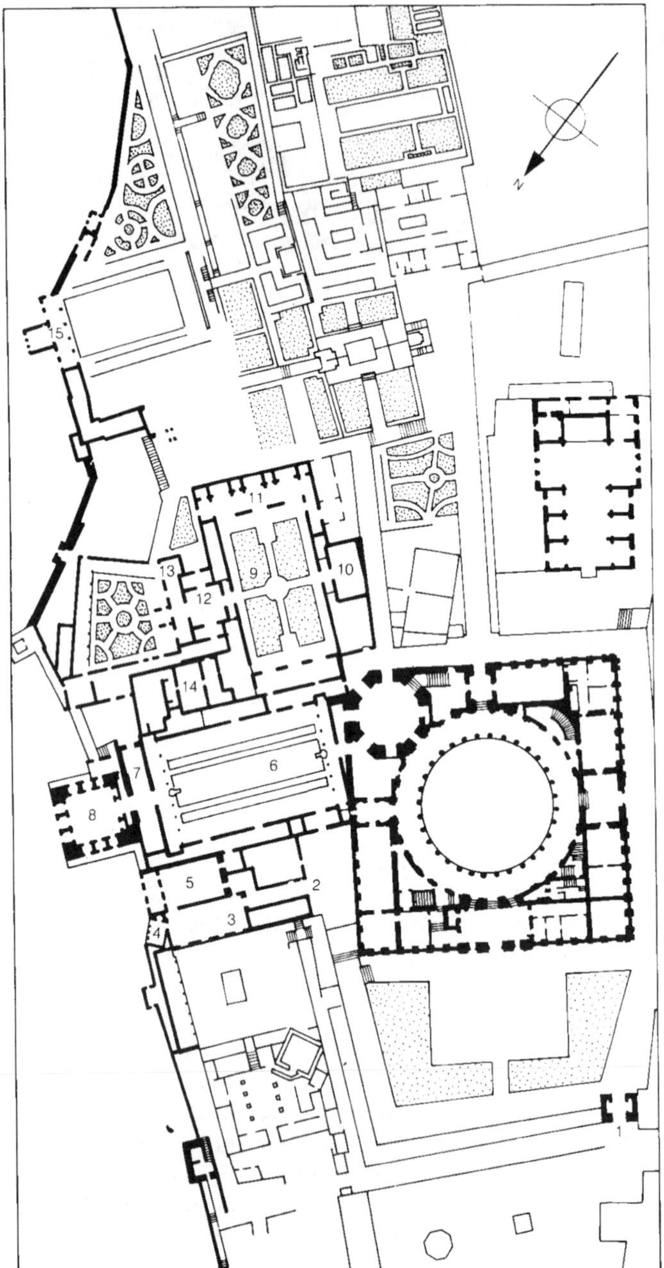

The Alhambra
1 Puerta del Vino
2 Tourist entrance
3 Mexuar
4 Oratory
5 Cuarto Dorado
6 Patio de los Arrayanes
7 Sala de la Barca
8 Salón del Trono
9 Patio de los Leones
10 Sala de los Abencerrajes
11 Sala de los Reyes
12 Sala de las Dos Hermanas
13 Sala de los Ajimeces
14 Hammam
15 Palacio del Partal

world', and for anyone coming to Granada from Seville it is certainly striking how generally more dour and conservative the people here are. However, Granada has a far more animated university life than Seville, and the town's countless lively student bars help partially to compensate for the place's inherently sober character. Moreover, Granada has the attraction of being a much cheaper place than Seville, and the renowned food of this area can be had in bars and restaurants at ridiculously low prices (particularly good are the hams, sausages, and broad bean dishes; see pages 182 and 183). Finally, for the sightseer, Granada still has a vast amount to offer quite apart from the Alhambra. This gazetteer can only rush rapidly through the town's main attractions, and anyone with a knowledge of Spanish who requires a thorough guide to Granada should purchase Antonio Gallego y Burín's excellent and beautifully illustrated *Guía Artistica de Granada*.

Most tours of Granada begin in the Alhambra, and many people come to the town without visiting any other monument. The popularity of this large complex has now grown to such proportions that entry is possible only with a 'timed' ticket, which should be purchased either in advance (tel: 958 220912) or, failing that, in the late afternoon, when the crowds of visitors begin significantly to disperse. The ticket office – once conveniently situated above the beautiful Torre de la Justicia of Falla fame – has now been relocated to a prison-like modern building next to the main car park, which lies in between the Alhambra and the Generalife, and is the point of departure for all coach tours. The most enjoyable and tranquil approach to the Alhambra is on foot from the lower town, following one of the three itineraries described overleaf. Once inside you could begin your visit by walking around the battlements of the Moorish Alcazaba, which date mainly from the late 13th century and take up the western corner of the Alhambra hill; the views are wonderful, particularly from the Torre de la Vela, which directly faces the Albaicín hill and is the highest point of the Alcazaba. After descending from the tower, follow the signs to the Nasrid palace, which is the most popular attraction of the Alhambra and was constructed largely in the late 14th century. Visitors are now obliged to stick closely to a signposted itinerary inside the palace, much of which is now closed to the public. After passing through the newly

Jarrón de la Alhambra

restored reception hall or Mexuar you will be faced by the wonderfully elaborated façade of the Palace of Comares. Steps lead from here up to the enormous Courtyard of the Myrtles (de los Arrayanes), which is dominated by a long narrow fishpond and has at one end the two-storeyed Hall of the Ambassadors (the largest room in the Alhambra). The next courtyard is that of the Lions (de los Leones), off which stand the two rooms of the Alhambra with the most intricate honeycomb domes, the Sala de las Dos Hermanas and the Sala de los Abencerrajes; the former, overlooked by the shuttered windows of the harem, has a dome with an estimated 5,000 cells. Off another side of the courtyard is the narrow Sala de los Reyes, so called because of the representation of what are possibly ten Moorish kings painted on leather on the ceiling; this extraordinary work, so unusual in an Islamic context, was probably by a Christian artist. You are now obliged to leave the Court of the Lions through a door off the Sala de las Dos Hermanas, and from there proceed to the Patio de Daraxa. The apartments on the upper level of this patio were used first by Charles V and then by Washington Irving (to visit these you need special permission from the Alhambra authorities). After descending to the lower level, you will come to an entrance leading into the palace's marble baths, one of the quietest corners of the Alhambra, but currently closed for restoration. The signposted tour will eventually deposit you in the Alhambra's gardens.

Before heading east in the direction of the Generalife you should go inside the Palace of Charles V, if only to see its powerfully impressive round courtyard. The ground floor rooms have now been converted into the beautifully and spaciously arranged Museo de la Alhambra, which has a superb series of locally-found Islamic treasures, including a marble basin stolen from Medina Azahara, the original wooden doors from the Sala de las Dos Hermanas, and the celebrated 'Jarrón de la Alhambra' – a nearly one-and-a-half metre high vase in white, blue and gold, decorated with gazelles. The same building houses on its upper floor the recently re-hung but still little-frequented Museo de Bellas Artes which, though predominantly mediocre and provincial, contains a few pleasant surprises by artists who were either born or lived in Granada. There are some quietly realistic paintings and sculptures by Alonso Cano (see page 115), and a characteristically haunting and enigmatic still life by Sánchez Cotán, this one featuring chard against a dark plain background. Also of interest are the colourful local landscapes and figure scenes by turn-of-the-century painters such as José-María Rodriguez-Acosta, José-María López Mezquita (an impressionistic view of a deserted Patio de los Arrayanes) and Picasso's first master, Antonio Muñoz Degrain (a glowing landscape of the Sierra Nevada).

Walking east towards the Generalife along the street flanking the southern side of the Palace of Charles V, you will pass first the 16th-century church of Santa María (built on the site of the Alhambra mosque; see page 96) and then the tiny

The Generalife

building (open now on Wednesdays) containing the charming if much restored baths of the former mosque, as well as a museum devoted to the turn-of-the-century musician Angel Barrios, whose father owned the bar-restaurant opposite, the Polinario; this latter establishment, though packed today with tour groups, was once at the centre of the Alhambra's intellectual life, and attracted painters such as the Catalan Santiago Rusiñol and the American John Singer Sargent, both of whom are represented in the Barrios Museum by minor works.

Further east are two of the most sought-after places to stay in Granada: the doll-like Hostal América (which has only fourteen rooms), and the celebrated Parador Nacional de San Francisco, which was built within a 16th-century Franciscan monastery over the site of a Moorish palace (fragments of this palace can be seen in one of the courtyards). A path hemmed in by trees and box hedges takes you to a modern bridge connecting the Alhambra with the Generalife. The buildings within the Generalife have been heavily restored, and the interest of the place lies essentially in its gardens, an enchanting mixture of Moorish and renaissance elements. Once back again into the Alhambra, you can return to the Nasrid Palace by following the path along the Alhambra's northern walls. The unreal stage-set quality of both the Alhambra and the Generalife is heightened should you visit these places at night, which is possible between 10 and 12 on Wednesdays and Saturdays.

From the Alhambra car park there is a wonderful and surprisingly little used footpath that will take you down to the eastern end of the Carrera del Darro (see below): this shaded path, known as the Cuesta del Rey Chico, runs in between the Alhambra and the Generalife, and passes underneath the bridge connecting the two sites. If you decide instead to walk down to the lower town from the Torre de la Justicia, you will pass through the wooded park that covers much of the southern slopes of the Alhambra hill. In the upper reaches of the wood stands the famous Hotel Washington Irving, which was thought in the late 19th century to be one of the most luxurious hotels in Spain; today the place has a gloomy, run-down character. More cheerful is the nearby Hotel Alhambra Palace, which stands just outside the wood and enjoys a magnificent panorama over southern Granada; this hotel, put up in 1910, is unfortunately a considerable eyesore from the outside, a monstrous neo-Moorish structure in garish ochre.

At the end of the narrow and very pretty Antequerela Alta, which runs east from the latter hotel, is Manuel de Falla's simple and evocative home (see page 225), immediately above which is a concert hall bearing the composer's name. The tiny street to the west of the hotel, the Callejón Niño del Royo, has in it the Fundación Rodríguez Acosta, a remarkably original house and garden of the early years of this century, now functioning as a cultural centre and a residence for artists. Next to it is the Museo Gómez Moreno, an excellent but virtually unvisited museum opened in 1982. Within its white and strikingly modern interior is displayed in random fashion, and to a musical accompaniment, a very eclectic collection of works of art, including a fascinating group of Iberian figurines, a powerful *Lamentation* by Hugo van der Goes, and an outstanding small sculpture by Alonso Cano of *San Diego de Alcalá.*

From the Hotel Washington Irving, the Alameda de la Alhambra descends to the Cuesta de Gomerez, which will take you to the Plaza Nueva; you leave the park through the 16th-century Granadas gate, the sides of which have been much damaged by coaches. An alternative way down is to make the steep descent from the Hotel Alhambra Palace to the Plaza del Príncipe, the lower side of which is lined with open-air bars and is a favourite meeting-place at night. Running parallel to the square's lower side is the Calle de los Molinos, where you will find the Cafeteria de las Flores (a celebrated breakfast haunt), and – at the street's western end – the tiny Bar López Correa, an evocative eccentric survival from the early years of this century, its walls plastered with bizarre objects and newspaper cuttings. To the south is the beautiful square and early 16th-century church of Santo Domingo, the façade of which features a triple-arched portico covered in frescos. West of the square, on the Calle Pavaneras, is the attractive 16th-century Casa de los Tiros, which has a modest museum and a collection of documents relating to Washington Irving;

behind the building a maze of streets lined with Moorish houses and gardens climbs up to the Alhambra hill. The Calle Pavaneras leads west from the museum to the Plaza Isabel la Católica, an ugly modern square at the southern end of the turn of the century Gran Vía de Colón (see page 226). Before reaching this square you will pass near the Casa de Vinos, a wine bar standing next to where the gate of the old Jewish quarter once was; the bar itself, very popular with students, has an excellent range of wines and a friendly atmosphere.

The Plaza Nueva, a few minutes' walk east from the Plaza Isabel La Católica, is surrounded by cheap hotels and has a number of open-air bars favoured largely by tourists. At the northwestern corner of the square are the Bodegas Castañeda, a famous old bar that has now been divided into two separate institutions as a result of a family dispute (ill. page 185); both do an excellent house aperitif which is strong enough to bring a day's sight-seeing to an end. As you head east up the square you will pass on your left what is now the town's Law Court (originally the Chancellery). The building, one of the finest renaissance structures in Granada, is in a majestic Italianate style and has a most elegant courtyard, perhaps designed by Diego de Siloe. Siloe was certainly responsible for the two structures that dominate the eastern and southern sides of the square into which the Plaza Nueva leads, the Plaza de Santa Ana; to the east is the church of Santa Ana (with a tall and stylish bell-tower), and to the south is Siloe's last known work, the Pilar del Toro (before 1559) – a renaissance fountain with elegant if faded classical carvings. By now you have left modern commercial Granada and are suddenly back in a quiet part of town which has changed little since the time when it was admired for its picturesqueness by travellers of the Romantic era.

Behind the church of Santa Ana runs the fast-flowing stream of the Darro, which divides the Alhambra hill from that of the Albaicín. Walking up the delightful Carrera del Darro, you will pass first the extraordinary Moorish baths at No. 3 (see page 86) and then the Calle Zafra, on which stands an evocatively decayed 14th-century Moorish house built around a pool (this house, the Casa Zafra, is soon to be turned into a museum, but in the meantime the caretaker will be please to show you around). Just beyond this street is the elaborate classical plateresque façade of the Casa de Castril, a renaissance house with a recently renovated interior displaying a selection of archaeological finds from the prehistoric to the Moorish period.

The Carrera del Darro comes to an end at the shaded promenade popularly known as the Paseo de los Tristes ('The Sad People') on account of the priests who once recited their rosaries here; containing today the bulk of the street's numerous attractive bars, it is overlooked on the other side of the river by the verdant slopes of the Alhambra hill. At its eastern end is the Cuesta del Chapiz, which climbs up to the Casa de Chapiz, a Moorish house which is now a centre for Moorish studies. East from here you leave the boundaries of the town and reach the gypsy cave

The Cathedral, Granada

district of Sacromonte, much visited by tourists on account of its appalling flamenco shows (see page 151).

Further to the east, in lonely isolation high above the narrow luxuriant valley of the Darro, is the austere 17th-century monastery of the Sacromonte, inside which is a small museum comprising a miscellaneous collection of documents and works of art, including an original letter written by Pizarro, and an *Immaculate Conception* by Sánchez Cotán.

The quiet and attractive heart of the Albaicín extends west from the Casa de Chapiz, and is an area covered in beautiful villas and gardens, all with superb views towards the Alhambra. One of these palaces has been converted into the Mirador de Morayma, a famous tourist restaurant (at Callejón de las Vacas 2). The most renowned viewpoint is the terrace in front of the church of San Nicolás, a place to which numerous people come at sunset; west from here is the 15th-century convent of Santa Isabel la Real, the church of which has a very fine gothic plateresque west portal, and a particularly elaborate mudéjar ceiling (see page 96). For the Cruces de Mayo celebrations, held in the first week of May, the entire Albaicín hill is alight with candles. You can walk back to the lower town on the shop-lined Calderería Nueva, which has now several Moroccan tea-rooms, small restaurants and crafts shops testifying to the recent Islamic influx into the district. This influx, sometimes referred to as 'the second coming of the Moors', consists not so much of Moroccans as of European converts to Islam, many of whom originate in the city's large hippy community; known generically as Sufis, these Muslims include many members of the international movement of the Murabitun, which is headed in Granada by the secretive Sheikh Abd al-Qadir, formerly Ian Dallas, the one-time Beatles manager who co-authored the screenplay of *Yellow Submarine*.

Incongruously tucked away behind the Plaza Isabel La Católica and the Gran Vía de Colón are the Royal Chapel and the cathedral (see page 98f), around which are to be found an extensive pedestrian and shopping district incorporating the 16th-century Plaza de Bibarrambla and the neo-Moorish bazaar (see page 86) known as the Alcaicería. At its southern end the Alcaicería leads into the Calle de los Reyes Católicos, on the other side of which is a narrow alley taking you to the Moorish Casa del Carbón (see page 86). The busy and unappealing Calle de los

Reyes Católicos connects the Plaza Isabel La Católica with the Puerta Real to the west. Turn left at the latter square and you will reach a wide thoroughfare which splits into the Carrera de Genil and the Acera del Darro. Off the former is the 18th-century building now housing the Town Council (*Diputación*), attached to which is the Café Restaurante Chikito of Lorca and Falla fame (see page 227). The Casa Bar Enrique, on the Acera del Darro, is an old-fashioned establishment well known for its hams, cheeses, and stock of sweetish Alpujarra wine known as the Vino de Costa.

The pleasant and narrow Calle de San Jerónimo runs north from the cathedral to the 18th-century Hospital de San Juan de Dios, passing by the shaded and intimate Plaza de la Universidad. Respectively to the west and east of San Juan de Dios are the monastery of San Jerónimo and the Hospital Real (now the main university building), two of the most majestic renaissance buildings in Granada (see pages 98-100). Granada's Charterhouse, containing perhaps the most elaborate and dynamic baroque decoration in the whole of Spain, lies in the western outskirts of the town, a good twenty-five minutes' uphill walk from the Hospital Real (see page 125). As well as its baroque decorations, it has an elegant early 16th-century cloister and a large collection of 17th-century paintings, including many clumsy figurative works by Sánchez Cotán, who was a monk here.

The most popular excursion from Granada is up into the **Sierra Nevada** by way of the well-graded GR420, which passes next to the excellently appointed skiiing resort where the World Skiing Championships were held in 1996. The road goes right to the summit of the Pico Veleta, though its last stretch is often closed because of snow. The spectacular descent down the other side into the Alpujarras is only practicable from July to September, and even so is slow and dangerous. The adventurous driver might also wish to ascend the Sierra Nevada on the beautiful but unasphalted Carretera de los Neveros, which begins to climb in earnest after the village of **Monachil**. If you lose heart at Monachil, you can always stop off at the Venta Bienvenido, an open-air inn on the outskirts of the village; here you will find outstanding home-made charcuterie, which you can wash down with the pleasant white wine from the adjoining village of **Huétor Vega**. Another possible trip by car is to follow what was once the tramline up into the Sierra (one of the original trams from the 1920's has been kept on display in Granada's Paseo del Salón): after leaving the city on the GR420, turn left 3 km after Cenes de la Vega on to the road marked Guéjar Sierra. Near the highest point that you can reach by car are two modest ventas well known for their garlic-flavoured dishes of rabbit, chicken and potatoes, cooked on an open fire.

The nearest important Moorish monument to Granada is the virtually unvisited 14th-century tower at the commuter village of **Las Gabias**, 8 km south-west of Granada on the Alhama road. This whitewashed tower, in the upper half of the village, is now attached to a Flamenco Club, and is locked with a venerable old key kept in the club's bar. The wooden door leading into the tower has warped, and some pushing is required to open it; before you go in you will notice outside a plaque recording that the place was captured in April 1491 by the Gran Capitán, who took thirty of its defenders prisoner. The outwardly bare structure is revealed inside to be extensively covered in Islamic plasterwork worthy of anything to be found in the Alhambra. In 1922 this jewel of Islamic architecture was rightly declared a 'National Monument', making it one of the first Spanish buildings to be awarded this status. Its present state of neglect, incomprehensible, appalling but also quite poignant, gives travellers an impression of what much of the Alhambra must have been like at the time of Washington Irving: the rich mosaic floors are covered in dust and bird skeletons, while the walls are scrawled with such unfortunate lines as *Paquita Puta* ('Paquita is a whore'). Before leaving you should climb up on to the roof terrace for extensive views embracing the Sierra Nevada and the distant Alhambra. The next village along on the Alhama road, **La Malaha**, was also important in Islamic times, and retains its Islamic salt flats and irrigation complex; at the end of the village is a track to the right leading to some hot pools where many Granadans come to bathe on autumn and winter nights.

Those in search of places in and around Granada closely associated with García Lorca would do well to buy Ian Gibson's excellent *Guide to the Granada of García Lorca* (1989). The major Lorca site on the outskirts of Granada is the **Huerta de San Vicente** (see page 237), which stood until recently in miraculous rural isolation only a few minutes' walk away from the junction of the Calle de Las Recogidas and the vile Camino de La Ronda; next to the ugly public park that has now been built around Lorca's family home is the Jardines Neptuno, a large and unwelcoming hall that puts on the best of the city's tourist flamenco shows. Further west, in the heart of the vega, are Lorca's childhood villages of **Fuentevaqueros** (where his birthplace has been turned into an informative if bland museum) and **Valderrubio**, both of which are accessible by a bus which you can catch outside Granada railway station (see page 227f). The commemorative park at **Víznar**, marking the probable spot where Lorca was assassinated, is best reached by taxi; a path to the left of the coldly formal monument at the park's entrance will take you down to an olive tree planted above the poet's reputed last resting-place. Continuing past the village of Víznar you will soon come to the pleasantly bosky recreational area of **Fuente Grande** (see page 239) where many Moors once had villas. The mineral spring here inspired several Moorish poets, who referred to it as the 'Fountain of Tears' on account of its gaseous bubbles; it is now enclosed within a large, tear-shaped pool.

GRAZALEMA [4D]: The subject of Pitt-Rivers' classic study, *People of the Sierra* (1954), is today one of the most visited villages in the Serranía de Ronda. Stretched over a mountain fold against a background of picturesquely protruding rocks, Grazalema is a beautiful if perhaps over-prettified place. The lower road into the village (the C344 from Arcos de la Frontera) passes the main local workshop specializing in blankets, an industry which has been practised here since Arab times; there is a small museum attached to the building. The road continues into the pleasant main square, from where you can walk up the Calle Mateos Gago to the prominently positioned 18th-century chapel of San José. There is a viewing balcony near the chapel, though in many ways the village is best seen from below. The village's swimming-pool, which you reach by continuing to drive along the lower road until you leave the village, has an especially good view of Grazalema, and indeed must have one of the finest situations of any pool in Andalucía.

Just above the village there is a camping site, the office of which will provide you with information about walks and horse-treks in the recently-created National Park of Grazalema. The drive through Zahara along the CA 531 goes through particularly impressive scenery. Before reaching the spectacular pass of **Las Palomas**, you will pass on the left-hand side of the road the entrance to a forest of *pínsapos*, a majestic pyramid-shaped pine of a type not found elsewhere in Europe (see page 10); to visit the forest special permission is required beforehand from the Dirección Provincial de la Agencia de Medio Ambiente b (Avenida Ana de Virgen 3-30, 11009 Cádiz; tel 956 274594/274629). After crossing the pass, the road descends in dramatic fashion to the village of **Zahara**, which hangs underneath a noble outcrop of rock. The tiny village's main square has a baroque church and an excellent viewing balcony; at the very top of the rock is the single remaining tower of a castle built by the Romans and renovated by the Arabs.

The C3331 south from Grazalema passes next to **Benaocaz**, where there is a small museum of local archaeology and ethnography. Eight winding kilometres further

View from the Alcazaba of Guadix towards the gypsy quarter of Santiago

on is **Ubrique**, famous for the leather industry which the Moors established here.

GUADIX [3G] has the strangest appearance of all Andalucían towns. Its old town, apparently covered in an orange-red dust, stands out against a background of rows of tufa pinnacles formed by savage erosion; in the far distance rise the snow-capped peaks of the Sierra Nevada. The prosperous Roman colony which existed here was converted to Christianity by St. Torquatus, and became one of the earliest and most important Visigothic bishoprics in Spain; the subsequent Moorish occupation lasted until 1489. Work was begun on the magnificent cathedral in 1510, on the site of the former mosque; it was not completed until 1796. The dark, late gothic interior was significantly altered by Diego de Siloe (see page 101), who also gave it the polygonal apse and the chapel of San Torcuato to the left of the chancel. Among the baroque additions are the fine choir and pulpit, and the west façade, which with its undulating cornices and rich plastic decoration, is one of the most dynamic of any Spanish cathedral. In front of the cathedral is the arcaded renaissance Plaza Mayor, which was largely rebuilt after the Civil War of 1936. A street at the far end of the square to the cathedral leads up to the whitewashed renaissance Peñaflor Palace, from which projects a charming wooden balcony. Below the palace a street descends to the church of Santiago, notable for its classical plateresque southern portal. The door of the building attached to the Peñaflor Palace takes you inside a 19th-century seminary, where arrows will guide you upstairs and outside into the courtyard of the 15th-century Moorish castle, or Alcazaba. The courtyard is parched and overgrown, and used as a squash court by pupils of the seminary. From the heavily restored battlements there is an excellent view of Guadix's northern outskirts, where dwellings - similar to those where gnomes live in fairy-tale illustrations - have been scooped out of the picturesquely shaped mounds, with tall white chimney-stacks pushing through the ground above. This is still a notorious gypsy district, and tourists can expect considerable attention from the local children.

Partially built into caves 6 km to the west, off the new motorway to Granada, is the village of **Purullena**. The village has a long-standing reputation for its ceramics industry, examples of which can be bought from the stalls lining the main street. The object to look out for is the increasingly rare traditional local piece known variously as the *jarra accitana* or the *jarra de los pajaricos*. This earthenware urn-like object, the lid of which is usually crowned by a hen, has an exceptionally intricate 18th-century design, and is one of the finest examples of the continuing baroque tradition in Andalucían folk art.

Façade of the Cathedral, Guadix

South-west of Purullena, and marked to Cortes y Graena and La Peza, is a quiet side road running through a narrow valley with green fields in between its scorched, pock-marked sides. For many centuries the main road linking Granada with Almería, this will take you after 3 km to the small spa of **Baños de Graena**, where the German traveller Hieronymus Münzer, passing through in 1494, found numerous Moors bathing in the 'clear and abundant' thermal waters issuing from a cave. Today old women with towels wrapped around their heads stand around a neo-Moorish and municipally-owned spa building of the 1920's; along the banks of the stream behind are the scant ruins of a 16th-century inn. The area abounds in caves, especially around the outlying hamlet of **Cortes**, which has several cave dwellings as well as a small church with a bell-tower that was once a minaret; above a Moorish irrigation channel just to the north of this hamlet is the *Cueva de la Tía Micaela*, one of the largest of the so-called *covarrones* – caves that had once been inhabited by Moors. At **Graena**, 3 km south of the spa, lives a Belgian archaeologist, Maryelle Bertrand, who has devoted many years to the study of the local caves. Continuing from Baños de Graena along the old road to Granada, you will soon reach (after 8 km) the attractive small village of **La Peza**, a place heavily fortified by the Moors, who built the now ruined 10th-century castle on the hill above it. Beyond, the road disappears into the dense forest covering the northern slopes of the Sierra Nevada.

HUELVA [3A]: A Phoenician settlement, and later the Roman colony of Onuba, Huelva has a long history but a largely modern appearance, the town having been extensively damaged in the 1755 earthquake that also destroyed Lisbon. The ugliest and least interesting of Andalucía's provincial capitals, Huelva is a heavily industrialized town with a flourishing port, which is used both by fishing fleets and boats exporting metals from the Río Tinto mines; the shrimps from Huelva are famous throughout Spain, and increasingly expensive.

One of the few pre-19th-century buildings to have survived in Huelva is the Convent of the Merced, which was founded in 1605; its church, dating mainly from the 18th century, has served as the town's cathedral since 1853, and is notable for its spacious and dazzlingly white interior. Following the Paseo Independencia east from the cathedral for ten minutes will take you to the heart of turn-of-the-century Huelva, a dirty and cramped area, with numerous seedy bars, particularly near the port. Many of the old buildings have been pulled down in recent years, but several splendid monuments remain, including the imposing Gran Teatro (1923) on the Calle Vázquez López, the art nouveau Clínica Sanz de Frutos (1911) at Calle Rico 26, and the neo-Moorish railway station (1880) at the eastern end of the town. South from the station is the town's greatest architectural monument, the now disused Río Tinto pier of 1874, an impressive if rather decayed iron-work construction designed by the British engineer George Barclay Bruce.

The main thoroughfare running through the northern half of the town centre is the Avenida Martín Alonso Pinzón, which is lined with fascist arcading. This avenue leads north into the Alameda Sundheim and into a quiet residential area. The Museo Provincial de Bellas Artes is situated off the Alameda, and occupies a pleasant modern building in the middle of a small shaded garden. This excellently arranged museum is particularly interesting for its ground-floor archaeological section, which features fascinating finds from the Río Tinto mines; the fine arts section on the floor above has a mainly mediocre collection of paintings dating from the 16th to 20th centuries. The best of the modern works are by the local painter Daniel Vázquez Díaz (1882-1969), who is best known for his murals in the nearby monastery of La Rábida (see page 91); one of his Cézanne-inspired canvases in the museum is a portrait of his poet friend Juan Ramón Jiménez (see MOGUER).

On a small hill just to the north of the Museum is a small residential district known variously as the Barrio Obrero or the Barrio Inglés. Built by the British in the early years of this century for their employees in the Río Tinto Mines, the architecture of this suburb is unmistakably suburban English, but with the difference that these incongruously situated houses have been painted in brilliant primary colours. Many of the Río Tinto employees had also half-timbered bungalows at the nearby coastal resort of **Punta Umbría**, which lies to the south of Huelva on the western side of the Odiel; this spacious high-rise resort, now the most popular on the Huelva coast, has a district known as the Punta de los Ingleses, where a handful of these British-built bungalows still survive.

To the north of Huelva, 3 km on the road towards Gibraleón, is the heavily restored **Sanctuario de Nuestra Señora de la Cinta**, to which a pilgrimage is made every year on 8 September. One of the tile decorations inside the church represents Columbus, who is supposed to have taken part in one of these pilgrimages. On the southern outskirts of Huelva, at the confluence of the estuaries of the rivers Odiel and Tinto, stands an enormous and ungainly statue of Columbus, which was given to the town in 1929 by its maker, an American sculptress called Whitney. From here it is but a short drive to the two main Andalucían sites associated with Columbus, the Monastery of La Rábida (see page 91) and PALOS DE LA FRONTERA.

HUÉRCAL-OVERA [3J], the main town in the far eastern corner of Andalucía, is a place of little charm in the middle of a dusty landscape speckled with orchards and ugly modern farm buildings. The holy processions of the town enjoy a certain fame for their exuberance and the beauty of their processional images, carved by artists of the Granada school. There is also a castle here of such cube-like simplicity that it resembles a child's building block.

A far more interesting castle is to be found at the top of the village of **Cuevas del Almanzora**, which stands in an eroded landscape about 20 km to the south: the building was put up in 1507 to protect the village from pirate attacks. During the morisco uprising of 1568-71, its leader al-Maleh made an unsuccesful attempt to besiege the castle; when the moriscos were eventually expelled from Granada by Philip II many stopped off here on their journey to Castille.

The most famous of the town's native moriscos was a eunuch called Yuder Pachá, who, on leaving Spain, ended up heading an army of Andalucían renegades that swept south over the Sahara to conquer the Songhai Empire for Morocco. In his honour, Cuevas is now twinned with the sub-Saharan township of Timbuktu.

Those interested in the history of nuclear disasters could head from Cuevas east to **Palomares** (see page 45), while pottery enthusiasts and gastronomes could go south to **Vera**. One of Vera's few attractive buildings, a late 18th-century warehouse, was recently pulled down to make way for a modern bank (the Banco Central), and the town's traditional earthenware of elegant Phoenician and Arab design is becoming increasingly difficult to find: mediocre examples of the engagingly simple and local jugs and pitchers can be bought from a man known as Bernardino, who lives at Calle Alfarería 11, and is the son of a well-known potter awarded a medal by King Juan Carlos. The ugly industrial town of **Albox**, 18 km west of Huércal-Overa, is also celebrated for its pottery industries, its traditonal crudely coloured and glazed ceramics being similar to those of NÍJAR. The most interesting monument nearby is the austere 18th-century **Sanctuario de Nuestra Señora de la Asunción**, 21 km to the north of Albox, high up on the impressively barren Sierra de las Estancias. The place, marking a spot where the Virgin made yet another of her miraculous appearances, is popular with Sunday excursionists, and there is a bar and restaurant at the side of the building.

HUÉSCAR [2H], at the northern edge of an eroded plateau, and immediately below the parched southern foothills of the Sierra de Segura, is one of the most isolated towns in Granada province. Situated near the end of the narrow strip of the province on which converge the territories of Jaén, Albacete, Murcia, and Almería, it is the largest town of a fascinating frontier zone between the former kingdom of Granada and the Levant. In the middle ages this whole area changed hands repeatedly between Moors and Christians. Huescar, together with the neighbouring settlements of Galera and Orce, were seized from the Moors in 1241 by the Master of the Order of Santiago, Don Rodrigo Iñiguez, who fortified them heavily so as to make a defensive barrier against the nascent Nasrid kingdom. Won back by the Moors in 1319, Huéscar became the Nasrids' easternmost stronghold, and as such was subject to constant Christian forays led by knights of the Order of Santiago. In 1347 the town was visited by the Loja-born polymath Ibn al-Khatib (see page 326) while accompanying the Nasrid king Yusuf I on a tour of inspection of the Nasrids' eastern defences. He found a place whose inhabitants had become so used to constant danger that they 'were prepared for any fate that God had in mind for them.' Though the Christians definitively captured the town in 1488, the area was to suffer enormously during the morisco uprising of 1570. Galera, after being briefly occupied by morisco rebels, was razed to the ground by Don Juan of Austria, who killed over 2,000 moriscos and devastated and sowed with salt land that had been praised by Ibn al-Jatib for its meadows, fertility and abundance of water. Huéscar itself, though not joining in with the rebels, lost over half its working population when the uprising was suppressed and the moriscos consequently expelled from Granada. A curious and rather absurd coda to the town's troubled history was that from 1809 right up to 1981 Huéscar was officially at war with Denmark: war had been declared by the town council as a patriotic gesture of support towards Spanish soldiers trapped in Denmark as a consequence of Spain's shifting allegiances during the Napoleonic wars. When this anomalous situation was finally righted with the signing of a peace treaty in 1981, Huéscar was twinned with the Danish town of Kolding.

Much damaged over the centuries, and with a number of ungainly buildings from the 1950's and 1960's in its centre, Huéscar is hardly an architectural jewel; but it is a lively survival of a largely vanished provincial Spain. Its main monument is its enormous and impressive collegiate church, which was partially designed by the great renaissance architects Covarrubias and Diego de Siloe (see page 101), and brought to completion in 1599 under the supervision of Vandelvira. Just off the adjoining main square, on the Paseo del Santo Cristo, is the long and sadly neglected facade of the Casa de los Peñalva – a rare and delightful example of art nouveau in Andalucía, and a reminder of the proximity of the Catalan-influenced regions of the *Levante* (Valencia and Murcia). Opposite the palace is the excellent Casa Felipe, an old-fashioned bar and restaurant where you can try two of the best known local specialities – *remojón* (a winter salad of salt cod, peeled roast potatoes, hard-boiled eggs and onions) and the *relleno*, a charcuterie dish made from pork, chicken, turkey, bread, rabbit, saffron, cloves, cinnamon, eggs, lemon juice and garlic.

The bizarre desert-like landscape south of Huéscar turns at sunset into an expanse of purples, oranges, reds, and lurid yellows. It is intercut with dried-up gorges lined at the bottom with citrus trees. Much of the landscape is pock-marked with caves, and on the southern outskirts of the village of **Galera**, 7 km to the south of Huéscar on the C3329, there is a picturesque district of cave dwellings, some of which have now been turned into tasteful, well-appointed holiday homes; a group of hill-top caves near these forms the important Iberian necropolis of Tútugi, dating from the 5th to the 3rd centuries BC. Some of the tombs have paintings representing battle and hunting scenes, but a local guide is needed to help you find these. A collection of Roman stones found in the area has been assembled in Galera's Town Hall.

A winding, desolate side-road west of Huescar leads after 8 km to the small village of **Orce**, which is built around a largely reconstructed Islamic castle. Within the archaeological museum arranged inside the castle's keep is a plaster cast of what was thought to be the oldest fragment of a human skull in existence. This prehistoric being, dubbed as 'The Man from Orce' but uncovered at nearby Venta de Micena, has recently been pronounced a goat. Orce and its famous 'Man' feature in the Portugese writer José Saramago's *The Stone Raft*, a humorously apocalyptic novel in which the Iberian penisula detaches itself from the rest of Europe and floats out to sea.

An entirely different and progressively greener and more mountainous countryside is to be seen if you drive north from Huéscar on the C330 to **Puebla de Don Fadrique**. Those in need of a swim could deviate after 2 km to **Fuencaliente**, a large and tepid thermal pool praised by the Moors and now encased in a characterless modern leisure centre. Puebla de Don Fadrique, 22 km further on, is like a smaller and yet more atmospheric version of Huescar, though with a more placid history (it was never incorporated into the Nasrid kingdom); its 16th-century church has fine classical-style reliefs above the portals. The landscape becomes particularly exciting if you continue north from here along the C321, and then turn left after 2 km on to the narrow road to **Cortijos Nuevos de la Sierra**. As you encircle the wild and wooded peaks of the Sierra Sagra, you will pass to your left a grove of sequoia trees planted early this century by a returning Spaniard from America.

JAÉN [2F], surrounded by an undulating expanse of olive trees, and backed by mountains, rises steeply up the slopes of a hill crowned by a massive cathedral. The capital of the Spanish province with the largest number of olive trees, Jaén has lived off its olive oil production since Roman times, a period when it also knew prosperity through silver-mining. Under the Moors the town became the centre of a small Moorish principality, and acquired the name of Geen or 'caravan route', a reference to the place's importance as a bridge between Castille and Andalucía. Ferdinand III captured the town in 1246, and its displaced Moorish ruler, Ibn Nasr, went to Granada to found the Nasrid Dynasty (see page 85). Much of the old town, including its walls, has now been destroyed, and in its stead has risen a seedy modern town, poor, parochial and stiflingly dull at night. Tourists come here mainly to see its cathedral or to stay in the parador above the town, but Jaén has a number of other attractions that deserve to be better known.

The Paseo de la Estación, the grand avenue which climbs up the hill from the railway station to the town centre, represents Jaén's attempt to imitate a major city such as Madrid. Half-way up, on the right-hand side of the road, is a large early 20th-century building, into which has been incorporated the west portal of the destroyed church of San Miguel. The museum's little-visited collections are paltry in comparison with the grandeur of the building in which they are housed. The archaeological section, which takes up the ground floor, contains what is undoubtedly the museum's most outstanding treasure, a group of Iberian sculptures discovered in 1975 at Obulco, a site on the outskirts of Porcuna (see BUJALANCE):

particularly exciting are the stones of fighting warriors, carved with great boldness and a feeling for form that is quite modern. In the first floor rooms are displayed the museum's paintings, which are mainly of the 19th and early 20th centuries. For the lover of kitsch and high-flown academic canvases, these rooms make for a most entertaining experience. The prize for the most absurd work must surely go to Moreno Carbonero's *Don Quixote and the Windmills*, a vast canvas dominated by a tumbling horse violently ejecting a skeletal Don Quixote. The other paintings include a large proportion of female nudes bordering on soft pornography, for instance a portrait of the actress Montserrat Güell, painted by a former director of the Prado, Sotomayor.

Jáen

Leaving the museum and continuing uphill on the Paseo de la Estación, you pass by a 20th-century sculptural group as monumentally awful as many of the works in the museum: known as the Monument of the Battles, it commemorates the battles both of Las Navas de Tolosa (see LA CAROLINA) and BAILÉN. At the far end of the Avenida is Jaén's ugly main square, the Plaza de la Constitución, but further uphill the town begins somewhat to improve. In between the square and the cathdral are three fine palaces: the 16th-century Palacio de los Vilches on the Plaza de los Vilches, the 17th-century Palacio de los Vélez on the Calle Dr. Ramón y Cajal, and the 17th-century Town Hall on the Plaza de San Francisco. This latter building, featuring an elegant arcaded coutyard, looks obliquely across its square towards the northern end of the cathedral. Attached to this side of the cathedral is the late 18th-century church of the Sagrario, which has a satisfyingly simple oval interior designed by Spain's leading neoclassical architect, Ventura Rodriguez (see MONTEFRÍO). The cathedral itself is on the site of the town's mosque, which was transformed into a place of Christian worship in the time of Ferdinand III. In the late 15th century work was started on a new cathedral, but the walls that were put up soon showed signs of cracking and were pulled down. The present structure, begun in 1548 under the supervision of the great Andrés de Vandelvira (see page 102), was not completed until the end of the 18th century. The most striking feature of the exterior is its baroque west façade of 1734, articulated by a giant order of columns, and flanked by towers: this majestic façade sensibly turns its back on the ugly lower town of Jaén, and looks up to the rugged castle hill. The cathedral's dark and heavy interior largely impresses more through size than detail. The renaissance structure has suffered from later additions, though you can see Vandelvira's style at its purest and most harmonious in the barrel-vaulted sacristy and adjoining chapter house. Of the cathedral's furnishings special mention must be made of the outstandingly lively and dynamic late baroque carvings in the choir, many of which are of gruesome martyrdoms. Among the characterful old bars in the vicinity of the Cathedral is the famous Gorrión, which has in its cellar a mummified ham dating back to the late 19th century. The Calle Maestra and its continuation, the Calle Martínez Molina, lead north from the cathedral into what remains of the old town of Jaén, and passes near the town's one surviving gate, the Puerta de San Lorenzo (on the Calle de los Almendros Aguilar). Heading off from the Calle Martínez Molina is the Calle Cañon, down which you will see a plaque recording the site of the parish church of San Pedro, where the guitarist Andrés Segovia was baptized on 24 March 1893; further on is the 16th-century convent of Santa Clara, with a west façade decorated with amusing if slightly unsophisticated classical carvings. A group of palms on the small Plaza de las Mujeres, on the northern end of the Calle Martínez Molina, shades the façade of the palace of Fernando Torres y Portugal. The building has recently been converted into a pleasantly laid out museum of popular crafts and 'international naïve art'. But its greatest attraction are the baths underneath it, discovered in 1914, which are shown to you by one of the museum's guides; these baths, the most extensive surviving ones in Spain, are traditionally thought to be the place where the Moorish King Alí was killed by his Moorish enemies in the 11th century. An underground passage connects the baths with the Moorish palace over which was built the monastery of San Domingo. The monastery, founded in 1392, later became a university and a seat of the Inquisition: it has an excellently preserved 16th-century courtyard, and a church with a façade designed by Vandelvira. The nearby gothic church of the Magdalena, at the northernmost end of the town, is Jaén's oldest church. It is erected over a mosque, the minaret of which forms part of its bell tower. The stagnant pool in the church's romantically overgrown courtyard is also Moorish, and was used for ritual ablutions.

Ascending the narrow and pretty Calle Santísima Trinidad, you will reach the Bar Sobrino Bigotes, in front of which is a path climbing steeply through rough and wooded terrain up to the town's castle. The path, though beautiful, is arduous and difficult to follow, and you might well prefer to go up to the castle by way of the much longer road. The 13th-century castle, built by al-Ahmar, has one of the most commanding positions of all the many castles in Andalucía. A drastically renovated part of it now houses the parador where de Gaulle wrote part of his memoirs. A path runs besides the ruined section of the castle and leads eventually to a spectacular view-point marked by a large cross: far, far below is the cathedral, standing up like a giant above its diminutive suroundings.

Eight kilometres to the east of Jaén is the pleasant village of **La Guardia de Jaén**, which has an important necropolis. At the top of the village are the ruins of a Moorish castle dating back to the 8th century, and the parish chuch of the Asunción built by Vandelvira. The church was originally that of the monastery of San Domingo, the ruins of which lie alongside it, and include the arcading and central fountain of its renaissance cloister. Next to the attractive 16th-century fountain of Las siete canas is a newly opened restaurant of that name, run by one of the most promising young Andalucían cooks of today, Juan Aceituno.

JEREZ DE LA FRONTERA [4C], in the middle of flat agricultural country, probably dates back to Phoenician times. Known to the Romans as Xeres, this name was corrupted to Sherrish by the Moors, who stayed in the town until 1264; as with many other places in this part of Andalucía, Jerez received the name 'de la frontera' around 1379 because it marked the western frontier of the Moorish kingdom of Granada. The fortified wines of the area, already famous in the middle ages, were first exported to England in the late 15th century. Thereafter numerous English and foreign merchants settled here, many, such as the Domecqs, becoming members of the Spanish aristocracy; the father of the English art critic John Ruskin was involved in the sherry trade in the early 19th century, and through this connection his son met the first great love of his life, Adèle Domecq. The presence in Jerez of these so-called 'sherry barons' gave the place a character totally unlike that of anywhere else in Andalucía, snobbish, aloof and with people apeing the social manners of the English. To most Andalucíans Jerez is essentially the home of the *señorito* or 'toff'.

Jerez is in fact a town of particularly sharp contrasts, and even in the Romantic period travellers commented on the contrast between the magnificence of its palaces and the dirt and squalor of many of its streets. Today it is a town with extensive and ugly modern development, spacious and verdant residential districts that could be in Florida, a ramshackle and run-down old part, and one of the most famous and intact of all of Andalucía's gypsy quarters. At the very centre of the town is the Plaza del Arenal, around which are to be found the town's most important monuments. To the south of the square, at the end of the Calle San Miguel, is the church of San Miguel, a building begun in an Isabelline gothic style, and with a splendidly ornate late 17th-century tower attached to the west façade. The much restored citadel or Alcázar, dating back to the time of the Almohads, rises up on a mound immediately to the west of the Plaza del Arenal; its most interesting feature is on its northern side,

The 18th-century palace of the Domecqs; a statue of one of the sherry barons is in the foreground

a small and well preserved mosque which was later made the chapel of Santa María la Real. Immediately below the chapel to the north is the former Collegiate Church of San Salvador (now the town's cathedral), a bizarre building dating from the 18th century but in a gothic style and with renaissance decorative features. Through an arch on the northern side of the Plaza del Arenal is a tiny passage on which is situated the lively Bar Juanito, renowned for its tapas. Nearby is the quiet and charming Plaza de la Asunción, dominated by the simple 15th-century church of San Dionisio, notable for its elegant gothic-mudéjar bell-tower. The Calle Calvo Sotelo heads from here to the town's most beautiful renaissance structure, the former Town Hall, which housed until recently an archaeological museum (now in the Plaza de San Mateo).

The least spoilt part of old Jerez stretches from north of the cathedral up to the gypsy quarter of Santiago. It is an area full of attractive churches and elegant palaces crammed into a maze of tiny streets and squares, some with a semi-abandoned look. Jerez, with its large gypsy population, is a famed centre of flamenco, and in the Palacio Pemartín on the Plaza San Juan is the Fundación Andaluza de Flamenco, Andalucía's major centre for the study and promotion of this music; the centre organizes festivals and conferences, and puts on regular exhibitions with material culled from its extensive archive. The Santiago quarter is a few minutes' walk from here, and has as its principal attraction the late 15th-century church of Santiago, Jerez's best preserved gothic building. It says much of the character of Jerez that this lively if slightly seedy district adjoins an area of grand late 19th-century villas grouped around an old-fashioned zoo

The busy Calle Larga heads north-west from the Plaza del Arenal through the commercial heart of Jerez. At the junction of the Calle Santa María is the Café Cena Cirullo, a splendid turn-of-the-century building that was once a celebrated meeting-place. Continuing further along the Calle Larga, you eventually reach the Plaza

Cristina, on which is the grand 18th-century palace built by the Domecq family, a statue to one of whom is to be found immediately in front of it. Shortly beyond the place begins Jerez's most elegant residential districts, in the middle of which are two of the town's most popular attractions, a Museum of Clocks (the Museo de Relojes, 'La Atalaya') and the Royal Andalucían Equestrian School, housed in an 18th-century building. Jerez is as famous for its horses as it is for its wines and flamenco, and the school puts on daily shows with riders dressed in 18th-century costume.

The main bodegas in Jerez are all in the centre of the town, and can be visited every weekday from 10.30 to 1.30; the Gonzalez Byass Bodega is particularly interesting on account of its 19th-century ironwork structure designed by Gustave Eiffel of the Eiffel Tower. Every year in September, the wine harvest is celebrated by the crushing of grapes on the steps in front of the cathedral. This festival is as phoney as the famous Horse Fair in June is élitist.

Southeast of the town, 5 km along the C440 to Medina Sidonia, is the **Charterhouse** of Jerez, well worth seeing if only for its sumptuous exterior and bosky surroundings (see page 119).

JIMENA DE LA FRONTERA [5D] is an attractive hill-village of Roman origin which is gradually being taken over by the British, many of whom work and do their shopping in nearby Gibraltar. Looming over the village is its large and ruined Moorish castle, which entered the possession of the Dukes of Medina-Sidonia after being captured by the Christians in 1434. The road north from Jimena to Arcos goes through wild and mountainous country densely covered with holm and cork oaks. After 14 km a dust track to the left climbs up the Puerto de la Yegua, near the top of which is an isolated farm; from here it is about a half-hour's walk through the trees and undergrowth to the fascinating rock shelter of **Laja Alta** (see page 57), but it is difficult to find without the services of a local guide.

Following the C331 south from Jimena in the direction of Gibraltar, you will reach after 22 km a turning to the right which leads steeply up to the extraordinary hill village of **Castellar de la Frontera**. This tiny place is entirely encased in its well-preserved fortress of Moorish origin. Captured by the Christians in 1434, the village was in such a primitive state by the 1970's that it was abandoned, its inhabitants being moved into the specially built Nuevo Castellar on the Gibraltar road. German hippies were later attracted to the place for the same reasons that forced its inhabitants to leave it: some of these Germans constructed ramshackle huts around the walls, and others took over the houses inside; soon graffiti began appearing in Spanish with the words 'German drug-addicted swine out'. The village is exceedingly picturesque, but claustrophobic and slightly threatening. From the balcony of its German-run bar there is a spectacular view towards Gibraltar. Following the recent draining of the artificial lake below, the corpses of two Germans were found, attached to each other by rope.

LACALAHORRA [3G], an austere village under the grey shingle slopes of the Sierra Nevada, is the capital of the Marquesado de Zenete, a largely flat and wild expanse whose strange character is enhanced to the west by the scars left by iron mines. This former fiefdom, created in 1489 from land newly conquered by the Christians, was a gift of the Catholic Monarchs to the all-powerful Cardinal Pedro Gonzalez de Mendoza, who in turn bequeathed it in 1491 to his illegitimate son Don Rodrigo de Vivar y Mendoza, the future patron of the pioneering renaissance palace at Lacalahorra (see page 104). This building, which seems to have been dropped like some children's toy on top of a grey, conical mound above the village, is one of the most remarkable if also little known monuments in Spain, and is worth a long journey to come and see.

The building's idiosyncrasies and haunting appeal are mirrored in the life story of Don Rodrigo, which reads like the most melodramatic of historical fictions, and was marked by constant problems arising out of the illegitimacy of his birth. In his early years these problems were eased by his enormously influential father, who successfully pleaded to make him his legitimate heir, and even managed to elevate his Granadan fiefdom into a Marquessate by marrying him off in 1493 to a daughter of the Duke of Medinaceli. But, despite the respectability conferred by this, the Spanish Church and aristocracy could never forget Don Rodrigo's bastard status, and became especially vindictive towards him after his father's death, which came fast on the heels of the wedding. When, shortly afterwards, Don Rodrigo's young and childless wife fell mortally ill, she was persuaded to transfer her rights to her father and not her husband. Don Rodrigo went off to Italy, where he became enamoured not only of Italian culture but also of Lucrezia Borgia, whom he unsuccessfully wooed. Back in Spain his mounting difficulties were compounded by an increasingly scandalous private life and a stubborn, proud and determined character. Falling passionately in love with a member of another of Spain's most powerful families, the Fonsecas, he secretly married this already betrothed woman, Doña María, and then, having consummated the marriage, immediately left her to face her father on her own. The father, refusing to accept the legitimacy of what had happened, made her go ahead with the contracted wedding to her cousin. Don Rodrigo, accusing the father of promoting bigamy, was promptly thrown into prison by Isabel la Católica, and he remained there until Isabel's death a few months later, in November 1504. Isabel's successor Philip I was better disposed to Don Rodrigo than she had been, and accepted his claim to be the legal husband of Doña Maria. After remarrying in public in 1506, Don Rodrigo enjoyed a few years of relative tranquillity in which he devoted himself to the construction of his palace at Lacalahorra. The palace was completed by 1512, but was lived in for an extremely short period thanks to Don Rodrigo having antagonized the authorities in Granada, who forced him to take refuge in Valencia, where he died in 1523, two years after his second wife.

The building abandoned by Don Rodrigo resumed its original function as a fortress during the second morisco rebellion, and soldiers were garrisoned here right up to the 19th century. Though empty and unlived in since then, it was bought early this century by the Dukes of Infantado, who were anxious that its interior should not end up in America, like that of the castle at VÉLEZ-BLANCO (see page 386); the Dukes have persisted in refusing to allow the State to undertake much needed restoration – a stance that will please visitors with a romantic taste for neglected monuments. Officially the place is only open on Wednesday from 10 am to 1pm , and 4 pm to 6 pm; but on other days you could try your luck with the helpful and informative caretaker, who lives in the village (tel: 958 677098) and has a daughter who runs the newly opened castellated restaurant on the outskirts. Recovering your breath after the steep, unshaded climb from the village, you can sit on a solitary remaining stretch of outer Moorish walls to admire the impressively stark and heavy exterior of the palace block. Flanked by round towers crowned by what appear to be observatory domes, the building from the outside is not unlike one of the futurist fantasies of the visionary French architect Ledoux. When work was begun on it, Don Rodrigo had apparently no intention of going to live there, and merely wanted to strengthen the existing Moorish castle. The Mendoza family architect, Lorenzo Vázquez, was brought in to design the building, but he was later thrown into prison by Don Rodrigo, probably as a result of disagreements following the decision to turn the castle into a palace. He was replaced by the Genoese sculptor and architect Michele Carlone, who worked here with a team of Italian craftsmen on the overwhelmingly beautiful courtyard that awaits you soon after entering the building. After the severity of the exterior, the delicacy of this double-arcaded courtyard – one of the earliest examples in Spain of the Italian renaissance style – comes as the most wonderful of surprises. Though much of the original marbling has been stripped off, exquisitely carved classical ornamentation and allegories remain around the portals and windows. The decorative programme, with its prominent Latin inscriptions and allegories of

La Calahorra

virtue, is the first in Spain to glorify the patron, who gives especial and understandable emphasis to his being a Mendoza who has married into the Fonsecas. The caretaker and his family have given a certain homely touch to the courtyard by decorating its staircase with plants and flowers; but the rest of the interior is poignantly bare and decayed, which adds to the child-like sense of discovery you might experience while wandering through the dark, shuttered rooms. Inscriptions identify the respective bedrooms of Don Rodrigo and his wife, which form part of a grand suite of rooms that still retain renaissance fireplaces and rotten *artesonado* ceilings; there is also a recognizable servant's quarter centred around a small, undecorated courtyard. The braver visitors will make their way down into the dungeon or up the collapsing staircases into the turrets.

The little-spoilt villages of the Marquesado de Zenete were extensively repopulated after 1492 (several have Galician-sounding names such as Ferreira, Lanteira and Aldeire), and have few Moorish remains other than a number of ruined baths that are difficult today to find. The best preserved, though crammed with hay and farming implements, are those in the cellar of a house in the Calle del Agua in **Hueneja**, 8 km east of Lacalahorra off the main road to Almería; the forcible closure of these and other local baths in 1566 was an important factor in sparking off the second of the morisco uprisings. For a truly memorable Moorish survival you have to go just beyond the Marquesado and into the province of Almería. Here, in the otherwise unexceptional village of **Fiñana**, 10 km further west along the N324, is an almost an intact 14th-century mosque, complete with elaborate stucco panels around the mihrab or prayer niche; the mosque survives as the small hermitage of Nuestro Padre Jesus Nazareno.

LA CAROLINA [1F], set back slightly from the main Madrid to Córdoba road was the most important of the foreign colonies founded in 1768 by Charles III and his minister Pablo de Olavide (see page 27). It is attractively laid out on a regular grid plan, and has a neoclassical parish church adjoining the elegant palace where Olavide lived until his fall from favour in 1775.

Just before reaching the small village of **Las Navas de Tolosa**, 4 km to the north of La Carolina on the Madrid road, you will see on the left-hand side of the road an unappealing modern memorial commemorating the celebrated battle which took place here on 16 July 1212 (see page 84). Represented in the over-life-sized sculptural group by Antonio González Orea are Alfonso VIII of Castille, Pedro II of Aragón, Sancho VII the Strong of Navarre, Don López de Haro, and the Archbishop of Toledo, Don Rodrigo Jiménez de Rada, all of whom participated in this decisive victory over the Moors; the bronze figure in front of them is that of a shepherd who guided them across the well-guarded Sierra Morena. The surviving Moors supposedly escaped through the beautiful pass to the north of here, which henceforth came to be known as the Pass of Despeñaperros ('overthrow of the dogs'; see page 11 and 25).

LANJARÓN [4G]: Visitors travelling directly to Lanjarón from Granada will be following the route that an excited Lady Louisa Tenison described in 1850 as the one 'which Boabdil chose when leaving his house and his kingdom for ever'. At **Durcal**, 30 km south of Granada on the N323, an enjoyable deviation from this can be made by descending a steep dust track into a delightful green and wooded valley, which forms a striking contrast to the arid mountains rising above it: there are various old mills here, one of which, the Molino de Lecrín, houses both a catering school and the headquarters of the Granada Gastronomical Society: elegantly jacketed trainee waiters will take you on a tour of a traditional Granadan kitchen before leading you into the dining-room of the Society's restaurant, which specializes in Hispano-Moorish dishes. Rejoining Boabdil's road to exile, you will pass 8 km further south the village of **Mondújar**, where Boabdil stopped to pay homage to his Nasrid ancestors in a cemetery (now gone) below the ruins of a Moorish castle. After another 5 km, after leaving the N323 and taking the modern road to Lanjarón, you will glimpse to your left an old bridge bearing what had once been the principal route into the Alpujarras. The moriscos, at the beginning of their second uprising, had pulled this bridge down in the hope of preventing the Christians from entering their Alpujarran territory. However, they had not reckoned with the fanatical determination of a Franciscan friar called Fray Cristóbal Molina, who – according to the chronicler Diego Hurtado de Mendoza – showed the Christian troops how they could negotiate the abyss by boldly leaping across it, a sword in one hand and a crucifix in another. Two soldiers followed his example, with fatal consequences for one of them; but the monk, aided by the other soldier, braved salvoes of arrows to put back the bridge's wooden beams. The present structure dates from around 1600.

Lanjarón is known as the 'Gateway to the Alpujarra', and a modern monument in

Lanjarón

the form of a Moorish arch with a half-opened door has recently been put at the entrance to this famous spa town, whose mineral water is drunk all over Spain. Behind the monument is a fountain inscribed with a line of poetry from Lorca, who enjoyed seeing from here the town extended like a balcony above the craggy, mountainous landscape. While staying at Lanjarón Lorca felt 'a wind from Africa', but you are unlikely to have the same sensation immediately on arrival here. Despite the neo-Moorish spa house, and the occasional Moroccan visitor who still comes here, the elegant hotels and spa residences at the western end of the town are more reminiscent of Marienbad than of Marakkesh. Only once you have reached the heart of this long town and walked beyond the main street will you find an old quarter in a traditional Alpujarran Berber style (see pages 41-2). The town's main Moorish monument is situated just below the houses, and is accessible along a dusty track winding through olive groves. This crag-top structure peering over a fearful chasm was taken by surprise by Ferdinand the Catholic during the first morisco uprising in 1500. The castle's valiant morisco leader – described by contemporaries as a 'terrible and notorious black man' – preferred to throw himself into this void rather than be made a prisoner.

LAUJAR DE ANDARAX [4H]: The eastern half of the Alpujarras is much less spoilt than the western half (see ÓRGIVA), but has a more barren landscape, and less obviously attractive towns and villages. Of these Laujar is one of the largest and most interesting. On the Plaza Mayor is an elegant late 18th-century Town Hall comprising three superimposed arcades. Next to this is one of the town's many charming fountains put up during the reign of Charles III. The village looks south to the stark and arid range of the Sierra de Gádor, but lies on the slopes of the Sierra Nevada, which is densely forested in its upper reaches. On the western outskirts of the town a steep asphalted road climbs up the latter range; the views are impressive, and there are a number of footpaths leading off into the forest. On the other side of the town is a popular picnic spot next to the shaded source of the River Andarax.

When Boabdil fled from Granada in 1492 he took refuge in the Laujar area, where he spent much of his time hunting, according to a letter written to the Catholic Kings by the royal secretary Fernando de Zafra. At the agricultural village of Fuente Victoria, 2 km east of the town, is a large brick residence traditionally known as 'The House of Boabdil'; the building can hardly be more than three centuries old, but credulous romantics might enjoy going inside to revel in thoughts of *Sic transit gloriae mundi* at the sight of the tomato crates, plastic buckets, egg boxes, discothèque speakers and other miscellaneous objects that are now kept in the fast decaying courtyard. The old woman who lives here is more cynical – 'a Moorish king wouldn't live in a tip like this,' she told me.

LEBRIJA [4C], in the middle of hilly agricultural landscape, was founded by the Turdetanians, who left here many traces of their civilization: the National Archaeological Museum in Madrid has various figurines and exquisite gold candlesticks from this area (see page 62). Under the Romans Lebrija was fortified and became an important centre of pilgrimage thanks to the cult of Venus and Bacchus celebrated here. Present-day Lebrija is not a place of great beauty but it does have considerable personality. It is one of the main Andalucían centres of flamenco, and every year in July there is held here one of the best of the region's flamenco festivals, the *Caracol* (see page 150). Of the local flamenco dynasties, the leading one is the Peña family, whose members include the singers La Perrata, El Perrate, and El Lebrijano (one of the most popular flamenco singers of today), and the guitarists Pedro Peña and Pedro Bacán. Another traditional speciality of the town is its earthenware, most notably its pitchers (*cántaros*), gazpacho bowls (*dornillos*) and water-carrying jugs with spout and handle (*botijos*). The main workshop of the town is that of Juan López Barrágan in the Calle Luis Recogado. López Barrágan, whose family have been potters as far back as he can remember, will happily give you a demonstration at his wheel. You can also buy from him earthenware at exceptionally cheap prices. The shape of the pitchers has remained unchanged since Roman times.

The parish church of Lebrija, Santa María de la Oliva, is also well worth a visit, and indeed is one of the outstanding churches of Seville province. Situated on top of a hill in the prettiest and oldest part of the town, the church was an Almohad mosque consecrated by the Christians in 1249. The west end of the church is still clearly recognizable as a mosque, and is like a miniature version of Córdoba's Mezquita, with exquisite Moorish decoration in its various domes. The chancel and crossing were a 16th-century addition, but have elaborate star-vaulting of Moorish character. The superb high altar of 1643 was the first major commission of Alonso Cano (see page 115) and is notable for the lifelike sculptures that he executed for it. The bell-tower dates from the 18th century, and is one of many in Andalucía inspired by the Giralda in Seville.

LINARES [2F]: In this large and ugly town known for it car factories and copper and lead mines, the guitarist Andrés Segovia was born in 1893 and the bullfighter Manolete was killed in 1947. The parish church of Santa María la Mayor was begun in the 12th century and has renaissance elements designed by the great local architect Andrés de Vandelvira (see ÚBEDA). There is a small archaeological museum which includes finds from the nearby Roman colony at Cástulo. But the main attraction of the town is the superbly ornate late baroque frontispiece of the former Hospital of San Juan de Dios (now the Palace of Justice).

LOJA [4F], lying along a narrow stretch of the fertile Genil Valley, occupies a position of great strategic importance at the western entrance to the fertile vega of

Granada. In recognition of this the Nasrid king Abd al-Hasan was forced in 1482 to abandon his attempt to recapture Alhama de Granada (see page 249) and rush to defend Loja from Christian invaders. The Christians eventually had to flee, leaving behind their artillery and siege equipment. In the meantime, however, Abd al-Hasan's son Boabdil, profiting from his father's absence, and apparently supported by both his mother and the rebellious Abencerrajes, rose up against him in Granada, thus compounding divisions within the Nasrid family that would lead to a fatal weakening of Islamic resistance to the Christian threat. The Christians returned to Loja four years later, and this time succeeded in taking it. Five thousand Muslims left the town to seek refuge in a Granada whose own collapse was now imminent.

Loja, which has been subject to much 20th-century development, has a cramped and untidy centre built around the fragmentary remains of its 9th-century citadel, once one of the most important Moorish fortifications in Spain. The entrance to the citadel, with its steeply ascending white-washed streets, is through an arch off the small, palm-shaded main square. Attached to this arch is a plaque commemorating the outstanding Islamic scholar Ibn al-Khatib, who was born in Loja in 1333, and not only excelled as a physician, historian, poet and philosopher, but also became vizier at the court of Granada; jealousy towards him led to his banishment in Morocco, where, in 1375, he was executed in Fez at the instigation of his former friend and protector in Granada, Muhammad V. On the square iself is a pastry shop where you can buy Loja's best known gastronomic delicacy – its ring-shaped, meringue-based sweets known as *roscos*. A large abandoned mill on the town's eastern outskirts has been turned into an unusual and fashionable night-time bar, which incorporates the mill workings into the decoration.

The town appears at its most beautiful when viewed from the opposite bank of the river Genil, preferably from the terrace of the pleasant restaurant called El Frontil. From here Loja is seen rising above fields, its buildings, and even the peeping battlements of its castle, framed against a background of barren peaks. Before crossing the Genil you should follow the river east until just beyond the outskirts of the town, where it runs in cataracts down a small gorge. This pleasant spot, known inappropriately as Los Infiernos, has a shaded picnic area with benches.

Further afield, 10 km to the west along the quiet C334, ironwork railings protecting a dense cluster of pines, cypresses, palms and other trees mark the entrance to the **Jardines Narváez** – among the finest of Andalucia's gardens. These gardens, so unexpected in the middle of the surrounding fields of olive trees, were laid out early in the last century by a landscape architect who had worked on the famous gardens of the royal palace at La Granja near Segovia. They are attached to a summer estate that had belonged to the Loja-born General Narváez, a ruthless military politician who became head of government under Isabel II, and was created 1st Duke of Valencia. Virtually unknown to tourists, these gardens are completely unpromoted by the present owners, who only allow visits on Wednesday mornings. Returning towards Loja on the same road, you can turn right at the isolated inn of the Venta Santa Barbara to reach the hamlet of **Ríofrío**, which is on the main road from Seville to Granada, 7 km to the west of Loja; a popular stopping-off place for drivers coming to and from Granada, it has good bars and restaurants where you can eat trout from the local trout farm. At **Estación de Salinas**, 12 km further west on the Seville road, a road to the north leads towards the Finca Bobadilla, a traditional finca which has been transformed into one of Spain' most luxurious hotels.

LORA DEL RÍO [3D] is a lively but unattractive market town with a pleasantly decrepit Town Hall (1730) in an extravagant baroque style; on the nearby calle Federico García Lorca is another interesting early 18th-century building, the Casa de los Leones. The modest ruins of the Roman settlement of **Arva** lie 10 km to the west of the town, off the C341 to Seville. More extensive, and beautifully situated are the remarkable Roman ruins of **Mulva** (see page 64), accessible only by a poor and unasphalted 8 km stretch of road from **Villanueva del Río y Minas**, a village 9 km further along the C431 from Arva.

LUCENA [3E], situated among hills covered in vines and olive trees, had a prosperous Jewish community in the middle ages, but was described by Gerald Brenan in the late 1940's as one of the poorest Spanish towns he had ever seen. The revival of small businesses in recent years has now turned the place into one of the wealthiest towns *per capita* in the whole of Andalucía – a development which has led to the pulling down of much of what was charming and old in favour of modern apartment blocks and pretentious shops and bars. However, a visit here is rewarded by a visit to the parish church of San Mateo, the Sagrario chapel of which, off the left aisle, is one of the exquisitely ornate masterpieces of the Andalucían baroque. The author of this chapel is anonymous, but it is appropriate that there should have been born in his town, in 1669, one of the most extravagant of Spain's baroque architects, Hurtado Izquierdo, who died at nearby PRIEGO DE CÓRDOBA (see page 125). Near the church are the much restored ruins of the castle where the unfortunate Boabdil – the last Moorish ruler in Spain – was briefly imprisoned by Isabella in 1483.

Brenan, finding the poverty of Lucena 'unendurable', escaped for a short while to the **Sanctuario de Nuestra Señora de Araceli**, 7 km to the south on top of a spectacular rock pinnacle. In addition to the superlative views, the sanctuary – a popular place to visit at weekends – has a small bar serving excellent sausages and other tapas.

An attractive drive along the C334 leads to the white village of **Rute**, overlooking the reservoir of Iznájar. The village is known for its dry and sweet anis. The poet Rafael Alberti (see page 229) spent much time in Rute in the 1920's, staying in the house of his brother-in-law, and producing a volume of verse entitled *Cuaderno de Rute* ('Rute Notebook').

MÁLAGA [4E]: Founded by the Phoenicians, a bishopric in the 6th century, and a flourishing town under the Moors, Málaga was captured by the Catholic Monarchs in 1487 and subjected to terrible reprisals. The town's economy, badly affected by the Christian conquest, was further damaged by the expulsion of the moriscos in 1568; it was not to recover until the 18th century. With its beautiful position between mountains and the sea, its balmy climate, and surrounding sub-tropical vegetation, Málaga developed in the early 19th century into a thriving winter resort, especially popular with the English. The poet García Lorca once described Málaga as his favourite town in Andalucía, but the place was badly damaged in the Civil War. In recent years the place has suffered even more at the hands of town-planners, who continue to this day to destroy most of the old and attractive parts of the town. The capital of the Costa del Sol, with an international airport famed for its cheap package flights, Málaga today overflows with tourists. The tolerance shown them by the exceptionally open and friendly people of Málaga is quite remarkable.

The town is divided in two by the seasonal torrent of the Guadalmedina, which in the summer months has a particularly unappealing aspect. The broad Avenida de Andalucía, lined with huge modern blocks, runs through the western part of town, slicing in half the district of El Perchel, which used to be the centre of Málaga's flamenco culture. The rest of this once delightful, ramshackle, district is slowly being pulled down, the most attractive of its remaining old and dilapidated streets being those in its northern half. At the western end of the Avenida de Andalucía are modern gardens containing the first monument erected in Spain (in 1978) to Málaga's most famous son, Pablo Picasso, born here in 1881; next to this modest work is a recent and highly energetic semi-abstract monument to Picasso by Ortiz Berrocal.

The continuation of the Avenida de Andalucía on the eastern side of the Guadalmedina is the shaded Alameda, an elegant promenade laid out in the 19th century, some of the trees being planted by the English consul William Mark (see page 196). Near the western end of the Alameda, at the junction of the Calle Comisa, is one of Málaga's few remaining old bars, the dirty, dimly lit Casa Guardia, founded in 1840, a long narrow room lined with barrels; this is an excellent place to try Málaga's famous sweet wines (see page 185). The commercial district to the north of here is pleasantly animated and has numerous interesting 19th-century buildings, such as the neo-Moorish market on the Calle Atarazanas. A lone 17th-century survival on the Pasillo de Santa Isabel, overlooking the Guadalmedina, is the Mesón de la Victoria, a charming building housing what is perhaps Málaga's most enjoyable museum, the Museo de Arte y Tradiciones Populares (Museum of Popular Art and Traditions).

At the very heart of commercial Málaga is the Plaza de la Constitución which has a shopping arcade known as the Pasaje Chinitas; in the middle of this is a clothes shop with a plaque marking the site of the Café Chinitas, a café frequented by bull-fighters and singers, and commemorated in a poem by García Lorca. East of the

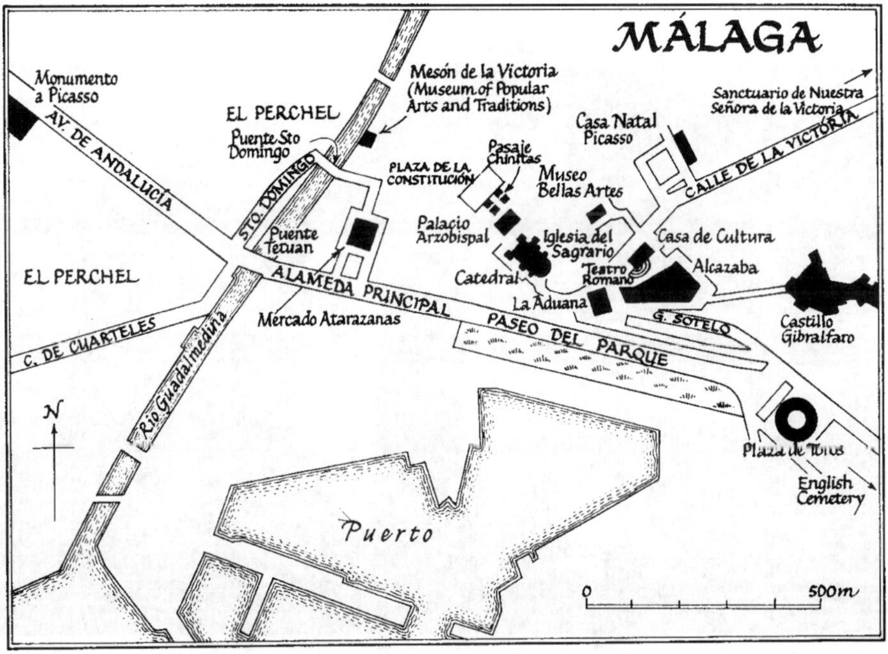

square, you come to what is left of medieval and renaissance Málaga, the principal monument being the cathedral, the oldest part of which is the Sagrario chapel on its northern side. The chapel, erected after 1487 on the site of a mosque, served as the town's cathedral until 1588; it has an Isabelline plateresque north portal and an exuberant renaissance high altar in gilded wood. The present cathedral, begun in 1528, has an oppressively marbled interior of gothic proportions but classical detailing. Opposite the cathedral's heavy late baroque façade, completed in 1783, is the late 18th-century Archbishop's Palace, inside which is the gloomy Museo Diocesano with numerous old master paintings of dubious attribution, and a series of modern works in quite execrable taste.

Continuing east from the cathedral, you will soon reach the hill supporting the Moorish Alcazaba or citadel, at the foot of which is a Roman theatre in a sadly neglected condition. The rebuilt Alcazaba, dating back to the Umayyad period, has beautiful views, pools, luxuriant terraces and an archaeological museum featuring mainly Moorish finds. On the high and verdant hill to the east of the Alcazaba rises the equally much restored Moorish castle of Gibralfaro, immediately below which is the town's modern parador.

A few minutes' walk north of the Roman theatre is Málaga's latest and most popular cultural attraction, the Museo Picasso, which is housed in a now sensationally

The neo-Moorish market, Málaga

modernised and extended 16th century palace that, in its dustier days, contained the town's modest Fine Arts Museum. Spaciously and elegantly arranged, the Museo Picasso is surely one of the finest European museums to have opened over the past decade, and certainly compensates for the city's previous neglect of of its most famous native son. Instead of just a handful of works executed when he was fourteen, the city now has a collection of his art ranging from an exquisitely detailed early portrait of his first wife Olga to some of the boldest and most colourful of his later compositions. The museum contains as well a large temporary exhibition space, which was inaugurated in 2003 with a massive exhibition bringing together works that had remained in the artist's personal collection.

The creation of the museum went hand in hand with the explosion of smart cafés, bars and arty shops in a now pedestrianized area stretching from the cathedral to the Plaza de la Merced, where Picasso's birthplace, No. 15, has become a small museum, with photographs of the artist's family and a reconstruction of the room where he spent his childhood. Near the square the long Calle de la Victoria leads to the Plaza Victoria, beyond which is the Sanctuary of Nuestra Señora de la Victoria. This church, begun in 1487 on the site where the Catholic Monarchs installed themselves during the siege of that year, was largely remodelled in the baroque period, and has as its principal attraction a small chapel, with exquisitely elaborate and joyful late baroque ornamentation. Near the Plaza Victoria, on the Calle Puerto Parejo, is the Bar Los Chulitos, renowned for its excellent fried fish and seafood.

The continuation of the Alameda to the east is the Paseo del Parque, which runs among trees and grass between the town's port and the Alcazaba hill. The most interesting of the buildings on its northern side is the large neoclassical customs house. The town's bullring stands at the Paseo's eastern end, and near this is the English cemetery, now hemmed in by modern development (see page 196). A No. 11 bus from the Paseo will take you east to Málaga's resort district of Pedregalejo, famed for its restaurants, nightlife and fashionable bars such as the Juan Sebastian Bar (reputedly popular with musicians!). On the Playa del Dedo, a few kilometres further east, is the famous Tintero, a large, cheap and popular fish restaurant, where the dishes are auctioned by the waiters as they hurry between the outdoor tables. Further east still along this much developed coastal road is the **Rincón de la Victoria**, on the slopes of which is the Cueva del Tesoro, where palaeolithic paintings have been found.

Málaga's airport is on the western side of the town, near the exclusive residential district of Churriana. Churriana boasts one of Andalucía's finest gardens, El Retiro, laid out in the 18th century with pools and classical statuary. The garden is overgrown with sub-tropical vegetation, and has a most unusual sundial. Until very recently the place was in aristocratic ownership and had been allowed to go evocatively to seed, but it has now been bought by a German chemical company, who have restored it with Prussian vigour, and turned it and the surrounding buildings into an ambitious tourist complex explaining man's relationship with the environment. Gerald Brenan lived for a long time in Churriana, and spent the last years of his life on the eastern outskirts of **Alhaurín el Grande**, 15 km to the west on the C344 (see page 241). His Alhaurín house, at La Cañada de las Palomas 20, is now the seat of the Gerald Brenan Foundation; there is also a Sala Gerald Brenan and a complete collection of his works in the Alhaurín library. Ten kilometres north of Alhaurín is **Cartama**,

The gardens of El Retiro, Churriana, 1989

known throughout Spain for its *morcilla* or blood sausage; you can buy excellent morcilla at Calle Pilar Alto 8, at the top of the village, between the ruins of a Moorish castle and the early 16th-century parish church.

The notoriously dangerous road between Málaga and Gibraltar takes you through some of the most depressing coastal development in Europe, starting with **Torremolinos** (shortened by the English to 'Torrie'). **Fuengirola**, which comes next, still has its Moorish castle, as well as a small Spanish district at the back of the town featuring some modest bars serving some of the best fish and sea-food on the coast (most notably the Bar la Paz Garrido on the Avenida de Mijas). On the slopes above Fuengirola stands the village of **Míjas**, where Manuel Cortes spent thirty years in hiding (see page 241); the village is now wholly given over to tourism, and has various ridiculous museums, such as one devoted to the 'smallest paintings in the world'. **Marbella**, 27 km west of Fuengirola, is the most up-market of the Costa del Sol resorts; the outlying luxury district of Puerto Banus – dominated by a grotesquely large statue donated by the Mayor of Moscow – attracts the coast's jet set, many of whom are drawn to the splendidly kitsch Olivia Valere discothèque, which has architectural features lifted from the Alhambra, and an appropriate situation behind the town's mosque. **Estepona**, 21 km further west, has Spain's oldest nudist beach, yet it has also kept the character of a fishing village more than any other resort on this coast.

MARCHENA [3D], at the heart of the fertile Guadalquivir basin, but away from the major routes that cross through it, is a lively, little-visited market town with various monuments reflecting an important past. Though the town suffered from considerable neglect and damage in the 19th and early 20th centuries, its present citizens have done their best to look after what they have left, and have made every effort to ensure that a visit here is an enjoyable experience. The surrounding walls, built by the Romans, and extended first by the Moors and then by the Christians after Ferdinand III's capture of the town in 1240, have partially survived, together with some of their gates and defensive towers. The most impressive gate is the Puerta de Sevilla off the Calle Rojas Marcos, while the best of the towers is the nearby Torre de Oro, the interior of which (entered from the Calle San Francisco) houses a recently opened and beautifully displayed archaeological museum, where you will be provided with an excellent map and brochure about the town. In the centre of the old town of Marchena is the late gothic parish church of San Juan, which has a superb intricately carved high altar containing panels of the life of Christ by Alejo Fernández (see page 113); in a room above the sacristy is kept a series of nine canvases by Zurbarán, commissioned in 1634 and completed in 1637. Nearby, on the edge of the walled town, is the vast precinct of the former Palace of the Dukes of Osuna. The magnificent plateresque palace was pulled down in the early years of last century by the Duke's creditors, and it is even said that parts of the masonry went into the making of the town's bullring. All that remains in the precinct are the 13th- to 15th-century church of Santa María, and the sorry remains of the town's castle.

Outside the walls, at Calle San Pedro 8 (an animated street leading off the Calle Rojas Marcos) is the town's Casino or Men's Club. This turn-of-the century building, incorporating a former Franciscan monastery, boasts a quite magnificent neo-Moorish exterior.

MARTOS [2F], a well-preserved small town overlooking a landscape of olive trees, has had an important history. Known to the Iberians as Tucci, the town later became a Roman settlement and then a Visigothic bishopric. It acquired the name of Martos after the Christians captured the town from the Moors in 1225, on St. Marta's day. Shortly afterwards the brothers Carvajal, accused of murdering the favourite of Ferdinand IV, Juan de Benavides, were thrown to their deaths from the now ruined castle which rises high above the town on a steep outcrop of rock. The brothers protested their innocence to the end, and, failing in their pleas, eventually begged God that the king himself should die within thirty days; their wish was to be granted. A stone tablet commemorating the brothers is to be found inside the church of Santa Marta, which also boasts an intricate Isabelline plateresque portal. The parish chuch of Santa María de la Villa dates back to the 13th century, but was extensively remodelled in the 15th, 16th and 19th centuries. Other attractions of the town include the renaissance Town Hall (originally a prison, and featuring representations of Wisdom and Justice), and a fountain known as the Fuente Nueva, which was designed in 1584 by a pupil of the influential Roman architect Vignola.

MEDINA SIDONIA [5C] occupies a prominent hill-top setting in the middle of a landscape of rolling wheatfields extending to the Serranía de Ronda. Originally the Roman colony of Assido, and later a Visigothic bishopric, the town was designated 'Medina' or city by the Arabs. The title of Duke of Medina-Sidonia was awarded to members of the family of Guzmán the Good, who had distinguished himself in the capture of the town in 1264. Today the place is one of the most dignified and least spoilt of the white hill-villages of Cádiz province. Its main monument of interest, the parish church of Santa María la Coronada, is near the top of the village's very steep hill, on a small, dusty and neglected square of considerable character: the building was erected over a mosque, the charming courtyard of which still survives, containing the entrance to the former minaret, which can be climbed. The gothic interior of the church dates mainly from the early 16th century, and has an enormous carved retable by Melchor Turín and Juan Bautista Vázquez. On the square below, steps lead down to a friendly bar and restaurant with a shaded outdoor terrace that has a superb view looking south. An even more extensive panorama can be had from the scant remains of the Moorish castle, reached by a rough path behind the church. The main survival of the Moorish fortifications is the beautiful and well-preserved Arco de la Pastora at the bottom of the village, next to the road marked to Jerez de la Frontera. The village's large and pleasant main square is half-way up the hill, and has a good cake-shop, the Sobrina de las Trejas, from which you can buy the village's celebrated bicuits and pastries: of particular renown is the honey and almond-based sweet known as *alfajor*, which dates back to Moorish times and on which a whole book has been written by the pioneering historian of Spanish food, Dr. Thebussem, a native of this town (see page 179).

A 20 km drive in a southeasterly direction will take you to the small village of **Benalup de Sidonia**, beyond which are two little visited sites of great interest: the prehistoric cave of **Tajo de las Figuras**, and the abandoned monastery of **El Cuervo**. To reach the first of these continue driving west on the CA 211 towards the Serranía de Ronda. After 10 km the cultivated fields on the left-hand side of the road give way to bracken, and you will find a metal gate: go through this and bear to the right as you walk up the hill in the direction of a crowning group of large rocks. At this stage you are almost certain to be intercepted by the shepherd responsible for guarding the rock shelter, who will lead you there himself; a rope is provided to assist in lifting yourself up to it. Back again on the road (a ten minutes' walk from the rock shelter), continue driving east, and, shortly beyond the 24 km post, at the top of a hill, you will see on the right-hand side of the road a cluster of trees and a white wooden gate. Beyond the gate is a clearly marked footpath which leads after an hour's walk to the Monastery of El Cuervo. The walk is a delightful one, and for much of its length follows a shaded stream, next to which you will find an abandoned mill (shortly beyond the mill this stream forms a pool where you can swim). To get to the monastery you have to turn sharply left at the hill, and climb up a steep path laid by the monks. The extensive ruins of the monastery constitute one of the most moving sites in all Andalucía. Begun in 1717, using sandstone quarried from the northern slopes of the Sierra Blanquilla on which it stands, the monastery belonged to the order of Discalced Carmelites. An Italian woodcarver was employed for the woodwork and statuary, though he never completed his work here, dying in Cádiz in 1755 in the tidal wave caused by the Lisbon earthquake. The monastery was occupied by French troops in 1810 and abandoned in 1835. Today stray cattle wander among its ruins. Of especial beauty is the crossing of the church: the dome has collapsed, but the ring that supported it has survived, overgrown with vegetation and even sprouting a tree. In the wooded slopes behind the monastery is a group of hermitages.

MINAS DE RÍO TINTO [2B]: The Río Tinto mines, reputedly the oldest in the world, form a cavity of sublime dimensions in the midst of the wild and forested mountains of the Sierra de Aracena; you can peer into them from the road between Nerva and Minas de Río Tinto. The latter village, in a forest clearing out of sight of the mines, was built at the turn of the last century as a replacement for a much older community destroyed during the rapid expansion of the mines under British ownership (see pages 16 and 36). The village proper, an unremarkable group of parallel white rows ascending a steep hill, has in its lower square a monument to oppressed miners that might induce a sense of guilt in British visitors, particularly those who buy the locally available reissue of Felix Lunar's mining memoirs, *A Cielo Abierto: De Río Tinto a Norteamerica* (1953). The former mining headquarters, where there once worked a director whom Lunar described as having probably come to Río Tinto 'from some colony in Africa', are housed in a elegant but much damaged Edwardian building just above the square; the row of ticket windows where the miners' wives collected their husbands' wages can still be seen. This building is now owned by the Río Tinto Foundation, which has a considerable archive relating to the history of the now dying mining industry, and has recently built a mining museum on top of the hill above the offices: the most exciting of its exhibits is the luxurious 'waggon of the Maharajah' which was acquired by the Río Tinto company after the cancellation of a trip to India by Queen Victoria. The ruins of the old railway station are visible further down the hill. Lower still, and completely hidden from the village, is the fascinating and beautifully maintained British colony of Bella Vista, with its Presbysterian neo-gothic church, and English-style village lawn with surrounding gabled houses and hedge-protected gardens. The houses today are mainly owned by the medical staff of the village's recently built General Hospital, the largest in Huelva province outside the capital. These new owners seem partly to be apeing the social manners of the departed British, to judge from a visit to what was once the social centre of the British colony – the former British Club. The clubhouse, fronted by tennis lawns, is still decorated inside in a traditional British style, complete with worn leather furniture, and a profusion of hunting trophies; in the room once used for concerts and amateur theatricals, there are even relics from Gilbert and Sullivan productions. Teas, for women only, are still held every Wednesday afternoon, possibly in retaliation for the continuing 'Men Only' bar, which is run by a man who worked for the British and is happy to show you the correct way of serving drinks while billiards are in progress.

Minas de Río Tinto villagers looking for a livelier and more traditionally Andalucían social life are forced to go to the pleasant large village of **Zalamea la Real**, 10 km to the west, off the main road to Huelva. This village, with its beautiful views over forested hills, is often identified (wrongly) as the setting of Calderón's play *The Mayor of Zalamea*; it is also famed for its aguardiente and anis. 21 km to the south of here, in the northern outskirts of the unattractive town of **Valverde**, is another interesting if recently much transformed relic of the British presence in Huelva - a pebbledash mansion built as the home of the director of the Liverpool-based railway company, The United Alkali Company Ltd.: the building, with its faint echoes of Charles Rennie Mackintosh, has recently been opened as a museum with photographs and other objects tracing the history of the local British colony.

MOGUER [3B]: Gently rising above a landscape of wheatfields, vineyards, orchards and olives, Moguer is the most beautiful and interesting village in the southern half of Huelva province. A dependency of NIEBLA until 1333, Moguer was entrusted in that year by Alfonso XI as a seigneury to Don Alonso Jofre Tenorio, Almirante Mayor of Castille. Close to the estuary of the Río Tinto, Moguer became prosperous not only through agriculture but also through its importance as a fishing and maritime centre: numerous famous figures associated with maritime history and the colonization of the New World came from Moguer, including Juan and Pedro Alonso Niño, who were respectively the captain and pilot of Columbus' ship, the Niña. The village today produces famous pastries, and an excellent sweet wine known as Vino de Naranja.

Moguer's medieval castle is now a decrepit ruin standing over a garage off the Calle Castillo, but many other monuments from the village's past survive in excellent condition, most notably the former convent of Santa Clara, which stands behind a white crenellated wall running the whole length of the narrow and charming Plaza de las Monjas. Founded in 1337/8 by Jofre Tenorio and his wife, Doña Elvira Álvarez, it served as a convent for sisters of the Order of St. Clare until 1898, and is now a museum, which you are obliged to visit with a guide. On entering you find yourself in a small brick cloister in a mudéjar style, beyond which is a much larger cloister, painted a brilliant white and lined with palms. Among the rooms that you are shown are the kitchen, the refectory, the sick room, and an enormous late 16th-century dormitory divided by rows of columns which once separated the beds and were hung with curtains. The highpoint of the visit is the church, which has various medieval and renaissance works of art, most notably the alabaster tomb of the convent's founder and some painted renaissance choir-stalls. An inscription in the right aisle records that Columbus said a prayer in the church on his return from his first journey to America.

Parallel to the convent of Santa Clara, off the Plaza de los Franciscanos, is the late 15th-century monastery of San Francisco, which sent numerous missionaries to America in the 16th, 17th and 18th centuries. The parish church of Nuestra Señora de la Granada, in the Plaza de la Iglesia, is a late 16th-century building with a bell-tower clearly inspired by the Giralda in Seville. The most important building of this later period in Moguer, and indeed the finest neoclassical building in the whole of Huelva province, is the elegant Town Hall on the adjoining Plaza del Cabildo.

In front of the Town Hall is a large memorial to the man who did more than anyone else to promote the fame of Moguer, the poet Juan Ramón Jiménez (see page 222ff). Moguer, with its quiet streets and elegant but decaying white houses has changed little since the time when Juan Ramón wrote his most popular book, *Platero y Yo* ('Platero and I'), extracts from which are quoted on ceramic plaques that mark the many surviving buildings and monuments associated with it. Born in 1881 at Calle de la Ribera 2, Juan Ramón later lived at what is now Calle Juan

Moguer: Convent of S. Clara

Ramón Jiménez 5. This house remained for a long time in the family's possession after the poet's death in 1958, and is now a delightfully old-fashioned museum, retaining much of the house's original furniture and decoration: among the many mementoes is the telegram announcing the poet's being awarded the Nobel Prize. On the eastern edge of the town is the cemetery where he and his wife Zenobia are buried, and nearby, off the Carretera San Juan del Puerto La Rábida, is the Casa de Fuentepiña, the country home where the poet wrote most of *Platero y Yo*.

MOJÁCAR [4J], the most popular resort on the Almería coast, is rapidly developing a character comparable to some of the Costa del Sol resorts, and has on its outskirts numerous signs in English advertising such implausible-sounding places as the Spotted-Turtle Inn. The old town, a Moorish honeycomb of white, flat-roofed houses rising on a hill, must have been enchanting when discovered by artists and writers in the 1950's; most of the houses in the upper end of town are now luxury residences, bars, restaurants or night-clubs. Walt Disney, who had distant Almerían blood, was rumoured for many years to have been born illegitimately in Mojácar to a woman called Antonia Suarez; this bizarre story, quashed by the recent discovery of a birth-certificate in Chicago, had even led to the placing outside the town of a road-sign marked 'Birthplace of Walt Disney'. Visitors to Mojácar can now indulge their fantasy by going at night to the extraordinary bar called Delfos, which is situated among fields on the town's northern outskirts. Created by an artist out of an old farm, the place features an endlessly diverting collection of junk, bric-à-brac and works of art within an ever-expanding and wholly decadent setting of plasterwork columns, capitals, cherubs and nudes.

The coast road south from Mojácar to the popular resort of **Carboneras** starts to climb after 10 km, and then heads inland, the coastline being at this point too steeply mountainous to skirt: just before the climb is a track leading off to the **Playa de Macena**, one of the most unspoilt beaches in the area. Five kilometres to the north of Mojácar is the coastal town of **Garrucha**, a place of little beauty, but none the less appealing for being more of a fishing port than a resort.

MONTEFRÍO [3F], a village of much character, lies between two rocky outcrops crowned by churches. The lower of the two churches, that of San Antonio, is on the eastern edge of the village, off the GR212 to Illora. Begun in the 16th century, perhaps to designs by Diego de Siloe, it was not completed until the 18th century; it has a finely sculpted west façade, and, in front of this, a terrace with an excellent view of Montefrío. The very centre of the town is dominated by the vast dome of the pantheon-like church of the Encarnación by Spain's leading neoclassical architect, Ventura Rodriguez; the structure is undeniably impressive even if totally inappropriate for an Andalucían village, both in its scale and architecture. Behind the building a street climbs up past the Town Hall towards the church perched on the village's eastern rock, the Iglesia de la Villa (stop off at the house at No. 11 to collect the keys). The street goes through the prettiest part of Montefrío, and, once above the roof level of the house, has excellent views over mountain and olive trees. The Iglesia de la Villa is Montefrío's oldest church and was built shortly after the Christian capture of the village in 1482; it stands on the site of a Nasrid castle pulled down by Ferdinand and Isabella.

The village enjoys a great reputation for its charcuterie, most notably its *morcilla* (blood sausage), *chorizo* (spiced sausage) and *salchichón*. Excellent home-made sausages can be tried at the Café Bar La Fonda near the church of the Encarnación; the salchichón here is especially good.

A fascinating and beautifully situated neolithic site, **Las Peñas de los Gitanos**, lies 10 km to the east of the village, off the road to Illora. A sign to it by the side of the road indicates a stony track which climbs up past a quarry. Bear left and follow the white-painted stones by the side of this track and you will eventually pass a small dolmen to your right, and reach what looks like a car park. Beyond this is a large field with various prehistoric tombs.

MONTILLA [3E], a town of unremarkable appearance set among gently rolling expanses of vineyards, is famous both for its dry white wines (see page 185) and historical associations. The place is now generally recognized as the site of the celebrated Battle of Munda, where Caesar defeated the sons and supporters of Pompey. It is also the birthplace of Gonzalo Fernández y Aguilar (1453-1515) who distinguished himself in various battles against the Moors, and earned the nickname 'El Gran Capitán' in the course of his campaigns in Italy against the French. Also connected with the town is the renaissance historian of Inca civilization, Garcilaso de la Vega ('El Inca'), to whom a small museum is dedicated. The son of the conquistador Sebastiano Garcilaso de la Vega and the Inca princess Isabel Chimpu Oclo, 'El Inca' was born in Peru in 1536 and came to Spain in 1560, where he entered the Church.

South of Montilla, 15 km in the direction of Antequera, is the attractive small town of **Aguilar de la Frontera**, also famed as a wine centre. Among its monuments are the elaborate baroque monastery church of the Discalced Carmelites, and the parish church of Santa María del Soterraño, dating mainly from the renaissance period. Of particular interest is the octagonal and poorly maintained square of San José (1806), which was certainly inspired by the Plaza Ochavada in nearby archidona. North of Montilla, 14 km along the N331 to Córdoba, is the town of **Fernán Nuñez**, which has an 18th-century Ducal Palace, an elegant group of brightly painted buildings arranged like a stage set around a fountain.

MONTORO [2E], built above a bend of the Guadalquivir, is one of the most attractive and least spoilt villages in Córdoba province. Of ancient origin, and occupied by the Arabs up to 1240, Montoro caught the attention of Isabel la Católica in 1480 when its inhabitants pooled their resources to construct a new bridge across the Guadalquivir and thus greatly improved the existing communications between

The bridge at Montoro

S. Bartolomé, Montoro

Castille and Andalucía. The women of the village even sold their jewellery to finance the bridge, which in consequence came to be known as the 'Bridge of Las Donadas' or 'the lay sisters'. From that time onwards Montoro was awarded numerous royal privileges. In 1986 King Juan Carlos was made honorary mayor of the village.

The village's main square, the Plaza de España, is especially delightful, dominated by the salmon-pink gothic-mudéjar portal of its parish church of San Bartolomé, and the classical plateresque façade of the former Ducal Palace (now the Town Hall); at No. 19 is a traditional inn (no longer in use) of a type rarely found today in Spain. The Calle B. Comacho, a tiny street to the north of the square, leads to the church of Santa María de La Mota, dating back to the 13th century; there are numerous pleasant little corners in this part of the village. The Calle Corredera, the village's main street, connects the Plaza de España with the Plaza L. Benitez, and at No. 73 is a dark, traditional village store selling excellent basketwork. Off the Plaza L. Benitez is the village's Casino or Men's Club, where you can enjoy good tapas of deep-fried pigs' testicles (*criadillas*) and brains *(sesos)* while seated in an elegant turn-of-the-century patio. Near this is a museum devoted to the locally-born contemporary artist, Antonio Rodríguez Costa, who is claimed to enjoy an international reputation.

The splendid bridge of Las Donadas, possibly designed by the celebrated Enrique de Egas, links the village with its run-down suburb of Retamar. The road which climbs up from here towards Cardeña (the CO510) provides some of the best views of Montoro.

MORÓN DE LA FRONTERA [4D], the centre of a Moorish city state in the 11th century, marks the approach of the Serranía de Ronda. Built on a hill, its highest point is its ruined 11th-century castle. Near this, in a small park with excellent views, is a statue of 1912 representing a plucked cock, an allusion to an unpopular 16th-century tax-collector nicknamed 'the cock', who one day was stripped bare and beaten up by the inhabitants of Morón: the phrase 'to end up like the cock of Morón' is still used in reference to people who make fools of themselves. (Interestingly, another version of this story, updated to the Batista era, is current in the Cuban town of Morón, which was founded in the 16th century by a native of its Andalucían namesake.) Immediately below the castle is the attractive parish church of San Miguel, which was constructed between 1503 and 1730 and has a west façade of 1726 in a pseudo-renaissance style. Wholly baroque is the magnificent early 18th-century west portal of the church of San Ignacio (La Compañía), which stands on a street to your left as you walk down the Calle San Miguel to the Plaza de Ayuntamiento, the lively juncion of the town's principal streets. Morón is famed as a flamenco centre, and hosts each summer a flamenco festival known as 'El Gazpacho'. A description of the flamencos of Morón forms the basis of *Flamenco: A Way of Life* (1967) by the American 'Flamencologist' Don Pohren, who in the 1960's ran a Flamenco Centre in the town's outskirts.

MOTRIL [4G], the largest town by the coast of Granada, lies 3 km inland in the middle of flat fertile land squeezed in between the sea and barren mountains. Vines, and almond and citrus trees grow here in abundance, and it is one of the only places in Spain suitable for the cultivation of such tropical fruits as the delicate custard apple (*chirimoya*). But the principal local activity is based on sugar cane, which was first cultivated here by Spanish planters fleeing from Cuba in 1898 (hence Motril's nickname of 'little Cuba'). The cane is used in the manufacture of an excellent rum known as *ron pálido*, which is rarely to be found outside Granada province.

The town of Motril is mainly modern and uninspiring, and the ruined castle which once belonged to the mother of the Moorish king Boabdil is of little interest; the equally unappealing port of Motril is a holiday resort particularly popular with the inhabitants of Granada. The nearby old village of **Salobreña** is a far prettier place than Motril, and rises up above the surrounding fields on a rock shaped like a ship. Further west from Salobreña the mountains come down directly to the coast;

the next important town and resort is **Almuñecar**, a long sprawling place dominated by the rock that supports its Moorish castle, inside which is the local cemetery. Laurie Lee stayed in the town at the end of the journey which was later to inspire *As I Walked Out One Midsummer's Morning*; he disguised the place under the name Castillo, but is now commemorated by a plaque in its centre. East from Salobreña the coast becomes increasingly arid and depressing the nearer it gets to Almería province. [3G]

NERJA [4F], a coastal town of sub-topical vegetation at the foot of the beautiful Sierra de Tejeda, must have been a paradise before being 'discovered' by the British in the late 1950's and turned into a vulgar resort with uncontrolled villa development behind it. Its finest feature is its 'Balcony of Europe', a small palm-lined belvedere jutting out into the sea; the view to the east is particularly attractive and takes in a rocky coastline overhung with palms and set against a background of wild mountains. The best beach is that of Burriana, on the eastern edge of the town.

The N340 east from Nerja to Almuñecar (see MOTRIL) is the most beautiful stretch of road along the Costa del Sol, and twists its way above small rock-lined coves and jagged capes. The **Cave of Nerja**, 3 km along this road, was discovered in 1957, conveniently just in time for the beginnings of the tourist boom; the cave is continuously packed with tourists, and, with its garish lighting, seems almost as artificial as that of St. George in Gibraltar. Only 10 km further on, however, a rough track to the right of the road winds steeply down to the beach of **Cantariján**, one of the most attractive and least spoilt beaches along Andalucía's Mediterranean coastline. The larger of its two rustic-looking bars produces an excellent paella.

The hill-village of **Frigiliana**, 6 km above Nerja, at the end of the MA 105, is exceedingly pretty and has magnificent views down to the coast; but the place is so spotlessly white and clean that it resembles a real village less than the cover of an estate agent's brochure. The English influence in the village is clearly evident in the ceramic plaques stuck to the walls of many of the houses and bearing rather fatuous historical information. At the top of the village is an English bar with a terrace and exotic garden.

There is a 15 km dust track leading from Frigiliana to **Cómpeta**, but if you are driving to the latter village, it is quicker and safer to head back to the coast, take the Málaga road for 8 km, and then turn north on to the MA 137. The climb proper to Cómpeta begins after **Torrox**, a village largely filled with Germans and Scandinavians; the road begins then dramatically to wind its way up the mountain, the slopes of which are covered with vineyards. The pretty old village of Cómpeta, from which the sea is visible in the far distance, is known for its sweet wines. The Danes and English now living in the village almost outnumber the

Fishermen's houses near Níjar

remarkably tolerant and friendly local population; at the time of writing there are three foreign-run estate agencies here, and two English-run bars. Behind the village the mountainside turns into the wild shrubland of the National Reserve of the Sierra de Tejeda.

NIEBLA [3B]: Surrounded by walls dating back possibly to Tartessian times, the small town of Niebla makes a most striking first impression when seen from the N431 between Seville and Huelva. Its exterior appearance bears witness to its rich past, and strategic importance. Known to the Romans as Ilupa, Niebla became a bishopric under the Visigoths, and was later the centre of a small Arab *taifa* or city-state; it was captured by Alfonso X in 1257. An English archaeologist, E. M. Whishaw lived here in the early years of this century, and wrote a strange and fanciful account of Niebla's origins entitled *Atlantis in Andalucía: a Study of Folk Memory*.

Niebla, at close quarters, may not quite live up to your initial impressions. The walls turn out to be in poor condition, and crudely restored in parts; on the other side of the town to the N431 they slouch down to a rubbish-strewn railway track

Niebla

and the sinister blood-red trickle of the Río Tinto. Inside the citadel is a friendly but unattractive town of mainly modern houses. Interesting archaeological finds have been made at Niebla, and certain guide-books refer to the town's archaeological museum, but of this there is now no trace. The one delightful monument here is the church of Santa María de la Granada, which stands on the other side of the main square to the Town Hall (where the key to the church can be had). You enter through a charming irregularly-shaped patio, which is probably what remains of a 10th-century Mozarabic church. The building was transformed into a mosque by the Almohads in the 13th century; the modest interior has elaborate late gothic vaulting, and Mozarabic brickwork. The castle of Niebla is attached to the perimeter wall facing the N431, and hosts a festival of theatre and dance every September. The local craft of basketwork is at present being revived.

NÍJAR [4J], an attractive small town by the standards of Almería province, is fringed by palm trees and orchards, and backed by the barren peaks of the Sierra Alhamilla; there are extensive views over the fertile Campo de Níjar to the parched mountains forming the CABO DE GATA. The place was given considerable notoriety by the writer Juan Goytisolo, whose travel book *Campo de Níjar* (1958) features a vivid account of the poverty of the area in the 1950's. The then mayor of Níjar, anxiously trying to develop his town, publicly expressed his desire to string up Goytisolo 'by the balls'. He need not have worried about the possible negative consequences of the book, for the town is now a fairly prosperous place drawing numerous visitors from the coast. The main attractions are the extremely cheap hand-made ceramics and textiles to be bought here. These crafts have been practised in the town since Moorish times, and their primitive designs, though very modern in appearance, have also changed little since then. The rugs are coarse-textured, while the ceramics are crudely glazed and painted in motley colours. Most of the town's crafts shops are situated on the Calle Real de las Eras, in the lower half of the town, near the post office.

OLVERA [4D]: *Mata a tu hombre. Y vete a Olvera* ('Kill your man and fly to Olvera') ran an old saying, coined at a time when Olvera was a notorious bandit's lair. It enjoys a magnificent hill-top situation in the middle of a landscape of jagged outcrops of rocks and rolling hills covered in olive-trees; the views to the south are dominated by the picturesque silhouette of the Serranía de Ronda. The village is laid out around a long main street which climbs up to the imposing 17th-century parish church of the Encarnación (which is best seen from the outside, the interior being somewhat bleak). On the square on which the church stands is a gate beyond which a path carved into the rock ascends steeply to the ruined castle (if the gate is closed, ask for the key at the house at No. 2 on the square). The castle was built by the Moors in the late 12th century, and then renovated by Alfonso XI after the

Olvera

Christian capture of the town in 1327. The views down to the church and village are quite vertiginous.

ÓRGIVA [4G], lying in the valley in between the Sierra Nevada and the Sierra de la Contraviesa, resembles an Alpine town gone somewhat to seed. Off the main street, which is lined with open-air bars, is the twin-towered façade of its baroque parish church, and the decrepit medieval tower of the castle of the Counts of Sástago. Órgiva is the most important town of the western Alpujarras, and is the traditional starting-point for a tour of this region made famous in recent times by Alarcón's *Viaje a la Alpujarra* and Gerald Brenan's *South from Granada* (see page 232f). Most of the villages are on the southern slopes of the Sierra Nevada, and are characterized by their flat-roofed wooden-beamed houses piled up on top of each other; in many of the villages you will find places to buy the beautiful rugs that have been made here since Moorish times. At the bottom of the spectacular, unasphalted road which descends from the Pico Veleta (see GRANADA), is the tiny 'Barranco de Poqueira', a steep and verdant river course, along which are arranged, one above the other, three of the most popular villages of the region, Capileira, Bubión and Pampaneira. **Capileira**, the highest and most spoilt of these, has various hotels and craftshops, and – in one of its picturesque old houses – a museum devoted to local traditons, the

Museo Pedro de Alarcón. The tiny village of **Bubión** shows fewer signs of tourism than the other two villages, but it has now a Sufi centre and an English-run school offering 'contact with Spanish rural society'. West of **Pampaneira**, 4 km along the Órgiva road, a track to the right marked *'O. Sel. Ling.'* ascends steeply to a famous Buddhist centre where those in need of a spiritual retreat can stay in small stone huts clinging to the upper slopes of the Sierra Nevada. The centre was founded by Tibetan monks in 1982, and served that year as the official Spanish residence of the Dalai Lama, who named it after the Tibetan for 'Place of the Clear Light'. Visitors are requested not to kill ('not even the smallest insect'), not to rob, not to lie, not to take drugs, cigarettes or alcohol, and not to indulge in 'inappropriate sexual conduct'. At the entrance is a dazzlingly painted Tibetan *stupa* commanding views over the Alpujarra that make you almost feel you are in Tibet.

The road east of Pampaneira runs above terraced fields with views over the range of the Alpujarras, the slopes of which have been made barren and arid by ruthless exploitation of their timber. After 5 km you could turn right to make a short detour to **Mecina Fondales**, where Gerald Brenan bought a house in his old age; outside, partly hidden among trees, is a bridge of possibly Roman origin built to carry the old road from Granada to Almería; further down is the hauntingly tranquil village of **Ferreirola**. Back on the main road and continuing east you will pass after **Portugos** the delightful Fonda de Los Castaños, an old-fashioned inn hidden among chestnut trees and run by an elderly couple who will cook home-made sausages for you on the open fire of their spacious bar-cum-sitting-room: though the rooms here are basic, there is no better place to stay in the whole of the Alpujarra. From a point slightly further along the road you can walk across fields and through bushes to a rocky outcrop known mysteriously as the *mezquita* or 'mosque'. This panoramically located site, poised high above the gorge of the Trevélez River, is sometimes thought to have been used in Moorish times as a rock-hewn minaret; more fanciful interpreters have seen in it the remains of a temple to Minerva erected by Greeks who had come to the area in search of precious minerals. Returning to the road and passing **Busquístar**, with its pleasantly quiet and little spoilt lower village, you come to **Trevélez**, which, at 1500 m, is the highest community not only in the region but in the whole of Spain (and one of the highest in Europe too). Numerous hippies settled here in the 1970's, and many tourists visit the place today, most of them attracted by its reputation for cured hams, which can be tasted in all the many village bars. To leave the tourist trail completely, head off 10 km after Trevélez on to the road leading to **Cástaras**, a parched and very poor village from which a narrow, unasphalted road leads to the similarly neglected village of **Nieles**. Heading east after Nieles you will join after 10 km the Alpujarra's principal road, the C332, which runs from here west to Órgiva (along the district's southern half) and north to Yegen and the province of Almería. You can deviate briefly towards Órgiva to visit the small town of **Cádiar**, which Brenan described as 'the navel of the Alpujarra'. This ordinary-looking place comes alive in early October with a popular wine festival in which wine is freely distributed from the fountain in the main square. The town is also associated with the instigator of the second morisco uprising, Fernando de Córdoba y Valor, who is better known under his adopted Moorish name of Aben Humaya: it was under a large olive tree half-way between Cádiar and the neighbouring village of Narila that he crowned himself in 1568 'King of the Andalucíans'. This event would inspire a pioneering work in the history of Spanish Romantic drama – Francisco Martínez de la Rosa's *Aben Humaya, or the Revolt of the Moors under Philip II* (1830). The reputed tree, or presumably a descendant of it, is hidden from the road in private property; but at Narila itself is a half-collapsed old house said to have belonged to the famous rebel.

Yegen, 15 km northeast of Cádiar, is the village so memorably chronicled in Brenan's *South from Granada* (1957): you can understand how Brenan was attracted less by the architecture (which he found ugly) than by the sweeping views over terraces of olive and chestnut trees towards the gaunt Sierra de Gador and the eroded wastes of the eastern Alpujarra. The house where Brenan stayed, marked by a plaque, is at the top of the village, and has been much altered in recent years. There is a small and pleasant shaded square in the lower part of the village, with a fountain, a parish church with a well preserved artesonado ceiling, and a Village Hall with a permanent exhibition of photographs of Brenan and other local celebrities. A larger and livelier place than Yegen is the neighbouring village of **Valor**, the central square of which is animated every September by the oldest and most famous of the Alpujarra's 'Moors and Christians' pageants; this community play of renaissance origin uses a 19th-century script incorporating the story of the morisco rebel Aben Humaya, who was born at Valor (his supposed birthplace is a modernized old house marked by a recent plaque referring to his role in seeking 'freedom for Al-Andalus'). Just beyond Valor, at **Mecina Alfahar**, is a road to LACALAHORRA by way of the Puerto de la Ragua; in the course of the ascent the sea becomes visible, seemingly suspended high over the range of the Alpujarras. The main road east from Mecina Alfahar takes you into the Almerían Alpujarra (see LAUJAR DE ANDARAX) after passing the town of **Ugíjar**, from where an adventurous short trip could be be made to **Las Canteras** (head south on the Murtas road, and then turn off on to the marked track to your left). This remote hamlet, probably unchanged since Brenan's day, looks south to a rocky peak towering over a loop in the Ugíjar River. The arduous forty minute walk to the top of the peak takes you to a virtually unvisited Moorish castle, the ruins of which, barely distinguishable at times from the rocks, include an intact Moorish water cistern. The truly sublime views embrace to the east a deep gorge lying under the shadow of the Sierra de Gador; the terrifyingly wild landscape falls within territory that Boabdil had secured for himself in a secret deal made with the Catholic Kings in 1491 (see LAUJAR DE ANDARAX).

OSUNA [3D], one of the most beautiful small towns in Andalucía, is also one of the best preserved. Bordered to the west by fertile plains, and to the east by arid hills, the town had barely been developed on its outskirts until very recently, when a large hospital and housing scheme were built on its eastern side. It was not so long ago that a horse-drawn cart led you from the railway station to the town centre, and even today the town's main laundry service is operated by the nuns of the Convent of Santa Catalina (appropriately of the order of the Immaculate Conception). More surprisingly, considering Osuna's artistic and architectural wealth, the place has as yet scarcely been affected by tourism.

An important town in Iberian times, Osuna became known to the Romans as Urso and took the side of Pompey in the Civil War against Caesar. Despite this, the town prospered more than ever after being finally subdued by Caesar, and enjoyed the privileges of being able to mint its own coins and having its own legislature: in the Archaeological Museum of Madrid are ten famous bronze tablets recording the town's statutes. Under the Moors the town lost much of its former importance, and only began to recover after Ferdinand III's capture of Osuna in 1239. Given by Alfonso the Wise to the Order of Calatrava in 1264, the seigneury of the town later passed into the hands of the commander of this order, Don Pedro Girón. It was in the 16th century, under Don Juan Téllez Girón, 4th Count of Ureña, that Osuna emerged as a major cultural centre, complete with a university founded in 1548. In 1562 the Girón family was elevated to the title of Dukes of Osuna. The presence of aristocrats and wealthy landowners led to the creation of numerous fine palaces

Tiles at Osuna

St. Jerome, by Ribera

here right up to the late 18th century. Osuna has still the reputation of being an élitist place, and it differs from many other towns in Seville province by the persistence here of a very rigid social structure.

Osuna is built on a steep slope, and its main square and principal street are in the upper part of town. As you walk up the Calle Sevilla towards the main square the horizon is dominated by the west façade of the town's Collegiate Church, which stands in isolation at the top of the hill. Just above the square is the Mesón del Duque, a most attractive restaurant with a considerable reputation for its traditional Andalucían food. Continuing up to the church, you will pass the town's small and recently opened archaeological museum, housed in a tower which once formed part of the town's walls: inside is a col lection of mainly Roman finds, including a fascinating display of medical instruments. The Convent of the Encarnación, founded in 1621 by the 4th Duke of Osuna, is further up the hill, and can be visited: its most remarkable feature is the cloister, extensively decorated with ceramic tiles featuring amusing figurative scenes of minimal religious content, such as those representing the five senses. The north façade of the massive Collegiate Church rises above the convent, occupying the site of a church belonging to the town's former castle.

The Collegiate Church was begun in 1534 and richly endowed by the 4th Count of Ureña, who provided it with an abbot, four dignitaries, ten canons, and at least thirty-four other functionaries. Though not fully complete until the 18th century, the greater part of the building is of the early 16th century, and is one of Andalucía's most harmonious renaissance structures. The exterior is largely undecorated, apart from its classical plateresque west portal, inspired by a work by the Florentine artist Benedetto da Maiano, and supporting a bas-relief damaged –

according to Richard Ford – by the pot-shots of French soldiers looking to amuse themselves. The terrace in front of this portal stands above a slope densely covered in cacti, and has wonderful views of Osuna and the surrounding countryside. This is a particularly good place to come to at sunset, for as the sun disappears below the plain, the portal facing it, known as the Puerta del Sol, turns from ochre to a deep gold. The light and spacious interior with elegant piers in pale grey stone has the simplicity of a Florentine renaissance church, with the exception of the late baroque chancel, a blaze of gold. The outstanding work of art inside the church is a dramatic *Crucifixion* by the leading 17th-century artist José Ribera. A series of four saints by Ribera can be seen in the renaissance sacristy, which is visited as part of a guided tour around the rooms adjoining the church. These paintings are of exceptionally high quality, the canvases representing *St. Jerome and the Angel* and *The Martyrdom of St. Bartholomew* being among the finest in this artist's œuvre: Ribera's characteristic emphasis on realistic detail such as wrinkles and veins is here combined with compositions of startling directness. Other highpoints of the guided tour are the tiny and enchanting plateresque cloister, and, quite especially, the Ducal Pantheon below it (see page 104). This burial place of the Dukes of Osuna takes the form of a church in miniature, and has some of the most exquisite renaissance ornamentation in Andalucía: of the sculptures here, one of the most interesting is an anonymous polychromed relief of *St. Jerome*, the saint's angular body having something of the realism and expressive pathos of Torrigiano's *St. Jerome* in the Museo de Bellas Artes in Seville (see page 113).

Behind the Collegiate Church is Osuna's former University (now a school), a simple renaissance structure with an unornamented arcaded courtyard, and an attractive small chapel. The path heading north from here passes near the former monastic church of the Merced, which has a most intricately carved late baroque tower; at present the rooms surounding the cloister are used by ceramic artists, but there have been plans for many years to turn the place into a hotel. Continuing along the path you will eventually reach the town's old and impressive quarries, a surrealistic landscape crowned by the ruins of a 16th-century hermitage. Returning from the quarries you can head back into the town centre by walking down the attractive Calle Granada, which heads on to the Calle Carrera, the town's animated main street. If you turn left in the direction of the town's main square you will pass the church of Santo Domingo, another of Osuna's renaissance buildings founded by the 4th Count of Ureña. On the opposite side of the street is the sharply descending Calle de San Pedro, on which stand the two most splendid of Osuna's many baroque palaces. The higher of these is the former Collegiate Chapter House, which has a frontispiece of 1776 featuring lively, undulating ornamentation framing an image of Seville's Giralda. Further down the street is the Palace of the Marqueses de Gomera, with a dazzlingly white façade topped by an agitated, asymmetrical skyline inspired by German rococo illustrations (see page 126). The excellently preserved interior has now been turned into a sumptuous hotel.

Collegiate Chapter House, Osuna

PALOS DE LA FRONTERA [3A] A friendly but characterless and heavily modernized village on the Río Tinto estuary, Palos attracts visitors purely through its associations with Christopher Columbus (see page 89ff). Columbus set sail from Palos on his first journey to America on 3 August 1492, and returned here on 15 March of the following year; the village is now known as 'the cradle of the Americas'. Immediately before setting off, Columbus attended mass at the 15th-century parish church of San Jorge, which stands at the northern end of the town. He is supposed to have left the church through its southern portal (attractively decorated in a mudéjar style) and to have sailed from the bay immediately below; beside the bay is a medieval well ('la Fontanilla') around which a hideous small park was built for the quincentenary celebrations of 1992. The main village street is named the Calle Colón (Columbus Street), and as you walk south along it from San Jorge to the Town Hall, you will pass at No. 24 the house which belonged to Palos' most famous son, Martín Alonso Pinzón, who accompanied Columbus on his first voyage (see page 91). This house, the most distinguished in the village, has been turned into a museum. On the southern outskirts of the town is the Avenida de América, which is lined with ceramic decorations listing all the countries of the Americas. The road south from here goes through fertile agricultural countryside before reaching a magnificent forest of pines, in the middle of which, surrounded by luxuriant gardens, is the 15th-century monastery of **La Rábida**, where Columbus spent much time before his first journey to America (see page 91). Replicas of the three ships he used are harboured immediately below, at La Muella de las Caravelas.

PEAL DEL BECERRO. In the Town hall of this unremarkable large village you should ask for the keys to the outlying Iberian tomb, which is the oldest of its kind in Spain, and enjoys a hill-top site commanding a magnificent panorama embracing the Sierras de Cazorla and Mágina.

PEÑARROYA PUEBLO NUEVO [1D], a depressed coal-mining town with a neo-gothic parish church in brick, an overall covering of soot, and numerous abandoned buildings, has the atmosphere of an industrial town of northern Europe transposed to an incongruously sunny setting. **Bélmez**, 7 km to the south on the N432 towards Córdoba, is a sinister small village with a Moorish castle dramatically thrust up on a tall pinnacle of rock; steps cut into the rock lead up almost vertically into the castle, from the top of which those not prone to vertigo can appreciate an extensive view over the bleak and parched surounding landscape.

PRIEGO DE CÓRDOBA [3F], built at the edge of a plateau, underneath the highest mountain in Córdoba province, is surrounded by a landscape of ravines, olive trees, and picturesque rock escarpments. Roman in origin, captured by the Christians in 1226, recaptured by the Arabs in 1330, the town was definitively in

Christian hands by 1370. In the 18th century Priego enjoyed an international reputation for its textiles, and it was during this period of great prosperity that this small town became one of the outstanding baroque centres of Andalucía, if not of Spain.

From the lively main square, the Plaza de Constantina, situated in an area of 19th- and early 20th-century buildings, it is an easy walk to the town's principal monuments. Standing some way from the others are two great 18th-century fountains that occupy a large and quiet square at the end of the Calle Rio. This square slopes gently up a hill, and at its lower end is the Fuente del Rey, divided into two basins, the largest of which is lined with 139 grotesque masks spouting water at a sculptural group representing a lion struggling with a dragon (by J. Álvarez Cubero); the other basin has at its centre a group of Neptune and Aphrodite. While this fountain takes its inspiration from the work of Italian baroque artists such as Bernini, the upper, more modest fountain, the Fuente de la Virgen de la Salud, is in an Italianate renaissance style, with bas-reliefs featuring Venus, Neptune and the Hydra.

Make your way back to the main square by way of the Calle Río (where there is an excellent restaurant of that name, serving such local specialities as *collejas*, a type of chard) and turn left onto the Calle Solana, which leads into the Plaza San Pedro. The church of San Pedro, a conventional 17th-century structure, is of interest mainly for its extravagant high altar designed by the great master of the Spanish baroque, Hurtado Izquierdo (see page 124f). Izquierdo, who was born at nearby LUCENA in 1669, died at Priego in 1728; his only work here is his San Pedro altar, which, by comparison with some of the anonymous baroque creations of the Priego school, is a very rational affair. The Plaza de San Pedro backs on to the town's much restored castle of Roman origin (this is now being restored again by the Town Hall, this time with a view to opening part of it to the public), the main façade of which overlooks the Plaza Abad Palomino, a square dramatically renovated in recent years in questionable taste. At the far end of this square is the parish church of the Asunción, which on the outside is a modest 16th-century structure with an attractive but unexceptional renaissance south portal. Nothing prepares you for the shock of its 18th-century interior, the finest in Priego and quite magnificent even in a European context. The ceiling of the simple 16th-century structure has been covered in an exuberant white stucco decoration, whipped up to a frothing frenzy over the chancel. But the best is yet to come: the chapel of the Sagrario of 1784, entered through a door off the left aisle, is a circular structure ringed by a balcony supported by angels, the whole overwhelming in its size, lightness, the vitality and complexity of its ornamentation, and the overall brilliance of its dazzlingly white and recently restored stucco-work (see page 126).

None other of the various 17th- and 18th-century churches of Priego is decorated to quite the same fanciful degree as that of the Asunción, though the stuccos

Santa Maria, Priego de Córdoba

in the chapel known as the Aurora are also well worth seeing. This chapel stands at the end of the Carrera de Álvarez, a street running off the Plaza Abad Palomino. Behind the chapel begins the most beautiful part of Priego, a corner of the town which hangs directly over a cliff and embraces the tiny medieval quarter of La Villa, an area of narrow white streets behind the church of the Asunción. The street which hugs the cliff is popular with evening strollers and has wonderful views over the unmistakably Andalucían landscape below.

The surrounding countryside has become increasingly exploited in recent years by rural tourism, as is exemplified in the Las Villas hotel complex outside **Zagrilla**, 6 km to the north. Zagrilla itself is a charming small village cooled by pools and fast-running streams.

QUESADA [2G] has an attractive hill-top position directly underneath the highest peak of the Cazorla range, Mt. Cabañas (2028 m). On the main square, housed in an unattractive modern building of make-shift appearance, is a museum opened in 1960 to display the works of the local painter, Rafael Zabaleta, who spent most of his life in Quesada. His own paintings, mainly of nudes and local scenes, are in a decorative sub-cubist style and would not look out of place in a tacky restaurant. But in the course of his life he seems to have made many important artist friends, and the museum has a photograph of him in the company of Salvador Dalí, and a room filled with lithographs dedicated to him by artists such as Picasso, Miró, Tapiès and Rafael Alberti; the key to this dire but curious museum can be had from the police station opposite.

The C323 south of Quesada leads up to the **Sanctuary of Tíscar**, impressively situated above rocks and olive trees, and erected over a Moorish fortress captured by the Christians in 1319; inside is a much venerated image of the Virgin, and a painting by Zabaleta representing the annual pilgrimage to the Sanctuary of Quesada. A stony track 5 km beyond Tíscar, manageable in a strong car, climbs up through forest almost to the summit of Mt. Cabañas and then descends to the **source of the Guadalquivir**. The source itself, marked by an inscription (see page 29), is of sentimental rather than aesthetic interest, but the fast-flowing river into which it turns runs through the beautiful forested valley which constitutes the heart of the National Park of Segura and Cazorla (see CAZORLA). Another, faster way of reaching the source from Quesada is to head north towards Cazorla, and then turn off to the right, passing by the hamlet of El Chorro. This road is also unasphalted, but is in better condition than the other one. Before it disappears into the pines there are magnificently extensive views over an apparent infinity of olive trees.

RONDA [4D], celebrated for its dramatic position, became one of the highpoints of the Romantic traveller's tour of Andalucía. This town, epitomizing Romantic ideals of the Sublime and the Picturesque, took on in the late 19th century the character of a genteel mountain resort; today the place is overrun with tourists, and its old quarter seems more like a large museum than a real town.

Standing on top of an amphitheatre of rock, Ronda is cleft in twain by the narrow vertiginous gorge of the Guadelvin. The gorge, spanned by a late 18th-century bridge (the Puente Nuevo), divides the old Moorish town from the Christian district of Mercadillo, founded after the Christian capture of Ronda in 1485. Virtually all the town's hotels are in the Mercadillo district, including the Edwardian-looking Hotel Reina Victoria, built by an English company in 1906 and occupying a spectacular position at the edge of the town's cliff. The German poet Rainer Maria Rilke stayed here between January and February of 1913, occupying Room No. 208; if you ask for the key to this room, you will find yourself in a small Rilke museum, containing documents of his stay, including his bill, which reveals that he drank

Tajo de Ronda, by J. F. Lewis

much tea and coffee, but no alcohol. There is a statue to Rilke in the hotel's beautiful grounds. Near these grounds, but separated from them by a locked gate, is the Paseo de los Ingleses, a spectacular path that heads south along the cliff to the turn-of-the-century gardens of the Merced, adjoining which is the second oldest bullring in Spain. Ronda occupies a critical position in the history of Spanish bull-fighting (see page 167), and an important museum of the sport is attached to the ring; every September, for the Ronda festival, a fight in 18th-century costume (a *Corrida Goyesca*) is put on here.

David and Lilian Bomberg near Ronda, 1956

Once across the bridge and into the old town, turn left down the steep Calle Mario de Paredes, and you will pass on your left the so-called Casa del Rey Moro, built in 1709 over a Moorish palace. Further down on the right is the curious renaissance façade of the Casa del Marqués de Salvatierra, which features carvings of Native American Indian inspiration; the interior, which can be visited, is crammed with renaissance to 19th-century antiques and pictures; an excellent view of the town's eastern fortifications can be had from its garden, which is shaded by a large *pínsapo* pine (see page 10). Below the palace you leave the town, passing in turn a renaissance and Moorish bridge; at the bottom of the hill turn right along the river and you will come to the enchanting remains of some Moorish baths. Returning to the Casa Salvatierra, make your way back up the hill along the Calle de Mario de Salvatierra, at the top of which is the minaret of a former mosque. Nearby, within another mosque, is the 16th-century hall church of Santa María la Mayor, with an interior inspired by that of Granada Cathedral. A few minutes' walk to the east takes you to the Casa Mondragón, originally the house of Ronda's last Moorish king, and later turned into the finest of the town's renaissance palaces. Next to this is a terrace containing an open-air bar much loved by tourists on account of its cliff-side views towards the Puente Nuevo. Even finer views are to be had from the Art Deco terraced gardens of the nearby Casa Don Bosco (Calle Tenorio 20); this early 20th-century building is now a Salesian College, and visitors are welcome.

A further opportuniy to admire Ronda's situation is provided by the rough path which descends steeply down from the river from below the Casa Mondragón.

However, the best walk you can do outside Ronda is to the **Hermitage of the Virgen de la Cabeza**, a walk much admired by Rilke. From Santa María la Mayor go south on the Calle Nuñez, and leave the town by what was originally its main gate, the Puerta Almocabar (before reaching this you will pass the attractive late 15th-century church of the Espiritu Santo). On the other side of the gate you enter the modern Barrio San Francisco, the main building of which is the monastery church of San Francisco, adorned with an attractive Isabelline plateresque portal. Heading west from the church you will immediately come to the main road to the coast. Turn left, and just before passing the last house turn right on to the path leading through fields of olive trees to the Hermitage (about half an hour's walk). The views towards distant Ronda are superb, particularly in the late afternoon or early evening, when the sun's rays directly illuminate the town's cliff-face. The English painter David Bomberg lived in a farm-house off this path during the 1950's, having first stayed in the town in 1933. His expressive views of Ronda, like his ones of Toledo, are among the finest landscapes ever painted of Spain, though they were little appreciated in his time. Unable to speak Spanish, and ridiculed locally for going everywhere on a donkey, he divided his last years in Ronda painting passionately and sharing his philosophy of art with a handful of British devotees, one of whom, the painter Miles Richmond, had to rush him to Gibraltar when he fell fatally ill early in 1957; he died two days after his return to England.

Two of the most popular excursions from Ronda are to the extraordinary prehistoric caves of **La Pileta** (15 km southwest, past Benaoján; see page 56), and to the Roman ruins of **Ronda la Vieja**, 16 km northwest along the MA 449 (see page 63).

SABIOTE [2G], a pretty, unspoilt, hill-village with cobbled streets, is still largely surrounded by its medieval walls, from which there are beautiful views over olive trees to the nearby Sierra de Cazorla (see CAZORLA). In the centre of the village, at its highest point, is the parish church of San Pedro Apostól, which has a charming if crudely carved south portal in a classical plateresque style. The Calle Castillo descends from here to the castle and has two houses (Nos. 1 and 3) with impressive 16th-century façades. The ruined castle, Roman in origin, but rebuilt by the Moors, is particularly striking for its massive renaissance additions, with crumbling classical detailing of Piranesi-like proportions; Andrés de Vandelvira (see page 102) is said to have been responsible for these. The nearby main road from Úbeda to Albacete (the N322) runs parallel to the Sierra de Cazorla and hugs the summit of a long ridge in between the valleys of the the Rivers Guadalimar and Guadalquivir; there are excellent views on either side. Even more extensive views are to be had from the village of **Iznatoraf**, which lies just off this road, about 33 km east of Sabiote. The village is perched on top of an exceptionally steep hill, and, with its maze of alleys lined with tall white houses, has a distinctly Moorish character.

SANLÚCAR DE BARRAMEDA [4B]: Lying at the mouth of the Guadalquivir, directly in front of the wild, tree-fringed expanses of the Coto Doñana, Sanlúcar de Barrameda has the character of a colonial town thrown up on some tropical coast. Vegetation pushes through the crumbling masonry of its convents, churches and palaces, its many vestiges of an impressive history. Yet Sanlúcar is not a sad place absorbed in nostalgic dreams of its past. The life which is led here is so lively, enchanting and special that it is easy to imagine the town as the setting of a novel by a 'magical realist' from Latin America.

A small agricultural village in Roman times, and then given its castle by the Moors, Sanlúcar was captured by the Christians in 1264 and entrusted as a fief to Guzmán the Good, whose descendants were the powerful Dukes of Medina-Sidonia. With its strategic position on the Guadalquivir, Sanlúcar became one of the major ports of Spain after 1492: Columbus embarked from here on his third journey to America in 1498, and for Magellan the place was the point of both departure and return on his pioneering voyage around the world in 1519-22. The commercial prosperity and cosmopolitan life led here in the 16th century were quite remarkable, and the population even reached about 50,000 at a time when Madrid's was only 12,000. The town's decline set in by the early 17th century, but was almost halted once and forever two centuries later, when Charles IV's infamous minister Godoy, who had a mistress here, was seriously considering turning the place into the capital of Spain. In the mid 19th century the French Duke of Montpensier had a summer palace built here, and since then the town has been very popular as a summer resort.

A quiet place for much of the year, Sanlúcar becomes congested with holiday-makers in August, though few of these are from further away than Seville, let alone from abroad. Sanlúcar is not a place for those who love clean beaches and good swimming. Its appeal as a resort is for those who are happy to spend most of their days sitting in bars, talking and observing people, sipping the excellent local fortified wine known as Manzanilla (see pages 184-5), and tasting what must surely be among the best food in Spain. A great variety of vegetables are cultivated in the fields behind the town, while a magnificent and celebrated range of fish and seafood is brought in daily to the adjoining port of Bonanza: particularly famous are the *acedías* (small sole), *pijotes* (whiting), *cazón* (dogfish), *rape* (angler fish), and, above all *langostinos* (prawns), for which people make a special journey to Sanlúcar. Almost every one of the town's countless bars serves the most excellent food, sometimes at ridiculously cheap prices.

Sanlúcar is divided into an upper and lower town (El Barrio Alto and El Barrio Bajo), the former traditionally living off agriculture, the latter off fishing: it is often thought that the town's finest meat and vegetable dishes are to be found in the Barrio Alto, and the best fish ones in the Barrio Bajo. The oldest part of Sanlúcar is in any case set quite some way from the coast, and begins near the town's principal commercial thoroughfare, the Calles Ancha and San Juan. The axis of these two

Sanlúcar at the turn of the century

connecting steets is the town's main square, which is an excellent place to begin a tour of Sanlúcar. The square's only drawback as a starting-point is that you may find it difficult to leave it, for it is a charming and animated place lined on all sides with tempting open-air bars and cafés: one of the cafés is the Ibense, which was the original of a famous chain of Spanish ice-cream parlours founded in the early years of this century. From the Plaza head south past the Town Hall towards the upper town, and you will arrive almost immediately at the small square of San Roque: a small plaque on the chapel of this name records that Velázquez's teacher, Antonio Pacheco, was born at Sanlúcar (see page 115). If you look to your right at the end of the square you will see the convent of the Madre de Dios, where you can buy another local speciality, *Tocinos de Cielo*, which are tiny and very rich versions of crème caramel. In the mornings the Plaza de San Roque is a particularly animated place, for it adjoins the town's market building, which is one of the best in Andalucía, both for its beautifully white interior, and the staggering range of produce on offer. The market can be entered from the Calle Bretones, the continuation of which, the Cuesta de Belén, climbs into the upper town, passing a low building adorned on the outside with some strange and badly eroded late gothic arches (this is thought by some to have been a group of shops). Near the top of the hill, on the right-hand side, are the gates leading into the amusing neo-Moorish Palace of the Dukes of Montpensier: the entrance lodge, inexplicably in the style of a Swiss chalet, is now used by the very friendly local police, who will gladly allow you to wander around the place's small park and into its fantastical courtyard. Turn left at the top of the hill, on to the Calle Luis de Eguiluz, and you will find yourself in front of the church of Santa María de la O, which has a finely decorated gothic plateresque façade, and an interior featuring a splendid artesonado ceiling. The church is attached to the Palace of the Dukes of Medina-Sidonia, which can be visited officially on Sunday afternoons or by trying your luck with the doorbell on other days: quite apart from its atmospheric 16th- to 18th-century interior, and the wonderful views over the Coto Doñana, the palace has one of Spain's richest private archives, containing a vast amount of documentation relating to the Armada (the archive can be consulted on previous application to the Duchess).

The Calle Luis de Eguilaz, as it heads east towards the castle, passes bodegas on both sides. At No. 11 is the house belonging to the largest manzanilla-producing firm, Antonio Barbadillo: the house has a charming courtyard adorned with a bust of the firm's founder; on the first floor are the firm's offices, where you can arrange to go on a tour of their bodegas. The large Moorish castle at the end of the street is in a ruinous condition, but a pleasant flight of steps by its side leads you down into the lower town, depositing you eventually on the Calle Ancha. Every 15th August this street is covered with a brilliant 'floral carpet' made out of salt and coloured sawdust; the townspeople are up for most of the previous night watching and taking part in its assembly. At the eastern end of the street is the imposing renaissance church of San Domingo.

North from the main square is a wide tree-lined promenade which leads down to the coast; many amusing and impressive turn-of-the-century villas can be seen in this part of the town, particularly if you head off to the right towards the end of the promenade and walk to the fishing district of **Bajo de Guía**. Bajo de Guía has recently been tidied up by the construction of a modern promenade, but still retains its friendly, ramshackle character. Its row of sea-facing bars includes that of the Restaurant Bigote, which has its own fishing fleet and a reputation as one of the best places to eat fish and sea-food in the whole of Andalucía. You should certainly try the tapas in its perpetually animated bar (no seating), but if you want to have a sit-down meal you might be better off in the neighbouring Mirador de Doñana, which now rivals the Bigote in quality and has the advantage of magnificent views from the upstairs dining room. For a few days towards the end of August the Sanlúcar beach, right up to Bajo de Guía, is the scene of horse-racing, a tradition which goes back to the late 19th century, and makes for an exciting spectacle.

At Bajo de Guía itself there are motor boats and a ferry service to take you across to the **Coto Doñana**. Landrovers on the other side will drive you along the Coto's wide sandy beach and deposit you at a place where the water is cleaner than it is at the actual mouth of the Guadalquivir; the beach, however, is dirty for the whole of its twenty kilometres. The pleasures of coming here are its quiet seclusion, beautiful views and wonderful array of shells; in the early evening you might even be surprised by the arrival of deer at the water's edge. In theory it is possible at low tide to drive your own car all the way to the popular modern resort of **Matalascañas**, but skill, bravery and a very strong car are ideally required to do this. To visit the interior of the Coto, you have to go on a guided tour by Landrover (tickets for these are available fom the Hotel Guadalquivir in Sanlúcar; it is advisable to book a long time ahead in the summer months).

A small road following the Guadalquivir north from Sanlúcar leads, after 4 km, to **Bonanza**, which is well worth visiting for its afternoon fish auction; further north still are salt flats and the haunting pine wood of **La Algaida**. The popular resort of **Chipiona**, 9 km to the west of Sanlúcar, has clean though impossibly crowded beaches; the coast to the south of here includes the pleasant **Playa de la Ballena**, but this whole area is soon to be transformed into a massive holiday centre.

SANTA OLALLA DEL CALA [2B/C]: The extensive, well-preserved battlements that stand in isolation above the village of Santa Olalla del Cala make a powerful impression on those travelling between Seville and Extremadura along the N630. At the foot of this castle is an attractive 14th-century church with a horseshoe-shaped west portal. From here you reach the castle by clambering up a small rock face, entering through a hole in its walls. The castle, dating from after 1293, was heavily remodelled in the 1460's and used as the local cemetery in the last century. The north side of the hill falls down directly to stark, rolling countryside.

Some 15 km to the west of the village along the C435 is the beautifully situated village of **Zufre**, which clings to the top of a hill, and has extensively preserved sections of its original 12th-century fortifications. Its large parish church in brick and pink stone is flanked by palm trees, and perched on the hill's edge. On its northern side is an enchanting small square with a fountain and a quaintly arcaded 16th-century Town Hall.

SEGURA DE LA SIERRA [1H], at a height of over 1,100 m, is a charming small village with panoramic views over the wild, mountainous and densely pine-forested landscape of this extreme northeastern corner of Jaén province. As soon as you enter the village through its medieval gate, you will find on the right-hand side of the street the Town Hall, a 16th-century building which was originally a Jesuit College; ask in here for the keys to the castle and to the Moorish baths. The village's tiny central square is shortly beyond the Town Hall, and you can descend from here to the small Moorish baths (in the basement of a house below the bakery), passing by an attractive 16th-century fountain adorned with the coat of arms of Charles V. Above the square is the village's only official accommodation, a cheap and beautiful old hostal tastefully decorated inside with antiques. Its little-spoilt look notwithstanding, the village attracts numerous holiday-makers in the summer months, and, directly above the village is the sort of modern bar (the Bar Terraza Ben Issam) which you would expect to find in a sea resort; the views from its terrace are magnificent. An unasphalted road behind this winds its way up to the large, well-preserved castle at the very top of the mountain on which the village is built.

Twenty kilometres south of Segura is the village of **Hornos**, which sits on a steep outcrop of rock above the northern shores of the reservoir of El Tranco (see CAZORLA); there is a good viewing balcony next to the Town Hall. From Hornos the C321 meanders east through mountainous and sparsely populated countryside in the direction of Granada and Almería provinces; once across the Segura range, the forest thins out, and the landscape becomes increasingly arid. At the village of **Pontones**, 35 km from Hornos, a short, unasphalted road to the right leads to the source of the River Segura, now enclosed in a particularly ugly picnic area.

SETENIL DE LAS BODEGAS [4D] seemed until comparatively recently one of the lost corners of Spain. When I first came here in 1974 the stream that runs through its centre was little more than an open drain, and a popular diversion among the local children was to throw a stone at a bush to see how many rats would jump out; the neighbouring village of **Torre-Alhaquime** was then so inbred that its population appeared mainly to consist of the physically and mentally deformed. The area now shows signs of new prosperity, and a growing number of tourists are coming here from nearby RONDA. But Setenil will always be one of the most curious villages in Andalucía on account of its being bizarrely situated within the bend of a gorge formed by the River Trejo. A great many of the houses are actually tucked away in the gorge's caves and seem almost to be supporting the rock above them.

Setenil de las Bodegas

As the name 'Setenil de las Bodegas' suggests, all the old houses in the village have wine cellars, for at one time the place lived largely off viticulture; the phylloxera epidemic at the end of the last century killed off all the vines, and caused the economic slump from which the village has only just emerged.

The layout of Setenil is slightly baffling, though you will have a clearer idea of it if you walk up to its parish church, which stands in the middle, and commands some of the best views of the town. The building itself has a dull, modern exterior but a fine late gothic interior with splendid vaulting: the vestry reputedly contains an item donated by Isabel La Católica. Slightly lower down from the church is the local Assize Court, situated in the old Tribunal: it has an excellent artesonado ceiling surrounded by an inscription recording the victory of Ferdinand and Isabel over the Moors. On the upper outskirts of the village is the welcoming Venta Mirabueno, which produces outstanding home-made charcuterie and cheese.

SEVILLE [3C], (map in back cover) the capital of Andalucía and the fourth largest town in Spain, has a long and distinguished history going back to Iberian times. Greeks, Phoenicians, and Carthaginians settled here, and, after 47 BC the place became one of the leading towns in Roman Baetica. Julius Caesar stayed here, and the emperors Hadrian and Trajan were born in the neighbouring settlement of Itálica. The Visigothic archbishop St. Isidore turned Seville in the 6th century into a major European centre of learning, and when the Moors first came to Spain in 732 they made the town briefly the capital of al-Andalus. In the 11th century Seville was the most important of Spain's *taifa* or city-states, and in the late 12th and 13th centuries the town enjoyed enormous prosperity under the Almohads. Captured by Ferdinand III in 1258, Seville later became a favoured residence of Spanish kings, in particular Pedro the Cruel. But it was not until after 1492, with the discovery of the New World, that Seville entered the most important phase in its history, becoming in the 16th century one of the liveliest and most cosmopolitan cities of the western world (see page 104ff). Economic and political decline set in in the early 17th century, but this was also the period when such remarkable artists as Velázquez, Zurbarán and Murillo worked in Seville (see page 115ff). When in the 19th century travellers started flocking to Spain from all over Europe, Seville emerged as one of the country's major tourist centres, attracting people not simply because of its monuments and superlative 17th-century paintings, but also because it represented to these travellers all that was most attractive about Spain. It was a city of jasmine-scented sensuality, the birthplace of Carmen and Don Juan, and the scene of endless exuberant secular and religious festivities.

For most of the 19th century Seville remained surrounded by its medieval walls, and these looked out directly on to the Guadalquivir river and to the surrounding fertile plains. By the end of the century most of the walls had been pulled down, and the city had begun to expand outwards to the detriment of its old core. The

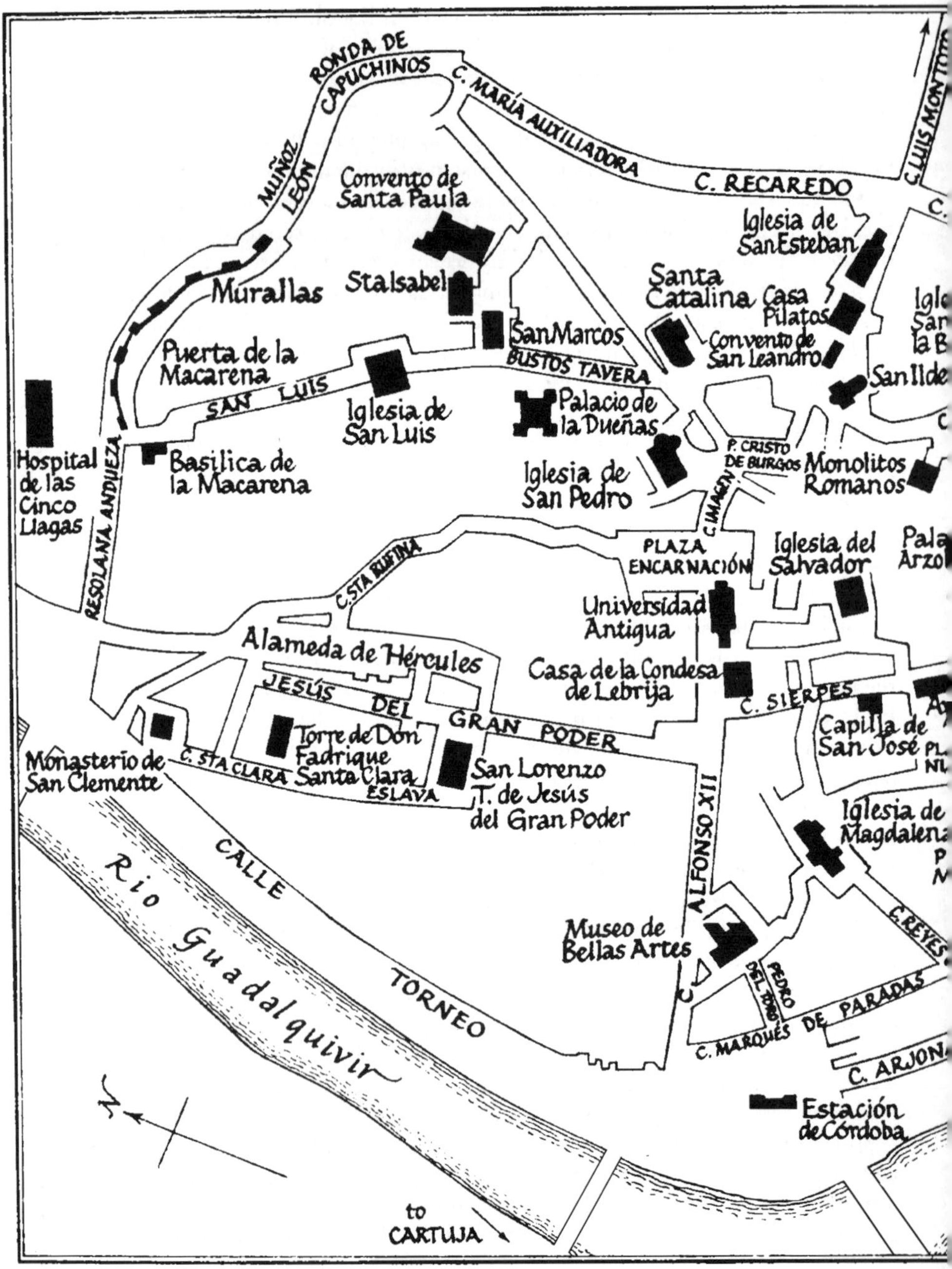
RONDA DE CAPUCHINOS
C. MARÍA AUXILIADORA
C. RECAREDO
MUÑOZ LEÓN
Convento de Santa Paula
Iglesia de San Esteban
Santa Catalina
Casa Pilatos
Convento de San Leandro
Murallas
Sta Isabel
San Marcos
BUSTOS TAVERA
Puerta de la Macarena
SAN LUIS
Iglesia de San Luis
Palacio de la Dueñas
Hospital de las Cinco Llagas
Basilica de la Macarena
RESOLANA ANDUEZA
Iglesia de San Pedro
P. CRISTO DE BURGOS
Monolitos Romanos
C. IMAGEN
C. STA RUFINA
PLAZA ENCARNACIÓN
Iglesia del Salvador
Universidad Antigua
Alameda de Hércules
Casa de la Condesa de Lebrija
C. SIERPES
Capilla de San José
JESÚS DEL GRAN PODER
Torre de Don Fadrique
Santa Clara
ESLAVA
San Lorenzo
T. de Jesús del Gran Poder
Monasterio de San Clemente
C. STA CLARA
C. ALFONSO XII
CALLE TORNEO
Rio Guadalquivir
Museo de Bellas Artes
PEDRO DEL TORO
C. MARQUÉS DE PARADAS
C. REYES
Estación de Córdoba
to CARTUJA
N

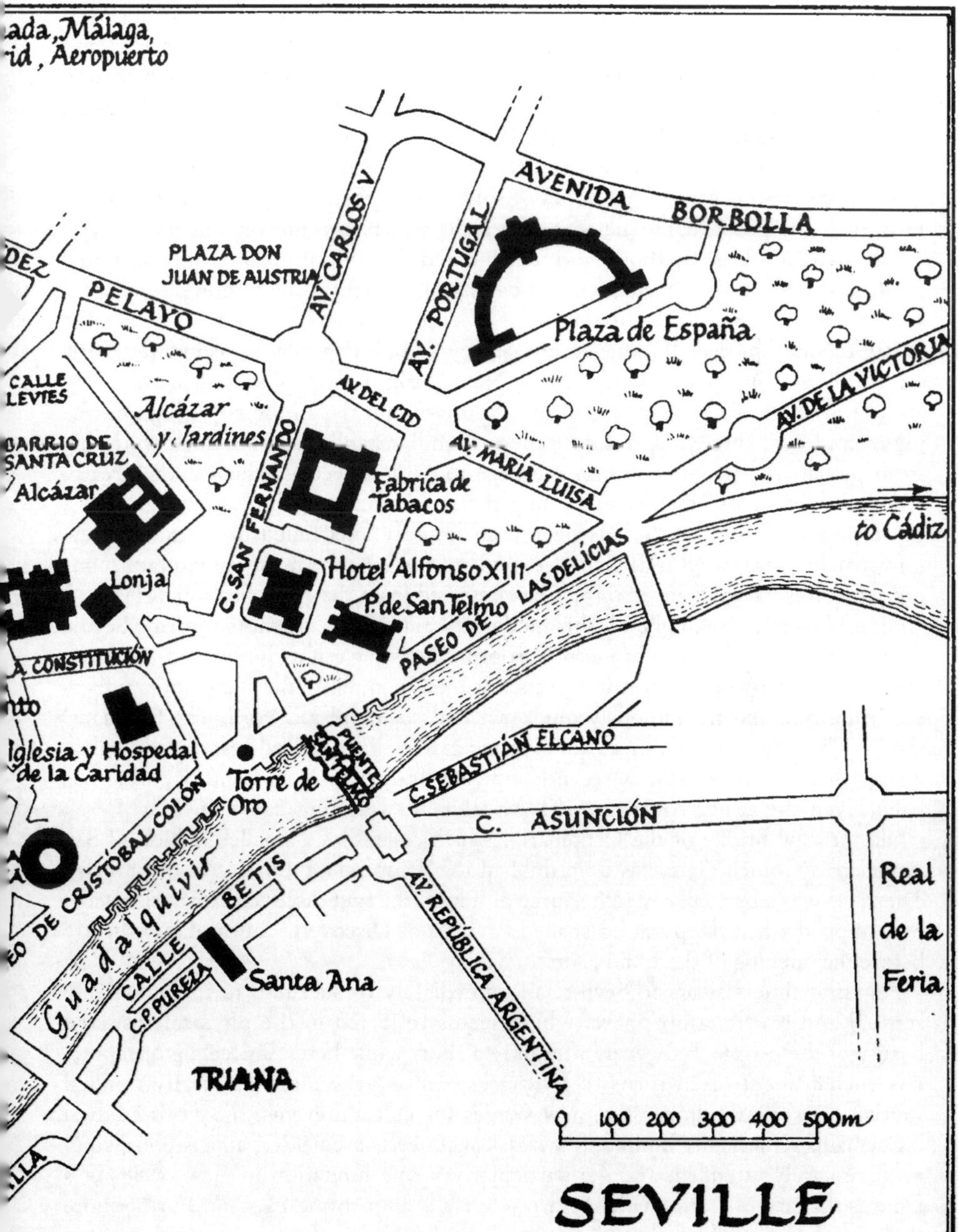

ada, Málaga,
rid, Aeropuerto
AVENIDA BORBOLLA
PLAZA DON JUAN DE AUSTRIA
PELAYO
AV. CARLOS V
AV. PORTUGAL
Plaza de España
AV. DE LA VICTORIA
CALLE LEVIES
Alcázar y Jardines
AV. DEL CID
AV. MARÍA LUISA
BARRIO DE SANTA CRUZ
Alcázar
C. SAN FERNANDO
Fabrica de Tabacos
to Cádiz
PASEO DE LAS DELICIAS
Hotel Alfonso XIII
Lonja
P. de San Telmo
A CONSTITUCIÓN
Iglesia y Hospedal de la Caridad
Torre de Oro
PUENTE SAN TELMO
C. SEBASTIÁN ELCANO
C. ASUNCIÓN
PASEO DE CRISTÓBAL COLÓN
Guadalquivir
BETIS
CALLE
C.P. PUREZA
Santa Ana
AV. REPÚBLICA ARGENTINA
Real de la Feria
TRIANA
0 100 200 300 400 500m
SEVILLE

Ibero-American Exhibition of 1929 promised to bring new life to Seville, and indeed gave to the city an elegant new focus in the enormous area of parkland and luxury residences created to the south of the cathedral. But the rush of workers into Seville in search of jobs initiated the unplanned urban sprawl that would bring chaos and congestion to the city by the 1970's.

The decision to hold in Seville in 1992 one of the most important World Exhibitions this century raised hopes of solving the worst of these urban problems. However, the prospect of the so-called EXPO was by no means universally welcomed here, not least by those who remembered that the city had been bankrupted by the Exhibition of 1929 and was still paying off its debts. Many thought the occasion would primarily benefit the more corrupt members of the ruling Socialist Party; others doubted the long-term viability of building new transport terminals on a scale worthy of London, Paris or New York; most people looked anxiously ahead to the EXPO's aftermath, and the almost certain rise in the city's high unemployment level. These fears did not prove groundless; and the city today is suffering from perhaps its worst recession ever, a noticeable effect of which is the greatly reduced number of Sevillians parading the streets on weekday nights. Yet, on a more positive note, Seville has been considerably smartened up, a radical new infrastructure has eased traffic congestion, and some of the most stunning of modern structures have enhanced rather than deterred from the city's perennial elegance. And, no less encouragingly, all this modernity and all the attempts to bring Seville more into line with other modern European cities have not diminished the more endearingly idiosyncratic features of its inhabitants, notably their late hours, inherent hedonism, and the famously quick wit that so impressed Ford. The Sevillians' sense of humour and genius at devising nicknames have indeed responded well to recent changes and crises. A recently opened branch of Marks and Spencers has been given the easier-to-pronounce Andalucían-sounding name of 'Mari Pere', while the new bridge of the Centenario, which resembles a smaller version of San Francisco's Golden Gate, has been dubbed the 'Paquillo' (a diminutive of Francis). The EXPO was a particularly rich source of jokes: 'the first discovery was fire' everyone quipped when the pyramid-shaped Pavilion of Discoveries burnt down shortly before the opening of the Exhibition.

Few first-time visitors to Seville fail immediately to succumb to its pervasively sensual and exotic atmosphere, which seems reflected in the physical ease and beauty of the people. However, after only a short while here, this feeling of rapturous enchantment often turns to frustration among the more culturally-minded tourists. Despite the impressive new venues for cultural events, the city's cultural life remains remarkably limited: few classical concerts are held, drama is poor, cinemas are barely attended, and – a particularly ironic limitation in view of Seville's fame as the city of Carmen and Figaro – opera is almost non-existent. Furthermore there is a scarcity of good guide-books to lead you through the labyrinth of little

The Giralda

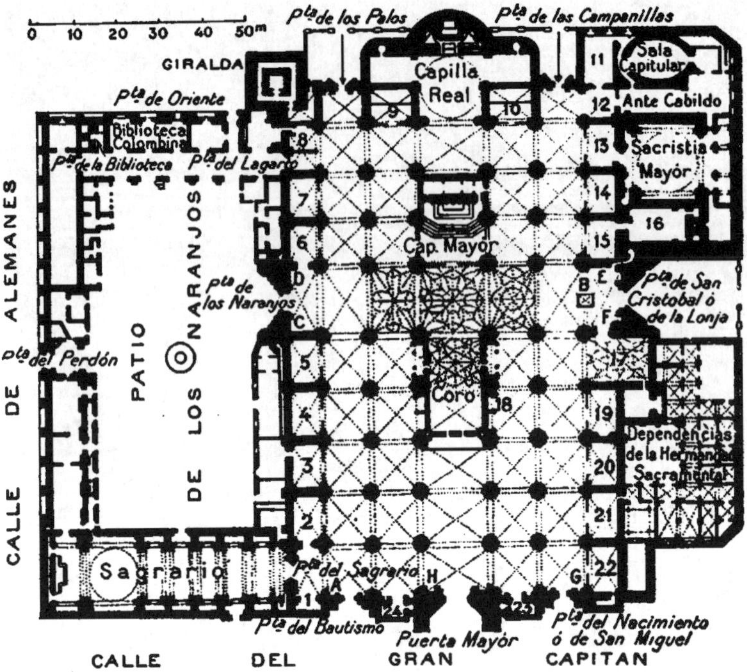

Seville Cathedral

A. Altar de la Visitación
B. Tomb of Christopher Columbus
C. Altar de la Virgén de Belém
D. Altar de la Asunción
E. Altar de la Santa Cruz
F. Altar de la Gamba
G. Altar de la Nacimiento
H. Altar de N. S. del Consuelo
1. Capilla de los Jacomes
2. Capilla del Bautisterio
3. Capilla de Escalas
4. Capilla de Santiago
5. Capilla de San Francisco
6. Capilla de las Doncellas
7. Capilla de los Evangelistas
8. Capilla del Pilar
9 Capilla de San Pedro
10. Capilla de la Concepción Grande
11 Contaduria Mayor
12. Capilla del Mariscal
13. Antesala
14. Capilla de San Andrés
15. Capilla de los Dolores
16. Sacristia de los Cálices
17. Capilla de la Antigua
18. Capilla de la Concepción Chica
19. Capilla de San Hermengildo
20. Capilla de San José
21 Capilla de Santa Ana
22. Capilla de San Laureano
23. Capilla de San Isidro
24. Capilla de San Leandro

known attractions to be found beyond the city's relatively small tourist district: Seville, like its inhabitants, is far more difficult to get to know than its apparent openness suggests, and has a large hidden side that is symbolized by the extent to which its old centre is occupied by the grounds of private palaces and closed order convents. In the pages that follow I have given only the most hurried overview of what the city has to offer, but in doing just this I have probably mentioned several places unknown even to the Sevillians themselves. Finally, I should add that the more you enjoy Seville the less time you will probably devote to conventional sightseeing. This famed city of endless socializing and lingering in bars is a place where the best of intentions are liable to go astray: the moment when visitors can guiltlessly abandon much of what they have set out to do and happily move on to the after-lunch drink marks an important step in adapting to the life of this most infuriating but entrancing of cities.

The one part of the city that not even the laziest tourist will miss is the southeastern corner of the old town taken up by the Cathedral, the Alcázar and their immediate surroundings. The **Cathedral** itself is so vast, and so filled with treasures that at least half a day is needed to see it (see page 109). The main entrance portal, the Puerta Mayor, is on the cathedral's western façade, and is adorned with naturalistic late 15th-century carvings by Pedro Millán and Lorenzo Mercadante, who were also responsible for the carvings on the two flanking portals (the Puertas del Bautismo and del Nacimiento); early 16th-century carvings by Miguel Perrin decorate the portals of the eastern façade, while the northern Puerta del Perdón (the entrance to the Patio de los Naranjos) is a superb example of mudéjar craftsmanship incorporating elements of the original Almohad mosque. The tourist entrance to the cathedral is now through a door next to the Giralda bell tower, on the building's northeastern side. Once inside, it is easy to become disoriented in the cavernous gloom, and much persistence and good eyesight are needed to track down the numerous scattered works by artists such as Pedro de Campaña, Alejo Fernandez, Morales, Murillo, Zurbarán, Valdés Leal, Juan de Arce and Martínez Montañes. The one unavoidable work is the late gothic high altar, begun in 1482 by Dancart and said to be the largest and most elaborate in Spain. A selection of paintings, including one by Goya, has been gathered together in the Sacristía de los Calices on the southern side of the cathedral. Adjoining this, and far too rarely visited, are the Sacristía Mayor and the oval Chapter House, two impressive renaissance structures designed by the great Diego de Siloe (see page 101).

The Sevillians, while generally critical of the functions that take place within the cathedral, are enamoured of the building, and think that its one ugly feature is the crocodile carcase (known as the *legarto* or 'lizard') that hangs, curiously, in a side chapel off the Patio de los Naranjos. They are not too keen either about climbing their beloved **Giralda** (see page 84), and have the reputation for doing so only when they want to commit suicide; the view of Seville from the top of this former minaret is in fact well worth the climb. In between the cathedral and the Alcázar is the former Exchange or *Lonja* (see page 110), an austere late 16th-century building now housing the **Archivio de las Indias** (a selection of old documents about Spain's colonial empire is always on show here). Directly facing the southern side of the Lonja, on the Calle Santo Tomás, is the recently created **Museo de Arte Contemporaneo**, which puts on little-visited exhibitions, and has

Tapestry on display in the Alcázar

a small permanent collection of 20th-century Spanish art. The **Alcázar** and its gardens are entered from the adjoining Plaza de la Contratacción (see page 110).

The Alcázar overlooks to the east the **Barrio de Santa Cruz**, which was the town's Jewish quarter, and is as much of a showpiece as is CÓRDOBA's Judería, but with fewer of the latter's offending tourists shops. With its maze of narrow streets, white walls covered in flowers, elegant black balconies and pervasive smells of jasmine, this is exactly how Romantic travellers liked to picture Seville, and it is appropriate that one of the squares has been given a statue of Don Juan Tenorio.

At the heart of this district is Leonardo de Figueroa's **Hospicio de los Venerables Sacerdotes**, a late 17th-century hospice that has recently been restored to its original shining whiteness; the rooms around its ceramic-lined courtyard are now used for temporary art exhibitions. But the tourists who come to the Barrio de Santa Cruz are mainly happy to wander around the well-kept streets, stopping only to sit outside at bars and restaurants frequented almost exclusively by other tourists.

The church of **Santa Maria la Blanca**, on the northern edge of the Barrio, was originally a synagogue, and has a gothic west portal surviving from this building; the interior was radically altered in an exuberant baroque style in the 1650's and has two outstanding canvases by Murillo (see page 121). Also contained at one time within the old Jewish quarter was the nearby Calle Levies, on which stands the palace of Miguel Mañara of Don Juan fame (see page 124), and the Carbonería, a spacious bar which has played an important role in Seville's cultural life, and where you can hear flamenco every Thursday night (see page 152). Behind the church runs a wide and ugly street which marks the site of the city's old walls, and is popularly referred to as La Ronda.

North of the Barrio de Santa Cruz the architecture of Seville retains many of the Barrio's features but becomes increasingly run-down. In the Calle Marmoles stand, above a stagnant rubbish-strewn pool, three enormous columns, the main survival of Roman Seville. Further north you are in the district known as the **Alfalfa**, which has, at Calle Góngora 7, one of Seville's most unusual bars, the Garlochi. This late-night bar is distinguished by a remarkable baroque decoration of flowers and religious images that changes according to the festive season; no blasphemy is intended in the cocktails bearing such names as 'Blood of Christ'. East of here is the 17th-century **Convent of San Leandro**, where you can buy famous egg-yolk sweets known as *Yemas*. Walking from the convent east towards the Ronda, you will reach after a few minutes the **Casa de Pilatos**, the most remarkable of Seville's renaissance palaces (see pages 114).

A corner of the garden, Casa de Pilatos

In the streets immediately to the north of the cathedral are a whole series of animated bars, including the Casa Bar Robles, well known for its tapas, and Antigüedades, the façade of which is adorned with ghoulish maquettes; of interest purely for its elegant setting is the Bar Abades in the Calle Abades, a bar arranged with great style around a beautiful small *patio*. Some of the best views of the Giralda are to be had from the rooftop bars of the Bar Placentines (on the Calle Placentines) and the Hotel Doña María (on the Calle Don Remundo). The main street leading north from the cathedral is the wide Avenida de la Constitución, which ends by the town's plateresque **Town Hall** (see pages 110). West of this street are Mañara's **Hospital de la Caridad** (see pages 123f) and, on the Guadalquivir, the Almohad **Torre de Oro** (now a small maritime museum) an early work by the successful contemporary architect Rafael Moneo (the Edificio de "Prevision Espanola"), the new, gasometer-shaped **Teatro de la Maestranza** (its austere walls hide an exciting interior), and the 18th-century **Maestranza** itself or Bull-Ring (see page 167f). The street at the southern side of Moneo's building contains the cavernous Bodegon de Torre de Oro, popular with both tourists and such a strange medley of people as 'Papa Clemente' (see page 384), the travel and style journalist Robert Elms, and the distinguished writer Norman Lewis, who has mysteriously singled it out as one of his favourite cheap restaurants in Europe; more interesting are the ruins of Almohad walls to be seen off the courtyard behind it.

The square on the western side of the Town Hall, the Plaza Nueva, is large and characterless, but that on the eastern side, the Plaza San Fernando, has considerable charm and elegance. North from this square is a pedestrian shopping district, the main steet of which is the narrow and lively **Calle Sierpes**, shaded in the summer by awnings. Walking along this you should turn west down the Calle Gallegos to see the small chapel of **San José,** which has one of the more elaborate late baroque altars in Andalucía (see page 125). Turning east along the Calle Gallegos you will come to the delightful **Plaza del Salvador**, dominated by the large early 17th-century church of that name; in a side chapel is a celebrated polychromed statue of *Christ Carrying the Cross* by Martínez Montañés, a monument to whom is in the middle of the square. The square has several open-air bars, including the Bar Alicantina, one of the most pleasant places to sit outside in Seville, and an establishment famous for its justifiably expensive sea-food tapas. Continuing north along the Calle Sierpes, turn east on to the short Calle de la Cerrajería, where you will find the **Edificio Ciudad de Londres**, a turn-of-the-century Moorish pastiche by the architect responsible for Seville's Hotel Alfonso XIII (see page 230). The building abuts on to the Calle Cuna, which runs parallel with the Calle Sierpes; at Calle Cuna 18 is the Palacio Lebrija, an 18th-century palace incorporating in its three patios magnificent Roman mosaics pilfered from Itálica. The Calle Sierpes comes to an end at the Campana, around which are a number of Seville's large shopping stores. The Campana forms part of a long thoroughfare which extends west to the Puente de Isabel II and east to the Ronda; it effectively divides the northern and southern halves of Seville's old town.

To the west of the Campana are the profusely marbled and polychromed **Church of the Magdalena** by Leonardo de Figueroa (see page 124), and the town's **Museo de Bellas Artes**, the best in Spain outside the Prado and housed in the attractive early 17th-century Convent of La Merced (see page 115ff). Having been scandalously closed for unnecessarily protracted restoration this place has now partly redeemed itself with its new and spacious layout, which makes the most of the cheerful and colourful architectural setting, and allows for a particularly dramatic display in the large and sumptuous convent church. Though the Velázquez holdings are meagre, the other Sevillian School artists are well represented, above all Zurbarán, whose series of canvases from the city's Charterhouse (see page 119) provide the place with its artistic climax; all that is lacking in the new highly selective display is the exuberant chaos of 19th- and 20th-century works that lent so much character to the old museum. To the east of the Campana is the 16th-century **University Church**, where you can admire in its spacious, simple interior two exquisitely carved Italian renaissance tombs by the obscure Genoese artists Antonio Aprile and Pace Gagini; the church has also a monument to the poet Gustavo Adolfo Bécquer, who, together with his painter brother Valeriano, is buried in the crypt here (see page 213). The **Plaza de la Encarnación**, in which the church stands, was until recently a featureless and slightly shabby square containing a market and a terminus for Seville's buses. It is now occupied by what is likely to remain – during the present economic crisis – Seville's last major example of modern architectural extravagance: a giant, honey-combed and undulating canopy-like structure resembling and popularly known as **Las Setas**, 'the Mushrooms'. Designed by the German architect Jürgen Mayer, and the subject of intense criticism, it is a spectacular piece of organic design that has managed to revitalize the whole area. Much of it is taken up by a shopping centre, but there are also an 'Antiquarium' (containing Roman finds uncovered during the construction work), a panoramic gastrobar, and a rooftop walk offering some of the finest views to be had of Seville. Further east, past the rather quieter and more pleasant Plaza de Cristo de Burgos, is the church of **Santa Catalina**, which has much 14th-century mudéjar work as well as a lavishly baroque 18th-century Sagrario chapel. The Bar El Rinconcillo, facing the church on the Calle Sol, is a famous bar with a splendid interior which has remained virtually unchanged since the late 19th century.

The northern and traditionally poorer half of Seville's old town attracts far fewer visitors than the southern half, but has nonetheless numerous fascinating monuments and corners. Heading north from Santa Catalina, you soon reach the attractively simple medieval church of **San Marcos**, the parish of which was once largely made up of gypsies (see page 108); the gypsies still identify with this district and often crowd to its bars. It is typical of the great contrasts that are to be found in Seville that immediately to the west of San Marcos are the vast 18th-century palace and gardens belonging to the wealthiest and most distinguished of the town's aristocrats, the Duchess of Alba. Behind the church to the east are grouped the 15th-century **Convents of Santa Isabel** and **Santa Paula**. The latter's church is entered through a large, pleasantly rustic courtyard, one of many such places in Seville where you suddenly feel far away from any city; the west portal has a polychrome renaissance lunette by the Florentine Niculoso Pisano (see page 113). Santa Paula is the only closed convent in Seville that can be officially visited, and the nuns take it in turns to show members of the public their small, atmospheric museum of ecclesiastical bric-à-brac; perhaps one of the best reasons to visit this convent is to buy the nuns' delicious home-made marmalade and other jams.

The church of **San Luis**, one of the most exciting buildings by Leonardo de Figueroa, is reached by continuing north from the church of San Marcos. The pompous exterior, imitating that of San Agnese in Rome, offers little hint of the colour and ornamental vitality of the interior, which is now attached to a drama school and has regular opening hours. Continuing north, through a once exclusively working class area famous for its popular traditions, you reach the chapel where the celebrated processional image of the Macarena is kept (see page 122). The 19th-century chapel of the Macarena adjoins the largest stretch of the town's old walls. Outside the walls, facing the chapel across a large square, is the enormous 16th-century **Hospital of the Five Wounds** (*Cinco Llagas*), which has been converted into the seat of the Andalucían Parliament. A No. 11 bus will take you north from here to the **Cemetery of San Fernando**, which has a small section reserved for both Protestants and atheists, but the great interest of which is the array of early 20th-century monuments, in particular the large and superb sculptural group by Manlliure representing the burial of the bull-fighter Joselito; one of the bearers carrying the coffin is García Lorca's friend, the poet and bullfighter Iganacio Sánchez Mejías, who himself lies buried at Joselito's side.

Back again inside the city walls you should explore the part of the city which lies to the west of the street running between the Macarena and Santa Catalina. Due west of the church of San Marcos is the **Calle Feria**, which has a lively flea-market on Thursday mornings. This market now extends to the west of here to the long 18th-century promenade known as the **Alameda de Hercules,** a once forlorn area next to a traditional red light district. The prostitutes have now gone, and the Alameda and its surroundings have been transformed out of all recognition, with the Alameda itself being pedestrianized, lined with smart open-air bars, and adorned with designer street lights, water features, and modern structures in questionable taste. West of the Alameda, you find yourself in the **Barrio de San Lorenzo**, one of the most pleasant residential districts of Seville; the large neoclassical chapel adjoining the **Church of San Lorenzo** houses Roldán's celebrated processional image of the Christ of the Gran Poder (see pages 122 and 161). North of this church, at the northern end of the Calle Santa Clara is one of the most remarkable of Seville's forgotten monuments, the 14th-century **Tower of Don Fadrique**, which stands in peaceful, enchanting grounds attached to the convent of Santa Clara; from the top of the tower you have perhaps the finest of all views of Seville. A few minutes walk away is the **Monastery of San Clemente**, a 13th-century foundation remodelled in the late 16th century, and given its present main cloister in 1632; the building was completely renovated in connection with the EXPO, and has been used since then as a place for art exhibitions. On its western side it faces a part of Seville that will be initially unrecognizable to anyone who has not been back to the city since 1992. The once seedy **Calle Torneo**, where a stagnant branch of the Guadalquivir used to come to an end amidst defaced walls and railway sidings, has been transformed into an elegant, designer-lit thoroughfare running alongside a freely flowing river. On summer nights the street has now become a haunt of the city's young, who flock to its many open-air bars or *kioscos*; the formerly tacky bar called the Joven Costalero (at No. 18), which used to have silver-foil decoration and a constant video-show of highlights from the *Semana Santa*, is now a smart local popularized by teenagers and *yuppís*.

Directly opposite the monastery are the **EXPO grounds**, which are accessible from here by crossing the Puente de la Barqueta. This bridge is popularly known as the *Puente del Lepero* ('Bridge of the Man from Lepe') in reference to the Andalucían town that features in so many local jokes (see page 263): the structure in itself is wholly unremarkable but provoked its nick-name for having been built before there was any water underneath it. Far more interesting are the bridges on either side by the Swiss-based Spanish architect Santiago Calatrava, which are perhaps the greatest architectural legacy of the EXPO. The one to the north, the Punta del Alamillo, is an enormous, daringly angled structure that was originally planned to counterbalance a similarly shaped bridge on the other side of the EXPO grounds; the Puente de la Cartuja, to the south, has the form of a poised crossbow, and has already become as much of a symbol of the new Seville as the Giralda is of the old city. The vast space once occupied by the EXPO now features some desultory public gardens, a white elephant of a hotel (the Hotel EXPO), and a Cruzcampo brewery. Most of the pavilions, including Nicholas Grimshaw's much praised British pavilion, were taken down after 1992, and the space was converted into what the EXPO had best functioned as – an amusements park. The park was closed down in the summer of 1995 but a southern section of it was reopened as the Puerta de Triana, a theme park incorporating the finally unveiled Pavillion of Discoveries (the fire damage to which had not been righted in time for the EXPO) and the famous 16th-century **Charterhouse**, which had lain romantically abandoned for many years before being radically restored to house, during the EXPO, an ambitious exhibition devoted to world art in 1492. The Charterhouse, with its associations with Columbus and Zurbarán, still retains its surrounding conical chimneys dating from the place's conversion in the 19th century into a ceramics factory founded by the Englishman Charles Pickman: workers in this factory were sometimes referred to as *Cartujanos* or 'Carthusians', which explains the popular sevillana that opens with the apparently baffling words, 'My boyfriend is a *Cartujano*'.

The Puente de la Cartuja links the Charterhouse with the southern end of the Calle Torneo, near where the street joins up with the Plaza de Armas: here you will find a bold new bus station (which, despite its size, serves only the province of Huelva) and the neo-Moorish **Estación de Córdoba**, a former 19th-century railway station which was turned in 1992 into yet another exhibitions venue.

Further south is the Puente de Isabel II, a 19th-century ironwork bridge that acquires a special beauty during the *Semana Santa*, when the much venerated image of the Virgin of Esperanza (see page 123) is carried across it. On its western side, and considered sometimes as a separate township from Seville, is the former gypsy district of **Triana**, from the embankment of which are beautiful views across the river to the Maestranza, the Torre de Oro and the Cathedral. The district is no longer the poor ramshackle place it used to be, and indeed becomes increasingly smart the further south you walk in the direction of the modern district of **Los Remedios**. The main street crossing though the northern half of Triana is the Calle Castilla, which passes at its northern end next to the ugly neoclassical church of **Nuestra Señora de la O**, worth a visit only for its famous processional image of the *Dead Christ*. This much loved work, carved in 1682 by Francisco Ruiz Gijón, is known popularly as the Christ of 'El Cacharro', and was reputedly inspired by the dead body of a handsome gypsy singer who had been killed in a street brawl outside the church. On the other side of the street to the church is the Sol y Sombra, one of the city's outstanding tapas bars. The Calle Castilla leads south towards the Plaza Alozano, next to which is the **Triana market**, occupying the site of the notorious Castle of the Inquisition (see pages 93 and 104). Opposite the market is a handsome turn-of-the-century shop decorated with and selling the elaborate tiles and ceramics for which Triana is traditionally famous; nearby, at the corner of the Calles Pages del Coro and Antillano Campos, is a beautifully tiled bar where guitarists and singers often meet in the evenings. The **Calle Betis**, which hugs the riverside in between the Puente Isabel II and the Puente San Telmo, is the fashionable heart of present-day Triana, lined with bars, restaurants and nightclubs. A curiosity at its northern end, and a survival of the old Triana, is the eccentric barbershop called Los Pajaritos ('the Little Birds'), the exterior of which is covered by day with bird cages.

South of the Puente de San Telmo, on the Seville side of the river, is a spacious, luxurious area of town incorporating the **Parque María Luisa**, the luxury **Hotel Alfonso XIII** (see page 230), and the eclectic pavillions put up for the Ibero-American exhibition of 1929 (see pages 220 and 230); two of the architectural pastiches in the park contain, respectively, the town's enjoyable **ethnography museum** and the extensive **archaeological museum**, the latter boasting a most striking horde of Tartessian jewellery from Carambolo (see page 62). On either side of the Hotel Alfonso XIII are the old **Tobacco Factory** (see page 214f) and the 18th-century **Palace of San Telmo**, the frontispiece of which is one of the most elaborate of Leonardo de Figueroa's works (see page 124).

East of the Ronda extend the main commercial districts of the modern city, within which is the new railway station of Santa Justa, which is comparable in its austerity, spaciousness and massive proportions to the new airport building by Rafael Moneo on the city's eastern outskirts.

The most popular excursion in the immediate vicinity of Seville is to the dusty and shabby Roman site of **Itálica**, situated in and around the unprepossessing village of **Santiponce** (see page 64). On the southern ouskirts of the village is the impressive monastery of San Isidro del Campo. The monastery which can now be visited on a guided tour, has numerous murals from the gothic period onwards, and a magnificent high altar of 1613 by Martínez Montañés.

The hilly land to the west of Santiponce is known as the **Aljarafe**, and is regarded with great affection by most Sevillians, many of whom chose to live here. Its appeal to the foreign visitor is less obvious, and its numerous villages include such unglamorous places as Camas, Valencina de la Concepción and **Castilleja de la Cuesta**, the latter being incongruously the ancestral home of Rita Hayworth, whose family name of Cansinos is still associated with the sweet aniseed-flavoured *tortas* (wide, thin biscuits) for which the village is famous. **Olivares**, the home village of the famous 17th-century Count-Duke of Olivares, has a beautiful and intimate arcaded

The ethnography museum, Seville

square, while **Umbrete** has a large and impressive 17th-century church, and a reputation for its young sweetish wine known as *mosto* (see page 184); between these two villages, near **Villanueva del Ariscal**, are the distinguished Bodegas Góngora, which have good table and fortified wines, an excellent brandy, and a cellar dating back to the middle ages. Near the village of **Bolullos de la Mitación**, in the southernmost part of the Aljarafe, are some outstanding 18th-century *haciendas* (most notably the Hacienda Torquemada; see page 18), and one of the district's most attractive sites. This, the isolated hermitage of **Cuatrovitas**, is notable for its well preserved Almohad tower, which was probably once the minaret of a mosque.

Just to the south of the Aljarafe, beyond the town of **Coria del Río**, begins the marshland of the Guadalquivir estuary. The road from Coria comes to an end at the strange small village of **Villafranca del Guadalquivir**, right in the middle of a vast and flat marshy expanse that, on a rainy day, looks almost like Holland. Such days are now much needed here, for the recent drought has had disastrous effects on the local rice industry, originally set up by rice-growers from Valencia. The village restaurant serves a curious Andalucían-Valencian cuisine featuring most of the many birds that fly into the area.

SORBAS [4J] occupies a dramatic site in the middle of one of the most dramatic landscapes in Europe. The old town stands high above its extensive modern suburbs and clings to the top of a high gorge which bites its way through an eroded landscape of primeval appearance. The desert which you are in continues west beyond TABERNAS. To the north is the little visited **Sierra de los Filabres**, which can be crossed on the C3325. From the south these mountains appear to be peaks on the moon, but, high up, they turn out to be surprisingly wooded. One of the most attractive of the villages is that of **Cóbdar**, which lies in a narrow steep-sided valley underneath a massive rockface from which marble used to be quarried.

TABERNAS [4H]: The ruins of the castle where Ferdinand and Isabel stayed during the siege of Almería rise on a barren mound above the town. But the main interest of Tabernas is its bizarrely eroded surroundings. This landscape takes on a futuristic aspect at the nearby Central Solar (off the small road north to Senes), where row upon row of solar panels stand in the desert as if in some science fiction film. Film-makers have indeed been favouring Tabernas for many years. Seven kilometres south of the town on the Almería road is 'Mini-Hollywood', the oldest and most famous of several local recreations of American villages of the 'Wild West'. This one was built originally for Sergio Leone's *A Fistful of Dollars*, and later used for spaghetti westerns such as Leone's *The Good, Bad and the Ugly*. Extras from the latter film decided to save the set as a tourist attraction, and today run the place themselves. Even without having to dress up in cowboy costumes the men who work here look convincing as gangsters: at regular intervals during the day they stage mock fights and hold-ups in the village (the main scene of the action is the saloon bar of the hotel). The more serious sightseer should head north from here along the C3326 to **Gérgal**, where there is an excellently preserved castle comprising a quadrangular block with round towers at each corner; the mountain above the village is crowned by a German/Spanish-built observatory with the largest telescope in Spain. South from Mini-Hollywood on the Almería road, there is a turning to the right marked to **Santa Fe de Mondújar**. Before reaching the village, you will see on the right the entrance to Europe's most extensive Bronze Age site, **Los Millares** (see page 60). For the key to this you have to continue on to Santa Fe, which lies beneath the site and is reached by a narrow ironwork bridge perched perilously above the sinister landcape: the key is to be had from the bar in front of the Town Hall at the end of this God-forsaken village.

Just after the Santa Fe turning a road to the left slowly ascends into the eastern Alpujarra (see LAUJAR DE ANDARAX), passing after 2 km the ugly spa town of **Alhama de Almería**,which is built around a ruined Nasrid castle of the 13th century. In the courtyard of the modern spa hotel of San Nicolas a Roman marble basin stands forlornly as a sole testimony to the spa's antiquity; but the visitor's attention is soon drawn again to the strange landscape outside, which extends in its surreal magnificence right across the hotel dining-room's panoramic window.

TARIFA [6C], named after the Moorish leader Tarif ibn Malik, was the first Moorish possession in Spain (see page 67). The town, entered by a Moorish gate from the Cádiz to Algeciras road (E25) is filled with narrow streets that are congested with tourists. The heavily restored Moorish castle dating back to the 10th century (and rebuilt in the 13th) now belongs to the Spanish navy and cannot be visited; the best view of it is from the port. The town was captured by the Christians in 1292, but was subject to several counter-attacks, during which the town was defended by Alonso Pérez de Guzmán. In an action foreshadowing that of General Moscardó's at Toledo in 1936, Pérez de Guzmán allowed his son to be killed rather than surrender the town: 'I prefer honour without a son, to dishonour with one,' he is supposed to have said. For this questionable gesture he received his name of the 'Good'.

The long sandy beaches east of Tarifa are very popular with wind-surfers; a particularly attractive stretch of dunes is to be found 10 km outside the town at **Punta Paloma**. The road west from Tarifa to Algeciras climbs up a barren mountainside and has wonderful views over to Morocco.

TEBA [4D]: On a barren hill rising above the village of Teba and the reservoir of Guadalteba-Guadalhorce stands an impressive and extensive castle, built by the Moors and dating back to Phoenician times. In 1330 Sir James Douglas, on his way to Jerusalem, took part here in a battle against the Moors. He was carrying with him a casket containing the heart of Robert Bruce, which he flung into the foray, swearing to follow after it. The casket fared rather better than he did, being afterwards recovered and taken to Melrose Abbey in Scotland, where it still lies.

ÚBEDA [2G], built on the slope of a hill, looks out over a landscape of olive trees towards the imposing Sierra de Cazorla. The main road which runs along the top of the hill, through the northern outskirts of the town, was in ancient times a major line of communication between Andalucía and eastern Spain. It later fell into disuse, and Úbeda acquired a reputation for being cut off from the rest of the country. Today it still has an isolated character, and it is certainly one of the least visited of Andalucía's towns of major architectural and historical interest. The town's reputation for remoteness is reflected in the popular expression 'to wander off on the hills of Úbeda' (*irse por los cerros de Úbeda*), meaning to 'wander off the point' or 'to be distracted'. The origin of this expression is also connected with the apocryphal story of Alvar Fañez, a Christian knight who fell in love with a Moorish girl, and as a result missed the critical battle that took place at Úbeda. Asked by Ferdinand III where he had been at the time, Fañez replied: 'On those hills, sire...'

Despite its ancient origins, Úbeda did not develop into an important town until the arrival of the Moors, who encircled it with walls and built a castle here. After the Christian victory at nearby Las Navas de Tolosa in 1212 (see LA CAROLINA), the Moors from Baeza took refuge here, believing the town to be more secure than their own. It fell to the Christians eight days later, but was not definitively captured until 1234, by Ferdinand III ('the Holy'). Numerous noble families were established by Ferdinand in Úbeda, twelve of whom are represented by the twelve lions in the town's coat of arms. Úbeda's period of greatest fame and prosperity was the 16th century, when its textiles were exported throughout Europe, and when members of its nobility held leading positions in the Spanish court. The most renowned of these noblemen was Francisco de los Cobos y Molina, who by 1529 was secretary to Charles V. He gained vast wealth and was the virtual ruler of Spain during Charles V's absences abroad, but eventually his greed for money and power led to his being replaced as Charles V's secretary by Juan Vázquez de Molina, who was also from Úbeda and to whose family indeed Francisco's mother belonged. The Cobos and the Molinas, linked by various marriages, dominated the life, culture and patronage of 16th-century Úbeda, and it was through them that the town became one of the renaissance jewels of Europe. Their principal architect was Andrés de Vandelvira, who was born near Albacete in 1509, and died in Jaén in 1575.

The prosperity of Úbeda declined dramatically in the early 17th century, and the town has few monuments of note after that date. In the 20th-century the town's fortunes have revived with the establishment of new industries and the expansion of old ones. The town has grown considerably beyond its former walls, and its northern, upper part, including the main square (the Plaza de Andalucía), is a rather unprepossessing district crammmed with tall dingy blocks. The most important old monument in this part of town is Vandelvira's **Hospital of Santiago**, which stands on the Calle Obispo Cobos, the main street leading from the town's bus station to the Plaza de Andalucía. Founded in the mid-16th century by Don Diego de Los Cobos y Molina, Bishop of Jaén, this vast, little-ornamented building shows Vandelvira at his most austere, and is sometimes referred to as the 'Andalucían Escorial'. Also of interest in this northern part of town is the **Church of San Nicolas de Bari** (Plaza San Nicolas), about a ten minute walk uphill from the Plaza de Andalucía. Dating mainly from the 14th century, it has a playful late gothic south portal of 1509, and a superb west portal designed by Vandelvira; within its gothic interior you will find one of Vandelvira's earliest works, the Chapel of Dean Ortega Salido, the elaborate decoration of which forms a striking contrast to the simplicity of the Hospital of Santiago.

The Plaza de Andalucía lies just outside the town's former walls, and a tower on its southern side, the **Torre del Reloj**, is a survival of the old fortifications. Next to it, in the square's southeastern corner, the narrow Calle Real descends into the old and peaceful heart of Úbeda. Half-way down, to your right, at the corner of the Calle Juan Pasquau Lopez, is the **Palace of the Counts of Guadiana**, crowned by a richly sculpted renaissance tower; in any other town this would be a building of

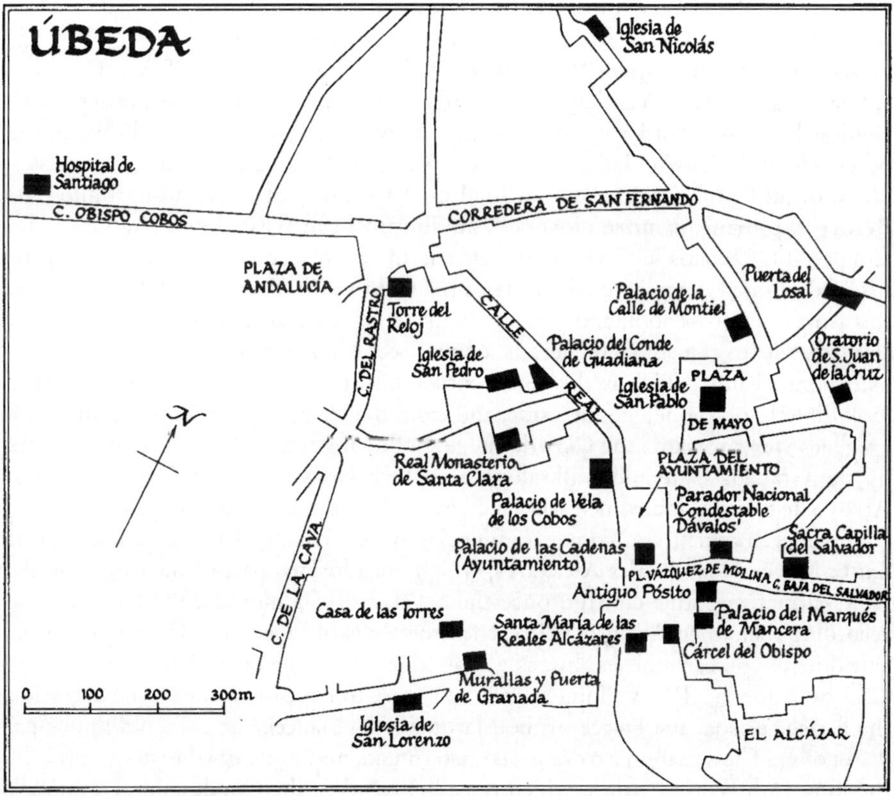

major importance, but as you continue to wander around Úbeda, you will find countless other palaces like it. Opposite, at Calle Real 45, is a large shop, Artesanía Blanco, which specializes in traditional local crafts, most notably basketwork and ceramics: the traditional Úbeda ceramics, produced here since Moorish times, are characterized by a dark green glaze. A short detour down the tiny Calle Juan Pasquau Lopez will take you to the medieval **Church of San Pedro** and the **Convent of Santa Clara**, where you can buy a wide range of cakes, biscuits and pastries. Continuing downhill along the Calle Real, you will reach at the end of the street, on the right hand side, the **Palace of Vela de Cobos**, which is crowned by an upper arcaded gallery, a typical feature of Spanish renaissance architecture and a space where the women of the household could exercise without being observed from the street.

The Calle Real opens out into the Plaza del Ayuntamiento, dominated at its southern end by the free-standing **Palacio de las Cadenas**, which was built originally as the Palace of Juan Vázquez de Molina, and is now the Town Hall: the secular masterpiece of Vandelvira, it is a relatively sober building attempting a conventionally classical ordering of its façades. Extending to the south and east on the other side of the Town Hall is the Plaza de Vázquez Molina, one of the most aristocratic of all Spanish squares, and lined on all sides with outstanding buildings. Before exploring it more closely, you should head west down the Calle del Condestable Dávalos until you reach the charming small square containing the profusely decorated twin-towered façade of the **Casa de las Torres** (mid-16th century; this is now an art school, and you can walk freely around its beautiful courtyard). Immediately to the south of here is a small section of the town's southern walls, incorporated into which is the 16th-century **Church of San Lorenzo**. The walls look directly onto open countryside, and from the terrace of San Lorenzo there are excellent views towards the Cazorla range. Following the walls to the east you pass by the Granada Gate and walk along a rubbish-strewn path until you reach the Arroyo de Santa María, which will take you back to the Plaza de Vázquez Molina.

The church which you come to immediately on arriving at the square is that of **Santa María de las Reales Alcázares**, which once formed part of the town's walls. In its attractive gothic cloister, once the courtyard of a mosque, there is a plaque recording that when Alfonso VII reached the walls of Úbeda in 1157 he placed his shield here; you can still see this, as well as a nearby statue of the Virgin left here in 1212 by Alfonso VIII. Walking round the square to the east, you pass in succession the former prison, the Palace of the Marqueses de Mancena and the old municipal warehouse. The square narrows in its eastern end, and in its northeastern corner is the long 16th-century palace which once belonged to the Condestable Dávalos: it was turned in 1930 into what is still one of the most impressive of Andalucía's luxury paradors (it is also the only hotel in the old town of Úbeda). Adjacent to it, proudly standing at the eastern end of the square, is the most interesting of all Úbeda's monuments, the **Chapel of San Salvador** (see page 103). This was originally intended as the private chapel of Francisco de Cobos, and was designed by Diego de Siloe and executed, with considerable modifications to the original design, by his great successor, Andrés de Vandelvira. The chapel is entered through a door on the narrow Calle Francisco de Cobos, on which street can also be seen the side façade of Cobos' palace: the rest of the palace was largely destroyed by fire. Crossing a courtyard, you enter the chapel through its large and splendid sacristy, which was built by Vandelvira at an angle to the chapel, resulting in a curiously shaped door between the two spaces. Siloe would undoubtedly have favoured a more classical solution. Within the sacristy is a photograph of a statue by Michelangelo given as a gift to Cobos by the Venetian state, but destroyed during the Civil War. During this same war the chapel itself suffered much damage, but it is

Chapel of San Salvador

being patiently restored, and is still one of the finest renaissance ensembles in Spain. The tall chancel, with elegant coffering in its vault and late baroque gilding, is divided from the nave by a splendid renaissance grille designed by Master Bartolomeu. The high altar, modified during the baroque period, features a carved and polychromed *Transfiguration* by one of Spain's most remarkable renaissance artists, Alonso de Berruguete. Berruguete was trained under Michelangelo, and his style is notable for its pathos and expressiveness. This masterly *Transfiguration* is a characteristically agitated work, but, sadly, it was badly damaged during the Civil War, and only the Christ is original, the rest being skilful restoration.

To the east and south of the chapel the town comes to an abrupt end, suspended over a sea of olive trees. Heading north along the Calle Francisco de los Cobos, you will eventually come to the **Monastery of San Juan de la Cruz**, where the saint and poet St. John of the Cross died of gangrene in 1591. Only a small part of this building is as it was in the 16th century, and its church (the first to be dedicated to the saint) was rebuilt after having been destroyed in the Civil War. The monastery houses a museum to the saint, with numerous documents and objects relating to his life, including the actual writing desk which he used; also displayed is a selection of the many books written about him, one of which is by Gerald Brenan. The museum has a singularly depressing atmosphere, complete with gloomily designed information panels in imitation peeling leather.

North of the monastery is the horseshoe-arched **Puerta del Losal,** the town's northeastern gate; beyond this runs the Calle de Valencia, lined with shops selling ceramics. To the west of the monastery is the large and pleasant **Plaza 1 de Mayo,** which has a bandstand in the middle; in its southwestern corner is the former 16th-century Town Hall, while on the northern side is the **Church of San Pablo,** an engagingly anarchic blend of gothic and renaissance elements, with a beautiful late gothic portal of the Virgin facing the square. North of the church is a 14th-century house containing a small **archaeological museum**: the collections are well arranged but unremarkable, and the interest of the museum lies primarily in its enchanting mudéjar courtyard. Still further north is the wide Corredera de San Fernando, a busy commercial street whch will lead you back to the Plaza de Andalucía.

UTRERA [3C], a flat, dusty, and ugly town, was very important in Moorish and Roman times, and even today is a place of considerable vitality and character. It is one of the main Andalucían centres of flamenco, and two of the most established contemporary flamenco singers live in the town, the sisters Fernanda and Bernarda de Utrera. Every year in July the flamenco festival known as the *Potaje* is held in the small modern park alongside the sad fragments of the town's Moorish castle. Next to the park is the church of Santiago, which dates back to the late 15th century and has an exuberantly decorative, if rather worn, Isabelline plateresque west portal. A good example of the classical plateresque style is the west portal of the Church of Santa María de la Asunción, which stands in the small and shaded Plaza Enrique de la Cuadra: the portal takes the form of a triumphal arch with classical coffering framing a tympanum of the Assumption of the Virgin. In front of this church stands a modern monument to the poet, humanist and pioneering archaeologist Rodrigo Caro, born in Utrera in 1573 (see page 64). At **El Palmar de Troya,** 13 km to the south of Utrera on the N333, a basilica of monstrous proportions and hideousness is being erected for the dissident Christian sect of the Holy Face, which was founded after a supposed series of apparitions of the Virgin to four girls in 1968; the head of this sect – which lives mainly off the gullibility of foreigners, and is regarded as a great joke among the Andalucíans – styles himself 'Pope Clement'.

VALDEPEÑAS DE JAÉN: Though much marred by unappealing blocks from the 1950's onwards, the isolated and remote Valdepeñas de Jaén is an enchanting and

Vejer de la Frontera

especially animated large village with a spectacular mountain setting and an as yet barely exploited potential as a summer resort. Within the village itself you can undertake a beautiful short walk in the luxuriant parkland known as 'Las Chorreras', which is named after a series of cascades and waterfalls. Another attraction is the restored and functioning water mill (now an excellent museum) built in the 16th century by one of the village's founding colonists from Flanders. 5 kms outside the village, in a Tuscan-like setting of cypresses, is the delightful Hermitage of Chircales, which has a 16th century votive painting commemorating the miraculous appearance of Christ in the adjoining cave. The lush abandoned garden next to the church will appeal to the romantically inclined.

VEJER DE LA FRONTERA [5C], rising steeply behind the fishing town of BARBATE, is a sprawling village very popular with day-trippers from the coast. Occupied by the Moors up to 1250, it has a strong Moorish character and a maze of narrow white streets. You enter the upper part of the village through the original Moorish gates. Inside is the 16th-century parish church, which was built over a mosque. Near this, hidden by the surrounding houses, is a Moorish castle, with a horseshoe gate and recently uncovered Moorish plasterwork; the castle is now used by boy scouts, who will lead you on to its terrace to see the wonderful views of the village and surrounding countryside. Just outside the villlage gates is the charming, palm-lined Plaza de los Pescaítos with 19th-century ceramic decorations in a Triana style. As at ARCOS DE LA FRONTERA, a bull with padded horns is let loose through the streets here on Easter Sunday.

VÉLEZ-BLANCO [2J]: The drive from the Sierra de Segura (see SEGURA) leads through a lonely landscape of parched wheatfields framed by bleached rocky peaks. Both Vélez-Blanco and the neighbouring Vélez-Rubio are at the centre of the major cereal-producing area in Almería province, and supplied grain to the troops of Ferdinand and Isabel during the last stages of the Reconquest. Vélez-Blanco, the smaller and more attractive of the two towns, extends under the rocky hill on which stands its famous castle (see page 104, and the colour photographs on the cover), which from the outside is one of the most impressive in all Andalucía. The original Moorish castle is a simple block connected by a bridge to a large polygonal structure built between 1506 and 1515 by an Italian architect, F. Florentini. The 16th-century bridge linking the Moorish and renaissance structures was destroyed by the French during the Peninsular War, and only recently rebuilt. The most serious damage suffered by this castle, however, was to its renaissance section, and was to be perpetuated by a descendant of the man who had commissioned it, Pedro Fejardo, Marquis of Vélez. The Marquis' descendant, fallen on hard times, sold off the castle's magnificent renaissance bronze door, and its entire marbled courtyard to a French antique dealer; the door ended up in a private collection in Paris, and the courtyard was eventually reconstructed in the Metropolitan Museum of Art, New York. The interior of Florentini's castle, patched up now with steel beams and concrete walls, has only the smallest fragments left of its original renaissance decoration. It is worth a visit primarily for the views from the top of its tallest tower, and for the informative commentary provided by the energetic old man who looks after the building. This man, known to everyone in the town as 'Tío Perez' spends most of his day in the castle, and should you want to look inside, you need only stand under the

Vélez-Blanco

bridge and shout out his name as loudly as possible; if he is not there, he can usually be found in the Círculo de los Pensionistas in the town centre.

Just outside the village to the south, off the C321 to Vélez Rubio, is a sign marked **Cueva de los Letreros** (see page 57). Turn right down a dust track, take the first turning to the left, and then the first one to the right. Up to now the track is just about manageable by car, but from now on you must walk. The prehistoric rock shelter of Los Letreros lies half way up the cliff in front of you, and is reached by concrete steps carved into the rock. The very faint red and brown sketches inside, consisting of stylized representations of men and animals, have been dated to 4,000 BC. The shelter is closed off by a metal grille, but the paintings – insofar as they can be made out at all – are visible from the outside. 'Tío Perez' might well offer to accompany you here and to open the grille, but he should be discouraged from doing so, as he is prone to throw water at the paintings to bring out the colour.

The principal monument of **Vélez Rubio** is the large late baroque parish church of 1753, the most important monument of this period in Almería province. The majestic, richly carved façade is dominated by the huge coat of arms of the Marquesses of Vélez, who had the church built at their expense.

VÉLEZ-MÁLAGA [4F], one of the last Moorish strongholds to be taken by the Christians, lies in a fertile valley at the foot of a steeply mountainous district known as the Axarquía. The town, only 4 km inland from the characterless coastal resort of Torre del Mar, is a large place with a prosperous and mainly modern look. The elegant and recently restored Palacio del Marques de Beniel is the seat of the recently inaugurated International University of the Axarquía, a summer school intended to give the town a new intellectual prestige. The old town of Vélez-Málaga rises up on a hill crowned by trees and the much restored tower of a Moorish castle. The church immediately below the tower is that of Nuestra Señora de la Encarnación. Originally a Visigothic church, it was used by the Moors as a mosque before being transformed back into a church after the Christian capture of the town in 1487.

ZUHEROS: Heading west from Doña Mencía (see Alcaudete) on the attractive CV241, you will pass near the isolated Hacienda Minerva (a beautifully situated estate imaginatively transformed into a hotel and restaurant by a local politician and historian), before reaching after 9 km the prettily maintained village of Zuheros, famous for its herb-flavoured goat cheeses marinated in olive oil, and which has a toy-town atmosphere, complete with what appears to be a papier-mâché castle. The view from the top of this is over an uninterrupted expanse of olive trees. In the barren mountains in which the village is built is to be found the Cueva de los Murciélagos ('the cave of the bats'), where major prehistoric finds were made at the end of the last century (see page 57). There are now a number of long and daily guided tours of the cave for a limited number of people.

Further Reading

The literature on Andalucía has increased enormously since I first wrote this book, with an especially large number of books having appeared in recent years on Granada and Islamic Andalucía. Though this bibliography still remains a select one, I have tried to make it the most extensive as yet available on the region. To make it less daunting I have used a starring system for the non-fiction works, with two stars being given to the relatively small number of books that are essential and entertaining reading for anyone coming to Andalucía for the first time; a single star indicates major works of reference or scholarship. Where possible I have listed titles in their English versions.

General

* Acery, D., *Not on Queen Victoria's Birthday, The Story of the Río Tinto Mines,* London, 1914

Amezcua Martínez et al., *Enfermedad y muerte en la cultura andaluza*, 1994

Artola, M., *El latifundio*, Madrid, 1978

Baird, David, *Inside Andalucía*, Málaga, 1990

Bernal, A., *La propriedad de la tierra y las luchas agrarias andaluzas*, Madrid, 1974

Bernaldo de Quiros, C., *El bandolerismo andaluz*, Madrid, 1973

Brandes, Stanley, *Metaphors of Masculinity*, University of Pennsylvania Press, 1980

Buck, Walter *and* Chapman, Abel, *Unexplored Spain*, London, 1910

Buck, Walter *and* Chapman, Abel, *Wild Spain*, London, 1893

Burgos, Antonio, *Andalucía ¿tercer mundo?*, Esplugas de Llobregat, 1976

Caro Baroja, *Los Pueblos de España, Ensayo de etnología*, Barcelona, 1946

Cuenca Toribio, José Manuel, *Andalucía*, Madrid, 1982

Díaz del Moral, J., *Historia de las agitaciones campesinos andaluces*, Madrid, 1979

Drain, Michel (ed.), *Los andaluces*, Madrid, 1980

Elms, Robert, *Spain: A portrait after the General*, London, 1992

Epton, Nina, *Andalusia*, London, 1968

Espinosa de los Monteros, Patricia, *Houses and Palaces of Andalucía,* with photographs by Francisco Fernández, London, 1998

Fraser, Ronald, *The Pueblo*, London, 1973

* Fundación March, *Tierras de España, Andalucía* (2 vols.), Madrid, 1980

Gilmore, David, *The People of the Plain. Class and Community in Lower Andalusía*, New York, 1980

Gilmore, David, *Aggression and Community in Andalusía*, New Haven, 1987

Hooper, John, *The New Spaniards*, London, 1995

Infante, Blas, *El ideal andaluz*, Madrid, 1976

* Javierra, José María (ed.) *Gran Enciclopedia de Andalucía* (10 vols.), Seville, 1979

Josephs, Allen, *White Wall of Spain. The Mysteries of Andalusian Culture*, Iowa City, 1983

Lépidis, Clément (ed.), *Andalousie*, Paris, 1985

Luard, Nicholas, *Andalucía, a Portrait of Southern Spain*, London, 1984

Martínez Alier, J., *La estabilidad del latifundismo*, Madrid, 1968
Martínez Alier, J., *Labourers and Landowners in Southern Spain*, London, 1971
Medina Molera, A., *Historia de Andalucía*, Seville, 1980
Mountfort, Guy, *Portrait of a Wilderness*, London, 1958
Muñoz Molina, Antonio, *El Robinson urbano*, Barcelona, 1993
Ortega y Gasset, José, *Teoría de Andalucía*, Madrid, 1944
Pareja López, Enrique (ed.), *Historia del arte en Andalucía* (8 vols.), Sevilla, 1988
Pemán, José María, *Andalucía*, Barcelona, 1958
Pitt-Rivers, Julian, *The People of the Sierra*, London, 1954
Praz, Mario, *Unromantic Spain*, London, 1928
Ramos y Espejo, *Andalucía de Fuente-Obejuna a Marinaleda*, Seville, 1985
Reig, Ramón, *Religión y religiosidad popular en Andalucía*, Madrid, 1989
Rodríguez Barberán, Javier, *Cementerios de Andalucía*, Seville, 1993
Sermet, Jean, *España del Sur*, Madrid, 1954
Urbano, M., *Andalucía en el testimonio de sus poetas*, Madrid, 1976
Zugasti, Julián, *El bandolerismo*, Madrid, 1876

Guide Books and Local History

Alcaide Aguilar, *Marchena, Guía basica, histórico-artística de Marchena*, Marchena, 1985
Ayuntamiento de Alcalá la Real, *Alcalá la Real: Patrimonio archítectónico y urbano*, Alcalá la Real, 1993
Ayuntamiento de Sevilla, *The City of Seville for the Enlightened Traveller*, Seville, 1995
Molina Hipólito, J., *Baeza, histórica y monumental*, Córdoba, 1985
Barrenetxea, J. L., *and* Muñoz, K., *La Alpujarra en Bici*, Bilbao
Bejarano, F., *Las calles de Málaga. De su historia y ambiente*, (2 vols.), Málaga, 1984
Bendala, M. et al., *Almonaster la Real*, Huelva, 1991
Bernaldo de Quirós, *Sierra Nevada* (1923), Granada, 1993
Burns, Tom, *Spain, Everything under the Sun*, London, 1988
Caba, Ruben, *Rutas literarias de España*, Madrid, 1990
Carandell, Juan *Sierra Nevada, Montblanc de España, y otros escritos (1920-35)*, Granada, 1994
Caro Romero, J., *Ronda*, Léon, 1980
Castellano, Ramón, *Monumentos artísticos de Morón*, Seville, 1988
* Castro, Eduardo, *and* Díaz, Juan Antonio, *Guía general de la Alpujarra*, Granada, 1992
Collomb, Robin, *Gredos Mountains and Sierra Nevada, Central and Southern Spain*, Goring (Colorado), 1987
Craggs, Chris, *Andalusian Rock Climbs*, Milnthorpe, *c.* 1992
Cuevas, J *and* J de las, *Arcos de la Frontera*, Cádiz, 1985
Diputación Provincial de Cádiz, *Algeciras*, Cádiz, 1983
Diputación Provincial de Cádiz, *Barbate*, Cádiz, 1988
Diputación Provincial de Cádiz, *Castellar de la Frontera*, Cádiz, 1983
Diputación Provincial de Cádiz, *Chipiona*, Cádiz, 1985
Diputación Provincial de Cádiz, *Conil de la Frontera*, Cádiz, 1988
Diputación Provincial de Cádiz, *Grazalema*, Cádiz, 1982

Diputación Provincial de Cádiz, *Jimena de la Frontera*, Cádiz, 1984
Diputación Provincial de Cádiz, *El Puerto de Santa María*, Cádiz, 1985
Diputación Provincial de Cádiz, *Rota*, Cádiz, 1985
Diputación Provincial de Cádiz, *Ubrique*, Cádiz, 1982
Diputación Provincial de Cádiz, *Zahara de la Sierra*, Cádiz, 1985
Diputación provincial de Córdoba, *Catálogo artístico y monumental de la provincia de Córdoba, Córdoba*, (5 vols.), Córdoba, 1981-1987
Diputación Provincial de Sevilla, *Guía artística de Sevilla y su provincia*, Seville, 1989
Ellingham, Mark, et al, *Rough Guide to Andalucía*, London, 1997
Equipo 28, *La Opera y Sevilla,* Seville, 1991
Evans, Sarah Jane, *Seville,* London, 1982
Facaros, Dana *and* Paul, Michael, *Cadogan Guide to Southern Spain*, London 1994
Fernandez, Fidel, *Sierra Nevada* (1931), Granada, 1994
Fernandez, J., *Guía de Málaga*, Málaga, 1989
Fitton, Mary, *Málaga, Portrait of a City*, London, 1971
Ford, Richard, *Handbook for Travellers in Spain* (1845) ed. Ian Robertson (3 vols.), Arundel, 1966
Gallego y Burin, Antonio, *Granada, Guía artística e historica de la ciudad*, Granada, 1987
García, Ernest *and* Paterson, Andrew, *Where to Watch Birds in Southern Spain*, London,
García Barrón, Luis Fernando *and* Márquez Rodríguez, María J., *Sierra de Aracena y Picos de Aroche*, Madrid, 1998
García Gómez, J. M., *Huelva*, Léon, 1987
García de Paredes Muñoz, A. *and* Fernández Segura, F. J., *Baza. Guía*, Baza, 1985
Germond de Lavigné, A., *Itinéraire général de l'Espagne et du Portugal*, Paris, 1881
Gilmour, David, *Cities of Spain*, London, 1992
Guías Anaya, *Andalucía*, Madrid, 1994
Hoces Pérez, Santiago, *Moclín, Escudo de Granada Nazarita*, Granada, 1992
Junta de Andalucía, *Andalucía America, Catalogo Bibliografico*, Seville, 1990
Junta de Andalucía, Consejería de Obras Publicas y Transportes, *Guías de arquitectura de Andalucía (colección)*, Seville, 1995-the present
Junta de Andalucía, Consejería de Obras Publicas y Transportes, *Cortijos, haciendas, y lagares, Arquitectura de las grandes explotaciones agrarias de Andalucía (colección)*, Seville, 2001-2011
Junta de Andalucía, Consejería de Cultura, *Guías oficiales de Madinat Al-Zahra; Museo de Bellas Artes de Sevilla; Museo Arqueologico de Sevilla; Italica*, Seville, various dates
López, Nicolás María, *En Sierra Nevada* (1900), Granada, 1992
Lowe, Alfonso, *The Companion Guide to the South of Spain*, London, 1973
Marín, Diego *and* Pelayo, Elias, *La Suiza Andaluza* (1894-5), Granada, 1992
Márquez Cruz, Francisco Solano, *Pueblos cordobeses de la A a la Z*, Córdoba,
Martínez Punzano, Gregorio, *Huescar a tu alcance*, Granada, 1992
Mead, Rowland, *Andalucía Handbook*, Bath 1997
Mena, José Enrique de Salamanca de, *Jaén*, Léon, 1981
Mena, José María de, *Arte y curiosidades en el cementerio de Sevilla*, Barcelona, 1987
Ministerio de Cultura, *Inventario artístico de Málaga y su provincia* (2 vols.), Madrid, 1985
Ministerio de Cultura, *Inventario artístico de Sevilla y su provincia* (2 vols.), Madrid, 1985

Moreno, Alonso M., *La vida rural en la Sierra de Huelva,* Huelva 1979
* Moreno, Arsenio, *Guía artística de Úbeda*, 1994
* Olmedo, Fernando, *and* Rubiales, Javier *(edd.)*, *Historia de la Cartuja de Sevilla*, Seville, 1989
Orti Belmonte, Miguel Angel, *Córdoba monumental artística e historica* (2 vols.), Córdoba,
Pelaez del Rosa, M. *and* Rivas Carmona, J. *Priego de Córdoba: Guía histórica y artística de la ciudad,* Salamanca, 1980
Rioja López, Concha, *La tienda tradicional Sevillana*, Seville, 1992
Robertson, Ian (ed.), *Blue Guide to Spain*, London, 1989
Rodríguez Barberan, Javier, *Cementerios de Andalucía*, Seville, 1993
* Rodríguez-Buzón, Calle, *Guía artística de Osuna*, Osuna, 1986
Rodríguez Gómez, Miguel, *Galera; oasis de la altiplanicie*, Galera, 1993
Salinas, Manuel, *Parques y jardines cordobeses*, Córdoba, 1991
Selecciones del Reader's Digest, *Guía Illustrada de Andalucía*, Madrid, 1984
Serrano Pérez, J., *Guía de Jaén y su provincia*, Jaén, 1895
Seymour-Davies, Hugh, *Andalusia*, with photographs by Charlie Waite, London, 1990
Sierra Fernandez, Alonso de la , *Guía artística de Cádiz*, Cádiz, 1987
Spahni, Jean Christian, *L'Alpujarre, L'Andalousie secrete*, Paris, 1959
Suárez Japón, J. M., *Olvera*, Cádiz, 1982
Tapia Garrido, José Ángel, *Almería piedra a piedra: Biografía de la ciudad,* Almería, 1970
Tapia Rodríguez, Javier, *Humor de Lepe*, Barcelona, 1989
Titos Martínez, Manuel, *Nuevos Paseos por Granada y sus contornos* (3 vols), Granada, 1992-4
Tornay Roman, Francisco, *Ronda, Situación, historia y monumentos*, Barcelona, 1978
Turner, Christopher, *Seville, Step by Step*, Harmmondsworth, 1992
Vazquez Consuegra, Guillermo, *Guía de Arquitectura de Sevilla*, Seville, 1992
Valdés, Manuel, *Hinojosa del Duque*, Córdoba, 1981
Valdivieso, Enrique et al., *Guía artística de Sevilla y su provincia*, Seville, 1981,
* Valdivieso, Enrique, *Historia de la pintura sevillana. Siglos XIII al XX*, Seville, 1986
Valdivieso, Enrique, *and* Morales, A., *Sevilla Oculta*, Seville, 1986
Vázquez Otero, D., *Pueblos Malagueños*, 2 vols., Málaga, 1966
Willkomm, Moritz, *Las Sierras de Granada* (1882), Granada, 1993

Travellers' Accounts

Alarcón, Pedro Antonio de, *Alpujarra*, Madrid, 1874
Alberich, José, *Del Támesis al Guadalquivir. Antología de viajeros ingleses en la Sevilla del siglo XIX*, Seville, 1976
Amicis, Edmondo de, *Spain and the Spaniards,* London, 1885
Badcock, Lowell, *Rough Leaves from a Journal*, London, 1835
Baxter, H. William, *Spain: Art-Remains and Art-Realities, Painters, Priests and Princes* (2 vols.), London 1875
Bernal Rodríguez, M., *La Andalucía de los libros de viajes del siglos XIX*, Seville, 1985
Blanco White, *Letters from Spain*, London, 1822
Bourgoing, J. F., *Travels in Spain* (vol. 3), London, 1789

Boyd, Alastair, *The Road from Ronda. Travels with a Horse through Southern Spain*, London, 1969
Boyd, Alastair, *The Sierras of the South. Travels in the Mountains of Andalusia*, London, 1992
Brenan, Gerald, *The Face of Spain*, London, 1950
* * Brenan, Gerald, *South from Granada*, London, 1957
Burns, Jimmy, *Spain: A Literary Companion*, London, 1994
Byrne, William Pitt, *Cosas de España* (vol. 2), London, 1866
Carter, Francis, *A Journey from Gibraltar to Malaga*, London, 1772
Cela, Camilo José, *Primer viaje andaluz*, Barcelona, 1959
Chetwode, Penelope, *Two Middle-Aged Ladies in Andalusia*, London, 1963
Cook, Samuel E., *Sketches in Spain*, London, 1834
Cook, Samuel E., *see also* Widdrington
Dennis, George, *A Summer in Andalusia* (2 vols.), London, 1839
Didier, Charles, *Un viaje a la Alpujarra en 1936*, Granada, 1993
Doré, Gustave *and* Davillier, Charles, *Spain...* (1874), London, 1876
Dumas, Alexandre, *De Paris à Cadiz*, Paris, 1846
Enzensburger, Hans Marcus, *Europe, Europe*, London, 1990
Eslava Galán, Juan, *Las rutos del olivo: Masaru en el Olivar*, Jaén, 2000
Ford, Richard, *The Letters of Richard Ford, 1797-1858*, ed. Prothero, Rowland E., London, 1905
* García Mercadal, J., *Viajes de extranjeros por España y Portugal, desde los tiempos más remotos hasta fines del siglo XV* (3 vols.), Madrid, 1952
* * Gautier, Théophile, *Voyage en Espagne* (1846), translated by C. A. Phillips as *A Romantic in Spain*, London, 1926
* * Goytisolo, Juan, *Campo de Níjar* (1959), ed. Peter Bush, London , 1984
Goytisolo, Juan, *La Chanca*, Paris, 1959
Grosso, Alfonso, *Por el río abajo*, Paris, 1966
Havelock Ellis, W. *The Soul of Spain*, London, 1929
Hopkins, Adam, *Spanish Journeys*, Harmondsworth, 1992
Hutchinson, Marjorie, *Málaga Farm*, London, 1956
Irving, Washington, *Diary. Spain, 1828-29*, New York, 1926
Jacob, William, *Travels in the South of Spain in 1809-10*, London, 1811
Jacobs, Michael, *Between Hopes and Memories: A Spanish Journey*, London, 1994
Jacobs, Michael, *In the Glow of the Phantom Palace: Travels from Granada to Timbuktu*, London, 2000
Jacobs, Michael, *The Factory of Light, Tales from my Andalusian Village*, London, 2003
* * Lee, Laurie, *A Rose for Winter*, London, 1955
* * Lee, Laurie, *As I Walked Out One Midsummer Morning*, London, 1969
Lewis, Norman, *To Run across the Sea*, London, 1989
López-Burgos, María Antonia, *Viageros ingleses en Andalucía, Granada (1800-1843)* Granada, 1994
Macaulay, Rose, *Fabled Shore*, London, 1949
Meier-Graefe, Alfred Julius, *The Spanish Journey*, London, 1926
Mitchell, David, *Travellers in Spain: An Illustrated Anthology*, London, 1990
Murdoch, Nina, *She Travelled Alone in Spain*, London, 1935

Murray, E. Dundas, *The Cities and Wilds of Andalusia* (2 vols.), London, 1849

Noteboom, Cees, *Roads to Santiago*, London 1997

Nuñez, Estuardo (ed.), *España vista por viajeros Hispano-Americanos,* Madrid, 1985

Ottensheim, Franck Pfendler d', *Madera, Niza, Andalucía, Sierra Nevada y Los Pirineos* (1848), Granada, 1994

Pérès, Henri, *L'Espagne vue par les voyageurs musulmans de 1610 à 1930*, Algiers, 1937

Peyron, Jean-François, *Nouveau Voyage en Espagne* (2 vols.), London, 1782

Ponz, Antonio, *Viaje de España*, (vols. 16-18), Madrid, 1791-94

Ritchie, Harry, *Here We Go: A summer on the Costa del Sol*, Harmondsworth, 1993

Robertson, Ian, *Los curiosos impertinentes, viajeros ingleses por España, 1760-1855*, Madrid, 1976

Scott, C. Rochfort, *Excursions in the Mountains of Ronda and Granada* (2 vols.), London, 1838

Seymour-Davies, Hugh, *The Bottlebrush Tree, A Village in Andalusía*, London 1988

Sitwell, Sacheverell, *Spain*, London, 1950

Slidell, Alexander, *Spain Revisited* (2 vols.), London , 1836

Standish, Frank Hall, *Seville*, London, 1840

Starkie, W. F., *Don Gypsy. Adventures with a Fiddle in Barbary, Andalusia and La Mancha*, London, 1936

Stewart, Chris, *Driving over Lemons: An optimist in Andalucía*, London, 1999

Stewart, Chris, *A Parrot in the Pepper Tree*, London, 2002

Stewart, Chris, *The Almond Blossom Appreciation Society*, London, 2009

Swinburne, H., *Travels through Spain in 1775 and 1776*, London, 1779

Taylor, Baron, *Voyage Pittoresque en Espagne, en Portugal et sur la Côte d'Afrique, de Tanger à Tetoan*, Paris, 1827

Thomas, R. M., *The Alpujarra: Notes of a Tour in the Andalusian Highlands*, London, 1903

Ticknor, George, *The Life, Letters and Journals of George Ticknor*, London, 1876

Titos Martínez, Manuel, *La aventura de Sierra Nevada, 1717- 1915*, Granada, 1990

Titos Martínez, Manuel, *Textos primitivos sobre Sierra Nevada (1754/1838)*, Granada, 1991

Townsend, Joseph, *A Journey through Spain in the Years 1786 and 1787*, London, 1791

Tracy, Honor, *Silk Hats and No Breakfast. Notes on a Spanish Journey*, London 1957

Trend, J. B., *Spain from the South*, London, 1928

Walker, Ted, *In Spain*, London, 1987

Webster, Jason, *Duende, A journey in search of Flamenco*, London, 2003

Webster, Jason, *Andalus, Unlocking the secrets of Moorish Spain*, London, 2004

Widdrington (formerly Cook), S. E., *Spain and the Spaniards*, London, 1844

Fiction and Poetry

Pedro de Alarcón, *The Three-Cornered Hat (1874) and Other Stories*, translated by Michael Alpert, Harmondsworth, 1975

Ali, Tariq, *Shadows of the Pomegranate Tree*, London, 1992

Bates, Ralph, *The Olive Field*, London, 1936

Bécquer, Gustavo, *Rimas*, trans. as *Stories and Poems*, ed. W. S. Hendrix, New York, 1931

Blasco Ibañez, Vicente, *La Bodega*, Madrid, 1905

Boehl von Faber, Cecilia ('Fernan Caballero'), *La Gaviota,* 1856

Cervantes, Miguel de, *Exemplary Stories* (1613), translated by C. A. Jones, Harmondsworth, 1972
Cervantes, Miguel de, *Don Quixote*, translated by Burton Raffel, 1995
Day, Douglas, *Journey of the Wolf*, London,1988
Enrique, Antonio, *Kalat-Horrat, Tres mujeres solas en un castillo*, Granada, 1991
Gala, Antonio, *El manuscrito carmesí* Barcelona, 1990
García Lorca, Federico, *Romancero Gitano*, translated by Carl W. Cobb, Jackson (Mississipi), *c.* 1983
Góngora, Luis de, *The Solitudes of Don Luis de Góngora* (1627), a text with verse translation by Edward Meryon Wilson, Cambridge, 1965
Goytisolo, Juan, *Count Julian* (1969), translated by Helen Lane, London, 1989
Goytisolo, Juan, *Juan the Landless*, translated by Helen Lane, London, 1990
Hemingway, Ernest, *For Whom the Bell Tolls*, London, 1940
Jiménez, Juan Ramón, *Platero and I* (1914), translated by G. M. Walsh, London, 1922
Maalouf, Amin, *Leo the African*, (Paris, 1986), London, 1994
Merimée, Prosper, *Carmen* in *Carmen and other stories*, translated by Nicholas Jotcham, Oxford, 1989
Morante, Elsa, *Aracoeli*, Turin, 1982
Muñoz Molina, Antonio, *El jinete polaco*, Barcelona, 1991
Pérez-Reverte, Arturo, *The Seville Communion*, London, 1998
Potocki, Jan, *The Manuscript found at Saragossa*, (*c.* 1815), translated by Ian Maclean, London, 1995
Rushdie, Salman, *The Moor's Last Sigh,* London, 1996
Sánchez-Albornoz, Claudio, *Ben Ammar de Sevilla*, Madrid, 1972
Sender, Ramón, *La tesis de Nancy*, 1962
Valera, Juan, *Pepita Jiménez* (1874), translation by H. de Onis, New York, 1964
Valera, Juan, *Doña Luz*, Madrid, 1879
Valera, Juan, *Juanita la larga*, Madrid, 1895
Warner, Sylvia Townsend, *After the Death of Don Juan*, London, 1938

Prehistory

Breuil, Henri, *Rock Paintings of Southern Andalusia*, Oxford, 1929
Góngora y Martínez, M. de, *Antigüedades prehistóricas de Andalucía*, Madrid, 1968
Maluquier de Montes, *La civilización de Tartessus*, Granada, 1985
Rothenerg, Beno, *Studies in Ancient Mining and Metallurgy in South-West Spain*, London 1981
Whishaw, E. M., *Atlantis in Andalucía. A study of folk memory*, London, 1929

Roman Andalucía

Abad Casal, L., *Pinturas romanas en Sevilla*, Seville, 1979
Bendala, M., *La necropolis romana de Carmona* (2 vols.), Seville, 1976
Blanco Frejeiro, A., *Mosaicos romanos de Itálica* (I), Madrid, 1978
Blázquez, J. M., *Mosaicos romanos de Sevilla, Granada, Cádiz y Murcia*, Madrid, 1982

Bonsor, G. E., *An Archaeological Sketch-Book of the Roman Necropolis at Carmona*, New York, 1931

Corzo Sánchez, Ramón, *Osuna de Pompeyo a Cesar*, Seville, 1977

Corzo Sánchez, Ramón, *and* Toscano San Gil, Margarita, *Las vías romanas de Andalucía*, Seville, 1992

García y Bellido, *Andalucía Monumental. Itálica*, Seville, 1984.

Gil Albarracín, A., *Construcciones romanas de Almería*, Almería, 1983

Gómez Moreno, M., *Monumentos romanos y visigoticos de Granada*, Granada, 1988

Gozalbes Craviato, *Las vías romanas de Málaga*, Madrid, 1986

Ibáñez Castro, A., *Córdoba Hispano-Romana*, Córdoba, 1983

* Keay, S. J., *Roman Spain*, London, 1988

Luzón Nogue, J. M., *La Itálica de Adriano*, Seville, 1989

Knapp, Robert, *Roman Córdoba*, Berkeley, 1983

Rios, D. de los, *Anfiteatro de Itálica*, Seville, 1988

Islamic Andalucía

Al-Andalus, The Arts of Islamic Spain (exhibition catalogue), Alhambra, Granada, and Metropolitan Museum, New York, 1992

Al-Mutamid, *Poesia*, Spanish translation by Miguel José Hagarty, Barcelona, 1979

Arberry, A. J., *Moorish Poetry, A translation of the Pennants, an anthology compiled in 1243 by the Andalusian Ibn Sa'id*, Cambridge, 1953

Arié, Rachel, *L'Espagne musulmane au temps des Nasrides (1232-1492)*, Paris, 1990

Arjona Castro, A., *El Reino de Córdoba durante la dominación musulmana*, Córdoba, 1982

Barrucan, Marianne *and* Bednorz, Achim, *Moorish Architecture in Andalusia*, Cologne, 1992

Bermúdez Pareja, J., *Pinturas sobre piel en la Alhambra de Granada*, Granada, 1987

Bosch-Vila, J., *La Sevilla islámica (712 -1248)*, Seville, 1984

Bosch-Vila, J., *Andalucía islámica*, Granada, 1980

* * Burckhardt, Titus, *Moorish Culture in Spain*, London, 1972

Caro Baroja, Julio, *Los moriscos del reino de Granada*, Madrid, 1991

* Chejne, Anuar, *Muslim Spain*, Minneapolis, 1974

Fernández-Puertas, Antonio, *The Alhambra*, London 1997

Fletcher, Richard, *Moorish Spain*, London, 1992

Franzen, Cola, *Poems of Arab Andalusia*, San Francisco, n.d.

Frishman, Martin, *and* Khan, Hassan-Uddin (edd.), *The Mosque*, London, 1994

Goldstein, David (ed.), *The Jewish Poets of Spain, 900-1250*, Harmondsworth, 1971

* Goodwin, Godfrey, *Islamic Spain* , London, 1990

Grabar, Oleg, *The Alhambra*, London, 1978

Guillen Robles, F., *Málaga musulmana*, Málaga, 1880

Hagarty, Miguel José, *Ajimez, Antología de poesía Andalusí*, Jerez, 1983

Harvey, L. P., *Islamic Spain 1250-1500*, Chicago, 1990

Irving, Washington, *A Chronicle of the Conquest of Granada* (2 vols.), London, 1986

Irving Washington, *Legends of the Alhambra*, London, 1832

Jacobs, Michael, *Alhambra*, with photographs by Francisco Férnadez, London, 2000

Jayyusi, Salma Khadra (ed.), *The Legacy of Muslim Spain* (2 vols.), New York, 1994

Ladero Quesada, Miguel, *Granada, Historia de un país islámico (1232-1571)*, Madrid, 1989
El Legado Andalusí, *El agua en la agricultura de al-Andalus*, Granada, 1995
El Legado Andalusí, *Al-Andalus y el caballo*, Granada, 1995
El Legado Andalusí, *Al-Andalus y el Mediterraneo*, Granada, 1995
El Legado Andalusí, *Arquitectura en el-Andalus, Documentos para el siglo XI*, Granada, 1995
El Legado Andalusí, *La arquitectura del Islam occidental*, Granada, 1995
El Legado Andalusí, *Casas y Palacios de al-Andalus, siglos XII y XIII*, Granada, 1995
El Legado Andalusí, *Itinerario cultural de Almorávides y Almohades: Magreb y Península Ibérica*, Granada, 1999
El Legado Andalusí, *Música y poesía al sur de al-Andalus*, Granada, 1995
El Legado Andalusí, *El Mudéjar Ibero-Americano: Del Islam al Nuevo Mundo*, Granada, 1995
El Legado Andalusí, *El Zoco: Vida económica y artes tradicionales de al-Andalus y Marruecos*, Granada, 1995
Falcón Márquez, T., *La Torre de Oro*, Seville, 1983
García del Moral, A., *La Giralda, 800 años de historia, de arte y de leyenda*, Seville, 1987
Guillen Robles, F., *Málaga Musulmana*, (2 vols.), Málaga, 1984
Menocal, María Rosa, *The Ornament of the World, How Muslims, Jews, and Christians created a culture of tolerance in Medieval Spain*, New York, 2002
Montgomery Watt, W., *A History of Islamic Spain*, Edinburgh, 1965
Nieto Cumplido, M., *La mezquita-catedral de Córdoba*, Córdoba, 1976
Pareja-López, E., *El arte en el Sur de Al-Andalus*, Seville, 1989
Pérès, Henri, *La Poésie Andalouse en Arabe classique au XIème siècle*, Algiers, 1953
Sánchez-Albornoz, C., *La España musulmana según los autores islamitas y cristianas medievales*, Paris, 1985
Smith, Colin, *Christians and Moors in Spain* (2 vols.), Warminster, 1988, 1989
Tibi, Amin T., *The Tibyan Memoirs of Abd Allah ibn Buluggin, last Zirid amir of Granada*, Leiden, 1986
Torres-Balbas, L., *Ciudades Hispano-Musulmanas*, Madrid, 1985
Vines Millet, C., *La Alhambra de Granada, Tres siglos de historia*, Córdoba, 1988
Whishaw, Bernard, *Arabic Spain*, London, 1986

Medieval Christian Andalucía

AA. VV., *La Catedral de Sevilla*, Seville, 1984
Collantes de Teran, A., *Sevilla en la Baja Edad Media. La ciudad y sus hombres*, Seville, 1984
Lomax, D. W., *The Reconquest of Spain*, London, 1978
Marin Fidalgo, A. *Arquitectura gótica del sur de la provincia de Huelva*, Huelva, 1982
Morales Martínez, A., *Arquitectura medieval en la Sierra de Aracena*, Seville, 1986
Parejo Delgado, M., *Baeza y Úbeda en la Baja Edad Media*, Granada, 1988
El retablo mayor de la Catedral de Sevilla, Monte de Piedad y Caja de Ahorros de Sevilla, Seville, 1981

Sixteenth-, seventeenth- and eighteenth-century Andalucía

Angulo, Diego, *Alejo Fernandez*, Seville, 1946

University of Granada, 'Arquitectura de los siglos XVII y XVIII en Andalucía Oriental', in *Cuadernos de Arte, Universitad de Granada, 23. XII'* Granada, 1975
Banda y Vargas, Antonio de la, *La escultura Sevillana del Siglo de Oro*, Madrid, 1978
Bernales Ballesteros, J., *Alonso Cano en Sevilla*, Seville, 1976
Bernales Ballesteros, J., *Pedro Roldán*, Seville, 1983
Bernales Ballesteros, J., *and* García de la Concha, F., *Imagineros andaluces de los Siglos de Oro*, Seville, 1986
Bonet Correa, Antonio, *Andalucía barrocca, arquítectura y urbanismo*, Barcelona, 1978.
* Bonet Correa, Antonio, *Andalucía monumental. Arquitectura y ciudad del Renacimiento al Barrocco*, Seville, 1986.
Brown, Jonathan, *Murillo and His Drawings*, Princeton, 1975
Brown, Jonathan, *Velázquez, Painter and Courtier*, New Haven and London, 1986
Domínguez Ortiz, Antonio, *La Sevilla del Siglo XVII*, Seville, 1984.
Elliott, J. H., *Imperial Spain, 1469-1716*, London, 1963
* Gallego y Burín, A., *El barrocco granadino*, Madrid, 1956.
García Cano, Maria Isabel, *La colonización de Carlos III en Andalucía, Fuente Palmera*, Córdoba, 1982
García Fuentes, Lutgardo, *El comercio español con America, 1650-1700*, Seville, 1980
Garrido Domínguez, F., *La plaza de toros de la Real Maestranza de Ronda*, Ronda, 1985
Gilman, B., *Martínez Montañés. Sevillian Sculptor*, New York, 1967
Gómez Moreno, M., *Diego de Siloe*, Granada, 1988
Hagarty, Miguel José, *Los plomos del Sacromonte*, Madrid, 1981
Hernández Díaz, J., *Arte y artistas del renacimiento en Sevilla*, Seville, 1983
Hernández Díaz, J., *Martínez Montañés.*, Seville, 1987
Junta de Andalucía, *Andalucía Americana. Edificios vinculados con el Descubrimento y la Carrera de Indias*, Seville, 1989
Kamen, Henry, *Spain in the later seventeenth century*, London, 1980.
Kinkead, Duncan, *Juan Valdés Leal (1622-1680). His Life and Work*, New York and London, 1978
Ladero Quesada, M. A., *Granada después de la conquista. Repobladores y mudejares*, Granada, 1988
Lleo Canal, V., *Nueva Roma: Mitología y Humanismo en el Renacimiento Sevillano*, Seville, 1979
López Guzmán, *Tradición y clasicismo en la Granada del XVI. Arquitectura civil y urbanismo*, Granada, 1987
Morales Padrón, Francisco, *La ciudad del quinientos. Historia de Sevilla*, Seville, 1977
Morales Martínez, A., *La obra renacentista del Ayuntamiento de Sevilla*, Seville, 1981
Orozco Díaz, E., *La Capilla Real de Granada*, Granada, 1968
Orozco Díaz, E., *La Cartuja de Granada*, Granada, 1972
Palomero Paramo, J. M., *El retablo sevillano del Renacimiento: analisis y evolucion. 1560-1629*, Seville, 1983
Peláez, Manuel, *and* Rivas Carmona, Jesús, *El Barroco en Andalucía*, Córdoba, 1982
* Perry, Mary Elizabeth, *Crime and Society in Early Modern Seville*, Hanover, NH, 1980
* Pike, Ruth, *Aristocrats and Traders: Sevillian Society in the 16th century*, Ithaca, NY, 1972

Pike, Ruth, *Enterprise and Adventure. The Genoese in Seville and the Opening of the New World*, Cornell, 1966
Raya Raya, M.A., *El retablo en Córdoba durante los siglos XVII y XVIII*, Córdoba, 1980
Rivas Carmona, J., *Arquitectura barroca cordobesa*, Córdoba, 1982
Rodríguez Vázquez, Antonio L., *Ricos y pobres: Propriedad y vida privada en la Sevilla del siglo XVI*, Seville, 1995
* Rosenthal, Earl, *The Cathedral of Granada. A Study in the Spanish Renaissance*, Princeton, 1961
* Rosenthal, Earl, *The Palace of Charles V in Granada*, Princeton, 1985
Ruiz Lagos, *Ilustrados y reformadores de la Baja Andalucía*, Madrid, 1974
Sanchez-Montes González, F., *El Realejo (1521-1630), Los inicios de un barrio cristiano*, Granada, 1987
* Sancho Corbacho, A., *Arquitectura barroca sevillana del siglo XVIII*, Madrid, 1984
Sanz Serrano, M. J., *La orfebrería sevillana del Barroco* (2 vols.), Seville, 1976
Sitwell, Sacheverell, *Spanish Baroque Art*, London, 1931.
Valdivieso González, Enrique, *Juan de Roelas*, Seville, 1978
Valdivieso, Enrique, *and* Serrera, J. M., *El Hospital de la Caridad de Sevilla*, Seville, 1980
Valdivieso González, Enrique, *and* Serrera, J. M., *La época de Murillo, Antecedentes y consecuentes de su pintura*, Seville, 1982
Valdivieso Gonzalez, Enrique, *and* Serrera, J. M., *Pintura sevillana del primer tercio del siglo XVII*, Madrid, 1985
Velázquez (exhibition catalogue), Museo del Prado, Madrid, 1990
Velázquez in Seville (exhibition catalogue), National Gallery of Scotland, Edinburgh, 1996
Velázquez y Seville (exhibition catalogue), Monasterio de la Cartuja de Santa María de las Cuevas, Seville, 1999
Wethey, H. E., *Alonso Cano. Pintor, escultor y arquitecto*, Madrid, 1983
* Zalama, Miguel Ángel, *El Palacio de La Calahorra*, Granada, 1990
Zurbarán (exhibition catalogue), Museo del Prado, Madrid, 1988

Nineteenth-century Andalucía

AA. VV. *Arquitectura modernista en Córdoba*, Córdoba, 1985
Alfageme Ruano, P., *El Romanticismo sevillano. Valeriano Bécquer, ilustrador*, Seville, 1989
Bernaldo de Quirós, *Colonialización y subversión en la Andalucía de los siglos XVIII-XIX*, Seville, 1981
* Carr, R., *Spain, 1808-1939*, Oxford, 1966
Corbin, John R., *The Anarchist Passion, Class Conflict in Southern Spain 1810-1965*, Aldershot, *c.* 1993
El Legado Andalusí, *La imagen romántica del legado Andalusí*, Granada, 1995
Estébanez Calderón, Serafín, *Escenas Andaluzas*, Madrid, 1883
Fernández López, J., *La pintura de historia en Sevilla del siglo XIX*, Seville, 1985
* Hempel, Lipschutz, *Spanish Painting and the French Romantics*, Cambridge, Mass., 1972
Herr, Elena Fernández, *Les origines de l'Espagne Romantique, les récits de voyage, 1755-1823*, Paris, 1973

Hoffmann, Léon-François, *Romantique Espagne, l'image de l'Espagne en France entre 1800 et 1850*, New Jersey, 1961
Hutchinson, Marjorie, *The English Cemetery at Málaga*, Málaga, 1964
Kaplan, T., *Anarchists of Andalusia, 1818-1903*, Princeton, 1976
Martín Rodríguez, M., *La Gran vía de Granada*, Granada, 1986
Pérez Calero, G., *Gonzalo Bilbao, El pintor de las cigarreras*, Madrid, 1989
Pérez Mullet, F., *La pintura gaditana (1875-1931)*, Córdoba, 1983
Porlán, Rafael, *La Andalucía de Valera*, Seville, 1980
* Raquejo, Tonia, *El palacio encantado, la Alhambra y el arte Británico*, Madrid, 1989
Reina Palazón, Antonio, *La pintura costumbrista en Sevilla, 1830-1870*, Seville, 1979
Ruiz Lagos, M., *Política y desarrollo social en la Baja Andalucía*, Madrid, 1976
Santos García Felguera, Marín de los (ed.), *Imagen romántica de España*, exhibition catalogue, Palacio de Velázquez, Madrid, 1981
Torres Martín, R., *La pintura costumbrista sevillana*, Madrid, 1980
Valdivieso González, Enrique, *Pintura sevillana del siglo XIX*, Seville, 1981
Villar Movellán, A., *Arquitectura del modernismo en Sevilla*, Seville, 1973

Twentieth-century Andalucía

Alberti, Rafael, *The Lost Grove*, Berkeley, 1976
Ayuntamiento de Sevilla, *La Exposición Universal de 1992 en Sevilla*, Seville, 1987
Balbontin de Arce, *Sevilla 1992, Crónica de una transformación urbana*, Seville, 1992
* Brenan, Gerald, *Personal Record*, London, 1974
Chalmers Mitchell, Sir Peter, *My House in Málaga*, London 1938
Cheka Godoy, Antonio, *Andalucía después del 92*, Málaga, 1994
Cuenca Toribio, *La Andalucía de la transición, c. 1975-1984*, Madrid, 1984
Fraser, Ronald, *In Hiding - The life of Manuel Cortés*, London, 1962
García Lorca, Federico, *Selected Letters*, ed. and translated by David Gershator, London, 1984
* Gibson, Ian, *The Assassination of Federico García Lorca*, London, 1979
* Gibson, Ian, *En Granada, su Granada. Guía a la Granada de Federico García Lorca*, Barcelona, 1989
* Gibson, Ian, *Federico García Lorca. A Biography*, London, 1989
Grard, Dominique, *Imágines de Andalucía y sus habitantes en la narrativa andaluza de principio del siglo XX, 1900-31*, Seville 1992
Monks, Joe, *With the Reds in Andalusia*, London, *c.* 1985
Morales Folguera, J. M., *La arquitectura del ocio en la Costa del Sol*, Málaga, 1982
Morris, Brian, *Son of Andalusia, The Lyrical Landscapes of Federico García Lorca*, Liverpool, 1997
Nicholson, H., *Death in the Morning*, London, 1936
Pérez Escolano, V., *Anibal Gonzalez*, Seville, 1973
Richardson, John, *A Life of Picasso, Volume I: 1881-1906*, London, 1991
Santa Cruz, Juan José, *La carretera de Sierra Nevada y otros escritos*, Granada, 1993
Tussell, Xavier, *Oligarquía y caciquismo en Andalucía, 1890-1923*, Barcelona, 1976
Tussell, Xavier, *La crisis del caciquismos andaluz 1923-31*, Madrid, 1977
Woolsey, Gamel, *Death's Other Kingdom*, London, 1939

Gypsies and Flamenco

Álvarez Caballero, Ángel, *Historia del cante flamenco*, Madrid, 1986

Barrios, Manuel, *Ese Difícil mundo del flamenco, Semblanzas*, Seville, 1972

* Borrow, George, *The Zincali: or an Account of the Gypsies of Spain* (2 vols.), London, 1841

Brown, Irving, *Nights and Days on the Gypsy Trail through Andalusia and on other Mediterranean Shores*, New York, 1922

Brown, Irving, *Deep Song*, London, 1929

Clébert, Jean-Paul, *The Gypsies*, London, 1967

Falla, Manuel de, 'Cante Jondo' in *On Music and Musicians*, London, 1970

García Lorca, Federico, *Deep Song and Other Prose*, New York, 1980

García Ulecia, Alberto (ed.), *Las confesiones de Antonio Mairena*, Seville, 1976

Grande, Félix, *Memoria del flamenco* (2 vols.), Madrid, 1979

Howson, Gerald, *The Flamencos of Cadiz Bay*, London, 1965

Infante, Blas, *Orígenes de la flamenco y secreto del cante,* Seville, 1980

Jones, Jo, *Paintings and Drawings of the Gypsies of Granada*, London, 1969

Machado y Alvarez (Demófilo), *Cantes flamencos*, Seville, 1881

* Mairena, A., and Molina, R., *Mundo y formas del cante flamenco*, Seville, 1979

* Mitchell, Timothy, *Flamenco Deep Song*, Yale, 1991

Molina, R., *Misterios del arte flamenco*, Seville, 1986

Nuñez de Prado, G., *Cantaores andaluces,* Barcelona, 1904

Ortiz de Villajos, C. G., *Gitanos de Granada, La Zambra*, Granada, 1949

Pohren, D. E., *Lives and Legends of Flamenco*, Madrid, 1975

Pohren, D. E., *A Way of Life*, Madrid, 1980

Pohren, D. E., *The Art of Flamenco*, Shaftesbury, 1984

Quintana, Bertha B., *and* Floyd, Lois, *¡Que Gitano! Gypsies of Southern Spain*, London, 1972

Sackville-West, Vita, *Pepita*, London, 1937

Sánchez, María Helena, *Los gitanos españoles*, Madrid, 1977

Woodall, James, *In Search of the Firedance: Spain through Flamenco*, London, 1992

Fairs and Festivals

Burgos, Antonio, *Folklore de las cofradías de Sevilla*, Seville, 1972

Burgos, Antonio, *La Romería del Rocío*, León, 1974

Conrad, Barnaby, *Gates of Fear* (on bull-fighting), New York, 1957

Epton, Nina, *Spanish Fiestas*, London, 1968

Gómez Lara, M. J., *and* Jiménez Barrientos, J., *Guía de la Semana Santa en Sevilla*

Hemingway, Ernest, *Death in the Afternoon*, New York, 1932

Herrero, José Sánchez et al., *Las cofradías de Sevilla, historia, antropología, arte,* Seville, 1985

Junta de Andalucía, *Plazas de Toros*, Seville, 1992

Mateos de los Santos, G., *Un siglo de carteles festivo-religiosos en Sevilla, 1881-1987*, Seville, 1988

Mena, José María de, *Todas las Vírgenes de Sevilla*, Seville, 1994

* Rodríguez Becerra, Salvador, *Guía de fiestas populares de Andalucía*, Seville, 1982

Salas, Nicolás, *Las Ferias de Sevilla*, Seville, 1974

Siurot, Manuel, *La Romería del Rocio*, Huelva, 1918
Willoughby, David, *Guide to Semana Santa, Holy Week in Seville*, Seville, 1974

Food and Wine

Alonso, Juan Carlos, *La cocina de Sevilla en su salsa*, Seville, 1988
Alonso, Juan Carlos, *De tapas por Sevilla*, Madrid, 1995
Amate, Pablo, *De tapas por Granada*, Madrid, 1996
Briz, José, *Breviario del gazpacho*, Madrid, 1989
* Capel, José Carlos, *Comer en Andalucía*, Madrid, 1981
Casas, Penelope, *The Foods and Wines of Spain*, Harmondsworth, 1985
Diputación Provincial de Córdoba, *Nuestras Tabernas*, Córdoba, 1987
* Fraga Iribarne, María Luísa, *Guía de dulces de los conventos sevillanos de clausura*, Córdoba, 1988
Jeffs, Julian, *Sherry*, London, 1982
Luard, Elizabeth, *The Flavours of Andalucía*, London, 1991
March, Lourdes *and* Ríos, Alicia, *The Art of Spanish Cooking*, 1993
* March, Lourdes, *and* Ríos, Alicia, *El libro del aceite y la aceituna*, Madrid, 1990
* Martínez Llopis, Manuel, *Historia de la gastronomía Española*, Madrid, 1989
Maspellí, López, *Gran libro de cocina andaluza*, 1990
Pérez, Dionisio (Post-Thebussem), *Guía del Buen Comer Español*, Madrid, 1929
Read, Jan, *The Wines of Spain*, London, 1986
Salcedo Hierro, Miguel, *La cocina andaluza*, 1979
Spinola, Carlos, *Gastronomía y cocina gaditana*, Cádiz, 1990

Practical Information

General information

Covering 87,268 sq. kms, Andalucía occupies 17.3% of Spanish territory, and is thus the second largest of Spain's seventeen autonomous regions; it is divided into the provinces of Almería, Cádiz, Córdoba, Huelva, Granada, Jaén, Málaga and Seville. A meeting point of Europe and Africa, and of the Mediterranean and the Atlantic, Andalucía is a region of exceptional geographical diversity. The wide and fertile expanse of the Guadalquivir basin, with its accumulation of mud, clay, gravel, loam and coastal sand, acts as the backbone to a region where more than a third of the land is over 600 m in altitude. The mountainous districts fall into two main zones of distinct geological make-up: to the north runs the Sierra Morena, with its predominance of slate, quartzite and intruded rock such as granite, while to the south and east extend the Baetic ranges – a series of intersecting ranges formed principally of limestone, mica, schist and volcanic rock, and centred around the Sierra Nevada, which has Spain's two highest peaks, the Veleta (3392 m) and Mulhacen (3481 m). Throughout the region there is an abundance of ilex, cork oak, wild olive, gall oak, pine trees and a wide variety of bush.

With its annual average temperature of 16.8° C, Andalucía represents a transitional zone between the typically temperate climates in medium latitudes with an Atlantic influence, and the sub-tropical climates nearer the Equator; however, it is also a region of climatic extremes which manages to combine desert-like areas (around Almería) with a mountainous district (the Sierra de Grazalema) that has the highest rainfall in Spain. The average rainfall in the summer is less than 350 mm in the coastal zones, and not quite 600 mm in the rest of the region. Together with the south of Portugal, Andalucía has the highest number of hours of sunshine in the Iberian peninsula, with an annual average of over 3,000 hours in the lower Guadalquivir Valley, and along the Atlantic coast, and the coast of Granada and Almería.

The population of Andalucía is nearly seven million, with most of this being concentrated along the coast and in the towns of the Guadalquivir Valley. The regional economy is dependent to a great extent upon tourism, fishing and farming (wheat, olives, grapes, cotton, sugar-beet, tobacco, sun-flower, rice, tomato, and citrus are among the principal crops, while pigs, horses and fighting-bulls are the basis of the region's live-stock farming); mining (iron, copper, lead, zinc, gold and silver) has declined greatly in recent years. The main industries are shipbuilding and aeronautical building, followed by car manufacture, the chemical industries, telecommunications, steel and electricity.

Chronology

2500 BC First use of metal in Andalucía
1500 BC Trojan War
Eighth century BC Phoenicians establish colonies in Andalucía, including Cádiz
Sixth century BC Greeks establish colonies in Andalucía. Carthaginians arrive as heirs to Phoenician interests. Last Celtic invasion in strength. Decline of Tartessus
219 BC Hannibal attacks Saguntum (near Valencia), leading to Second Punic War, bringing Romans to the Peninsula
206 BC Rome takes control of Hispania after fall of Cádiz
151 BC Foundation of Córdoba, centre of Roman administration
45 BC Caesar defeats Pompey
19 BC Romans complete conquest of peninsula. Establishment of province of Baetica
98 AD Accession of Trajan
117 AD Accession of Hadrian
409 Peninsula overrun by Vandals, Alans and Suevi; collapse of Roman power
410 Sack of Rome
414 First incursion of Visigoths
426 Sack of Seville by the Vandals
456 Visigoths control all peninsula
622 Flight (*hegira*) of Muhammad to Medina. Beginning of Muslim calendar
711 Arrival of Muslims in Spain with capture of Gibraltar by Tarik
c. **718** Christian victory at Covadonga initiates reconquest
720 Walls and Roman bridge at Córdoba rebuilt
723 Muslim advance into Europe halted at Poitiers
756 Independent Umayyad emirate of al-Andalus established by Abd al-Rahman I, fugitive from Damascus
784 Work begins on mosque at Córdoba
800 Charlemagne crowned emperor
822 Accession of Abd al-Rahman II, beginning of period of prosperity. Mosque of Córdoba enlarged, mosques built at Seville and Jáen
851 Mozarab uprising in Córdoba
928 Abd al-Rahman III proclaimed Caliph, independent of Baghdad. Beginning of Caliphate of Córdoba
936 Work starts at Medina Azahara
955 Foundation of Almería
961 Al Hakam II creates famous library
1031 Collapse of Caliphate and disintegration of al-Andalus into taifa kingdoms
1035 Castile and Aragón emerge as monarchies
1042 Work starts on Alcázar of Seville
1064 Work starts on Alcazaba of Málaga
1085 Reconquest of Toledo
1086 Almoravid dynasty under the King of Seville, al-Mutamid, re-unites al-Andalus and defeats Christians at battle of Sagrajas
c. **1130** Alfonso VII founds school of translators in Toledo through which Arabic and Jewish learning reaches western Europe
1146 Almohad invasion from Africa
1163 Seville declared capital of al-Andalus
1184 Work starts on the Giralda in Seville
1195 Defeat of Alfonso VII by Almohads at Alarcos
1212 Battle of Las Navas de Tolosa opens the valley of the Guadalquivir to the allied Christians of Castile, Aragón and Navarre
1231 Al-Ahmar Ibn Nasr appointed

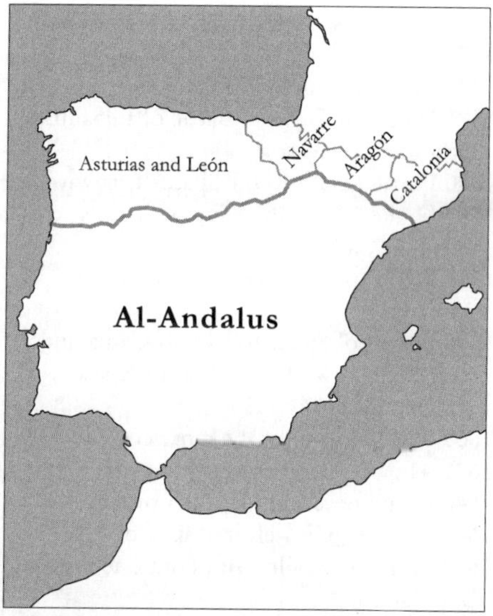

711-1031 AD
Emirate and Caliphate of Córdoba

1065 AD
Taifa Kingdoms

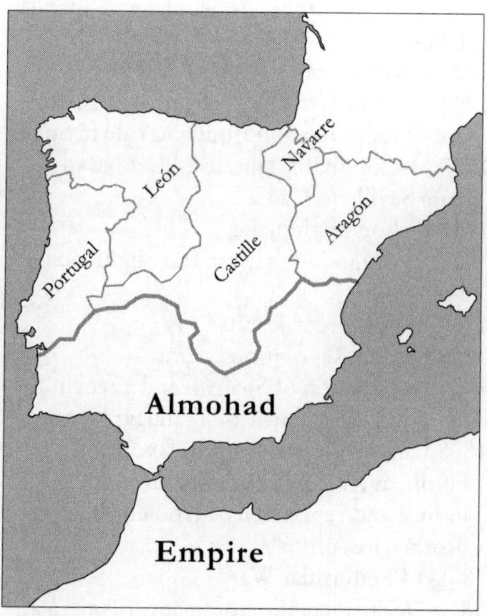

1212 AD
Almoravid and Almohad Empires

Before 1492 AD
Nasrid Kingdom of Granada

The territorial evolution of al-Andalus

governor of Arjona, soon extends sway to Jaén and Guadix, and founds Nasrid dynasty
1236 Ferdinand III takes Córdoba
1237 Emergence of Moorish kingdom of Granada. Work starts on the Alhambra
1246 Ferdinand III takes Jaén and Arjona
1248 Ferdinand III takes Seville
1314 Work starts on the Generalife
1348 Black Death
1369 Civil War and murder of Pedro I, dynasty of the Trastamara
1403-84 Canary Islands conquered from the Andalucían ports
1453 Fall of Constantinople
1469 Marriage of Isabella of Castile to Ferdinand of Aragón
1478 Inquisition founded in Castile
1482 Boabdil dethrones his father in Granada
1487 Málaga falls to the Christians
1489 Baeza and Almería surrender to Ferdinand and Isabella
1491 Boabdil surrenders Granada
1492 Ferdinand and Isabella enter Granada. Discovery of New World by Columbus (known as America from 1507)
Expulsion of the Jews from Andalucía
1502 Muslims in Castile offered choice of expulsion or conversion
1503 Monopoly of American trade given to Seville
1516 Accession of Charles I, first Hapsburg monarch
1519 Charles elected Holy Roman Emperor as Charles V
1519-22 Magellan starts circumnavigation of globe from Sanlúcar de Barrameda
1519-22 Cortés seizes Mexico ('New Spain')
1526 Wedding of Charles V in Seville
1527 Sack of Rome
1531-4 Conquest of Peru by Pizarro
1535 Capture of Tunis by Charles V
1554 Marriage of Philip and Mary Tudor
1556 Charles V abdicates in favour of his son Philip II
1568-70 Morisco uprising in Alpujarras
1570 Visit of Philip II to Andalucía
Morisco rebellion in Granada
1571 Defeat of Turks at Battle of Lepanto by Don Juan of Austria
1580 Portugal falls to the Spanish crown
1587 Drake 'singes the King of Spain's beard' at Cádiz
1588 Defeat in Channel of 'Invincible' Armada
1596 Defeat of Spanish fleet off Cádiz and sack of the town by the Earl of Essex
1598 Death of Philip II
1609-11 Expulsion of the moriscos
1621-41 Ascendancy of Olivares
1640 Portuguese and Catalan uprisings
1643 Catastrophic defeat at Rocroi
1649 Plague in Seville wipes out one third of population
1655 English capture of Jamaica, key to Caribbean
1702-13 War of Spanish Succession, involving most of Europe. Bourbons win Spanish throne
1704 Gibraltar captured by British
1713 Peace of Utrecht confirms British control of Gibraltar and Bourbon rule in Spain
1717 Monopoly of American trade passes from Seville to Cádiz
1755 Lisbon earthquake
1759-88 Reign of Charles III: enlightened despotism
1767 Expulsion of Jesuits
1789 French Revolution begins
1805 Destruction of Spanish and French naval power at Battle of Trafalgar
1808 Charles IV abdicates in favour of Ferdinand VII but both are lured to France and replaced by Napoleon's brother Joseph
1808-14 Peninsular War
1810-26 Emancipation of Spanish America, beginning with uprising in Buenos Aires
1812 Constitution proclaimed in Cádiz;

birth of liberalism and anti-clericalism in Spain

1814 Return from France of Ferdinand VII, who abolishes Constitution of 1812

1823 French army helps Ferdinand VII restore absolutist rule

1833 Isabella II proclaimed queen on death of her father Ferdinand VII

1833-9 First Carlist War, disputing Isabella's right to the throne

1834 Andalucía divided into eight provinces

1846 The 'Spanish Marriages' leading to fall of Louis Philippe in France

1847 Feria de Seville

1868 Abdication of Isabella II. The Cortes proclaims a constitutional monarchy and in 1870 invites Amadeo of Savoy to be king. Search for successor leads to Franco-Prussian War

1872-6 Second Carlist War

1873-74 First Republic

1874 Bourbon restoration under Alfonso XII, son of Isabella II

1898 Spanish-American War over Cuba marks the end of empire for Spain with loss of Cuba, Puerto Rico and the Philippines

1902 Sixteen year-old Alfonso XIII ascends the throne

1912 Protectorate established in Morocco

1917 Social agitation in Andalucía. War in Morocco

1923-30 Dictatorship of Primo de Rivera

1929 Ibero-American Exposition in Seville

1930 Primo de Rivera forced into exile

1931 Fall of Alfonso XIII. Second Republic proclaimed

1932 Rebellion in Seville led by General Sanjurjo

1933-35 Primo de Rivera's son José Antonio forms the Falangist party

1936-39 Civil War, ending in victory for the Nationalists under Franco over the loyalist Republicans. Franco's dictatorship begins

1947 Franco declares Spain a kingdom, with himself as regent

1953 Spain receives US aid in exchange for defence bases

1956 Moroccan independence, but with Spain retaining Ceuta and Melilla

1968 Spain closes border with Gibraltar

1975 Death of Franco. Accession of Juan Carlos I, grandson of Alfonso XIII

1981 Attempted military coup collapses on personal intervention of Juan Carlos

1982 Socialists, under Sevillian Felipe González, return to power for first time since Civil War. Autonomy granted to Andalucía. Establishment of a Parliament

1985 Frontier between Spain and Gibraltar reopens

1986 Spain joins European community

1992 EXPO in Seville

1996 Socialists defeated in elections; José-María Aznar becomes Prime Minister

1996 Partido Popular comes to power, with Jose Maria Aznar as prime minister.

2000 Partido Popular re-elected.

2004 Jose Luis Zapatero and the P.S.O.E (Socialists) come to power as a result of Madrid bombings. Zapatero wins subsequent election in 2008 and remains prime minister until 2011.

2011 Partido Popular elected; Mariano Rajoy becomes prime minister.

Principal Islamic rulers in Andalucía

Emirs of Córdoba	AD
Abd al-Rahman I	756
Hisham I	788
Hakam I	799
Abd al-Rahman II	822
Muhammad I	852
Mondhir	886
Abd Allah	888
Caliphs of Córdoba	
Abd al-Rahman III	912
Hakam II	961
Hisham II	976
Muhammad II	1008
Sulayman	1009
Hisham II (second time)	1010
Sulayman (second time)	1012
Ali Ibn Hamud	1017
Al Qasim	1022
Abd al-Rahman V	1022
Muhammad III	1023
Yahya Ibn Ali	1024
Hisham III	1027
Almoravid Sultans	
Yusuf Ibn Teshufin	1067
Ali Ibn Yusuf	1107
Teshufin Ibn Ali	1144
Almohad Sultans	
Abd al-Mumin	1147
Yusuf Abu Yacub	1163
Yacub Ibn Yusuf	1178
Muhammad Ibn Yacub	1199
Abu Yacub	1213
Abu Malik	1223
Mamun	1225
Kings of Granada	
Muhammad I	1238
Muhammad II	1273
Muhammad III	1303
Nasr	1309
Ismail I	1312
Muhammad IV	1325
Yusuf I	1333
Muhammad V	1354
Ismail II	1359
Abu-Said	1361
Muhammad V (second time)	1362
Yusuf II	1391
Muhammad VI	1396
Yusuf III	1408
Muhammad VII	1425
Muhammad VIII	1427
Muhammad VII (second time)	1429
Ibn Alhamar	1431
Muhammad VII (third time)	1432
Ibn Ostman	1445
Ibn Ismail	1454
Muley Hacen	1456
Abu Abdallah (Boabdil)	1482

Christian Rulers of Spain

Kings and Queens of León and Castille

Ferdinand I	1037
Sancho II	1065
Alfonso VI 'the Brave'	1072
Doña Urraca	1109
Alfonso VII 'the Emperor'	1126

Kings of León

Ferdinand II	1157
Alfonso IX	1188

Kings of Castille

Sancho III	1157
Alfonso VIII	1158
Enrique I	1214
Doña Berenguela	1217

Kings and Queens of León and Castille

Ferdinand III 'the Saint'	1217
Alfonso X 'the Wise'	1252
Sancho IV	1284
Ferdinand IV	1294
Alfonso XI	1312
Pedro I 'the Cruel'	1349
Enrique II	1369
Juan I	1379
Enrique III	1390
Juan II	1406
Enrique IV 'the Impotent'	1454
Isabel 'the Catholic' m. Ferdinand II of Aragón (r. 1479-1516)	1474

Queen of Castille and Aragón

Juana 'the Mad'	1504

Kings of the House of Habsburg

Philip I	1504
Charles I, Holy Roman Emperor as Charles V	1516
Philip II	1556
Philip III	1598
Philip IV	1621
Charles II	1665

Kings and Queens of the House of Bourbon

Philip V (abdicated)	1700
Luis I	1724
Philip V (reinstated)	1725
Ferdinand VI	1746
Charles III	1759
Charles IV	1788
[Joseph Bonaparte]	1808
Ferdinand VII	1814
Isabel II (abdicated)	1833
[interregnum]	1868
Amadeo of Savoy	1870
[republic]	1873
Alfonso XII	1875
Alfonso XIII (abdicated)	1886
[republic]	1931
[Gen. Francisco Franco]	1939
Juan Carlos I	1975

Language

Pronunciation

Spanish is a phonetic language, so the indications below should always hold good. In Castilian, which is regarded as standard Spanish, differences from English include the *r*, which is rolled; *h*, which is always silent; *c* before *e* or *i,* and *z*, which are pronounced as *th* in *thanks* (but not always in Andalucía; see below); *g* before *e* or *i,* and *j*, which are pronounced *ch* as in lo*ch*; *v*, which is pronounced like *b*; *ll*, which is pronounced as *y* in *yes*.

As a general rule, words ending in a vowel, *n* or *s* are stressed on the penultimate syllable; other words are stressed on the last syllable. The stress may also be indicated by a written accent, e.g. Andalucía.

The Spanish spoken in Andalucía differs from that of Castille in two important respects: the *c* before *e* or *i,* and the *z*, are not always pronounced as *th* but often instead as *s*, (a phenomenon known as the *seseo*, which has no hard and fast rules); and pronunciation is frequently clipped, with the last syllable in a word often omitted: eg. *manteca colorada* becomes *manteca colorá*.

Vowels

a	as in f*a*ther; e.g. patata
e	as in b*e*g; e.g. peseta
i	as in pol*i*ce; e.g. t*i*nto
o	as in g*o*t; e.g. pollo
u	1) as in f*oo*d; e.g. mucho 2) before another vowel as *w* as in *w*ater; cuando)
y	as Spanish *i*; e.g. yo

Consonants

b	soft, with lips slightly apart; e.g. sá*b*ado
c	1) hard, as in *c*at; e.g. catorce; 2) before *e* or *i* as the *th* in thin; e.g. doce
d	between vowels and at end of word as the *th* in thus; e.g. comedor
g	1) hard, as in *g*et; e.g. gracias 2) before *e* or *i*, as the *ch* in loch, e.g. gente
h	always silent; e.g. hotel
j	as the *ch* in loch; e.g. abajo
ñ	as the *ni* in onion; e.g. mañana
r	rolled; e.g. tarde
v	like Spanish b; e.g. vino
x	1) like the *x* in box; e.g. próximo 2) between *e* and a consonant, as an *s*; e.g. exportación
z	as the *th* in thin; e.g. diez

Letter Groups

cc	*kth*; e.g. dirección
ch	as in *ch*urch; e.g. derecho
ll	as in mi*lli*on; e.g. allí
qu	as in *c*at; e.g. queso
rr	strongly trilled; e.g. cerrado

Essential Vocabulary

January *enero*
February *febrero*
March *marzo*
April *abril*
May *mayo*
June *junio*
July *julio*
August *agosto*
September *septiembre*
October *octubre*
November *noviembre*
December *diciembre*

Monday *lunes*
Tuesday *martes*
Wednesday *miércoles*
Thursday *jueves*
Friday *viernes*
Saturday *sábado*
Sunday *domingo*

Christmas (Christmastide) *Navidad(es)*
Easter (Eastertide) *Pascua (Semana Santa)*

1 *uno*
2 *dos*
3 *tres*
4 *cuatro*
5 *cinco*
6 *seis*
7 *siete*
8 *ocho*
9 *nueve*
10 *diez*
11 *once*
12 *doce*
13 *trece*
14 *catorce*
15 *quince*
16 *dieciséis*
17 *diecisiete*
18 *dieciocho*
19 *diecinueve*
20 *veinte*
21 *veintiuno*
22 *veintidós*
31 *treinta y uno*
32 *treinta y dos*
40 *cuarenta*
50 *cincuenta*
60 *sesenta*
70 *setenta*
80 *ochenta*
90 *noventa*
100 *cien*
200 *doscientos*
500 *quinientos*
1,000 *mil*

first *primero, -a*
second *segundo, -a*
third *tercero, -a*
fourth *cuarto, -a*
fifth *quinto, -a*

Good morning *buenos días*
Good afternoon *buenas tardes*
Good night *buenas noches*
Hello/ goodbye *hola/ adiós*
See you later *hasta luego*

Yes/ no *sí/no*
Please/ thank you *por favor/ gracias*
I'm sorry *lo siento/ perdón*
Excuse me *perdóneme*
Not at all/ you're welcome *de nada*
morning/ afternoon *mañana/ tarde*
night *noche*
today *hoy*
yesterday *ayer*
tomorrow *mañana*
next week *la semana próxima*
last week *la semana pasada*
month *mes*
year *año*
early/ late *temprano/ tarde*

and/ but *y/ pero*
big/ small *grande/ pequeño, -a*
expensive/ cheap *caro, -a/ barato, -a*
good/ bad *buen(o), -a/ mal(o), -a*
here/ there *aquí/ ahí, allí*
hot/ cold *caliente/ frío, -a*
left/ right *izquierda/ derecha*
more/ less *más/ menos*
near/ far *cerca/ lejos*
now/ later *ahora/ más tarde*
open/ closed *abierto, -a/ cerrado, -a*
straight ahead *todo seguido*
this/ that *esto/ eso*
very *mucho*
what/ how much *qué/ cuánto*
where/ when *dónde/ cuando*
with/without *con/ sin*

Pleased to meet you *Encantado/a, mucho gusto*
How are you? *¿Cómo está usted?* (formal); *¿Cómo estás? ¿Qué tal?* (familiar)
Very well, thank you *Muy bien, gracias*
Do you speak English? *¿Habla usted inglés?*
I don't speak Spanish *No hablo español*
I don't understand *No comprendo/ no entiendo*
I don't know *No sé*
Please speak more slowly *¿Puede usted hablar más despacio, por favor?*
My name is... *Me llamo...*
I am English/ American/ Australian/ Canadian/ Irish *Soy inglés(a)/ americano(a)/ australiano(a)/ canadiense(a)/ irlandes(a)*
What is this called in Spanish? *¿Cómo se llama esto en español?*
Where is/are...? *¿Dónde está/ están...?*
Is there a...? *¿Hay un/ una...?*
I would like... *Quisiera/querría...* (Except to order food/drink e.g. *Quiero una cerveza por favor)*
Do you have...? *¿Tiene usted...?*
Just a moment *Un momento*
That's fine, that's OK *Está bien*

At the Hotel
bath: *baño*
dining room/ restaurant: *comedor, restaurante*
double bed: *cama matrimonial*
key: *llave*
lounge: *salón*
overlooking the sea: *con vista al mar*
a quiet room: *una habitación tranquila*
shower: *ducha*
wash basin: *lavabo*
WC: *váter*
I have a reservation: *Tengo una reserva*
Have you got a room? *¿Tiene usted una habitación?*
Come in! *¡Adelante!/ ¡Pase usted!*
This room is too small/ cold/ noisy *Esta habitación es demasiado pequeña/ fría/ ruidosa*
What time is breakfast/dinner? *¿A qué hora se sirve el desayuno/la cena?*

Shopping

credit card: *tarjeta de crédito*
travellers cheque: *cheque de viaje*
Where is the nearest...? *¿Dónde está ... más cercano, -a?*
Can you help me? *¿Puede usted ayudarme?*
Can you show me...? *¿Puede usted enseñarme...?*
I'll take it *Me lo llevo*
I'll leave it *No me lo llevo*
That's too expensive *Eso es demasiado*
This is faulty *Este tiene una falta*
Can I have a replacement? *¿Puede cambiármelo?*
Can I have a refund? *¿Puede devolverme el dinero?*

Shops
antique shop: *tienda de antigüedades*
art gallery: *galeria de arte*
baker: *panadería*
bank: *banco*
barber: *barbería*
beauty parlour: *salón de belleza*
bookshop: *librería*
cake shop: *pastelería*
camera/photographic shop: *tienda de fotografía*
chemist: *farmacia*
clothes store: *tienda de moda*
delicatessen: *charcutería; delicatessen; tienda donde se venden alimentos selectos*
department store: *grandes almacenes*
fishmonger: *pescadería*
florist: *florería*
greengrocer: *frutería*
grocer: *tienda de ultramarinos*
hairdresser: *peluquería*
jeweller: *joyería*
market: *mercado*
newsstand: *quiosco de periódicos*

optician: *óptico*
perfumery: *perfumería*
post office: *oficina de correos* (letter: *carta*; postal order: *giro postal*; string: *cuerda*)
shoe shop: *zapatería*
souvenir shop: *tienda de recuerdos*
stationer's: *papelería*
supermarket: *supermercado*
tailor: *sastrería*
tobacconist: *estanco*
tourist office: *oficina de turismo*
toy shop: *juguetería*
travel agency: *agencia de viajes*

At the Bank

I would like to change some pounds/ traveller's cheques/ dollars *Quisiera cambiar unas libras esterlinas/ unos cheques de viaje/ dólares*
What is the exchange rate? *¿A cuánto está el cambio?*
Can I get cash with this credit card? *¿Puedo sacar dinero con esta tarjeta de crédito?*
Can you cash a personal cheque? *¿Puede usted cobrarme un cheque personal?*
Do you need to see my passport? *¿Quiere usted ver mi pasaporte?*

At the Chemist

antiseptic cream: *crema antiséptica*
aspirin: *aspirina*
bandages: *vendas*
condoms: *preservativos*
cotton: *algodón*
diarrhoea/ upset stomach pills: *píldoras para diarrea/ el estómago trastornado*
indigestion tablets: *tabletas para indigestión*
insect repellant: *repelente para insectos*
laxative: *laxante*
plaster: *esparadrapo*
sanitary towels: *compresas*
shampoo: *champú*
shaving cream: *crema de afeitar*
soap: *jabón*
sun cream: *crema para quemaduras del sol*
tampons: *tampones*
tissues: *pañuelos de papel*
toothbrush: *cepillo de dientes*
toothpaste: *pata de dientes*
travel sickness pills: *pastillas para el mareo*

Clothes

bra: *sostén*
coat: *abrigo*
dress: *vestido*
hat: *sombrero*
headscarf: *pañuelo*
gloves: *guantes*
jacket: *chaqueta*
pullover: *suéter; jersey*
shirt: *camisa*
scarf: *bufanda*
shoes: *zapatos*
skirt: *falda*
socks: *calcetines*
stockings: *medias*
swimsuit: *traje de baño*
tie: *corbata*
tights: *leotardos*
trousers: *pantalones*
T-shirt: *camiseta*
underpants: *bragas* (for women); *calzoncillos* (for men)

Transport

aeroplane: *avión*
airport: *aeropuerto*
bus: *autobús*
bus stop: *parada de autobús*
car: *coche*
coach: *autocar*
ferry/boat: *ferry/ barco*
ferry port: *puerto*
hovercraft: *aerodeslizador*
railway station: *estación*
service station: *estación de servicios; gasolinera*

train: *tren*
ticket: *billete*
one-way: *de ida*
return: *de ida y vuelta*
ticket office: *taquilla*

Car

battery: *batería*
brakes: *frenos*
exhaust: *tubo de escape*
fan belt: *correa de ventilador*
lights: *luces*
windshield: *parabrisas*
My car has broken down *Tengo un coche averiado*
My car has got a flat tyre *Tengo un neumático pinchado*
My car won't start *Mi coche no arranca*
How long will it take to repair? *¿Cuánto tardará en repararlo?*
Where can I hire a car? *¿Dónde puedo alquilar un coche?*
By what time must I return it? *¿Para qué hora debo devolverlo?*
Is full insurance included? *¿Está incluido un seguro a todo riesgo?*
Is it insured for another driver? *¿Es asegurado para otro conductor?*
Is the petrol tank full? *¿Está lleno el depósito de gasolina?*
deposit: *depósito*
unlimited mileage: *kilometraje ilimitado*

Road signs

all directions: *todas direcciones*
caution: *cuidado*
danger: *peligro*
detour: *desviación*
drive slowly: *conduzca despacio; con moderación; al paso*
emergency exit: *salida de emergencia*
level crossing: *paso a nivel*
no parking: *prohibido aparcar*
one way: *dirección única*
other directions: *otras direcciones*
parking permitted: *aparcamiento permetido*
road blocked: *calle bloqueada*
road works: *obras*
slow: *despacio*
stop: *¡alto!*
toll: *peaje*
town centre: *centro ciudad*

Public Transport

first/second class *primera/segunda clase*
sleeper/couchette *coche-cama/litera*
Do I need to change anywhere? *¿Tengo que hacer transbordo?*
Is it direct? *¿Es directo?*
Is there a dining car? *¿Hay un coche-comedor?*
Is this the...for...? *¿Es éste el...para...?*
Please tell me where to get off *¿Me diría usted cuando tengo que apearme?*
Take me to... *Lléveme a...*
What time does it arrive? *¿A qué hora llega?*
What time is the last...for...? *¿A qué hora sale el último...para...?*
What time is the next...for...? *¿A qué hora sale el próximo...para...?*
Where does it stop? *¿Dónde para?*
Which gate/platform/quay? *¿Qué barrera/andén/muelle?*

Glossary

ajimez: small pairs of windows divided by a column or pier
alameda: park or park-like promenade
alcazaba: Moorish castle
alcázar: Moorish fortified palace
aljibe: cistern or water supply, usually of Moorish origin, occasionally Roman
almadraba: tuna fish hunt
Almohads: Berber invaders who replaced the Almoravids and ruled Andalucía in the late 12th and early 13th centuries
Almoravids: Berber rulers of Spain in the 11th and 12th centuries
artesonado: elaborate inlaid ceiling of Moorish or mudéjar style
atalaya: watch tower
ayuntamiento: Town Hall
azulejo: glazed ceramic tiles used as decoration in Moorish and later architecture
barrio: town district or suburb
bodega: cellar, wine bar or warehouse
bracero: landless agricultural worker
calle: street
camarín: shrine in church holding a venerated image
cante jondo: 'deep song', a form of flamenco; see p.145ff
capilla mayor: chapel with high altar
capilla real: royal chapel
carmen: villa with a garden, esp. in Granada
carnicería: butcher's
carretera: main road
Cartuja: Carthusian monastery
casino: social and gambling club
castillo: castle
chiringuito: beachfront restaurant
ciudad: city, town
ciudadela: citadel
colegiata: collegiate church
convento: monastery or convent
converso: Jew converted to Christianity
coro: choir of a church, normally walled and in middle of building
coro alto: raised choir in a church, usually above west door
correos: post office
corrida de toros: bull-fight
cortijo: rural farmhouse
coto: hunting reserve
cuesta: slope, hill
cueva: cave
custodia: monstrance
duende: a magical quality (a figurative meaning of the word usually used in reference to flamenco); see page 147f
embalse: artificial lake or reservoir
ermita: hermitage
esgrafiado: façade decoration, made by scratching patterns into stucco, or implanting small bits of coal
feria: annual fair
gitano: gypsy
granja: farmstead
iglesia: church
Isabelline: elaborately ornamental late gothic style developed under the Catholic monarchs
jornalero: landless agricultural day labourer
judería: Jewish quarter
juerga: shindig
Junta de Andalucía: government of the Autonomous Region of Andalucía
latifundio: large estate
Levante: the provinces of Valencia and Murcia; also the sharp wind from the east

lonja: exchange or Bourse building
mampostería: rough concrete made of rubble
maqsura: elevated platform, usually with grilles
marismas: marshes
matanza: pig slaughter
medina: Moorish town
mercado: market
mezquita: a mosque, but especially that of Córdoba
mihrab: prayer niche in mosque, showing direction of Mecca
mirador: viewing place, belvedere
mocarabes: ornamental moorish ceiling decoration, usually painted stucco
monasterio: monastery or convent
morisco: Muslim converted to Christianity, at least nominally
mozarab: Christian under Muslim rule, normally benefiting from religious tolerance
muqarnas: hanging masonry effect in Moorish architecture, achieved with multiple support elements
palacio: mansion
panadería: bakery
parador: luxury hotel, government run, sometimes in historic buildings
paseo: evening stroll; the promenade where it takes place
paso: float used in the *Semana Santa* processions
patio: courtyard
pescadería: fishmonger's
piscina: swimming pool
plateresque: elaborate early Renaissance style named for its resemblance to the work of silversmiths (*plateros*)
plaza: square
plaza de toros: bull ring
plaza mayor: main square of a town
posada: inn (old term)
preservativo: condom
pueblo: village or town
puerta: gateway, mountain pass
puerto: port
rambla: dry river bed
Reconquista: the Christian reconquest of Spain culminating in the fall of Granada (1492)
reja: iron screen or grille
retablo: carved or painted altarpiece
río: river
romería: pilgrimage to rural shrine
sacristía: sacristy
saeta: song in honour of Virgin or Christ (see page 161)
sala capitular: chapter house
señorito: toff
sevillana: rhythmic flamenco dance
SIDA: AIDS
sierra: mountain range
sillería: choir stalls
solar: aristocratic town mansion
solera: blending system for sherry and brandy
Solomonic column: twisted column, after its supposed use in Solomon's temple
tablao: flamenco show
taifa: small Moorish kingdom, of a type that emerged after the collapse of the Córdoba caliphate
trascoro: end wall of the choir
vega: cultivated fertile plain
venta: roadside inn

Bad language

Listed here are some of the more common words that never feature in guidebook glossaries, but that will frequently be heard by anyone lingering in a Spanish bar.

acojonado: bowled over
acojonante: absolutely incredible
bacalao: dance music, usually techno
cabrón: bastard
cachondeo, estar de: to have a laugh
camello: drug dealer
canuto: joint
chocolate: marijuana
chorizo: delinquent
chungo/a: seedy, ill
chupar: to practice oral sex/ to drink heavily
cojonudo/a: absolutely wonderful
colgarse: to become dependent on drugs; to become obsessed with
coño: although referring to female genitalia, this is a common expletive used even in polite conversation to give emphasis to a phrase; eg. *¿que coño haces?* what the hell are you doing?
¡cóñole!: bloody hell!
copas, estar de: out drinking
correrse: to have an orgasm
corrida: ejaculation
cutre: tacky
descolgarse: to come off drugs
enchufado: well connected
flipado/ a: high on drugs
flipante: amazing
flipar: to be amazed
follar: to f**k
frito/a: worn out
gamberro: thief
gilipollas (also *gil* and *gilí*): a w**ker
gilipollez: a completely stupid act
guay: fantastic
guiri: foreigner
¡hostia!: an expression of pleasant surprise referring to the holy wafer
joder: to f**k, also common expression of surprise
ligar: to pick up (a man or a woman)
ligue: one night stand
macarra: a lout
marica (also *mariquita* and *maricón*): homosexual
paja, echar una: to masturbate
pijos: the Spanish equivalent of the English 'Sloanes'
polvo, echar un: to f**k
polvos: cocaine, heroin
porro: a joint
puta madre, de: absolutely wonderful
rácano: mean
reventar, estar para: to be absolutely wonderful/dreadful
sinvergüenza: a complete rogue
tío: guy
tortillera: lesbian

Language of Food

At the Restaurant

breakfast: *desayuno*
lunch: *almuerzo*
dinner: *cena*
set menu: *menú fijo*
Do you have a table for...? *¿Tiene usted una mesa para...?*
I'd like to reserve a table *Quisiera reservar una mesa*
Can I see the menu? *¿Puedo ver la carta o el menú del día*
Can I see the wine list? *¿Puedo ver la lista de vinos?*
What do you recommend? *¿Qué recomienda usted?*
Can you bring me another...? *Tráigame otro/otra... por favor*
I didn't order this *No he pedido esto*
I'll have... *Tomaré...*
Can I have the bill, please? *La cuenta, por favor*
Is service included? *¿Está incluido el servicio?*

Essential words

beer/lager: *cerveza*
bottle: *botella*
bread: *pan*
butter: *mantequilla*
carafe: *jarra*
cheese: *queso*
chocolate: *chocolate*
coffee: *café*
cold: *frío, -a*
dry: *seco*
fizzy drink: *gaseosa*
fruit juice: *zumo de fruta*
glass: *vaso*
hot: *caliente*
iced: *con hielo/frío, -a*
lemonade: *limonada*
milk: *leche*
mineral water: *agua mineral*
  sparkling: *con gas/gaseosa*
  still: *sin gas/sin carbonato*
mustard: *mostaza*
oil: *aceite*
orangeade: *naranjada*
pepper: *pimienta*
salt: *sal*
steak: *filete*
  medium: *regular*
  rare: *poco hecho*
  well done: *muy hecho*
  very rare: *muy poco hecho*
sugar: *azúcar*
sweet: *dulce*
tea: *té*
vinegar: *vinagre*
wine: *vino*
  white: *vino blanco*
  red: *vino tinto*
  rosé: *vino rosado*

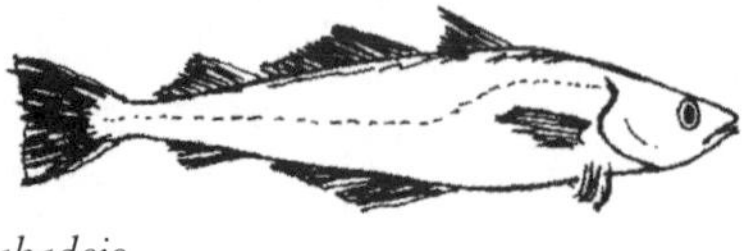

abadejo

acedia

aguja

anchoa

Menu glossary

Asterisks denote tapas and other dishes typically to be found in Andalucían bars and taverns; the Andalucían names have been used wherever possible. Sweets and pastries are covered more fully in the section 'Convent Confectionery' on page 435.

abadejo: fresh cod
**acedia*: flat fish resembling tiny sole
aceite (de oliva): (olive) oil
aceitunas: olives
acelgas: Swiss chard
achicoria: chicory
(en) adobo, adobado: marinated, pickled
aguacate: avocado
**aguja palá*: swordfish
ahumado: smoked
ajillo, ajo: garlic
**ajo blanco*: white gazpacho made from almonds
ajos tiernos: young garlic shoots
albaricoques: apricots
**alboronía*: a type of *pisto* stew (see below) with aubergines
alcachofa: artichoke
alcaparras: capers
**alcaparrones*: large capers
**alcauciles*: artichokes
alfajor: sweet made with almonds, sugar, cinnamon and lemon juice
al(l)ioli: garlic mayonnaise
almejas: clams
almendras: almonds
**almendritas*: small cuttlefish, often found in the bars of Huelva and Cádiz; especially good when fried whole with garlic and parsley
en almíbar: (in) syrup
**almóndiga*: the Andalucían word for meatball (can also be made from cod); derived from the Arabic 'al bunduga' (little ball)
alubias: dried beans
anchoas: anchovies
**anchoba*: a metre-long blue fish comparable to what is known in English as a 'trevally' (a type of horse mackerel); very common in the Bay of Cádiz, and usually served either marinated or stewed with tomato
anguila: eel
angulas: baby eels
apio: celery
arrope: syrup
arroz: rice
asado: roast
**asadura*: chopped up liver served as a tapa
atún: tuna
avellanas: hazelnuts
aves: poultry
azafrán: saffron
azúcar: sugar
bacalao: dried salt codfish
baila: type of sea perch with yellow head, orange body, and tasty blue flesh

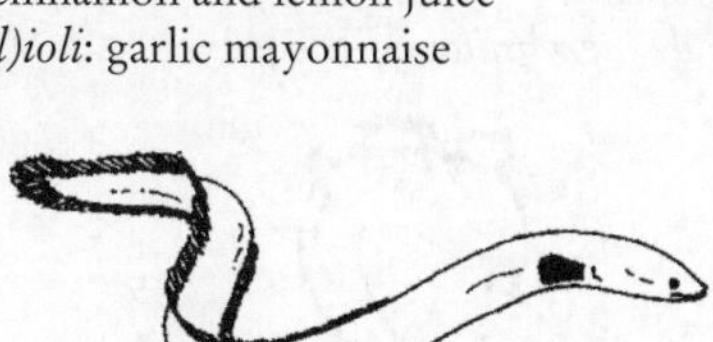

anguila

atún

baila

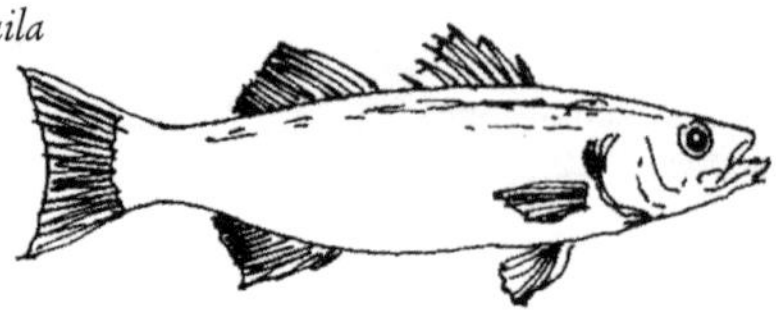

besugo

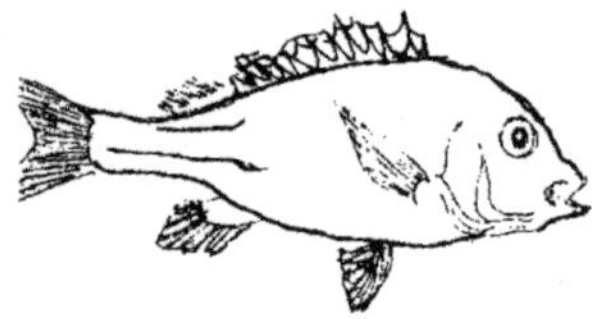

**berdigones*: cockles
berenjena: aubergine, eggplant
besugo: sea bream
**bienmesabe*: literally 'taste-me-well', a term used in Seville and Cádiz for marinated fried fish
biftec, bistec: steak, beefsteak
bocadillos: sandwiches
**bocas*: crab claws
bodega: wine cellar or shop
bogavante: lobster
bonito: a fish very similar to tuna but with whiter meat
boquerones: a kind of anchovy
boronia: another word for *alboronía* (see above)
botijo: clay pot with handle and two openings, one for filling vessel with water, the other for drinking from
(a la) brasa: charcoal broiled
braseado, -a: braised
**brazo gitano*: usually a dessert made with eggs, flour and jam, resembling a Swiss roll; sometimes a savoury concoction made with tuna wrapped in potato and mayonnaise (literally: *gypsy's arm*)
(en) brochetas: skewered
**buchón*: a Córdoban speciality: a fried and breaded fish roll (usually hake or Mediterranean sea bass) stuffed with ham; fish equivalent of a *flamenquín* (see below)
buey: ox
bullab(v)esa: Mediterranean fish soup
buñuelitos, buñuelos: fritters with a wide variety of fillings
**burgaillo*: a large sea snail
**burgajo*: a snail
butifarra: seasoned pork sausage
caballa: mackerel
cabra: goat
**cabrilla*: medium-large white snail (in Seville and Cádiz)
cabrito: kid
calabacín: baby marrow, courgette, zucchini
**calamares de campo*: thin slices of green pepper fried in batter
calamares (en su tinta): squid (in their own ink)
**caldereta*: lamb stew with vegetables
caldeirada: poached fish in garlic and paprika sauce/ fish and seafood stew
caldo: broth or soup-stew of meat and vegetables
callos: tripe
camarones: shrimps
caña de lomo: the finest kind of *chacina* or dried salt pork
**cañaíllas de la isla*: large sea snails commonly found in the Bay of Cádiz
cangrejo de mar, de río: crab, crayfish
**caracoles*: small snails
cardo, cardillo: cardoon, artichoke
carne: meat
carne de membrillo: quince jelly

boqueron

botijo

butifarra

caballa

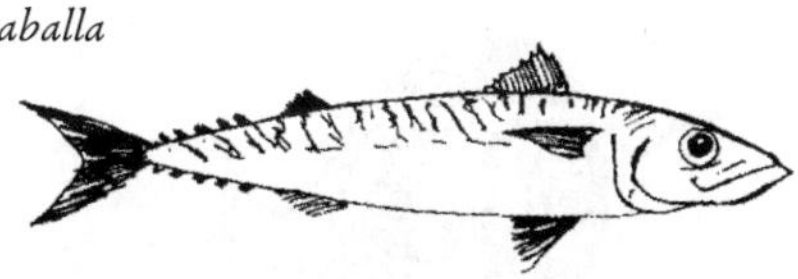

carnero: mutton
(de la) casa: of the restaurant
castaña: chestnut
**castañuela*: type of cuttlefish common to the coasts of Huelva and Cádiz
caza: game
**cazón*: dogfish
cazuela, cazuelita: casserole
cebolla: onion
cebón: steer/fattened beef
centolla: (large) crab
cerdo: pork
cerezas: cherries
chacina: dried salt pork
champiñones: mushrooms
**chícharos*: peas (in Huelva and Cádiz); chickpeas (in Seville)
chicharrón: pork crackling
chile: chili red pepper
chilindrón: thick tomato sauce made with ham and red peppers
chipirones: squid
chirimoya: custard apple
**chochos*: salted and vinegar-steeped lupins, served as tapas in some bodegas
choco: cuttlefish
chocolate: chocolate
chorizo: spiced pork sausage
chuleta: chop, usually veal or pork
chuletón: large beef or veal rib steak
chumbera: prickly pear
churrería: shop selling *churros* (see below)
churro: doughnut fritter
cigalas: crayfish
ciruela: plum
cochinillo: suckling pig
cocido: stew of meat and vegetables with many regional variations
cocido, -a: cooked, boiled
cogollo: heart (of vegetable)
col: cabbage
coliflor: cauliflower
conejo: rabbit
**coquinas*: small clams
corazón: heart
corb(v)ina: sea bass or perch
cordero: lamb
corzo: roebuck
costra: crust
crema: cream
criadillas: testicles
croquetas: croquettes
crudo, -a: raw
cuajada de leche: milk product like yoghurt
dorada: gilthead bream
dulces: sweets, desserts
duro: hard (-boiled)
embutidos: charcuteries
empanada: meat, fish or seafood pie
empanado, -a: fried in breadcrumbs
encebollado: cooked with onions
ensalada: salad
entremeses: appetizers
erizo de mar: sea urchin

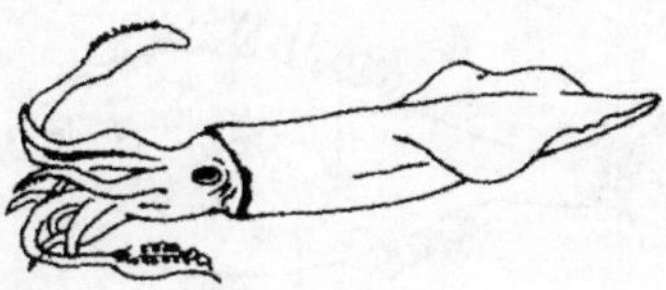

calamar

cañaílla

caracol

cardillo

(en) *escabeche, escabechado*: pickled, marinated
escalfado: poached
escarola: endive
espárragos: asparagus
espinacas: spinach
estofado: stew(ed)
esturión: sturgeon
faisán: pheasant
fiambres: cold cuts
fideos: pasta, noodles
filete: fillet, usually steak
flamenquín: roll of meat filled with ham and cheese
flan: baked caramel custard
frambuesas: raspberries
fresas, fresones: strawberries
fresco, -a: fresh
frío: cold
frito, -a: fried
fritura: fried dish/ fritter
**fritura mixta de pescados*: a selection of fried white fish
fruta: fruit
gachas: savoury oatmeal, often with garlic
galletas: biscuits
gallina: hen
gallo: rooster; also a flat fish like sole
gambas: large prawns
ganso: goose
garbanzos: chickpeas
garum: a Roman fish paste comparable to Gentleman's Relish
gazpacho: chilled garlic and tomato soup
girasol: sunflower
**gitana*: large white snail (in Huelva), comparable to the Sevillian *cabrilla* (see above)
gorullos: home-made lumps of pasta, often found in Almerían cooking
gratinado, -a: browned, with cheese or breadcrumbs
guindillas: hot red peppers
guisado: stew
guisantes: peas
**gurumelo*: a wild mushroom that usually grows among brambles; served as a tapa in some of the Huelva bars
habas: broad beans
**habas enzapatás*: large, end-of-season broad beans
habichuela: bean, kidney bean
helado: ice cream
hervido, -a: boiled, poached
hierbabuena: mint
hígado: liver
higo: fig
higo chumbo: prickly pear
hinojo: fennel
hoja: leaf
(al) horno: baked
hueso de santo: small roll of marzipan filled with candied egg yolk, angel's hair or jam
huevas: fish roe

cazón

dorada

gallo

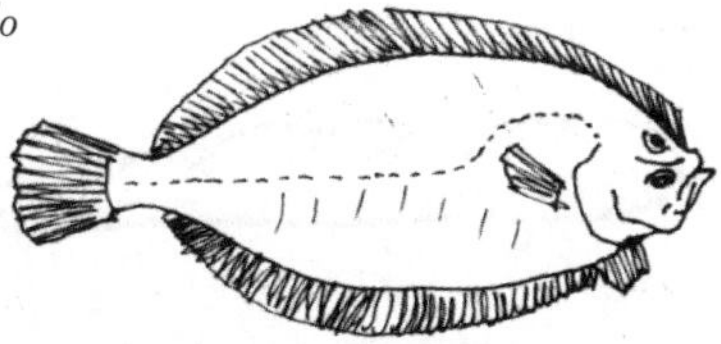

higos chumbos

huevos: eggs
  al plato: fried or baked
  revueltos: scrambled
**huevos de choco*: soft, egg-like forms found inside cuttlefish
jabalí: wild boar
jamón: ham
**japuta*: small oval flat fish known in English as 'pomfret'
judías: beans
(en su) jugo: (in its own) juice
(sopa) juliana: soup of thin-sliced vegetables
lacón: pork shoulder
langosta: spiny lobster
langostino: large prawn
laurel: bay leaf
lechazo: young lamb
leche frita: literally 'fried milk': a popular baked custard cream dessert
lechón: suckling pig
lechuga: lettuce
lengua: tongue
lenguado: sole
lentejas: lentils
liebre: hare
limón: lemon
lombarda: red cabbage
lomo: loin (usually of pork)
lubina: sea bass
magras: lean, air-cured ham
manolete: bread stick like French baguette
manteca: lard
**manteca colorá*: lard flavoured with pimiento
mantecado: enriched ice cream
mantequilla: butter
manitas: pig's trotters
manzana: apple
**mariquitas*: small sardines served fried
mariscada: mixed grill of seafoods
mariscos: seafood
mejillones: mussels
melocotón: peach
melva: type of tuna
menestra de legumbres/ verduras: mixed sautéed vegetables flavoured with ham
**menudillos*: chicken livers and sweetbreads cooked with onions
menúo: Andalucían form of tripe, often cooked with chickpeas
merluza: hake
mero: Mediterranean sea bass
miel: honey
migas: fried bread crumbs
mojama: dried salted tuna fish, from the Arabic 'musamma' (to dry)
mollejas: sweetbreads (usually veal or lamb)
**moraga*: the frying of sardines over a wood fire; a speciality of the beaches of the Costa del Sol
morcilla: blood sausage, black pudding
morcillo: shank
morcon: large blood sausage
mortero: mortar

jurel

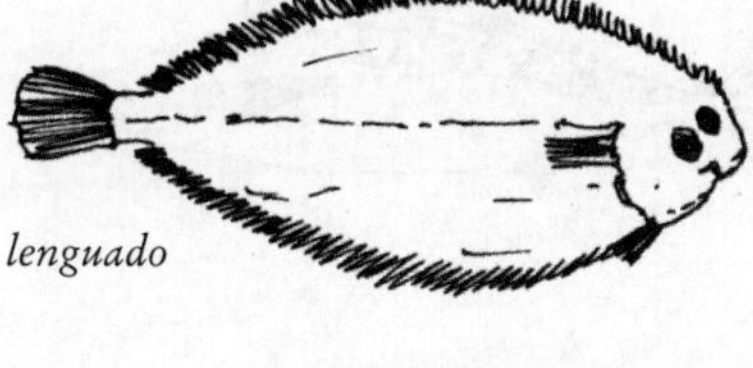

lenguado

lubina

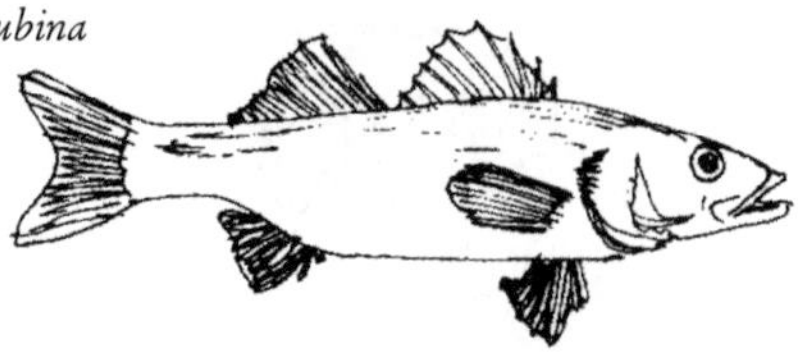

manolete

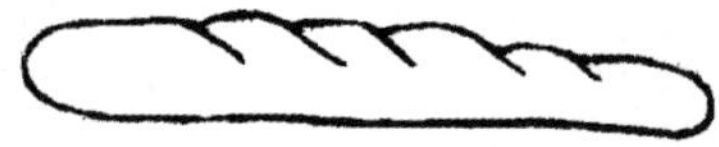

mosto: must, unfermented grape juice
**muergo*: razor fish, abundant in Cádiz and Huelva
mújol: mullet
naranja: orange
navaja: razor fish
nécoras: small crabs
níspero: wild mushroom
nueces: nuts, walnuts
nuez moscada: nutmeg
oca: goose
olla: pot, pan
olla gaditana: stew with white beans, pork and vegetables
ostión: a large oyster of metallic taste found in Andalucía's Atlantic coast
ostras: oysters
paella: saffron rice dish with meat, fish or seafood
**pajaritos*: small birds; in Almería the word refers also to small green peppers fried in batter
palometa: small oval flat fish comparable to *japuta* (see above)
pan: bread
pan integral: wholemeal bread
**papa*: potato, usually served as a tapa cold, sliced and dressed with oil, vinegar, green pepper and onion
**papandúas*: fried small pieces of salt cod
pargo: type of bream or porgy
(a la) parilla: grilled, broiled
parillada (de mariscos, de pescados): grilled or broiled seafoods or fish
pasas: raisins
pastel: pâté/pie, pastry, cake
**pastel de olla*: diced leftovers of meat from stew, usually served on fried slices of French bread
patatas: potatoes
pato: duck
**pavías de pescado*: fritters made from either hake or salt cod
pavo: turkey
pechuga: breast (usually chicken)
pepinillos: gherkins
pepinos: cucumber
pera: pear
perca: perch
percebe: goose barnacle
perdiz: partridge
**perdiz de huerta*: lettuce cut into quarters and dressed with oil, salt and vinegar
perejil: parsley
pescadillas: whiting/ small hake
pescado: fish
pestiño: anis and honey biscuit
pez espada: swordfish
picadillo: salad of finely diced vegetables, usually tomato, onion, pepper and cucumber
pichón: pigeon
pierna: leg
pijota: whiting or small hake, served fried

melva

merluza

mero

muergo

pimienta: (black) pepper
pimientos: sweet peppers
piña: pineapple
pinchitos de carne: kebab
piñon: pine kernel
**pinchos morunos*: lamb kebabs marinated in wine
**pipirrana*: salad of tomato, onion, tuna and black olives, very common in the roadside inns of Almería
**pirinaca*: salad of tomatoes, peppers and onions
pisto: stew of mixed vegetables, often with egg
(a la) plancha: cooked on a flat metal hot plate
plátano: banana
platija: plaice
pollo: chicken
**polvorones*: a powdery sweetmeat made from icing sugar and ground almonds, a speciality of Estepa
pomelo: grapefruit
potaje: soup
pringá: mixed handminced meats from a *cocido*
puchero: cooking pot for fire; used for the stew known as *cocido* (see above)
puerros: leeks
pulpitos: tiny octopuses
pulpo: octopus
puntillitas: tiny squid
queso: cheese
quisquillas: small shrimps
rábanos: radishes
rabo de toro/ buey: oxtail
ración: portion, helping (tapas)
raia: angler fish
rape: monkfish
rascacio: scorpion fish
raya: ray, skate
rebozado, -a: fried in batter
relleno, -a: stuffed
remolacha: beetroot
repollo: cabbage
repostería: cakes, pastries, sweets, tarts
**revoltillos*: tripe dish rolled up and held together by the intestines of the animal; often flavoured with ham and mint
revuelto: any dish with a basis of scrambled eggs
riñones: kidneys
(de) río: freshwater
róbalo: sea perch
rodaballo: turbot
(a la) romana: deep-fried
ropa vieja: literally 'old clothes'; meat leftovers in tomato sauce
rosquilla: doughnut
rubio: red gurnard
sal: salt
salado, -a: salted
(en) salazón: cured
salchicha: sausage
salchichón: salami

palometa

pargo

pez espada

rape

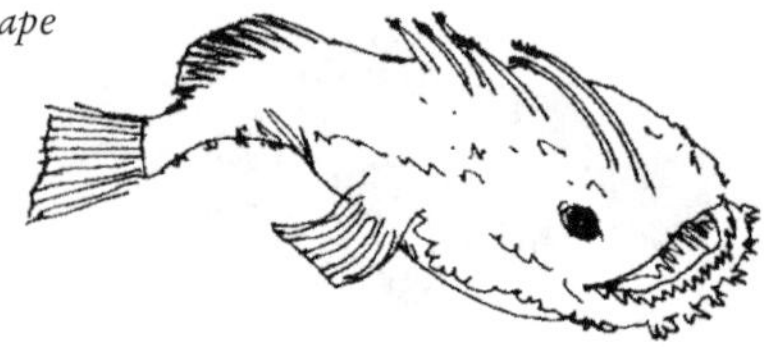

salmonete: red mullet
**salmorejo*: cold tomato soup, a Córdoban speciality
salpicón: finely chopped seafood or chicken salad
salsa: sauce
salteado, -a: sautéed
sandía: watermelon
santiaguiño: tiny, clawless lobster-like crustacean known variously as 'Galician lobster' and 'sea cricket'
sardina: sardine
sargo: bream
sesos: brains
setas: wild mushrooms
solomillo: tenderloin
sopa: soup
surtido: assortment
**tabernero*: a tapa of *pisto* (see above) served on a slice of French bread, a speciality of Almería
tapa: snack, aperitif
tartaleta: savoury or sweet tart
ternasco: baby lamb
ternera: veal; beef
tinaja: large earthenware jar with wooden lid
tocino: bacon
tocino de cielo: a small crème caramel (literally 'heavenly bacon')
**tollo*: small, marinated, sun-dried dogfish, usually served cooked with tomatoes and cumin
tomate: tomato
toro (de lidia): beef (from the bullring)
tortilla: omelette
**tortillita de camarones*: shrimp omelette served in small portions
tortitas: waffles
tortuga: turtle
tostado, -a: toasted
tronco: slice
trucha: trout
trufas: truffles
turrón: nougat
urta: type of bream
uvas: grapes
uvas pasas: raisins
vaca: beef
(al) vapor: steamed
venado: venison
verduras: vegetables
vieiras: scallops
vinagreta: dressing made with onion, parsley, oil, salt and vinegar
yema: sweet made with egg yolk and syrup
zanahorias: carrots
zarzuela: stew of fish or shellfish

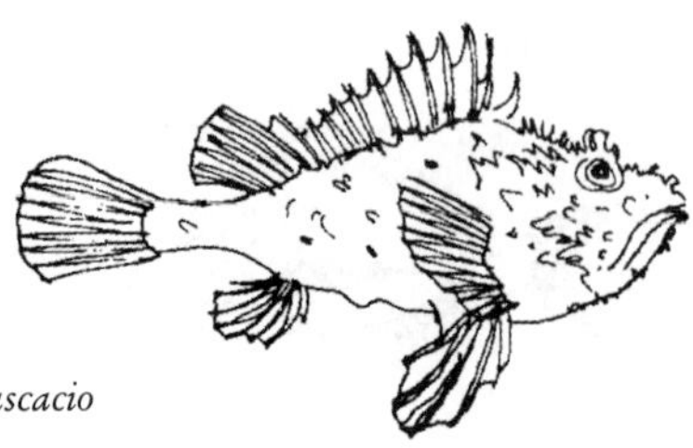

rascacio

róbalo

rodaballo

sargo

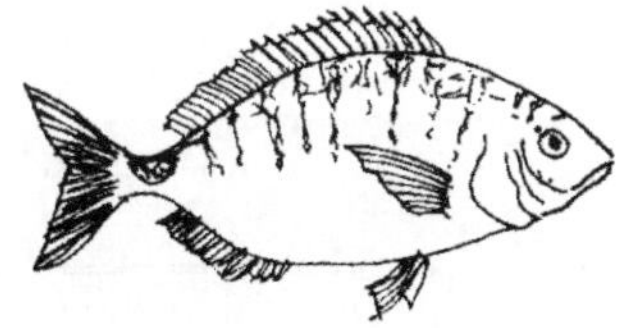

Drink Glossary

agua mineral: mineral water
 con gas: sparkling
 sin gas: still
aguardiente: liquor, brandy
amontillado: dry, amber-coloured sherry
anis: aniseed spirit
botella: bottle
café: coffee
caña: long, narrow glass; also the expression for a small glass of beer on tap
carajillo: coffee to which a drop of brandy has been added
catavino: fine, tulip-shaped sherry glass
cava: sparkling wine from Catalonia
cerveza: beer, lager
cerveza de barril: draft beer
cosecha/vendimia: vintage
dulce: sweet
fino: pale, straw-coloured, light, dry sherry
gaseosa: bottled sweet fizzy drink, like lemonade
jarra: flask, carafe
jerez-xeres-shery: sherry
leche: milk
limonada: lemonade
litrona: litre-sized glass of beer, popular mainly with foreign 'lager louts'
manzanilla: fortified wine from Sanlúcar, very similar to fino sherry
media botella: half-bottle
moscatel: sweet, aromatic white wine
naranjada: orangeade
oloroso: dark-gold, full-bodied, semi-sweet sherry
Pedro Ximénez: a type of *oloroso* (see above)
ponche: a blend of brandy with orange and herbs
sangria: cold red wine with fruit, lemonade and cointreau
seco: dry
té: tea
tinto de verano: iced red wine and *gaseosa* (see above)
tubo: draught beer served in a long narrow glass
vendimia/cosecha: vintage
vino: wine
 vino blanco: white wine
 vino rosado: rosé wine
 vinto tinto: red wine
zumo de fruta: fruit juice

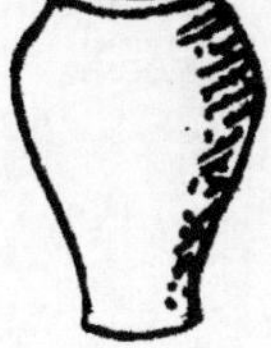

tinaja

caña

All the information in this book has been checked with care. However, no responsibility can be taken for any possible inaccuracies.

We are always most grateful to readers who can draw attention to errors and omissions, or who would like to suggest improvements. Please contact us at the addresses mentioned on the copyright page

A-Z of Practical Information

Accommodation A full listing of accommodation in Andalucía can be had at tourist offices; the Michelin *Red Guide to Spain and Portugal* has a selection of the more expensive hotels, while the *Rough Guide to Andalucía* gives useful advice on a wider range of places. Best of the Spanish hotel guides is the one published annually by Campsa, though the website TripAdvisor should also be consulted.

Many tourists come to Spain intending to stay solely in government-run *paradors (www. parador.es),* which are reliable in quality, and often have wonderful architectural settings, but are impersonal in character and remarkably similar in their furnishings. The most sought-after in Andalucía is Granada's Parador de San Francisco (Real de la Alhambra, tel 958 22 14 40), which is in a 16th-century monastery within the Alhambra, and is certainly more appealing than the majority of Granada's upmarket hotels. Second in popularity is Carmona's Parador Alcázar del Rey Don Pedro (Alcázar s/n, tel 95 414 10 10), which is frequently used as a base for tourists and businessmen visiting nearby Seville. The only other Andalucían paradors in historical buildings are the Parador Casa de Corregidor in Arcos de la Frontera (Pl. Cabildo, s/n, tel 956 70 05 00); Parador Castillo de Santa Catalina in Jaén (tel 953 23 00 00); the Parador Condestable Dávalos at Úbeda (Pl. Vazquez de Molina, 1, tel 953 75 03 45); the Parador de Ronda (Plaza de España, s/n., tel 95 287 75 00). There are modern paradors at Antequera (Málaga), Ayamonte (Huelva), Cádiz, Córdoba, Málaga and Mazagón (Huelva).

Those wishing to stay in an old and stylish setting can do much better than going to a parador. For old-fashioned luxury, Seville's Alfonso XIII (San Fernando, 2, tel 95 91 70 00) remains without equal in Andalucía. The region has also a growing number of palaces that have been converted into hotels, for instance, Carmona's Casa de Carmona (Pl. Lasso de la Vega, 1, tel 954 19 10 00), Sanlucar de Barrameda's Posada del Palacio (C/Caballero 11, tel 956 36 48 40), Osuna's architecturally breathtaking Palacio de los Marqueses de la Gomera (San Pedro, 20, Osuna, tel 954 812 223) and Écija's Palacio de los Granados (C/Emilio Castelar, 42, tel 955 90 53 44). Monastic accommodation is not available in Andalucía as it is in other parts of Spain; however, the coastal town of El Puerto de Santa María has a luxuriously converted monastery, the Monasterio San Miguel (tel 956 54 04 40); cheaper and wholly eccentric is the converted Charterhouse at Cazalla de la Sierra, the Hospedería de la Cartuja (Ctra. Cazalla-Constantina, tel 954 88 45 16). Special to Andalucía are the numerous converted *haciendas* or estates, including, near Seville, the Hacienda de San Rafael at Las Cabezas de San Juan (Ctra. Nacional IV, km. 594, tel: 954 22 71 16) and the Cortíjo Aguila Real at Guillena (Ctra. Guillena-Burguillos, tel 955 78 50 06); near Castellar de la Frontera is the Casa Convento La Almoraima (tel 956 69 30 02). Anyone wishing to experience life in one of the region's numerous caves can now stay in one of many converted 'self-catering' cave dwellings at the Granadan village of Galera (information and reservations from

Promociones Turísticas de Galera, tel/fax 958 73 90 68). Other cave-hotels can also be found at Guadix. The concept of 'village-style' hotels arranged as clusters of small dwellings is relatively new to Andalucía, and is being promoted by the regional government; the most recent of these is La Villa Turística de Priego at Aldea de Zagrilla (14816 Priego, Córdoba, tel 957 70 35 03).

The budget traveller will find extensive cheap and clean accommodation throughout the region, particularly away from the coast; the most basic places to stay are the *fondas*, which are marked outside with an F. In many of the villages it is also worth askingif anyone has any *camas* or guest rooms available, as these are generally of excellent value and very friendly. The highest concentration of cheap places to stay in Granada is off the Plaza Nueva, while a surprising number of attractive and very low-priced pensions still survive in Seville's Barrio de Santa Cruz and Córdoba's Judería. The regional government produces a list of the region's 130 official camp sites, the majority of which are along the coast and very noisy. Reservations can be made through the Federación Española de Camping y Caravanas.

Rented property around Mojácar and the main resorts of the Costa del Sol can easily be arranged through travel agencies or the internet; those interested in renting traditional dwellings in the Andalucían interior should search the internet for *alojamientos rurales* or *casas rurales*. An excellent agency for Alpujarran rentings is the Bubión-based Rustic Blue (tel 958 76 33 81, www.rusticblue.com). If you wish to rent a place through local enquiries, the person to approach in a village or small town is the *corredor*, who traditionally conducts his business in one of the local bars: the corredor of Sanlúcar de Barrameda, Francisco Salazar Romero (known as 'Curro') has a visiting card putting as his address and office hours: Bar 'Los Monaguillos'/Bar 'El Cura' 10-2, 5-9.

Bars and Restaurants The serious gastronome will have to purchase a copy of Gourmetour's annually updated *Guía gastronómica y turística de España*, which describes all the region's most sophisticated restaurants, together with the best shops selling food and wine, and some of the more fashionable bars; this information can be supplemented with a copy of José Carlos Capel's excellent if now hard-to-find book on eating in Andalucía, *Comer en Andalucía* (Madrid, 1981). Also useful are the guides to the best tapas bars in Seville, Granada, Málaga, Marbella, Torremolinos, Cádiz and Jerez published by El País in their pocket series, *Guías con encanto.* A full glossary of food terms, including many of the region's unique tapas, is given on page 419. Convent confectionery is discussed in a special entry below.

Most bars with normal opening hours serve food in Spain, beginning with breakfast, from as early as six o'clock in some of the seedier establishments popular with all-night drinkers; breakfast continues to about midday, the hour between 11 and 12 being traditionally the time favoured by office-workers; from about 1.30 onwards the bars begin to fill up with people having pre-lunch drinks and tapas, which will usually be available for the rest of the day, and even throughout the whole night in the case of a handful of generally insalubrious-looking bars. Many of the bars are attached to restaurants, and a tapa at the counter might help you decide whether you want to go on afterwards to have a full meal sitting down. The bars calling themselves *bodegas, bodegones,* or *tabernas* exist primarily to sell wine kept in barrels behind the counter; but food of some sort, if only cheese, ham and olives, will always be on hand. Roadside bars-cum-restaurants are known as *ventas* (literally inns), and are often some of the best places to eat good, simple fare.

Exclusively late-night bars, where tapas are rarely provided, are referred to as *bares de copas*, and frequently bear the name *pub*: these places, so different in character to their British namesakes, are where you come to drink generously-sized, post-supper *cubatas* (spirits) in settings ranging from ones of calm and comfort to others sometimes indistinguishable in their crowds and loud music to *discotecas* (to where Spaniards of all ages often go just to have a drink). *Cokteleriás* speak for themselves, but *whiskerías* do not cater for the Glenfiddich connoisseur: they are brothels or *puti-clubs* (and are generally known today simply as Clubs).

Beaches With its Mediterranean and Atlantic coast lines, Andalucía offers a greater variety of beaches than any other Spanish region. The beaches in the province of Huelva are flat, sandy, and so long that it is possible to find many secluded stretches. The greatest concentration of beautiful, little-spoilt Andalucían beaches is between Conil de la Frontera and Tarifa (Cádiz), and along the Cabo de Gata (Almería); their drawbacks are the often vicious *levante* wind which blows in the former, and the parched austerity of the latter. The Costa del Sol, the coastline of the provinces of Málaga and Granada, has an excellent climate and a number of clean beaches of fine sand (especially to the west of Málaga), but its resorts are among the most commercially exploited in Spain: Harry Ritchie's *Here We go: A Season on the Costa del Sol* (1993), though a welcome attack on the sort of cultural tourist who would not go near the place, is likely to confirm prejudices about high-rise horrors, and embarassingly behaved foreigners.

The main beaches for those needing sun-loungers, parasols etc include:

Cádiz (Playa de la Victoria)
Playa de Valdegrana (El Puerto de Santa María, Cádiz)
Mazagón (Huelva)
Punta Umbria (Huelva)
Matalascañas (Huelva)
Estepona (Málaga)
Marbella (Málaga)
Fuengirola (Málaga)
Torremolinos (Málaga)
Nerja (Málaga)
Motril (Granada)
La Garrucha (Almería)
Roquetas (Almería)
Mojácar (Almería)

Wilder and less frequented are:

La Antilla (Isla Cristina, Huelva)
Los Caños de Meca (Cádiz)
Bolonia (Cádiz)

Zahara de los Atunes (Cádiz)
Tarifa (Cádiz)
La Barrosa (Chiclana, Cádiz)
La Ballena (Chipiona, Cádiz)
Cantariján (Nerja, Málaga)
San José (Almería)
Los Escullos (Almería)
San Pedro (Almería)
El Plomo (Almería)
La Macena (Mojácar, Almería)
Puerto Rey (La Garrucha, Almería)

Toplessness is common on all beaches, and nudity is still prevalent in the more secluded ones, though less so now than in the early 90's; Spain's first and largest nudist resort is at Estepona. Beach bars or *chiringuitos* are to be found in most of the beaches, though recent regulations have greatly restricted their number. All Spanish beaches are free.

Bull-fighting Nearly all the ferias and fiestas listed on page 436ff include bull-fights. Outlined below are the main fights of the bull-fighting year, which begins in Seville with the Spring feria and ends there with the Columbus Day festival of October 12.

April/May: Seville, Jerez de la Frontera
May: Córdoba, Sanlúcar de Barrameda, Écija, Ronda
June: Granada, Algeciras
June, July, and August: El Puerto de Santa María
July: La Línea de la Concepción
August: Huelva, Málaga, Almería, Antequera
September: Ronda (*goyescas*, or bullfights in 18th-century style), Priego de Córdoba, Cabra, Pozoblanco, Linares
October: Jaén, Úbeda, Baeza, Seville

Novilladas, which are held throughout the bull-fighting year, are fights involving apprentice fighters and smaller bulls.

The oldest and most beautiful of the main bull-rings are the ones at Seville and Ronda; however, there is a well-known group of old and rustically picturesque small rings in the Sierra de Huelva, notably at Campo-frío, Higuera de la Sierra, Aroche and Almonaster la Real (the last two are sometimes claimed as the oldest in Spain). The most important bull-fighting museums are at Seville, Ronda and Córdoba.

One of the best-known Andalucían bull-fighters is Jesulín de Ubrique, who has tried to maintain his popularity with such gimmicks as holding fights only for women or pensioners. Another name to look out for is that of Francisco Rivera, the subject of Edward Lewine's *Death and the Sun: A Bullfighter's Season in the Heart of Spain*, who comes from a famous Andalucían bull-fighting family but never lived up to his remarkable early promise.

The success of a fight depends to a great extent on the quality of the bulls, and *aficionados* always note the name of the stock farm or *ganadería* where the bulls were raised. The main Andalucían ganaderías are in the provinces of Seville and Cádiz, and include the most prestigious one in all of Spain – that of Eduardo Miura (at the Finca Zahariche at Lora del Río Seville), which was founded in 1849, and has an almost mythical reputation for the ferocity of its bulls. Others include those of Murube (at the Finca La Cobatilla, Utrera Seville, founded 1848), Jandilla (at the Finca Jandilla, Vejer de la Frontera Cádiz), Torrestella (at the Finca Los Alburejos, Medina-Sidonia, founded 1951), Juan Pedro Domecq (at the Finca Los Alvaros, Castillo de las Guardas Seville, founded in 1790 and acquired in 1830 by Ferdinand VII), Joaquín Buendía (Santa Coloma Seville, founded 1906), Pablo Romero (at the Fincas La Herrera and Partido de Resima, Sanlúcar la Mayor and Villamanrique Seville, founded 1888), and Hermanos Nuñez (at the Finca El Grullo, Véjer de la Frontera Cádiz, founded 1941). Those, like Hemingway, who are interested in the processes of branding, separation from the mothers, and selective breeding, should visit the estates during the early spring.

Business Hours Most shops are open between 10 am and 1.30 or 2 pm and between 5 and 7.30 or 8 pm; groceries and newsagents open around 8 am. Banking hours are usually 9 am – 2 pm Mondays to Fridays, with occasional banks open also on Saturday mornings. Office-workers are often difficult to contact between 11 and 12, when they're frequently out for breakfast. Government offices and Town Halls usually remain open to 3, but are closed thereafter.

Convent Confectionery In Andalucía, as throughout Spain, much of the best confectionery can be bought in the closed order convents, especially around Christmas time and Easter. The correct procedure in buying sweets from the nuns is to ring the bell next to the grille and greet the nuns with the words, '*Ave María Purísima*', to which you will receive the reply, '*sin pecado concebida*' ('without inherited sin'); after putting in your order for, say, half a dozen doughnuts ('*media docena de roscos*'), you place your money in the rotating drum or *torno* which lies behind the grille, and then wait until your product is delivered to you; it's best to have the correct money, as accidental short-changing on the nuns' part can lead to a moral quandary on yours. The list of products is appended on a notice besides the grille; opening hours are the same as most shops, though with slightly earlier closing hours in the evenings.

María Luisa Fraga Iribarne's *Guía de dulces de los conventos sevillanos de clausura* (1988), an excellent short introduction to the subject, features a complete guide to the confectionery- selling convents in the province of Seville. Listed below are some of the better known places, with occasional reference to sweets for which they are particularly famed. Most of the sweets have no English equivalent, and can only be roughly translated. The ones you'll be most likely to encounter are:

bizcochos (sponge fingers)
bollitos (soft doughnuts)
roscos (crisp, deep-fried doughnuts)
huesos de santo (boudoir biscuits, literally 'saints' bones')
yemas (sweetened egg yolks)
palmeras (palm feuilletes)
pestinos (honey-coated fritters)
magdalenas (madeleines)
merengues (meringues)
hojaldre (mille-feuille pastries)
tortas de aceite (thin, oil-fried biscuits)
mazapan (marzipan)
polvorones (crumbly, almond-flavoured biscuits)
mantecados (butter-cakes)
tocino de cielo (small crème caramels, literally 'heaven's bacon').

Seville Province

Seville: Convento de San Leandro (*yemas)*
Convento de Santa Ines (*bollitos de Santa Inés*, particularly good when heated up)

Convento de Santa María la Real
Convento de Santa Paula (nineteen types of jam and marmalade; also quince jelly (*dulce de membrillo*))
Alcalá de Guadaira: Convento de Santa Clara
Carmona: Convento de Santa Clara
Écija: Convento de la Purísima Concepción (*bizcochos marroquíes*)
Estepa: Convento de Santa Clara
Lebrija: Convento de la Purísima Concepción
Marchena: Convento de San Andrés (*tortas de hoja*)
Convento de Santa María (*obleas*, wafers)
Morón: Convento de la Asunción
Osuna: Convento de Santa Catalina
Convento de la Encarnación
Utrera: Convento de la Inmaculada Concepción

Jaén Province

Jaén: Las Carmelitas Descalzas (*ochios*)
Alcaudete: Las Claritas de Jesús (*empanadillas de sidra*, cider turnovers)
Alcalá la Real: Las Trinitarias
Las Dominicas (*cuajadas*, milk curds)
Martos: Las Madres Trinitarias
Úbeda: Convento de Santa Clara

Granada Province

Granada: Las Agustinas Recoletas (*higos*, a fig-based sweet)
Las Comendadoras de Santiago (*huesos de chocolate*

Córdoba Province

Córdoba: Las Clarisas de Santa Isabel: (*mojicones* sponge cakes)
Las Madres del Cister

Cádiz Province

Sanlúcar de Barrameda: Convento de Madre de Dios (*tocinos de cielo*)

Cultural Festivals Andalucía's, if not Spain's, leading music festival is the annual Festival Internacional de Música y Danza de Granada, (June/July), with most of the concerts and performances taking place in and around the Alhambra (information can be obtained from Festival Internacional de Música y Danza, tel 958 27 62 00).

Second in importance is Seville's *Festival de Danza de Itálica*, which runs through July, and has as its setting the Roman ruins of outlying Itálica. Seville frequently hosts other festivals, but it is important to find out the most recent information online. One of Spain's greatest festivals, dedicated to 'World Music', is Etnosur (www.etnosur.com) which is held in late July at Alcalá la Real and attracts hippies from all over Spain (there is no entrance fee to any of the concerts or other activities).

There are two major theatre festivals in Andalucía: the bi-annual *Festival Iberamericano de Cádiz,* which brings together diverse companies from all over Spain, Portugal and Latin America, and the *Festival de Teatro de Málaga*. There are puppet festivals in Seville and Almería (information can be obtained from the town halls and on the internet).

Fiestas and Ferias So numerous are Spanish festivals that anyone travelling around Spain (particularly in the spring and summer months) is highly likely to come across at least one town or village that is '*en fiesta*'. For a complete list of every Andalucían festival, together with a brief description of what they comprise, the traveller needs to consult beforehand Rodríguez Becerra's *Guía de las fiestas populares de Andalucía* (1st edition, Seville, 1982), which is far too large and heavy to be carried around. Listed below by region is a selection of some of the better known and more distinctive ones.

Almería Province

Albox: Romería de la Virgen del Saliente; 8-17 September

Almería: Fiestas de San Juan Bautista: 24 June; singing and fires on the beach; young girls traditionally wash their faces in the water.

Feria de Agosto: 22-31 August

Carboneras: Fiestas de Moros y Cristianos en Honor a San Antonio de Padua: 10-13 June

Cuevas de Almanzora: Carnival: February

Cádiz Province

Arcos de la Frontera: Holy Week

Benamahoma (Grazalema): Easter Sunday, with fireworks, songs and a bull tied to a rope and teased until eventually brought to the slaughter-house.

Moros y Cristianos en Honor a San Antonio, 1st week of August

Cádiz: Carnival: February

Holy Week

Jerez de la Frontera: Holy Week

Horse Fair: April/May

Fiesta de la Vendimia: September

Olvera: Romería de Nuestra Señora de los Remedios: second Monday after Easter (known curiously as 'Quasimodo Monday')

Puerto Real: Fiesta de la Cruz: 1st or 2nd week in May

Feria de Puerto Real: 4-8 June

Puerto de Santa María: Holy Week

Puerto de Santa María: Feria de Primavera (Feria del vino fino): 21-25 May

Rota: Fiestas de la Urta: 6-13 August; created in 1982, largely with tourists in mind, this gives the spectator a free opportunity to judge the best prepared fish dish known as *urta a la Roteña.*
San Fernando: Carnival: February
Sanlúcar de Barrameda: Feria de la Manzanilla: last week of May
Trebujena: Carnival: February
Véjer de la Frontera: Easter Sunday, with bull-running through the streets
Zahara de la Sierra: Corpus Christi

Córdoba Province

Aguilar de la Frontera: Holy Week
Baena: Holy Week, famous especially for its massed ranks of drummers who begin playing on Maundy Thursday
Córdoba: Carnival: February
Holy Week
Cruces de Mayo (first days of May)
Feria de Nuestra Señora de la Salud: 25 May–2 June
Corpus Christi
Doña Mencía: Holy Week
Fuente Carreteros (Fuente Palmera): Fiesta de los Santos Inocentes: 28 December: known as 'the Day of the Mad', this festival involves groups of 'mad dancers'.
Fuente Tójar: Fiestas de San Isidro y Feria Real de Ganado: 15-17 May; the fame of this festival is due to the secular dancing that accompanies the procession of San Isidro on the afternoon of the 15th.
Lucena: Holy Week
Montilla: Holy Week
Obejo: Romería de San Benito: 21 March, with men executing a curious 'sword dance'.
Puente Genil: Holy Week

Granada Province

Albondón: Moros y Cristianos Festival: 23-26 August
Baza/Guadix: Fiestas Patronales de la Virgen de la Piedad: 6-15 September; famous, above all, for the arrival at Baza from Guadix, on the afternoon of 6 September, of the so-called 'Cascamorras', who attempts to steal the local devotional image of the Virgin (see page 271).
Granada: Holy Week
Cruces de Mayo: last week in May, and largely centred on the Albaicín, which is beautifully decorated but also filled with large and drunken crowds of students
Corpus Christi: the most famous Corpus Christi processions in Andalucía are followed by an eight-day feria.
Moclín: Romería del Cristo del Paño: 5 October
Quentar: Moros y Cristianos: 1st Sunday in October
Válor: Moros y Cristianos: mid-September

Huelva Province

Alajar: Romería de la Reina de los Ángeles: 7-8 September
Almonte: Romería del Rocío: Saturday, Sunday, and Monday of Pentecost
Rocío Chico: 19 August
Huelva: Holy Week
Isla Cristina: Carnival
Puebla de Guzmán: Romería de la Santísima Virgen de la Peña: last Sunday of April

Jaén Province:

Andújar: Romería en Honor de la Virgen de la Cabeza: last Sunday of April
Jaén: Holy Week

Málaga Province

Alfarnate: Moros y Cristianos: 12-16 September
Antequera: Holy Week
Benalauria: Moros y Cristianos: 4-5 August
Benamocarra: Moros y Cristianos: last week of October

Fuengirola: Fiestas de San Juan: 21-24 June
Feria: 6-12 October
Málaga: Carnival: February
Holy Week
Feria de Málaga: First half of August
Fiesta de los Verdiales: 28 December. Costumed dancing and singing to celebrate the winter solstice: the name derives from a type of olive that always remains green.
Marbella: Feria: 15-19 October
Ronda: Holy Week
Feria y Fiestas de Pedro Romero: 31 August–10 September

Seville Province
Alcalá de Guadaira: Holy Week
Alcalá del Río: Holy Week
Bolullos de la Mitación: Romería de la Virgen de Cuatrovitas: 4th Sunday of October
Carmona: Carnival: February
Holy Week
Castilleja de la Cuesta: Holy Week, particularly interesting for the rivalry shown between the various Brotherhoods on Easter Sunday
Constantina: Holy Week
Romería de la Virgen del Robledo: last Sunday of October
Coripe: Burning of Judas: Easter Sunday
Écija: Holy Week
Feria de Primavera: 8 May
Estepa: Holy Week
Fuentes de Andalucía: Carnival: February
Lebrija: Holy Week
Feria: 8-13 September
Lora del Río: Romería de la Virgen de Setefilla: 17 May, and 8 September
Mairena del Alcor: Feria de Abril: the first feria of the Andalucían year, as well as the oldest, this is usually timed for the week after Easter.
Morón de la Frontera: Carnival, February
Holy Week
Osuna: Holy Week
Feria: 13-15 May
Sanlúcar la Mayor: Feria: 13-16 May

Seville: Holy Week
Feria: either one or two weeks after Easter
Cruces de Mayo
Velada en honor de Santa Ana y Santiago Apostol: end of July. Popular festival of 15th-century origin held in the Barrio de Triana.
Umbrete: Fiestas del Corpus Christi, Feria; 2-8 August
Utrera: Holy Week

Fishing All fishing in Spain requires a *Licencia Estatal de Pesca* from ICONA; foreigners must apply for a special category licence (*Especial*); an additional licence is needed for sea fishing (apply to the *Dirección General de Pesca Marítima*).

The best trout fishing in Andalucía is in the Sierra Nevada (the Vallades, Frades and, above all, Genil rivers), the Sierra Morena (the Cabrera, Grande and Sardinilla rivers), and the Sierra de Segura (the Beas river).

Flamenco Most tourists in search of flamenco end up at one of the region's commercial spectacles known as *tablaos:* two of the most popular are Seville's Los Gallos (Pl. Santa Cruz, 11, tel 954 22 40 02) and Granada's visually unappealing Sala de Neptuno (Paseo de la Ronda). A far more pleasant and intimate environment for flamenco is Seville's Carbonería bar (C/Leviés, 18, tel 954 21 44 60), which was co-founded by Esperanza Flores whose tasteful flamenco costumes are prized today; as well as informal flamenco recitals on Thursday evenings, there are spontaneous performances on other days.

Recitals are also frequently held in Andalucía's two hundred or so flamenco clubs or *peñas*, the main ones being at Almería (Peña Taranto), Cádiz (Enrique El Mellizo, tel 956 22 19 85), Jerez de la Frontera (Los Cernícalos, Sancho Vizcaíno, 23, tel 956 33 38 71), Córdoba (Callejón Niño Perdido 14008), Granada (La Plateria, Placeta de Toqueros, 7), Huelva (Peña Flamenca de Huelva, Adoratrices, 24), Jaén (Peña Flamenca de Jaén, Maestra, 11, tel 956 23 17 10), Málaga (Juan Parera, Callejón del Picador), and Seville (Torres Macarena, Torrijano, 29).

The most sophisticated of the flamenco festivals is the *Bienal de Arte Flamenco Ciudad de Sevilla*, which is held in September and organized by the Consejería de Cultura de la Junta de Andalucía in collaboration with the Junta de Sevilla. A festival of classical flamenco, concentrating mainly on guitar music, takes place every summer in Córdoba, organized by Paco Peña's Flamenco School. Flamenco events also feature in Granada's summer music festival (see under Cultural Events)

Andalucía's other important flamenco festivals are listed below in calendar order:
Second half of May: Córdoba: *Concurso Nacional de Arte Flamenco* (a ten day competition held every three years).

June: Alhaurín de la Torre (Málaga): *Torre del cante*
Lebrija (Seville): *Caracola*
First half of July: Marchena (Seville): *Fiesta de la Guitarra*
Alora (Málaga): *Festival del Cante Grande*
Utrera (Seville): *Potaje Gitano*
Moguer (Huelva): *Festival de Arte Flamenco*
Second half of July: Alcalá de Guadaira (Seville): *Festival Flamenco*
Almería: *Festival de Cante Jondo*
Morón de la Frontera (Seville): *Gazpacho Andaluz*
Punta Umbría (Huelva): *Festival Flamenco 'Rumbo al Mar'*
Chiclana (Cádiz): *Festival Flamenco 'La Parpuja'*.
First half of August: La Puebla de Cazalla (Seville): *Reunión del Cante Jondo*
Pegalajar (Jaén): *Festival de Arte Flamenco*
Jerez (Cádiz): *Festival Flamenco de Jerez*
La Rambla (Córdoba): *Botijo Flamenco*
Baena (Córdoba): *Salmorejo Flamenco*
San Fernando (Cádiz)
Puente Genil (Córdoba): *Festival Cante Grande*
Second half of August: Écija (Seville): *Noche Flamenca Ecijana*
Linares (Jaén): *Concurso Nacional de Tarantos*
Ronda (Málaga): *Festival Cante Grande*
Montilla (Córdoba): *La Cata Flamenca*
First Saturday in September: Mairena de Alcor (Seville): *Festival de Cante Jondo 'Antonio Mairena'*

For those wishing to study flamenco guitar, the best courses are those offered by Paco Peña in Córdoba and by the Centre of Flamenco Studies in Jerez de la Frontera. A leading dance school is the Escuela de Danza Matilde Coral, Castilla (pasaje interior derecha, 82-40, 41010 Seville, tel 954 33 97 31). Flamenco singing is not at present taught anywhere.

Some great recent names in flamenco are:

Singers: Fosforito, El Cabrero, the late Camarón de la Isla, El Lebrijano, Menese, Enrique Morente, Antonio Nuñez ('Chocolate'), Curro Albaycin and Manuel Agujeta;
Dancers: Antonio Gades, Mario Maya, Matilde Coral, Cristina Hoyos, Rafael El Negro, Farruco (Antonio Montoya Flores), Manuela Vargas, Manuela Carrasco, Blanca del Rey, Merche Esmeralda, La Tolea, Carmen Cortés;
Guitarists: Paco de Lucía, the late Pedro Bacán, the Habichuelas, Quique Veneno;
Pianist: Pedro Romero.

Golf Golf is especially popular along the Costa del Sol, with various hotels catering almost exclusively for golfers, for instance the Parador de Golf, which is located between Málaga and Torremolinos (www.parador.es, tel 952 38 12 55). A golf guide to the region is published by the Andalucían tourist board; see also their website: www.juntadeandalucia.es, and further information is provided in the monthly magazine *Costa Golf*, which is available from most of the coast's newsagents.

Hunting Andalucía, with its extensive wildernesses, is a rich land for hunters, and includes what was the favourite Spanish hunting ground of Francisco Franco – the Sierra de Cazorla y Segura.

The season for small game (mainly rabbit and red partridge) is from the third Sunday in October to the third Sunday in January; hunting is usually restricted to Thursdays, Saturdays, Sundays and holidays. The season for acquatic birds lasts a week longer but is liable to sudden interruptions resulting from droughts and ecological accidents. Deer, roebuck, and wild boar can be hunted from the third Sunday in October up to the fourth Sunday in February; roe-deer from the second Sunday in September to the second

Sunday in November; and moufflon and *arrui* from the second Sunday in September to the first Sunday in December. Mountain goat cannot be hunted outside hunting reserves and other restricted areas. Licences have to be obtained from the Instituto Andaluz de Reforma Agraria (IARA) de la Junta de Andalucía, Calle Tabladilla, s/n, 41013 Seville, tel 955 03 22 71). Insurance documents from your country of origin are needed, together with a licence to transport sporting guns, and an International Yellow Health Certificate for hunting dogs.

Islamic Heritage The principal courses in Andalucía on Spanish Islamic culture are offered by the Universities of Córdoba and Granada; Granada has also the Centro de Estudios Islámicos, which is housed in the beautiful Carmen de Chápiz, and features an excellent library.

The recently founded El Legado Andalusí (Corral del Carbón, Mariana Pineda, s/n, 18009, Granada, tel 958 22 59 95, www.legadoandalusi.es) is dedicated to the revival of Spain's Islamic heritage, and, as well as organizing and publishing books on this theme, has created a series of ten Islamic cultural itineraries (*Las Rutas de Al Andalus*) that include not only the region's major Islamic monuments but also a host of hitherto neglected and frequently fascinating sites. All the routes end in Granada and bear such names as *La ruta de Ibn Batuta* or *La ruta de Washington Irving*; individually outlined in pamphlets available from local tourist offices, they are also the subject of an attractive guide-book published by El País Aguilar (in English and Spanish) and romantically subtitled 'Ten routes across Andalucía to help you discover the traces of a lost civilization that illuminated Europe'.

Museums and Archaeological Sites: A complete list of Andalucía's museums is given here, together with opening times where available. Please note that this information is subject to change. If in doubt, check with the local tourist office, or your hotel. There are three official websites which give information about museums in English: www.juntadeandalucia.es; www. andalucia.org; and www.museosdeandalucia.es.

Most of the more interesting, eccentric or characterful of these places are described in the main body of the text; the others will appeal mainly to dedicated specialists, in particular those who love prehistoric shards and dusty ecclesiastical bric-à-brac. Opening times vary widely, but as a rule museums are shut on Mondays and in the middle of the day. Times have only been given for the most significant in each province.

Almería Province

Almería: Museo de Almería, Ctra. de Ronda, 91, tel 950 26 44 92; Tues 2.30 pm-8.30 pm, Weds–Sat 9 am-8.30 pm, Sun 9 am–2.30 pm, Mon closed.

Cádiz Province

Algeciras: Museo Municipal, Calle Ortega y Gasset, s/n, tel 956 57 06 72

Arcos de la Frontera: Museo-Tesoro Parroquial, Plaza de España, tel 956 70 16 08

Bolonia: Conjunto Arqueologico Baelo Claudia; Ensenada de Bolonia, s/n, 11380, Tarifa, tel 956 68 85 30, fax 956 68 85 60

Cádiz: Museo Catedralicio, Plaza Fray Felix, Casa de la Contaduna, tel 956 25 98 12

Museo de Cádiz, Plaza Mina, tel 956 21 22 81; Tues 2.30 pm–8.30 pm; Weds–Sat 9 am–8.30 pm; Sun 9 am–2pm; closed Mon.

Museo Histórico-Municipal, Santa Inés, 9–11, tel 956 22 17 88

Jerez: Colección de Relojes, La Atalaya, Cervantes, 4, tel 956 18 21 00

Museo Arqueológico Municipal, Plaza del Mercado, s/n, tel 956 33 33 16

Bodega-Museo, Casa del Vino, Avda. Álvaro Domecq, tel 956 33 20 50

La Línea de la Concepción: Archivo-Museo Histórico, Plaza de la Constitución, tel 956 69 06 57

Puerto de Santa María: Casa-Museo Rafael Alberti, Sto. Domingo 25

Museo Municipal, Pagador, 1, tel 956 54 27 05

Museo Taurino, Fernán Caballero, 7, tel 956 85 14 48

San Fernando: Museo Histórico, Calle Real, 63, tel 956 88 26 31

Sanlúcar de Barrameda: Colección Mariana (religious art), Convento de Capuchinos, Plaza Capuchinos; tel 956 36 02 01

Córdoba Province

Cabra: Museo Municipal, Casa de Cultura, Calle Martin Belda, 25; tel 957 52 01 10

Cañete de las Torres: Museo Histórico Local, Plaza España, 8, Casa de Cultura, tel 957 18 30 00

Córdoba: Alcázar de los Reyes Cristianos, Calle Caballerizas Reales, s/n, tel 957 42 01 51

Museo Arqueológico, Plaza Jerónimo Páez, 7, tel 957 47 40 11

Museo de Bellas Artes, Plaza del Potro, 2, tel 957 49 19 09; Tues-Sat 10 am-2 pm and 5.30 pm-7.30 pm; Sun 9 am-2.30 pm; closed Mon.

Tesoro Catedralicio de Córdoba, Calle Torrijos, 12, tel 957 47 05 12

Museo Julio Romero de Torres, Plaza del Potro, 2, tel 957 49 19 09

Museo Monográfico Madinat al-Zahra, Medina Azahara (8 miles outside Córdoba), tel 957 23 40 25; 10.30 am–12 pm & 3.30 pm–5 pm (winter); 10.30 am–12 pm & 5.30 pm–7 pm (summer)

Museo Municipal Taurino (including memorabilia of Manolete), Plaza Maimónides, s/n, tel 957 20 10 56

Palacio-Museo de Viana, Plaza de Don Gome, 2, tel 957 48 01 34

Tesoro, Cathedral, tel 957 47 05 12

Torre de La Calahorra, Puente Romano, tel 957 29 39 29

Doña Mencía: Museo Histórico-Arqueológico, Calle Juan Ramón Jiménez, 6, Casa de Cultura, tel 957 67 61 52

Espejo: Museo Parroquial, Iglesia de San Bartolomé, tel 957 37 61 34

Montemayor: Museo de Ulía (Roman archaeology), Iglesia de la Asunción, tel 957 38 40 40

Puente Genil: Museo Arqueológico Municipal, Calle Ancha, s/n, Convento de los Padres Franciscanos, tel 957 60 00 25

Torrecampo: Casa-Museo Posada del Moro, Nudo 13; write in advance.

Granada Province

Almuñecar: Museo Arqueológico, Cueva de Siete Palacios, tel 958 63 11 25

Fuente Vaqueros: Casa-Museo Federico García Lorca, Calle Poeta F. G. Lorca, 4, tel 958 51 69 62/958 51 64 53

Granada: Museo de la Alhambra, Palacio de Carlos V, Alhambra, tel 958 02 79 00/29; Sun and Tues: 8.30 am–2.30 pm; Wed-Sat: 8.30 am-6 pm (winter), 8.30 am–8 pm (summer); closed Mon and public holidays

Basílica de San Juan de Dios, San Juan de Dios, 23, tel 958 27 57 00

Monasterio de Cartuja, Paseo de Cartuja, tel 958 16 19 32; Mon-Sat 10 am–1 pm & 3.30 pm–6 pm, Sun 10 am-12 pm, 4 pm-7 pm.

Casa de los Pisa, Convalecencia, 1, tel 958 22 21 44

Casa-Museo Ángel Barrios, Real de la Alhambra, tel 958 02 79 07

Casa-Museo Federico García Lorca, Virgen Blanca, 6, tel 958 25 84 66

Casa-Museo Manuel de Falla, Ante-queruela Alta, 11, tel 958 22 21 88

Colección del Observatorio de Cartuja, Campus Universitario Cartuja, tel 958 20 10 33; by appointment only

Colección Municipal, Ayuntamiento, tel 958 22 75 68

Fundación Rodríguez Acosta, Callejón Niños del Rollo, 8, tel 958 22 74 97; by appointment only

Museo Gómez Moreno, Callejón Niños del Rollo, 8, tel 958 22 74 97

Museo Arqueológico Provincial, Carrera del Darro, 43, tel 958 22 56 40

Museo Catedralicio, Cathedral, tel 958 22 29 59

Museo de Bellas Artes, Palace of Charles V, Alhambra, tel 958 56 35 08; Tues 2.30 pm-6 pm; Wed-Sat 9 am-6 pm; Sun 9 am-2.30 pm; closed Mon.

Museo de los Reyes Católicos, Capilla Real, tel 958 22 78 48

Museo del Sacromonte, Abadía del Sacromonte, tel 958 22 14 45

Museo Nacional de Arte Hispano-Musulmán, Casa Real de la Alhambra, tel 958 22 62 79; 9 am-2 pm, Sat 9 am-1 pm, closed Sun, Mon.

Real Monasterio de San Jerónimo, Rector López Argüeta, 9, tel 958 27 93 37

Guadix: Museo Catedralicio, Cathedral, tel 958 66 51 08

Huelva Province

Aroche: Colleción del Santo Rosario, Paseo Ordoñez Valdés, tel 959 14 02 61

Museo Municipal, C/Cilla 2, tel 959 14 02 61; by appointment only

Huelva: Museo de Huelva, Alameda Sundheim, 13, tel 959 65 04 24; Tues–Sat 10 am–8.30 pm (winter); 10 am–3.30 pm (summer); Sun 10 am–5 pm; Mon closed

Moguer: Casa Museo Zenobia–Juan Ramón, Juan Ramón Jiménez, 10, tel 959 37 21 48

Palos de la Frontera: Monasterio de La Rábida, Carretera a Huelva, tel 959 35 04 11

Río Tinto: Museo Ferroviario de Riotinto, tel 959 59 00 25, http://www.parque-mineroderiotinto.com/

Valverde del Camino: Museo Minero, Plaza del Museo, tel 959 59 00 25

Museo Mineralógico, Casa de Cultura

Jaén Province

Baeza: Museo Catedralicio, Plaza Santa María, 1, tel 953 74 41 57

Cazorla: Museo del Alto Guadalquivir (ethnology collection), Calle Camino del Castillo, s/n, tel 953 71 16 38

Jaén: Museo Catedralicio, Cathedral, tel 953 23 42 33

Museo de Artes y Costumbres Populares y Museo Internacional de Arte Naïf, Palacio de Villardompardo, Plaza de Santa Luisa de Marillac, s/n, tel 953 24 80 68

Museo Provincial de Jaén, Ronda Estación,

27, tel 953 10 13 67; Tues-Sat 10 am -8.30 pm (winter), 9 am-3.30 pm (summer); Sun: 10 am-5 pm; closed Mon.

Linares: Museo Arqueológico, General Echagüe, 2, tel 953 10 60 74

Porcuna: Museo Arqueológico Municipal de Obulco, Torréon de Boabdil, tel 953 54 40 0

Quesada: Museo Zabaleta, Plaza Cesáreo Rodríguez Aguilera, tel 953 73 42 60

Santisteban del Puerto: Museo Jacinto Higueras, Plaza Mayor 8, tel 953 40 21 11

Úbeda: Museo San Juan de la Cruz, Calle del Carmen, 13, tel 953 75 06 15

Málaga Province

Antequera: Museo Municipal, Palacio Nájera, tel 952 84 18 27

Museo Arqueológico Municipal, Avda. J. L. Peralta, 43, tel 952 84 85 93

Málaga: Museo Catedralicio, Cathedral, tel 952 21 59 17

Museo Diocesano de Arte Sacro, Palacio Episcopal, tel 952 22 25 52

Museo Mesón de la Victoria (ethnology), Pasillo Santa Isabel, 10, tel 952 21 71 37

Museo Picasso, Palacio de los Condes de Buenavista, C/San Agustin, 8, tel 902 44 33 77; Tues-Thur and Sun 10 am-8 pm, Fri-Sat 10 am-9 pm

Museo-Tesoro Cofradía de la Expiración, Plaza Enrique Narraro, 1, tel 952 24 91 16

Ronda: Museo Taurino, Plaza de Toros, tel 952 87 41 32

Seville Province

Carmona: Museo y Necrópolis Romana, Jorge Bonsor 9, tel 954 14 08 11

Gerena: Colección Taurina, Calle Canteras 12, tel 955 78 28 15

Lebrija: Museo Tesoro Parroquial, Plaza Rector Merina, tel 955 97 23 37

Los Palacios: Museo Taurino Antonio Urquijo, Cortijo Juan Gómez Km 575 Ctra. Madrid–Cádiz, tel 955 86 50 00

Marchena: Museo Parroquial, Iglesia de S. Juan Bautista, tel 95 484 32 57

Osuna: Museo Arqueológico, Torre del Agua, Plaza de la Duquesa, tel 95 481 12 07

Museo del Arte Sacro (with Ducal mausoleum), Iglesia Colegial, tel 95 481 04 44

Paradas: Museo Parroquial, Parroquia de San Eutropio, tel 954 84 90 39

Santiponce: Museo Arqueológico de Itálica, Ctra. Mérida, tel 955 62 22 66/99 73 76

Seville: Casa de las Dueñas, Dueñas, 5, tel 954 22 09 56

Casa de Pilatos, Plaza Pilatos, 1, tel 954 22 52 98; open 9 am-7 pm; closed Tues am.

Centro Andaluz de de Arte Contemporáneo, Monasterio de la Cartuja de Santa María de Las Cuevas, Avda. Américo Vespucio, 2/ Camino de los Descubrimientos, s/n, tel 955 03 70 70

Colección de Mineralogía, University, Palos de la Frontera, 1, tel 954 62 50 60

Hospital de la Caridad, Temprada, 3, tel 954 22 32 32; Mon-Sat 9 am-1.30 pm, 3.30 pm-6.30 pm, Sun 9 am-1 pm

Hospital de los Venerables Sacerdotes, Plaza Venerables, 8, tel 954 56 26 96

Museo Arqueológico Provincial, Plaza de América, tel 955 12 06 32

Museo Catedralicio y Giralda, Cathedral, tel 954 21 49 71

Museo Conventual de Santa Paula, Santa Paula, 11, tel 954 53 63 30

Museo de Arte Contemporáneo, Calle Santo Tomás, 5, Palacio de la antigua Cilla del Cabildo, tel 954 21 58 30

Museo de Artes y Costumbres Populares, Pabellón Mudéjar, Plaza de América, 3, tel 955 54 29 51.

Museo de Bellas Artes, Plaza Museo, 9, tel 955 54 29 42/600 160 885 Tue-Sat 9 am–8.30 pm, Sun 9 am – 2.30 pm

Museo Naval, Torre del Oro, tel 954 22 24 19

Museo Taurino, Paseo Cristóbal Colón, 12, tel 954 22 45 77

Museo-Tesoro de la Basílica de la Macarena, Bécquer, 1, tel 954 90 18 00, 954 37 01 95
Museo-Tesoro del Templo del Gran Poder, Plaza San Lorenzo, 13, tel 954 91 56 86
Palacio de Lebrija, Cuna, 8, tel 954 22 78 02
Reales Alcázares, Plaza del Triunfo, tel 954 50 23 23

Nature Reserves There are two National Parks in Andalucía, the Coto Doñana (where access is strictly regulated, and motor transport forbidden) and the Sierra Nevada (open to the public, but much of it accessible only by foot or on bicycle). However, the regional government, in collaboration with the national Ministry of the Environ-ment, has had an impressive policy of nature conservation which has led to the creation of a number of protected areas amounting to 17% of the region, and bearing the official titles of *Paraje Natural*, *Reserva Integral*, and *Parque Natural*. For up-to-date information, consult www.andalucia.com. The *Parques Naturales* are generally easy to access; they consist of:

Almería Province
Cabo de Gata-Níjar
Sierra de María

Cádiz Province
The cliffs and pinewoods of Barbate
The Bahía de Cádiz
Los Alcornocales
Sierra de Grazalema
Estrecho

Córdoba Province
Sierra de Cárdena y Montoro
Sierra de Hornachuelos
Sierras Subbéticas

Granada Province
Sierra de Baza
Sierra de Castril
Sierra de Huétor

Huelva Province
The environs of Doñana
Sierra de Aracena y Picos de Aroche

Jaén Province
Despeñaperros
Sierra de Andújar
Sierras de Cazorla, Segura y Las Villas
Sierra Mágina

Málaga Province
Montes de Málaga
Sierra de las Nieves
Sierras de Tejeda, Almijara y Almara

Seville Province
Sierra Norte

Newspapers: Spain's leading national newspapers are *El País*, *El Mundo* and the conservative *ABC*, all of which have Andalucían editions; the last of these is probably unrivalled for its detailed coverage of traditional fiestas.

Of the various English-language publications, the monthly magazine *Lookout*, published in Fuengirola, was even said – by one of its frequent contributors, Ian Gibson – to have impressed Anthony Burgess. It is now, however, an advertising free paper. The Málaga newspaper *Sur* publishes a weekly *Sur in English* (online www.surinenglish.com) and *The Olive Press* (www.theolivepress.es) calls itself Spain's No. 1 English-language newspaper; www. costanews.com provides a breezy take on local news. For English language radio stations broadcasting in Andalucía see www.andalucia.com/media/ radio/home. htm. There are many English language radio stations in Andalucía, especially for interviews, women's magazine type programmes, sport, weather and news.

Opening Times (except museum opening times; see above): Cathedrals are usually open in the mornings from 9 am to 1 pm, and in the afternoons from 5 to 7 pm. Only a handful of the churches have the same opening times as the cathedrals, the others being open only for services that usually take place between 8 and 10 in the morning or in the evening between 6 and 8. As a rule parish churches have their services exclusively in the evenings, and those attached to convents or monasteries only in the mornings; at other times of day you can sometimes get to see the parish churches if you succeed in tracking down the parish priest or *párroco*. Nuns and monks are generally less obliging than priests in showing you their buildings, and in any case most of the nuns belong to closed orders and can only address you from behind a grille. Ironically, men stand a better chance of getting in to the convents than women, possibly because of the tradition of the priest confessor. A woman journalist disguised as a man became the first known woman to have visited the Charterhouse at Jerez.

The countless castles of Andalucía mainly belong to their respective towns or villages and can be visited by asking for the key from the local Town Hall or *Ayuntamiento*, which tend to be open in the mornings only (that is, between 10 am and 3 pm).

Riding Andalucía is famous not only for its Jerez horses, but also for the importance given to riding in its culture. Riders, predominantly *señoritos* or 'toffs', are to be seen in large numbers in the Rocío pilgrimage and in all the ferias. The main horse centre is Jerez, which has been the seat since 1973 of *La Escuela Andaluza de Arte Ecuestre*, Europe's most famed riding school after that of Vienna; horse shows take place here regularly; for the scheduled programme see www.realescuela.org/home.htm. Jerez also holds in May Spain's most prestigious equine event, the *Feria del Caballo*, which includes numerous competitions. In nearby Sanlúcar de Barrameda, there is racing on the beach in late August, an especially beautiful tradition dating back to the late 19th century.

Two of the most popular places for riding holidays are the interior of Málaga province and the Alpujarras. Information on riding holidays in Andalucía can be had from *Equiberia*, tel 920 34 83 38, www.equiberia.com).

Skiing The Sierra Nevada (see www.sierranevada.es) Europe's southernmost ski resort, gained considerable publicity and outstanding modern facilities through hosting the World Alpine Ski Championships in 1996 (these were intended for 1995 but had to be postponed owing to an uncharacteristic lack of snow). For general information on winter sports contact *Federación Española Deportes de Invierno,* Madrid (www.rfedi.es).

Spas The prospect of staying in a spa resort might well seem appealing after long periods of indulging in the more hedonistic aspects of Andalucían life. There are several such resorts in the region: see www.andalucia.org/en/health-and-beauty. If your primary concerns are luxury and ultra-modern facilities then you should go to those along the Costa del Sol, such as the ones at Marbella, Benahavis and Mijas; if, instead, you are more interested in historical settings and old-fashioned charm (sometimes to the point of evocative decay), then you should aim for those in the interior of Granada and Málaga provinces, notably the ones at Alhama de Granada, Graena, Lanjarón, Carratraca and Tolox.

Telephone If you want to call Andalucía/ Spain from overseas, you should dial your country exit code, + 34 (the code for Spain), followed by the 9-digit telephone number.

If you want to call another country from Andalucía/Spain, dial 00 followed by the country code and the telephone number. You can make calls from phone boxes. These work with coins or cards available from post offices, kiosks and 'estancos' (licensed outlets for tobacco/stamps).

If you wish to make calls from Andalucía to the rest of Spain you should dial the number with no prefix. This number should comprise 9 digits, regardless of whether it is a landline or mobile.

If you wish to use your mobile phone in Andalucía/Spain, you should be aware that Spain uses GSM 900/1800 technology (not compatible with that of some countries such as the USA and Japan). If you have a compatible handset, you should contact your mobile operator to make sure you can use your phone in Andalucía/Spain (some operators will have to activate the international roaming service). Once you have taken these steps at home, you will be able to use your mobile in Andalucía/Spain as if it were a Spanish handset: i.e. you should dial 00 + the country code to make international call

Some useful numbers

'900' numbers and some emergency numbers are free of charge.
National Police: 091
Local Police: 092
Guardia Civil: 062
Emergencies: 112
Ambulance: 061
Fire brigade: 080
Maritime Rescue and Safety: 900 20 22 02
Regional Government of Andalusia, information: 902 50 55 05
Youth Tourism Information (INTURJOVEN): 902 51 00 00
Women's Line: 900 20 09 99
Child Line: 900 50 61 13
Consumers' Line: 900 84 90 90
Healthcare Line: 902 50 50 60
Post Office Information: 902 19 71 97
AENA (Spanish airports) Information: 902 40 47 04
RENFE – National Rail Services, Information and Bookings: 902 24 02 02
RENFE – International Rail Services, Information and Bookings: 902 24 34 02
Highways Agency (Dirección General de Tráfico (DGT)) – Roadside Assistance: 900 12 35 05

Tipping There are no hard and fast rules about tipping in Spain, and tips are generally little more than a token gesture. In taxis, restaurants and bars it is customary merely to round off the bill to the nearest convenient sum.

Tourist Offices

See: www.andalucia.org

Almería: Parque Nicolás Salmerón, tel 950 17 52 20; email: otalmeria@andalucia.org; web: www.almeria-turismo.org

Cádiz: Avenida Ramón de Carranza, s/n; tel 956 20 31 91; email: turismo@ dipucadiz.es; web: www.cadizturismo.com

Córdoba: calle Torrijos 10 (Palacio de Congreso); tel: 957 35 51 79; email: otcordoba@andalucia.org; web: www.cordobaturismo.es

Granada: Calle Santa Ana, 4, Bajo; tel: 958 57 52 02; email: otgranada@andalucia.org; web: www.granadatur.com/en/

Huelva: Calle Fernando El Católico, 18; tel: 959 25 74 67; email: turismo@ diphuelva.es; web: www.turismohuelva.org

Jaén: Calle Maestra, 8; tel: 953 19 04 55; email: otjaen@andalucia.org; web: www.promojaen.es

Málaga: Avenue de Cervantes, Casita del Jardinero, tel: 952 20 96 03
Plaza de la Marina, 11, tel: 952 122 020

email:info@malagaturismo.com; web: www.malagaturismo.com

Seville: Plaza del Triunfo, 1; tel: 954 50 10 01/ 78 75 78; email: otsevilla@ andalucia.org; web: www.andalucia.org/en/destinations/ provinces/sevilla/

Transport For travellers from the UK with easy access to Eurostar, high-speed rail travel to Seville or Córdoba compares well in terms of real time and cost with flying, and is of course incomparably more comfortable. There are sleeper trains from Paris to Madrid, and then the high-speed AVE takes only two hours to Seville; or one can stay overnight in Barcelona and take a direct AVE from there. For best timings and deals, see www.seat61.com. Much slower, but more charming, is the TALGO from Madrid to Granada, which takes about six hours. Within Andalucía it is usually faster and more convenient to travel by coach than by train; however, some of the train journeys are worthwhile for the scenery alone, notably the stretches between Algeciras and Ronda, Málaga and Antequera, and Seville and Cazalla de la Sierra. Almost every place of interest in Andalucía is accessible by coach, although travellers with little time to spare might be frustrated by the irregular services to many of the lesser destinations; tourists generally might also be irritated by the ubiquitous videos that are shown on the longer journeys. Road travel between the major towns has become much faster (if less picturesque) as a result of the whole new network of dual carriageways and other main roads that were constructed from the mid-1980's onwards. By far the cheapest places to hire cars are in Málaga and along the Costa del Sol; if you are using one of the international car companies it is usually cheaper to pay for your car before coming to Spain. Sadly, boat travel is no longer a viable possibility: the services between the main coastal resorts have all been suspended, and the riverboat service between Seville and Sanlúcar de Barrameda is ever more irregular.

There are international airports at Seville, Málaga and Gibraltar, the last two places being the cheapest destinations to fly to from abroad; in addition, internal flights can be made to Jerez de la Frontera, Córdoba, Granada and Almería.

Walking: Walking has never been a popular Andalucían activity; and, outside the Parques Naturales, there seem to be few paths that do not come to an end in the middle of a stony, sun-scorched wasteland. The English hiker seen walking uphill in the heat of the day is the butt of many a local joke and only confirms Noël Coward's famous line about 'Mad dogs and Englishmen'. Appropriately most of the agencies that organize hiking tours of Andalucía are British-run, including the Alpujarra-based Rustic Blue (tel 958 76 33 81, www.rusticblue.com). For general information about hiking, contact the Federación Española de Deportes de Montaña (934 26 42 67, www.fedme.es)

Watersports: Almería's Cabo de Gata offers exceptional skin-diving, while Tarifa, with its famous *levante* wind, is a world-famous centre for wind-surfing. There is a much-repeated local story about a man who was dragged on his wind-surfer all the way to the Canary Islands.

Websites A selection of the more useful websites about Andalucía:

General reference:

www.andalucia.com: a mass of information on customs and culture and with subsections for each province.

www.andalucia.org: the official regional website with information on just about every town and village of note in Andalucía

www.idealspain.com: what to look out for if you are thinking of moving to Spain.

www.juntaandalucia.es: regional government site.

www.livinginspain.co.uk: serving English-speaking expatriates.

www.okspain.org: USA site of Spanish tourist board.

www.parador.es: official guide to the state run *parador* hotel chain.

www.red2000.com: tourist guide to Spain.

www.renfe.es/ingles: Spanish national rail website.

www.tourspain.co.uk and **www.spain.info** official tourism portal in the UK

Leisure and Culture

www.asoliva.com: site dedicated to Spanish olive oil.

www.equiberia.com: wide range of information on horses and riding in Spain

www.flamenco-world.com: global information about this quintessentially Andalucían art form.

www.legadoandalusi.es: site filled with fascinating information about Andalucía's Islamic past.

www.rfedi.es: information about skiing in Spain–in Spanish only.

www.mundo-taurino.org: links to bull fighting sites.

www.reddeparquesnacionales.mma.es: information on the national parks of Spain

www.sherry.org: devoted to Andalucía's most famous export.

www.brindisa.com: a wonderful source of Spanish delicacies in the UK; www.rgarcia andsons.com and www.ibericalondon.co. uk also specialise in Spanish food in the UK

Towns and cities

www.aboutgranada.com: city guide to Granada.

www.almeria-turismo.org: tourist guide to Almería

www.aboutsevilla.com: city guide to Seville.

www.cadiznet.com: provincial guide to Cádiz.

www.costasol.com: information about the Costa del Sol.

www.gibraltar.gi: information on Gibraltar.

www.guiadehuelva.com: guide to Huelva province.

www.malaga.com: city guide to Málaga.

www.marbella.com/eng/: golf courses, property, hotels and restaurants.

www.turiscordoba.es: tourist guide to Córdoba

Index

First American edition published 2013 by
INTERLINK BOOKS
An imprint of Interlink Publishing Group, Inc.
46 Crosby Street, Northampton, Massachusetts 01060
www.interlinkbooks.com

Book design by James Sutton
Map design by Ted Hammond
Cover design by Pam Fontes-May

Library of Congress Cataloging-in-publication Data available
ISBN 978-1-56656-951-4

Printed and bound in China

Publisher's Acknowledgements: The publisher would like to thank the Spanish Tourist Office and Caterina Busquets, Barbara Fyjis-Walker, Lynette Quinlan, Jenny Wilson, Kicca Tommasi, Richard Fyjis-Walker, Sean Swallow, Angela de Pablos, Fernando Olmedo and Tom Bean for all the help they have given with this book. For this new edition we are indebted to Carmen Suarez for her meticulous research and Isobel Ramsden for her careful proof-reading

Front cover photo: Wonderful light inside the Torre de Cemares © Fotografiecor | Dreamstime.com)
Picture on page 1, Looking from the Tocador della Reyna, Alhambra, by George Vivian; colour photographs of Guadix by Maximo Lopez; of Coto Doñana and Bar in Seville by Nacho Pintos; of Jaén Cathedral by Firesmile; of the Grenadine Semana Santa procession and Virgin by Michal Osmenda. Many thanks for these contributions. Frontispiece: Velez-Blanco (Tony Sonte Images/Robert Everts)
Pictures on pages 30, 40, 126, 159, 165, 166, 172, 175, 228, 236, 250, 254, 266, 281, 303, 307, 318, 330, 331, 364, 373, and colour plates 18, 19 and 20 by Michael Jacobs. Pictures on pages 21, 43, 47, 48, 87, 97, 142, 148, 151, 153, 162, 185, 233, 284, 298, 304, 358, 438 and 440 courtesy of Michael Jacobs
Picture on page 45 courtesy of Carmen de la Guardia
Pictures on pages 14, 49, 100, 139, 145, 194, 200, 210, 221, 295, 367, 368, 371, 430, 432, 435, 437, 447 and colour plates 2, 3, 4, 5, 11, 12, 13 and 16 courtesy of Alexander Fyjis-Walker
Pictures on pages 295 and 367 by A. F. Kersting
Pictures on pages 8, 11, 15, 24, 37, 49, 56, 62, 71, 73, 78, 82, 87, 94, 108, 110, 130, 133, 136, 144, 160, 168, 169, 178, 183, 189, 193, 197, 199, 212, 213, 215, 216, 217, 224, 259, 262, 285, 287, 299, 301, 321, 323, 339, 346, 349, 350, 357 and 361 courtesy of Equipo 28, Seville. With special thanks to Fernando Olmedo
Pictures on pages 53, 65, 75, 77, 90, 99, 100, 103, 112, 122, 123, 157, 223, 243, 253, 267, 268, 269, 272, 277, 288, 289, 308, 315, 337, 340, 344, 345, 352, 355, 370, 377, 383, 385, 386 and colour plates 1, 6, 7, 8, 14, 15, 17 and 21 by courtesy of the Spanish Tourist Office, London. With special thanks to Caterina Busquets
Picture on p. 117 by courtesy of the V&A Picture Library. Copyright the Board of Trustees of the Victoria and Albert Museum
Pictures on page 120 and 125 by courtesy of the Trustees of the Wallace Collection
Picture on page 207 courtesy of Sir Brinsley Ford and the Courtauld Institute of Art
Colour plate 9 by Tony Stone Images/John Lawrence
Colour plate 10 by Tony Stone Images/Robert Frerck